From Silents to Sound

Janine, Marissa and Dennis —
from "Daddy" with love

From Silents to Sound

A Biographical Encyclopedia of Performers Who Made the Transition to Talking Pictures

by
Roy Liebman

McFarland & Company, Inc., Publishers
Jefferson, North Carolina and London

British Library Cataloguing-in-Publication data are available

Library of Congress Cataloguing-in-Publication Data

Liebman, Roy.
From silents to sound : a biographical encyclopedia of performers who
made the transition to talking pictures / by Roy Liebman.
p.   cm.
Includes bibliographical references and index.
ISBN 0-7864-0382-9 (library binding : 50# alkaline paper) ∞
1. Motion picture actors and actresses — United States — Biography —
Dictionaries.   I. Title.
PN1998.2.L52   1998   791.43'028'092273 — dc21 [B]
97-41808 CIP

Manufactured in the United States of America

*McFarland & Company, Inc., Publishers
Box 611, Jefferson, North Carolina 28640*

Contents

Introduction

Garbo talked, Gilbert self-destructed and Chaplin refused. That is roughly the extent of what most people know about the performers who made the transition from silent films to talkies. Most also know that the "revolution" began with Warner Bros.' *The Jazz Singer* in October 1927. By 1929, Hollywood moguls had embraced what they had first hoped was a passing fad, and theaters were rapidly being wired for sound.

Yes, Greta Garbo made a successful talkie debut, while John Gilbert's was disastrous and Charles Chaplin did not deign to make talkies for a decade. But there were scores of other major silent stars and literally thousands of lesser lights who also made at least a single sound picture. Many actually made hundreds.

Some background on the transition period might be useful. For one thing, it is probably true that a majority of silent actors and actresses experienced varying degrees of career decline after sound came. It is also true that some went on to even greater heights than they would have achieved had the cinema remained silent.

What were some of the reasons for their success or failure? The performers certainly had widely divergent backgrounds. Some had previous theater experience; some had none. They were from all parts of the United States and the world, so their accents varied widely. There was no readily apparent common thread and, contrary to popular lore (and the film *Singin' in the Rain*), they did not necessarily have voices like fingernails being dragged across a blackboard.

In truth, many factors influenced their fates, for good or ill. Perhaps most importantly, the addition of spoken dialogue to film created a new art form, or at the very least, a new medium. Actors had to do more than just recite the lines that previously would have appeared on intertitles. Acting styles needed to be adjusted, and the interaction between actors and audience was entirely and forever altered.

As the 1920s drew to a close, there were still a large number of performers who had been around since the early teens and even before. There was an inevitable desire for fresh faces. In addition, some of these veterans were now getting too old to play the type of roles they were known for. This was especially true of the actresses who had reached their mid-thirties, an age when romantic leads for women got scarcer.

The advent of sound gave the studios new leverage over their stables of stars. When contracts expired, studio heads seized the opportunity to cut the salaries of some of their high-priced stars under the threat of dismissal. Some were indeed released and had to freelance, generally at lower salaries and with lesser studios. Some may even have chosen to freelance, thinking that they would do better. This choice was to their disadvantage in most cases.

Another ploy used by studios was to cite problems of "temperament." In the late 1920s and very early 1930s, many performers were released for that all-purpose reason. Certain stars who believed themselves indispensable probably did play into the moguls' hands with behavior that could be described as uncooperative. News accounts are replete with stories of "nervous breakdowns" and other physical problems, real or imaginary. Underneath many such problems one could no doubt discover the bottom line. Studio financial motives were probably behind most of these dismissals.

It is obvious that some actors and actresses had little going for them besides their physical appearance. They had "faces," to paraphrase Norma Desmond in *Sunset Blvd.*, and many had been proficient silent players, but the demands of roles in which they had to use their voices were simply beyond their talents.

It is important to note that despite years of development, the apparatus used in the earliest talkies was seriously unreliable. Many voices were recorded improperly and made to sound worse than they were. For example, the lisping, sibilant Vitaphone "s" was notorious. Equipment often malfunctioned in theaters, and many critics reviewed the sound quality of films as well as their content.

The wise performers, if they could manage it, delayed their sound debuts until 1929 or even 1930, by which time the technology had improved. By then actors no longer all had to huddle around a microphone concealed in a potted plant.

Of course, some performers simply did have unsuitable voices. Sometimes a voice did not correspond with the actor's physical image or persona. Some voices had heavy regional or foreign accents. There may have been an actual speech impediment, or at least an amusingly odd pitch or nasal twang. In many cases the vocal problem was less definable. A performer's voice simply lessened his or her appeal. In particular, women and men with beautiful faces often found that the addition of even technically good voices turned them from screen luminaries into ordinary actors and actresses. Ironically, efforts to improve their elocution often made matters worse because their now "cultured" voices were even further out of synch with their personas.

In the early days of talkies, some fine-sounding voices coming from the screen were not actually the stars' own voices. A few of the stars, especially actresses, had their voices dubbed by others. That practice obviously could not have continued over the course of an individual's entire career. Many stars went on vaudeville tours or had plays written for them so they could gain stage experience and prove they could "talk." These efforts usually did little to enhance their screen popularity.

In some cases there just was no discernible reason for the decline of a film career. There was only a belief that the performer was "through," even though looks and talent may have been undiminished. In Hollywood — then as now — perception was frequently the reality. Once performers were perceived to be through, they *were* through. Their careers may have continued limping along but when they appeared on the screen they were referred to as "silent" or "former" stars or were described as attempting a "comeback."

The 1936 film *Hollywood Boulevard* brought many of the veteran faces back to the screen. While some reviews looked upon this favorably, *The New York Times* probably expressed the view of most of the oldtimers involved: "We felt pathetically embarrassed for the former stars and featured players who appeared as extras, bit players and background. Hollywood, having neglected them all these years, at least should have had the decency and good taste not to make them parade themselves as Exhibits A, B and C of the Forgotten Men and Women of Filmdom."

Silent film star Betty Blythe, who made over 120 films, spoke of those like herself who had risen high and fallen far: "We pass out suddenly and cruelly, still in the full vigor of our youth, just when we have mastered the technique of film acting. Often … we are dead some time before we realize it. One day we hold Hollywood in our hand, and the next moment we are out of it. We are condemned without a hearing, and execution often comes without warning."

Although this is a poignant statement, and was unfortunately ofttimes true, some went on to flourish in talkies. This book describes the fate of 500 of those who crossed the chasm: great and lesser silent film performers who became the "one-shot" wonders, the fabulously successful, and the everything-in-between of the talkies.

The Entries

This biographical encyclopedia includes those actors and actresses who made at least *three* silent films and who had some starring or supporting roles in sound. An attempt has been made to include all the major stars of the silents, and there are numerous more obscure players as well.

Some stars are not included because they made fewer than three silents: for instance, Claudette Colbert, Edward G. Robinson, Joan Bennett and Lew Ayres. Others, such as Clark Gable, John Wayne and Jean Harlow, were essentially bit players or extras in silent films. Stars whose silent careers were entirely in foreign countries, like Marlene Dietrich, and those who made films in America but who returned to a foreign country for their talkie careers, like Emil Jannings, Percy Marmont and Carlyle Blackwell, are also not included.

Each entry contains a place of birth or, occasionally, more than one if the birthplace is not known with certainty. Birth and death dates are provided; if a birth date is not firmly established, a range is provided. Although it can be assumed that the earliest year is the accurate one, this is not always the case.

Every attempt has been made to provide real names, nicknames, and stage names for each performer as appropriate. Nicknames appear in quotation marks, e.g. Roscoe Arbuckle ("Fatty"). A performer best known by a stage name is listed under that name, with the real name following in parentheses.

Many of the entries begin by citing a source or sources for a filmography of the performer, usually film periodicals or biographies. Although not cited in the entries, there are several books available that contain nothing but filmographies. It must be cautioned that some of these sources are not always completely accurate.

Following the filmography source note is a capsule account of the performer's silent and sound careers. The title and year of the performer's last silent film was determined by consulting filmographies or the *American Film Institute Catalog of Motion Pictures Produced in the United States*. The film cited is the last silent released, not necessarily the last made. Again, caution must be taken. The information is based on the documentary record available at the time the sources were produced, and there may be inaccuracies.

Because this reference book is intended to be a record of how performers made the transition, excerpts from selected reviews (10 or fewer) of *sound films only* are provided. Brief comments on the performer's career follow these review citations. The information in each entry is intended only to provide an overview of the performer's career and is not meant to be comprehensive.

More About Reviews

This book contains paraphrased judgments or comments made by contemporaneous (and occasionally later) reviewers of sound films. These can provide clues as to whether players were succeeding in talkies. Sometimes a performer was not mentioned at all even when he or she was the nominal lead. This tells its own story.

The author attempted to locate reviews from various periods of a performer's talkie career, although the earlier sound films are favored. If a performer's career was brief, reviews of all the sound films may be excerpted.

It should be noted that sometimes films were produced by very minor and even fly-by-night studios. Some pictures were so obscure that no reviews were found at all for a few players. Westerns, in particular, often were not reviewed widely.

Reviewers mostly wrote for the moviegoing public, but sometimes they aimed at other audiences. *Harrison's Reports and Reviews* (abbreviated as *Harrison's Reports* in the excerpts), which was published from 1919 to 1963, was directed to the theater managers who booked the films. Harrison's reviews often referred to the moral content of a film and whether it would appeal to "high class" audiences or the "masses."

If the reader is interested in seeing other reviews of these performers' films, such works as James M. Salem's *A Guide to Critical Reviews* (Scarecrow Press, 1971) and Patricia and Stephen Hanson's *Film Review Index* (Oryx Press, 1986–1987) provide sources for reviews. The latter covers the years from 1882.

The author hopes you will enjoy reading about these players as much as he enjoyed writing about them. As more films are rediscovered and restored, these mostly long-forgotten actors and actresses will be rediscovered as well. Whether they successfully leaped the chasm or were effectively silenced by sound, they can be appreciated for what they contributed to the art of the cinema.

The Encyclopedia

Adorée, Renée (Renée La Fonte or de la
Fonte), Lille, France, 1896/98–1933
Filmography: *Films in Review* (June/July 1968)
Silent: Renée Adorée arrived in New York from
Europe in 1919 and appeared in several Broadway
musicals. Her first American film role was in *The
Strongest* (1920); there may have been an earlier
Australian film as well. Her first major dramatic
role came in *The Eternal Struggle*. She appeared in
various genres, including westerns, before her
memorable portrayal of the French peasant girl in
1925's *The Big Parade* which teamed her with frequent co-star John Gilbert.

For a brief while Adorée was considered top
MGM star material, leading to her pairing with
Lon Chaney in *The Black Bird* and, most notably,
in *La Bohème* with Gilbert and Lillian Gish. The remainder of her silent career was not very distinguished although she was occasionally top-billed.
Included in Renée Adorée's more than 35 silent
films were *Mr. Wu* (with Chaney), *West of Chicago*,
The Bandolero, *On Ze Boulevard*, *Man and Maid*
and *The Exquisite Sinner*. Her last silent: *The Pagan*
(1929), technically a silent with singing sequences,
including the popular "Pagan Love Song" sung by
Ramon Novarro.

Sound: There were only three roles in Renée
Adorée's talkie career, all in support. The first was
in the part-talkie *The Spieler* (1928). A 1929 film,
Redemption, was her last teaming with John
Gilbert; because of its perceived poor quality, it
was not released for a year. Adorée's last role was
in the musical melodrama *The Call of the Flesh*
(1930), again with Novarro.

Comments: The height of Renée Adorée's brief
stardom came in the mid–1920s. After *La Bohème*
her films were run-of-the-mill and it was not likely
she would have prospered in starring roles in
sound. Her accent began to limit her possibilities
in talkies although her English was clearly understandable.

By 1929 Adorée was already ill with the tuber-
culosis which finally claimed her life. In her last
talkie her thinness was a stark contrast to the
plump figure she often exhibited (and had to fight
against) during the 1920s. She collapsed during the
shooting of *The Call of the Flesh* and barely completed her role, although she gave a nice lighthearted performance.

Reviews

The Spieler: Adorée's accent is captivating and
she looks unusually attractive. Her performance is
charming and classy. *Harrison's Reports* 1/26/29,
New York Times 2/25/29, *Variety* 2/27/29.

Redemption: Adorée is a gypsy and she declaims
her lines. *New York Times* 5/3/30. *Harrison's Reports* 5/10/30.

Call of the Flesh: Adorée plays a Spanish dancer.
She is good in her light comedy interludes in sup-
port of Ramon Novarro. *New York Times* 9/13/30,
Variety 9/17/30, *Harrison's Reports* 9/20/30.

Agnew, Robert (Bobby), Dayton, Kentucky,
1899/1900–1983
Silent: One of the popular juveniles of the early
1920s was handsome former "Arrow Collar Boy"
Robert Agnew. He entered pictures about 1920 in
The Frisky Mrs. Johnson and *The Valley of Doubt*.
His first lead was in 1921's *The Highest Law* and in
that year he appeared in films with Norma Talmadge.

Throughout the '20s, Agnew played supporting
roles and beginning in mid-decade had leads in
*Gold Heels, Troubles of a Bride, The Taxi Mystery,
Tessie* and *The College Hero* for Universal, Famous
Players-Lasky and Fox. Other films included *The
Sign on the Door, Bluebeard's Eighth Wife, Wine,
Private Affairs* and *Snowbound*. Last silent: *The
Heart of Broadway* (1928).

Sound: Just as Bobby Agnew's career as a romantic lead was beginning to find success, sound
came in and his prospects almost immediately
began to wane. His first talkie was Warner Bros.'

Midnight Taxi (1928), one of the early Vitaphone pictures, in 1928. He did not make another until 1930's *Extravagance* and *The Woman Racket*.

Agnew's last major role was as second lead (with Myrna Loy) in *The Naughty Flirt* in 1931. His roles in his last two, *Gold Diggers of 1933* and *Little Man, What Now?* (1934), were mere bits. (He was cast as the "dance director" in the former.)

Robert Agnew did not break all ties with the industry. After his on-camera career had ended, he became a production manager at Warners and in the 1950s worked behind the scenes on many well-known television series.

Reviews

The Midnight Taxi: Agnew plays a minor role but his voice allows him further opportunities in talkies. *Variety* 10/31/28.

Albertson, Frank, Fergus Falls, Minnesota, 1909–1964

Filmography: List of films in *Films in Review* (Apr. 1964), with additional films (May–Sept. 1964)

Silent: Frank Albertson began his lengthy career behind the scenes in Hollywood as a prop boy in the early '20s and also did extra work from 1922. Ultimately his all–American boy freshness placed him before the cameras. Signing with Fox, he made only three silents, the first two, *The Farmer's Daughter* and *Prep and Pep*, coming in 1928. Last silent: *Blue Skies* (1929), with synchronized music and sound effects.

Sound: For the first 20 years of the sound era, there was rarely a year without several Frank Albertson roles (eight in 1930 alone). Some of these were leads or second leads but his was mainly a supporting career. His first talkie was the musical revue *Words and Music* (1929), followed that year by *Salute* and *Happy Days*.

Albertson's films included *Midshipman Jack, Navy Blue and Gold, Spring Is Here, Wake Island, Dr. Christian Meets the Women, Here Comes Elmer, Arson Squad* and *Bachelor Mother*. Among his more prestigious efforts were *Alice Adams* (in an atypical and convincingly performed role as Katharine Hepburn's ne'er-do-well brother), *The Plainsman, It's a Wonderful Life, Psycho* and *The Last Hurrah*. He also appeared in the 1932 serial *The Lost Special*.

Albertson was less active after the late 1940s. He was not on the screen at all from 1949 to 1955 but returned in 1956 to make a few more films. His last came in 1963; in that year he appeared in *Papa's Delicate Condition, Johnny Cool* and *Bye Bye Birdie*. He was also much seen on television.

Comments: Frank Albertson had the kind of looks and high-pitched, yet husky, voice that made him ideal for callow or earnest youth roles. Early in his career he frequently played characters with names like Skeet, Kicker and Junior. He was equally adept at comedy or melodrama and eventually proved to be a most competent actor.

Albertson's richly comic turn as Katharine Hepburn's brother Walter in *Alice Adams* (1935) is probably one of his best-remembered. As he aged, his roles got smaller but he became one of Hollywood's dependable supporting actors and always brought a touch of color to his characterizations, however brief.

Reviews

Salute: Albertson, in his role as the proverbial fresh plebe, shows good future potential with dialogue. He is a stand out, even funnier than black comedian Stepin Fetchit. *Variety* 8/21/29.

Alice Adams: Albertson turns in a fine performance. *Variety* 8/21/35.

Bachelor Mother: Albertson is prominent in support, with an excellent portrayal. *Variety* 7/5/39.

The Enemy Below: In a lesser role, Albertson is very good. *Variety* 11/27/57.

Alden, Mary, New Orleans, Louisiana, 1883–1946

Silent: After theater experience, Mary Alden became part of the D. W. Griffith "stock company" in the early 'teens. Her feature appearances began about 1914 with such films as *The Battle of the Sexes* and *The Lily and the Rose*, and the next year she made *Birth of a Nation* in which she played her best-remembered role as the scheming mulatto housekeeper.

Alden was a busy supporting actress (and in occasional leads, e.g., 1925's *Siege*) through the '20s, playing many mother roles. Her films included *Macbeth, The Land of Promise, The Narrow Path, Erstwhile Susan, Notoriety, The Plastic Age, Brown of Harvard* and *Ladies of the Mob*. Last silent: *Someone to Love* (1928).

Sound: *Girl Overboard*, a 1929 part-talkie, was Mary Alden's first. In talkies her roles diminished to small parts (sometimes very small, including briefly seen maids) and she did not make another feature appearance until 1931. Among her films were *Politics, Strange Interlude, Rasputin and the Empress, The Great Hotel Mystery, Gentle Julia* and 1937's *That I May Live*, her last known film.

Alexander, Ben (Nicholas Alexander),
Goldfield, Nevada, 1910/11–1969

Filmography: Academy of Motion Picture Arts and Sciences

Silent: It is perhaps hard to imagine that Jack Webb's jowly sidekick on the popular TV series *Dragnet* was a golden-haired child star with page boy haircut and bangs. But Ben(nie) Alexander was just that in the 'teens. He began at the age of about three for C. B. DeMille (*Each Pearl a Tear*) and then appeared in such well-known later films as D.W. Griffith's *Hearts of the World* and Mary Pickford's *The Little American*.

Other early features included *Little Orphan Annie*, *Tangled Threads*, *The Family Honor* and *The Triflers*. In the 1920s he continued his sometimes top-billed appearances in *The Heart Line*, *Boy of Mine*, *Penrod and Sam* (as Penrod), *Pampered Youth*, *A Self-Made Failure*, *Frivolous Sal* and others. He also was seen in the 1926 serial *Scotty of the Scouts*. Last silent: *The Highbinders* (1926).

Sound: Ben Alexander made his sound debut in style as one of the German soldier-comrades in *All Quiet on the Western Front* (1930). Subsequent, mostly supporting roles came from 1931 to '38 and there were a few scattered thereafter. They included *This Day and Age*, *Stage Mother*, *Are These Our Children?*, *Many a Slip*, *The Life of Vergie Winters*, *Western Gold* and *It's a Wise Child*.

Alexander had a fine baritone voice and he eventually drifted into radio announcing interspersed with occasional small film roles. *Dragnet*, both the television show and the film, and the series *Felony Squad* brought him his last taste of fame in the 1950s and 1960s. He had been out of films from 1941 to 1954.

REVIEWS

Dragnet: Laughs might be provoked by a fight scene in which Jack Webb and his police sidekick, Ben Alexander, are involved. Otherwise Alexander is seen to advantage. The unwelcome laughs would no doubt be due to the physical shape, or lack thereof, of Ben Alexander. *Variety 8/25/54.*

Alvarado, Don (also known as Don Page,
Jose Page or Paige), Albuquerque, New Mexico, 1900/04–1967

Silent: Don Alvarado had his first small roles in 1925's *Satan in Sables* and *The Pleasure Buyers*. Handsome and Hispanic, he sometimes found himself in "Latin lover" and other exotic roles. Among his films, including a couple for D. W. Griffith, were *The Battle of the Sexes*, *Loves of Carmen*, *The Scarlet Lady*, *Driftwood*, *The Night Cry* and *Drums of Love*. Last silent: *The Apache* (1928).

Sound: Alvarado continued his "Latin" roles in the 1929 part-sound *The Bridge of San Luis Rey* and the popular RKO musical *Rio Rita*. He never achieved stardom and his 1930s films were generally mediocre. They included *Beau Ideal*, *Black Beauty*, *Sweet Adeline*, *Rio Grande Romance*, *A Trip to Paris*, *Cafe Society* and *One Night in the Tropics*.

Don Alvarado also made a few Spanish language versions of Hollywood films in the mid–1930s and then became an assistant director at Warner Bros. in 1937. He appeared in an occasional '40s film; his final one may have been *The Big Steal* in 1949.

REVIEWS

The Bridge of San Luis Rey: Although the film is condemned and there is very little dialogue, the cast is of high quality and special excellence is shown in the playing of Don Alvarado as a twin brother. *Variety 5/22/29, Harrison's Reports 5/25/29.*

Beau Ideal: Not comparable to *Beau Geste*. Don Alvarado struck poses as the leading heavy. *Harrison's Reports 1/17/31, Variety 1/21/31.*

Rio Grande Romance: Don Alvarado is of secondary interest, getting about three minutes of screen time, all of them show him registering worry. *Variety 5/12/37.*

Ames, Robert, Hartford, Connecticut, 1889–
1931

Silent: Suavely handsome Broadway star Robert Ames made his first film *What Women Want* in 1920. He returned in '25 and '26 for a few more including *The Wedding Song*, *Without Mercy* and *The Crown of Lies*.

Ames played the romantic lead in the silent version of the Marion Davies starrer *Marianne* (1929) but the film was remade in sound with a different actor. Last silent: *Voice of the City* (1929).

Sound: With his smooth voice, Robert Ames became more popular when talkies arrived and most of his 1929 pictures were sound. His most prominent role was probably as Gloria Swanson's unworthy beloved in her talkie debut *The Trespasser*. Others that year included *Nix on Dames* and *Rich People*.

Ames made 12 films in 1930 and '31, including *Holiday*, *A Lady to Love*, *Madonna of the Streets*, *Behind Office Doors*, *Millie* and *War Nurse*. His final film *Tomorrow and Tomorrow* was released in 1932 after his suicide.

REVIEWS

The Trespasser: Robert Ames does not quite get over being out-acted and out-spoken by Gloria

Swanson in most of his scenes. *Variety* (U.K. review) 10/2/29.

Nix on Dames: It is considered to be a poor film with no boxoffice names, but Robert Ames is adequate in his part. *Variety* 11/27/29, *Harrison's Reports* 11/30/29.

A Lady to Love: Although none of the characters is considered sympathetic, as the hired hand Robert Ames is very good. *Variety* 3/5/30, *Harrison's Reports* 3/8/30.

Directed by Swedish great Victor Seastrom (Sjostrom), this was based on Sidney Howard's *They Knew What They Wanted.*

War Nurse: Ames has very little to do in this but the cast all does good acting. *Variety* 10/29/30, *Harrison's Reports* 11/1/30.

Millie: Robert Ames does well enough. *Variety* 2/11/31.

Smart Woman: Ames, as the hero, is presented as a person with little common sense. *Variety* 10/13/31, *Harrison's Reports* 10/17/31.

Tomorrow and Tomorrow: Already referred to as "the late Robert Ames," he plays the husband. *Variety* 2/2/32.

Anderson, G(ilbert) M(axwell)

("Broncho Billy") (Max Aronson), Little Rock, Arkansas, 1882–1971

Silent: Between 1909 and 1915 G. M. Anderson is said to have made over 350 one- and two-reelers (one or more each week), most them featuring the good-bad man character Broncho Billy. The first picture starring Billy may have been *Broncho Billy's Redemption* (circa 1910).

Anderson had bought the rights to the Peter Kyne character for some $50, an investment well worth making considering the financial return on the popular films. Each story was self-contained. Billy may have been married, or even killed, in one installment but the next one was a whole new story.

Anderson's screen debut could have come as early as 1902 in *The Messenger Boy's Mistake* and he can be seen in several roles in Edwin Porter's epochal *The Great Train Robbery* in 1903. Among other early films were *Broncho Billy's Christmas Dinner, The Cowboy Coward, Broncho Billy's Last Spree, Broncho Billy and the Redskin* and *Broncho Billy's Sentence.*

Anderson also directed many of his films. He attempted an acting comeback in 1919 with a series of five-reel westerns which were not successful. That year he starred in the final Broncho Billy movie, the feature *The Son-of-a-Gun.* A co-founder in 1907 of the Essanay Film Company (he was the "ay," his partner George K. Spoor was the "Ess"), Anderson also was involved in making other people's films, including those of Charlie Chaplin. He continued to direct and produce until about 1922. When he was at Metro he produced the films of Stan Laurel. Last silent: *Lucky Dog* (1919).

Sound: G. M. Anderson was presented with an honorary Academy Award in 1958 for his contributions to the film industry. Several years later he set what must be a record for the length of time between a last silent appearance and a first sound film appearance: He made his talkie debut more than 45 years after his last silent in 1965's *The Bounty Killer,* in which he had but a single line in one scene.

Because he was a true pioneering actor and a studio owner, very few others in the history of cinema can claim as much distinction as G. M. Anderson. A tall, burly man with a profile resembling carved granite, he made westerns that were truly redolent of the real West. While the stories may have been fanciful, their costuming and dusty, humble settings were certainly realistic enough.

As a businessman Anderson perhaps was less successful, although Essanay was a profitable studio for many years. He was endowed with a prickly personality which caused problems not only with his partner Spoor but also later when he was an employee of other studios.

For decades Anderson lived in obscurity, a mere footnote to film history. The Oscar redressed this to some degree. Being back in harness and finally being able to speak aloud from the screen was undoubtedly a major thrill for the old man.

Arbuckle, Roscoe ("Fatty"), Smith Center, Kansas, 1887–1933

Silent: After many years of stage, carnival and vaudeville experience, Roscoe "Fatty" Arbuckle entered films about 1908 or '09 with Selig. He eventually moved to Keystone where, for Mack Sennett, he became an extremely popular star in many one- and two-reelers in 1913–15.

Arbuckle's teaming with Mabel Normand in opuses like *Fatty and Mabel's Wash Day* and *Fatty and Mabel's Simple Life* was very successful. Although very obese, he was a natural athlete who had tremendous coordination and agility. He utilized these gifts well when he left Sennett to found his own company Comique, for which he made successful two-reelers throughout the remainder of the 1910s. He also directed and produced many of them.

It was in one of Comique's 1917 comedies, *The Butcher Boy,* that Buster Keaton made his debut. He stayed with the hefty comic until Arbuckle signed with Paramount and moved into features about 1920. His first was *The Round Up,* a comedy with many straight dramatic elements. Others were *Brewster's Millions* and *The Life of the Party*. *Crazy to Marry* (1921) proved to be his last feature released.

Some of Arbuckle's films were still awaiting release when the 1921 sex scandal around the death of bit player Virginia Rappe broke. It was the end of his silent acting career, although some of his later films had European showings.

The public was outraged over Arbuckle's presumed guilt and the studios blacklisted him, although he could be spotted briefly in a 1923 film. After three trials he was finally acquitted, but he remained a pariah on-screen.

Arbuckle did not remain completely inactive, however, eventually working behind the scenes directing films under the pseudonym of William B. Goodrich (possibly an ironic version of Will Be Good?). Among his work was *The Red Mill* with Marion Davies and *Special Delivery*, an Eddie Cantor starrer. There were also some Educational shorts starring his nephew Al St. John.

Sound: With the passage of the years, Arbuckle began to find his way back into favor and was signed by Warner Bros. to appear in a series of comedy shorts in 1932. The first of these was *Hey, Pop!* in November of that year.

Others in the Arbuckle series included *How've You Been?*, *In the Dough*, *Close Relations*, *Bussin' Around* and *Tomalio*. He had just been signed to a feature contract when death claimed him. In the 1960s some of the comic's work was seen in the compilations *When Comedy Was King* and *Days of Thrills and Laughter*.

Roscoe Arbuckle was a shadow (albeit not physically) of his former self when he made his sound shorts. His clowning, often so inspired when he was at the top, seemed somewhat forced and mirthless. While it is unlikely that he would have been a major star in talkies, he proved that he could "talk" and he certainly might have been effective as a character actor. It is generally agreed that as a director he was uninspired.

Would "Fatty" Arbuckle have been content to be some western star's sidekick after his glorious years at the top? He had, after all, been one of the highest paid performers of his day. It will never be known for sure but, after the years in the wilderness, he probably would have accepted almost any work.

There is no doubt that Arbuckle was badly treated by Hollywood. Those who knew him well said he was a kind and generous man who had been utterly destroyed by his ordeal. Perceptive as usual, Louise Brooks said of him: "He had been very nice and sweetly dead ever since the scandal that ruined his career."

Perhaps Roscoe Arbuckle would not, after all, have been allowed to pursue his career. Even at the last, when he had been "forgiven" by Hollywood, his films still were banned in Great Britain.

Arlen, Richard (Richard Van Mattimore),
Charlottesville, Virginia, 1898/1900–1976
Filmography: *Films in Review* (June/July 1979); *Classic Images* (July 1990)

Silent: After working as an extra from the early 1920s, Paramount player Richard Arlen had his first lead (under the name Van Mattimore) in 1923's *Vengeance of the Deep*. Then it was back to bit and extra work until a supporting role in *In the Name of Love* (1925) began his career in earnest. Not counting his extra/bit work, he had roles in more than 20 silent films.

The most famous of Arlen's pictures was most certainly *Wings* (1927), an enormously popular tale of World War I fliers directed by William Wellman. Among his silent film co-stars were Clara Bow, Louise Brooks (*Rolled Stockings*, *Beggars of Life*) and Bebe Daniels (*She's a Sheik*, *Feel My Pulse*). Last silent: *The Four Feathers* (1929), with synchronized music and sound effects, released after his first talkie.

Sound: Richard Arlen's first sound film was *The Man I Love* (1929). He made about 100 in all, most in starring roles. A notable early talkie was 1929's *The Virginian*. He appeared in many other westerns including a well-made series based on Zane Grey stories.

Undoubtedly Arlen's best-remembered talkie is *Island of Lost Souls* (1932), which has become a minor classic of the horror genre. Another well-received film of the early '30s was *Tiger Shark*. In his active career, lasting about 40 years, he made pictures in all genres, including over 35 westerns, but his specialty was the action-adventure.

Beginning about 1939, Richard Arlen appeared in a long string of melodramas, many with plots involving flying, wartime heroics, and other rugged enterprises. These included such revelatory titles as *Power Dive*, *Submarine Alert*, *The Devil's Pipeline*, *Legion of the Lost Flyers*, *Forced Landing*, *Flying Blind*, *The Wrecking Crew* and *Speed to Spare*.

After Arlen left his longtime home, Paramount, in 1944, his career began to falter, but his appearances for other studios (including Republic, PRC and Universal) continued fairly steadily through the rest of the 1940s. Roles became more sporadic in the 1950s but he was still to be seen in supporting and small parts through much of the 1960s.

Richard Arlen's later pictures were generally westerns but there were also films such as *The*

Mountain and *The Best Man*. His final film appearance — the year of his death — was in a cameo in the unsuccessful spoof *Won Ton Ton, the Dog Who Saved Hollywood*.

Comments: In the opinion of many, Richard Arlen was never more than a journeyman actor, yet his career lasted far longer than that of almost all his silent film (*and* talkie) contemporaries. True, his deep voice proved suitable for talkies and he had, in his younger days, matinee-idol looks, but then so did many who completely dropped out of sight.

It may be paradoxical, but probable, that Arlen's very blandness as a performer helped to prolong his career. He did not have an easily identifiable persona as an actor and thus could readily fit into almost every genre except possibly comedy.

Arlen read his lines competently enough and was convincing as a rugged tough guy or even a villain. He apparently did not aspire to top stardom and was content to work in "B" films, for which there was a heavy demand when double features were the rule.

Arlen aged fairly well and so could play heroes well into his forties. It certainly helped that his films were generally short and packed with action and that colorful supporting players like Andy Devine (the comic relief in several of Arlen's melodramas) were present.

Of course, it also helped more than a little that Richard Arlen projected a likable image. This image persisted when Arlen, by then white-haired and noticeably aged, was seen in character roles which stressed his innate decency.

Reviews

The Man I Love: Arlen plays a fighter named Dum Dum. His acting is mildly praised but the story is mediocre at best. *New York Times* 5/29/29, *Harrison's Reports* 6/1/29.

Island of Lost Souls: The film is based on H. G. Wells's popular *The Island of Doctor Moreau*. Arlen's acting is acceptable. *New York Times* 1/13/33, *Variety* 1/17/33.

Hell and High Water: "Mediocre" is the kindest word used for the story, and both Arlen's on-screen character and amateurish characterization are panned. *Harrison's Reports* 12/16/33, *New York Times* 12/18/33.

She Made Her Bed: The picture is roundly condemned and Arlen struggles with a poorly written character. *New York Times* 4/27/34, *Variety* 5/1/34.

Flying Blind: In one of his numerous adventure-melodramas, Arlen is praised and given a good chance for regaining his popularity. *Variety* 8/20/41.

The Phantom Speaks: In this thriller Arlen is pleasing. *Variety* 6/13/45.

Speed to Spare: Another fast paced thriller in which Arlen performs well. *Variety* 2/18/48.

The Blazing Forest: The acting is generally good, including Arlen's ingratiating performance as a ne'er-do-well. It was one of his last important roles. *Variety* 10/1/52.

Warlock: In this adult western Arlen is outstanding in a small role. *Variety* 4/8/59, *New York Times* 5/1/59.

Arliss, George (George Andrews), London, England, 1868–1946

Filmography: Films in Review (Nov. 1985)

Silent: Following a lengthy theater career distinguished thespian George Arliss made his film debut in *The Devil* in 1921. It was based on one of his stage characterizations.

Arliss made only six silents in all. Three of them — *The Man Who Played God*, *Disraeli* and *The Green Goddess* (also based on his stage play) — were redone as talkies. Last silent: *$20 a Week* (1924).

Sound: George Arliss's plummy voice, with its perfect elocution of seemingly every separate syllable, was first heard in Warner Bros.' 1929 remake of *Disraeli*. It proved to be a major success and earned him an Academy Award as Best Actor.

That film can be credited (or blamed) for setting Arliss off on a series of biographical films which included *Voltaire*, *Alexander Hamilton* and *Cardinal Richelieu*. He later played the Duke of Wellington (in *The Iron Duke*) in England. The remake of the melodrama *The Green Goddess* was actually his first completed talkie but its release was withheld until the debut of *Disraeli*.

Arliss also made several comedies like *A Successful Calamity*, *The King's Vacation*, *The Working Man* and *The Last Gentleman*. One of his more popular films was *The Man Who Played God*, a melodrama that was credited with making a viable film actress of Bette Davis. *Voltaire* (1933) proved to be his last Warner Bros. film whereupon he went to Twentieth Century Pictures for *The House of Rothschild*, another big success.

In the mid-1930s, Arliss returned to England to make a film and then came back to the U.S. to play the crafty *Cardinal Richelieu*, his final American film. The last few of his approximately 20 talkies were made in England, his cinema swan song coming in *Doctor Syn* (1937).

Comments: George Arliss was an unlikely leading man for American talking pictures. He was past 60 at the time *Disraeli* was made and he seemed not to be the type who could attract contemporary American audiences just emerging from the Jazz

Age. Certainly his silent films had not been notable successes.

In addition, Arliss had a long horsey face and in contemporary photographs his fastidiously groomed appearance and monocle make him seem like a refugee from another century. Everything seemed to be against his becoming a major star but he defied the odds and did just that.

Although Arliss could be said to have reached his peak with his first talkie, with the right roles (many based on tested stage plays) he did continue to find success. Notwithstanding the theatricality—some said hamminess—which he brought to his film performances, he was an actor of some charm and likability.

Arliss's beautifully modulated voice was made for sound. He also had another advantage: considerable control over the making of his films, even director approval. He carefully crafted his basic screen image as a wily and cunning but kindly man who always seemed to be assisting young lovers.

Probably Arliss is best-known (but not necessarily praised) for the handful of biographical films he did. A wag said every famous man in history looked like George Arliss and he was criticized for being "The Man with One Face."

Arliss said in his own defense, "I am strongly of the opinion that no actor who is playing a long and important part should have his features monkeyed with." Audiences of the early 1930s did not mind that he was always "George Arliss"; they came to the theater to see his larger-than-life characterizations just as they were.

REVIEWS

Disraeli: Arliss is on his mettle and he lends to the role an artistry and vigor that is a joy to behold. In his first talking film he realizes that it is but one performance and it must be his best work. His voice is smooth and he betrays not the slightest anxiety concerning the microphone. He makes the role vivid and appealing, and he rises to the same heights that he rose to in the play. *New York Times* 10/3/29, *Variety* 10/9/29, *Harrison's Reports* 10/12/29.

The Green Goddess: Arliss gives his usual polished performance, and he is as artistic as ever, but the average American does not relish seeing an oriental trying to win over a white woman. *New York Times* 2/14/30, *Harrison's Reports* 2/22/30.

Arliss played the Rajah of a mythical Himalayan kingdom.

Alexander Hamilton: Even though it's dull entertainment, Arliss wins other feather for his cap and gives a fine sensitive portrayal with consummate skill. *New York Times* 9/17/31, *Variety* 9/22/31.

The Man Who Played God: Mr. Arliss delivers another of his effective and meticulous portrayals. He does good acting but is unconvincing as a man who is loved by two women, for he is not a young, romantic figure. This is one of the reasons why the pictures in which he appears do not draw young people and the masses. *New York Times* 2/11/32, *Harrison's Reports* 2/20/32.

A Successful Calamity: Arliss's saccharine outlook and hoyden ways continue. It would be well for him not to try his fans' patience much further with this sort of fluff. *Variety* 9/27/32.

The King's Vacation: George Arliss gives another of his pleasing impersonations, and plays his role in his usual suave, quiet fashion. One drawback is that the romance of the story is built about Arliss, who is not a romantic figure. For the majority of his followers he won't be missed in stories such as this. *New York Times* 1/20/33, *Harrison's Reports* 1/28/33, *Variety* 1/31/33.

Voltaire: Opinion was divided. Some thought the picture creaks with staginess and even Arliss seems to be overacting. Others said that he added to his histrionic laurels by a thoroughly intriguing portrait and that it was as effective as Mr. Arliss's previous historical portrayals. His acting is smooth and painstaking. *Harrison's Reports* 8/19/33, *New York Times* 8/23/33.

The House of Rothschild: In a superb characterization, Arliss outshines any performance he has contributed to the screen; his acting is of the highest order. His diction is smooth and admirably suited to his work. His artistry makes of the character a proud man, at times cunning, but always sympathetic. *New York Times* 3/15/34, *Harrison's Reports* 3/17/34, *Variety* 3/20/34.

Arliss played a dual role in this film, probably the greatest hit he had after *Disraeli*.

The Last Gentleman: In his role as a crotchety old man, Arliss drops into this featherweight comedy a genuinely ingratiating gaiety. *Harrison's Reports* 7/28/34, *New York Times* 10/18/34.

Doctor Syn: Critical opinion differed. One review said that with Arliss in the name part it doesn't ring true, is hardly suitable for American audiences, and is below the level of entertainment one expects of a George Arliss picture. Others thought it charming and played as only Arliss can. *Variety* 9/8/37, *Harrison's Reports* 10/30/37, *New York Times* 11/15/37.

Arliss somewhat improbably played an ex-pirate and smuggler in his last film.

Arthur, George K. (Arthur George Brest),
Littlehampton, Surrey or Aberdeen, Scotland, 1899–

Filmography: *Films in Review* (Mar. 1962)

Silent: George K. Arthur had a hit with his first English film *Kipps*. A follow-up film, *Paddy the Next Best Thing*, one of two made in England with Mae Marsh, was also a success. His first American role came in *Madness of Youth* (1922).

It was Arthur's appearance in von Sternberg's 1925 oddity *The Salvation Hunters* that led to an MGM contract. There he spent his most successful years appearing in support in prestigious "A" productions like *Irene*, *Kiki*, *Bardelys the Magnificent* and *The Student Prince* opposite most of the leading actresses, including Norma Shearer, Marion Davies, the Talmadge sisters and Joan Crawford.

Arthur had leading roles in "B" films as well. The diminutive comic actor was teamed in several popular comedies with hulking Karl Dane, including *Rookies*, *Detectives*, *Circus Rookies*, *Baby Mine* and *All at Sea*. Last silent: *China Bound* (1929).

Sound: After his sound debut with Dane in a brief comedy turn in *The Hollywood Revue of 1929*, George K. Arthur was seen in MGM films like *The Last of Mrs. Cheyney* and *Chasing Rainbows*. The studio did not renew his contract and afterwards he and Dane appeared in a series of two-reelers, first for RKO and then for Paramount in 1930–31.

Arthur tried a comeback via vaudeville but to little avail. After a further handful of ever-decreasing parts in features, including more for MGM and an English picture, he left the screen in 1935. His last role was that of a railway porter in *Vanessa: Her Love Story* in which his face was not even seen on camera.

Arthur made a worthy return to the film business in the 1950s, this time as a producer of many well-regarded short films (e.g., *The Bespoke Overcoat* and *The Caller Left No Card*) and a few features. He was successful in that endeavor for many years, garnering several awards.

Comments: The virtual end of George K. Arthur's flourishing career came swiftly. Although other actors with English accents made the transition smoothly enough, Arthur was not so fortunate. Perhaps it was his "guilt by association" with Karl Dane which linked his name with failure. They had become an established film duo and Dane had major problems with the English language.

Perhaps Arthur just did not want to play the character roles which many of his countrymen found themselves doing to their profit. But more likely perhaps, as the *New York Times* review of *The Last of Mrs. Cheyney* suggests, he simply was not a very good talkie actor.

REVIEWS

The Last of Mrs. Cheyney: The voices would be all the better if they were more natural. George K. Arthur is one of those who tries to act as he would for the silent screen and still speak his lines. What he does say is extravagant and silly. *New York Times* 8/12/29.

Arthur plays a Cockney page boy.

Chasing Rainbows: George K. Arthur has a small part in the repetitious story. *Variety* 2/26/30.

This was an unsuccessful attempt to recreate some of the magic of *The Broadway Melody*.

Looking Forward: George K. Arthur contributes good work. *New York Times* 5/1/33.

Blind Adventure: Arthur does a walk-on as an inebriated guest. *Variety* 11/7/33.

Riptide: Arthur makes the most of a minor role. *New York Times* 3/31/34.

Arthur, Jean (Gladys Greene), New York or
Plattsburgh, New York, 1898/1908–1991

Filmography: *Films in Review* (June-July 1966), *Classic Images* (Mar.-Apr. 1984), *Hollywood Studio Magazine* (Sept. 1987), *Journal of Popular Film and Television* (Spring 1989); List of films: *Film Dope* (Dec. 1972), added films (Mar. 1988); *Sweethearts of the Sage*

Silent: Before she came to films in 1923, Jean Arthur had been a model, primarily in print advertising. Her early efforts on-screen included one- and two-reel comedies, *Somebody Lied* presumably being the first. She was also seen in westerns after her feature debut in John Gilbert's *Cameo Kirby* and she appeared in the 1927 serial *The Masked Menace*.

A role in 1927's *The Poor Nut* led to a Paramount contract, during the course of which Arthur appeared mainly in supporting roles. She was dubbed a 1929 Wampas Baby Star after having made about 30 features that included *The Drug Store Cowboy*, *Seven Chances*, *Tearin' Loose*, *The Fighting Cheat*, *The Broken Gate*, *Wallflowers* and *Sins of the Fathers*. Last silent: *Stairs of Sand* (1929), made after her first talkie.

Sound: *Brotherly Love*, a 1928 part-talkie, marked Jean Arthur's sound debut. It starred the popular MGM comedy team of George K. Arthur (no relation) and Karl Dane. *The Canary Murder Case* was her first fully sound picture in 1929. She made four other talkies that year including *The Greene Murder Case* and *The Mysterious Dr. Fu Manchu*.

It was obvious that sound was not proving a boon to Arthur's career despite her unique voice.

Her film parts continued to be insignificant ingenues — *The Gang Buster, The Ex-Bad Boy, Street of Chance* and *The Silver Horde* (a good film but a conventional role). When she left Hollywood in 1931 to (as she put it) "learn to act," she landed on the Broadway stage.

When Arthur returned in 1933 for the second, and vastly more successful, phase of her 40-plus film talkie career, it was as a blonde. (She had previously appeared with her natural brunette hair color.) And she *had* gained new acting skills. Although her first few films were no better than the earlier ones (*The Past of Mary Holmes, The Defense Rests*), the big time was about to arrive with a Columbia contract.

The defining year was 1935. Two of Arthur's roles were in the successful comedies *If You Could Only Cook* and *The Whole Town's Talking*, the latter her breakthrough picture. She became a full-fledged star in Frank Capra's 1936 classic *Mr. Deeds Goes to Town*. Other notable comedy and drama roles were in *Mr. Smith Goes to Washington, Only Angels Have Wings, You Can't Take It with You* and *The More the Merrier* (she received an Academy Award nomination for Best Actress of 1943).

Jean Arthur's roles decreased, apparently by her own choice, in the mid–1940s and she was offscreen completely from 1945–47. She returned for only two more appearances, both well-regarded, in 1948's *A Foreign Affair* and 1953's *Shane*. During the hiatus she returned to Broadway for the popular success *Peter Pan* and also starred in *Saint Joan*, which did not come to Broadway.

Arthur became almost as well-known for signing on for plays in which she ultimately did *not* appear, *Born Yesterday* being the most notorious example. She made her television bow in a 1965 episode of *Gunsmoke* and the next year had her own series, the short-lived *Jean Arthur Show*. Later she taught drama in college.

Comments: Because Arthur was to become so famous for her remarkable voice, it is somewhat puzzling that the advent of sound did not immediately result in a dramatic career boost. It clearly did not, although she made the transition readily enough. Paramount, who dropped many of their top stars, considered her another minor silent actress and she was in danger of slipping irretrievably into quickies.

Arthur may have been quite correct in saying that she really was not a very good actress at that point; her silent career had certainly been mediocre. Her absence from the screen in the early '30s, subsequent stage experience and physical makeover enabled her to return as virtually a new face. Suddenly Jean Arthur's husky, melodious voice was considered a remarkable instrument and was compared to "a thousand tinkling bells." She was able to work with such outstanding directors as Frank Capra and George Stevens and co-stars like Jimmy Stewart and Gary Cooper.

Stewart said of Arthur that she "was the finest actress I ever worked with. No one had her humor, her timing." Stevens called her "one of the greatest comediennes the screen has ever seen." Others were less kind, calling her moody, temperamental and uncooperative.

It seems both views may have been right. On the screen, Arthur portrayed independent and liberated women who could be warm, likable and sympathetic. Off-screen she apparently was almost pathologically shy and subject to extreme stage fright. She had to force herself to face a camera or a live audience, but once "on" she truly came alive.

Besides her remarkable voice, Arthur brought a consistent persona to the screen. She almost cornered the market on women who were at the same time hard-boiled yet goodhearted, clear-seeing yet dreamy. "Bemused" is a word often applied to her characters.

The "real" Jean Arthur is perhaps irrelevant. She created a body of memorable roles in screwball comedies like *The Devil and Miss Jones, You Can't Take It with You, Easy Living* and *The More the Merrier*. She will always be thought of as the ideal Capra-esque heroine.

REVIEWS

The Defense Rests: Jean Arthur does not look and sound like a lady lawyer but she tries hard to make her assignment seem authentic. *Variety* 8/21/34.

Diamond Jim: Jean Arthur is a first-rate trouper, as well as being decorative in a dual role. *Variety* 8/28/35.

Mr. Deeds Goes to Town: Jean Arthur's attempts to play a female reporter are realistic even if it's still Hollywood in some respects. *Variety* 4/22/36.

Mr. Smith Goes to Washington: Jean Arthur is excellent as the wisely cynical senatorial secretary. *Variety* 10/11/39.

Arthur received top billing over Jimmy Stewart in the title role.

Talk of the Town: Arthur adds another clean-cut comedy characterization. *Variety* 7/29/42.

A Foreign Affair: Jean Arthur is back in a top-flight characterization after a considerable screen absence. *Variety* 6/16/48.

Shane: Arthur gives the character her special brand of acting skill, which shows through the very dowdy costuming and makeup. *Variety* 4/15/53.

Arthur, Johnny (John Williams), Scottdale, Pennsylvania, 1883–1952

Silent: Diminutive Johnny Arthur was a vaudeville and Follies performer when he was signed by Sennett in the early 1920s. Besides his many appearances in two-reelers, he played supporting roles in a few features such as *The Unknown Purple*, *Daring Love* and *Mademoiselle Midnight*. Last silent feature: *The Monster* (1925), in which he had a lead opposite Lon Chaney.

Sound: Because of his distinctive voice and prissy persona, Johnny Arthur was a popular supporting player in talkies. *On Trial* (1928) marked his sound debut and all his 1929 films were talking as well. They included *The Desert Song*, *The Aviator*, *The Gamblers*, *Divorce Made Easy* and *The Show of Shows*.

Arthur remained busy through the 1930s in a series of Educational and Christie shorts as well as Our Gang comedies. He also made the Vitaphone shorts *Stimulation* and *Paper Hanging*. There were many feature appearances, with an occasional leading role, in such films as *Going Wild*, *Personality*, *She Couldn't Say No*, *Twenty Million Sweethearts*, *Crime and Punishment* and *Pick a Star*.

In the 1940s less was seen of Johnny Arthur and by the middle of the decade he was gone from the screen. He played a Japanese arch-fiend in the serial *The Masked Marvel* (1943) as well as acting in a few features like *Singapore*, *Shepherd of the Ozarks* and *That Natzy Nuisance*, in which he played another Japanese villain, Suki Yaki.

REVIEWS

On Trial: Johnny Arthur does good work. His ability to turn from comedian to tragedian adds the final dramatic touch. *Variety* 11/28/28.

Personality: This light programmer owes everything to Johnny Arthur, who is the star. *Variety* 2/26/30.

Easy Millions: Arthur ably supports the lead. *Variety* 9/26/33.

Jeepers Creepers: Playing a character bit, Arthur is amusing but sometimes overdoes his role as the rich man's secretary-valet. *Variety* 11/1/39.

Asher, Max (also Ascher), Oakland, California, 1880/85–1959

Silent: Dubbed "The Funniest Dutch Comedian in Pictures," Max Asher starred in the "Mike and Jake" series in 1913 and '14 and appeared in numerous one-reelers for Keystone, Universal and Sterling, among others, throughout the 'teens. His first feature appearance may have been in a small role in 1919's *A Yankee Princess*.

In the 1920s, Asher was a popular character actor, usually in small roles, in a variety of pictures including *Rip Van Winkle*, *Trigger Finger*, *The Snob Buster*, *We're in the Navy Now*, *Avenging Fangs*, *The Shooting of Dan McGrew* and *Play Safe*. He also continued to be seen in two-reelers, including the "What Happened to Jane" series. Last silent: *The Kid's Clever* (1929).

Sound: *Show Boat*, a 1929 part-talkie, was Max Asher's first sound endeavor. In features he was next seen in 1930's *Trigger Tricks* and *Sweethearts on Parade* and then there were scattered, brief roles over the next few years. He was also seen in shorts and the mid-'30s remake of the serial *The Perils of Pauline*.

Among Asher's other films were *Soul of the Slums*, *Subway Express*, *Rider of Death Valley* (he was a "Citizen"), *Crashin' Broadway*, *Jealousy* and finally *Little Man, What Now?* in 1934, in which he had a bit. After leaving acting he became a make-up artist.

Asther, Nils, Hellerup, Denmark or Malmo, Sweden, 1897–1981

Filmography: *Films in Review* (Aug.-Sept. 1979)

Silent: Nils Asther made his film debut about 1916 acting in Swedish and German films. His introduction to American audiences came with *Topsy and Eva* (1927) followed by the major success *Sorrell and Son*. He was a supporting player in *Our Dancing Daughters*.

Asther co-starred with Greta Garbo in two of her late silents. In one of them, *Wild Orchids*, he portrayed a Javanese prince. He was seen in 11 American silent films altogether. Last silent: *The Single Standard*, with Garbo.

Sound: Along with numerous other MGM stars, Nils Asther made the first of his 30 or so talkie appearances in the "all-singing, all-dancing" *The Hollywood Revue of 1929*. *The Sea Bat* (1930) marked his first dramatic feature role.

After a two-year absence from the screen, Asther returned to do a few supporting roles for MGM (e.g., *Letty Lynton*) and thence to RKO, Universal, Fox and Columbia where his most memorable sound film, Frank Capra's *The Bitter Tea of General Yen*, was made. Other films of the period included *If I Were Free*, *Madame Spy* and *Love Time*.

Asther was again absent from the American screen from 1934–1940, during which time he made several English films. His U.S. career resumed in 1941 with a series of films for studios such as Monogram, Universal and PRC. Among them were *Doctor Kildare's Wedding Day*, *Sweater Girl*, *Night Monster*, *Son of Lassie*, *Alaska*, *Mystery Broadcast* and *The Feathered Serpent*.

In the 1940s Asther generally appeared in "B" picture supporting roles and an occasional lead, as in *The Man in Half Moon Street* and *That Man from Tangier*, his last American film. Produced abroad, the latter picture was made in 1953. He was seen in some early 1950s TV programs and appeared in Swedish and Danish films as late as the 1960s.

Comments: Nils Asther was a handsome Swede who, because of his dark looks, was not confined to Aryan types. He readily could play exotic roles such as the one in *Wild Orchids*. His heavy accent had been a potential problem at the end of the silent era but he apparently took speech lessons and his accent became pleasantly continental. Its origin could have been from many European countries; for instance, he convincingly played Frenchmen in *Letty Lynton* and *Bluebeard*.

But Asther unquestionably did have an accent and it limited his parts in the talkie era. He rarely had starring roles and those were only in "B" pictures after the mid-'30s. His physical appearance, while romantic (he was dubbed "The Masculine Garbo"), also made him a natural for villains' roles, of which he played his share.

Asther remained a distinguished-looking and dependable presence in talkies and he did have his one chance at a really juicy part with the title role, and a fine performance, in Frank Capra's offbeat *The Bitter Tea of General Yen*. Unfortunately it led to little but mediocre roles in largely undistinguished films.

REVIEWS

The Sea Bat: In this entertaining sea story Asther is the brother. *Variety* 8/13/30.

Letty Lynton: Asther plays a South American villain and invests the role with more menace than the average love story of this type. To some extent he overplays his assignment, but nonetheless he turns in a performance that is strikingly potent. *Variety* 5/3/32.

The Bitter Tea of General Yen: A love affair between people of two dissimilar races, particularly when the woman is white, is particularly distasteful to American audiences. Also, most of the action revolves around the doings of a villain, played by Asther. However, he gives a conspicuously good performance in the title role. *Harrison's Reports* 1/7/33, *New York Times* 1/12/33, *Variety* 1/17/33.

Love Time: Asther does a nice job as Franz Schubert. *Variety* 11/6/34.

The Man in Half Moon Street: Asther plays a man over 100 years old who is kept alive with the glands of murdered young men. He portrays the mad scientist with a restraint that almost makes him appear normal, but his performance points out the incredible nature of the story even more. *New York Times* 1/20/45.

Jealousy: Asther plays the particularly unpleasant part of the heroine's husband, a man who is unbelievably selfish and cruel. *Harrison's Reports* 7/28/45.

That Man from Tangiers: Asther fills the bill neatly as the dashing and romantic count, although the film is a tedious and mediocre comedy-melodrama. *Variety* 4/15/53, *Harrison's Reports* 4/18/53.

Astor, Gertrude, Lima, Ohio, 1887–1977

Filmography: Partial filmography *Classic Images* (July 1990)

Silent: In 1915 Gertrude Astor was one of the first actresses to be put under contract when Universal Studios was established. She had begun appearing in films about a year before, making numerous one- and two-reelers as well as features throughout the silent era.

Astor's films included *Hurricane's Gal, The Impossible Mrs. Bellew, Alice Adams, Flaming Youth, The Verdict, The Cat and The Canary, Kiki* and *Synthetic Sin*. Among her serials were *The Lion's Claw* and *The Lion Man*. Last silent: *The Naughty Duchess* (1928), made after her first sound film.

Sound: After her part-talkie debut in *Hit of the Show* (1928), Astor was usually to be found far down in the cast list, except in two-reel comedies of the 1930s. A member of John Ford's "stock company," she worked steadily though the '30s, more sporadically in the '40s, and made only a handful in the next decade.

Astor's last appearance was possibly in *All in a Night's Work* (1961). Among her talkies were *Be Yourself, Wine, Women and Song, Empty Saddles, Great Guy, Misbehaving Husbands* and *All Over Town*. She was also (briefly) seen in such major films as *Dragonwyck, Around the World in Eighty Days, Jolson Sings Again* and *Sunset Blvd*.

Comments: Gertrude Astor was never a major star but she was an enduring and much-loved figure in the film industry. The statuesque blonde was tall in an era of generally petite actresses, usually being relegated to character roles as the "other woman," comedy relief or even villains.

Astor's voice was perfectly adequate for talkies and she was still attractive although no longer particularly young. The versatility she had shown throughout her career enabled her to continue on until her 70s and in 1975 she was honored with a luncheon at Universal. All her surviving directors were present, a reminder that she was not forgotten by the Hollywood of which she had been so much a part.

REVIEWS

Untamed: A romantic melodrama in which Gertrude Astor plays a vamp and the romantic rival of Joan Crawford in the latter's first starring talkie. *Harrison's Reports* 12/7/29.

Be Yourself!: In one of Fannie Brice's few films, the blonde gold digger is played stereotypically by Gertrude Astor. *Variety* 3/12/30.

Carnival Lady: Astor impresses as a palm reader. *Variety* 12/5/33.

Astor, Mary (Lucille Langehanke), Quincy, Illinois, 1906–1987

Filmography: List of films: *Film Dope* (Mar. 1973), *Stars* (Mar. 1990)

Silent: Mary Astor was one of the very few actresses who turned a beauty contest win into a really distinguished career. Starting in 1920 there were two-reel comedies for Tri-Art, then supporting roles in early features such as *The Man Who Played God* and *The Bright Shawl*.

Although she had played leads in minor films (e.g., *Puritan Passion*), Astor's first real starring role was in 1924's *Beau Brummell* opposite John Barrymore. There were off-screen fireworks between them as well.

Others of Astor's mostly undistinguished silents included *Inez from Hollywood*, *Don Juan*, *Don Q, Son of Zorro*, *The Sea Tiger*, *Two Arabian Knights* and *Romance of the Underworld*. Last silent: *The Woman from Hell* (1929).

Sound: *Ladies Love Brutes* (1930), starring George Bancroft, marked Astor's introduction to sound and she made films almost without letup until the end of the '40s and then intermittently thereafter.

Astor's 1930s films included several prestigious ones like *Red Dust*, *The Prisoner of Zenda* and especially the classic *Dodsworth*, starring Walter Huston. It was made right after a divorce and sex scandal that miraculously did not derail her career. She appeared in many major films in the '40s as well. Among them were the famous *The Maltese Falcon*, *The Great Lie* (for which she won the Best Supporting Actress Academy Award), *The Palm Beach Story* and the charming musical *Meet Me in St. Louis*.

Astor's other films included *The Lash*, *Behind Office Doors*, *The Kennel Murder Case*, *Trapped by Television*, *Paradise for Three*, *Young Ideas* and *Cass Timberlane*. She was seen in no films from 1950–55 and then made a few thereafter, among them *Youngblood Hawke*, *A Kiss Before Dying*, *A Stranger in My Arms* and *Return to Peyton Place*.

Lastly there was the gothic melodrama *Hush … Hush, Sweet Charlotte* in 1964. In it Astor, her beauty gone, had little screen time but she was ultimately revealed as the axe murderess who had propelled the action. She subsequently wrote two frank and well-received autobiographies as well as several novels.

Comments: Raven-haired Mary Astor was undeniably one of the most beautiful of silent film actresses but her roles mostly called for pretty posing, not great acting skill. That was to come in the talkies, immeasurably enhanced by her deep and melodious voice. Her off-screen lover John Barrymore apparently helped her to develop her acting ability, inculcating his theory that acting is not self-expression but expressing the idea of the writer. (He later perhaps forgot this himself.)

In the mid–1930s came the notoriety of a messy divorce and child custody battle spiced with a sex scandal. Astor's widely publicized diary revealed a vividly described and torrid love affair with, of all people, dyspeptic playwright George S. Kaufman. Rather than destroying her, the furor over the revelations may have enhanced her career by changing her virginal image forever.

The 1940s saw Astor alternating between leading and supporting roles. After signing with MGM she was relegated largely to supporting and even mother roles for which she was still far too young but which she played with charm. By and large the studio did not know what to do with her.

In her last few films, Astor still retained the quiet dignity she brought to her best screen roles. That quality may well have sprung from the misfortunes and angst of her private life about which she was refreshingly honest. Her travails may have been hell for her but they unquestionably helped to make her the really fine actress she became.

REVIEWS

Ladies Love Brutes: Mary Astor is the outstanding player in her parts as a high-bred society woman. She plays with a grace and certainty that are most engaging. *Variety* 5/21/30.

Smart Woman: Instead of building her up or carrying her along, the script wears Astor down. *Variety* 10/13/31.

Dodsworth: In her first major release since the scandal, Astor is the sympathetic other woman. Even though her footage is limited, her performance is varied and mature. *Variety* 9/30/36.

The Maltese Falcon: Astor is skillful in the role of an adventuress. Legend has it that director John Huston made Mary Astor run around the set before delivering her lines as Brigid O'Shaughnessy, in order to give them a breathless (and presumably untrustworthy) quality. *Variety* 10/1/41.

Meet Me in St. Louis: In this tuneful, merry comedy-drama, Mary Astor is the mother. *Harrison's Reports* 11/4/44.

Blonde Fever: Only Astor manages to make her somewhat thankless role as a faithful wife jell. *Variety* 11/22/44.

Act of Violence: Astor is a standout as the brassy, blowzy woman of the streets. *Variety* 12/22/48.

August, Edwin (Edwin von der Butz), 1883–1964

Silent: Beginning about 1910, "The Biograph Man" Edwin August was a matinee idol in D. W. Griffith films and later in such 1915–18 features as *Evidence, The Perils of Divorce, The Yellow Passport* and *A Broadway Scandal.* He may have made over 300 films, mostly one- and two-reelers.

August also was in the serial *The Lion's Claw* and he directed 1919's *The Poison Pen.* There were only four films in the 1920s including *The Idol of the North* and *The Blonde Vampire.* Last silent: *Scandal Sheet* (1925).

Sound: August's first talkie was *Side Street* (1929), followed by 1930's *Romance of the West.* He appeared in only a few films thereafter, mostly in the years 1935 to 1938, when he was seen in *Orchids to You, The Music Goes Round* and *The Rage of Paris.* He may have had a few very minor roles in the early 1940s as well.

Ayres, Agnes (Agnes Hinkle), Carbondale, Illinois, 1898–1940

Filmography: Films in Review (Apr. 1986)

Silent: Agnes Ayres began as an Essanay extra about 1914 in Chicago. By 1917 she was a supporting player at Vitagraph in New York, becoming known as the "O. Henry Girl" because of her appearances in two-reelers based on the author's stories. Her career took a turn upward after her arrival in Hollywood in 1919.

Ayres was soon appearing in Paramount/DeMille films such as *Held by the Enemy, The Affairs of Anatol* and *Forbidden Fruit.* In addition, she co-starred with popular Wallace Reid in several pictures. Nineteen twenty-one was the year she secured her latter-day recognition as one of the best-known of the minor silent actresses, starring opposite Rudolph Valentino in *The Sheik.*

Other silents with Ayres included *Clarence, The Ten Commandments, The Awful Truth* and *Morals for Men.* Her career began to slow in the latter '20s and she appeared in only three films in 1926–'28. One was a cameo role in *The Son of the Sheik* (she was Valentino's *mother* this time), and one was a two-reeler. Last silent: *Into the Night* (1928).

Sound: Agnes Ayres made three films in 1929. The first two, in which she had starring roles, were the part-talkies *Bye-Bye Buddy* and *Broken Hearted.* They were produced by small companies and were not reviewed, and very little is known of them. She played a supporting role in her first all-talking film *The Donovan Case,* Frank Capra's first talkie.

Ayres apparently made no further screen appearances until her return in 1936 and '37 for uncredited bits in *Maid of Salem, Small Town Girl, Midnight Taxi* and *Souls at Sea.* Although her parts were very small, there were newspaper stories about her "comeback." A role in the two-reeler *Morning, Judge* (1937) apparently marked *finis* to her career.

Comments: Pretty Agnes Ayres reached the apogee of her career in the early 1920s with her DeMille films and appearances with all–American boy Wallace Reid. It is, of course, her role opposite Valentino, anything *but* an all-American boy, that is best-known to modern audiences.

Ayres's feeble attempts to fend off the perfervid advances of the sheik as they galloped over the desert sands on horseback is one of the iconographic images of the silent cinema. Millions of women undoubtedly envied her, possibly cursed her, and would have given anything if they could be in her place. It was a career-high few actresses, minor or major, could boast of.

REVIEWS

The Donovan Affair: Agnes Ayres impersonates the young wife, and she appears to be putting on some weight in what may be her talking picture debut. *New York Times* 4/29/29, *Variety* 5/8/29.

Baby Peggy *see* Montgomery, Peggy

Baclanova, Olga, Moscow, Russia, 1896/99–1974

Silent: After appearing on the stage with the Moscow Art Theatre, statuesque and blonde Olga Baclanova traveled to the United States with the company in the mid–1920s. They were seen on Broadway and later she also had roles in plays on the West Coast.

A veteran of some Russian silents from about 1914 to 1918, Baclanova (sometimes grandly billed by her surname alone) played a few bit roles in American movies. Her first lead in American films came in Mauritz Stiller's *Street of Sin.* The Josef von Sternberg success *Docks of New York* followed; other films included *Three Sinners, The Woman Disputed, The Man Who Laughs* and *Forgotten Faces.* Last silent: *Avalanche* (1928).

Sound: Olga Baclanova's talkie career consisted

of a handful of forgotten films and one cult classic. Her first talkie role in *The Wolf of Wall Street* (1929) was followed by a lead in the overheated melodrama *A Dangerous Woman*. She soon slipped into supporting roles in *The Man I Love* (her final Paramount film), *Cheer Up and Smile*, *Are You There?* and *The Great Lover*.

Although some of her films were comedies, Baclanova was by now firmly typecast as a deep-dyed villainess, "moll" or aristocrat, which her "exotic" mien allowed her to portray convincingly. Her sometime casting as a diva presumably was inspired by her own singing voice which was displayed in several of her roles.

In 1930 Olga Baclanova appeared in a British film, *The Life of Beethoven*. Her cult classic was MGM's *Freaks* (1932) in which she played the scheming trapeze artist and would-be murderess Cleopatra. It was a most unusual film for MGM and a unique experiment which they did not repeat in light of the almost universal condemnation it received.

Baclanova made one more for MGM, *Downstairs*, starring John Gilbert, and thence to *Billion Dollar Scandal* (1933), her last film for ten years. She returned to the stage and also was heard on the radio. In 1943, there was a final screen role: another opera singer in the filmization of the hit Broadway play *Claudia*, in which she had appeared.

Comments: Although it could be speculated that Olga Baclanova's accent derailed her film career, she apparently had an easily understandable accent and reviews refer to it as "charming." She also had a serviceable singing voice, one which she had used to good advantage on Broadway.

It is more probable that Baclanova's "vamp" persona was the immediate reason for her decline. Beginning in the late '20s, she inherited the mantle of Pola Negri to become the latter-day incarnation of the foreign-born "vampire." (One writer characterized her persona as that of a "vicious predator.")

The exaggerated characterization of the femme fatale which had become popular in the early 1910s eventually killed off more than a few careers and by the early talkie period this kind of characterization was somewhat risible.

Freaks arguably was the culmination of Baclanova's "vamp" persona. Many silent players found themselves in horror films but none was ever quite like *Freaks*. Despite her two or three notable silents, she probably would be totally unremembered today but for the cult status of that film.

Of course, it probably was not the kind of work for which the classically stage-trained Olga Baclanova would have wanted to be remembered. At the time of its release, the film was reviled by critics who called it loathsome. It was also a financial failure and even was banned entirely in some countries.

Freaks has since found its audience and Baclanova is a legitimate part of its fame (or infamy); she is described as "moving like a huge, sleek, devouring animal." Her film career did not long outlast this most famous role but she had made her mark and her final film *Claudia* was a worthy farewell.

REVIEWS

Wolf of Wall Street: Baclanova, as the hero's wife, has a fascinating accent but some of her lines are indistinctly recorded. Reviewers are divided on her performance. *New York Times* 1/28/29, *Variety* 1/30/29, *Harrison's Reports* 2/2/29.

A Dangerous Woman: The film is considered somewhat unpleasant, but Baclanova acts and sings Russian folk songs impressively and speaks with a charming accent. *New York Times* 5/21/29, *Variety* 5/22/29, *Harrison's Reports* 5/25/29.

The Man I Love: Baclanova plays her usual bad woman, this time a Baroness, and she sings well in this picture about boxing starring Richard Arlen in his first talkie. *New York Times* 5/28/29, *Variety* 5/29/29.

Cheer Up and Smile: In this frothy Arthur Lake musical programmer Baclanova is the female menace. It is a waste of her talents. *Variety* 8/6/30.

Are You There?: This picture is so terrible that it has been withdrawn from wide release and shown only in a few second-run theaters. (It contained one of Bea Lillie's few film roles and no doubt did much to persuade her that the theater was her proper milieu.) *Harrison's Reports* 2/21/31.

The Great Lover: Baclanova is again a heavy as a catty, temperamental opera singer. She is good in some of her scenes. *New York Times* 8/24/31, *Variety* 8/25/31.

Freaks: The reviewers do not know what to make of this controversial film but think that Baclanova was acceptable in some of it. She plays a circus trapeze artist who, in cahoots with her strong man lover, marries a midget for his money and then tries to poison him. A terrible revenge is exacted on her by the circus sideshow performers (the "freaks") and she is left looking like a half-woman, half-hen — herself a freak. *New York Times* 7/9/32, *Variety* 7/12/32.

(The film was a total failure. MGM's effort to recoup some of its losses by re-releasing the film under a new title, *Nature's Mistakes*— hardly a snappy title — was also not successful.)

Billion Dollar Scandal: The story about the Teapot Dome scandal is weak. The third-billed Baclanova plays the moll of a gangster named Fingers. *Variety* 1/10/33.

Claudia: Baclanova repeats the opera diva caricature she gave in the sentimental play. *Variety* 8/18/43.

Baggot, King (sometimes Baggott), St. Louis, Missouri, 1879–1948

Filmography: Partial list of films *Film Dope* (Mar. 1973)

Silent: King Baggot was both a popular star in silents (dubbed "The Most Photographed Man in the World") and a prolific director. His first appearance came about 1910, possibly in *The Wishing Ring*. Among the films in which he appeared (perhaps as many as 300 by 1923) were *The Man Who Stayed Home*, *Life's Twist*, *The Better Man*, *Bubbles*, *Lady Raffles*, *The Corsican Brothers* and *Doctor Jekyll and Mr. Hyde*. Most were one- or two-reelers.

Baggot did not appear in pictures for the rest of the 1920s but continued to direct and write scenarios until the end of the decade. One notable film he directed was *Tumbleweeds* (1925), William S. Hart's final feature. Last silent: *Thrill Chaser*(?) (1923).

Sound: King Baggot once again appeared before the cameras in 1930 to play small roles in several features until the middle part of the decade. They included *The Czar of Broadway*, *Afraid to Talk*, *Father Brown, Detective* and *Mississippi*. In the latter he had a very minor role as a gambler. After a six-year hiatus, he reappeared in 1941's *Come Live with Me*, in which he played a doorman, and there were two further brief roles.

REVIEWS

The Czar of Broadway: King Baggott is good in a lesser role. *Variety* 7/2/30.

Once a Gentleman: Among the many veterans in the cast is King Baggott. *Variety* 10/8/30.

Baird, Leah, Chicago, Illinois, 1883/91–1971

Silent: Stage actress Leah Baird was first seen onscreen about 1911, possibly in *The Wooing of Winifred*, for the Vitagraph studio. She came to Universal-Imp a couple of years later and co-starred with King Baggot in several, including *Ivanhoe*. In 1914–16 she was back at Vitagraph for a series of domestic dramas, mainly two-reelers. The pinnacle of her popularity came before 1920, one of her major roles being in the serial *The Wolves of Kultur*.

Among Baird's other films were *The Echo of Youth*, *The Volcano*, *The Lights of New York*, *The Heart Line*, *The Devil's Pay Day* and *When Husbands Deceive*. After 1920 her on-camera career waned and by 1925 she was retired from acting but was writing scenarios such as *Devil's Island*, *Spangles* and *Stolen Pleasures*. She continued in this pursuit until the mid–1930s. Last silent: *The Unnamed Woman* (1925), for which she was also the scenarist.

Sound: Leah Baird returned for some bit parts in several films, beginning in 1941. In at least two of them, *Bullets for O'Hara* and *Lady Gangster*, she was cast as a prison matron. Her other '40s movies included *Yankee Doodle Dandy*, *Air Force* and *My Reputation*. Her last known appearance was in *Around the World in 80 Days*.

Bakewell, William, Los Angeles, California, 1908–1993

Silent: William Bakewell began his career in 1925 playing supporting roles. As he progressed to juvenile leads, among his films were *The Latest from Paris*, *Harold Teen*, *West Point*, *The Waning Sex* and two for D. W. Griffith, including *The Battle of the Sexes*. He signed with First National in 1928, co-starring with Alice White in several pictures. Last silent: *Annapolis* (1928), with synchronized sound effects and music.

Sound: Griffith's 1929 *Lady of the Pavements*, a part-talkie, was William Bakewell's first sound film although he played only a bit part. *The Iron Mask* and *Hot Stuff* also had talking sequences. There were also a few musicals like *On with the Show*, *The Show of Shows* and *The Gold Diggers of Broadway*.

Bakewell's best role came in the classic anti-war drama *All Quiet on the Western Front* (1930), in which he was seen as one of the young German protagonists. He began to freelance in 1931 and was busy throughout the decade, appearing in MGM films like *Dance, Fools, Dance*, *Reducing*, and *Politics* (the latter two with Marie Dressler), as well as those for other studios, some of the Poverty Row variety.

Bakewell's other '30s pictures included *Three Cornered Moon*, *Quality Street* and *On Probation*. A bit as a Union officer was his contribution to *Gone with the Wind* in 1939. He was seen in support in the 1940s in such features as *Seven Sinners*, and he played the lead in the serial *Hap Harrigan*.

In the 1950s, Bakewell's roles became fewer, his last major parts being in a Davy Crockett film and in 1958's *Hell's Five Hours*. There were also TV appearances. His last parts were bits, the final one in *The Strongest Man in the World* (1975).

Comments: William Bakewell was handsome enough to be a conventional leading man, mostly in "B" films, and rugged enough to be convincing in authoritative roles. It was undoubtedly his essential blandness as an actor which kept his career going as long as it did, even though it reached its apex with two films when he was only 21 or 22 years old. Those films were *The Iron Mask* (in which

Bakewell played both the King of France and his twin brother) and, of course, *All Quiet on the Western Front*. He made over 100 films in all and it certainly did not hurt that his voice was fine for talkies and that he retained some vestiges of his good looks well into middle age.

REVIEWS

Hot Stuff: In this 30% talking picture about jazzing college students, William Bakewell is good as the young hero. *Harrison's Reports* 5/4/29.

Dance, Fools, Dance: Bakewell never loses sight of the fact that his part is that of a hard-drinking young weakling, Joan Crawford's brother. (Perhaps the most memorable feature of this pre–Code film is the scene where the characters all strip to their underwear to take a swim.) *New York Times* 3/21/31.

Quality Street: A mediocre performance is given by William Bakewell. *Variety* 4/14/37.

Bancroft, George, Philadelphia, Pennsylvania, 1882–1956

Filmography: List of films in *Eighty Silent Film Stars*; *Film Dope* (Mar. 1973)

Silent: Stage-trained George Bancroft made his first film, *The Journey's End*, in 1921. He was generally a featured player specializing in villain roles for which his 6'2" burliness made him a natural. Among his films in the early and mid–1920s were *The Pony Express*, *White Gold*, *The Rainbow Trail*, *Old Ironsides*, *The Rough Riders* and *Teeth*.

Bancroft became a star in 1927 with the leading role in the very successful gangster melodrama *Underworld*, directed by Josef von Sternberg. This was followed in 1928 by the popular *The Drag Net* and *The Showdown*. Last silent: *The Docks of New York* (1928).

Sound: George Bancroft retained his star status through his first few talkies, his sound debut coming in *The Wolf of Wall Street* (1929). This was followed by *The Mighty*, *Thunderbolt* (for which he received an Academy Award nomination), *Derelict* and *Ladies Love Brutes*.

Bancroft was soon back in supporting roles, with an occasional lead. His work in the 1930s was clustered in the early and latter parts of the decade; between 1933 and 1935 he was only seen in one film, the against type and poorly-received *Elmer and Elsie*.

Among the major pictures in which Bancroft appeared were *Stagecoach*, *Mr. Deeds Goes to Town*, *Each Dawn I Die*, *Angels with Dirty Faces* and *North West Mounted Police*. He made three in 1942, his final year in films, the last of which was *Whistling in Dixie*.

Comments: George Bancroft had the makings of a fine actor. His physical presence was commanding, his strong face was interesting and his theater-trained voice an asset. However, his talkie starring career was not helped by the fact that he was considered arrogant and temperamental. He apparently let stardom go to his head and his habitual lateness and other discourtesies caused a backlash. Directors refused to work with him.

Nonetheless, Bancroft did have a distinguished talkie career, although not as the star he had once been, however briefly. Certainly many of his films were "A" pictures and his roles were substantial. He convincingly portrayed both rectitude and menace and could always be depended on to deliver a solid performance.

REVIEWS

The Wolf of Wall Street: It is well acted by Bancroft and undoubtedly his greatest job for the screen. His good acting coupled with his strong but pleasing personality make it an outstanding picture. His powerful voice, in particular, registers well. *New York Times* 1/28/29, *Variety* 1/30/29, *Harrison's Reports* 2/2/29.

Ladies Love Brutes: This is a picture that Bancroft will have to carry. (His leading lady is Mary Astor, in her very first talkie.) *Variety* 5/21/30.

The Derelict: Different from any other film of Bancroft's in the past. He not only looks like a real ship's mate but also acts like one. *Harrison's Reports* 11/22/30.

Lady and Gent: This deftly hoked-up sentimental drama is the best story the heavyweight star, who plays a boxer, has had in a long time. *Variety* 7/19/32.

Elmer and Elsie: The ordinarily virile Bancroft is given the role of a sap. It is almost embarrassing watching him act at times like a bashful schoolboy and a Milquetoast. *Harrison's Reports* 8/4/34, *Variety* 8/7/34.

Hell-Ship Morgan: The film marks the return of George Bancroft to the screen. He looks thinner and only occasionally displays the hefty vigor associated with his work. The part doesn't afford great opportunities. *Variety* 3/11/36.

Banky, Vilma (Vilma Konsics, Lonchit, Baulsy and various other versions, including Banky), Budapest or Nagydorog, Hungary, 1898/1904–1991

Filmography: *Films in Review* (Aug.-Sept. 1977)

Silent: After appearances in several Austrian, French and Hungarian films from 1920, beauteous, blonde Samuel Goldwyn protégée Vilma Banky (dubbed "The Hungarian Rhapsody") made her

Hollywood debut with *The Dark Angel* (1925). It was her first teaming with suave Ronald Colman.

Banky made ten American films altogether, including three more with Colman and two (*The Eagle* and *Son of the Sheik*) with Rudolph Valentino. In the latter, now her most revived film, she portrayed Yasmin, a most unlikely looking Arab temptress.

Among her very few pictures with other leading men, Vilma Banky had the title role in the popular western *The Winning of Barbara Worth*, one of Gary Cooper's earliest films. Last silent: *The Awakening* (1928), with synchronized music and sound effects.

Sound: The first of Vilma Banky's two American sound films was the part-talkie *This is Heaven* (1929). Her second was 1930's *A Lady to Love*, based on the play *They Knew What They Wanted*, co-starring Edward G. Robinson and directed by Victor Sjostrom (Seastrom).

Following this, Banky appeared in only one other motion picture, the German film *The Rebel* (*Der Rebell*) in 1932. Before she retired, she and her husband Rod LaRocque toured in the play *Cherries Are Ripe* in 1930–31.

Comments: This Is Heaven was successful enough for the studio to try Vilma Banky in an all-talking production. Once again she played a foreign-born person, obviating any need to explain away her accent. In her film roles, where everything was carefully scripted, her speech was understandable and not grating to American ears.

But Banky's accent was undeniably heavy. Her fractured English was the object of fun to friends and her mispronunciations were dubbed "Bankyisms." Although still at the height of her blue-eyed beauty, it was apparent that her future roles would be severely limited.

Vilma Banky had played "exotic" roles, such as in *The Son of the Sheik*, but she had also played American girls and what came from her mouth was simply not in keeping with the audience's expectations. Understandably, she did not wish to become "the source of drollery" proposed in the *Variety* review.

REVIEWS

This Is Heaven: One laugh that Banky got suggests the possibility of Goldwyn doing an all-talker with her garbled English as the source of drollery. As to whether her talk will prove effective is questionable. She has a decided but charming accent, but her enunciation is not very good, although generally understandable. She is always radiant. *Variety* 4/3/29, *Harrison's Reports* 4/6/29, *New York Times* 5/27/29.

A Lady to Love: Banky is radiant and much too beautiful ever to have juggled a tray in her role as a waitress. She possesses too much charm and not enough of the believability that might have made the role realistic. Nevertheless, despite her handicap of too much beauty and her heavy Hungarian accent, she does exceedingly well. *New York Times* 3/1/30, *Variety* 3/5/30, *Harrison's Reports* 3/8/30.

The Rebel: Banky has been absent from the screen for a long time so it will be difficult to tell how much help she will be to the box-office of this adventure of the Napoleonic Wars. She's more beautiful than ever although English is still difficult for her. *Harrison's Reports* 7/1/33, *Variety* 8/1/33.

Barnes, T(homas) Roy, Lincoln, England,
1880–1937

Silent: T. Roy Barnes came from vaudeville to make his first films in 1920 and he remained busy throughout the decade. Although he played many leads, mostly in comedy, he was seen increasingly in supporting roles by the end of the decade.

Barnes's films included *Her Face Value*, *Adam and Eva*, *Reckless Romance*, *The Price of Pleasure*, *A Regular Scout* and *Smile, Brother, Smile*. Last silent: *The Gate Crasher* (1928).

Sound: T. Roy Barnes remained busy in mostly minor roles until 1935. His first talkie appearance came in *Dangerous Curves*, a Clara Bow vehicle; other films of 1929–30 were *Sally*, *Caught Short* and *Wide Open*. In subsequent years he was seen in *Women of All Nations*, *Riptide*, *Life Begins at 40* and *The Virginia Judge*.

In the 1934 W. C. Fields classic *It's a Gift*, Barnes is the natty but annoying salesman who disturbs Fields's early morning efforts to sleep by inquiring about "Carl LaFong." In the face of the irascible comic's protests that he knows no such person, the salesman insists on lengthily spelling out the name: "Capital L, small a, capital F…" It is a neat comic cameo which ensures at least one talkie appearance by Barnes will be remembered.

REVIEWS

Sally: T. Roy Barnes plays a theater manager and is only occasionally out of the ordinary. *New York Times* 12/24/29, *Variety* 12/25/29.

Wide Open: In this very good farce comedy T. Roy Barnes is the blustering salesman. *Harrison's Reports* 3/29/30.

Barriscale, Bessie, New York, New York, ca.
1884–1965

Silent: From about 1913 to 1920, stage actress

Bessie Barriscale was a popular star for Ince and other studios; at one point she had her own production company. Among her features were *Rose of the Rancho*, *The Devil*, *Honor's Altar*, *Borrowed Plumage*, *The Cast-Off*, *Beckoning Roads*, *Maid o' the Storm* and *A Woman Who Understood*. After her starring career ended, she played in vaudeville. Last silent: *The Breaking Point* (1921).

Sound: Barriscale's first talkie was the part-sound *Show Folks* (1928). Although she did not have a large role she delivered an important speech in the sound portion of the picture. She also appeared in a number of 1933–34 films including *Above the Clouds*, *Bondage*, *Beloved* and *The Man Who Reclaimed His Head*. In *Secrets* (1933), along with other former silent stars, she played one of Mary Pickford's unsympathetic middle-aged children.

REVIEWS

Show Folks: In the part where the characters talk, Barriscale in a small part as the old down-and-out actress is excellent. Perhaps many of the old picture-goers would want to see her in talking pictures because she has not lost any of her old acting ability. *Harrison's Reports* 12/22/28.

Barry, Wesley, Los Angeles, California,
1906–1994

Silent: Freckle-faced, red-haired Wesley Barry began his career about 1918 in Mary Pickford films like *Amarilly of Clothesline Alley*, *Johanna Enlists*, *How Could You Jean?* and *Daddy-Long-Legs*. For a while he was one of the most popular child actors of the silents in supporting and starring roles.

Among Barry's films were *Male and Female*, *Dinty*, *Bob Hampton of Placer*, *The Country Kid*, *The Fighting Cub* and *In Old Kentucky*. His most famous part was probably the title role in 1922's *Penrod*. Last silent: *Top Sergeant Mulligan* (1928).

Sound: Like most child actors, Wesley Barry had to cope with picture roles becoming scarcer as he aged. He was top-billed in one of his first sound films, 1930's *The Thoroughbred*, and had supporting roles in his others that year, *Sunny Skies* and *Border Romance*. Eventually he found himself being cast in bits as newsboys and messenger boys in many of his 1930s films, although he still played an occasional top supporting role.

Among Barry's motion pictures in the '30s were *Hell Bent for Frisco*, *The Life of Vergie Winters*, *Night Life of the Gods*, *The Plough and the Stars*, *Spring Madness* and *Man About Town*. His on-camera career did not long outlast the end of the decade but he eventually became an assistant director and then a director and producer.

REVIEWS

Thoroughbred: Barry is the hero of this nice little program picture which has heart interest and some thrills. *Harrison's Reports* 9/6/30.

Barrymore, Ethel (family name was originally Blythe), Philadelphia, Pennsylvania, 1879–1959
Filmography: *Films in Review* (June-July 1963); List of films *Film Dope* (Mar. 1973)

Silent: Part of a famed English-based theatrical family and sister of Lionel and John Barrymore, Ethel Barrymore made her stage debut in 1894 and became a star with *Captain Jinks of the Horse Marines* in 1901. She also appeared in the British theater.

Nineteen fourteen's *The Nightingale* was the first of Barrymore's 13 silents, most of which were made for Metro-Rolfe. She interspersed films and plays for the next several years; her busiest on-screen year was 1917 when she made seven features. Ethel Barrymore's films included *The Kiss of Hate*, *The Awakening of Helena Richie*, *The Call of Her People*, *The White Raven*, *The Lifted Veil* and *An American Widow*. In the '20s she played on Broadway to great acclaim and toured in vaudeville with her perennial showcase *The Twelve Pound Look*. Last silent: *The Divorcee* (1919).

Sound: Barrymore returned to the screen for only one feature film in the 1930s, portraying Russian Empress Alexandra in *Rasputin and the Empress* and co-starring for the only time in films with her brothers. It was not well-received but it gave the public a chance to hear that inimitable voice. She may also have appeared in a 1933 short called *All at Sea*.

Barrymore was not seen again in movies until 1944's *None but the Lonely Heart*, starring Cary Grant. It was the film which garnered her an Academy Award as Best Supporting Actress for her role as the dying pawnbroker Ma Mott. In that decade she played some of her finest Broadway roles as well.

Among Ethel Barrymore's 20-plus other films were *The Spiral Staircase*, Alfred Hitchcock's *The Paradine Case* (another Academy Award nomination), *The Red Danube*, *The Farmer's Daughter*, *Deadline USA*, *Just for You* and *Young at Heart*.

The 1951 melodrama *Kind Lady* was the only talkie in which Barrymore had a top-billed starring role. She made her final film *Johnny Trouble* in 1957 at a time when her health was seriously declining. She also appeared frequently on radio and television.

Comments: Although Ethel Barrymore's throaty,

authoritative voice was a distinct asset to talkies, her greatest successes came on the stage. Dubbed the "First Lady of the American Theater" (along with several others at one time or another), she found fame in such dramas as *Declassee*, *The Kingdom of God*, *Whiteoaks* and especially *The Corn Is Green*.

Barrymore lived to laugh at a critic who reviewed her first starring play thusly: "If the young lady who plays Madame Trentoni had possessed beauty, charm or talent this play might have been a success."

A distinguished film presence, Ethel Barrymore never became a major one. She appeared in several worthy talkies but her roles were most often subsidiary, usually those of a tough but goodhearted matron. In these parts, her underlying humor was sometimes allowed to surface.

Although essentially always playing "herself," Barrymore could diversify her parts a bit. She was a murderess in *Moss Rose*, for instance. In silents she had been a leading lady but was already quite mature, both in age and physical appearance, when she essayed her first sound film.

Undoubtedly a fine actress (a Broadway theater was named for her), Ethel Barrymore was almost equally as famous for being a member of an endlessly fascinating trio. About her family she said: "Both my brothers and I were born under a dark star."

Barrymore's often unhappy personal life was grist for society columnists and her vaudeville tag line "That's all there is, there isn't any more" was widely imitated. She definitely was, and was famous for being, a "personality" as well as an American theater icon.

REVIEWS

Rasputin and the Empress: One reviewer thought that Barrymore is able to impart to the spectators the grief her character feels, but another thought Lionel Barrymore's domination of the film makes a mere stooge of her. (There was apparently spirited competition between the siblings which sometimes broke out into squabbling and temperament on the set. Ethel Barrymore did not care for her performance, which she characterized as resembling Tallulah Bankhead's wickedly-done impression of her.) *Harrison's Reports* 11/31/32, *Variety* 12/27/32.

The Spiral Staircase: Ethel Barrymore's performance in the picture will get praise for her role of a wealthy, bed-ridden eccentric. (In this suspenseful mystery Barrymore kills the murderer herself.) *Variety* 1/9/46.

The Paradine Case: Barrymore skillfully imparts her performance as Charles Laughton's half-crazed wife. *Variety* 12/31/47.

The Red Danube: Barrymore calls on her usual alchemy to transform her lackluster lines, but the effort doesn't pay off. *Variety* 9/21/49.

Just for You: Barrymore, in a lesser role, is a standout as the school dean with a delicate sense of humor. *Variety* 2/15/50.

Kind Lady: In the title role Barrymore demonstrates the acting authority that makes even a throwaway line a standout piece of dialogue. *Variety* 6/20/51.

Johnny Trouble: Barrymore offers a warm and penetrating characterization and is happy casting for the part. (This is an upbeat, if implausible, story of a wealthy widow who takes charge of a boys' dormitory and is called Nana by them.) *Variety* 9/11/57.

Barrymore, John (family name was originally Blythe), Philadelphia, Pennsylvania, 1882–1942

Filmography: *Films in Review* (Dec. 1952); *Film Fan Monthly* (July-Aug. 1966); *Focus on Film* (Winter 1972)

Silent: Already establishing himself as a theater idol, John Barrymore made his first film, *An American Citizen*, in 1913 or '14 for Famous Players-Lasky. A series of light comedies followed, interspersed with stage performances. The films included *Are You a Mason?*, *The Lost Bridegroom*, *The Incorrigible Dukane* and *The Man from Mexico*.

Barrymore's popularity rose with the 1920 tour de force *Doctor Jekyll and Mr. Hyde*, in which he seemed to be metamorphosing to the grotesque Hyde in full view of the camera. Another of his popular films was as the title character in the 1922 version of *Sherlock Holmes*.

After signing with Warner Bros. in 1924, "Jack" Barrymore seemed to find his niche in a series of costume dramas such as *Beau Brummell*, *Don Juan*, *The Beloved Rogue* and *The Sea Beast*, a version of *Moby Dick*. Last silent: *Eternal Love* (1929), with synchronized music and sound effects.

Sound: The great Barrymore voice was first heard from the screen in Warner Bros.' all-star melange *The Show of Shows*. Seemingly costumed as a hunchback, he performed a scene from *Richard III*. His first full talkie was *General Crack* (1929), yet another costume melodrama.

Before Barrymore departed from Warner Bros. in 1932 he made the hit films *Moby Dick* and *Svengali*. It was as a freelancer that he made such prestigious pictures as *Grand Hotel*, *Dinner at Eight*, *Twentieth Century*, *Counsellor-at-Law* (considered to be his finest screen performance), *Topaze* and *A Bill of Divorcement*.

Barrymore was off the screen for most of 1934 to 1936. When he returned, he alternated major films such as *Romeo and Juliet* and *Maytime* with "B" efforts like *Night Club Scandal* and *Bulldog Drummond Comes Back* and its three sequels. His last decent roles came at the end of the decade.

John Barrymore had the lead in the bittersweet comedy *The Great Man Votes*, made in 1938, and a strong and worthy supporting part in the sophisticated screwball comedy *Midnight* the next year. His remaining films were unworthy or completely awful efforts like *Personal Appearance*, *The Invisible Woman*, *The Great Profile* and *Playmates*, mercifully his last film in 1941.

Comments: John Barrymore was more than capable of understated performances, but many of his roles had a certain bravura hamminess about them. In his last years this tendency became outright parody in films, on radio and on the stage. It is this period of terrible physical and emotional decline that he is unfortunately so often remembered for.

The 1920s saw Barrymore's greatest theater performances in *Hamlet* and *Richard III* but his 22 silent films, especially those of the Warner Bros. period, were often mediocre. They were expensively mounted and prestigious but sometimes dull and not always successful at the box office. Lavish productions and swashbuckling failed to make up for the lack of spoken dialogue, without which Jack Barrymore could not be seen at his best. With his mellifluous voice, he was made for talkies. The early to mid-'30s were his golden screen years.

Barrymore was cast in a series of roles which brought out his acting ability, not necessarily his physical attributes as had been the emphasis at Warners. His looks were, in truth, beginning to deteriorate anyway. He was willing to subsume his considerable screen charisma in character roles when called for.

Unfortunately, Barrymore never received an Academy Award for any of his performances. Although Howard Hawks called the Oscar Jaffe character in *Twentieth Century* "the world's *second* biggest ham," (Barrymore supposedly being the biggest), his quizzical schoolmaster in *Topaze* and gentlemanly criminal in *Grand Hotel* are certainly examples of effective underplaying.

Barrymore's rapid decline in the late 1930s was tragically witnessed by the world. He suffered from headaches and other physical ailments and some believe his alcoholism was caused by a fear of going insane like his father Maurice.

Not being able to remember lines, John Barrymore was forced to have cue cards prominently placed around his sets. He sometimes can be seen to be reading from them in his later movies. Hopefully those last awful years of self-parody and indeed self-loathing do not dim the luster of those of his films which are undying classics.

REVIEWS

General Crack: Barrymore's best performance since *Beau Brummell*. Aside from a tendency to display his profile too much, he acts powerfully and gives a fine performance although he is wasted in a poor movie. His voice is incisive and is one that suits the Vitaphone method of recording. His speech dominates the scenes. *New York Times* 12/4/29, *Variety* 12/11/29, *Harrison's Reports* 12/14/29.

Svengali: Barrymore is excellent. He dominates the film, playing a disgusting-looking character in broad strokes. *Variety* 5/6/31, *Harrison's Reports* 5/9/31.

Grand Hotel: The movie is something of a screen epic. Barrymore is back where he belongs as the down-at-heel but glamorous baron and hotel thief, playing opposite Greta Garbo. *Variety* 4/19/32.

A Bill of Divorcement: Barrymore gives a fine performance and distinguishes himself anew in a part far from his accustomed range, if indeed anything is beyond his range. *Variety* 10/4/32.

Topaze: Barrymore is in probably the best bit of character comedy he has ever done. His performance is flawless and is a simple but arresting characterization. *Variety* 2/14/33, *Harrison's Reports* 2/18/33.

Counsellor-at-Law: The lead is physically unsuited to Barrymore and he contributes his usual screen tricks. *Variety* 12/12/33.

Twentieth Century: It's Barrymore's picture and it's a pleasure to see him go off his nut — but not too much. (He portrayed Oscar Jaffe, a temperamental play producer, in this early screwball comedy that brought Carole Lombard to the fore.) *Variety* 5/8/34.

The Great Man Votes: Barrymore is provided with a part particularly suited to his talents, even if his characterization is slightly overstressed in several spots. His general performance is one of the best he has turned out in some time. *Variety* 1/11/39.

Playmates: Barrymore clowns his way through the picture in his customary style, except for the one scene in which he begins reciting the soliloquy from *Hamlet*. In that short scene he proves he can still hold an audience spellbound. *Harrison's Reports* 11/15/41.

Barrymore, Lionel (family name was originally Blythe), Philadelphia, Pennsylvania, 1878–1953

Filmography: *Films in Review* (Apr. 1962), additional films (May 1962); List of films *Film Dope* (Mar. 1973)

Silent: "Hollywood's Grand Old Man" Lionel Barrymore came from a prominent stage family, among whose members were his sister Ethel and brother John. Although he wanted to be a painter, he succumbed to his genes and made his stage debut in 1893. He went to work for D. W. Griffith before 1910 writing scenarios and eventually acting.

Among Barrymore's earliest films, many one- and two-reelers, were *The New York Hat* (1912) co-starring Mary Pickford, *Friends, Brutality, The Sheriff's Baby* and *The Woman in Black*. He was also in *Judith of Bethulia*, in which he played multiple roles. Other studios for which he worked were Metro-Rolfe, Chadwick and Goldwyn.

Until 1925 Lionel Barrymore alternated between films and plays such as *The Copperhead, The Jest, The Claw* and *Macbeth*. His motion pictures, in which he played both leads and supporting roles, included *The Barrier, The Bells, Sadie Thompson, The Copperhead, Fifty-Fifty, Drums of Love, America* (a villain role), *The Master Mind, The Seats of the Mighty, A Modern Magdalen* and *The Thirteenth Hour*.

Barrymore also appeared in the Pearl White serial *The Exploits of Elaine* in 1915 and its sequel, and he directed a few pictures as well. Last silent: *West of Zanzibar* (1928), with synchronized music and sound effects.

Sound: *The Lion and the Mouse* (1928), a Vitaphone part-talkie, was Lionel Barrymore's first. He also appeared in the part-sound *The River Woman* that year. Nineteen twenty-nine was devoted mostly to directing although he was seen in *The Mysterious Island* and *Alias Jimmy Valentine*, part-talkies, and had a cameo in *The Hollywood Revue of 1929*.

Barrymore's first sound directorial effort was the short *Confession*, followed by *Madame X, The Unholy Night* and the ill-starred (in more ways than one) *His Glorious Night*. On the business side of the cameras he played "himself" in 1930's *Free and Easy* and he returned to real acting for the 1931 MGM film *A Free Soul*, for which he won the Academy Award for Best Actor.

That year Lionel Barrymore also directed for the last time with *Ten Cents a Dance*. His film appearances to 1953 included *Broken Lullaby, Christopher Bean, David Copperfield, The Road to Glory, Captains Courageous, Dinner at Eight, You Can't Take It with You, Saratoga, The Valley of Decision, It's a Wonderful Life, Key Largo* and *Main Street to Broadway*, his last.

The role that is considered Barrymore's best, and one fairly free of his mannerisms, came in *Grand Hotel* (1932). He played Otto Kringelein, the bookkeeper who comes to the hotel to die. That year he played opposite both his siblings for the only time in *Rasputin and the Empress*. During his career he supported most of the top MGM stars such as Jean Harlow, Joan Crawford, Greta Garbo and Norma Shearer.

Although Lionel Barrymore made numerous prestigious films (and over 150 in all), he is well remembered for playing Dr. Gillespie, the gruff but kindly physician, in the lengthy Dr. Kildare "B" series which lasted until 1947. He also originated the role of Judge Hardy in *A Family Affair* (1937), the year he began appearing before the camera in a wheelchair.

Barrymore also appeared on radio, memorably as Scrooge in *A Christmas Carol*, for several years. His other talents included painting and composing music. Several of his pieces were performed by symphony orchestras, including his tribute to brother John, "In Memoriam." A novel, *Mr. Cantonwine*, was published in 1951, and there also was a book of non-revealing memoirs.

Comments: Lionel Barrymore was one of the most shameless and successful scene stealers in cinema history. It was probably in his blood; his siblings certainly had the knack as well. He had a panoply of facial and other gestures (eyebrow wiggling, hand rubbing), and his deep, resonant voice could assume all sorts of inflections and a variety of chuckles and growls.

It is perhaps an open question as to how good a cinema actor Barrymore really was. He certainly had presence and panache but he was inclined to hamminess, to over-reliance on his "shtick" and ultimately to replaying the same character over and over. As his films appeared in the 1930s there was increasing notice taken by critics of his oft-repeated mannerisms. His stage career undoubtedly was distinguished.

This is not particularly true of Barrymore's directing career. As a director he is remembered, if at all, for 1929's *His Glorious Night*, the film that was anything but glorious for its star John Gilbert (making his first talking feature). The story still persists that the film was sabotaged at the order of Louis B. Mayer to ruin Gilbert's career.

Would Barrymore do such a thing? There is no question that he was particularly close to MGM mogul Louis B. Mayer and that the actor had a lengthy and secure berth at the studio that few others enjoyed. Legend has it that Mayer supplied him with drugs to keep him pliable. There is therefore a shadow, however nebulous and unwarranted, over the actor's reputation.

REVIEWS

The Lion and the Mouse: Barrymore's voice accomplished many of the things he sought to make it do, but due to mechanical difficulties it was not always distinct. It was the most clear when he spoke in low tones. *Variety* 5/30/28 (1st review), *Variety* 6/20/28 (2nd review).

The Mysterious Island: The performance of Lionel Barrymore as the inventive genius is predominant. He never fails to hold tense interest. (He was top billed but only 5% of the picture had spoken dialogue.) *Variety* 12/25/29.

A Free Soul: From the standpoint of performance this is unquestionably Lionel Barrymore's picture. He has never done better acting in his role as a lawyer making a heart-rending plea to the jury and then dying. *Variety* 6/9/31, *Harrison's Reports* 6/13/31.

Carolina: The performance by Lionel Barrymore is excellent. He is a sympathetic character, arousing pity. *Harrison's Reports* 2/10/34.

The Devil Doll: Barrymore has a field day in the leading part. (This Tod Browning–directed film had much in common with Lon Chaney's *The Unholy Three*, including the villain's [Barrymore] impersonation of an old lady. He is supposed to have quipped, when he saw himself in drag, "My God, it's Ethel.") *Variety* 8/12/36.

Captains Courageous: Barrymore plays "himself" as usual. *Variety* 5/19/37.

Dr. Kildare's Strange Case: Barrymore dominates the picture with a persuasive characterization. (The Kildare series relied heavily on the interplay between the idealistic Dr. Kildare, essayed by Lew Ayres, and Gillespie. It began in 1937 with *Internes Can't Take Money*.) Variety 4/17/42.

It's a Wonderful Life: As a Scrooge-like banker, Lionel Barrymore lends a lot of luster. *Variety* 12/25/46.

Key Largo: Barrymore shows up strongly. *Variety* 7/7/48.

Barthelmess, Richard, New York, New York, 1895–1963

Filmography: Films in Review (Jan. 1958); *Classic Images* (May 1989); Academy of Motion Picture Arts and Sciences; List of films: *Eighty Silent Film Stars*.

Silent: Richard Barthelmess's first notable film work was in 1916's *War Brides* starring Alla Nazimova, who happened to be a friend of his mother's. He subsequently co-starred in several films with popular Marguerite Clark before signing with D. W. Griffith.

Barthelmess's appearances for that famous director led to stardom in the 1919-20 duo of *Broken Blossoms* and *Way Down East*, both co-starring Lillian Gish. Superstardom then quickly came with the great success of Henry King's rural melodrama

Tol'able David, made for Richard Barthelmess's own company, Inspiration Pictures, in 1921. Other notable silents were *The Enchanted Cottage* and *Soul Fire*.

Barthelmess remained a major silent star throughout the 1920s, eventually signing with First National. For that studio *The Patent Leather Kid* proved to be another great hit and he was nominated for the first Best Actor Academy Award for that film and *The Noose*. Emil Jannings won but Barthelmess received an award for distinguished achievement. Last silent: *Scarlet Seas* (1929), with synchronized sound effects and music.

Sound: The first of Richard Barthelmess's 20 sound films was the successful part-talkie *Weary River* (1929) in which he played a convict and supposedly sang a song. The domestic drama *Drag*, his first all-talking picture, was also a success. Nineteen thirty's *Son of the Gods* proved to be a misstep but his next, the World War One flying drama *Dawn Patrol*, director Howard Hawks's first talkie, was the high-point of his sound career. It was widely considered that he did fine work in that film, in which he played a British flying ace.

About Richard Barthelmess's role in the offbeat 1931 film *The Last Flight* it was said: "Perhaps never before or since have those longing — even aching eyes — been put to such good use in a film. They stare out at emptiness or shift with anxious suspicion." Unfortunately this interesting picture was not a big success nor did any of his remaining sound films match the success of *The Dawn Patrol*.

Films like *The Lash*, *Cabin in the Cotton*, *Alias the Doctor* and *Central Airport* (another pilot role) did little to maintain Barthelmess's stardom. He (or First National) then made an effort to change his image and he began playing anti-heroes and even gangsters in such films as *The Finger Points*, *A Modern Hero*, *Midnight Alibi* and *Four Hours to Kill*.

Warner Bros., which had absorbed First National, released Barthelmess from his contract in 1934 and his final starring role came in England with *Spy of Napoleon*, in which he was miscast. He then was off-screen for about three years. During that time he appeared in his first Broadway role, an unsuccessful adaptation of James M. Cain's *The Postman Always Rings Twice* (1936).

Barthelmess made a worthy return to the screen as a supporting player in Hawks's well-regarded 1939 ensemble film *Only Angels Have Wings*, which starred Cary Grant and Jean Arthur. As yet another pilot, this time with a secret (and an alias), he gave a low-key but effective performance and he once again revealed his talent for portraying character through subtle body movement.

Barthelmess made only three more supporting appearances — in each one portraying a villain — in *The Man Who Talked Too Much* (1940), *The Mayor of 44th Street* and a remake of the popular *The Spoilers* (the latter two both in 1942) before leaving the screen for good.

Comments: Richard Barthelmess's early sound films proved that he was a very good actor and not just a silent screen "pretty" face. (Lillian Gish considered him to be the most beautiful man in silent pictures.) His understated acting style stood him in good stead in the ensemble films in which he found himself; this may be one of the keys to his early sound success.

On the other hand, Barthelmess's acting technique did not work to his benefit when he was performing one-on-one with flamboyant personalities such as Bette Davis. As the reviews indicate, his underplaying sometimes came through as a lack of vigor or even interest.

Barthelmess's starring films after *The Dawn Patrol* were generally not well-received. Even such interesting efforts as *The Last Flight* and the overwrought, campy *Cabin in the Cotton* were not films that the public wanted to see. He was undeniably getting (and appearing) too old for some of the roles he was playing.

Almost 35 at the time that talkies came in, Barthelmess had lost the youthful innocence of his premier silent days. He apparently tried plastic surgery in an effort to prolong his boyish appearance but seemed to age rapidly anyhow. His voice, although not bad, was a bit on the light tenor side and it retained a touch of a New York accent. It was not too well-suited to heroic roles and certainly not to the villainous ones.

Despite the ultimate fading of his starring career, Richard Barthelmess was one of the few male leads of the earlier silent days who maintained a leading position in talkies through the mid–1930s. He still managed to appear on at least one poll of the most popular film stars of 1931. Whatever his ultimate lack of sound film success, he remains one of the top cinema stars of all time.

REVIEWS

Weary River: Among its merits is the revealing of Barthelmess's melodious vibrant tenor. He emerges as possibly the first of the veteran film stars to register a clean-cut triumph in talkies. His voice has a human warmth and he uses it with an unexpected range of effect. Always he is natural, sincere, nicely repressed, conveying by deft suggestion the shades of meaning. However the picture is a waste of his talent. *New York Times* 1/25/29, *Variety* 1/30/29, *Harrison's Reports* 4/6/29.

Son of the Gods: Barthelmess cannot do much with the characterization allotted to him in this uninspired film and he does not excel in speaking his lines. Also, he is miscast as a supposed Chinese man (shades of *Broken Blossoms*?). (Constance Bennett (misidentified by one critic as Constance Talmadge), got the bulk of the good reviews.) *New York Times* 1/31/30, *Variety* 2/5/30, *Harrison's Reports* 2/8/30.

The Dawn Patrol: Barthelmess contributes another of his dependable performances in this air picture. *Variety* 7/16/30.

The Last Flight: A curious but often brilliant study of the post-war psychology of four injured American aviators in which Barthelmess acts well and surrounds himself with an ensemble of good actors, as has been his wont. (Not very successful in its time, this picture has gained latter-day appreciation.) *New York Times* 8/20/31, *Variety* 8/25/31, *Harrison's Reports* 8/29/31.

Cabin in the Cotton: Barthelmess gives a careful but hardly an inspired performance. His general demeanor lacks the desired spontaneity and often he speaks his lines in a monotone and without vigor. Bette Davis's rising popularity is really the film's best chance for business.

(Surely this will be forever memorable as the film in which she uttered to Barthelmess her famous line "I'd love to kiss yuh, but I just washed mah hair," in her best Southern accent. She also shocked his character by [off-screen] appearing before him in the nude.) *New York Times* 9/30/32, *Variety* 10/4/32.

Heroes for Sale: This film is not very good but Barthelmess carries on bravely under the afflictions which fall to the lot of his character. The role of the businessman turned hobo is probably one of the toughest roles he has ever had. *New York Times* 7/24/33, *Variety* 7/25/33.

Midnight Alibi: Barthelmess turns in a good performance as a gambler. *New York Times* 7/4/34.

Only Angels Have Wings: Reviewers differed, some not appreciating Barthelmess's understated acting. Most think he is impressive with his deadpan performance and he steals this movie. (He was third-billed and played the husband of pre-fame Rita Hayworth.) *Hollywood Reporter* 5/11/39, *Variety* 5/17/39, *Rob Wagner's Script* 5/20/39, *The Spectator* 10/20/39 (Graham Greene).

The Spoilers: Barthelmess gives a creditable performance as the gambler named the Bronco Kid. *Variety* 4/15/42, *New York Times* 5/22/42.

Barton, Buzz (William Lamoreaux), Gallatin, Missouri, 1913–1980

Silent: An appealingly freckle-faced redhead and

a crackerjack rider, Buzz Barton was doubling as a stunt "man" by the age of 11 for child stars such as Frankie Darro. In 1926 he acted under the names of Billy Lamar and Red Lennox in a Rayart series starring Jack Perrin. Among those films were *Hi-Jacking Rustlers*, *West of the Rainbow's End*, *Thunderbolt's Tracks* and *Splitting the Breeze*.

The young man's potential brought him his own FBO series and a new name: Buzz Barton. His first starring feature *The Boy Rider* (1927) proved to be popular and he was soon billed as "the screen's youngest western star." His pictures, in which his character was invariably named "Red," included *The Slingshot Kid*, *The Fightin' Redhead*, *The Little Buckaroo*, *Young Whirlwind* and *The Freckled Rascal*. Last silent: *Pals of the Prairie* (1929), with synchronized music and sound effects.

Sound: Buzz Barton's starring career was pretty much ended by a combination of sound and simply growing up. In his first talkie, *Canyon Hawk* (1930), he shared the lead and he was starred in 1931's *The Cyclone Kid* but that was just about his last hurrah. Although he worked fairly steadily up to the time of World War Two, his latter roles were bits.

Besides the serials *The Lone Defender* (1930) and *Mystery Trooper* (1931), Barton appeared in such films as *Riders of the Cactus*, *Tangled Fortunes*, *Fighting Pioneers*, *Saddle Aces*, *Phantom Gold* and *Wild Horse Valley*. He made no films at all in 1933 and '34. In the 1950s he returned to Hollywood as a stuntman and wrangler.

REVIEWS

Canyon Hawks: Barton is too big for cute kid parts and does not do much in this picture. *Variety* 10/15/30.

Cyclone Kid: One of those impossible stories that has Barton making narrow escapes. *Variety* 11/24/31.

Human Targets: Barton puts over his fight with an adult bad man convincingly and he looks like a real comer in westerns. Still a young man, he has sincerity and wistfulness. *Variety* 1/26/32.

Basquette, Lina (Lena Baskett or Baskette),
San Mateo, California, 1907–1994

Filmography: List of films in *Classic Images* (May-June 1983); *Sweethearts of the Sage*

Silent: In 1916 young Lina Basquette was signed for a series of "Lena Baskette features" by Universal. The first was possibly *Juvenile Dancer Supreme*. After making numerous films including *Polly Put the Kettle On*, *The Gates of Doom*, *The Weaker Vessel* and *Penrod* (1922 version), she went to Broadway to appear in the 1923 Ziegfeld Follies as a dancer.

It was in New York that her name was changed to the more glamorous Lina Basquette. By 1927 she was back in Hollywood making features which included *The Noose*, *Ranger of the North* and *Wheel of Chance*. Last silent: *Celebrity* (1928).

Sound: *Show Folks* (1928) was Basquette's first part-talkie. Others followed in 1929, including *Come Across* and *The Younger Generation*; her biggest film that year (although not a successful one) was Cecil B. DeMille's *The Godless Girl* with which her career reached its peak.

Basquette's films in the 1930s were mainly westerns and "B" melodramas and some of her parts were undeniably small. She made no film appearances at all in 1933–34 and 1939–41. Among her motion pictures were *The Dude Wrangler* (her sole 1930 effort), *The Arizona Terror*, *Hello Trouble*, *Ebb Tide*, *The Buccaneer* (1938 version) and *The Midnight Lady*.

In the 1940s Basquette apparently made only one film, 1942's *A Night for Crime*, in which she had a major role as a murderess. After almost 50 years she returned for a small role in *Paradise Park* (1991), which had very limited regional release. It was a story about a trailer park visited by God; she played one of the residents.

Comments: Why did Lina Basquette's career plummet so rapidly? She was still quite young and undeniably a brunette beauty. The reasons seem to lie with her personal life rather than her suitability for talkies. She had married Sam, one of the Warner Bros., and when he died she claimed his family had her blacklisted. They gained custody of her daughter in a bitter legal battle.

Basquette's off-screen temperament matched her on-screen persona. She was involved in tempestuous relationships with Jack Dempsey and others, apparently tried to commit suicide, and generally made scandalous headlines of which 1930s Hollywood did not approve. In the latter part of that decade, she even hinted at an indecent proposition from Adolf Hitler himself.

Although journalist Adela Rogers St. John had once dubbed her "The Tragedy Girl," Lina Basquette came back. She later became a successful dog breeder (Great Danes), wrote two dog care books and her autobiography, and seems to have made her peace with life.

REVIEWS

Show Folks: Basquette is best when she is dancing as part of the vaudeville team in this film. Her voice registers well in the film, in which only the last 1,000 feet has spoken dialogue. *Variety* 12/12/28, *Harrison's Reports* 12/22/28.

Arizona Terror: In this Ken Maynard western

Basquette is the leading lady but hasn't much to do. *Variety* 9/29/31.

Morals for Women: Basquette, down at the bottom of the cast list, plays a gold digger. *Variety* 11/17/31.

Phantom Express: Basquette has a small part in this poorly made melodrama. *Variety* 9/27/32.

Rose of the Rio Grande: Basquette makes the best impression in this uninteresting picture. *Variety* 7/13/38.

Baxter, Warner, Columbus, Ohio, 1889/91–1951

Filmography: List of films in *American Classic Screen* (Jan.-Feb. 1983); *Classic Images* (Sept.-Nov. 1989); *Eighty Silent Film Stars*

Silent: Stage-trained Warner Baxter made his screen debut in *All Woman* (1918), but it was in 1921 that his film career really began. It was a career which was to last almost 30 years. Among his 43 silent films in various genres were *Those Who Dance*, *The Female*, *The Golden Bed*, *Aloma of the South Seas* and *Miss Brewster's Millions*.

Baxter's more prestigious efforts were the first versions of *The Great Gatsby* (title role), *Craig's Wife* and *Ramona*, opposite Dolores Del Rio. Some of his costars were Agnes Ayres, Florence Vidor and Ethel Clayton at studios that included Goldwyn, Realart, Universal, Vitagraph, Fox, First National and MGM.

For much of his early career, Baxter was primarily a Paramount player but he freelanced for the final two years of the silent era. Last silent: *West of Zanzibar* (1928) starring Lon Chaney, with synchronized sound effects and music.

Sound: Baxter's maiden talkie *In Old Arizona* (1929) highlighted his deep and fine voice. The picture's novelty was that it was one of the very first sound films to be shot at least partially outdoors. His role of the Cisco Kid won him an Academy Award for Best Actor. Although the character was featured in several subsequent films, Baxter only repeated it twice: *The Cisco Kid* (1930) and *The Return of the Cisco Kid* (1939).

During the 1930s, Baxter was under contract to Twentieth Century–Fox and was one of the highest-salaried actors in Hollywood. He appeared in over 60 sound films, among them major efforts like *Forty-Second Street*, *Stand Up and Cheer*, *Penthouse*, *Kidnapped* (Freddie Bartholomew was the young hero), *Daddy Long Legs* with Janet Gaynor and *Broadway Bill*, directed by Frank Capra.

The Prisoner of Shark Island (1936) is usually considered Baxter's best sound performance. By the 1940s his stardom was clearly on the wane. After *Adam Had Four Sons*, with a young Ingrid Bergman, he was off-screen until 1943, apparently having suffered a nervous breakdown. His only other "A" picture of consequence in that decade was a supporting role in the unsuccessful *Lady in the Dark*; he was one of Ginger Rogers's love interests.

The "Crime Doctor" series, based on a radio show, supplied the bulk of Baxter's roles in the '40s. They included *Just Before Dawn*, *The Millerson Case* and *The Devil's Henchman*. He also made a few other "B" melodramas, the last of which was *State Penitentiary* (1950).

Comments: Warner Baxter was undoubtedly one of the successes of the transition from the silents to talkies. He was if anything more popular in sound films; they indeed may have saved his career. Although his silent oeuvre was reasonably successful, he was little more than a dependable leading man, not a major star. About 40 years old in 1929, he could not have expected to maintain a starring career much longer.

Baxter was certainly a competent actor and his speaking voice was an asset. It was perfectly suited to his persona and it was that persona which proved to be his continuing strength. As he had in his silents, he usually projected innate decency, dependability, solidity and, if the truth were known, *stolidity*.

It is no wonder that one of his favorite roles was as Dr. Mudd in *The Prisoner of Shark Island*. It encapsulated everything that summed up "Warner Baxter." To modern audiences, that honor belongs to the iconographic figure of theater director Julian Marsh in *Forty-Second Street*.

If he is remembered for nothing else, Baxter certainly had the distinction of uttering one of the most quoted (and misquoted) lines in cinema history to Ruby Keeler: "You're going out a youngster, but you've got to come back a star!"

REVIEWS

In Old Arizona: This picture is enlivened by Warner Baxter who does the best work of his career, and possibly the best talkie performance of any actor to date. He has never done anything to compare with his acting in this. His broken English is captivating. (He [presumably] sings the song "My Tonia," later recorded to great popularity by tenor Nick Lucas.) *New York Times* 1/21/29, *Variety* 1/23/29, *Harrison's Reports* 1/26/29.

Six Hours to Live: In this offbeat fantasy about a murder victim returning to life for six hours, Baxter does an excellent piece of acting. *Harrison's Reports* 10/22/32, *Variety* 10/25/32.

Forty-Second Street: A good and realistic performance by Warner Baxter as the neurotic showman. *Variety* 3/14/33, *Harrison's Reports* 3/18/33.

Under the Pampas Moon: Baxter is unable to overcome the plot defects, and his role forces him to act in almost a coy manner. *Harrison's Reports* 6/8/35.

The Prisoner of Shark Island: Perhaps his best acting part as Doctor Samuel Mudd who was accused of being in league with John Wilkes Booth. Directed by John Ford. *Variety* 2/19/36.

Crime Doctor: In this program mystery melodrama, Warner Baxter, as the victim, gives a convincing performance. *Harrison's Reports* 7/10/43.

State Penitentiary: The performers enact their roles with force and conviction. Baxter acts with restraint. *Harrison's Reports* 5/20/50.

Bedford, Barbara (Violet Rose — — —?),

Prairie du Chien, Wisconsin, 1900?–

Filmography: *Classic Images* (Nov.-Dec. 1984); List of films in *Sweethearts of the Sage*.

Silent: Barbara Bedford made a hit in one of the first of her 50 silent films, *The Last of the Mohicans* (1920). Her first known film was *The Cradle of Courage*, a William S. Hart western, in the same year. She also appeared opposite John Gilbert several times in 1920 to '22. Among her better-remembered motion pictures were *Tumbleweed* (Hart's final film in 1925), *Cinderella of the Hills* and *Mockery*, co-starring Lon Chaney.

Bedford also appeared in the 1923 version of *The Spoilers*. Among her other silents were *Forbidden Love*, *The Mad Whirl*, *What Fools Men*, *Life of an Actress*, *The Girl from Gay Paree* and *Bitter Sweets*. Last silent: *The Heroic Lover* (1929), with synchronized music and sound effects.

Sound: Despite her good voice, all of Barbara Bedford's 1929 films were silent and she did not appear in a talkie until her supporting role in 1930's *The Lash* with Richard Barthelmess. She was in only a single feature between 1931 and 1934.

In the latter year Bedford returned in the lead of *Found Alive*, a cheapie jungle melodrama distributed by Ideal Pictures. Its truly horrible reviews and probably limited distribution doomed any chance of a comeback as a leading lady.

From then on, Barbara Bedford's name was to be found lower down in the cast lists of her films at studios such as Peerless, Monogram and Chesterfield. Many of her later roles were in "Our Gang" and "Crime Does Not Pay" shorts.

Bedford's last known appearance was in 1944's *Meet the People*; other features included *Desert Vengeance*, *The Death Kiss*, *On Probation*, *The Midnight Phantom*, *The Mine with the Iron Door* and *Three Comrades*.

Comments: Barbara Bedford was an intelligent-looking actress possessed of a cool beauty, and she proved to be a dependable leading lady or second lead in silents. She appeared in every genre from comedy to westerns to (in the sound era) musicals.

Possessing a voice that was pleasantly, though surprisingly, low-pitched, Bedford was perhaps more suited for talkie villainy than for routine leads. It may be why she was not more successful in talkies, although she still remained a handsome woman into her mid–30s. In any case, her best days lay in the time before movies found their voice.

REVIEWS

The Love Trader: Bedford appears in the supporting cast. *Harrison's Reports* 11/1/30.

The Lash: The supporting cast is excellent, including Barbara Bedford who plays the Mexican Lupe. *Harrison's Reports* 1/3/31.

Desert Vengeance: A Buck Jones western with Barbara Bedford as the leading lady. She will be remembered from silent days. *Variety* 3/11/31.

Found Alive: The acting is less than adequate. The picture might better have been left undiscovered. *New York Times* 2/12/34.

Beery, Noah (Noah Beery, *Jr.*, the name by

which his son [born 1915] was later known), Kansas City, Missouri, 1883/84–1946

Filmography: List of films in *Eighty Silent Film Stars*

Silent: From at least 1916 to the end of the silent era, Noah Beery was exceedingly active in character parts of all kinds. In many of those years he was seen in at least ten films and in one year (1923) he made 17! Among his earliest films were *The Social Highwayman*, *The Clever Mrs. Carfax*, *Believe Me Xantippe* and *A Mormon Maid* (with Mae Murray).

Beery's burly physical presence and beetle-browed countenance made him a natural for villainy and he shone in such films as *The Mark of Zorro*, *The Coming of Amos*, *Beau Geste* and numerous westerns. Other films included *The Call of the North*, *Tillie*, *The Destroying Angel*, *To the Last Man*, *Lily of the Dust*, *Lord Jim*, *Hellship Bronson* and *Beau Sabreur*. Last silent: *The Four Feathers* (1929), with synchronized music and sound effects, made after his first part-talkie.

Sound: Noah Beery kept up his hectic pace at the dawn of talkies, appearing in 24 films in two years, 1929 and 1930. His deep voice was first heard in the part-talkie *Noah's Ark* (1928) and he was on-screen steadily through the early '40s, although slackening his pace somewhat after 1936. In the last few years of his life he was seen even less frequently.

Beery continued his evil ways in many films, sometimes dastardly, sometimes just unsavory.

Often, though, he was avuncularly sympathetic or, at least, had his tongue planted firmly in cheek. He could sing too, and did in early musicals like *The Golden Dawn* (1930). His films included *Careers*, *Tol'able David* (1930 version), *She Done Him Wrong*, *David Harum*, *The Girl of the Golden West*, *The Tulsa Kid*, *Isle of Missing Men* and *Barbary Coast Gent*.

As in the silent days there were numerous westerns as well. *This Man's Navy* (1945), starring his brother Wallace, was Noah Beery's last film. He also appeared in the serials *Ace Drummond*, *Zorro Rides Again* and *Adventures of Red Ryder*. Shortly before the time of his death he was playing a major role as Boss Tweed in the Broadway musical *Up in Central Park*.

Comments: Noah Beery often tended toward scenery-chewing but usually did so with a twinkle in his eye that made him likable in almost any role. His basso profundo voice was a perfect complement to his other physical characteristics (like his homely, lived-in face), and it enhanced his status as a portrayer of villainy.

It certainly helped to extend Beery's career well into the sound period although his sound films were generally of lesser quality than the silents. In this new medium it was his slightly younger brother Wallace who, at MGM, had the lion's share of the Beery family glory.

Reviews

Noah's Ark: Beery is great in a dual role as the Russian spy and the King. *Variety* 11/7/28, *Harrison's Reports* 3/23/29.

Careers: The recorded voices of the supporting cast, especially Noah Beery as the villain, are up to par. *Variety* 6/12/29, *Harrison's Reports* 6/22/29.

The Show of Shows: Beery has just the voice one expects from him, a deep, resonant bass. He could acquit himself favorably in a musical comedy role. *New York Times* 11/21/29.

Panamint's Bad Man: In this good western Beery is the proprietor of a casino. *Harrison's Reports* 7/9/38.

Torpedoed: Beery's caricature of the republic's president is as bad as his Spanish. *New York Times* 9/26/39.

Beery, Wallace, Kansas City, Missouri,

1884/89–1949

Filmography: *Film Fan Monthly* (July–Aug. 1967), *Films in Review* (July–Sept. 1973), *Classic Images* (Nov.–Dec. 1987)

Silent: Following a varied career that included — or so the story goes — a stint as a circus elephant trainer, Wallace Beery came to show business in stock and Broadway musicals. He debuted in films about 1913 and soon was mildly popular playing an oversized Swedish maid in the "Sweedie" series. He also worked with wife-to-be Gloria Swanson.

For most of the 'teens Beery worked in one- and two-reelers and is said to have directed a few. Among his features in that decade were *The Slim Princess*, *Johanna Enlists*, *The Love Burglar* and *The Unpardonable Sin*. The latter film, in which he played a brutish Hun, proved to be a big break for his career. He also appeared in the serial *Patria*.

The films in which Beery appeared in the first half of the 1920s, mainly for Paramount and First National, continued to move him up toward minor character stardom. His 1920 performances in *The Last of the Mohicans* and *The Virgin of Stamboul* were well-received. Other Beery silent films included *The Four Horsemen of the Apocalypse*, *Robin Hood*, *The Lost World*, *The Sea Hawk* (1924 version), *Old Ironsides*, *Beggars of Life*, *So Big* and *Casey at the Bat*. His starring role in 1923's *Richard, the Lion Hearted* was another career booster.

Beery's teaming with Raymond Hatton in the 1926 comedy *Behind the Front* resulted in their reteaming in *We're in the Navy Now*, *Now We're in the Air*, *Fireman Save My Child* and *Partners in Crime*. Eventually, diminishing interest in this teaming as well as some indifferent films began to slow his career even though he was frequently top-billed. Last silent: *Stairs of Sand* (1929), made after his first part-talkies.

Sound: Beery's talkie career did not get off to an auspicious beginning. His first was the 1928 part-sound *Beggars of Life*, followed by the 1929 melodrama *Chinatown Nights*, also a part-talkie. This in turn was followed by the all-sound *River of Romance*, in which he played a supporting role.

Beery was released by Paramount, as were so many of their silent stars, and he was off the screen for almost a year before being rescued by MGM. A meaty and impressive second lead as Butch, the murderer, in 1930s *The Big House* (a role originally slated for Lon Chaney), resulted in his first Academy Award nomination.

That year's *Min and Bill*, in which Beery co-starred with Marie Dressler, cemented his new-found stardom. Other pictures in the '30s were *The Secret Six*, *The Champ* (a 1931 Academy Award for Best Actor shared with Fredric March), *Billy the Kid*, *Tugboat Annie* (reteamed with Dressler), *Viva Villa!*, *Treasure Island*, *Dinner at Eight* and *Ah, Wilderness*.

It is generally agreed that Wally Beery reached the apex of his career in the first half of the '30s. Although he remained a bankable star, the importance of his roles declined after Irving Thalberg died. He no longer was paired with other important MGM stars, no doubt as a result of Louis B. Mayer's antipathy towards him.

In the 1940s Beery tended to be cast as the "good bad man" in minor "A" westerns like *Wyoming, Jackass Mail, Bad Bascomb* and *Bad Man of Brimstone*. He was sometimes teamed with raucous Marjorie Main in a vain effort to recreate the Beery-Dressler magic. In the last few years of that decade, his output was sparse and none of his films memorable. He was heard on the radio as well.

Beery had an atypical role in the 1948 color musical *A Date with Judy*, his penultimate film. He joined in singing "A Most Unusual Day" and even danced a little. Shortly after completing *Big Jack* (1949), he died, still in harness.

Comments: Apparently Wallace Beery offstage was the same rather slovenly and profane person he was on camera. What he did not transfer to his private life was his on-screen sweetness, if reports from co-stars like Jackie Cooper are to be believed. He could be remote and unfriendly on and off the set and he mugged, ad-libbed freely and stole scenes with wild abandon. He also loudly condemned others for doing the same things.

Talkies revealed that Beery's voice perfectly fit his face and screen persona. It was a voice which brought a more lovable Wallace Beery to the fore, though he could still play "nasty" with conviction. (Many of his silent roles had been villainous.)

As time went on, Beery came to rely more heavily on his mannerisms, both physical and verbal, and by the end of his career he was basically playing "Wallace Beery," or at least the cinema version of him. This included a winsome hesitation in his speech, running his hand over his jowly face with a boyish "Aw shucks" and other "shtick."

Beery appeared in almost 170 silents, including numerous one- and two-reelers, and about 50 talkies. During the height of his career he was one of the top box office attractions and in the Top Ten for several years in the '30s and 1940. There was no one quite like him. He was both a great screen character and one of the most disliked men in Hollywood.

REVIEWS

Chinatown Nights: Beery has not been given a choice assignment. But he has a powerful screen personality with a manly, stentorian voice. *Variety* 4/13/29.

The River of Romance: A new and different Wallace Beery without his familiar tricks, but no less interesting as a talkie player. *Variety* 7/31/29.

The Big House: Moviegoers have been accustomed to good acting on the part of Beery, but he

has never done better work. *Harrison's Reports* 7/5/30.

Min and Bill: An excellent performance by Beery as Bill. *Harrison's Reports* 11/29/30.

The Secret Six: Beery has been hurt by his casting as a ruthless gang leader, a repulsive role. It's a bad gangster film in every way except for the bit of natural humor he cannot help but inject into it. *Variety* 5/6/31.

The Champ: Understanding, adult piece of work by Beery, who had to hustle to keep up with Jackie Cooper. *Variety* 11/17/31.

Dinner at Eight: Beery is at home as the millionaire vulgarian. He is made to order for this type of role. He is excellent; every time he appears there are laughs. (The inspired, though on the surface unlikely, teaming of Beery with Jean Harlow was a highlight of this all-star MGM extravaganza. He did a variation of his sleazy businessman impersonation from *Grand Hotel* a year earlier.) *Variety* 8/29/33, *Harrison's Reports* 9/2/33.

Viva Villa!: Reviewers differed. Some thought Beery's performance was excellent. Another said that his characterization let Villa down and that Beery is a hybrid dialectician, neither Mexican nor Gringo, and with a vacillating accent. *Variety* 4/17/34, *Harrison's Reports* 4/28/34.

Sergeant Madden: This raises new possibilities for Beery's screen future. He has hitherto been typed by making smirking facial contortions whenever confronted with an embarrassing or dramatic moment. Josef von Sternberg presents him in a straight portrayal that is refreshing and Beery does a neat job, even down to the Irish brogue. *Variety* 3/22/39.

Rationing: Beery is as good as could be expected with an inferior role. *Variety* 1/26/44.

A Date with Judy: Beery does a very good job, with little of his customary mugging. *Variety* 6/23/48.

Bellamy, Madge (Margaret Philpott), Hillsboro, Texas, 1900/04–1990

Filmography: List of films in *Films in Review* (Apr. 1970), additional films (May-July 1970); *Classic Images* (Sept.-Oct. 1983, Feb. 1990); *Sweethearts of the Sage*

Silent: Madge Bellamy's career began with a supporting role in *The Riddle Woman* (1919). By 1921 she was in films such as *The Cup of Life* and *Blind Hearts*, and remained a popular star throughout the 1920s, her best-remembered role coming in John Ford's 1924 railroad epic *The Iron Horse*.

Other Bellamy films of the period included *Lorna Doone, The Parasite, Bertha the Sewing Machine Girl, The Wings of Youth, Lightnin'* and *Colleen*, one of her big hits. Last silent: *Fugitives* (1929), with synchronized music, made after her first talkie.

Sound: *Mother Knows Best*, a 1928 part-talkie, marked Bellamy's sound debut. Her first all-talking production was *Tonight at Twelve* (1929), in which she got top billing. She made no film appearances in 1930 or '31. Her few other talkies in the 1930s included leading roles in the now-cult film *White Zombie* and *Gigolettes of Paris*.

Bellamy played supporting or bit parts in other movies, including *Charlie Chan in London*, *The Great Hospital Mystery*, *The Daring Young Man* and *Under Your Spell*. There was also a serial, *Gordon of Ghost City*, in 1933. By 1937 her career was virtually over, although she made a final appearance in 1945's *Northwest Trail*.

Comments: Madge Bellamy's career in talkies could not be deemed a success. As the reviews indicate, her voice was not strong, even though she essayed a few songs in her films (assuming that it was actually her voice). The public did not buy her as talkie star and she slipped rapidly. *Gigolettes of Paris* (1933), in which her performance was quite acceptable, was her last starring film.

Today Bellamy is undoubtedly best-known through *White Zombie*, a cheaply-made but atmospheric 1932 horror film with Bela Lugosi. Unfortunately, both her odd Kewpie doll-like makeup and her laughably hesitant and underplayed performance (in a film full of otherwise over-the-top acting) lead viewers to the inevitable conclusion that she simply was not a good actress, or at least not a good *sound* film actress. She did later claim that her voice had been dubbed in this film because she had lost her own voice.

REVIEWS

Mother Knows Best: Bellamy gives an admirable performance and even though her voice is none too strong, she acquits herself favorably in the sound passages. She also sings and does celebrity imitations, but these vocal efforts are not to be compared with her acting. *New York Times* 9/17/28, *Variety* 9/19/28.

White Zombie: Bellamy is lovely to look at but is not called upon for much dramatic exertion. *Variety* 8/2/32.

Gigolettes of Paris: The acting is stilted; Bellamy's performance is unexciting. (She played a nightclub entertainer and sang in this film. It was originally called *Gold Diggers of Paris* but this title was changed when Warner Bros. produced *The Gold Diggers of 1933*.) *Variety* 10/17/33.

The Great Hotel Murder: Most decorative of the women is Madge Bellamy as a cigar counter girl. Miss Bellamy was formerly a star at Fox in silent days. Her voice is good and she looks great. *Variety* 3/6/35.

Bennett, Alma, Seattle, Washington, 1889–1958

Silent: Alma Bennett was a '20s version of the "vamp" in numerous features like *Long Pants*, *A Fool and His Money*, *Don Juan's Three Nights* and *Why Men Leave Home*. In westerns and action films she sometimes played straight leads and she appeared in two-reelers with Ben Turpin. Her debut had come about 1919, possibly in *The Right to Happiness*.

Bennett was active through the 1920s, although some of her last roles were small. Other films included *The Lost World*, *Flaming Hearts*, *Three Jumps Ahead* and *The Face on the Barroom Floor*. Last silent: *The Head of the Family* (1928).

Sound: *My Lady's Past* (1929), a part-talkie, marked Bennett's sound debut. This was her last full year on screen and, although she had the lead in *New Orleans*, the remainder of her roles were small.

The other Bennett films, both part-talkie and full sound, were *Painted Faces*, *Two Men and a Maid*, both 1929, and 1930's *Midnight Daddies*. The latter was her final feature (her character was billed as "A vamp"), but she may have appeared in some comedy shorts as well.

REVIEWS

New Orleans: Alma Bennett is the heroine and is deserving of special attention. Her portrayal of passion is of the Greta Garbo type, only far more concentrated. If given a real break Alma would compare favorably with other vamps of the screen. *Harrison's Reports* 8/10/29, *Variety* 8/28/29.

Bennett, Belle, Milaca, Minnesota, 1890/91– 1932

Silent: Belle Bennett began her career on her family's showboat and eventually came to the movies about 1914. Her early films included *Mrs. Wiggs of the Cabbage Patch*, *Sweet Kitty Bellairs*, *Mignon*, *Fires of Rebellion* and *The Reckoning Day*. From 1919 to 1924 she was on-screen only sporadically, alternating film roles with Broadway appearances where she played to acclaim.

Nineteen twenty-five was the year Belle Bennett became the very symbol of sacrificing motherhood; *Stella Dallas* was the vehicle. It made her a star throughout the remainder of her life. Other films included *East Lynne* (1925 version), *Mother*, *The Way of All Flesh*, *Mother Machree*, *The Reckless Lady* and *If Marriage Fails*. Last silents: *The Battle of the Sexes*, with synchronized sound effects and music, and *The Power of Silence*, released about the same time in 1928.

Sound: *The Iron Mask* (1929) was Bennett's initial part-talkie. All her other 1929 films had at least some talking in them as well: *Molly and Me*, *My Lady's Past* and *Their Own Desire*. She continued to "suffer" in such 1930 films as *Courage*, *Recaptured Love* and *The Woman Who Was Forgotten*. *The Big Shot* (1931), in which she had a supporting role, was her final picture.

Comments: Belle Bennett was considered little more than an ordinarily competent leading woman until *Stella Dallas*. It made her a major star but also placed her firmly in mother roles at the age of 35. Although it is very likely that she was not happy about the typecasting, it gave her a career niche.

Bennett's stage-trained voice was suitable for sound and she continued to be top-billed up to her last film, in which she was down the cast list. She had become a specialist in "weepies" but perhaps moviegoers were becoming less tolerant of such roles. Her stardom probably would not have continued much longer, but a solid career in character roles was surely in the offing.

REVIEWS

Molly and Me: Bennett does good acting in her role as a burlesque queen, but her voice is only fair in this back stage melodrama. Her stage experience stands her in good stead. *Harrison's Reports* 4/20/29, *Variety* 6/19/29.

My Lady's Past: Bennett's appearance is too maternal for the role. *Variety* 8/2/29.

Their Own Desire: Bennett has another suffering role in marital drama. (She played the mother of Norma Shearer, a woman less than ten years her junior.) *Variety* 1/29/30.

The Woman Who Was Forgotten: Bennett is excellent in this teary melodrama, first as the carefree happy girl and finally as the poor old scrubwoman. *Harrison's Reports* 2/1/30.

Courage: Bennett has been in many a mother part, but this is the best one yet She put her whole soul into it and plays with quiet assurance. *Harrison's Reports* 5/31/30, *Variety* 6/11/30.

Recaptured Love: It is a little different role for this actress of the silent days. *Variety* 8/13/30.

The Big Shot: A rural comedy that possesses a cast of little marquee value. (Bennett was billed no higher than fifth in this insignificant film.) Variety 1/5/32.

Bennett, Constance, New York, New York,
1904/05–1965
Filmography: *Films in Review* (Oct. 1965); List of films in *Film Dope* (Aug. 1973)

Silent: After working as an extra in one-reel comedies, blonde Constance Bennett, daughter of stage and film actor Richard Bennett, played her first small role as a chorus girl in 1922's *Reckless Youth*. There were a dozen or so other features, in some of which she had supporting roles.

Bennett's motion pictures included *Cytherea*, *What's Wrong with the Women?*, *The Goose Hangs High*, *Code of the West*, *My Son* and *The Pinch Hitter*. She had a major success as one of the three leads, along with Joan Crawford, in *Sally, Irene and Mary*. She also appeared in the 1924 serial *Into the Net*. Last silent: *Married?* (1926).

Sound: Constance Bennett found her niche in the early talkies and from 1930 to '33 was one of Hollywood's most popular (and highest paid) actresses. She may have only been second to the great Garbo herself in screen popularity.

Bennett's talkie debut came in the romantic comedy *This Thing Called Love* (1929). Most of her films were melodramas which saw her struggle upward through adversity. Despite her sophistication, her *métier* was playing shopgirls; it was not until the later '30s that she played roles closer to her own "real life" persona.

Bennett's major success, at least in retrospect, was probably George Cukor's *What Price Hollywood?* in 1932. After 1933 her vehicles became tiresome to her formerly rabid public and her career declined while that of her younger sister Joan was on the ascendancy.

Bennett found brief popularity once again with *Topper* and its first sequel in the later '30s but soon was back in dreary melodramas or as support in comedies like *Two-Faced Woman*, Greta Garbo's final movie. She remained fairly active through most of the 1940s, however.

Among Bennett's 40 talkies were *Son of the Gods*, *Common Clay* (her first major hit), *The Easiest Way*, *Bought*, *Bed of Roses*, *Outcast Lady*, *Law of the Tropics*, *Madame Spy*, *The Unsuspected* and *As Young As You Feel*. After a 13 year hiatus she returned for one last role in the 1965 remake of *Madame X*. She appeared on the stage off and on from the late '30s and also had night club act in the 1950s.

Comments: Constance Bennett found relatively fleeting fame in early talkies with her weepy tales of woe that often co-starred Joel McCrea. Her playing against type was, for a while, accepted by audiences though her brittle voice and sleek (occasionally bulimic) blonde looks bespoke sophistication.

The studio moguls were not always pleased with their difficult star. Bennett was a shrewd businesswoman and had what today would be called an "in your face" attitude towards the Hollywood pow-ers-that-be and even the press. Tact obviously was not first on her list of character traits; hauteur per-haps was.

As long as Bennett's films proved successful, she was tolerated; once she began to slip, she had little studio support. Sister Joan compared her to a "sil-very comet" and "an overwhelming and volatile mixture ... shot from a cannon." Sometimes that came across on the screen and very often it came across in the publicity about her somewhat tem-pestuous private life. She always made good copy.

REVIEWS

This Thing Called Love: Bennett is an engaging performer and gives a consistently good perfor-mance. Her good acting causes the comedy. *Vari-ety* 7/18/29, *Harrison's Reports* 12/21/29.

Bought: Constance Bennett's leading role will make this a success because her hosts of women followers will want to see her. They like the fact that she is never bested by men. This is the first talkie in which she has displayed an aptitude for acting, rather than being an automaton. *Variety* 8/18/31.

What Price Hollywood?: The heroine is an extremely sympathetic character because of the excel-lent performance given by Constance Bennett. For a little while it looks as if there's going to be a new Miss Bennett but it doesn't last. In the following scene she is again assumes her very familiar screen persona. *Harrison's Reports* 6/25/32, *Variety* 7/19/32.

Bed of Roses: As a rapacious female, Bennett's characterization hews close to the line almost all the way. *Variety* 7/4/33.

Topper: Bennett carries out her assignment with great skill. (She received top billing as the ghostly Marion Kerby in this classic comedy opposite Cary Grant and Roland Young in the title role.) *Variety* 7/14/37.

Law of the Tropics: The presence of Constance Bennett may draw some interest. Although she isn't exactly young and doesn't look it, it doesn't hurt the picture. Her slight brassiness fits the character. It's good casting and a skillful performance. (The allusion to Bennett's age stems from the fact that Miriam Hopkins turned the part down saying she was too old to play against the leading man, Jeffrey Lynn.) *Variety* 9/3/41.

Madame Spy: The Bennett name may produce some marquee voltage. She is decorative as the spy-wife and does what she can with the material given to her. *Variety* 12/9/42.

Angel on the Amazon: Miss Bennett is okay. (The degree to which Bennett's film fortunes had declined is evident by the fact that she was billed below the legendarily untalented ex–ice skater Vera [Hruba] Ralston.) *Variety* 12/22/48.

Bennett, Enid, York, Western Australia, 1895–1969

Silent: From 1917, Enid Bennett was a popular star. Among her earlier films were *Happiness, Coals of Fire, The Vamp, Naughty Though Married* and *Silk Hosiery*, and she later had leading roles in Dou-glas Fairbanks's *Robin Hood* and Milton Sills's *The Sea Hawk*.

Bennett remained active through 1924 but then made only two more pictures in the silent period. Other films were *The Courtship of Miles Standish* (starring Charles Ray), *The Red Lily* and *A Woman's Heart*. Last silent: *The Wrong Mr. Wright* (1927).

Sound: In 1931 Enid Bennett returned for a handful of character roles. In *Skippy* she was the mother of the title character (Jackie Cooper); she repeated the role in *Sooky*, its same-year sequel. *Waterloo Bridge* was her other motion picture that year.

Bennett was not seen again until 1939 when she appeared in *Intermezzo* and *Meet Dr. Christian*. The Mickey Rooney-Judy Garland musical *Strike Up the Band* (1940) contained what may have been her last film role. She played the mother of one of the numerous children in the cast.

REVIEWS

Skippy: The stars are ably assisted by Enid Ben-nett. *Harrison's Reports* 1/11/31.

Sooky: Enid Bennett is excellent as Skippy's mother. She plays with a reticence that is a great asset. *New York Times* 12/21/31, *Variety* 12/22/31.

Bennett, Richard, Beacon Mills, Indiana, 1870/73–1944

Silent: A flamboyant Broadway star in the old style, Richard Bennett made his film debut top-billed in 1913's *Damaged Goods*. He starred in sev-eral others as well in the 'teens, including *Philip Holden — Waster, The Valley of Decision, The Gilded Youth* and *The End of the Road*.

Because Bennett was primarily a stage actor, his silent film appearances were few. A supporting role in 1923's *The Eternal City* was his first in four years although he had been credited with writing a sce-nario and "technical direction" on a few films pre-viously. He also was seen in *Youth for Sale*. Last silent: *Lying Wives* (1925).

Sound: Richard Bennett's first talkie was *The Home Towners* (1928), in which he received top bill-ing. From 1931 to '34 he played character parts in a handful of pictures, among which were *Arrowsmith,*

Bought, Madame Racketeer, This Reckless Age and *Nana*. He then returned to the theater.

By the 1940s Bennett was becoming better known as the father of the actresses Constance and Joan Bennett (daughter Barbara also had a brief show biz career) than as a star in his own right. He had his last major role as the patriarch in Orson Welles' *The Magnificent Ambersons* (1942) and was also seen in Welles' *Journey Into Fear*.

REVIEWS

The Home Towners: Richard Bennett is limited to carrying the story as a straight man. (He performs well, looks good on-screen and his diction is invariably clear.) *Variety* 10/31/28, *New York Times* 12/24/28.

Bought: Bennett plays his role in a subdued manner but gives a supreme performance. He supported the star, his daughter Constance. *Variety* 8/18/31, *Harrison's Reports* 8/22/31.

No Greater Love: Richard Bennett, in little more than a bit, is hardly recognizable behind a beard and speaking with a dialect. *Variety* 5/17/32.

Big Executive: Richard Bennett's performance strikes a strong note. He has a part that he carries out powerfully. *Variety* 10/3/33.

Nana: Bennett seems to overact occasionally, but overall he handles it with restraint. *Variety* 2/6/34.

The Magnificent Ambersons: Richard Bennett evinces none of the scenery-chewing for which he was once known. *Variety* 7/1/42.

Besserer, Eugenie, Marseilles, France, 1870–1934

Silent: Before Eugenie Besserer became an archetypal mother figure, she played mature leads in two-reelers for Selig from 1911 and was known as "The Ellen Terry of the Screen." She also was a D. W. Griffith player in films like *Scarlet Days* and *The Greatest Question*.

Among Besserer's numerous other films were *The City of Purple Dreams, Auction of Souls, Anna Christie* (1923 version), *Molly O', The Coast of Folly* and *When a Man Loves*. Last silent: *Speedway* (1929), with synchronized music and sound effects, made considerably after her first part-talkie.

Sound: The first sound film in which Eugenie Besserer appeared was the very first commercially successful part-talkie, *The Jazz Singer* (1927). She was Mrs. Rabinowitz, the cantor's wife, and mother of the star Al Jolson. Although she did not actually have spoken dialogue, she uttered some muffled sounds in the first talking scene with Jolson. (He playfully accused her of acting "kittenish.")

Another early Besserer part-talkie was 1928's *A Lady of Chance*, and all but one of her nine 1929 films had some talking, including *The Bridge of San Luis Rey, Illusion, Madame X, Fast Company* and *Mr. Antonio*. After 1930's *In Gay Madrid* and *A Royal Romance* she had few billed appearances and these were small. Other films to 1933 were *Six Hours to Live* and *To the Last Man*, her last known role.

REVIEWS

The Jazz Singer: The supporting cast stands out in the person of Eugenie Besserer, as the mother. *Variety* 10/12/27.

In Gay Madrid: The acting is charming throughout, including that of Eugenie Besserer in the supporting cast. (With her "all-purpose" accent, Besserer played a Spanish señora.) *Harrison's Reports* 6/14/30.

Bevan, Billy (William Harris?), Orange, Australia, 1887–1957

Silent: Before coming to America in 1912, Billy Bevan had been a staple in Australian stock companies and vaudeville. Sporting his signature walrus mustache, he was featured in Universal and Christie one- and two-reelers and for ten years appeared for Sennett. His first credited feature was the 1920 Sennett production *Love, Honor and Behave*.

In the '20s Bevan made a few other appearances in full-length films interspersed with numerous two-reelers. His features included *A Small Town Idol, The Crossroads of New York, The Extra Girl, The White Sin* and *Easy Pickings*. Last silent feature: *Riley the Cop* (1928), with synchronized sound effects and music.

Sound: Although he was not from England, Billy Bevan assumed a realistic Cockney accent for many of his sound roles, and they were numerous. Although seldom noted in reviews, he supplied authentic local color, most often in small roles as porters, barkeeps, bobbies and similar working class persons, in features of the 1930s and '40s.

Bevan did occasionally have better parts in films such as *Journey's End* (1930), one of his first sound features. Other appearances that year were in *For the Love o' Lil* and *Peacock Alley*. Another of his more important roles came in the popular 1934 adventure *The Lost Patrol*, directed by John Ford.

Among Bevan's pictures in the very active '30s were *Payment Deferred, Vanity Fair, Alice in Wonderland, A Tale of Two Cities, Dracula's Daughter, Lloyds of London* and *Bringing Up Baby*.

In the 1940s Bevan appeared on-screen in *Tin Pan Alley, Suspicion, Dr. Jekyll and Mr. Hyde, Forever and a Day, The Picture of Dorian Gray* and *The Black Arrow*, among others. His final year in films may have been 1950 but he was glimpsed in two silent comedy compilations of the early '60s.

Sky Hawk: Bevan turns the cockney comedy role to good account. He plays the airplane mechanic and gives an excellent performance in a sympathetic part. *New York Times* 12/12/29, *Variety* 12/18/29.

Sky Devils: Bevan contributes to the general amusement. *New York Times* 5/4/32.

Billington, Francelia, Dallas, Texas, 1895–1934

Silent: Francelia Billington worked briefly at Kalem and Thanhouser before becoming a leading lady at Reliance-Majestic from 1913 to '15 and then at Universal from 1916. She was teamed with such male stars as Carlyle Blackwell, William Russell and Tom Mix. She was especially active prior to 1920, made a few pictures in each of the years from 1920–22 and only three or four more during the rest of the silent era.

Billington specialized in dramas and westerns. Among her films were *Bettina Loved a Soldier, The Frame Up, Sands of Sacrifice,* Erich von Stroheim's *Blind Husbands* (perhaps her best-known), *The Great Air Robbery, Desert Love* and *Blue Blazes.* Last silent: *Tex* (1926). A film entitled *A Rough Shod Fighter* was shown in 1927 but may have actually been produced ten years earlier.

Sound: *The Mounted Stranger,* a 1930 Hoot Gibson western, appears to have been Billington's sole talkie. She played a supporting role.

The Mounted Stranger: The dialogue, and its recitation by the cast, is easy and natural. *Variety* 2/12/30, *Harrison's Reports* 2/15/30.

Blane, Sally (Elizabeth Jane Jung or Young), Salida, Colorado, 1910–1997

Filmography: *Classic Images* (Sept. 1982); List of films in *Sweethearts of the Sage*

Silent: After appearing in a small role in the 1917 film *Sirens of the Sea,* Sally Blane returned to the screen as Betty Jane Young in "The Collegians" series about 1926. She became Sally Blane when she began making features, the first of which were *Casey at the Bat, Rolled Stockings* and *Shootin' Irons,* all 1927. Other films, in some of which she co-starred with Tom Mix, included *A Horseman of the Plains, Fools for Luck, The Vanishing Pioneer* and *King Cowboy.* Last silent: *Eyes of the Underworld* (1929).

Sound: Blane was especially busy in 1929, a year in which she made eight films, three of them silents and the rest sound. Her first talkie was *The Very*

Idea which was followed by *The Vagabond Lover* with Rudy Vallee. In *The Show of Shows* she briefly danced and sang with her sister Loretta Young in the "Meet My Sister" musical number.

Blane worked steadily until about 1935 in westerns and action melodramas and was somewhat less active in the last part of the decade. She played leads or top supporting roles in "B" films such as *Silver Streak, The Phantom Express, The Great Hospital Mystery, Against the Law, Crashin' Thru, Numbered Women* and *Charlie Chan at Treasure Island.*

Sally Blane was also seen in support in major productions like *I Am a Fugitive from a Chain Gang* and *The Story of Alexander Graham Bell.* The latter film marked the only joint appearance of all the Young sisters, including the eldest Polly Ann and their half-sister Georgianna. Blane's last film for many years was 1939's *Fighting Mad* but she returned for a small role in *A Bullet for Joey* (1955).

Comments: Closely resembling her sister Loretta Young, Sally Blane spent her career in films which generally played the lower half of the bill. Her younger sibling proved to be the major star. As was revealed in early talkies like *The Vagabond Lover* and *Tanned Legs,* she had quite a bit to learn about film acting and the use of her voice. Eventually she became a competent, if somewhat bland, actress in the course of her 1930s melodramas.

The Vagabond Lover: Sally Blane is a good leading lady. *Variety* 12/4/29, *Harrison's Reports* 12/7/29.

Shanghaied Love: Sally Blane is the girl. *Variety* 11/10/31.

Cross Examination: In the supporting cast is Sally Blane. It is a murder story in which she has little to do and which she does perfunctorily. *Harrison's Reports* 2/20/32, *Variety* 3/1/32.

Forbidden Company: Blane is handicapped with a weak part. *Variety* 7/12/32.

Advice to the Lovelorn: Except for the leading man no one else matters in the cast. Sally Blane, as the female lead, is merely a stooge. *Variety* 12/19/33.

Numbered Women: Sally Blane is the heroine. *Harrison's Reports* 5/28/38.

Bletcher, William (Billy), Lancaster, Pennsylvania, 1894–1979

Filmography: List of features in *Films in Review* (May 1970)

Silent: Billy Bletcher spent his first film years with Mack Sennett, including a stint as one of the raucous Keystone Kops. Subsequently, in four years at the Christie studio, he co-starred with Bobby Vernon in a series of comedies. Because they were about the same diminutive height (little more than five feet tall), much of the humor dealt with mistaken identities between them.

Bletcher made the transition to character actor in features in the late 'teens and '20s. Among his films were *The Love Hunger*, *The Wild Girl*, *One Hour to Love* and *Daredevil's Reward*. Last silent: *The Cowboy Kid* (1928).

Sound: With sound, William Bletcher's voice led to an expansion of his career. He appeared in features and shorts such as the "Our Gang" comedies and a series with hefty Billy Gilbert. The latter teaming was possibly an attempt to recreate Laurel and Hardy. They came to be known as "The Schmaltz Brothers," speaking with a "Dutch" dialect *à la* Weber and Fields. Among their comedies were *Rhapsody in Brew* and *Call Her Sausage*.

Bletcher performed on the radio and in 1950 even substituted for the actor who played "The Lone Ranger." He also was heard in numerous Disney and Warner Bros. cartoons and was the voice of "The Big Bad Wolf" in the famous *The Three Little Pigs*. Other vocal achievements included dubbing for other performers (some of the "Munchkins" in *The Wizard of Oz*) and dubbing English dialogue in several foreign films.

Bletcher also continued character appearances in features such as *Top Speed*, *Diplomaniacs*, *Babes in Toyland*, *Lash of the Penitents* and *Destry Rides Again*. One of his largest roles came as the arch villain's henchman in the 1934 serial *The Lost City*, among the oddest and campiest of '30s chapterplays. He also played a sidekick in some westerns, did some directing, and was active on-screen in bit roles as late as the 1960s in films like *The Patsy*, *The Chase* and *Harlow*.

Comments: Sound revealed William Bletcher to have a pleasantly deep and exceptionally resonant voice that sounded almost out of place coming from such a small man. It sounded, oddly, almost as if his own voice were dubbed. But he made that asset work for him throughout his sound career. His short stature and beetle-browed appearance kept him from leading man roles but he actually was lucky. His career lasted much longer than that of any mere romantic actor.

Reviews

Branded Men: The hero Ken Maynard is assisted by a runt. Bletcher's big voice coming out of his small body gets most of the laughs. *Variety* 12/15/31.

Blue, Monte (Gerard or Gerald Montgomery Blue), Indianapolis, Indiana, 1887/90–1963

Filmography: List of films in *Films in Review* (Oct. 1963); *Classic Images* (Spring-Summer 1971)
Silent: One of Monte Blue's earliest-known films

was *Birth of a Nation*. He was an actor-stuntman for D. W. Griffith as early as 1914 and continued in supporting roles through the 'teens. By 1921 he had achieved better parts in films like *The Affairs of Anatol* and *Orphans of the Storm* and, co-starring with actresses such as Mae Murray, he reached stardom in the Ernst Lubitsch comedies *The Marriage Circle*, *Kiss Me Again* and *So This Is Paris*.

Among Blue's other 70 silents were *Tents of Allah*, *Loves of Camille*, *The Kentuckian*, *Brass Knuckles*, *Dark Swan* and *Mademoiselle Midnight*. The many studios for which he appeared included Triangle, Vitagraph, Fox, Bluebird, Hodkinson, Metro, Famous Players-Lasky and Realart. Last silent: *Across the Atlantic* (1928).

Sound: Monte Blue's first film with sound, and possibly still his best-remembered, was the part-talkie *White Shadows in the South Seas* (1928). That year's *Conquest* was the first of his all-talkies. He remained a leading man for a very few years but then his decline was rapid. In the mid–1930s and the 1940s he was often seen in small roles and bits in which he continued until the mid–'50s.

Among Blue's large number of sound films were *Isle of Escape*, *The Thundering Herd*, *Spawn of the North*, *New York Town*, *That Way with Women* and *Rebellious Daughters*. He also could be spotted (albeit briefly) in prestige pictures like *Juarez*, *Johnny Belinda*, *Lives of a Bengal Lancer* and *The Palm Beach Story*.

Blue also had roles in such serials as *Secret Agent X-9*, *Hawk of the Wilderness*, *Riders of Death Valley* and *Undersea Kingdom*. In his final movie he played the Native American chief Geronimo in *Apache*. All told, he appeared in about 130 sound films and was also seen on TV.

Comments: Monte Blue was a versatile actor who may have made 200 films. His deep voice was certainly made for talkies but could record poorly at times, as in 1929's *The Show of Shows*. Part of a sequence in *White Shadows in the South Seas* was reportedly dubbed by another actor whose voice did not match his. A rumor that Blue's voice was unsuitable made the rounds but it was only a temporary setback.

As he aged, Blue's face hardened in a way which made him most suitable for villain roles. He was supposedly part–Native American and he indeed played many Indians and "half-breeds" in westerns (and usually was up to no good). The peak of Blue's stardom was the period during which he was at Warner Bros. from the early 1920s to the early '30s.

When he returned from appearing on the stage, Blue was no longer considered a star. In later films his parts were generally small (e.g., "Cannery official" in *Spawn of the North*, "Doorman" in *The*

Palm Beach Story), and he frequently was not mentioned in reviews. But he could always be depended upon to give a good performance and lend color to his roles — even as a hissable bad man.

REVIEWS

White Shadows of the South Seas: Blue does his part well. *New York Times* 8/1/28, *Variety* 8/8/28, *Harrison's Reports* 8/11/28.

Conquest: Monte Blue's following and the all-talkie label may carry the picture. *Variety* 2/13/29.

The Isle of Escape: Monte Blue makes a better railroad man or sea captain than the South Sea lover he plays here. He can't help himself since he has to recite lines as they are written. *Variety* 4/2/30.

Young Bill Hickok: The veteran Monte Blue does well in a minor part as a marshal. *Variety* 10/2/40.

Blythe, Betty (Elizabeth Blythe Slaughter),
Los Angeles, California, 1893–1972

Silent: Debuting at Vitagraph studios, 5'9" Betty Blythe made about 20 of her 60+ silent films there; later she worked at Goldwyn. Her first picture was possibly *Her Own People* (1917). In 1921 the major hit *The Queen of Sheba* brought her acclaim and popularized the word "Sheba" as the female equivalent of "Sheik." After its success, she formed her own production company and received a reputed 10,000 letters a week. Her period of fame was relatively brief, however.

Blythe's other silents included *How Women Love, Sinner or Saint, Nomads of the North, Garden of Desire, The Darling of the Rich, In Hollywood with Potash and Perlmutter* and *Eager Lips*. She went to Europe to appear in *Chu Chin Chow, A Daughter of Israel* and *She*. Last silent: *Stolen Love* (1928), made after her first part-talkie.

Sound: *Glorious Betsy*, a 1928 part-talkie, was Blythe's first film with spoken dialogue. She was out of features from 1929 to '32 and then played mainly supporting and small roles until the late 1940s. She also had an occasional lead, as in the 1941 "B" film *Misbehaving Husbands* with Harry Langdon co-starring.

Other Blythe pictures included *Back Street* (1932 version), *Only Yesterday, Money Means Nothing, Anna Karenina, Rainbow on the River, Conquest, The Women* and *Where Are Your Children?* She was last seen as an extra in 1964's *My Fair Lady*. By the time she left the screen, she had appeared in about 120 films.

REVIEWS

Lena Rivers: No names worthy of box office excitement. Betty Blythe is good looking but pre-

sumptuous in the role of a society woman. *Variety* 5/24/32.

Western Courage: Blythe is adequate in a supporting role. *Variety* 3/18/36.

Misbehaving Husbands: One of the only redeeming features of this absurd comedy-drama is Betty Blythe's re-entry to the Hollywood scene as a promising actress. The former beauty of the silent films appears to be a future bet. (There was a plan to co-star Blythe and Harry Langdon in a series of marital comedies but the renewal of both their careers was very brief.) *Variety* 1/15/41.

Boardman, Eleanor, Philadelphia, Pennsylvania, 1898/99–1991

Filmography: *Films in Review* (Dec. 1973)

Silent: After a modeling and brief stage career, aristocratically beautiful Eleanor Boardman had her first film role in *The Stranger's Banquet* (1922), the year in which she was named a Wampas Baby Star. Her first important appearance was in the following year's *Souls for Sale*. She made 25 silents, mostly for MGM, several directed by her husband King Vidor.

Among Boardman's films were *Bardelys the Magnificent, Wife of the Centaur, Sinners in Silk, The Only Thing, Wine of Youth, Vanity Fair* (1923 version) and *Tell It to the Marines. The Crowd*, directed by Vidor, is by far her most remembered film and an acknowledged silent masterwork. In this affecting "kitchen sink" drama, she played the wife of an anonymous working-class family beset by tragedy. Last silent: *Diamond Handcuffs* (1928).

Sound: Boardman's only 1929 film, and her first part-talkie, was *She Goes to War. Redemption*, made in 1929 and co-starring John Gilbert, was actually her first completed full sound film but it was released after *Mamba* in 1930. This was due to Gilbert's perceived problems with talkies.

Boardman made only a handful of talkies, the best of which was probably *The Great Meadow* (1931), a tale of pre–Revolutionary Virginia and Kentucky. Her other talkies were *The Flood, Women Love Once* and *The Squaw Man*, her last American film. *The Three-Cornered Hat*, made in Spain and also known as *It Happened in Spain*, was directed by her second husband Harry d'Abbadie d'Arrast in 1934. It may not have been released in the U.S.

Comments: In Boardman's greatest film role, *The Crowd*, she played against type successfully. She tried this again in *The Great Meadow* to lesser success. Somehow her privileged background came through; it was difficult to believe her in tatty clothing and straitened circumstances.

Boardman's sound career was certainly no triumph. Although her natural speaking voice was rather low and cultured, her on-screen voice was colorless and the films were of little interest to moviegoers. She basically was an indifferent actress and showed no charisma as a talking star. But there's always *The Crowd*.

REVIEWS

She Goes to War: Reviewers did not agree on this. One stated that Boardman gave a fine and sensitive performance and that her beauty and intelligent acting were too good for the story. Another said that the supporting players stole the film away from Boardman, who was hampered by an unsympathetic part. New York Times 6/10/29, *Variety* 6/12/29, *Harrison's Reports* 6/15/29.

Mamba: In one or two scenes Miss Boardman is near bewitching. *Variety* 3/19/30.

The Great Meadow: Eleanor Boardman gets all the worst of the dialogue, but she looks good in any situation. *Variety* 3/18/31.

The Flood: Boardman fails to register and her voice reproduces colorlessly. *Variety* 4/29/31.

Women Love Once: Boardman looks well, arouses sympathy, and her performance would be impressive except for a heavily affected English accent. *Variety* 6/30/31, *Harrison's Reports* 7/4/31.

The Squaw Man: Some awkward moments of Eleanor Boardman's performance may be forgiven because she plays an English beauty. *Variety* 9/22/31.

Boland, Mary, Philadelphia, Pennsylvania, 1880–1965

Filmography: List of films in *Films in Review* (Aug.-Sept. 1965)

Silent: An actress in stock and then on Broadway from about 1905, Mary Boland specialized in heavy drama. She was considered a most versatile performer, once playing seven roles in a play. Her handful of silent dramas, in which she generally played leads, were made from 1915 on.

Boland's films began with *The Edge of the Abyss* and included *The Price of Happiness*, *A Woman's Experience*, *Mountain Dew*, *The Stepping Stone* and *The Prodigal Wife*. Last silent: *His Temporary Wife* (1920).

Sound: After another decade of theater work, this time including some comedies, Boland returned in 1931 for *Secrets of a Secretary*. She remained primarily a character comedienne in such films as *Personal Maid*, *The Night of June 13th*, *Three Cornered Moon*, *Six of a Kind*, *The Big Broadcast of 1936* and, notably, *Ruggles of Red Gap*, *The Women* and *Pride and Prejudice*.

Boland's major fame came in a series of marital comedies co-starring character actor Charlie Ruggles, with whom she also appeared in *Ruggles of Red Gap*. She returned to the theater in the early '40s and was off-screen from 1941 to '43 and then was seen in only a few more pictures until her last, *Guilty Bystander*, in 1950. In that "B" melodrama, she essayed a villainous role.

Comments: Mary Boland's talkie persona was the essence of the chattery, overbearing and perhaps not too bright wife and/or mother, a type often seen in 1930s cinema. Her voice was well-suited to this characterization, its tone usually demanding, hectoring, scolding or even shrewish.

Perhaps the epitome of Boland's "silly" side was as Mrs. Bennet, out to marry off her five daughters, in 1940's *Pride and Prejudice*. It's perhaps a shame she rarely got to reveal her dramatic skills in sound films but she compensated audiences, if not always herself, by delivering some delightful performances.

REVIEWS

Personal Maid: The moviegoers will go for Mary Boland. She should have that chance to do bigger things than here. Anything and everything she pulls as the neurotic and slightly eccentric rich society mother will win the customers. She's a really fine actress. *Variety* 9/8/31, *Harrison's Reports* 9/12/31.

Early to Bed: Mary Boland, by her expert handling of the comedy lines, makes more of the material than it really offers. She and Charlie Ruggles individually are excellent comics and together they're twice as good. *Harrison's Reports* 6/13/36, *Variety* 7/22/36.

Julia Misbehaves: Boland registers strongly as the tipsy mother. *Variety* 8/18/48.

Guilty Bystander: Mary Boland, best known as a comedienne, plays a blowzy flop-hotel operator, and the top heavy. *Variety* 2/15/50, *New York Times* 4/21/50.

Boles, John, Greenville, Texas, 1895/1900–1969

Filmography: *Hollywood Players: the Thirties*

Silent: After studying singing in Paris and New York, John Boles appeared in operetta and musical comedy on Broadway. He had roles in two films in 1924–25 before starting his film career in earnest with Gloria Swanson's unsuccessful 1927 vehicle *The Love of Sunya*. This was probably Boles's best-known silent film.

Other Boles silents included *Shepherd of the Hills*, *The Water Hole*, *What Holds Men?*, *Virgin Lips* and *Fazil* (called "Fizzle" by wags of the day). His 11-film career in this medium could well be said to have been unmemorable. Last silent: *Man-Made Woman* (1928).

Sound: John Boles appeared in the part-talkie

The Last Warning before warbling his way through the lead of *The Desert Song*, the first talkie operetta. It was a big success and was followed by more than 40 other sound films. His next musical *Rio Rita* was also a major hit. Other 1930–31 musicals included *Captain of the Guard*, *The Song of the West*, *King of Jazz* (he was one of a large ensemble) and *One Heavenly Night*.

When the vogue for musicals died about 1930, Boles was cast in *Seed* (1931), which established his viability as a dramatic leading man. For studios like Twentieth Century–Fox, Universal and Columbia he alternated between melodrama, romance and a later wave of musicals, including three with Shirley Temple (*Stand Up and Cheer*, *Curly Top* and *The Littlest Rebel*).

There was also *Bottoms Up*, *Music in the Air* (reunited with Gloria Swanson) and *Rose of the Rancho* in which diva Gladys Swarthout made her film debut. Boles's straight dramatic roles included *White Gold*, *Six Hours to Live*, *Resurrection*, *The Life of Vergie Winters*, *A Message to Garcia* and *Only Yesterday* (Margaret Sullavan's film debut).

Among the more popular films in which Boles was seen as the leading man were the first version of *Back Street* with Irene Dunne and *Craig's Wife*. He also played the second male lead in *Frankenstein* (third, if one counts the Monster). *Stella Dallas* was his last major film (he was completely overshadowed by Barbara Stanwyck in the title role).

Boles's starring career petered out in 1938 after *Sinners in Paradise*. He was back in 1942 for three supporting roles, including such undistinguished fare as *The Road to Happiness* and *Between Us Girls*. His last, after a nearly ten-year hiatus, was the dismal Spanish-made *Babes in Bagdad* (1952). He also performed on concert stages.

Comments: John Boles was obviously one silent player whose career was resuscitated by the advent of sound; indeed, his talkie career far exceeded his minor splash in silents. His professionally trained voice put him in excellent stead during the brief flowering of early sound musicals and operettas, albeit his latter attempts in that genre were not too successful. He was more fortunate than some of his singing counterparts like Charles King, Alexander Gray and Stanley Smith who all faded with the musicals of the early 1930s. His being cast in "serious" drama gave him a new lease on life.

Boles was handsome, he could portray decency and sincerity well, and undoubtedly he was valued as the type of leading man who did not overwhelm his leading ladies (quite the contrary in fact). Unfortunately, that very strength was also a weakness which helped to end his starring career.

Boles was bland and uncharismatic and was not a strong actor. "Colorless" was a word seen often in reviews, even during the silent period. He found himself most often overshadowed by his leading ladies up to and including the irrepressible Shirley Temple.

John Boles was undoubtedly at his best in his early stage and talkie appearances and in his post-film concertizing which highlighted his most agreeable baritone singing voice. When the same mellifluous baritone was used for dramatic acting purposes, he ofttimes fell short.

Reviews

The Desert Song: Mr. Boles, as The Red Shadow, does exceptionally well on the screen and has a good baritone voice. *Variety* 4/10/29, *New York Times* 5/2/29, *Harrison's Reports* 5/11/29.

Rio Rita: The melodies are rendered admirably by John Boles. Reviewers differed on his acting ability, some opining that his acting was fine. Another stated that as an actor he suggested an amiable choir singer trying to cut up at a fancy dress party. *New York Times* 10/7/29, *Variety* 10/9/29, *Harrison's Reports* 10/12/29, *Cinema* 1/30.

Song of the West: John Boles fares a little better than the leading lady but the story, in which he is entrusted with the heroic role, is apt to arouse undue mirth. He is cast in a part that suggests action, dash and glamour but it is static, stuffy and unpersuasive. *New York Times* 2/28/30, *Variety* 3/5/30.

Seed: Reviews differed on Boles's performance but tended to be critical. One said that he was not bad in his role as the selfish husband. Another stated that his performance was no better than it was in other portrayals, his interpretation was too placid to be convincing. A minority view held that he was much improved over previous work. (He played opposite Bette Davis in one of her first pictures.) *Harrison's Reports* 5/2/31, *New York Times* 5/15/31. *Variety* 5/20/31.

Back Street: Again reviewers were split. Some stated that Boles in his role as the adulterous husband was not convincing, and was even stodgy in his playing. Others believed him to be effective and to be doing his best work to date. *Rob Wagner's Script* 8/13/32, *New York Times* 8/29/32, *Variety* 8/30/32, *Photoplay* 9/32.

Rose of the Rancho: Reviewers could not seem to agree on Boles's abilities. Some thought he made the best of what was a bad film, others disliked him. One said that Boles was always unsympathetic and never more so than in this film. *New York Times* 1/9/36, *Variety* 1/15/36, *Spectator* 3/6/36 (Graham Greene).

Craig's Wife: Boles, although sincere and natural in the role of the husband, is unable to keep the audience from jeering in that dramatically feeble moment of rebellion. On the other hand his restrained playing brought sympathy to his role. (In any case he was overshadowed by Rosalind Russell in her first important characterization.) *New York Times* 10/2/36, *Variety* 10/7/36.

Stella Dallas: Boles is a good choice for the leading male role for which a gentlemanly personality is essential. (Unfortunately, he was gentlemanly to the point of colorlessness and was again outshone by a leading lady, this time Barbara Stanwyck in an Oscar-nominated role.) *Hollywood Spectator* 7/31/37, *New York Times* 8/6/37, *Rob Wagner's Script* 8/28/37.

Between Us Girls: John Boles is competent and adequate. *Variety* 9/2/42, *New York Times* 9/25/42.

Babes in Bagdad: Boles gives his part the proper ridiculous touch, sometimes too much so. (In some areas the film was released two years after its completion.) *Variety* 12/10/52, *New York Times* 4/5/54.

Bonomo, Joe, Brooklyn, New York, 1901/02–1978

Filmography: Classic Images (June 1991)

Silent: Dubbed "The Mightiest Man in the Movies," Joe Bonomo broke into films as a stunt man. A weight lifter and wrestler, he was capable of truly amazing feats of strength which were often showcased in his films. He primarily appeared in serials, his first being 1919's *Hurricane Hutch*.

Other silent serials in which Bonomo appeared, and sometimes starred, were *The Eagle's Talons, Beasts of Paradise, The Iron Man, Wolves of the North, The Great Circus Mystery, Perils of the Wild, The Fighting Marine, The Golden Stallion* and *The Chinatown Mystery*.

Bonomo also made several features beginning in 1926, including *The Flaming Frontier, You Never Know Women, The Sea Tiger, The King of Kings* and *Vamping Venus*. His roles in features were generally small. He also may have made at least one two-reeler. Last silent: *Phantom of the North* (1929), made after his first talkie.

Sound: *Noah's Ark*, the 1928 part-talkie, was Joe Bonomo's first. His first full sound film was the 1929 comedy *Courtin' Wildcats* in which he literally played a gorilla, an impersonation he was to repeat in *Murders in the Rue Morgue* three years later.

Most of Bonomo's sound roles were in serials, as they had been in the silents, but now he was strictly a supporting player. Among them were *Heroes of the Flames* (his first in 1931), *The Sign of the Wolf, The Vanishing Legion, The Phantom of the West, Battling with Buffalo Bill, The Last Frontier* and *The Lost Special*.

The burly Bonomo apparently only had small parts in two other features: *The Sign of the Cross* and *Island of Lost Souls* in 1933. He was the "Tiger Man."

Borden, Olive (Sybil Tinkle), Timpson,

Texas or Richmond, Virginia, 1906/07–1947

Filmography: Classic Images (Feb. 1991)

Silent: Sultry Olive Borden paid her dues with Mack Sennett and with small roles in films such as *Ponjola* and *Children of Jazz* (1923). She was a Wampas Baby Star of 1925 and soon thereafter began appearing in co-starring roles with Tom Mix (*The Yankee Señor* and *My Own Pal*), as well as in John Ford's *Three Bad Men*, all 1926.

A Fox contract led to starring roles in *Fig Leaves, The Monkey Talks, Virgin Lips, Yellow Fingers, The Joy Girl* and other films in which she generally exemplified the lady who lived fast. With the end of her Fox days in 1928, she began appearing in lower-budget films like *The Albany Night Boat* for Tiffany-Stahl. Borden then went on to Columbia, FBO and First National. Last silent: *The Eternal Woman* (1929), made after her first sound picture.

Sound: *Gang War*, a 1928 film with a talking prologue, was Olive Borden's first effort with sound although she did not appear in the sound portion. All her 1929 films, except for *The Eternal Woman*, were either partly or full sound. They included *Half Marriage, Dance Hall, Love in the Desert* and *Wedding Rings*.

Borden's last good role was probably in 1930's *The Social Lion*. She sometimes had supporting roles in her other talkies on the way to obscurity, including *The Divorce Racket, Hotel Variety* and (her last) *Chloe: Love Is Calling You* (1934).

Comments: Olive Borden flamed briefly across the Hollywood sky and just as quickly faded. She was released by Fox for "temperament," a reason provided for the dismissal of many stars but one which in her case may have been true. By all accounts she led a tempestuous private life and was difficult to work with after she attained stardom.

Although talkies were not the immediate cause of her downfall, they did not help either. She could be an exciting silent star but her talkie presence was mediocre as were the melodramas in which she appeared. She got little work in the early '30s and her quickie last film was made in Florida for a company called Pinnacle.

After much sad wandering, including a stint in the military, Olive Borden came back to the public eye at the time of her early death — destitute, with her beauty gone — in a Los Angeles mission for the down-and-out.

Gang War: Borden makes a good heroine. *Harrison's Reports* 7/28/28.

Half Marriage: A starless feature but Borden is a revelation in dialogue. She is natural and modern. She does her best screen work. *Variety* 8/14/29, *Harrison's Reports* 8/17/29.

Wedding Rings: Olive Borden is excellent as the heavy. She even sings a jazzy song and does it well. *Harrison's Reports* 1/18/30, *Variety* 5/14/30.

The Social Lion: Borden can take a bow for her performance. *Variety* 6/18/30.

Bosworth, Hobart, Marietta, Ohio, 1867–1943

Filmography: Classic Images (July 1985)

Silent: Affectionately called "The Dean of Hollywood," Hobart Bosworth was a cinema pioneer from about 1908 and he may have starred in the first film actually made in Hollywood about 1909. Most of Bosworth's films between that year and the early 'teens were Selig outdoor adventures; he formed his own company in 1913 to picturize Jack London stories. The first of these was *The Sea Wolf* and he also appeared in a stage version of this story.

From 1913, Bosworth made some of the earliest four- and five-reelers and he was seen in many westerns and adventure-melodramas. Among his films were *Burning Daylight, The Border Legion, Behind the Door* (a 1919 hit which re-established his stardom), *The Sea Lion, Odyssey of the North, Fatherhood, The Big Parade* and *My Best Girl*.

The studios for which Bosworth appeared included Universal, Fox, Ince, Goldwyn, Selznick, Metro, MGM, Pathe, Columbia, Tiffany and Lasky-Paramount. His output diminished in 1918 and '19 but he returned the next year with a full slate. He freelanced throughout the '20s in leading and supporting roles, making nearly 60 films and over 230 in his silent career. Last silent: *Eternal Love* (1929).

Sound: Bosworth appeared in *The Show of Shows* (1929), his first sound feature, followed by *General Crack* the same year. His initial sound endeavor apparently had been the Vitaphone short *A Man of Peace* the previous year. He made almost 40 talkies in supporting parts, although the busiest years were those from 1929–1932.

Bosworth's movies, in which he very occasionally was starred, included *Abraham Lincoln, County Fair, Lady for a Day, One Foot in Heaven, Steamboat 'Round the Bend, Bullets for O'Hara* and *Wolves of the Sea*. There were also serials like *The Last of the Mohicans* and *The Secret of Treasure Island*. His final effort was *Sin Town* in 1942, a year in which he made three films.

General Crack: Bosworth gives a fair performance as a government minister. *New York Times* 12/4/29.

Sit Tight: Hobart Bosworth is unconvincing due to the inferiority of the script. *Variety* 2/25/31.

The Dark Hour: Bosworth struggles to rise above some impossible situations. *Variety* 8/5/36.

Wolves of the Sea: Excepting for Hobart Bosworth, as the old captain, the cast is unknown. (At the age of about 70, he received top billing in this quickie Guaranteed Pictures release.) *Variety* 2/2/38.

Boteler, Wade, Santa Ana, California, 1888/91–1943

Silent: In stock from 1913, Wade Boteler came to films in 1919 and eventually appeared for such studios as Paramount, Ince, First National, Warner Bros., Fox and Sennett. Beginning as a supporting player (*23½ Hours Leave, A Very Good Young Man*), he went on to a solid career in the '20s, mostly as a character actor but with an occasional lead. He specialized in blue collar roles, often as a tough military noncom or lawman.

Among Boteler's films were *Let's Be Fashionable, Seven Keys to Baldpate* (1925 version), *High School Hero, Deserted at the Altar, The Whipping Boss* (title role), *Top Sergeant Mulligan* (title role), *Hold That Lion* and *Let 'er Go Gallegher*. He was also seen in the serial *Around the World in Eighteen Days*. Last silents: *Baby Cyclone, The Crash* and *The Toilers*, the latter with synchronized music and sound effects, released about the same time in 1928.

Sound: The Leatherneck, a 1929 part-talkie, marked Wade Boteler's sound bow. All his 1929 pictures had some sound including *Big News, The Godless Girl* and *Close Harmony*. He remained a top supporting actor, and one of the busiest, in films of the 1930s, including westerns, and was active to the time of his death.

Among the films in which Boteler appeared were *Kick In, Silver Dollar, The Death Kiss, She Done Him Wrong, Manhattan Melodrama, Black Fury, Counterfeit, Love Is News, The Rage of Paris, Mr. Smith Goes to Washington, High Sierra, It Ain't Hay* and *Gentleman Jim*. Amazingly, he sometimes acted in as many as 25 or more a year.

Boteler somehow also found the time to appear in such serials as *Red Barry, The Green Hornet, The Green Hornet Strikes Again* and *Don Winslow of the Navy*. His last films were released posthumously, a fitting monument to his frenetic activity which almost made his death from a heart attack seem like an inevitability.

REVIEWS

Missing Daughters: Wade Boteler brings some distinction to the nondescript part of a police officer. *Variety* 6/14/39.

Bow, Clara, Brooklyn, New York, 1904/05–1965

Filmography: *Films in Review* (Oct. 1963); List of films in *Film Dope* (Mar. 1974)

Silent: Clara Bow came to the screen as a result of winning a magazine beauty contest. Her first role in *Beyond the Rainbow* (1922) was left on the cutting room floor, later to be reinstated upon its re-release after she became famous. It was her role in the whaling saga *Down To the Sea in Ships* the following year that brought her some notice.

After coming under the tutelage of producer B. P. Schulberg, Bow made a long string of films for Preferred Pictures in 1924–25 (14 in 1924 alone), including *Black Oxen*, *The Plastic Age*, *Kiss Me Again* and a western with Tom Mix. In some of these she had starring roles; in others she was in support.

Bow went to Paramount with Schulberg, her first film there being *Dancing Mothers*; with *Mantrap* she became a big star and established her "flapper" image. Other hits included her archetypal film *It* (she was dubbed "The It Girl" by novelist Elinor Glyn), *Wings*, *Children of Divorce*, *Get Your Man* and *Red Hair*.

Bow appeared in about 45 silents, at least 30 of them before reaching major stardom. Last silent: *The Fleet's In* (1928), with synchronized musical score.

Sound: Nineteen twenty-nine's *The Wild Party* marked Clara Bow's sound debut, the first of 11 talkies. A change in her image was essayed for her second film *Dangerous Curves* (1929), a circus picture in which she played a sweeter and more sentimental role. Her sound film persona thereafter alternated between a slightly less jazzy version of her old image and a more subdued one.

In 1930 and '31 Bow appeared in such pictures as *The Saturday Night Kid*, *True to the Navy*, *Her Wedding Night* and *No Limit*. She also essayed a little dance routine and sang a song in Paramount's "all talking, all singing" extravaganza *Paramount on Parade*.

By the time *Kick In* was made, Clara Bow's career was on the decline because of poor vehicles and also her highly publicized erratic behavior. There was a high-profile messy trial in which her one-time secretary told "all"—and there was much to tell. The story about her servicing the entire USC football team, including Marion Morrison (later known as John Wayne), may not have been true, but she was hardly a girl scout.

Bow was absent from the screen for about a year and by the time she appeared in Fox's steamy melodrama *Call Her Savage* in 1932, it was already being described as a comeback. One further film, *Hoopla* (1933), marked the end of her career.

Bow did remain in the public eye off and on, marrying cowboy actor Rex Bell and opening an ultimately unsuccessful restaurant. In 1947 there was a much-publicized radio contest to identify "Mrs. Hush." It proved to be none other than Clara Bow.

Comments: Clara Bow's silent screen image was not much in tune with the grim reality brought on by the Depression of the early 1930s, but she was only 25 years old in 1930 and might have survived somewhat longer. She was a good actress in the right role and she seemed to be capable of improving.

Bow's voice was by no means unpleasant, although her first talkie revealed the need for some speech training. Low-pitched and with a noticeable but not overpowering Brooklyn accent, her voice was even suitable for musicals like *Love Among the Millionaires*, in which she again sang.

Bow's problems stemmed from different sources. The poorly-scripted melodramas she was appearing in certainly did not help and she was not at ease with the mechanics of talkies. Used to the freedom of motion which silent filmmaking provided, the relative restrictions of the new medium did not suit her.

But the major problem came from within. Clara Bow's personal demons and the resulting scandals attached to her name made carrying on a career too difficult for her essential fragility. She had weight problems and suffered a breakdown on the set of one of her 1931 movies. The carefree Bow image as projected on the screen was just that.

REVIEWS

The Wild Party: Bow's voice is better than the story, although there is room for improvement. She has proved she can "talk." It is not over-melodious in delivery but it suits her personality. Sometimes it is distinct and sometimes it isn't. *New York Times* 4/2/29, *Variety* 4/3/29, *Harrison's Reports* 4/6/29.

Dangerous Curves: This new chapter in Bow's career bodes well. Fans had begun to tire of the star in the flaming sex roles. The dialogue is the best thing this star has had. *Variety* 7/17/29, *Harrison's Reports* 7/20/29.

True to the Navy: Bow has seldom been so unimportant. Her studio doesn't seem to be looking after her interests. This is a typical picture in which she is a flirtatious soda fountain clerk with a sweetheart in every ship. The picture is just fairly entertaining with no particular outstanding performance. *Variety* 5/28/30, *Harrison's Reports* 5/31/30.

Her Wedding Night: Clara Bow is in a highly entertaining farce-comedy. She needs something good after the kind of publicity she is getting. *Variety* 10/1/30, *Harrison's Reports* 10/4/30.

No Limit: Clara Bow seems more improved physically than histrionically. She's looking better now than ever but the dramatic assignment isn't her metier. Detouring from the light comedy path is what has harmed her the most. *Variety* 1/21/31.

Kick In: In her performance Bow reveals her limitations. She is the least effective member of the cast. *New York Times* 5/25/31.

Call Her Savage: She plays with a new and engaging restraint and seems to be one of the few stars that are nearly story proof. She has shown a greatly improved acting technique. However, whoever has chosen this material for her comeback has certainly shown poor judgment. With good material she might have had an opportunity to come back; with such bad material this is doubtful. *Variety* 11/29/32, *Harrison's Reports* 12/3/32.

Hoopla: Reviews differed. One thought that Bow gave a more mature performance, one which showed her to be an improved actress. She seemed set to come back strongly. Another said that she did not appear at her best either in acting or in appearance. *Variety* 12/5/33, *Harrison's Reports* 12/9/33.

Bowers, John, Garrett, Indiana, 1899–1936

Silent: In films from 1915, John Bowers became a popular leading man and for the next 12 years top-billed numerous films, both drama and comedy. Among them were *Easy Money*, *Joan of the Woods*, *The Pest*, *Godless Men*, *The Sky Pilot*, *Quincy Adams Sawyer*, *When a Man's a Man*, *Chickie* and *Whispering Smith*. Last silents: *Heroes in Blue* and *The Opening Night*, released at about the same time in 1927.

Sound: In his first sound role in *Skin Deep* (1929), Bowers had a supporting role as a district attorney. He starred in his one other independently-made talkie, *Mounted Fury*, in 1931 but its muddled story and poor reception finished his film career.

Comments: To paraphrase Shakespeare, nothing became John Bowers's life like the leaving of it. All but forgotten for what he did during his career, his apparent suicide by drowning in the Pacific Ocean is memorialized in Norman Maine's similar death in the classic film *A Star Is Born*, made the following year.

The fictional Maine and the real Bowers had both been stars but there the similarity ends. In the film Maine was married to a rising star (played by Janet Gaynor). Bowers was married to actress Marguerite de la Motte whose popularity had peaked many years before in the silents.

Reviews

Skin Deep: Reviews referred to this film as hackneyed and uninteresting. Bowers was mentioned as being in the cast. *Variety* 10/2/29, *Harrison's Reports* 10/5/29.

Mounted Fury: The 65-minute story is long, drawn out and boring. The audience laughed at some of the situations. In the cast is John Bowers. *Harrison's Reports* 12/19/31, *Variety* 12/22/31.

Boyd, William, Hendrysburg or Cambridge, Ohio, 1895/98–1972

Filmography: List of films in *Eighty Silent Film Stars*

Silent: Beginning as an extra about 1916 or perhaps later, William Boyd gradually garnered bits, then larger roles, and by the mid–'20s he was being starred. Nineteen nineteen's *Why Change Your Wife?* was among his first major films.

Among Boyd's other motion pictures were *Moonlight and Honeysuckle*, *Bobbed Hair*, *The Young Rajah*, *The Temple of Venus*, *Dress Parade*, *Tarnish*, *Two Arabian Knights* and *Skyscraper*.

Bill Boyd was much used by C. B. DeMille, for whom he appeared in supporting and leading roles in films such as *Manslaughter*, *The Road to Yesterday*, *The Volga Boatman* and *The King of Kings*. By the end of the decade he was specializing in adventure-melodramas. Last silent: *Power* (1928).

Sound: The part-talkies *Lady of the Pavements*, directed by D. W. Griffith, and *The Leatherneck* were Boyd's first in early 1929. Other films that year were the melodramas *The Flying Fool*, *High Voltage*, *His First Command* and *The Locked Door*.

Boyd had a full complement of pictures in 1930, including the Vitaphone short *The Frame*, a new version of *The Spoilers* (starring Gary Cooper), *Officer O'Brien*, *Derelict* and *The Benson Murder Case*. It was the year he also began playing some second leads, an ominous turn in his career.

By 1931 Boyd's star was noticeably waning. A further jolt came from a scandal involving an eccentric actor who was billed as William (Stage) Boyd in order to avoid confusion between the two men. Unfortunately, confusion did arise in the public's mind between them, especially after a newspaper photo showed the *wrong* William Boyd.

Among Boyd's other early '30s films were *The Big Gamble*, *The Painted Desert* (in which Clark

Gable played his first major role as the villain), *Suicide Fleet*, *Emergency Call*, *Carnival Boat* and *Sky Devils*. His roles proceeded to grow even less worthy and by 1935 he was considered to be a washed-up ex-matinee idol.

At this low point Bill Boyd was providentially rescued by a hard-drinking, profane and limping hero named Hop-a-Long (later Hopalong) Cassidy. After other actors had turned down the part, he became (almost literally) Hoppy, the protagonist of a series of western stories by Clarence Mulford.

The casting proved to be fortuitous, to say the very least. Boyd's characterization changed the image of the grungy Cassidy to that of a polite and gentlemanly figure. It was a character he was to play in 66 films over a 13-year period. Among the Cassidy films were *Bar 20 Rides Again*, *North of the Rio Grande*, *The Frontiersman*, *Santa Fe Marshal*, *Lost Canyon*, *Hoppy Serves a Writ*, *In Old Mexico* and *Border Vigilantes*. Boyd began producing the series himself in 1943. As the titles below indicate, many later entries in the series were rather atypical westerns, incorporating mystery and other unusual elements. None were made between mid–1944 and early '46.

William Boyd's last "Hoppys" gradually lost popularity with his primarily juvenile audience. Among these were *Forty Thieves*, *The Devil's Playground*, *Masquerade*, *Unexpected Guest*, *The Dead Don't Dream* and *Sinister Journey*. The final entry was *Strange Gamble*.

After the last features were made in 1948, Bill Boyd appeared in a TV series of 39 half-hour Cassidy programs and made one last appearance for his old mentor DeMille in 1952's *The Greatest Show on Earth*, in which he played a cameo as "himself" playing Hoppy.

Comments: To the microphone William Boyd revealed a pleasing baritone voice that meshed well with the he-man roles he specialized in, but he was not an especially good actor. In silents, his rugged good looks and prematurely graying hair had made him a suitably romantic figure but his talkie future was in "B" quickies.

Ironically, the typecasting which had shortened other careers saved Boyd's. The Hopalong Cassidy series caught on in a big way with young audiences and he continued to play that role until the end of his career. To keep his juvenile fans content, Hoppy rarely had a love interest; that was left to a succession of young sidekicks.

Whether through luck or business acumen, Bill Boyd purchased the rights to the Hoppy character in 1946 and through sale of the films to TV and the accompanying merchandising he grew wealthy. In real life, four times married, a two-fisted drinker and a sometime hellraiser, he was not like the courtly Cassidy.

In truth, William Boyd may not have been very happy being so identified with his character that he became lost in it. But he was always a good manager of his public image. Many a slipping star was reduced to playing in westerns but none ever made such a lucrative virtue of necessity.

REVIEWS

Flying Fool: The comedy is caused by the fine acting of William Boyd as a two-fisted he-man. He has had many such roles by now. *Harrison's Reports* 8/10/29, *Variety* 8/28/29.

His First Command: Boyd is rather passive; he scarcely seems to take an interest in what is going on. *New York Times* 12/23/29.

Hop-A-Long Cassidy: Bill Boyd measures up as Hop-A-Long Cassidy, except when he forgets his southern drawl. His absence from the screen in recent months may be a hindrance at the box office. *Variety* 10/2/35.

Texas Trail: The Hopalong Cassidy series has finally hit its stride in the usual capable hands of William Boyd. He's more realistic in this than in recent vehicles. *Variety* 12/22/37.

Range War: William Boyd plays the same old character as before, even managing to surmount many implausible situations. *Variety* 8/30/39.

Bracy, Sidney (sometimes Bracey), Melbourne, Australia, 1877–1942

Silent: A leading man in two-reelers from 1910 and then a character actor, Sidney Bracy appeared in hundreds of films. Among his silents were *Robin Hood* (1913 version), *The Man Inside*, *Crime and Punishment* (1917 version), *An Amateur Devil*, *Is Matrimony a Failure?*, *So This Is Marriage* and *The Thirteenth Juror*.

In the 1920s the now gray-haired Bracy also appeared in such prestigious films as *Merry-Go-Round*, *Manslaughter*, *The Merry Widow*, *The Cameraman* (he was the news editor) and *Queen Kelly*. Last silent: *Sioux Blood* (1929).

Sound: The part-talkie *His Captive Woman* was Bracy's first in 1929. His sound film appearances, generally in minor roles, lasted until his death and included *Redemption*, *The Bishop Murder Case*, *Ten Cents a Dance*, *Isle of Fury*, *Anna Karenina*, *Les Misérables*, *The Little Princess*, *Lloyds of London*, *The Rage of Paris* and what was possibly his last, *The Body Disappears* (1941).

REVIEWS

Everybody's Happy: Sidney Bracey plays an interesting character. *Variety* 9/27/39.

Brady, Alice, New York, New York, 1892–1939
Filmography: Films in Review (Nov. 1966)
Silent: Before essaying films, Alice Brady was a musical and dramatic star on Broadway. The daughter of theater impresario William Brady, she made the first of her more than 50 starring silent dramas in 1914's *As Ye Sow*. Her second film, *The Boss* (1915), established her as a film star.

Brady made more than ten films in some years for studios like William A. Brady Picture Plays, World, Select and Famous Players. Other silent films included *Bought and Paid For, Betsy Ross, The Gilded Cage, A Woman Alone, The Whirlpool, The New York Idea* and *Anna Ascends*. Last silent: *The Snow Bride* (1923).

Sound: After another decade devoted to the theater, Brady brought her multiple talents back to the cinema in 1933's *When Ladies Meet*. Now primarily a comedienne in supporting parts, with occasional top billing, she became celebrated for her portrayals of dizzy society matrons in films like *The Gay Divorcee, 100 Men and a Girl, My Man Godfrey, Gold Diggers of 1935* and *Three Smart Girls*.

There were also meaty dramatic roles like that in *Stage Mother* among Brady's 25 talkies. In 1938 she won the Academy Award for Best Supporting Actress playing Mrs. O'Leary of the great Chicago fire fame in *In Old Chicago*. Her final role in *Young Abe Lincoln* (1939) was also a heavily dramatic one.

Comments: Film viewers familiar with Alice Brady only through her often inconsequential sound comedies would be surprised to discover her considerable dramatic fame. She alternated film and theater roles with ease, appearing in such high-powered and deeply serious stage plays as O'Neill's *Mourning Becomes Electra*.

The exaggeratedly "cultured," fluttery persona which Brady assumed for her more farcical roles was only one facet of her talent. Despite the straitjacket into which Hollywood usually forced her, she was an intelligent and versatile actress who somehow managed to occasionally rise above her typecasting.

REVIEWS

When Ladies Meet: Alice Brady, as a nitwit socialite, is dangerously close to running away with the film and is responsible for a major portion of laughs from her silly behavior. She is a delight. *Variety* 6/27/33, *Harrison's Reports* 7/1/33.

Stage Mother: One feels both sympathy and dislike for Alice Brady as the mother; she is hard and relentless. *Harrison's Reports* 10/7/33.

The Gay Divorcee: Some of the comedy is brought about by the nitwit behavior of Alice Brady. *Harrison's Reports* 10/13/34.

Lady Tubbs: Alice Brady makes plenty of the juicy title role. Occasionally there's a tendency on her part to overclown, but by dint of adroit acting she manages to prevent things from taking on an air of burlesque. *Variety* 7/24/35.

My Man Godfrey: Alice Brady does a bang-up job with another tough part. *Variety* 9/23/36.

Three Smart Girls: Brady just skirts dangerous shoals in her overplaying. *Variety* 1/27/37.

In Old Chicago: Alice Brady gives the outstanding performance as Mrs. O'Leary, with a pleasing Irish brogue. Her scenes depicting the struggle of the young widow are compelling and sincere. *Variety* 1/5/38.

Young Mr. Lincoln: Alice Brady is excellent. She almost steals the picture. *Variety* 6/7/39.

Brady, Edwin (also known as Edward), New York, New York, 1889–1942
Silent: A veteran of the stage and vaudeville, Edwin Brady began a long career as a character actor about 1916 in such films as *The Mainspring, The Devil's Bait, The Sultana* and *Mutiny*. He also had an occasional early lead (*The Gun Woman, Wild Sumac*) and was in the serials *Neal of the Navy* and *The Great Radium Mystery*.

In the 1920s Ed Brady was a popular supporting player in numerous films including *Cheated Love, To the Last Man, The Rose of Kildare, The King of Kings, Harold Teen* and *The Trail of the Lonesome Pine*. Last silent: *The Bushranger* (1928).

Sound: *Alibi* (1929) was Brady's introduction to sound. That year he also was seen in *The Delightful Rogue*, followed by 1930's *The Texan, Cameo Kirby* and *City Girl*. Throughout the 1930s he appeared in numerous films, often as a policeman, and he was in many westerns as well.

Among Ed Brady's other motion pictures were *The Conquering Horde, South of Santa Fe, George White's Scandals, Treasure Island, Public Hero No. 1, Klondike Annie, The Buccaneer, Union Pacific* and *Saps at Sea*.

Brendel, El (Elmer Brendel), Philadelphia, Pennsylvania, 1890/98–1964
Silent: A Swedish dialect comedian in vaudeville, El Brendel was notable as being among the first, with his partner, to do an act lip synching to recordings. He appeared in Broadway musicals and came to Hollywood in 1926 with roles in such films as *The Campus Flirt, Arizona Bound, Rolled Stockings, You Never Know Women, Man of the Forest* and *Wings*. Last silent: *Ten Modern Commandments*(?) (1927).

Sound: In 1929 Brendel brought — or possibly inflicted — his patented catch phrase "Yumpin' yiminy" to the talkies. He appeared in musicals that year (*Sunny Side Up*, *Happy Days* and *Hot for Paris*) as well as the melodramas *Frozen Justice* and *The Cock-Eyed World* and the Vitaphone short *Beau Night*.

Brendel's musicals continued the next year with *Fox Movietone Follies of 1930*, *The Golden Calf* and the sci-fi fantasy *Just Imagine*, possibly his most remembered film. He also made the western epic *The Big Trail*. He continued his string of features throughout the decade, mostly in support but with a few starring roles (*Mr. Lemon of Orange*, *Olsen's Big Moment* [also known as *Olsen's Night Out*]).

El Brendel's other films included *The Spider*, *Delicious*, *Six Cylinder Love*, *Blonde Trouble*, *Code of the Streets*, *Valley of the Giants* and *Career Woman*. In the mid–1930s he was seen in two-reelers for Vitaphone (some even were in color) and at Columbia from the late '30s he was teamed with several comics including Harry Langdon and Tom Kennedy.

The quality of Brendel's shorts kept declining, however, and he was dropped by the studio after 1945. By the early '40s his feature output had dropped as well; the public had tired of his exaggerated "Swedish" persona. His latter films included *The Beautiful Blonde from Bashful Bend*, *I'm from Arkansas*, *Paris Model* and *The She-Creature*, possibly his last, in 1956.

REVIEWS

The Cock-Eyed World: To El Brendel falls the honor of razzing the star Victor McLaglen and he does it well. *Harrison's Reports* 8/10/29.

Just Imagine: The "Swedish" comic gets a bit further away from dialect comedy than in previous efforts and is the outstanding personality of the film, although not a rave. *Variety* 11/26/30.

Mr. Lemon of Orange: Brendel, still doing the same Swede that was successful in vaudeville, now rates with or near Jack Oakie among new comics with personal followings. This is Brendel's first time out without dialect. He played a dual role, in one of which he still retained the Swedish accent. The other role was Silent McGee. *Variety* 4/1/31.

Risky Business: Brendel is good for an important bit and gets his usual quota of chuckles. *Variety* 3/29/39.

Brent, Evelyn (Mary Elizabeth Riggs),

Tampa, Florida, 1899–1975
Filmography: List of films in *Monthly Film Bulletin* (May 1966); *Films in Review* (June 1976); *Classic Images* (Jan.-Feb. 1983); *Sweethearts of the Sage*

Silent: After extra work at Fort Lee, New Jersey, studios beginning about 1914, Evelyn Brent had her first recognizable supporting roles in *The Shooting of Dan McGrew* and in the films of English actress Olga Petrova. This was under her real name of Betty Riggs; she adopted her stage name in 1916 after she signed with Metro.

Brent's career progressed slowly. In 1920 she went to England where in two years she made about 12 films. She was named a 1923 Wampas Baby Star and the following year, after a prolonged period off screen, she signed with FBO to appear in a series of films in which she was either a "moll" or a chorus girl. These included *Silk Stocking Sal*, *Smooth as Satin* and *Three Wise Crooks*.

After 13 years, "overnight" success finally arrived for Brent at Paramount in 1927 with *Underworld*, *The Last Command* (co-starring Emil Jannings) and *The Drag Net*. Others of her 65 silent films included *The Plunderer*, *Queen o'Diamonds*, *Flame of the Argentine*, *Blind Alley*, *The Glorious Lady* and *A Night of Mystery*. Last silent: *The Mating Call* (1928).

Sound: Evelyn Brent's first talkie was the all-star *Interference* in 1928. Like so many other high-priced Paramount players, she was released in 1930 after *Paramount on Parade*, in which she did a musical comedy sketch with Maurice Chevalier.

Afterward Brent freelanced at various studios (Majestic, Invincible, Liberty, Republic, Monogram, Universal, Metropolitan, Columbia, Warner Bros. and RKO). At one point she had her own production company but its one film, *The Pagan Lady*, was unsuccessful. She only appeared in a single film during 1933–34 and in the latter year undertook a vaudeville tour.

Brent was never a major star again but she worked fairly steadily in leads and supporting roles during the rest of the 1930s and into the early '40s. Noticeably aged, she returned in 1944 for several pictures and then made a few in 1947–48. Her last commercially released film was a Charlie Chan picture, *(The Mystery of) the Golden Eye*. Her final film appearance apparently came in the religious picture *Again, Pioneers* (1950).

Other Brent sound films included *Slightly Scarlet*, *The World Gone Mad*, *Penthouse Party*, westerns (*Hopalong Cassidy Returns*, *The Law West of Tombstone*), *Emergency Landing*, *Spy Train*, *The Seventh Victim* (a Val Lewton thriller in which she was a member of a devil-worshipping cult) and the 1941 serial *Holt of the Secret Service*. There were also some 1950s television roles.

Comments: Of dark and exotic mien, Evelyn Brent did not look like the average leading lady of the '20s and '30s. She had a certain toughness in her aspect that consigned her to "bad girl" parts, but it was typecasting that cut two ways. It gave her the niche which led to stardom; on the other hand, it was a box that eventually ended her starring career.

Brent's voice fit her brassy persona and did not impede her transition to talkies. The major blow to her career was her release by Paramount, an apparent effort to save on salary money. As a freelancer she suffered the fate of most former leading actresses and when she was top-billed it was invariably in poor films. She was a watchable actress who probably deserved better.

REVIEWS

Interference: The voices are extraordinarily fine and Evelyn Brent does fine work considering her lack of stage training. She has top billing in Paramount's first all-talking picture. *New York Times* 11/17/28, *Variety* 11/21/28, *Harrison's Reviews* 11/24/28.

Fast Company: Brent is a little out of character as the heroine in a role that called for a less icy persona. *Variety* 10/9/29, *Harrison's Reviews* 10/12/29.

The Silver Horde: Brent plays a woman of questionable character. *Variety* 10/29/30.

The Pagan Lady: None of the characters are sympathetic, not even the heroine. She is an immoral woman, on the type of Sadie Thompson, but does not look the part and seems miscast. *Harrison's Reports* 9/5/31.

Symphony of Living: Top-billed Evelyn Brent is badly miscast as the ungracious mother. *Variety* 7/3/35.

Daughter of the Tong: Top-billed for perhaps the last time, the veteran Evelyn Brent plays the head of a smuggling ring, a part that is highly suited to her. She looks good and carries out her assignment very capably. *Variety* 8/16/39.

Brian, Mary (Louise Dantzler), Corsicana, Texas, 1908–

Filmography: *Classic Images* (Dec. 1982); List of films in *Sweethearts of the Sage*

Silent: "The Sweetest Girl in Pictures" debuted as Wendy in the 1924 success *Peter Pan*. This was dark-haired Mary Brian who became a Wampas Baby Star in 1926 and who, at Paramount from 1924 to 1931, generally was called upon to do little else but play the virginal leading lady.

Other Brian silents included *The Air Mail*, *The Enchanted Hill*, *High Hat*, *Beau Geste*, *Brown of Harvard*, *Under the Tonto Rim* and *Harold Teen*. Last silent: *Someone to Love* (1928), made after her talkie debut.

Sound: Beginning her sound career with *Varsity*, a part-talkie, in 1928, Brian went on to appear in such prestigious films as *The Virginian*, *The Royal Family of Broadway* and *The Front Page*. Throughout most of the 1930s she freelanced at Fox, Warner Bros., Universal, Columbia, RKO and later at Monogram, Allied and Remington. Her films were mainly of the "B" variety; in better pictures she generally served as pretty window-dressing.

Brian made films steadily until 1937, then sporadically through '43. One more, *Dragnet*, followed in 1947. Others included *Manhattan Tower*, *Moonlight and Pretzels*, *Three Married Men*, *Calaboose*, *College Rhythm* and *Blessed Event*. There were also several westerns and in the 1950s she appeared in a TV series.

REVIEWS

The Man I Love: Mary Brian handles her role to perfection, although the sound projection system makes the characters talk through their noses. *Variety* 5/29/29, *Harrison's Reports* 6/1/29.

The Virginian: Brian, as the school ma'am, is given a chance to show what a good actress she is. *Harrison's Reports* 12/14/29, *Variety* 12/25/29.

The Front Page: Mary Brian does nicely enough as the reporter's sweetheart but has nothing to do. *Variety* 3/25/31.

The Runaround (also known as *Lovable and Sweet*): It is the most beautiful colored picture that has been produced to this day; however no one in the cast is of box-office importance and there is no outstanding performance. Mary Brian, the heroine, looks better in black and white. *Harrison's Reports* 6/27/31, *Variety* 8/11/31.

Shadows of Sing Sing: A program gangster melodrama which is amateurishly produced. Top-billed Mary Brian is a sympathetic character, but that is not enough to hold the interest. She has little to do. *Harrison's Reports* 1/20/34, *Variety* 2/27/34.

Killer at Large: Mary Brian is a store detective. She is pleasing enough without once impressing. *Variety* 10/28/36.

Brockwell, Gladys (Gladys Lindeman), Brooklyn, New York, 1894–1929

Filmography: Academy of Motion Picture Arts and Sciences

Silent: Gladys Brockwell's first films may have been made as early as 1913 for Lubin; one of her earliest was *The Ambassador's Envoy*, made in 1914. She reached stardom with Fox, primarily in "vamp" roles, including *Flames of the Flesh* and *The Scarlet Road*.

Brockwell also appeared in character roles, working steadily throughout the silent era in films such as *Thieves*, *A Sister to Salome*, *Paid Back*, *The Darling of New York*, *So Big*, *The Restless Sex*, *Skyrocket* and *Long Pants*. Last silent: *The Woman Disputed* (1928), with synchronized sound effects and music, made after her first talkie.

Sound: The first all-talkie *Lights of New York* (1928) featured Brockwell, as did another 1928 talking effort, *The Home Towners*. That year she also made the Vitaphone short *Hollywood Bound*.

Sound was featured in all of Brockwell's 1929 efforts: *From Headquarters* and *Hardboiled Rose* (part-talkies), and *The Argyle Case*, *The Drake Case* and *The Hottentot*. Some of her roles were leads and others quite small.

Comments: An automobile accident put an end to the career and life of Gladys Brockwell. She was a stage-trained, talented actress who effectively played older character roles even in her youth. Her voice was well-modulated and, if enthusiastic reviews are to be credited, she no doubt would have had a promising future ahead of her in talkie supporting roles.

REVIEWS

Lights of New York: The picture has a standout in Gladys Brockwell as the mistress. She evidences stage training somewhere and runs far ahead of the rest of the cast. *Variety* 7/11/28, *Harrison's Reports* 7/14/28.

The Home Towners: Gladys Brockwell, as the wife, is the standout and is excellent all the way. She's in talkies permanently and belongs there. *Variety* 10/31/28, *Harrison's Reports* 11/3/28.

The Drake Case: No name to draw with but the late Gladys Brockwell does her top-billed role to perfection. *Variety* 9/18/29, *Harrison's Reports* 9/21/29.

Bronson, Betty (Elizabeth Bronson), Trenton, New Jersey, 1906/07–1971.

Filmography: *Films in Review* (Dec. 1974)

Silent: After appearing as an extra in a few films and in a small role in *Java Head* (1923), Betty Bronson's title role in *Peter Pan* made her an "overnight" star at Paramount in 1924. The next year's *A Kiss for Cinderella* proved to be a worthy follow-up and probably the apex of her career. She also played a cameo in MGM's *Ben-Hur*.

Bronson went to Warner Bros. in 1927. Other roles included *Not So Long Ago*, *Paradise*, *Brass Knuckles*, *Ritzy*, *Open Range*, *Everybody's Acting* and *The Cat's Pajamas*. Last silent: *The Companionate Marriage* (1928).

Sound: The sensational Al Jolson success *The Singing Fool* marked Bronson's talkie debut in 1928. This was followed in 1929 by the part-talkies *The*

Locked Door and *One Stolen Night* and the talkies *The Bellamy Trial* and *Sonny Boy*. Other early pictures were *The Medicine Man* and *Lover Come Back*.

Bronson's output slowed thereafter until 1932's *Midnight Patrol* marked her departure from the screen. She returned to Hollywood only once for a conventional western leading lady role in Gene Autry's *The Yodelin' Kid from Pine Ridge* (1937). She had been off the screen for well over 25 years when she essayed some small roles in a few films, the last of which was *Evel Knievel* (1971).

Comments: "Fey" is a good word to describe tiny Betty Bronson's pretty, offbeat looks. At one time she actually was considered as a possible "new" Mary Pickford. *Peter Pan* was a perfect match for her physically but her other films were generally undistinguished and her roles could have been played by any young starlet. Bronson's persona needed special handling but there seemed to be little effort to tailor roles to her particular talents. Her career was already beginning to languish by the end of the silent period.

Nor was her first talkie appearance in *The Singing Fool* a propitious one, although the film was a huge moneymaker. In that film Betty Bronson's voice was small and her acting was unmemorable, although contemporaneous reviews were encouraging. Perhaps she was overwhelmed by her boisterous co-star Al Jolson. It is said that he was not discreet in his criticism of her (in his opinion) lack of talent.

In truth, Bronson revealed little of the screen presence in her talkies which would sustain a lengthy career. Indeed, she made fewer than 25 films from 1924 to 1932. In her last "starring" part in the Gene Autry film, the cowboy star literally rode off with her into the sunset. Her career went there as well.

REVIEWS

The Singing Fool: Betty Bronson is the cigarette girl who ultimately wins Al Jolson. Her voice from the screen is quite appealing but her lines are not always as natural as they might be. *New York Times* 9/20/28, *Variety* 9/26/28, *Harrison's Reports* 10/13/28.

Sonny Boy: Charmingly played and well acted by the youthful and pleasant Betty Bronson. The conversation is splendidly handled, particularly by her, and her voice registers quite well. *Variety* 3/6/29, *New York Times* 3/9/29, *Harrison's Reports* 3/16/29.

One Stolen Night: Bronson is a charming and appealing heroine but while the talk is intelligible enough, the voices are not always pleasant to listen to. Sometimes they sound very harsh. *Harrison's Reports* 5/4/29.

The Locked Door: Betty Bronson plays the sister-in-law. *Harrison's Reports* 1/25/30.

The Medicine Man: A mediocre entertainment despite the fine acting. Betty Bronson is a charming heroine as the father-beaten heroine. *Harrison's Reports* 6/7/30, *Variety* 6/25/30.

Lover Come Back: Betty Bronson is not impressive in a role that makes her effort to act too obvious to be appealing. It is a shame that Columbia should take such a young actress, who appears as if she had just left her mother's arms, and put her in a role as a deceitful wife. It is a lack of good judgment and good taste. *Variety* 6/9/31, *Harrison's Reports* 6/13/31.

Yodelin' Kid from Pine Ridge: Bronson never played a less important or less convincing part than her role as a hillbilly. *Variety* 10/13/37.

The Naked Kiss: Betty Bronson of early film fame radiates in a landlady bit. *Variety* 1/20/65.

Brook, Clive (Clifford Brook), London, England, 1887/91–1974

Filmography: *Films in Review* (June-July 1975); List of films in *Film Dope* (July 1974), with corrections (Oct. 1975)

Silent: After a successful theater career, Clive Brook entered the British cinema in 1920 with *Trent's Last Case*, the first of about 30 films until 1924. Among his co-stars were American actresses Evelyn Brent and Betty Compson.

Brook came to Hollywood in 1924 to make his debut in *Christine of the Hungry Heart*. Numerous other pictures, most of them romantic melodramas, followed, including *Declassee*, *The Woman Hater*, *The Devil Dancer*, *Hula*, *Forgotten Faces*, *If Marriage Fails* and *For Alimony Only*. He also appeared in Josef von Sternberg's popular *Underworld* (1927).

Among Brook's co-stars were Mary Astor, Clara Bow, Corinne Griffith and Pola Negri, and among the studios for which he worked were RKO, Ince, DeMille, Warner Bros., Paramount and Fox. Last silent: *The Four Feathers* (1929), with synchronized music and sound effects, made after his first talkies.

Sound: The 1928 part-talkie *The Perfect Crime* marked the first time that Brook's upper crust English accent was heard on-screen. His first all-sound film was Paramount's *Interference* late that same year. He remained popular during the first years of talkies in such pictures as *Charming Sinners*, *Shanghai Express* (again directed by von Sternberg), *The Laughing Lady*, *East Lynne* (1931 version), *Sherlock Holmes* (1932 version), *Cavalcade* and *Gallant Lady*.

Brook's popularity began to wane in the mid–'30s and he returned to his homeland to make a few more films, the last in 1944. This was the comedy *On Approval* which he also directed; co-starring Bea Lillie, it is considered a minor classic of its genre. He also appeared in the British theater and on television. His final film, the American-made *The List of Adrian Messenger*, came in 1963. In the early '50s he appeared on the Broadway stage.

Comments: A wag once said that Clive Brook was so stiff in his films that he always was mistaken for the butler. His clipped pronunciation and cultured voice seemed to be what the moguls thought they wanted at the dawn of sound. He could "talk" in a way that was an elocution teacher's dream.

For a while, audiences seemed to agree but eventually Brook's perceived lack of on-screen emotion (i.e., his "stiff upper lip") was compared unfavorably to the charisma of the newer breed of American stars.

Apparently Brook's real personality was far different than his on-screen persona but he had been somewhat a victim of typecasting and was never given much opportunity to vary his roles. He seemed more appreciated back in England.

Reviews

Interference: Clive Brook knows his stuff thoroughly and reads lines with the easy naturalism of a stage-trained actor. *Variety* 11/21/28.

The Laughing Lady: The extremely smooth and yet virile performance of Clive Brook as the hero makes this a picture that will be highly appreciated. He gives a consistently finished and sincere performance. *Variety* 1/8/30, *Harrison's Reports* 1/11/30.

Anybody's Woman: Although some of the situations are not very logical, Clive Brook gives such an excellent performance as to make the picture interesting throughout. *Harrison's Reports* 8/23/30.

Scandal Sheet: One saving grace is the presence of Clive Brook because he plays an absurd character yet manages to look only moderately sheepish about it. *Variety* 2/11/31.

Shanghai Express: Clive Brook as the hero is unusually wooden in this and does not arouse much sympathy. *Variety* 2/23/32, *Harrison's Reports* 2/27/32.

Sherlock Holmes: The Holmes character does not show Brook at his best. He seems almost as uncomfortable as Calvin Coolidge in cowboy chaps and hat. (This seemed like perfect casting for Brook because he briefly spoofed the great detective in one of the comedy sketches in the all-star *Paramount on Parade* in 1930.) *Variety* 11/15/32, *Harrison's Reports* 11/19/32.

Gallant Lady: Brook is always reliable although making him an outcast is a little out of his line, but it is not an unreasonable character in his hands. *Variety* 1/23/34.

Brooks, Louise, Cherryvale, Kansas, 1906–1985

Filmography: *Classic Images* (Apr.-May 1973); List of films in *Monthly Film Bulletin Checklist* (July 1965); *Film Dope* (July 1974)

Silent: After musical and dancing experience, a bit in 1925's *The Street of Forgotten Men* was pretty Louise Brooks's entree into film. She had supporting or leading roles, often as a "jazz baby," in about a dozen silents altogether. Many of them were for Paramount and most of them were highly forgettable.

Brooks's pictures included *It's the Old Army Game* with W. C. Fields, *Rolled Stockings*, *A Social Celebrity*, *Evening Clothes* and *The City Gone Wild*. Last U.S. silent: *A Girl in Every Port* (1928).

Brooks went abroad and in 1929–30 made the German films *Pandora's Box* and *Diary of a Lost Girl*, both directed by G. W. Pabst, and the French-made *Prix de Beauté*. Little noted in America at the time of their release, the German pictures came to be wildly appreciated in later years.

Sound: Brooks's sound debut came in the part-talkie *Beggars of Life* (1928). Her second, *The Canary Murder Case* (1929), hastened the end of her American career. Because she was not available (i.e., supposedly refused) to do her own dubbing on *The Canary Murder Case*, her voice was dubbed by another actress (Margaret Livingston). Paramount dispensed with her services.

Always an iconoclast, Brooks apparently was blacklisted by the studio for her lack of cooperation. She also made no bones about her desire for better films, in the hope of which she had departed for Europe. Although the studio spread the story that her voice was not right for talkies, this was patently untrue.

Subsequently, Brooks had a small role in *It Pays to Advertise* in 1930, starred in a two-reeler directed by Roscoe Arbuckle (*Windy Riley Goes to Hollywood*) and then played another small part in *God's Gift to Women*. Returning in the latter part of the 1930s, she appeared in *King of Gamblers* but her role was cut.

After the routine western *Empty Saddles* in 1937, Brooks's final role proved to be that of a conventional (something she was definitely *not*) leading lady in the John Wayne "B" oater *Overland Stage Raiders* the following year.

Comments: Probably unique in the annals of Hollywood was Louise Brooks. She was an actress who appeared in a relative handful of mostly undistinguished American silent films — and no distinguished sound films, with the possible exception of *Beggars of Life*— and was considered no more than an average actress in her prime.

Brooks's present-day fame rests, most deservedly, on the remarkable performances in her two German silents, particularly *Pandora's Box*. In that now much-revived motion picture, she plays the world-weary prostitute-siren who cannot help destroying her lovers and who, in turn, falls victim to Jack the Ripper.

Brooks rose from total obscurity decades later almost as an icon, famously dubbed "The Girl in the Black Helmet" for her distinctive 1920s hair style. In the fulsomely expressed opinion of film historians and film buffs, she was a hitherto unrecognized genius.

French historian Henri Langlois said of Brooks: "Those who have seen her can never forget her. She is the modern actress par excellence.... She is outside of time." Another referred to her as "a magical presence."

The other leg upon which Brooks's latter-day reputation is built is her body of very perceptive writings on film and film personalities. These began appearing in the 1950s and were published in prestigious journals, particularly *Sight and Sound*.

In 1958, a writer said: "It is doubtful whether any film star ... is more completely forgotten in the United States than Louise Brooks." Totally washed-up in Hollywood at the age of 24, her triumphant resurrection finally came 30 years later.

Reviews

The Canary Murder Case: A perfect program picture in which Louise Brooks plays a merciless little gold digger and blackmailer who is the murder victim. *Variety* 3/13/29.

It Pays to Advertise: It is filled with advertisements and it may irritate people. (This apparently was an early example of what is now called product placement. In a separate editorial Harrison called the film "nothing but a billboard of immense size." Brooks, in a small role, may have been lost among the plugs for Listerine, Boston Garters, Murad Cigarettes, Arrow Collars, BVDs and many other consumer goods of the day.) *Harrison's Reports* 2/18/31.

Empty Saddles: Louise Brooks is not flattered by the camera but does a good bit of acting. She is the outstanding female player. *Variety* 2/3/37.

Overland Stage Raiders: Louise Brooks is the feminine appeal with nothing much to do except look glamorous in a shoulder-length straight-banged coiffeur. *Variety* 9/28/38.

Brown, John Mack (later Johnny), Dothan,
Alabama, 1904–1974

Filmography: *Film Fan Monthly* (June 1970–Mar. 1971, May–Aug. 1971)

Silent: Ex-University of Alabama football star John Mack Brown had bits in *Slide, Kelly, Slide* (probably his film debut), *Mockery* and *After Midnight* as well as in the western *The Bugle Call* (all 1927). His ascent was rapid; in the same year he was Marion Davies's leading man in *The Fair Coed*.

In 1928 Brown had supporting roles in two Garbo films — *The Divine Woman* and *A Woman of Affairs* — as well as appearing in *Our Dancing Daughters* as Joan Crawford's co-star. Other pictures included *The Play Girl*, *Square Crooks*, *Annapolis* (he was top-billed) and *Soft Living*. Last silent: *The Single Standard* (1929), with synchronized sound effects and music, a film in which he played Greta Garbo's husband, made after his first talkie.

Sound: The 1928 part-talkie *A Lady of Chance*, with Norma Shearer, was John Mack Brown's introduction to sound. Nineteen twenty-nine marked his acme as a dramatic actor when, besides co-starring with Garbo, he partnered Mary Pickford in *Coquette*, her Academy Award–winning role. In that year he also made *Jazz Heaven* and *The Valiant*, a part-talkie which was Paul Muni's screen debut.

Two of Brown's 1930 films took place in the West. In the first, *Montana Moon*, it was merely the setting for a modern story. The second was *Billy the Kid* which proved to be popular and set him on the course he was to follow for most of his career. He was released by MGM in 1931, seemingly a victim of Clark Gable's ascendancy. After 1934 almost every one of his pictures were westerns, the apparent sole exception being the 1944 drama *Forever Yours*.

Some of John Mack Brown's early '30s non-westerns were *Undertow*, *Hurricane*, *Belle of the Nineties*, *The Last Flight*, *The Secret Six* (with Gable) and *Flames*. He then starred in western series for Universal, Paramount, Republic and Monogram up to 1952 and in serials such as *Wild West Days*, *Fighting with Kit Carson*, *Flaming Frontiers*, *Rustlers of Red Dog* and *The Oregon Trail*.

Among Brown's over 100 features were *Born to the West*, *Lawless Land*, *Oklahoma Frontier*, *Little Joe the Wrangler*, *Raiders of the South*, *The Sheriff of Medicine Bow*, *Law and Order* and *Dead Man's Trail*. He interrupted his string of "B" westerns in 1942 for a supporting role in the modern western comedy *Ride 'Em, Cowboy* with Abbott and Costello.

After a bit in 1953's *The Marshal's Daughter*, Johnny Mack Brown was off the screen for 12 years, returning for character parts in *The Bounty Killer*

and *Requiem for a Gunfighter* in 1965 and *Apache Uprising* (1966), in which he portrayed a villain. He also did some TV work.

Comments: At the beginning of his screen career, John Mack Brown was a slim and handsome athlete who, although not a seasoned actor, could competently perform leading roles with strong female stars carrying the films. With the advent of sound, his lack of acting prowess was more evident as was his pleasant but noticeable Southern accent. He came across as amiable enough but his days as a romantic leading man were numbered.

Brown's later (and considerable) weight gain also would not have been suitable for "A" picture romance. It did not particularly mar his image as a western lead (between 1942 and 1950 he was among the top ten moneymaking western stars) but his beefiness occasionally strained credulity in action scenes. All things considered, his likability was his biggest asset and he had a most satisfactory career.

REVIEWS

A Lady of Chance: John Mack Brown is pleasing as the poor boy hero. He fits on appearance, wearing a gold football for those who remember his past, but he isn't a heavy weight on the acting side. *Harrison's Reports* 1/19/29, *Variety* 1/16/29.

Coquette: Brown lacks the maturity and power which the character needs but he has that necessary screen asset, appearance. *Variety* 4/10/29.

The Great Meadow: The players are competent and if one can forget Brown's sideburns and Virginny accent, one might like him. A better test will be in a better picture. *Harrison's Reports* 2/28/31, *Variety* 3/18/31.

Desperate Trails: Brown appears to be a sure bet as a cowboy star. He is bound to increase in popularity with western fans *Variety* 8/16/39.

Arizona Cyclone: Johnny Mack Brown stars in another western that will continue to keep his fans in tow. *Variety* 3/11/42.

Forever Yours: Brown is a little too stiff and solemn as the Army doctor. *Variety* 9/26/45.

The Lost Trail: Brown has developed a noticeable paunch since his all–American football days but still carries off his role as a western hero in convincing fashion. *Variety* 11/28/45.

Brunette, Fritzi(e) (Freda Samuels?), New
Orleans, Louisiana or Savannah, Georgia, 1890–1943

Silent: From about 1913, when she began at the Selig studio, to 1923, Fritzie Brunette appeared in two-reelers and features for several studios. Throughout much of that period she played leads; a frequent co-star was J. Warren Kerrigan.

Brunette's films included *Unto Those Who Sin, The Still Alarm, The Woman Thou Gavest Me, The Green Flame* and *The Butterfly Girl*. After being missing from movie screens for a while she returned for a couple in 1925. Last silent: *Driftwood* (1928).

Sound: In about 1937, Brunette began playing small roles and bits in several films including *Maid of Salem, $1000 a Touchdown, I'm from Missouri, Souls at Sea, City Girl* and *Edison the Man* (1940), which may have been her last appearance.

Burke, Billie (Mary W. Burke), Washington, D.C., 1885–1970

Filmography: Films in Review (June–July 1981)

Silent: After debuting on the English stage about 1900 and then on Broadway in 1907, Billie Burke made her film bow in *Peggy* (1916). This was followed by the not-too-successful serial *Gloria's Romance* and about 15 more silent films which she alternated with theater work.

Burke's films included *Arms and the Girl, Eve's Daughter, The Land of Promise, Sadie Love, In Pursuit of Polly* and *Good Gracious, Anabelle*. Last silent: *The Education of Elizabeth* (1921).

Sound: Billie Burke debuted as "herself" (i.e., Mrs. Florenz Ziegfeld) in an extremely fleeting non-speaking cameo in Ziegfeld's *Glorifying the American Girl* in 1929. She made some Pathe shorts in 1930 and her first real role in a feature was in *A Bill of Divorcement* in 1932.

One of Burke's signature roles came shortly thereafter in *Dinner at Eight*. This picture initiated her typecasting as a silly and nagging wife, a persona also memorably seen in *Topper* (1937) and its two sequels.

Surely best known to latter-day audiences as Glinda the good witch in *The Wizard of Oz*, Burke's almost 60 sound films included *Becky Sharp, Splendor, Craig's Wife, Navy Blue and Gold, The Man Who Came to Dinner, The Barkleys of Broadway* and *Small Town Girl*.

Burke was less active in films after 1943 but continued to be seen somewhat sporadically until 1960 when she made her last pictures, *Sergeant Rutledge* and *Pepe*. In the '40s she had a popular radio show and also was seen in some Columbia shorts. She returned to the stage and appeared on television in the 1950s.

Comments: Although she was highly regarded as a theater actress, Billie Burke was equally well-known as the often cheated-upon wife of impresario Flo Ziegfeld. Their battles over his alleged infidelities took on a legendary status.

Very wealthy at various stages of his career, Ziegfeld died in straitened circumstances. It was her debts more than her love for cinema acting

which turned Burke back to the financial rewards of the movies in the '30s.

Possessed of a lilting, almost musical voice and delicate red-haired beauty, Billie Burke played in both comedy and drama on stage as she later would in films. But she was of "character" age when sound came along and her voice was perceived as being more suitable for comedy.

Burke almost inevitably was typecast as a flighty, even scatterbrained and often overbearing wife. In the greatly fictionalized 1936 film *The Great Ziegfeld*, she was portrayed by Myrna Loy.

REVIEWS

A Bill of Divorcement: Billie Burke gives a fine performance and her name will be an asset on the marquee. The role held out small promise but she looks fresh and young and gives much charm to the character. *Variety* 10/4/32.

Dinner at Eight: Burke is more happily cast than in any of her previous screen roles and is eminently suited for the role of a fluttering society matron. *Variety* 8/29/33.

After Office Hours: Burke is again a fluttery matron and she eclipses most of the cast. *Variety* 3/13/35.

Topper Takes a Trip: The dialogue that is given to Burke is of a wacky, dumb Dora flavor, but it is exceedingly clever. *Variety* 1/4/39.

Dulcy: Billie Burke has a minor role that never gets going. *Variety* 10/2/40.

The Cheaters: Burke as the giddy extravagant spouse contributes a splendid performance. *Variety* 7/4/45.

Burns, Edmund (also known as Edward), Philadelphia, Pennsylvania, 1892–1980

Silent: After appearing in *Intolerance* (1916) and other early films like *Her Hour* and *Headin' South*, Edmund Burns was a popular DeMille leading player in such pictures as *Male and Female*. Afterwards he was primarily a supporting actor.

Burns's silents included *The Love Burglar, The Virgin of Stamboul, Sunny Side Up* (1926), *Jazzmania, Two-Fisted Jones* and *The Lavender Bath Lady*. Last silent: *Children of the Ritz* (1929), with synchronized music and sound effects.

Sound: Burns's first part-talkie was *She Goes to War* (1929). Other '29 sound films were *Tanned Legs, The Love Racket* and *After the Fog*. From 1931 to 1937 he had roles in several films, among them *Hell Bent for Frisco, The Westerner, Broadway Bill, It Happened One Night, Love Me Forever, Hollywood Boulevard* and *Follow the Fleet*. The quickie *Motor Madness* (1937) may have been his last.

Busch, Mae, Australia, 1891/97–1946

Filmography: *Films in Review* (Aug.-Sept. 1986)

Silent: It was about 1912 that Mae Busch made her first film appearance (possibly in *The Agitator*), and by 1915 she was working for Mack Sennett and co-starring with Eddie Foy. She went to Fox in 1917 to work in two-reelers and thence to Universal for the feature *The Devil's Passkey* (1919). Supporting appearances, usually in villainous roles, followed.

Film fame, such as it was, came with Busch's roles in Erich von Stroheim's *Foolish Wives* (1922) and *The Christian* in 1923. Her time as a star was brief due to sex scandals and a contract with MGM that she unwisely broke in 1926. She later returned there for *As the City Sleeps* with Lon Chaney, with whom she had appeared in the original version of *The Unholy Three*.

Thereafter for Busch it was small studios like Columbia (then part of "Poverty Row"), Tiffany, Gotham, Quality and Rayart. Her features included *Name the Man, Married Flirts, Nut Cracker, Tongues of Scandal, San Francisco Nights, Fazil* and *Sisters of Eve*. Last silent: *A Man's Man* (1929), with synchronized sound effects and music.

Sound: Mae Busch's first sound film was *Alibi* (1929). She returned to MGM for a series of shorts and features in 1929 to '31, one of them being Laurel and Hardy's first sound short *Unaccustomed As We Are*. Busch appeared in many other Laurel and Hardy shorts (including *Oliver the Eighth, Tit for Tat* and *Them Thar Hills*) and features (*Sons of the Desert*, and *The Bohemian Girl*).

Busch worked steadily through 1936 at Fox, Universal, Warner Bros. and some independents. From 1936 to 1945 she was on-screen in fewer than 10 features, the last of which was *Masquerade in Mexico* (1945). Other sound films included *Blondie Johnson, Stranded, Prison Farm, I Like It That Way* and the serial *The Clutching Hand* (1936).

Comments: Although not a star in talkies (nor had she really been one after the mid–1920s), Mae Busch proved to be a successful character actress in the sound era. Her very lightly accented voice fit her somewhat sharp features perfectly. While it could sound demure, it was also convincingly edged with menace or even shrewishness.

Her latter-day (1950s) designation by comic Jackie Gleason as "the ever-popular" Mae Busch ironically gave her 15 minutes of fame long after she was forgotten by most filmgoers. But that same flippant designation made it appear as if she had been "*never*-popular" and was totally inconsequential in films.

Those seeing Busch's major silent films and her delightful supporting roles with Laurel and Hardy know differently. She was a versatile actress before her voice was ever heard, and she could deliver a witty line with the best of them in talkies.

REVIEWS

Alibi: Mae Busch does quite well as the crook's mistress. *New York Times* 4/9/29.

Sons of the Desert: Busch gives a big boost to her scenes. *Variety* 1/9/34.

Prison Farm: As Trixie, Mae Busch of silent pictures heads the excellent supporting cast. *Variety* 7/20/38.

Bushman, Francis X(avier), Baltimore, Maryland, 1883–1966

Filmography: *Films in Review* (Mar. 1978)

Silent: One of filmdom's most popular leading men from 1914 to 1917, Francis X. Bushman made his first film (possibly *His Friend's Wife*) for Essanay in Chicago about 1911. His popular teaming with Beverly Bayne (later to be his wife) began in 1913. Among their many films together were *Graustark* (1915) and *Romeo and Juliet* (1916).

Bushman's career plummeted after the unsuccessful serial *The Great Secret* and, ironically, the uncovering of *his* own great secret: a wife and five children, all hitherto unpublicized. After about 130 films up to 1920, mostly one- and two-reelers, he made only 10 or so in the final decade of the silents from 1923–1928.

Among Bushman's films were *Their Compact, The Silent Voice, A Million a Minute, Daring Hearts, The Masked Bride, The Lady in Ermine* and, of course, 1925's *Ben-Hur* in which he played the villain Messala. Last silent: *The Charge of the Gauchos* (1928).

Sound: Bushman made three films in 1930. *The Call of the Circus* was his first talkie, followed by *The Dude Wrangler* and *Once a Gentleman*. Overall his output of sound films was not large, about 15 over the next three decades. Among those in which he played small character roles were *Hollywood Boulevard, Wilson* (he was Barney Baruch), *The Bad and the Beautiful* and *Apache Country*.

Bushman's final effort, *The Ghost in the Invisible Bikini*, came the year of his death. He also worked in radio and television, making perhaps thousands of radio broadcasts from 1932 to the 1940s. His son Ralph, renamed Francis X. Bushman, Jr., having inherited his father's good looks, made films in the 1930s.

Comments: Francis X. Bushman was a bonafide matinee idol of impressive physique and chiseled chin. His popularity in silent films was enormous and his ultimate fall all that much more precipitous. Even had his career proceeded normally, however, by the time sound arrived he was well into middle age and character roles were inevitable.

Fortunately Bushman's speaking voice was well-trained and well-attuned to his physical appearance. He had aged gracefully and handsomely, with lots of white hair, and he could believably play dignified men of substance. It no doubt would have been better to have stopped before his final grade–Z effort but the riches that had been his in the glory years were his no longer. He surely was happy just to be working.

REVIEWS

Call of the Circus: The cast does well except where the dramatics are overdrawn. Bushman as a man in love with a much younger woman, is at fault more often than the others. *Variety* 1/29/30.

Once a Gentleman: Among the many veteran names in the cast is Francis X. Bushman. He is no longer recognizable as the screen's former no. 1 sheik without a reading of the cast list. *Variety* 10/8/30.

Hollywood Boulevard: Its old-timers are used intelligently and plausibly; among them is Francis X. Bushman as a director. *Variety* 9/23/36.

Apache Country: Bushman is buried in the minor role of a U.S. commissioner in this Gene Autry western. *Variety* 5/21/52.

Calhern, Louis (Carl Vogt), Brooklyn, New York, 1894/95–1956

Silent: The face of Louis Calhern, with its strong Roman nose like that on some ancient coin, first appeared before the public in a Bronx stock company. The year was probably 1912. He spent the next few years in stock, vaudeville and repertory and, after service in the First World War, joined a Los Angeles stock company.

It was there that Calhern was discovered by Hollywood in the person of the early woman director Lois Weber. He was co-starred with her favorite actress Claire Windsor and made three pictures in 1921: *What's Worth While?*, *The Blot* and *Too Wise Wives*. In the following year he appeared in *Woman, Wake Up!*

Broadway finally beckoned to Calhern and he made his mark in George M. Cohan's *The Song and Dance Man*. He became a bona fide matinee idol after his performance in the 1924 play *Cobra*. Last silent: *The Last Moment* (1923).

Sound: The 1931 film *Stolen Heaven* was Calhern's first talkie and for much of the remainder of that decade he played top supporting roles. Often a suave villain, his 1930s pictures included *Night After Night* (Mae West's debut), *Duck Soup* (as a

foil for Groucho Marx's put-downs), *Sweet Adeline*, *The Last Days of Pompeii*, *The Life of Emile Zola* and *Juarez*.

Calhern continued to intersperse film and stage roles and in the early part of the 1940s he was mainly pursuing the latter, especially after his success in a road company of *Life with Father*. He did return to Hollywood on occasion in mid-decade for films such as *Heaven Can Wait*, *Up in Arms* and *The Bridge of San Luis Rey*.

In 1946 Calhern had his theater role of a lifetime playing Justice Oliver Wendell Holmes in *The Magnificent Yankee*. He repeated the title role in the movie version made in 1950. A smattering of films in the latter '40s included *Notorious*, *The Red Pony* and *Arch of Triumph*.

In 1949 Calhern was signed by MGM and he began the final stage of his career with top character roles in numerous films. First, he took time out to return to Broadway for his long-dreamed-of version of *King Lear*, a part that seemed a perfect cap to a distinguished stage career.

Among Calhern's films of the 1950s were *Annie Get Your Gun*, *The Asphalt Jungle* (in one of his most acclaimed roles as a greedy and crooked lawyer, with Marilyn Monroe as his mistress), the title role of *Julius Caesar*, *Executive Suite* and his last, *High Society*. In it he played the roguish Uncle Willie.

Comments: At 6'3" and, in latter days, with gray hair, Louis Calhern always presented an authoritative and usually dignified image in films. This was occasionally played against for laughs, as in his role as the Sylvanian prime minister and rival to Groucho Marx in *Duck Soup*, and his blustery Colonel in Danny Kaye's *Up in Arms*. In truth, though, it did not always seem like he got the humor.

This distinguished image was maintained by Calhern even when he played a bad man, as he often did, and the characterization was rendered all the more interesting. He was seen in every genre, including musicals, and always provided a strong center for each picture in which he appeared. Still in harness when he died, he was filming what would have been almost his 70th picture role.

REVIEWS

Blonde Crazy: Louis Calhern uses his long experience to good effect in a cheater part. *Variety* 12/8/31.

Duck Soup: Louis Calhern gives an adequate interpretation as Trentino. *New York Times* 11/23/33.

The Man with Two Faces: The arch-villainy of the Svengali-like menace, as played by Louis Calhern, is hardly credible. *Variety* 7/17/34.

The Last Days of Pompeii: Calhern is good casting as the haughty Roman prefect. *Variety* 10/23/35.

The Red Danube: The neatest performance is turned in by Louis Calhern as a Soviet colonel. Sticking consistently to his accent, Calhern has just the right combination of warped integrity, hardened purpose and meticulous adherence to the rules of the game. *Variety* 9/21/49.

The Asphalt Jungle: Calhern's role is the most stereotyped of the assorted types in the script but it has the advantage of his acting skill. *Variety* 5/10/50.

Julius Caesar: Reviews disagreed on Calhern's Caesar. One said it was a triumph, and that he played him with restraint and feeling. Another stated that his Caesar was puffed and pompous. *Variety* 6/3/53, *New York Times* 6/5/53.

High Society: The late Louis Calhern is top drawer. *Variety* 7/18/56.

Calhoun, Alice, Cleveland, Ohio, 1904–1966

Silent: Among the studios for which pretty and popular Alice Calhoun starred in about 50 films were Vitagraph and Warner Bros. Beginning about 1919 they included *The Sea Rider, Masters of Men, Flowing Gold, The Happy Warrior, The Power of the Weak, The Trunk Mystery* and *The Man on the Box.* One of her best-known was *The Little Minister* (1922). Last silent: *Isle of Forgotten Women* (1927).

Sound: The 1929 "B" western *Bride of the Desert* marked Alice Calhoun's sound debut and her one talkie leading part. Her one other known appearance in sound pictures was *Now I'll Tell* (1934), based on the life of gambler Arnold Rothstein, in which she had a small role.

Reviews

Bride of the Desert: In this inexpensively produced western, Alice Calhoun has no sex appeal in a housewife's apron. *Variety* 11/10/29.

Canutt, Yakima (Enos Canutt), Colfax, Washington, 1895/96–1986

Filmography: List of films in *Film Dope* (Nov. 1974), with corrections (June 1977)

Silent: Yakima Canutt came to films via rodeos in which he was the World Champion cowboy for three years, the last being 1923. It was about that year that he began doing stunt work and playing small parts after previously appearing in the 1919 serial *Lightning Bryce* as well as an occasional feature.

Canutt was signed by Arrow for a series of starring westerns and he appeared for that studio, FBO and others in nearly 50 pictures. They included *Romance and Rustlers, Desert Greed, Branded a Bandit, The Human Tornado, The Strange Rider, The Devil Horse, The Three Outcasts* and *The Cactus Cure.* He also made the 1924 serial *The Days of '49.* Last silent: *Riders of the Storm* (1929).

Sound: The late 1929 film *A Texan's Honor* was Canutt's first venture into sound. Although he was to have an occasional starring role in talkies (1930's *Canyon Hawks* was one), he very soon fell into support and then villain roles. In many films he often doubled for the hero (John Wayne, Roy Rogers, Gene Autry) and also appeared in his own part.

Among Canutt's films were *Westward Ho, King of the Pecos, Pueblo Terror, Westward Bound, The Ranger and the Lady, The Great Train Robbery* and *In Old Oklahoma.* He also appeared in *Gone with the Wind* and the serials *The Vigilantes Are Coming* and *The Mysterious Pilot* (1937).

While Canutt still was seen on camera as late as the 1950s, he increasingly was involved behind the scenes. From 1939 to 1970 he directed a few films and was second unit director on numerous others. His famous stunts were seen in such films as *Ben-Hur, Stagecoach* and *Boom Town.*

In 1966 Yak Canutt won a special Academy Award for being the virtual creator of the profession of stunting and in 1978 he received a tribute from the Academy of Motion Picture Arts and Sciences.

Comments: Sound was not kind to Yakima Canutt as a western star. His voice was on the piping side (and was unkindly compared to that of a hummingbird!), but he found his niche playing villains and perfecting and performing the stunts for which he was vastly famous among the cognoscenti.

Indeed, Canutt's stern visage and narrow eyes were perhaps more suited to "bad" men. He also played Native American roles and was thought by many to be at least part–Indian, but he was not.

Despite the sometimes perilous stunts which Canutt originated and performed (including the renowned *Stagecoach* stunt of falling under the galloping horses and the coach) and the many injuries he sustained over the years, he lived to a ripe old age.

Yak certainly was among the most admired men in the "old" Hollywood and his Academy Award was a fitting tribute to his pioneering work in professionalizing, and therefore, hopefully making safer, the art of stunting.

Carewe , Arthur Edmund, (sometimes Carew), Trebizond, Armenia, 1894–1937

Silent: Arthur Edmund Carewe was tall and dark with an intensely brooding face. This made him suitable for either romantic leads or villains, both of which he played. Beginning about 1919, he appeared in such films as *Dangerous Waters*, *Burning Daylight*, *Bar Nothin'* and *Trilby* (he was a convincing Svengali).

Other Carewe motion pictures included *The Phantom of the Opera*, *The Cat and the Canary*, *The Torrent* and *The Silent Lover*. Last silent: *Uncle Tom's Cabin* (1927), in which he played a slave.

Sound: Carewe's first two talkies were *The Matrimonial Bed* and *Sweet Kitty Bellairs*, released about the same time in 1930. He made only about ten sound films among which were *The Life of the Party*, *Doctor X*, *Mystery of the Wax Museum*, *Thunder in the Night* and *Charlie Chan's Secret*, his final film in 1936. That was the year Carewe suffered a paralytic stroke; after a year of failing health, he registered at a Santa Monica auto camp under an assumed name and there took his own life.

It is said that Carewe was considered for the role of Dracula, a part in which he certainly would not have been miscast. *NOTE*: He also was billed as Arthur Carew and Arthur Carewe. He is not to be confused with director Edwin Carewe.

Reviews

The Matrimonial Bed: Arthur Edmund Carewe as the doctor-hypnotist is always stentorian in tone. *Variety* 8/27/30.

Doctor X: Arthur Edmund Carewe, who years ago gave a striking performance as Svengali in a silent film of *Trilby*, is in his element as one of the scientists. *New York Times* 8/4/32.

Thunder in the Night: Several lesser parts are ably performed, among them Arthur Edmund Carewe. *Variety* 9/18/35.

Charlie Chan's Secret: A uniformly fine performance is contributed by Carewe. *Variety* 1/22/36.

Carey, Harry (Henry Carey II), The

Bronx, New York, 1878–1947

Filmography: List of films in *Eighty Silent Film Stars*

Silent: Beginning in 1909 or perhaps somewhat later, Harry Carey appeared in over 100 one- and two-reel Biograph films for D. W. Griffith. Coming to Hollywood in 1914, he ultimately teamed with director John Ford to make about 25 films. His film debut had come in a 1908 picture called *Bill Sharkey's Last Game* (there are other versions of the character's surname).

Carey had also written and acted in a stage play. He went to Universal in 1915 where, after making some dramas, he appeared in the western *A Knight of the Range* in 1916. For the next decade he was seen almost exclusively in westerns for Universal

(which he left in 1922), Hodkinson, Pathe, FBO and other studios.

Carey's features included *Judith of Bethulia*, *Just Jim*, *Straight Shooting* (John Ford's first directorial effort), *Bare Fists*, *Bullet Proof*, *Man to Man*, *The Night Hawk*, *Driftin' Thru* and *Silent Sanderson*. He also appeared in the 1915 serial *Graft*.

In 1927 Carey began his career as a character actor with roles in films like *A Little Journey* and *Slide, Kelly, Slide*, as well as continuing his western heroics. Realizing his career was slipping somewhat, he embarked on a vaudeville tour with his wife Olive in 1928. He had made some 200 pictures to that point. Last silent: *The Trail of '98* (1929), with synchronized music and sound effects, in which he played a villain.

Sound: Carey had his last starring role in a major motion picture in the popular *Trader Horn* (1931), the first feature shot almost in its entirety in Africa. He continued to play leads in "B" westerns while at the same time establishing a niche as a respected character actor in better features of the '30s and '40s.

Carey's films included *Law and Order*, *The Prisoner of Shark Island*, *Souls at Sea*, *Mr. Smith Goes to Washington* (Academy Award nomination for Best Supporting Actor), *The Spoilers* (1942 version), *Air Force*, *Duel in the Sun* and *The Angel and the Badman*. His last films, *So Dear to My Heart* and *Red River*, were posthumously released in 1948.

Harry Carey appeared in such serials as *The Devil Horse*, *The Vanishing Legion* and *The Last of the Mohicans*. He also played on Broadway, notably in Eugene O'Neill's *Ah, Wilderness*. Although John Ford had used him in only one sound film, the director dedicated 1948's *The Three Godfathers* to his old star. He had appeared in a 1916 version of the same story.

Comments: In his westerns Harry Carey exemplified the grittier side of western life, much like William S. Hart in the silents and Gary Cooper and Clint Eastwood in later decades. His stern, even dour countenance would have seemed out of place in the slickly produced Tom Mix pictures.

Too old in talkies for much western-style heroics, Carey's deep voice, apparent decency, and honesty in acting well-suited him for the character roles he played. Although the persona he adopted for westerns would not be in favor again for many years, his work influenced later stars, among them John Wayne.

Wayne acknowledged his debt to Harry Carey at the close of John Ford's 1956 classic *The Searchers*. He was photographed framed within a doorway holding his left arm with his right. It was a typical Carey gesture and a moving tribute to one of the pioneers of Hollywood's West.

Trader Horn: There were differing opinions of Carey's playing. One review stated that he mostly walked through the film. Others praised him as a real human being who is in the picture just what he is in real life, a regular fellow. His voice is manly and yet melodious and he will long be remembered as Horn. *Variety* 2/11/31, *Harrison's Reports* 2/14/31.

Wagon Trail: Carey is in his glory in this excellent vehicle. He does a fine job. *Variety* 5/29/35.

King of Alcatraz: Carey, who has successfully removed himself from westerns during the past several years, is fine. *Variety* 10/5/38.

My Son Is Guilty: There is a good character study by Harry Carey of a veteran cop. *Variety* 1/17/40.

The Great Moment: In a supporting role of a doctor, Carey expertly handles it. *Variety* 6/7/44.

So Dear to My Heart: The late Harry Carey, in his last screen role, is an understanding judge. *Variety* 12/8/48.

Carey, Olive (Olive Fuller Golden; also
known as Olive Golden), New York, New York, 1896–1988

Filmography: List of films in *Sweethearts of the Sage*

Silent: Pretty Olive Golden joined the D. W. Griffith stock company to make comedies, and then for Universal, Famous Players and Lubin she appeared in supporting roles in such features as *Tess of the Storm Country* (1914 version), *The Frame-Up, Just Jim* and *A Knight of the Range.*

In some of her pictures Golden supported Harry Carey, who was eventually to be her husband, and whose name she would assume professionally. Her numerous two- and three-reelers made in 1915 and '16 included *For the Love of a Girl, The Night Riders* and *The Committee on Credentials.* Last silent feature: *Love's Lariat* (1916).

Sound: In 1931 Olive Carey played a role in her husband's *Trader Horn* and the next year in his *Border Devils.* She apparently also had a role in the first Jeanette MacDonald-Nelson Eddy operetta *Naughty Marietta* (1935). In these '30s efforts, she was still billed as Olive Golden.

Much plumper now, Carey returned in 1950 to play a string of supporting roles into the next decade. Among her pictures were *Gunfight at the OK Corral, The Cobweb, Pillars of the Sky, Rogue Cop, The Wings of Eagles, The Alamo, The Searchers* (as mother to her real-life son Harry Carey, Jr.), *Two Rode Together* and her last, *Billy the Kid Versus Dracula.* She was a favorite of director John Ford, in whose first film her husband had appeared.

Trader Horn: Mrs. Harry Carey plays the missionary. Her part is small but her acting is so good that more should have been given her to do. *Harrison's Reports* 2/14/31.

The Bride Comes to Yellow Sky: Carey is exactly right in her role. *New York Times* 1/14/53.

Pillars of the Sky: Olive Carey does well in carrying out the plot requirements. *Variety* 8/8/56.

Carol, Sue (Evelyn Lederer), Chicago, Illinois, 1906–1982

Silent: The screen persona of pert Sue Carol was as one of the late '20s archetypal flappers, a perennial college girl always looking for a good time. Her career began in 1927 with *Slaves of Beauty* and many of her films teamed her with husband-to-be Nick Stuart.

Other Carol films were *Girls Gone Wild, The Air Circus, Soft Cushions* and *The Cohens and the Kellys in Paris.* Last silent: *The Exalted Flapper* (1929), with synchronized music, made after her first sound film.

Sound: The part-talkie *The Air Circus* (1928) marked Sue Carol's first sound film, and aside from two silents her 1929 films were all- or part-talking. They included *Chasing Through Europe, Fox Movietone Follies of 1929* and *Why Leave Home?*

Nineteen thirty saw Carol in a full menu of films in which she generally portrayed her usual screen character. These included *Dancing Sweeties, She's My Weakness* and *The Big Party.* There was also a western, *The Lone Star Ranger,* which perhaps gave an indication that Carol's screen type, and indeed her career, was beginning to wane.

Among Carol's pictures of the '30s, many of them quickie melodramas, were *Graft, In Line of Duty, Secret Sinners* and *Straightaway.* Her last film was 1937's *A Doctor's Diary* in which she had a small supporting role. She later became an agent.

Comments: Brunette Sue Carol is perhaps best remembered now as the Hollywood agent whose major client was her husband, Paramount star Alan Ladd. She made his career the centerpiece of her life and always preferred to be known as Sue Carol Ladd.

Never a big star, nor indeed a big talent, Carol was perkiness personified; the perennial standard "Sweet Sue" was supposedly written for her. Although she sang and danced fetchingly, she freely admitted she was not trained in either and it sometimes showed on the screen.

The Air Circus: Carol does nicely and is at all times attractive. *Variety* 9/5/28, *Harrison's Reports* 9/15/28.

Why Leave Home: Carol sings the theme song. She has a pleasing talking and singing voice. *Variety* 9/18/29, *Harrison's Reports* 9/21/29.

The Big Party: It is Sue Carol who has top billing but it's Dixie Lee who runs away with top honors. Carol is entirely subordinated. *Variety* 4/16/30.

Dancing Sweeties: One review said that Sue Carol lisped her way ineffectually through her scenes, while another said she did a convincing job. *New York Times* 8/16/30, *Variety* 8/20/30.

Secret Sinners: The efforts of a group of good actors go for little but Carol almost manages to make her part seem human. *Variety* 12/26/33.

Carr, Alexander, Russia, 1878–1946

Silent: Alexander Carr came to Hollywood to recreate his popular 1916 stage role in *Potash and Perlmutter* (he was "Mawruss Perlmutter"). He had previously been a circus clown and burlesque comic. The film, made in 1923, was the first of a small handful of silents.

Carr's other silent movies included the sequel *In Hollywood with Potash and Perlmutter, Partners Again* (yet another "P&P" sequel) and *The Beautiful Cheat.* Last silent: *April Fool* (1926), another "Jewish" role, in which he was top-billed.

Sound: In 1932 Carr returned and made nine more films through 1934. In all but one his roles were supporting and he was usually the stereotypical '30s "Hebrew." He was the star of the schmaltzy 1932 melodrama *No Greater Love,* in which he gave what is considered his finest film performance.

Among Carr's other pictures were *Hypnotized, The Death Kiss, Uptown New York, I Hate Women* and his last, after a lengthy hiatus, 1940's *Christmas in July.* His brother Nat Carr was also a character actor.

REVIEWS

No Greater Love: Alexander Carr makes his role into a routine portrait of a sentimental Jew but the picture belongs to him all the way. *New York Times* 5/14/32, *Variety* 5/17/32.

Her Splendid Folly: Carr handles the comedy speaking in broken dialect as a film producer. *Variety* 11/14/33.

Carr, Mary (Mary Kennevan?), Philadelphia, Pennsylvania, 1874–1973

Silent: Best known for her starring role in 1920's *Over the Hill (to the Poorhouse),* Mary Carr became one of the cinema's archetypal mother figures. She may have been in films as early as 1905 for Lubin and other studios but her full-length features began

about 1916 with *Her Bleeding Heart* and *Love's Toll.* She continued to be active throughout the following decade.

Carr's numerous other films included *Mrs. Wiggs of the Cabbage Patch, You Are Guilty, Thunderclap, Why Men Leave Home, Big Pal, Painted People, The King of the Turf, Jesse James, A Million for Love* and *Pleasures of the Rich.* Last silent: *Some Mother's Boy* (1929), in which she had top billing, made after her first talkie.

Sound: The first all-talking film *Lights of New York* (1928) was also Mary Carr's first. She was on-screen, sometimes in small character parts, steadily through 1937; afterwards her appearances grew fewer. Her talkies included *Kept Husbands, Forbidden Trail, Bombshell, Love Past Thirty, The Country Doctor, East Side of Heaven, Hot Curves* and *Law of the Tong.*

Carr also appeared in shorts in the early '30s, at least one of them being with Laurel and Hardy. In the '40s her roles were sparse and she returned for her last, as "The Quaker Woman" in 1956's *Friendly Persuasion,* after a long absence.

Comments: Mary Carr was perhaps old enough to portray mothers convincingly when she entered films, but she certainly was not as old as she was usually made up to be. Her mothers always tended to look grandmotherly; perhaps her own six children provided her with experience.

Carr's voice proved be flat in accent and somewhat high-pitched but it did not detract from her screen image. It fit with her persona. Her sweet-featured, sympathetic face with its crown of white hair (perhaps a wig) made a welcome addition to any film in which she appeared.

REVIEWS

Lights of New York: Mary Carr in a bit as the mother gives an illustration of what may be accomplished by delivering dialogue with stage experience. *Variety* 7/11/28.

Second Wife: The faithful housekeeper is charmingly acted by Mary Carr. *New York Times* 2/10/30.

West of Rainbow's End: Mary Carr, the old timer, is pretty much wasted. *Variety* 3/9/38.

Carroll, Nancy (Ann La Hiff), New York, New York, 1904/06–1965

Filmography: Films in Review (May 1964)

Silent: Following a stint as a chorus girl in Broadway musicals, flame-haired Nancy Carroll entered films with a supporting role in 1927's *Ladies Must Dress.* A few more insignificant silents followed in 1928: *Easy Come, Easy Go, The Water Hole, Chicken à la King* and *Manhattan Cocktail.* The latter picture is referred to in at least one source as a part-talkie but this is uncertain. Last silent: *The Sin Sister* (1929), made after her first part-talkie.

Sound: The popular melodrama *The Shopworn Angel* premiered in the very last days of 1928. It was most probably Nancy Carroll's first picture with sound and definitely her first major success. The also up-and-coming Gary Cooper was her co-star.

That success was almost immediately followed by another part-sound hit in early 1929, *Abie's Irish Rose* with Buddy Rogers as Abie. Carroll's first full sound film was *The Wolf of Wall Street* in which she played the supporting role of a maid.

Carroll soon appeared in *Close Harmony*, the first of the musicals she made over the next couple of years which generally co-starred Buddy Rogers or Stanley Smith. Others included *The Dance of Life*, *Sweetie*, *Honey* and *Paramount on Parade*.

Nineteen thirty was probably Carroll's most spectacular year with such well-regarded dramas as *Laughter* and *The Devil's Holiday*, for which she received an Academy Award nomination. Until 1933 she remained one of Paramount's top stars, alternating between comedy and drama with ease. Carroll was seen on-screen until 1935 in such films as *Hot Saturday*, *The Woman Accused*, *The Kiss Before the Mirror* and *I'll Love You Forever*. With her popularity slipping she left the screen for some years, returning in 1938 for *There Goes My Heart*. Her comeback was inauspicious and her role in this film was severely edited down.

That year Carroll made her final screen appearance in a small part in Deanna Durbin's *That Certain Age*. After her picture career was over, she appeared in the Broadway drama *I Must Love Someone* and also did radio and television work, as well as continuing her stage appearances.

Comments: At the very beginning of her screen career, Nancy Carroll was apparently not looked upon as star material. Her films were minor and her characters invariably were given names like Maisie (or Mazie) and Babs. She rose above these expectations when sound arrived and is generally considered to be the first major star created by the talkies.

Carroll reputedly was the first woman to sing into a microphone and tap dance on a soundstage, but this may be debatable. Her speaking voice was fine and, although her singing could be called not more than adequate, she could dance with brio. She was possessed of natural red hair and bright blue eyes set in a round and expressive face believably ranging from perkiness to pathos.

Carroll was a good actress who could touch the spectator's heart with her emoting. Unfortunately she also exhibited the explosive temperament associated with her hair color and there were battles with the Paramount powers that did not endear her to them.

As long as she was making money for the studio, Carroll remained on top but her downfall began after an unsuccessful film, *The Night Angel*, in 1931. Although many of her later films were poor, the waiflike star is still remembered fondly by movie fans.

REVIEWS

The Shopworn Angel: The part Nancy Carroll plays is not very pleasant but she contributes excellent work and seems natural and lifelike. She also sings and her voice records surprisingly well in both efforts. *Harrison's Reports* 1/5/29, *Variety* 1/9/29.

Sweetie: Carroll gets less sympathy in this than in her previous roles but her performance is convincing. *Variety* 10/30/29.

Honey: Nancy Carroll is the heroine and she gives an excellent performance. *Harrison's Reports* 3/22/30, *Variety* 4/2/30.

Laughter: Nancy Carroll is starred and plays well in the comedy drama, but perhaps Frederic March's performance has smothered hers. She does not awaken any sympathy. *Variety* 10/8/30, *Harrison's Reports* 11/8/30.

The Man I Killed: Carroll handles herself capably in a role that gives her little opportunity. *Variety* 1/26/32.

A Kiss Before the Mirror: Nancy Carroll plays a more mature character than usual but in trying to go dramatic in a couple of scenes overplays badly. *Variety* 5/16/33.

Jealousy: Miss Carroll does nice work in spots with an assurance she did not display in her earlier days. *Variety* 11/27/34.

Atlantic Adventure: After failing to maintain an English accent at the outset, Nancy Carroll comes through. She looks particularly well. *Variety* 9/4/35.

Catlett, Walter, San Francisco, California, 1889–1960

Silent: A veteran of vaudeville, stock and the Broadway stage from 1911, including the long-running musical hit *Sally*, owlish Walter Catlett also appeared in English theater and music halls. He apparently made only three silents, the first of which was *Second Youth* in 1924, followed by *Summer Bachelors* in 1926. Last silent: *The Music Master* (1927).

Sound: Catlett returned for three talkies in 1929: *Happy Days*, *Married in Hollywood* and *Why Leave Home?* For the next 20 years or so he was busy in about 50 feature comedies, dramas and melodramas. About 1930 he was signed to direct and write comedy shorts but this did not turn out to be his métier. He also appeared in comedy shorts at Columbia from 1934 to '40.

From 1949 to '51 Catlett co-starred with Raymond Walburn in the low-budget "Latham" series, in which he portrayed a small town mayor. Other films included *The Floradora Girl, A Tale of Two Cities, Mr. Deeds Goes to Town, Cain and Mabel, Bringing Up Baby, Yankee Doodle Dandy, The Boy with Green Hair* and *Friendly Persuasion*. His last film, *Davy Crockett and the River Pirates*, was made in 1956.

Comments: Like many well-known character actors, Walter Catlett found his real cinema fame only in talking films. His fussy, excitable persona, characterized as "fidgety and google-eyed," could only be complete with the addition of the querulous voice which fit that persona as perfectly as did his tortoise shell glasses.

Catlett's roles were usually not large but were nonetheless often memorable, one example being that of the put-upon small town sheriff in the classic farce *Bringing Up Baby*. He always managed to live up to his apt description as "a low and wonderful American comedian." He also could be very effective when he occasionally played against type.

REVIEWS

Let's Go Places: Walter Catlett's humor does well on the screen as he impersonates the star director. *New York Times* 3/1/30.

Maker of Men: Catlett is very funny as a loyal alumnus. *New York Times* 12/19/31.

Rain: For the brief time that Walter Catlett is on the screen as a cockney quartermaster he makes the most of the part. *New York Times* 10/13/32, *Variety* 10/18/32.

Olsen's Big Moment (aka *Olsen's Night Out*): It's Walter Catlett's best picture and it ought to help him considerably. He does a swell drunk imitation and doesn't let up for a moment. His dialogue is much funnier than that of anyone else in the film. *Variety* 1/9/34.

A Tale of Two Cities: Catlett, abandoning his slapstick, is surprisingly good as the crafty and treacherous informer. *New York Times* 12/26/35.

Bringing Up Baby: Catlett gives an expertly comic portrayal. *Variety* 2/16/38.

Remedy for Riches: Walter Catlett's version of a local policeman causes laughs. *Variety* 3/12/41.

His Butler's Sister: Catlett plays a wacky stage producer. *Variety* 11/10/43.

Cawthorn, Joseph, England, 1868/69–1949

Silent: After much stage experience supposedly beginning at age three, German dialect comedian Joseph Cawthorn came to Hollywood in 1927 for such films as *The Secret Studio, Silk Legs, 2 Girls Wanted* and *Very Confidential*. Last silent: *Hold 'Em Yale!* (1928).

Sound: Cawthorn made liberal use of his ersatz German accent in many of the over 40 talkies in which he appeared. Five of them came in 1929 and included *Taming of the Shrew, Jazz Heaven, Speakeasy* and *Street Girl*. Among his others through 1936 were *Dixiana, Kiki, Love Me Tonight, White Zombie, The Cat and the Fiddle, Gold Diggers of 1935, Naughty Marietta* and *The Great Ziegfeld*.

Cawthorn still had an occasional top-billed role as in 1938's British-made *Crime Over London*, in which he played a dual role. He continued appearing on the stage and he returned for a few films in the early 1940s such as *Lillian Russell* and *So Ends the Night*.

The Postman Didn't Ring was apparently Cawthorn's last picture in 1942. In many of his later roles he portrayed kindly professor types, still disguising his own proper English accent with his version of a German one.

REVIEWS

Street Girl: Cawthorn, although an Englishman, speaks better broken German than the newest arrival from Germany. *Harrison's Reports* 8/10/29.

Jazz Heaven: If it makes the first run theaters it will have to be on the strength of Joseph Cawthorn and his Jewish comedy. It's entertaining and laughable as he does it and he does it all. Of course, RKO will sign up Cawthorn after this picture. *Variety* 11/6/29.

The Princess and the Plumber: Joseph Cawthorn won much laughter. *New York Times* 12/23/30.

Smart Girl: Most of the acting honors go to Cawthorn. *Variety* 8/21/35.

Chadwick, Helene, Chadwicks or Chadwick, New York, 1897–1940

Silent: The first features of Helene Chadwick came in the mid–1910s and included *The Challenge* (1916), *The Angel Factory, The Yellow Ticket, The Naulahka* and *Caleb Piper's Girl*. She remained active as a star through the end of the silent era in such films as *Godless Men, The Sin Flood, Reno, Her Own Free Will, The Woman Hater, Pleasures of the Rich, Stage Kisses* and *Say It with Sables*. Last silent: *Confessions of a Wife* (1928).

Sound: Chadwick must be counted among the victims of the talkies. After her initial part-talkie *Father and Son* (1929), she did not receive screen credit again until 1931 when she began playing a few small parts that continued to about 1935. Among them were *Hell Bound, Morning Glory, Ever*

Since Eve, *A Wicked Woman* and *Call of the Wild*. She may also have done extra work.

Father and Son: Helene Chadwick plays the good girl with restraint and wins a great share of the spectator's interest by her fine acting. *Variety* 6/5/29, *Harrison's Reports* 6/8/29.

Chandler, Lane (Robert Oakes), Culbertson, Montana or North Dakota, 1899–1972

Silent: Six foot-three Lane Chandler's entree into movies came as an extra and bit player about 1923; in 1927 he had his first lead in Paramount's *Open Range*. Although he went on to appear in films with Greta Garbo and Clara Bow, he generally was not top-billed in the silents, sometimes supporting leading men like Gary Cooper.

Among Chandler's films were *The Big Killing*, *The First Kiss*, *Red Hair*, *Legion of the Condemned* and *Love and Learn*. Last silent: *The Single Standard* (1929), with synchronized music and sound effects.

Sound: Nineteen twenty-nine's *The Studio Murder Mystery* was Chandler's first talkie and he appeared way down in the cast list. His other that year was *The Forward Pass*. After being released by Paramount he freelanced and had his first top billing in the western *Firebrand Jordan* (1930).

In 1931 Chandler was signed by Kent Pictures for a western series which included such alliterative titles as *Wyoming Whirlwind*, *Texas Tornado*, *The Hurricane Horseman* and *Reckless Rider*. He also had the lead in the 1930 serial *Lightning Express*.

Chandler's stardom, such as it was, was short-lived and he soon found himself in supporting roles in non-westerns, interspersed with oaters in which he occasionally played the lead. His parts eventually declined to bits.

Despite his general lack of success, Chandler seemed to be a DeMille favorite and played small roles in such films as *The Sign of the Cross*, *Union Pacific*, *The Buccaneer*, *Unconquered* and *The Greatest Show on Earth*. On the opposite extreme he was also in shorts, including those of The Three Stooges.

Others of Chandler's hundreds of film appearances included *Roman Scandals*, *Born to Sing*, *Calamity Jane*, *The Firefly*, *Laura*, *The Spider*, *Wells Fargo* and *The Sea Devils*. There also were many serial appearances, among them *The Black Coin*, *Buck Rogers*, *The Devil Horse*, *Deadwood Dick*, *Fighting with Kit Carson*, *Flash Gordon*, *The Green Hornet*, *Junior G-Men* and *The Phantom Creeps*.

Chandler was still to be seen in 1950s movies and even an occasional later one, as well as many TV series like *Maverick*, *The Restless Gun* and *Alfred Hitchcock Presents*.

Comments: For a brief time it must have seemed as if handsome and rugged Lane Chandler had a shot at becoming a major leading man. He had the kind of all–American looks and the non-threatening personality which many top silent actresses liked in their leading men. But the rise of Gary Cooper, a similar "strong, silent" type, and also a Montanan, seemed to overshadow his small gifts.

There was also the matter of Lane Chandler's voice. While suitably deep, it was flat and redolent of the prairie. It may have been satisfactory for the slim demands of cinema range riding but it only emphasized his almost total lack of charisma.

Chaney, Lon (Leonidas Frank Chaney; posthumously known as Lon Chaney, Sr.), Colorado Springs, Colorado, 1883–1930

Filmography: *Films in Review* (Dec. 1953)

Silent: Vaudevillian Lon Chaney's first-known screen appearances were in two-reelers in 1912. He made almost 100 films in the next five years, one notable role coming in William S. Hart's *Riddle Gawne* (1918). He also wrote and directed some films during that period, and even occasionally was a prop man.

Nineteen nineteen's *The Miracle Man* proved to be Chaney's breakthrough film. His physical contortions as a fake cripple foreshadowed his legendary roles, beginning with the legless character in *The Penalty* in 1920. During the next few years he was seen in a variety of character roles, often as a villain, before true stardom arrived with Universal's *The Hunchback of Notre Dame* in 1923.

Nineteen twenty-five was Lon Chaney's greatest year. He went to MGM to appear in *The Unholy Three*; this was followed by the classic and enormously popular *The Phantom of the Opera* back at Universal. He remained a major MGM star for the rest of the decade in such films as *The Road to Mandalay*, *London After Midnight*, *Tell It to the Marines*, *Laugh, Clown, Laugh* and *The Unknown*.

Many of Chaney's best films were directed by Tod Browning, whose inner demons seemed to mesh well with those of his star. Three of his silents in 1928–29, including *Where East Is East* and *West of Zanzibar*, were released with synchronized music and sound effects. Last silent: *Thunder* (1929), with synchronized music and sound effects.

Sound: Many MGM stars appeared in the all-talking, all-singing, all-dancing *Hollywood Revue of 1929*, MGM's contribution to that short-lived dawn of the talkies genre. Tribute was paid to Lon Chaney in the specialty number "Lon Chaney's Going to Get You If You Don't Watch Out," composed and sung by vaudevillian Gus Edwards. Several dancers wearing grotesque masks were featured and, at the number's conclusion, Master of Ceremonies Jack Benny greeted the supposedly real Chaney, who was mute and masked. After a handshake, "Chaney" left Benny holding a prop arm. This actually was not the actor himself.

Chaney apparently wished to make his sound debut in a more auspicious manner and that chance soon came. Tod Browning requested that the star be loaned out to Universal for his production of *Dracula*. However, producer Irving Thalberg wished Chaney's first talkie to be an MGM release. His eyes lit on *The Unholy Three*.

As a silent it had been a big moneymaker, and the leading role of the ventriloquist seemed eminently adaptable for talkies. This then became Chaney's sound debut. It opened in mid–1930 and was a success but by that time he was mortally ill of cancer. *The Unholy Three* was both his first and final sound film.

Comments: Although Lon Chaney made his reputation as a phenomenally successful master of the art of make-up and physical contortion, his first sound role did not rely as much on his bag of tricks. Still there was, not unnaturally, a good deal of hype around his sound debut.

Chaney supposedly declined to take voice lessons. "It ruins voices," he is reported to have said. "That's what's the matter with John Gilbert." Whether or not he actually did take voice lessons (and there *is* evidence he at least consulted some voice "experts"), his deep voice matched his role perfectly.

A perfectionist, Chaney undoubtedly tested and studied his voice as carefully as he always experimented with his makeup. His rendering of the other voices he used in the film was competent as well. In order to prove he did all the voices himself, he had the studio draw up an affidavit to that effect which was used in publicizing the film.

While all this may have helped to arouse curiosity, in the end it was Chaney who sold *The Unholy Three* with his performance. It is likely that his future career would have been largely in the gangster roles he often played in silents. (He was supposedly set for the role that Wallace Beery ultimately played, and for which he was Oscar-nominated, in *The Big House*.)

Of course, Bela Lugosi ended up with the career-making role of Dracula but there might well have been some horror roles in Lon Chaney's future as well. Perhaps he would have had the type of career that Boris Karloff enjoyed. Indeed, had Chaney lived Karloff might never have been heard from. The moviegoing public never had a chance to find out.

REVIEWS

The Unholy Three: While it is notable as a vehicle for the actor's vocal gymnastics, viewers might prefer the silent version to the present one. Its main asset is that it is the first Chaney talker, but while skill in makeup permitted Chaney to get away with the impersonation of an old woman in the silent version, his handling of five different voices in the dialogue destroys all plausibility. The finest thing about this picture is that it discloses Lon Chaney's natural voice just exactly as it should be — deep, vibrant and perfectly poised. *New York Times* 7/5/30, *Variety* 7/9/30, *Harrison's Reports* 7/12/30, *Photoplay* 8/30.

Chaplin, Charles, London, England, 1889–1977

Filmography: List of films in *Film Dope* (Nov. 1974), corrections (Dec. 1983)

Silent: The son of two down-at-heel music hall performers, Charlie Chaplin began his rise to worldwide fame and acclaim modestly enough as a young member, perhaps age seven, of the Eight Lancashire Lads. His contribution was apparently as a clog dancer. A few years later he was on the stage in *Sherlock Holmes* and other plays before joining Fred Karno's music hall troupe.

Chaplin accompanied the group, of which Stan Laurel also was a member, on a tour of the United States in *A Night in an English Music Hall*. After being signed by Mack Sennett as a potential replacement for comic Ford Sterling he appeared in his first Keystone one-reeler, *Making a Living* (1914), playing an English dandy.

In Chaplin's second film, *Kid Auto Races at Venice*, he began to experiment with elements of the "Little Fellow" tramp persona which he refined over the next year or so into what would become the world's most recognized persona and costume.

Other early Chaplin efforts included *Mabel's Busy Day*, *Between Showers*, *Tango Tangles*, *His New Profession* and *A Film Johnnie*, many co-starring Mabel Normand and Roscoe "Fatty" Arbuckle. After his twelfth or so film, *Caught in a Cabaret*, he was directing nearly all his pictures and writing them as well. He also appeared in his first feature, 1914's *Tillie's Punctured Romance* starring Marie Dressler.

By 1915 Chaplin was already becoming one of the most popular comics in the movies and he left Sennett to join Essanay at $1,250 a week. It was there that he perfected The Tramp in a 1915 film of the same name. It presaged the emotional overtones and social concerns of his mature work. His other Essanay movies included *His New Job*, *Work*, *By the Sea* and *Shanghaied*.

His popularity soaring, shrewd businessman Chaplin made another move in 1916, this time to Mutual. There he earned an astonishing $10,000 weekly plus a signing bonus of $150,000, a total of $670,000 the first year. For this handsome sum he was to make 12 pictures a year, but he failed to make the deadline.

Chaplin did ultimately turn out the 12 films but they were spread over parts of 1916 and '17. The "Mutuals" proved to be little gems, and his best to date. They included *The Rink*, *The Pawnshop*, *The Adventurer*, *Easy Street*, *The Cure* and *The Immigrant*.

Moving ever upward in the pantheon of world film stars, Chaplin built his own studio and took his talents to First National where his output slowed to one or two films a year. There he made the popular World War One feature *Shoulder Arms* as well as the briefer works *A Dog's Life*, *Sunnyside*, *A Day's Pleasure*, *The Idle Class*, *Pay Day* and *The Pilgrim*. He also appeared in the patriotic split-reeler *The Bond* to support the war effort.

It was with the enormously successful *The Kid* (1921), co-starring Jackie Coogan (soon to have his own great but brief starring career) that Chaplin sealed his pre-eminent status as the world cinema's greatest comic actor. During this period he also had a cameo in his great friend Douglas Fairbanks's *The Nut*.

Having joined Fairbanks and the latter's wife Mary Pickford as one of the founders of United Artists in 1919, Chaplin contributed his first film to that company (*A Woman of Paris*) in 1923. He directed it but only had a cameo role. It starred his longtime on- and off-screen leading lady Edna Purviance and, although it did nothing for her continued career, it ultimately influenced directors who followed. Largely unseen for 50 years, it resurfaced to modern-day acclaim.

Chaplin's acknowledged masterpiece *The Gold Rush* appeared in 1925, with Georgia Hale as his new leading woman. It also featured Mack Swain, who had been in numerous previous Chaplin films. This was followed by *The Circus* in 1928. He also made a brief cameo appearance in Marion Davies's *Show People* that year.

A holdout against what he considered to be the excesses of the dialogue film, Chaplin had the prestige and power to continue making silents after the talkies came to dominate the cinema. Two years after most theaters had been wired for sound films, he stunned the filmgoing public with yet another silent masterwork.

Nineteen thirty-one's *City Lights* proved to be a considerable success. A sentimental comedy, it contained only synchronized music and sound effects, the latter sometimes used mockingly to imitate speech. Last silent: *Modern Times* (1936), with synchronized sound effects, music and a singing sequence. Although there actually is a smidgen of spoken dialogue over a loudspeaker, this is generally considered a silent film because of the lack of dialogue spoken between characters.

Sound: The last appearance of the "Little Fellow" as an actual tramp came in *Modern Times*, but the character of the Jewish barber in the first of Chaplin's talkies, *The Great Dictator* (1940), had certain elements of his famous creation. In it he played a dual role: the barber and his look-alike Adenoid Hynkel, the tyrant of Tomania. The latter was obviously a satiric portrait of a certain German who had world conquest on his mind.

Chaplin received two Academy Award nominations: Best Actor and Best Writer of an Original Story. His voice was fine and his cultured British tones showed no trace of what must have once been a "lower-class," perhaps even Cockney, accent.

In a complete departure, Chaplin's next film, 1947's *Monsieur Verdoux*, was a black comedy about a French multiple wife-murderer. It was a daring movie to make at the time and it proved controversial. He seemed to be avenging himself on all the women who had created problems for him (including Joan Barry, who not too many years before had sued him in a lengthy paternity case). Of course, he was hardly an innocent bystander in his relations with women.

Chaplin made two films in the decade of the 1950s, the reasonably successful *Limelight* (1952) and the little-seen, satiric *A King in New York* (1957). The latter picture reflected his bitterness over having been barred from returning to the United States in 1952 because of his supposed Communist sympathies. His final screen effort was the misfire comedy *A Countess from Hong Kong* in 1966, which starred Marlon Brando and Sophia Loren and in which he had a cameo role.

After a long exile in Switzerland, Charlie Chaplin returned to Hollywood in 1972 to accept a special Oscar for "the incalculable effect he has had in making motion pictures the art form of this century." His greeting at the ceremony was overwhelming and the old man seemed overwhelmed by it. This was actually his second special Academy Award, the first coming in 1928 "for versatility and genius in writing, acting, directing and producing *The Circus*," probably the least known of his mature works.

Chaplin was far from forgotten even after he became professionally inactive. Some of his films were released with a new musical track and his own narration. The television series *The Unknown Chaplin*, an analysis of his directorial genius via a compilation of rehearsal scenes and outtakes, was aired to great acclaim in the 1980s. A Richard Attenborough film entitled simply *Chaplin*, purporting to be the story of his life, was released to a general lack of success in the early '90s.

The iconographic "Little Fellow" again became a successful media figure some 50 years after his last appearance in *Modern Times* when a popular IBM campaign utilized a Chaplin tramp look-alike in an ad campaign for its computers. Ironically, the man who had satirized the mechanization of society in *Modern Times* had become the unwitting spokesman for one of the largest corporations in the world.

Comments: To literally the whole world in the late 'teens and 1920s, Charles Spencer Chaplin was simply Charlie or Charlot or Carlito. His fame was a phenomenon likely never to be repeated. He was arguably the most famous man on the face of the earth, spawning a cottage industry of imitators (most successfully Billy West) and including at least one woman (Minerva Courtney). The product of a deprived Dickensian childhood had reached heights of adoration that no mere entertainer had ever reached before.

More books and articles, numbering in the thousands, have been written about Chaplin than any other cinema figure. Many writers search for the roots of his genius in those early life experiences in London where he and his older half-brother Sydney struggled to survive. Chaplin apparently had the ability to look at life through a child's eyes. His tramp character was by turns naive and knowing, gentle and aggressive, and seemingly had a child's freedom from much of civilization's notions of morality.

In his early one-reelers, the "Little Fellow"—to use Charlie Chaplin's own cognomen—was not a particularly sympathetic figure, in fact he could be malicious. Although poverty was often shown, there was little attempt to reflect social reality. That came later when he movingly portrayed what it was like to be the archetypal outsider, often defeated. In doing so, he created a character who was universal.

As in all great comic inventions, Chaplin's tramp had a series of readily identifiable characteristics: turning rapidly on one foot, a twitching mustache, cane swinging, mechanically raising his hat straight up. Early in his career, derrière-kicking seemed to be a favorite of his as well. He was extremely graceful and athletic, almost balletic, in his movements.

In later years, Chaplin's standing as a great direc-

tor diminished somewhat. He was accused, perhaps with some merit, of being overly sentimental and old-fashioned in his views. Another source of criticism was the open expression of his social tenets. An example is the much-noted final speech in *The Great Dictator* where a didactic plea for peace and understanding was delivered.

Chaplin certainly held strong beliefs. His great overriding theme of the individual versus an uncaring society had perhaps become too obviously stated. *A King in New York*, while having its share of amusing moments, was blatantly overloaded with his favorite *bêtes noire*.

On a technical level, it has been noted that Chaplin's directorial style had little obvious flair. He pretty much shot scenes straight on with a minimum of "tricks." Because of the other qualities of his best films this usually did not receive much attention. Whatever his stylistic shortcomings, more recently the pendulum has swung back and he is again recognized as a great director.

Chaplin's views on talking pictures were clearly expressed in his two 1930s films. In the renowned opening of *City Lights*, some local wardheelers are about to unveil a statue and the usual speechmaking is taking place. Instead of words the droning yet expressive sound of a saxophone issues forth.

In *Modern Times*, Chaplin's voice is heard for the first time on-screen when as a singing waiter he delivers a garbled song which starts out, "Señora ce la tima/Voulez vous la taxi meter." Those relatively brief satirical moments speak more than volumes could about his views on the "talkers."

Fashions in film acting and directing come and go but Chaplin's premier place in cinema history is largely undiminished and is likely to remain so. He has survived his personal reputation for stinginess, vindictiveness, lack of generosity and the more than occasional untruthfulness revealed in his own books.

The artist Chaplin, if not the person, survived being called a "little runt of a Svengali" and "a lecherous hound who lies like a cheap Cockney cad" in the wake of his highly publicized involvements in sordid scandals with underaged girls. His artistry survives his political views, which were perhaps only naive, and which were roundly and violently denounced by substantial segments of the American public.

Greatness tends to overcome such temporary, if violent, swings in the public mood. But in what does Chaplin's real greatness lie? One writer opined: "That Chaplin can cry until he laughs and makes us laugh with him is the measure of his genius."

Critic Andrew Sarris said: "Charles Chaplin is

arguably the single most important artist produced by the cinema.... He remains the supreme exemplification of the axiom that lives not lenses stand at the center of cinematic creation." The "life" to which he is referring may be the man Chaplin who undeniably was a great *auteur* and a superior all-around filmmaker, even providing his own music soundtracks.

To most people it is not really the flawed person of Charles Spencer Chaplin they may admire, or even revere, but his persona: Charlie, The Little Fellow, The Tramp. That little forlorn figure up there on the screen, walking into an uncertain tomorrow down a perilous road, has shown us some of the eternal verities.

Reviews

The Great Dictator: A controversy will arise as to its entertaining value, for it is not a comedy all the way through but rather a propaganda picture. His imitation of Hitler is a piece of art. *Harrison's Reports* 10/26/40.

Monsieur Verdoux: Chaplin will have to carry this one; the character generates little sympathy. His endeavor to get his "common man" ideology into the film militates against its comic value and the casting is all Chaplin, perhaps too much so and he has acted in questionable taste. *Variety* 4/16/47, *Harrison's Reports* 4/19/47.

Limelight: As the picture's star, author, producer, director, music composer and choreographer Chaplin does an outstanding job in every department, thus proving his genius. In some of the scenes Chaplin indulges in too much preaching and moralizing in what impresses one as an attempt to get over his personal philosophy. (His role as the has-been clown Calvero had a certain resonance to the real-life comic whose adoring American public had apparently forsaken him.) *Harrison's Reports* 10/11/52.

A King in New York: Chaplin stands revealed as an embittered man who permits his formerly good humor to be bogged down by personal prejudice. *Variety* 9/18/57.

Chase, Charley (sometimes Charlie;
Charles Parrott), Baltimore, Maryland, 1893–1940

Filmography: Film Fan Monthly (July-Aug. 1969)

Silent: Comedian Charley Chase started with Sennett in 1914, was a Keystone Kop for perhaps a brief while, and appeared with Chaplin, Arbuckle and others in the Sennett stable. He then gave up his performing career and began to direct about 1915 for studios such as L-KO, Fox, Paramount and Famous Players-Lasky.

In 1921, Chase went to Hal Roach studios and continued directing there under his real name. About 1923 he came back to the business side of the camera to star in a series of "Paul Parrott" comedies. He also played a character called "Jimmy Jump."

When Chase began performing for comedy director Leo McCarey in the mid–1920s, he finally came into his own. With his comic persona as a dapper, mild-mannered and well-intentioned bumbler, he was a man who just could not help getting into all manner of trouble.

Chase's roles were almost entirely in two-reelers like *At First Sight* (one of his first since the Sennett days), *Dog Shy, Bromo and Juliet, His Wooden Wedding, Crazy Like a Fox, Long Fliv the King* and the well-regarded *Mighty Like a Moose* and *Limousine Love.* Last silent: *Movie Night* (1929), a two-reeler.

Sound: Charley Chase's first sound feature was *Modern Love,* a 1929 part-talkie, in which he was the leading man. His *métier* remained the sound short of which he made nearly 100. By 1936 that form was no longer as popular and he provided solid support in a few features, among which were *Start Cheering* and *Kelly the Second.*

Chase had earlier appeared in the Laurel and Hardy classic *Sons of the Desert* as the obnoxious conventioneer. He ultimately returned to making shorts for Columbia. His films included *Fifty Million Husbands, Girl Shock, Dollar Dizzy, The Real McCoy, The Nickel Nurser, The Chases of Pimple Street* and two of his best, *Fallen Arches* and *Rattling Romeo.*

Comments: For a long while, Charley Chase was largely unappreciated. His output may have been major — over 200 short films — but his reputation was not; he was just one of the many comics who had had their day and were relegated to obscurity.

Chase's films now have been rediscovered by latter-day audiences to appreciative laughter, and he has been given his due as one of the best of the silent and sound comedians. Although he appeared in relatively few features, it was not because of his voice which was a well-regulated baritone, fitting his persona perfectly.

Indeed, Chase sang commendably well in some of his films, even as part of a barbershop quartet. It seemed that he could not (or the studios thought he could not) carry an entire feature as a leading man. His feature *Bank Night* apparently was not released (or was briefly released) in full-length form before being edited down into the short *Neighborhood House.*

Why Chase was not utilized in more feature character roles is somewhat of a mystery but his shorts stand as monument enough. They were generally well-written and produced and co-starred some of the best supporting comic actors of the day, including Billy Gilbert, Anita Garvin, Edgar Kennedy, Thelma Todd, Gertrude Astor and James Finlayson.

REVIEWS

Sons of the Desert: Charlie Chase has been cast to give movement to the more deliberate comedy of the stars Laurel and Hardy. He's the exuberant practical joker and he works too hard. *Variety* 1/9/34.

Kelly the Second: Charlie Chase is partially dwarfed but he garners his share of laurels with his familiar comedy routine. He gets a real chance to talk in several scenes and cashes in. (Chase played a druggist turned fight manager.) *Variety* 10/7/36.

Start Cheering: One of the specialty acts that should go over big with audiences is one which shows Charley Chase eating lit cigarette papers and anything else he can lay his hands on. *Harrison's Reports* 2/19/38.

Christy, Ann (Gladys Cronin), Logansport, Indiana, 1905?–1987

Silent: A beauty contest winner, petite Ann Christy appeared in Christie two-reel comedies in 1927 and then made her feature bow in that year's *The Kid Sister*. Her 1928 films were *The Water Hole* and the popular *Speedy*, in which she co-starred with Harold Lloyd as his last silent leading lady. She was also dubbed a 1928 Wampas Baby Star. Last silents: *The Lariat Kid* and *Just Off Broadway*, released at about the same time in 1929.

Sound: Christy's first sound feature was the melodrama *The Fourth Alarm* in late 1930 and she also appeared in shorts, one of which was Bing Crosby's first film for Sennett. Her only other known feature credit was the 1932 quickie *Behind Stone Walls*.

Clair, Ethlyne (Ethlyne Williamson), Talladega, Alabama, 1904?–1996

Filmography: List of films in *Sweethearts of the Sage*

Silent: After winning a beauty contest, Ethlyne Clair played some small roles and then appeared in the lengthy Universal comedy series "The Newlyweds and Their Baby." From 1927 her features were mostly westerns, several with Hoot Gibson and Tom Tyler. They included *A Hero on Horseback*, *Painted Ponies*, *Riding for Fame*, *Gun Law* and *Guardians of the Wild*.

Clair also appeared in melodramas like *Hey Rube!* and *Three Miles Up* and was starred in the serials *The Vanishing Rider* (1928) and *Queen of the Northwoods* (1929). In that year she also was

dubbed a Wampas Baby Star. Last silent: *The Pride of Pawnee* (1929), released after her first part-talkie.

Sound: Clair had no leads in talkies. A small role in the part-talkie *From Headquarters* (1929) marked her sound debut. Her first full talkie, in which she was merely one of the "crowd," was the all-singing, all-dancing Warner Bros.' extravaganza *The Show of Shows*. *Second Choice*, in which she appeared in support, was her single 1930 film.

In 1931 Clair played a brief role in *God's Gift to Women* and that apparently marked the end of her career. Although she sometimes claimed to have continued to make appearances in movies until the latter 1940s, there is no evidence of this. She may have been an extra.

REVIEWS

From Headquarters: A rather good cast does its best, including Ethlyne Clair who plays the tropical girl. *Harrison's Reports* 6/22/29, *Variety* 7/17/29.

Clayton, Ethel, Champaign, Illinois, 1884–1966

Silent: Ethel Clayton was a very popular star who began appearing in features in 1914. Some of her earliest ones were *The Lion and the Mouse*, *The College Widow*, *Broken Chains* and *Dollars and the Woman*. She had made her debut about 1910 and found fame with the Lubin studio.

In the '20s, Clayton's roles became more sporadic and she fell into supporting parts. Among her other films were *Whims of Society*, *A City Sparrow*, *Exit the Vamp*, *Can a Woman Love Twice?* and *The Princess from Hoboken*. Last silent: *Mother Machree* (1928), with synchronized music and sound effects.

Sound: *Hit the Deck* and *The Call of the Circus*, released about the same time in 1930, were Clayton's first sound films. In the latter she played the female lead, probably for the final time. She continued appearing in small parts, and then bits, at least through 1940.

One of Clayton's more interesting roles was in Mary Pickford's *Secrets* in 1933. With other former silent stars, she played one of Pickford's unsympathetic adult children. Her other sound films included *The All American*, *Let's Fall in Love*, *Easy to Take*, *Hold 'Em Navy*, *Scandal Street*, *Paris Honeymoon* and *Love Thy Neighbor*. She did not receive billing in any films during 1934 and '35.

REVIEWS

Hit the Deck: Ethel Clayton officiates and while one may take her scripted utterances as they come, the silly assertions don't in the least embellish the story. *New York Times* 1/15/30.

Clifford, Ruth, Pawtucket, Rhode Island, 1900–

Silent: After minor roles in Edison one- and two-reelers beginning about 1915, Ruth Clifford went to Universal in 1917 and became a star in the first of her approximately 25 films there, *A Kentucky Cinderella*.

Other Clifford films included *Butterfly*, *Abraham Lincoln* (1924 version), *Ponjola*, *Typhoon Love*, *Daughters of the Rich*, *Her Husband's Secret* and *The Devil's Apple Tree*. Last silent: *The Eternal Woman* (1929).

Sound: Clifford's first talkie was the all-singing, all-talking, all-dancing *The Show of Shows* (1929), in which she made the briefest of appearances surrounded by many other starlets. She apparently made no other talkies until 1933.

Clifford worked fairly steadily in supporting roles throughout the decade, except apparently for 1937. She was seen in such movies as *Elmer and Elsie*, *Dante's Inferno*, *She Married Her Boss*, *Four Men and a Prayer*, *Hollywood Boulevard* and *Wife, Husband and Friend*.

In later years Clifford could be briefly glimpsed in John Ford movies like *How Green Was My Valley*, *She Wore a Yellow Ribbon*, *Wagon Master* and *The Searchers*, as well as in TV programs and films of the 1950s that included *The Man in the Gray Flannel Suit*.

Cobb, Edmund, Albuquerque, New Mexico, 1892–1974

Filmography: *Filmograph* (v. 2, no. 2, 1971); Academy of Motion Picture Arts and Sciences; List of films in *Eighty Silent Film Stars*

Silent: Beginning about 1910, companies making films in New Mexico and Colorado used young Edmund Cobb in bit parts as a villain and in 1913 he appeared in the seminal serial *The Adventures of Kathlyn*. Working for early companies which included Lubin, Essanay and Selig, he made numerous two-reel westerns, sometimes in leading roles, sometimes in support.

Cobb also essayed an occasional feature and did stunt work. In the 1920s he continued making two-reelers and features and, in mid-decade, appeared in the serials *Days of '49* and *Fighting with Buffalo Bill*.

Among Cobb's features for Arrow, Universal and others were *Captain Jinks of the Horse Marines*, *The Desert Scorpion*, *Battling Bates*, *Blasted Hopes*, *The Burning Trail*, *General Custer at Little Big Horn*, *Wolf's Trail* and *The Four-Footed Ranger*.

Cobb's final silent leading roles were in a series of films with Dynamite, a dog, who received top billing. He probably made over 130 silents in all.

Last silent feature: *Young Whirlwind* (1928). Last silent appearance: *A Final Reckoning* (1929), a serial.

Sound: The talkies found Cobb mostly in supporting roles. As he aged, his face hardened and he made a most believable villain. He was seen in 1930's *The Indians Are Coming* starring Tim McCoy, the chapterplay that is generally considered to be both the last silent and the first sound serial. He also appeared that year in the feature *Beyond the Rio Grande*.

Cobb worked steadily as a dependable character player, and a very occasional western lead, in over 250 pictures until about 1950. His films included *Law of the Rio Grande*, *Gunners and Guns* (lead), *Law of the Plains*, *Blazing Six Shooters*, *I Was a Prisoner on Devil's Island*, *Song of the Range* and *Law of the Canyon*.

Cobb continued to appear in films sporadically until 1957 (e.g., *Lucy Gallant*, *The Amazing Colossal Man*) and then returned for a very few in the '60s, among them *The Bounty Killer* and *Requiem for a Gunfighter*. The 1966 *Johnny Reno* was his last.

Cobb also was seen (generally up to no good) in innumerable serials like *Gordon of Ghost City*, *Law of the Wild*, *Mystery Mountain*, *The Miracle Rider*, *Zorro Rides Again*, *Fighting Devil Dogs*, *The Spider's Web*, *Jesse James Rides Again*, *G-Men Never Forget* and *Government Agents vs. Phantom Legion*.

Cody, Lew (also Lewis; Louis Cote), Berlin, New Hampshire or Waterville, Maine, 1884/87–1934

Silent: Mustachioed smoothie Lew Cody began his film career about 1915 in such films as *Should a Wife Forgive?*, *The Cycle of Fate* and *The Mating*, and soon became a popular player. Although he often portrayed villains, he was also an accomplished light comedy actor, as in his co-starring appearances in popular MGM marital comedies with Aileen Pringle.

Cody's other films included *The Beloved Cheater*, *The Butterfly Man*, *The Secrets of Paris*, *The Gay Deceiver*, *Beau Broadway*, *The Sporting Venus* and *Time, the Comedian*. Last silent: *A Single Man* (1929).

Sound: Age, more than sound, affected Cody's career. And it was not much affected; he was on-screen until the time of his death, albeit sometimes as a supporting player.

Cody's first talkie was Gloria Swanson's 1930 comedy *What a Widow!* Other of his efforts included *The Common Law*, *Sporting Blood*, *The Crusader*, *The Unwritten Law*, *Wine, Women and Song* and his last, *Shoot the Works* (1934).

What a Widow!: Cody, as a famous dancer, is pretty heavy even as a harmless drunk who is always fried. *Variety* 9/17/30.

Meet the Wife: Pretty good work from Lew Cody who is sufficiently suave. *Variety* 6/23/31.

X Marks the Spot: The dapper type managing editor is top-billed Lew Cody. *Variety* 12/8/31.

File 113: The top-billed Cody plays a detective briskly but does not impress as a mental genius, rather a prosperous stockbroker. *Variety* 2/23/32.

Sitting Pretty: Lew Cody plays a picture producer. *Variety* 9/16/30.

Shoot the Works: A member of the cast, Lew Cody, is now dead. *Harrison's Reports* 7/14/34.

Coghlan, Frank ("Junior"; also billed as Coughlan and Coughlin), New Haven, Connecticut, 1916/17–

Silent: As a freckle-faced little boy with a Jackie Coogan haircut, Junior Coghlan was an extra for a few years, perhaps going as far back as 1919's *To Please One Woman*. He received occasional billing in features beginning in 1922 and was also in some two-reelers as well as the serial *The Great Circus Mystery*. Among his earlier films were *Bobbed Hair, Cause for Divorce* and *The Darling of New York*.

Young Coghlan signed to appear in Cecil B. DeMille productions about the mid–20s and was seen in features the rest of the decade. They included *The Road to Yesterday, The Last Frontier, Mike, The Skyrocket, The Yankee Clipper* and *A Harp in Hock*. He had a very few starring roles at the end of the decade including *Let 'Er Go Gallegher*. Last silent: *Marked Money* (1928).

Sound: The 1929 part-talkie *Square Shoulders* was Junior Coghlan's first sound film and it continued his brief string of starring roles. *River's End* and *The Girl Said No* followed in 1930. The usual problems of adolescent actors did not seem to affect him and he appeared in a series of films throughout the decade, but the importance of his roles gradually declined.

Among Coghlan's features were *Penrod and Sam* (he was Sam), *Hell's House, Alibi Ike, Make Way for a Lady, Brother Rat, Boy's Reformatory* and *Knute Rockne, All-American*. He also was in the serials *The Last of the Mohicans* and *Scouts to the Rescue*.

It is for his portrayal of Billy Batson in the 1941 serial *Adventures of Captain Marvel* that Frank Coghlan is best-known today. Because he was dimin\utive and still boyish-looking at 25 and his voice was also young, he could convincingly be the teenage boy who turned into the muscular superhero (played by Tom Tyler) with the cry of "Shazam!"

Before going off to the service during World War Two, Coghlan made a few other film appearances, among them *The Man Who Came to Dinner, Murder Over New York* and *Follow the Band*. He ultimately decided to make the U.S. Navy his career and eventually became the head of the Motion Picture Section of the Navy's Office of Information.

In that capacity, Coghlan was the liaison between the military and Hollywood on the making of several Navy-related pictures. He made a half-dozen on-screen appearances (including a brief part in *The Sand Pebbles*) in the '60s, and he later was active in TV commercials. He wrote his autobiography *They Still Call Me Junior* for McFarland in 1992.

Square Shoulders: The voices sound harsh and are very unintelligible. As the hero, Junior Coghlan is manly looking and acts well but falters during the single talking sequence, an emotional bit. *Harrison's Reports* 6/15/29, *Variety* 7/3/29.

Penrod and Sam: Coghlan is seldom without self-consciousness but he tops the actor who plays Penrod; he is the more natural throughout. *New York Times* 9/26/31, *Variety* 9/29/31.

Collier, William, Jr. ("Buster"), New York, New York, 1900–1988

Silent: Handsome, clean-cut William Collier, Jr. (his adoptive father William, Sr. ["Willie"], was a well-known character actor), was a natural for the youth-oriented films of the latter '20s. He made his first picture in 1916 but his career began seriously in 1920 with such movies as *Everybody's Sweetheart* and *The Soul of Youth*.

Real popularity came a bit later in the decade. "Buster" Collier's other films included *Wine of Youth, Pleasure Mad, The Wanderer, Backstage, Eve's Secret* and such "college" films as *The College Widow* and *The Floating College*. Last silent: *Tide of Empire* (1929), with synchronized sound effects and music, made after his first part-talkie.

Sound: Collier's initial part-talkie was the early Vitaphone *The Lion and the Mouse* (1928); others that year were *Beware of Bachelors* and *Women They Talk About*. Of his ten 1929 films, all but two were fully or part-talking. He went steadily onward until 1933 in films such as *The College Coquette, The Donovan Affair, The Show of Shows, Lummox, Reducing, The Story of Temple Drake* and *Up the River*.

In the sound era, Collier continued playing leads and also had supporting roles in musicals, comedies and dramas. He even essayed a few unsympathetic character roles. After appearing in some major pictures (*Little Caesar, Cimarron, Street Scene*) his career began fading.

Nineteen thirty-three was the last year Collier made a full complement of films, and he made only one thereafter: *The People's Enemy* (1935). Although contemporary reviews were often favorable to him, latter-day viewings of his films do not reveal him to have been a very good talkie actor.

REVIEWS

The Lion and the Mouse: Young Collier's voice sounded differently in different sequences, in one place as if someone else were speaking the lines. His voice is okay. *Variety* 5/30/28, 6/20/28, *Harrison's Reports* 6/23/28.

Beware of Bachelors: Collier as the hero is only fair. *Harrison's Reports* 1/26/29, *Variety* 2/6/29.

The Donovan Affair: William Collier, Jr., supplies the love interest. *Harrison's Reports* 5/4/29.

Rain or Shine: Collier capably handles his light assignment as the wealthy family's son in this Frank Capra film. *Variety* 7/23/30.

Little Caesar: William Collier, Jr., contributes real trouping to a part that seemed out of his line. *Variety* 1/4/31.

Street Scene: Collier plays splendidly opposite the heroine, playing his quieter scenes with emphasis and rising to the more emotional ones with satisfying vigor. *Variety* 9/1/31.

Exposed: Collier plays the ambulance surgeon and is top-billed. *Variety* 9/27/32.

The People's Enemy: Lots of overacting is done by William Collier, Jr., as the brother of the head mobster. *Variety* 5/1/35.

Colman, Ronald, Richmond, England,
1891–1958

Filmography: *Films in Review* (Apr. 1958), *Focus on Film* (Sept.-Oct. 1970), *Classic Images* (Winter 1970)

Silent: After a few years on the London stage, Ronald Colman made a handful of English films in 1919 and 1920, including *The Black Spider, The Toilers, Snow in the Desert* and *A Son of David*. In them he played supporting roles.

Colman arrived in America in 1920. He had small roles in a few plays and a couple of insignificant films, one of which was *Handcuffs or Kisses*. His real break came with the Lillian Gish starrer *The White Sister* in 1923. He played an Italian officer, the first of the lushly romantic roles in which he then specialized.

Colman's signing with Sam Goldwyn and subsequent teaming with Vilma Banky in several films from 1925 cemented his success. They appeared together in *The Dark Angel, The Winning of Bar-bara Worth, The Magic Flame, The Night of Love* and *Two Lovers*.

Among the 20 or so U.S. silent films in which Colman appeared were *Romola, Stella Dallas, Beau Geste* (a huge success), *Lady Windermere's Fan, Her Sister from Paris, Kiki* and *His Supreme Moment*. Besides Gish and Banky, he partnered both Norma and Constance Talmadge and Blanche Sweet. Last silent: *The Rescue* (1929), with synchronized sound effects and music.

Sound: Colman's first sound film was 1929's *Bulldog Drummond*. In playing the character as gentlemanly, urbane and witty, he not only differed from the author's conception but he established a persona different from that of his silent days. For *Drummond* and that year's *Condemned* he was nominated for an Academy Award as Best Actor.

With his extraordinary voice, Colman's fame in talkies exceeded his silent stardom and many of his films proved to be enduring classics. Among these were *Lost Horizon, The Prisoner of Zenda* and *A Tale of Two Cities*. Some of his other talkies were not quite up to those standards, although there were schmaltzily enjoyable ones such as *If I Were King, Clive of India* and *The Light That Failed*.

In 1934, nearing the apex of his fame, Colman was voted the "Handsomest Man on the Screen." His other pictures included *The Devil to Pay, Raffles, Under Two Flags, Lucky Partners, The Late George Apley, The Talk of the Town* and *Random Harvest*, a major hit co-starring Greer Garson and for which he garnered another Oscar nomination.

In the mid–40s Colman was off the screen for about two-and-a-half years. His role as the mad Shakespearean actor in his penultimate starring film *A Double Life* (1948) finally garnered him the Best Actor Academy Award for which he had been nominated four times.

Colman went on to make the quiz show comedy *Champagne for Caesar* in 1950, his intellectual character being named Beauregard Bottomley. He finished out his distinguished career with a cameo in *Around the World in 80 Days* and the ill-conceived but star-filled *The Story of Mankind* (1957), in which he played the Spirit of Man.

Colman also performed on numerous radio programs (frequently guesting with Jack Benny), the television series *The Halls of Ivy*, in which he appeared with his wife Benita Hume, and he made several recordings including a reading of Shakespeare's sonnets.

Comments: It was, of course, the sublime Ronald Colman voice which led the way to his success in talkies. It was cultured, beautifully modulated and so flexible that with little change in emphasis and intonation he could portray courage, roguishness, deep sincerity, passion or humor. Perhaps best of all was the way he could enunciate through his nose so gloriously.

Colman also was usually fortunate in the choice of stories given to him. The change in persona from his dark romantic roles, in which he played gypsies and other "exotics," seemed to be deliberate. The lesson of the failure of most of the silent screen's great lovers, especially John Gilbert, was not lost on him or Goldwyn. In his first sound films he made sure he did not make smoldering love and declaim flowery words.

It was not all smooth sailing for Colman. In 1933 there was a much-publicized breakup with Goldwyn over the latter's charge that his star was sometimes drunk on the set. Some of his films were not so good, particularly his later comedies, and he had lingering health problems as revealed in his prematurely aged face. In the 1940s he attempted to broaden his image but made only eight films during the entire decade.

Colman seemed to understand what his limitations were as an actor and, except for *A Double Life*, rarely strayed beyond certain boundaries. Apparently a gentleman in real life as well as on the screen, he did have some well-known idiosyncrasies. One of them was always being photographed on his left profile. Another was that he, plain and simply, was a camera hog!

Colman was adept at mild swashbuckling, comedy and romance but he was especially good at conveying a sense of duty, honor and even self-sacrifice. These qualities were often leavened with a sardonic touch, which is just what his best roles required. Perhaps that is why they *were* his best roles.

REVIEWS

Bulldog Drummond: Considering it is Colman's first talkie, with his surprisingly good performance and his drawing power the film looks safe enough. The hero is excellently impersonated by Colman and the voices have registered well. *Variety* 5/8/29, *Harrison's Reports* 5/11/29.

Raffles: In the hands of the bland Colman, it gets a persuasive reading that makes it fresh. *Variety* 7/30/30.

Arrowsmith: It is hard to believe Ronald Colman in the title role; he is unable to convince as the intense scientist. His performance is all on one plane and he either lacks the strength to play such a part or has been permitted to seem to be in over his head. (His performance which seemed at the time wooden and passionless is thought by latter-day critics to have been a deliberate choice on his or director John Ford's part.) *Variety* 12/15/31.

A Tale of Two Cities: Colman makes his Sydney Carton one of the most pathetic figures in screen history. Gone are his drawing room mannerisms, shaved along with his mustache. *Variety* 1/1/36.

Lost Horizon: Ronald Colman, with fine restraint, conveys the metamorphosis of the diplomat. *Variety* 3/10/37.

If I Were King: Colman's delineation is excellent, carrying through it a verve and spontaneity for an outstanding performance. *Variety* 9/21/38.

Talk of the Town: Plenty of meaty lines and situations handed to Colman, who manages the transition from the stuffy professor to a human being with the least amount of implausibility. *Variety* 7/29/42.

A Double Life: Colman realizes every facet of the demanding part in a performance that is flawless. It's an acting gem of unusual versatility. *Variety* 12/31/47.

Compson, Betty (Eleanor Compson),
Beaver, Utah, 1897–1974

Filmography: *Films in Review* (Aug.-Sept. 1966), *Classic Images* (Feb.-Apr. 1985); List of films in *Sweethearts of the Sage*

Silent: Beginning inauspiciously in Christie comedies about 1915 after vaudeville experience, Betty Compson hit her screen stride with *The Miracle Man* in 1919. (The film advanced not only her career but those of Lon Chaney and Thomas Meighan as well.) She formed her own production company and eventually signed with Paramount, appearing in such films as *The Little Minister* and *To Have and to Hold*.

Compson was released two years later and in 1922 she made some films in England, including *Woman to Woman* (remade as a talkie). She was subsequently re-signed by Paramount, once again being released about 1925. Freelancing for a while in the latter 1920s, she made several "quickies" for Poverty Row studios such as Chadwick.

After a stint at Columbia, a return to stardom for Compson came in 1928 with *The Docks of New York* and *The Big City* (a reteaming with Chaney). Others of Compson's numerous silent features included *Ladies Must Live*, *The White Shadow*, *New Lives for Old*, *The Pony Express*, *Twelve Miles Out* and *Cheating Cheaters*. There was also a serial, *The Terror of the Range*. Last silent: *Scarlet Seas* (1929), with synchronized music and sound effects, made after her first part-talkie.

Sound: Compson's stardom was reaffirmed with the part-talkies *The Barker* (1928) and *Weary River* the following year. For the former role, she was nominated for the Academy Award for best Actress; Mary Pickford won it for *Coquette*. Other early sound films were *The Great Gabbo* and *The Case of Sergeant Grischa.*

Although signed with RKO, for whom she made one of their earliest all-talkies *Street Girl,* a considerable success, Compson appeared in many "Poverty Row" films with studios like PRC, Imperial, Victory, Kent, Chesterfield and Monogram. She worked also for majors like Warner Bros., Republic, Universal and Paramount. Her last notable film is generally agreed to have been *Destination Unknown* in 1933.

Compson worked steadily in films (with time out for a vaudeville tour) throughout the 1930s and into 1941; her output lessened thereafter and she appeared in only about a half-dozen more until 1948. Her almost 60 sound films included *The Spoilers* (1930 version), *Hollywood Boulevard, Under the Big Top, Mad Youth, Hard Boiled Mahoney* and her last, *Here Comes Trouble* (1948).

Comments: In the silent era, Compson saw her career rise and wane more than once but she always fought back. (She was dubbed "The Girl Who Came Back" by Hollywood scribe Adela Rogers St. Johns.) She reinvented herself more than once as well, accompanied by changes in her hair color from brown to blonde and back again.

The Compson voice was satisfactory, but possibly no more than that, and in talkies after 1929 she was just another leading lady with no special charisma. At the age of 32 she was a bit beyond her prime by Hollywood standards, a fact alluded to by reviewers of the time. She also had an unfortunate mannerism of unprettily moving her mouth in awkward ways when she spoke, something that was apparently more noticeable in talkies.

When Compson declined into quickies once again in the early '30s, it was for the remainder of her career. She never could top *The Miracle Man,* about which she said: "The terrible thing with doing something outstanding once is that people remember that one act and no matter what you do afterward ... it is never considered as good." Nevertheless she had a lengthy career and, in its totality, a worthy one.

REVIEWS

The Barker: Well supplied with 'It' is Betty Compson. If the studio featured players on merit, her name would be on the same line as the leads. *Variety* 12/12/28.

Street Girl: Compson troupes so excellently that she almost overcomes certain not-to-be slighted physical shortcomings. She makes you laugh and cry, however the role really called for a younger person. *Variety* 8/7/29, *Harrison's Reports* 8/10/29.

The Case of Sergeant Grischa: Betty Compson is the heroine but one can't get rid of the idea that she should not have been played by Compson, even with her name, whatever that may now mean. *Harrison's Reports* 3/8/30, *Variety* 3/12/30.

Notorious But Nice: Compson breaks through the crust of incompetence at times to project her vivid personality. *Variety* 3/6/34.

Two Gun Justice: Although Betty Compson shares the top billing she is not seen in this Tim McCoy western very much. *Variety* 6/8/38

Here Comes Trouble: Betty Compson, a veteran of the silent era, does nicely as the newspaper publisher's wife. *Variety* 4/14/48.

Compton, Joyce, Lexington, Kentucky, 1907–1997

Filmography: *Classic Images* (June–July 1982); List of films *Sweethearts of the Sage*

Silent: Nineteen twenty-six Wampas Baby Star Joyce Compton made a small number of silents beginning in 1925 with *Broadway Lady* and *What Fools Men.* She had been an extra previously and was to remain a supporting player throughout her career. Among her films for First National, Fox and Universal were *Syncopating Sue, Ankles Preferred* and *The Border Cavalier.* Last silent: *Soft Living* (1928).

Sound: All Joyce Compton's 1929 films were talking, the first also being Clara Bow's sound debut, *The Wild Party.* The others that year were *Dangerous Curves* (also starring Bow), *Salute* and *The Sky Hawk.* She went on to appear in over 100 features for Fox and other studios.

In 1933 Compton was signed by Sennett for comedy shorts but generally played the straight woman in these. She also appeared with Charley Chase in a series of shorts. Her features, in some of which she played bit roles, included *Love Before Breakfast, Women of All Nations, They Drive by Night, Magnificent Obsession* (1936 version), *Mildred Pierce, Mighty Joe Young, Sky Murder* and *The Best Years of Our Lives.*

Compton's best-known film role nowadays is probably her bimbette in 1937's *The Awful Truth.* After 1949 she appeared in only three films: *The Persuaders* and *Jet Pilot* (1957) and *Girl in the Woods* the following year. She did some TV work until 1961, the last being *The Pete and Gladys Show,* and then retired.

Comments: Joyce Compton was always considered a competent comedienne but it was not until the latter '30s that she became typecast as the first in a string of archetypal "dumb blondes" (although she was actually a redhead). Her Southern accent, which she never completely lost, was a strong asset to this characterization.

Those who assumed Compton's mantle in the 1950s and afterwards may have brought their own strengths to the stereotype but they never quite radiated the likability that this most charming actress did in her numerous films.

REVIEWS

Salute: The dialogue is rather sappy but it is neatly managed by Joyce Compton. *Variety* 10/9/29.

The White Parade: Compton registers with one of those Una Merkel–like Dixie drawls. *Variety* 11/13/34.

Murder with Pictures: Compton is entirely sufficient. *Variety* 11/25/36.

Honeymoon Deferred: Joyce Compton turns in another of her expert secretary portrayals. *Variety* 2/21/40.

Scattergood Meets Broadway: Compton catches the attention as a blonde gold digger. *Variety* 8/27/41.

Conklin, Chester, Oskaloosa, Iowa,
1886/88–1971

Silent: After working as a circus clown and in vaudeville, Chester Conklin, with his droopy walrus mustache, became one of the most recognizable of the famous Keystone Kops in 1914. He departed Keystone after five years to star in Fox's Sunshine comedies.

Conklin also was seen in very occasional 'teens features like *Tillie's Punctured Romance* and the later *Yankee Doodle in Berlin*. In the early '20s he became active as a character actor between his continuing stints in two-reelers for Kay Bee and others.

Chester Conklin supported W. C. Fields in a few films and also played a small number of leading roles. Among his numerous films were *Skirts*, *Souls for Sale*, *Where Was I?*, *The Duchess of Buffalo*, *Cabaret*, *Taxi 13* and *The Nervous Wreck*.

Conklin essayed serious roles in *Greed* and *Woman of the World* and also appeared in such prestigious pictures as *Anna Christie* (1923 version), *The Phantom of the Opera* and *Gentlemen Prefer Blondes*. Last silent: *Stairs of Sand* (1929).

Sound: Although he appeared in several 1929 talkies such as *The House of Horror* and *The Studio Murder Mystery*, sound proved not to be Conklin's medium. He apparently had problems adjusting to its physical limitations and his film output fell drastically. He made a dozen or fewer features in the 1930s and a scattering thereafter.

By the '50s Conklin had been reduced to bits and extra work which eventually also dried up. He did appear in short subjects, among them Vitaphone's *The Master Sweeper* in 1930. His films included *Her Majesty Love*, *Hallelujah, I'm a Bum*, *Call of the Prairie*, *Hotel Haywire*, *Zenobia* and *Hail the Conquering Hero*.

Along with other old-timers, Chester Conklin was cast in Hollywood's occasional, and usually exaggerated, homages to the silent days such as *The Perils of Pauline* (1947 version) and *Hollywood Cavalcade*. He returned from virtual retirement in the '60s for a couple of bits, the last being in *A Big Hand for the Little Lady* (1966).

REVIEWS

The Studio Murder Mystery: Chester Conklin receives a good spot in the billing, but he plays only a bit part of a studio gateman. *Variety* 6/12/29.

The Love Trader: Chester Conklin appears in the supporting cast. *Harrison's Reports* 11/1/30.

Her Majesty Love: Conklin has a minor role, scarcely a bit, and never gets the chance to build on it. (He once again is in support of W. C. Fields in the latter's talkie feature debut.) *Variety* 12/1/31.

Coogan, Jackie, Los Angeles, California,
1914–1984

Silent: As legend or fact has it, Jackie Coogan was introduced by his father Jack Coogan during the course of the latter's vaudeville act and was spotted by Charlie Chaplin. However it happened that young Coogan came to the great comedian's attention, he was cast by him in the spectacularly successful *The Kid* (1921). He had made his screen debut as an 18-month-old baby in *Skinner's Baby*.

For a few years, Coogan was very successful starring for his own production company and then he signed with Metro for a phenomenal half-million dollars a year. He was billed as the "Greatest Boy Actor in the World."

In the latter part of the decade, however, Coogan's popularity decreased and in 1928 he tried his luck in vaudeville. His films included *Peck's Bad Boy*, *Oliver Twist* (with Lon Chaney as Fagin), *Trouble*, *Circus Days*, *Daddy*, *Old Clothes*, *My Boy* and *Little Robinson Crusoe*. Last silent: *Buttons* (1927).

Sound: After a cameo as "himself" in 1930's *Free and Easy*, Jackie Coogan attempted a comeback with that year's *Tom Sawyer* and *Huckleberry Finn* in 1931. They were not too successful. His next film, and final pre-war lead, was in *Home on the Range* (1934). Then it was sporadic small roles for the rest of the decade (*Million Dollar Legs*, *College Swing*, *Sky Patrol*).

By 1937's *One in a Million*, Coogan was reduced to an uncredited bit. During the '30s he also had his own orchestra and made some minor stage appearances. He was then professionally inactive until the latter 1940s when he began making occasional quickie films and night club appearances. In one of his club dates, Jackie Coogan burlesqued his role as The Kid.

During the late '40s, Jackie Coogan co-starred in a couple of Monogram quickies, *Kilroy Was Here* and *French Leave*, with Jackie Cooper, another formerly popular child actor. After decades of struggle his career was finally rescued by television in 1956.

An Emmy nomination for a *Playhouse 90* role brought Coogan back to films in some worthy character roles, albeit sometimes he portrayed a villain. Among his later films were *The Proud Ones*, *The Joker Is Wild*, *The Buster Keaton Story*, *Lonely-hearts*, *A Fine Madness* and *Marlowe*. He also appeared, and occasionally overacted, in such grade–Z fare as *High School Confidential!*, *The Beat Generation* and *Sex Kittens Go to College*.

Perhaps (unfortunately) best known to modern mass audiences was Jackie Coogan's role as the ghoulish Uncle Fester in TV's *The Addams Family*. Aside from that dubious but no doubt profitable role, he continued making well-regarded TV and stage appearances up to the time of his death.

Comments: Undoubtedly Jackie Coogan was one of the most successful child actors ever to appear on the screen. He was extremely appealing-looking, with expressive dark eyes and a Dutch boy bob, and he could actually act. In the early '20s his popularity rivaled that of the biggest Hollywood stars; the song "Jackie" was written for him in 1922.

Unfortunately, little Jackie's roles had a sameness to them which began to wear on audiences. He was usually a sad-faced orphan who suffered but who ultimately found happiness. His inevitable fate was, of course, to grow up. And he did not grow up particularly cute.

Coogan's real life began to mirror the suffering of his screen characters. His father died early, in a car crash which also injured Jackie, and his mother and stepfather took charge of his finances. When he reached legal age he asked his mother for the vast sums he had earned, estimated at four million dollars, but he was refused.

A 1938 lawsuit resulted in Coogan's receiving part of his Hollywood earnings, but only a small portion remained. Although he did not personally benefit, the case had the salutary effect of the passage of the so-called Coogan Act to protect future child wage earners.

As an adult, Coogan was physically heavy and bald with a somewhat dour face; his voice also registered rather harshly. His appearance helped him to play meanies very convincingly but he could be a fine actor. Despite his latter-day identification with the Fester role, the beloved "Kid" will not be forgotten.

During the height of Coogan's career, playwright Robert E. Sherwood said, "Whatever else the silent drama may have accomplished … it can claim at least one distinction; it has provided the only possible medium for the expression of Jackie Coogan's altogether inexplicable genius." A tribute indeed!

REVIEWS

Tom Sawyer: Splendidly acted by a great group of youngsters, one of them being Jackie Coogan who plays Tom to the life. *Variety* 12/24/30.

Home on the Range: Coogan is not impressive. He is still pretty much of a kid. *Variety* 2/12/35.

Sky Pilot: For whatever marquee value it may have, Jackie Coogan is in the cast, in a semi-sympathetic, semi-cowardly role. His registering of emotion includes only one thing, a cloudy pout, and there his histrionics are exhausted. It's just another step backward on his much-publicized 'comeback' trail. *Variety* 11/29/39.

Kilroy Was Here: Coogan turns in an excellent performance. *Variety* 7/9/47.

French Leave: Coogan registers well enough as a bungling, irresponsible sailor. *Variety* 4/21/48.

Lonelyhearts: Excellent support is rendered by Jackie Coogan as a hack reporter. *Variety* 12/3/58.

Cook, Clyde, Fort McQuarrie, Australia,
1891–1984

Silent: After stage experience in England, thin and mustachioed Clyde Cook came to work for Mack Sennett beginning about 1915 and made numerous one- and two-reelers. In many of these the comedy sprang largely from his acrobatic ability. He later worked at Fox in "Clyde Cook Comedies."

In the early '20s, Cook branched out into features such as *Skirts*, *He Who Gets Slapped* and *So This Is Marriage*. He also worked in vaudeville and the Ziegfeld Follies. His feature career took off about 1926 and he appeared in support in numerous comedies and dramas like *Barbed Wire*, *The Winning of Barbara Worth*, *Good Time Charley* and *The Docks of New York*.

In many of his later silents, Cook was near the top of the cast list and he became a leading man in several films with comedienne Louise Fazenda, such as *Domestic Troubles*, *Five and Ten Cent Annie*, *Pay As You Enter* and *Simple Sis*. Last silent: *Strong Boy* (1929), with sound effects and music, made after his first part-talkies.

Sound: Talkies proved to be no problem for Cook. His physical appearance and accent suited him perfectly for Cockney-type supporting roles and characters with names such as Cocky, Flashlight and Pinkey. His sound debut came in one of two 1928 part-talkers, *The Spieler* or *Beware of Bachelors*, or that year's Vitaphone short *Lucky in Love*.

Among Cook's 1929 talkies were *The Taming of the Shrew*, *Jazz Heaven* and *In the Headlines*, and in 1930 he was seen in *The Dawn Patrol*. Among Cook's other features were *Barbary Coast*, *The White Angel*, *Wee Willie Winkie*, *The Sea Hawk*, *The Man from Down Under*, *To Each His Own* and *The Verdict*.

In 1932 Hal Roach attempted to duplicate the popularity of Laurel and Hardy by teaming various sets of comic actors together in the "Taxi Boys" shorts. The first of these combinations was Clyde Cook and Franklin Pangborn in *What Price Taxi?*

When this did not work out, Cook was teamed with others but eventually was himself replaced. He worked steadily in features into the 1940s and also was seen in a few during the next decade. His last appearance, after a lengthy hiatus, was in 1963's *Donovan's Reef*.

REVIEWS

Jazz Heaven: Cook has a role that just fits him, and he plays it with his own way of dumb fun making. *Variety* 11/6/29.

Women Everywhere: Cook does not make much of a mark as a cockney sailor. *New York Times* 6/23/30.

West of Singapore: Clyde Cook is cast as comedy relief and he manages fairly well. *Variety* 4/4/33.

Cooper, Gary (Frank Cooper), Helena,
Montana, 1901–1961

Filmography: *Films in Review* (Dec. 1959); List of films in *Film Dope* (Oct. 1975); *Stars* (Sept. 1991)

Silent: Tall (6'4"), rangy Gary Cooper began his distinguished career as an extra and bit player for small companies like Chesterfield in the mid–1920s. Because of his riding prowess, many of those appearances came in westerns. The first time his new Christian name appeared on the screen was in a two-reeler.

The Ronald Colman-Vilma Banky film *The Winning of Barbara Worth* provided Cooper with his first attention-getting role in 1926 and the next year's *Wings* saw him in another small but meaty part. Adopted both professionally and personally by Clara Bow, he was in the cast of two of her successful 1927 films, *Children of Divorce* and *It*.

Cooper's first leads came in such westerns as *Nevada* and *Arizona Bound* and he also advanced to starring roles in films like *The First Kiss*, *Doomsday*, *Beau Sabreur*, *Legion of the Condemned* and *Wolf Song*, technically a silent but with singing sequences.

A romantic tale of the First World War, *Lilac Time* (1928), co-starring Colleen Moore, proved to be Cooper's break-out hit. Last silent: *Betrayal* (1929), with synchronized sound effects and music, made after his first part-talkie. This was also Emil Jannings's final American film.

Sound: The part-talker weepie *The Shopworn Angel* premiered in the very last days of 1928 with Cooper and Nancy Carroll as the leads. He made only one talkie in 1929 but it was the successful *The Virginian* ("When you call me that, smile"), and his sound success seemed assured.

Seven 1930 pictures followed for Cooper, one being the Foreign Legion melodrama *Morocco*, co-starring Marlene Dietrich. This cemented his star status in sound pictures. Others that year included *Paramount on Parade*, *The Texan*, *Seven Days Leave* and yet another remake of *The Spoilers*.

As the '30s progressed, Cooper established his persona in film after film as the archetypal decent yet rugged All-American guy. He never played a real villain in any of his sound films. From 1936 to '57 he was among the top ten box office stars every year but three.

This enviable record began for Cooper in such '30s hits as *A Farewell to Arms*, *Lives of a Bengal Lancer*, *Mr. Deeds Goes to Town*, *The Plainsman*, *Beau Geste* and *The General Died at Dawn*. In 1939 he was the highest-paid man in the United States.

The 1940s dawned splendidly for Gary Cooper as well. He received his first Academy Award as Best Actor for 1941's *Sergeant York* and he also made Frank Capra's *Meet John Doe* that year. These were followed by the hit screwball comedy *Ball of Fire* and the popular biopic about Lou Gehrig, *The Pride of the Yankees*. The lean actor then reached what may have been his screen pinnacle in 1943's *For Whom the Bell Tolls*, co-starring Ingrid Bergman.

After the latter film, the quality and popularity of Cooper's pictures commenced to take a decided downward turn. Such dramas as *The Story of Dr. Wassell*, *Saratoga Trunk*, *Cloak and Dagger*, *Unconquered* and *Task Force*, and the comedies *Casanova Brown* and *Along Came Jones*, were generally not well-received. For almost ten years, it seemed as if his glory days were over.

The great success of 1952's *High Noon* brought Cooper back to the top ranks once more and also brought him his second Oscar as well. If none of his succeeding films were quite of the same caliber, some, like *The Court-Martial of Billy Mitchell*, *Friendly Persuasion* and *Love in the Afternoon* were certainly most respectable. The latter film did raise some eyebrows because the star was almost 40 years older than his leading woman Audrey Hepburn.

The final years of his 95-film career saw Cooper in several pictures which did little to advance his legend. They were mostly routine but large-scale westerns like *They Came to Cordura*, *Man of the West* and *The Hanging Tree* or melodramas such as *The Wreck of the Mary Deare* and his last, *The Naked Edge*. A final honorary Academy Award for his service to the film industry was accepted on his behalf by James Stewart because of Coop's terminal illness.

Comments: Gary Cooper said of his acting prowess in his early silent films that he was so embarrassed by his lack of talent that he literally fled the set after a scene. Viewers of *The Virginian*, his first all-talkie, would have probably agreed that his emoting had not improved much. To say the least, he was stiff.

Eventually Coop's acting improved to such an extent that he was often accused of playing himself (i.e., not acting at all). This actually was a tribute to his mastery of the *appearance* of being natural. It also was a tribute to the fact that he understood his range and stayed within it as much as he could.

It took enormous work to underplay. Director Billy Wilder said of Cooper: "Don't be deceived by Gary's naturalness. He's a great craftsman. It's a tribute to his vast technique that he makes it all seem so easy."

No less a master than John Barrymore agreed, calling Cooper "the world's greatest actor. He does without effect what the rest of us spend our lives to learn — namely to be natural." One possible advantage he had was not having to unlearn stage technique in films; he never had stage experience to start with.

Other directors were not so charitable when they had to work with Cooper. When he was before the cameras, he sometimes seemed to be underplaying so much that they despaired of his performance. It was only on film that his acting ability shone through. One director said simply, "The camera liked him."

It is fair to say that Cooper became *the* cinema icon of decency and quiet courage, with perhaps only James Stewart as a strong contender. In the great years of his career, there was no other actor who could match him in that image. Although in his private life he may have been more at home among high society than the working class, he always knowingly referred to his celluloid self as "the fellow down the block."

Cooper's image and longevity in talkies was certainly aided by the natural aging process in which the beautiful face of his youth transmogrified into the almost granite-like visage of his middle age.

His baritone voice, still redolent of the prairies (rather than the English schools which he attended), perfectly fit his established persona.

Interestingly, given his standing as one of the greatest male stars of all time, it is often said that Coop's films will never be revived as are those of Bogart, Cagney, Gable and other male superstars.

If that is true, it may be because the image that Gary Cooper created seems hopelessly old-fashioned in today's world. But it may well be that he is an ironic victim of the very skills he worked so hard to develop: He was just too believable as "the fellow down the block."

REVIEWS

The Shopworn Angel: It moves too slowly and this is owing to the part of Mr. Cooper but he contributes excellent work and seems natural and lifelike. He has a few brief lines of dialogue. *Harrison's Reports* 1/5/29, *Variety* 1/9/29.

A Farewell to Arms: Cooper is great. His sincerity is consistently impressive in a none too easy assignment. *Variety* 12/13/32.

Mr. Deeds Goes to Town: This film needs the marquee power of Gary Cooper but there are times when his impression is just a bit too scatterbrained for sympathy. *Variety* 4/22/36.

The General Died at Dawn: Gary Cooper as the daredevil American is at top form throughout. *Variety* 9/9/36.

Sergeant York: Cooper seems singularly well-suited and well-chosen; the role is made to order for him. It is unlikely he has ever been seen to greater advantage, or has given a better performance. *Variety* 7/2/41.

The Pride of the Yankees: Gary Cooper blends nicely into the hero's role and he makes his 'Gehrig' look and sound believable even if he's not a physical prototype. There's is however an evident awkwardness in Cooper's stance and swing at the plate. (This is considered the finest picture about baseball ever made. Cooper's rendition of Lou Gehrig's famous farewell speech was movingly rendered. The naturally right-handed actor could not believably bat left-handed so the expedient of printing the film in reverse was used. To complete the illusion Cooper actually ran to third base when, in the film, he was supposed to be heading for first.) *Variety* 7/15/42.

Good Sam: Cooper gives one of his by now standard performances, including the wan smile, the gawky naiveté and a sartorial manner that suggests Sam's pants need pressing. *Variety* 7/28/48.

The Fountainhead: Cooper is uneasy and is miscast as the hero. Given long speeches to deliver, he fails to sustain the mood demanded. His faltering delivery emphasizes his preference for the monosyllabic. *Variety* 6/29/49.

High Noon: Cooper does an unusually able job. *Variety* 4/30/52.

The Wreck of the Mary Deare: Gary Cooper is perfectly cast in a rugged role. He conveys a surprising range of emotion and reaction considering his usual taciturnity. *Variety* 11/4/59.

Corbin, Virginia Lee, Prescott, Arizona, 1910?–1942

Silent: Once a model and one of the most beautiful of the silent child performers, blonde and delicate Virginia Lee Corbin was in pictures by 1916 or so. She eventually appeared for Lasky, Metro, Universal and Knickerbocker.

At Fox, Corbin starred in the "Kiddie" features which included *Aladdin and the Wonderful Lamp*, *The Babes in the Woods*, *Jack and the Beanstalk* and *Treasure Island*. Other early films in which she had supporting roles were *Ace High*, *The Forbidden Room* and *The White Dove*.

In the '20s, Corbin gradually worked her way into flapper-type roles and was occasionally starred in such films as *North Star*, *Driven from Home*, *The Handsome Brute* and *Bare Knees*. Just as frequently she was far down the cast list. Among her other pictures were *Enemies of Children*, *Sinners in Silk*, *Lilies of the Streets*, *Hands Up!* and *The Little Snob*. Last silents: *Head of the Family* and *Jazzland*, released at about the same time in 1928.

Sound: Corbin's first sound film was *Footlights and Fools* (1929). She was billed in only four more, all in 1931, including the female lead in the western *Shotgun Pass*.

There were supporting roles for Corbin in *Morals for Women*, *X Marks the Spot* and *Forgotten Women*, her last. It was a rather aptly named farewell to a once-promising career. In the late '30s, she worked as an extra.

REVIEWS

Footlights and Fools: Virginia Lee Corbin is adept as a dumb chorine. *Variety* 11/13/29.

Morals for Women: In a role billed last in the credits, Corbin contributes as one of a trio of types for whom the Greeks had a word. *Variety* 11/17/31.

Cornwall, Anne, New York, New York, 1898?–1980

Silent: After stage experience, Anne Cornwall made her first credited film, *The Knife*, in 1918. Among her other early dramatic and comedy efforts were *The Indestructible Wife*, *The World to Live In*, *The Copperhead* and *La La Lucille*. She continued to play supporting roles through 1927 and also had some leads in westerns and melodramas, as well as appearing in Christie comedies in 1927–28.

Cornwall's films included *To Have and to Hold*, *Her Gilded Cage*, *Dulcy*, *Introduce Me*, *40-Horse Hawkins*, *The Flaming Frontier*, *Under Western Skies* and *Eyes of the Totem*. Last silent feature: *College* (1927), in which she had the lead opposite Buster Keaton.

Sound: Cornwall's first sound efforts were comedy shorts with Laurel and Hardy (*Men o' War*) and others. Her voice proved to be of average quality but sound unquestionably ended her career as a leading lady. Her first feature was 1930's *The Widow from Chicago* and she continued to play small roles in the 1930s (*True Confession*, *Mr. Smith Goes to Washington*) and then bits well into the 1950s.

Corrado, Gino (also known as Eugene Corey; Gino Lizerani), Florence, Italy, 1893/96–1982

Silent: Gino Corrado claimed to have worked in pictures as far back as *Intolerance*, but if so he received no billing until the early 1920s in such films as *The Guttersnipe*, *The Ordeal*, *My American Wife*, *Adam's Rib* and *Flaming Youth*.

Just when Corrado played the first of his multitude of waiter roles is not known but he appeared in colorful, and sometimes major, supporting roles throughout the '20s. His films included *La Bohème*, *Sunrise*, *Men*, *Women's Wares*, *Modern Youth* and *Speed Madness*. Last silent: *The One Woman Idea* (1929), with synchronized music.

Sound: With the advent of sound, Gino Corrado could no longer avoid playing "exotic" types; his accent was too noticeable. However, it did allow him to be an all-purpose ethnic, including a Mexican. His neatly-trimmed mustache, round face and curly hair perfectly fit such roles, as did his animated acting style. Among his first talkies in 1929 were the westerns *The Rainbow* and *Señor Americano*. *The Iron Mask* had a brief talking sequence as well.

Corrado was very active thereafter, although generally in smaller roles. He was the very prototype of the excitable waiter, maitre d' or other officious petty functionary in scores of '30s and '40s movies such as *A Notorious Affair*, *Song of the Caballero*, *Broadway Bill*, *Wonder Bar*, *Diamond Jim*, *Magnificent Obsession*, *The Bride Wore Red*, *Bluebeard's Eighth Wife*, *Mr. Smith Goes to Washington* and *Kitty Foyle*.

Corrado remained on-screen through the early 1950s in *Casablanca*, *My Wild Irish Rose*, *The Stratton Story*, *The Pride of the Yankees*, *Road to Rio*,

Harvey and *Three Coins in the Fountain*. He also appeared in comedy shorts, among them those of The Three Stooges. His last known appearance was in a television version of *A Bell for Adano* in 1954. In a case of life mirroring art, he actually worked as a headwaiter between pictures and eventually opened his own restaurant.

Cortez, Ricardo (Jacob Krantz, Kranze or Krantze), Vienna, Austria, or Alsace-Lorraine, France, 1899–1977

Filmography: *Classic Images* (Oct. 1990); List of films in *Eighty Silent Film Stars*

Silent: After being seen in a 1922 dance contest (or so the story goes), Ricardo Cortez was signed by Paramount apparently as a "Latin lover" threat to keep the balky Rudolph Valentino in line. He had done extra work since about 1918. Among his first films were *Call of the Canyon* and *Sixty Cents an Hour* in 1923.

Cortez made about 30 silents and co-starred with some of the leading actresses including Gloria Swanson, Bebe Daniels, Jetta Goudal, Betty Bronson, Betty Compson and Greta Garbo in her first screen role (*The Torrent*). He also was seen in D. W. Griffith's *The Sorrows of Satan* and appeared with Lon Chaney in *Mockery*.

Some other Cortez efforts were *Children of Jazz*, *Argentine Love*, *The Spaniard*, *The Pony Express*, *New York* and *Ladies of the Night Club*. After leaving Paramount about 1927, he made films at MGM, First National, Columbia, Tiffany-Stahl, Pathe and Warner Bros. Last silent: *The Gun Runner* (1928).

Sound: The part-talkie *The Younger Generation* (1929) marked Cortez's sound debut. His first all-talkie was *The Lost Zeppelin* and all his '29 films had some dialogue. Among the more than 65 sound films, in which he appeared quite steadily through 1942, were two with Irene Dunne, one of them the *Symphony of Six Million*, a tale of Jewish angst. It is considered one of his best roles.

Other Cortez pictures included *White Shoulders*, *The Phantom of Crestwood*, the first version of *the Maltese Falcon* in 1931, 1934's *Wonder Bar* (perhaps his biggest sound success), *The Torch Singer*, *Who Is Hope Schuyler?*, *The Californian*, *Man Hunt* and *Charlie Chan in Reno*.

Cortez turned to directing as well as acting in the late 1930s and directed six films for Fox from 1938 to 1941. After 1942 he was seen only in a relative handful of films through 1950's *Bunco Squad*. His last film role after many years was a character part in *The Last Hurrah* (1958).

Comments: Ricardo Cortez was dubbed "The Comeback Champ" because he was considered a fading star in the latter '20s but returned strongly in the talkie era. Although, with his "bedroom" eyes, he may have been the silent moviegoer's idea of a smoldering Latin, in talkies he looked more like, and was frequently cast as, a villain.

The Cortez voice, with a touch of The Bronx about it, was deep, smooth in timbre, and perfectly suited to his appearance. It also could carry a nice hint of menace, an invaluable adjunct to his bad guy or good-but-tough guy portrayals.

REVIEWS

Her Man: Cortez is fine in every way as the apache villain, a rough and hard role for anyone. *Variety* 9/17/30.

The Maltese Falcon: Ricardo Cortez plays the role as a nonchalant, although extremely odd, private detective. His performance is excellent. *Variety* 6/2/31, *Harrison's Reports* 6/6/31.

Symphony of Six Million: Cortez is good as the young surgeon. He keeps well in character, albeit the character itself is artificial. *Variety* 4/19/32.

Flesh: Cortez does a perfect job as a 100% unsympathetic character. *Variety* 12/13/32.

Wonder Bar: Cortez is effective as the heavy. *Variety* 3/6/34.

Her Husband Lies: Ricardo Cortez takes full advantage his characterization and the result is a finely polished portrayal. *Variety* 3/24/37.

Bunco Squad: The acting is competent and Ricardo Cortez plays a swindler. *Harrison's Reports* 8/12/50.

Costello, Dolores, Pittsburgh, Pennsylvania, 1904/05–1979

Filmography: *Focus on Film* (Winter 1972)

Silent: Dolores Costello was a child actress in Vitagraph films with her matinée idol father Maurice and her older sister Helen(e) from about 1910 until 1913. A beautiful blue-eyed blonde, she returned to the screen in 1923 for bit parts, including *The Glimpses of the Moon*.

Costello had her first major role for Warner Bros. in *The Sea Beast*, based on *Moby Dick* and starring her husband-to-be John Barrymore. Other films included *Mannequin*, *Bride of the Storm*, *The Little Irish Girl*, *When a Man Loves*, *Old San Francisco* and *The Heart of Maryland*. Last silent: *The College Widow* (1927).

Sound: All of Costello's 1928 roles were in part-talkies, the first of which was *Tenderloin*. The others were *Glorious Betsy* and *Noah's Ark*. Her first in 1929, *The Redeeming Sin*, was also only part-talking.

Costello's full sound films in that year included *The Glad Rag Doll*, *The Madonna of Avenue A* and *The Show of Shows*, in which she danced and sang in a musical number ("Meet My Sister") with

Helene, who had also become a Warner Bros. leading lady.

After marriage to Barrymore, Costello's screen appearances dwindled; from 1932–35 she was not seen on-screen. She came back the next year, sometimes billed as Dolores Costello Barrymore, for *Little Lord Fauntleroy* and then she made a few more insignificant pictures, the last in 1939.

There was a final "comeback" in 1942 for *The Magnificent Ambersons*, considered Costello's best performance, and a last brief appearance in 1943's *This Is the Army*. Among her other films were *Second Choice, Hearts in Exile, Whispering Enemies, Breaking the Ice* and *Outside These Walls*.

Comments: Dolores Costello was dubbed "The Belle of the Box Office" in the late 1920s. She was undeniably possessed of a Madonna-like beauty and was popular but, truth to tell, she was not a great actress. In her early sound roles her voice was tentative and it seemed to exhibit a slight speech impediment. The public's interest probably centered around her more as Barrymore's wife than for her acting abilities.

In her sporadic returns to the camera, Costello never possessed a commanding voice but she seemed to gain confidence and showed flashes of real talent. Certainly noteworthy was her affecting performance as Isabel Amberson in *The Magnificent Ambersons*. Perhaps it took a director of Orson Welles's stature to bring out the best in her.

However, Costello did not seem impelled to perform. For one thing, she probably was not keen on playing mothers of grown children. Whatever the reason, she did not have the chance to further develop her maturing talents after *Ambersons*.

REVIEWS

Tenderloin: Costello is not an elocutionist and her main fault in talking is the lack of agreement between her emotional expression and speech. "Talking" is just not her forte. However, she arouses sympathy because of her good acting. *Variety* 3/21/28, *Harrison's Reports* 4/21/28.

Glorious Betsy: Reviewers differed. One said that Costello, limited to two or three talking sequences, is again at a disadvantage, with her lines sounding unnatural. Another stated she does excellent work. *Variety* 5/2/28, *Harrison's Reports* 5/12/28.

Noah's Ark: The Costello voice is just not for the talkies and it hurts the impression made by her silent acting. *Variety* 11/7/28.

The Glad Rag Doll: Dolores Costello is well enough fitted for this story. *Variety* 6/5/29.

Expensive Women: Costello makes her screen return in this film and the acting is pretty low stuff. *Variety* 11/17/31.

Little Lord Fauntleroy: Dolores Costello Barrymore and Freddie Bartholomew are an ideal coupling in the two principal roles. (This was probably Costello's most popular talkie, due mainly to the presence of the then very popular Bartholomew. At the age of about 30 she really was too young to play his mother.) *Variety* 4/8/36.

Yours for the Asking: It doesn't do right by Dolores Costello Barrymore after her neat comeback in *Little Lord Fauntleroy.* The role is not especially sympathetic and seldom presents her with a real opportunity. She is as attractive as ever. *Variety* 8/26/36.

The Magnificent Ambersons: Dolores Costello is still very attractive and does as good an acting job as possible in a stilted role. (At the age of about 36, she played the mother of Tim Holt who was certainly in his mid–20s by then.) *Variety* 7/1/42.

Costello, Helene (Helen Costello), New York, New York, 1903/04–1957

Silent: With her younger sister Dolores, Helene Costello appeared in one- and two-reelers as early as 1909 with their father, the matinée idol Maurice Costello. After appearing in vaudeville and on the stage, she returned as an adult to star in Warner Bros. films beginning in 1925.

Costello's feature films included *The Man on the Box, The Honeymoon Express, Wet Paint, The Fortune Hunter, In Old Kentucky, Burning Up Broadway* and *Comrades.* She was named a Wampas Baby Star of 1927. Last silent: *When Dreams Come True* (1929), made after her sound debut.

Sound: Costello was the leading lady in the first all-talkie, *Lights of New York* (1928), produced by Warner Bros. with the Vitaphone process. Her only other starring sound film was *The Midnight Taxi* made the same year. *The Circus Kid,* also 1928, had a talking prologue in which she apparently was not seen.

Costello's final '20s appearance was a brief one singing and dancing (both awkwardly) with Dolores in the "Meet My Sister" number from Warners' all-singing, all-dancing *The Show of Shows* (1929).

Costello returned in the mid–1930s with appearances in at least two films: *Public Hero No. 1* (1935) and *Riff Raff* the following year. In the latter film she played a convict who helps Jean Harlow to escape from prison. She may also have done some extra work.

Comments: Helene Costello was the "dark" half of the Costello sisters in more ways than one. She was a very pretty brunette whereas Dolores was a beautiful blonde. There was also a personal dark side, although it emerged after her starring career was over. She had a tumultuous private life, was married several times, and was involved in a bruising and highly-publicized custody fight over her only child. And there was drug abuse.

Costello's silent career was largely undistinguished. What may have seemed like a golden chance, the starring role in *Lights of New York*, turned out to be a career dead end. Her performance engendered much criticism of her acting abilities, although perhaps some of the blame might have been fairly laid at the door of the primitive technology then in use.

REVIEWS

Lights of New York: Reviewers had a difference of opinion on Helene Costello in the female lead. One stated she was a total loss and that for talkies she should take speech classes right away. Another thought she was good. *Variety* 7/11/28, *Harrison's Reports* 7/14/28.

The Midnight Taxi: Helene Costello is carefully proficient, having been given much protection, it appears, on the dialogue. *Variety* 10/31/28, *Harrison's Reports* 11/3/28.

Costello, Maurice, Pittsburgh, Pennsylvania, 1877–1950

Silent: A true film pioneer, theater star Maurice Costello was in films for Vitagraph by 1907 and may have begun even earlier at the Edison studio. He was a matinée idol in one- and two-reelers at a time when stars received no screen credits. He was therefore dubbed "Dimples" or "The Dimpled Darling." After he left Vitagraph in 1917, his career diminished.

Among Costello's early features were *Mr. Barnes of New York* (1914), *The Crown Prince's Double, The Man Who Won* and *The Tower of Jewels*. Later films, mostly in support, included *Determination, The Glimpses of the Moon, Love of Women, The Mad Marriage, Wives of the Prophet* and *Wolves of the Air*. Last silent: *Black Feather* (1928).

Sound: Costello's first talkie was *Hollywood Boulevard* (1936), a film that featured many old-time silent stars. He went on to play small roles in several more from 1938 to about 1941, including *There's That Woman Again, It's a Wonderful World, Mr. Smith Goes to Washington, The Sea Hawk* and *Lady from Louisiana*, possibly his last.

Comments: Although almost 60 when he made his first sound film, gray-haired Maurice Costello was still distinguished-looking and he retained vestiges of his matinée idol appearance. Unfortunately it was not his screen "comeback" that garnered par-

ticular attention but his personal life. There were spats about finances with actress daughters Helene and Dolores that certainly gave that benighted family more publicity than they could ever have desired.

REVIEWS

Hollywood Boulevard: It introduces its old-timers intelligently and plausibly; one of them is Maurice Costello as the director in the studio scene. *Variety* 9/23/36.

It's a Date: A large group of old-time film stars and favorites are paraded briefly before the camera, including Maurice Costello. *Variety* 10/16/40.

Crawford, Joan (Lucille Le Sueur, later Billie Cassin), San Antonio, Texas, 1904/08–1977

Filmography: *Films in Review* (Dec. 1956), added films (June-July 1966); List of films in *Film Dope* (Oct. 1975), with corrections (June 1977), *Stars* (Mar. 1990)

Silent: It was a long way from the plumpish chorus girl and dancer Lucille Le Sueur had been in the early 1920s to the archetypal movie queen Joan Crawford became. Her pre-film days were modest enough: nightclubs and the chorus line of one Broadway show. Her early screen appearances were also modest, the first of which was in a minute role in *Lady for a Night* (1925).

She advanced to conventional leads at MGM quickly enough in *Old Clothes* (1925), a Jackie Coogan starrer, but Crawford's films were generally not the top of the MGM line. She did co-star with Lon Chaney in the interesting *The Unknown* and made a hit in *Sally, Irene and Mary* but it was several years before her break-out vehicle as the vivacious Charleston-dancing Diana in *Our Dancing Daughters* (1928).

At one point Joan Crawford was "punished" by being cast in westerns like *Winners of the Wilderness* and *The Law of the Range*. Others of her almost 25 silents included *The Boob, The Taxi Dancer, Tramp, Tramp, Tramp*, with Harry Langdon, *Across to Singapore, Four Walls* and *Rose-Marie*. Last silent: *Our Modern Maidens* (1929), with synchronized music and sound effects.

Sound: Crawford's introduction to sound was the all-star *The Hollywood Revue of 1929* in which she sang and, by today's standards, somewhat clunkily danced in one of the myriad musical numbers. Her first starring vehicle was the silly but successful *Untamed* later that year.

With *Paid* in 1930, Crawford discarded the silent "jazz baby" image to play the first of the melodramatic working girl roles that were to make her *the* star of the 1930s and the ideal of real working women throughout the land.

Among Crawford's films of the early '30s were *Letty Lynton*, *Possessed*, *This Modern Age*, *Sadie McKee*, *Chained* and *Forsaking All Others*. She had a change of pace in the musical *Dancing Lady* (1933) with frequent co-star Clark Gable, and two misfires with *Rain* and *Today We Live*. There was also a stand-out picture and a worthy performance in 1932's ensemble drama *Grand Hotel*.

In the middle of the decade, Crawford evolved into her "clothes horse" phase where her glamorous and much-imitated look (courtesy of the designer Adrian) was often more important than the plots of her pictures. It was during this time that her popularity began to decline with such pictures as *No More Ladies*, *Love on the Run*, *The Last of Mrs. Cheyney*, *I Live My Life* and *Mannequin*.

The low point of Crawford's MGM career probably came with *Ice Follies of 1939* but in that year there was also a high point: an unsympathetic — and supporting — role in *The Women*. In 1938 she and several other stars had been dubbed "box office poison" by the theater owners and her days at MGM were eventually numbered. With Norma Shearer and Greta Garbo retired, Greer Garson replaced her as MGM's leading dramatic female star.

Although she had a brief "dramatic actress" phase and a meaty role in *A Woman's Face* (1941), most of Crawford's remaining MGM films were mediocre. They included the interesting *Strange Cargo* (the last of her eight pictures with Gable), *Susan and God*, *When Ladies Meet*, *Reunion in France* and her last there, *Above Suspicion* (1943). Then for two years, except for a cameo in 1944's *Hollywood Canteen*, she was off the screen.

Finally Crawford was signed by Warner Bros. and it was there her career was rescued by *Mildred Pierce* for which she won the 1945 Best Actress Oscar. This began a new phase of high-gloss melodramas, in which she sometimes played "femmes fatales," to the early 1950s. Among them were *Humoresque*, *Possessed* (Academy Award–nominated), *Daisy Kenyon*, *The Damned Don't Cry*, *This Woman Is Dangerous* and *Flamingo Road*.

With 1952's *Sudden Fear*, for which she garnered another Academy Award nomination, Crawford entered what might be called a brief "woman in jeopardy" phase. This continued with *Torch Song*, *Autumn Leaves* and *Female on the Beach*. The offbeat "psychological" western *Johnny Guitar*, which possibly could be fit into the same category, was also made during this time.

With a single exception, after the mid–1950s Crawford was never again a star to be reckoned with. Although she continued to appear in leading roles, they were scattered and she made supporting, if top-billed, appearances as well. The late '50s movies *The Story of Esther Costello* and *The Best of Everything* did not register with fans but she came back with a vengeance in 1962's *What Ever Happened to Baby Jane?* Although her old rival Bette Davis had the showier role, she held her own and the film was a smash hit.

Thus was ushered in Crawford's final phase, that of a "scream queen." Most of her few remaining films were in the horror genre: *Strait-Jacket*, *I Saw What You Did*, *Berserk* and her final effort, 1970's *Trog*. She also appeared in an unsympathetic role in *The Caretakers*. During the 1960s and '70s she was seen on television as well. Some time after her death, her name once again became part of the public consciousness as a result of her daughter's (in)famous book *Mommie Dearest* and the subsequent film.

Comments: Few stars fought as hard for, and held on so long to, their careers as did Joan Crawford and never did any Hollywood star reinvent herself as often in an effort to stay on top. It is rumored that she even had her back teeth extracted to give her better cheekbones.

Crawford was a star 24 hours a day. It was a truly remarkable and incredibly single-minded feat. She was undeniably a great *star* so it is almost a secondary consideration as to whether she was a great, or even a good, *actress*. Her acting style certainly tended toward the unsubtle and the "wheels" were often seen turning.

Author F. Scott Fitzgerald, who knew something about pretense, said, "She can't change her emotions in the middle of a scene without going through a Jekyll-and-Hyde contortion of the face." An overwrought tenseness was sometimes substituted for emotion and her gestures could be oversized.

Later in her career, Crawford became even more "actressy" and mannered; often a star-like imperiousness was evident. It is fair to say that a mediocre director produced a similar performance and a good director like Frank Borzage or George Cukor could produce a better performance.

Crawford certainly made the transition to talkies with complete ease. Her deepish voice proved to be excellent although she undoubtedly had voice lessons which resulted in an accent midway between Culver City and an East Coast finishing school. Some of her performances were quite creditable, and occasionally one was even brave. On the other hand she walked through some roles with nothing but her magnificent eyebrows, generously made-up lips and padded shoulders to show for it.

Crawford established a recognizable persona, that of a basically strong woman always needing the love of, and sometimes the help of, a strong man. From what is known of her "true" self, that may have been descriptive of her real life as well.

It also has been said that there was no real Crawford outside the studio, that every facet of her life was "performance art with herself as her greatest creation." She herself stated, "I was born in front of a camera, I don't know anything else." And director George Cukor said of her, "The camera saw, I suspect, a side of her that no flesh and blood lover ever saw."

It is obvious that whether or not she was a good actress or even a good or "real" person, Crawford could not have stayed at the pinnacle of her craft without something to sustain her. Was it just because she was pretty and her talents were adequate? Was she merely providing what the audiences of the day wanted to see?

Crawford was certainly always attentive to her fans and worked at keeping them happy. She sent her fan clubs a schedule of where she was going to be at all times so they could catch a glimpse of their idol. They thought they really knew "her." If, in actuality, she abused her adopted children and was more like her role as the obsessive housecleaner in *Harriet Craig* than the gracious lady she seemed, it was perhaps immaterial to the fans.

Crawford fought and clawed and endured even when plum parts went to other actresses like Norma Shearer, the wife of MGM production chief Irving Thalberg. Perhaps the parts she yearned for and did not get were those she could not play. But despite all her shortcomings as an actress and person, she was memorable for a reason: The camera found in her that indefinable something vital to superstardom. That is rare and it is for that she should be remembered.

REVIEWS

Untamed: Joan Crawford's death scene is overdone with her wails seemingly endless. Her acting is generally excellent and her voice is very pleasing. *Variety* 12/4/29, *Harrison's Reports* 12/7/29.

Rain: It is a mistake to have assigned the Sadie Thompson role to Crawford. She is miscast and it shows her off unfavorably. The dramatic significance of it all is beyond her range and her appearance as the lady of easy virtue is extremely bizarre.

(Although the bad reviews caused even Crawford to disown her performance, in later years critics and she herself re-evaluated the merits of the film

and it has gained a better reputation.) *Variety* 10/18/32, *Harrison's Reports* 10/22/32.

Mannequin: One of the best Joan Crawford pictures in several seasons. It is splendidly acted by Miss Crawford and will revive the Crawford fan following. The Crawford-Tracy combination is good showmanship. Her role is closer to the kind of characterization which won her earlier big following. It should re-establish her as an important exhibitor asset. *Variety* 12/22/37.

Strange Cargo: The marquee power of Gable and Crawford will have to shoulder the burden of carrying this one. She is provided with a particularly meaty role as the hardened dance hall gal; it is a departure from those of the past several years and reminiscent of the earlier work that carried her to popularity originally. Her characterization will give studio executives an idea of proper use of her talents for the future. *Variety* 3/6/40.

Mildred Pierce: This justifies Crawford's two-year wait for the proper story. She generally underplays her role and reaches the peak of her acting career. *Variety* 10/3/45.

Flamingo Road: Crawford's portrayal of a demanding, many-sided part is handled with her usual resourceful technique. She imparts convincing personality shadings. *Variety* 4/6/49.

Johnny Guitar: Crawford should leave saddles and Levis to someone else and stick to city lights. It is a major disappointment to loyal Crawford fans. (As Vienna, she played in her first western since *Montana Moon* in 1930. A brooding and neurotic saga, this has become a minor cult classic and has been analyzed like few westerns before or since.) *Variety* 5/5/54.

Autumn Leaves: Crawford has a strong dramatic vehicle, her best in some time. *Variety* 4/18/56.

What Ever Happened to Baby Jane: Crawford gives a quiet, remarkably fine interpretation. Because her character is physically confined she has to act from the inside. She wisely underplays with Bette Davis. In one superb bit, she makes her face fairly glow with the remembrance of things past. A genuine heartbreaker. *Variety* 10/31/62.

Crisp, Donald, Aberfeldy, Scotland,
1880/82–1974

Filmography: List of films in *Film Dope* (Oct. 1975); *Eighty Silent Film Stars*

Silent: One of the most memorably horrific villains of the silents was Donald Crisp in his role as Battling Burrows in *Broken Blossoms* (1919). He had begun as an extra and then directed and acted in one-reelers at Biograph for D. W. Griffith from about 1910. Before that he was a stage singer and actor both in the U.K. and the U.S., to which he emigrated in 1906.

Among Crisp's very earliest film appearances were *The Miser's Heart*, *Her Awakening*, *The Battle* and *The Primal Call*. His feature appearances included the role of General Grant in *The Birth of a Nation*, but most of his work during the silent era was behind the camera. He directed an early version of *Ramona* in 1916, Buster Keaton's *The Navigator* and several Bryant Washburn and Douglas Fairbanks films.

Among the latter was *Don Q, Son of Zorro*, in which Crisp also acted; and he was on-screen in Fairbanks's *The Black Pirate* (1926) as well. Last silent (as a performer): *The Viking* (1929), in color with synchronized music and sound effects, made after his first part-talkie. He was top-billed as Leif Ericson.

Sound: *The River Pirate*, a 1928 part-talkie, marked Crisp's sound acting debut. His first all-sound film came with *Scotland Yard* in 1930, the year he directed his final film *The Runaway Bride*. He then began what was to be a distinguished career as a character actor.

Among Crisp's films were *A Woman Rebels*, *The Charge of the Light Brigade*, *Knute Rockne, All American*, *Mutiny on the Bounty*, *The Valley of Decision* and the 1941 John Ford film for which he won the Best Supporting Actor Academy Award, *How Green Was My Valley*.

After 1945, Crisp's roles grew sporadic but he established somewhat of a cottage industry appearing with the popular canine star Lassie the collie. His appearance in 1943's *Lassie Come Home*, was followed by most of the others in that series as well.

Crisp continued through the '50s (*Prince Valiant*, *The Last Hurrah*) and into the early '60s with some Disney films. His final appearance came in *Spencer's Mountain* (1963). He had made his TV debut when he was in his late 70s and at the time of his death was the oldest living Oscar winner.

Comments: In talkies, Crisp seemed to be Hollywood's archetypal Scotsman. He had an authoritative baritone voice, complete with a pleasant Scottish burr, that lent verisimilitude to his stern patriarchs, clergymen and other portrayals. As he aged, his face took on a kindlier cast; in the silents its gimlet-eyed intensity had been well used for villainy. He could now play decency most convincingly.

Crisp's claim to have appeared in over 400 films probably cannot be verified. Also not verified is his claim to have directed parts of *The Birth of a Nation*. In fact, his assertion has been largely rejected, and his most popular films, with Keaton and Fairbanks, were probably as much directed by their stars as by their nominal director. As an actor he was most competent; as a director he would have to considered conventionally adequate at best.

REVIEWS

The Old Maid: Donald Crisp is kindly and sympathetic as the family doctor. *Variety* 8/2/39.

How Green Was My Valley: Donald Crisp is inspired casting. *Variety* 10/29/41.

Lassie Come Home: Crisp is excellent. *Variety* 8/18/43.

The Hills of Home: Donald Crisp is unusually excellent in this Lassie picture. *Variety* 10/6/48.

The Long Gray Line: Donald Crisp is great. *Variety* 2/9/55.

Cunard, Grace (Harriet Jeffries), Columbus, Ohio, 1893/94–1967

Filmography: List of films in *Sweethearts of the Sage*

Silent: Following stage experience, serial queen Grace Cunard made her film debut about 1908 at Biograph in New York. She went to Hollywood in 1911 and appeared for Kaybee, Lubin and also Universal, for whom she wrote and starred in two-reelers.

Cunard co-starred with Francis Ford in many of her chapterplays and she also directed or co-directed several. They included *Lucille Love (Girl of Mystery)*, *The Broken Coin*, *Peg o' the Ring*, *The Purple Mask* and *Elmo the Mighty*. She made many features with Ford as well. Her pictures included *Lady Raffles Returns*, *His Majesty Dick Turpin*, *The Sham Reality*, *The Powder Trail* and *The Spawn*.

By the end of the 'teens, Cunard's starring career was faltering and she continued in mostly supporting roles, including *Emblems of Love*, *Outwitted*, *Exclusive Rights* and *The Denver Dude*. There was a sizeable role in *The Last Man on Earth* (1924) and another serial, 1928's *The Chinatown Mystery*. Last silent: *The Price of Fear* (1928).

Sound: After her sound debut in *Untamed* (1929), Cunard was still to be seen in small, bit and extra roles through the 1930s and possibly later. These included *Resurrection*, *The Magnificent Brute*, *Alias Mary Dow*, *Wings Over Honolulu* and *A Little Bit of Heaven*.

Dana, Viola (Violet, Viola or Virginia Flugrath), Brooklyn, New York, 1897–1987

Filmography: *Films in Review* (Mar. 1976)

Silent: After stage experience as a youngster in *The Poor Little Rich Girl* and other plays, Viola Dana entered films (possibly in *A Christmas Carol*) with the Edison Company about 1910. She was one of three actress-sisters, Edna Flugrath and Shirley Mason (*née* Leonie Flugrath) being the others.

Dana achieved stardom with 1915's *The Stoning*. From 1916–1924 she appeared in numerous Metro films and then worked at Paramount, FBO, Universal and First National. Among her at least 100 films were *God's Law and Man's*, *The Microbe*, *June Madness*, *Rouged Lips*, *The Necessary Evil*, *Revelation*, *Kosher Kitty Kelly* and *Naughty Nanette*. Last silent: *Two Sisters* (1929), made after her only talkie appearance.

Sound: Dana's only sound film appearance came with very brief glimpses of her in two musical numbers in Warner Bros.' *The Show of Shows* (1929). In one, she sang and danced with Shirley Mason (as Dutch girls) in the "Meet My Sister" number which featured several Hollywood sisters.

Comments: Despite her stage experience and previous screen popularity, Viola Dana made no starring sound features. According to her, there was nothing wrong with her voice, it was only that she was considered a "silent" actress. From television interviews many years later, it is clear that she did have a New York accent but it is by no means certain that that was the death knell of her career.

Dana was probably right in her assessment: She was simply shelved in favor of new and younger faces. About this traumatic time in her life she said: "After all those years in the movies as a star, it was terrible realizing you had become overnight a has-been. I was just past 30." (She was 32.) Like so many other fading stars, she did try a vaudeville tour. Although it was popular, it did not bring her back to the screen.

Dane, Karl (Rasmus K. Gottlieb), Copenhagen, Denmark, 1886–1934

Silent: Karl Dane's greatest cinema success began in 1925 but he had already been in Danish films and a few American films of 1918 and '19. Among these were *My Four Years in Germany*, *To Hell with the Kaiser* and *The Great Victory*. In all of these, oddly, he played the same role, that of German Chancellor von Bethmann-Hollweg. Then, for the first five years of the 1920s, he was off the screen.

Following his praised role as Slim in 1925's *The Big Parade*, the hulking Dane was cast in several prestigious MGM films including *Bardelys the Magnificent*, *La Bohème*, *The Enemy* and *The Scarlet Letter*. He also supported Rudolph Valentino in United Artists' *Son of the Sheik*.

Dane's 1927 teaming with diminutive English comic actor George K. Arthur brought him further screen success. Among their popular films together were *Rookies*, *Detectives*, *Circus Rookies* and *Baby*

Mine. Last silent: *Speedway* (1929), with sound effects and music, made after his first part-talkies.

Sound: The Dane-Arthur part-talkie *Brotherly Love* (1928) was Dane's introduction to sound, but almost all of his nine 1929 films were silent. In that year he was seen in the part-talkie *Alias Jimmy Valentine* and sang a snippet of a song with Arthur in *The Hollywood Revue of 1929*. His first featured sound appearance came in *Navy Blues* at the end of the year.

Dane played Scandinavian characters in a few more films at MGM (*Montana Moon*, *The Big House*, *Billy the Kid*) before the studio released him in 1930. In at least the latter two films he was essentially mute, seen in a few scenes but without any lines. With Arthur, who had also been terminated by MGM, he appeared in vaudeville and in a series of comedy shorts for RKO and Paramount in 1930 and '31.

These efforts failed to resuscitate Dane's career (or that of Arthur either) and he appeared in only one more feature, MGM's *Fast Life*, in which he played a small role as, not surprisingly, a Swede. Aside from an appearance in the serial *The Whispering Shadow* (1933), he was finished in the movies.

Comments: The fate of Karl Dane proved to be one of Hollywood's saddest stories. A most popular silent comic actor with his trademark, if unsavory, habit of tobacco chewing and spitting, he could not (or did not work hard enough to) overcome his unacceptably heavy accent. If he had been able to master it to some extent, his tall, muscular frame, mobile face and arresting light blue eyes might have allowed him to continue as an employable character actor for some time.

Dane had been a studio carpenter before hitting it big. In order to survive, he returned to the laboring ranks as well as doing various menial jobs. His damaged pride over being rendered virtually speechless on-screen and his depression over being forgotten must have been profound; he ended his life a suicide. MGM saved the once-famous actor from being burned in a pauper's grave, notifying the coroner that the studio would take charge of the funeral arrangements.

REVIEWS

Alias Jimmy Valentine: Karl Dane has a rich role as a dumb Swede and provides a wealth of comedy. *Variety* 11/21/28.

Navy Blues: Dane talks with a Swedish accent. *New York Times* 1/11/30.

Billy the Kid: Karl Dane hasn't one line to speak. He plays a dumb Swede and merely grunts. *Variety* 10/22/30.

Daniels, Bebe (Virginia Daniels), Dallas, Texas, 1901–1971.

Filmography: *Films in Review* (Aug. 1964)

Silent: Bebe Daniels was a child actress in one- and two-reelers for Selig and 101 Bison before signing with Hal Roach at about the age of 13. She was best-known in the early years as Harold Lloyd's leading lady for four years in his "Lonesome Luke" series. They may have turned out a film every week.

Daniels entered features under C. B. DeMille's aegis in a small role in *Male and Female*. Other DeMille pictures in which she appeared were *Why Change Your Wife?* and *The Affairs of Anatol*. From 1920–22 she was seen in Realart comedies (a subsidiary of Paramount) and then she went on to Paramount itself.

From 1922 to '28, Daniels was a major star in dramas, westerns and farces. Among her over 200 one- and two-reelers and more than 50 features were *One Wild Week*, *Sinners in Heaven*, *She's a Sheik*, *Swim, Girl, Swim*, *Heritage of the Forest*, *Brewster's Millions*, *Volcano* and *The Campus Flirt*. Last silent: *What a Night!* (1928).

Sound: Paramount seemed to have little interest in putting its highly-paid silent stars into talkers and Daniels had to buy out her contract. It proved to be a good move because she made her sound debut at RKO in one of the earliest screen musicals, *Rio Rita* (1929). It was a major smash and was followed by other films in which she also sang, including *Dixiana* and *Love Comes Along*.

Daniels ultimately signed with Warner Bros. and for them she appeared in the famous *42nd Street* (1932). She appeared the following year in Universal's *Counsellor-at-Law*, one of John Barrymore's best sound performances. Her American sound films, of which there were more than 15, included *Alias French Gertie*, *Reaching for the Moon* with Douglas Fairbanks, Sr., *Cocktail Hour*, *Registered Nurse* and her last, *Music is Magic* for Fox (1935).

The latter film must have been too uncomfortably close to real life for Daniels because she again played an over-the-hill musical star making way for younger talent. In this case it was Alice Faye at the beginning of her screen career. She had of course made a similar sacrifice for Ruby Keeler in *42nd Street*.

After 1933 Daniels's career began to decline and she emigrated to England with her husband, actor Ben Lyon. She appeared in a few British films like *The Return of Carol Deane*, and she and Lyon starred in a popular radio and then television series, *Life with the Lyons*. They also made some films as a couple, the last of which was *The Lyons in Paris* (1956). Daniels also appeared on the London stage.

Although their professional career in England was worthy, it was the patriotism they showed for their temporarily adopted country that won Bebe Daniels and Ben Lyon the greatest plaudits. They remained in England throughout most of the Second World War and became symbols of the American commitment to ultimate British victory.

Comments: Although Bebe Daniels was one of the biggest female stars in the late 1920s, Paramount apparently did not even give her a voice test. It is obvious from her success in *Rio Rita* that they had been shortsighted. Her singing voice was quite good and her speaking voice, though at times thin and high, was mostly acceptable.

Even after the vogue for musicals died in 1930, Daniels proved to have some staying power in talkies when her vehicles were worthwhile. This was due in large measure to her vivacious personality, honed through years of knockabout comedy. Today she is known primarily through her role as the temperamental musical star Dorothy Brock in *42nd Street*, much later parodied in the musical and film of *The Boy Friend*.

REVIEWS

Rio Rita: Bebe Daniels dominates the picture will receive the most attention. She has made a terrific comeback acting and singing. She has a great future ahead of her. *Variety* 10/9/29, *Harrison's Reports* 10/12/29.

Dixiana: Among the leading players is the inimitable Bebe Daniels. She sings nicely. *Harrison's Reports* 8/9/30, *Variety* 9/10/30.

My Past: Bebe Daniels gives an intelligent performance given the poor material. She co-stars with her husband Ben Lyon. *Harrison's Reports* 2/28/31, *Variety* 3/18/31.

The Maltese Falcon: The performance given by Bebe Daniels is excellent. (She plays the shady "heroine" Miss Wonderly, later so memorably portrayed by Mary Astor.) *Harrison's Reports* 6/6/31.

42nd Street: A good performance by Bebe Daniels, in a not particularly sympathetic assignment, as the washed-up musical comedy star. *Variety* 3/14/33.

Counsellor-at-Law: Daniels has an atypical role as the secretary whose affection for her troubled boss (John Barrymore) goes unrequited. (It was her last good role.) *Variety* 12/12/33.

Music Is Magic: Bebe Daniels is wasted in the unsympathetic role of a fading picture actress. *Variety* 11/20/35.

D'Arcy, Roy (Roy Giusti), San Francisco, California, 1894–1969.

Silent: One of the silents' villains you loved to hate was mustachioed Roy D'Arcy. His evil doings (sometimes tongue-in-cheek) were carried out in modern dress as well costume dramas like *The Merry Widow, Bardelys the Magnificent, Graustark, Beverly of Graustark* and *La Bohème*.

Among D'Arcy's other films were *Pretty Ladies, The Temptress, Adam and Evil, On Ze Boulevard, Forbidden Hours* and *Lovers?*. Last silent: *The Woman from Hell* (1929), in which he played a character named Slick Glicks.

Sound: The part-talkie *The Last Warning* (1929) was Roy D'Arcy's first; *The Black Watch*, made the same year, was his first all-sound effort. His roles grew smaller in talkies but he made appearances throughout the '30s. He was in the popular *Flying Down to Rio* but, interestingly, was mostly glimpsed as a shadow on the wall.

Among other motion pictures in which D'Arcy often chewed the scenery as a villain were *Kentucky Blue Streak, Discarded Lovers, Hollywood Boulevard, Under Strange Flags* and *Chasing Danger*, perhaps his last, in 1939.

REVIEWS

The Black Watch: Roy D'Arcy plays an acceptable menace but is permitted to overact. He reads his dialogue with the ultra-slow articulation generally associated with a scheming Hindu. *Variety* 5/15/29, *New York Times* 5/23/29.

Sherlock Holmes: D'Arcy is as jaunty as ever as a sinister aide to the villain. *Variety* 11/15/32.

Orient Express: Roy D'Arcy is still smiling, even as a murderer. *Variety* 3/6/34.

Captain Calamity: D'Arcy is too villainous even for a villain. *Variety* 12/23/36.

Darro, Frankie, (also known as Darrow; Frank Johnson), Chicago, Illinois, 1917/18–1976

Silent: One of the most popular of the child and teenage performers below star level, Frankie Darro made his debut in 1924. He usually was seen in action films, including numerous westerns and "B" melodramas and, although mostly a supporting player, he also had some leads. Among his earliest films were *Judgment of the Storm, Roaring Rails, The Cowboy Musketeer* and *Racing for Life*.

Among Darro's frequent co-stars was sagebrush hero Tom Tyler with whom he did a popular FBO series. His later silents included *The Arizona Streak, Born to Battle, Red Hot Hoofs, Phantom of the Range, Lightning Lariats* and *When the Law Rides*.

He also was to be seen in occasional big-budget pictures like *So Big, Kiki* and *Long Pants*. Last silent: *The Pride of Pawnee* (1929), made after his first part-talkie.

Sound: Nineteen twenty-eight's *The Circus Kid*, in which Darro was top-billed, had a talking prologue. *The Rainbow Man* (1929) was his first full talkie, followed by *Blaze o' Glory* the same year. The Rin Tin Tin serial *The Lightning Warrior* came in 1930.

As he matured, Darro remained short of stature and could believably play jockeys, which he did on several occasions. He also became somewhat of a prototype of a juvenile delinquent. His pictures included *Three on a Match, Way Back Home, The Mad Genius, Little Men, Tugboat Annie, The Ex-Mrs. Bradford, Saratoga* and *The Pride of Maryland*.

In the mid–30s Darro teamed with Kane Richmond for a series of melodramas, among them *Born to Fight, Headline Crasher* and *Tough to Handle*. He also stayed active in serials during the 1930s, acting in such chapterplays as *The Vanishing Legion, The Wolf Dog, The Devil Horse, Burn 'Em Up Barnes, The Great Adventures of Wild Bill Hickok* and, most notably, the very successful Gene Autry serial *The Phantom Empire* (1935).

Roles inevitably began to decrease for Darro but he was busy through 1941 for Poverty Row studios such as Monogram and Conn. Off the screen during some of the war years, he returned in '46 for the low-budget "Teenagers" films starring Freddie Stewart and June Preisser. Later in the decade he briefly became one of the Bowery Boys (*Angels' Alley, Trouble Makers, Hold That Baby*).

By 1950, Darro's career had virtually come to a standstill. Although he had parts in the "A" productions *Riding High* and *Across the Wide Missouri*, they were not large. His final film was one of the last "B" westerns, *The Lawless Rider* (1954). He later did some stunt work, was the man inside Robby the Robot in *Forbidden Planet* and appeared on television, notably The Red Skelton Show.

REVIEWS

Way Back Home: Frankie Darro plays an orphan boy. The acting of everyone is excellent. *Harrison's Reports* 12/19/31.

No Greater Glory: Practically all the Hollywood boy stars have been enlisted and Frankie Darro is the most nearly human of the group. *Variety* 5/8/34.

Mind Your Own Business: Darro is only so-so in a secondary role. *Variety* 2/17/37.

On the Spot: Frankie Darro is trapped in his characterization as a sharp-shooting kid. *Variety* 6/26/40.

Let's Go Collegiate: Darro, generally a good bet in programmers, has been relegated to what is virtually a subordinate role even though top-billed. *Variety* 11/19/41.

Fighting Fools: Darro is fair. *Variety* 4/27/49.

Darwell, Jane (Patti Woodward), Palmyra, Missouri, 1880–1967

Silent: After stock experience, Jane Darwell entered movies in 1914 and played supporting roles in fewer than ten films in two years before returning to the theater. She actually may have first appeared in a 1911 movie called *The Capture of Aguinaldo.*

Darwell's films included *Brewster's Millions, The Master Mind, Ready Money, The Goose Girl, After Five* and *Rose of the Rancho.* Last silent: *The Reform Candidate* (1915).

Sound: Jane Darwell returned with *Tom Sawyer* (1930), starring Jackie Coogan as Tom. Although usually cast as kindly mothers, grandmothers or domestics, she also could play acerbic characters well. Her first big role was in 1931's *Back Street* and she became a well-known character actress at Twentieth Century–Fox after *The White Parade* in 1934.

Other Darwell efforts included *Wonder Bar, Life Begins at Forty, Craig's Wife, Gone with the Wind, The Scarlet Empress, The Rains Came, The Ox-Bow Incident, Caged, There's Always Tomorrow* and *The Last Hurrah.* She also was a frequent co-star of child actresses Shirley Temple and Jane Withers.

Darwell was a favorite of John Ford in films such as *The Grapes of Wrath* (1940), for which she won an Oscar for Best Supporting Actress as Ma Joad, *My Darling Clementine* and *Three Godfathers.* Her last film was *Mary Poppins* (1963), and she also appeared in *The Real McCoys* and other TV shows.

Comments: Because of the fame her role in *The Grapes of Wrath* brought her, it might be assumed that Jane Darwell was one of the most important character actresses of her day. Although she was no doubt appreciated for her talent, the fact is that before and after her memorable role she was frequently cast in very insubstantial roles not worthy of that talent.

Nonetheless, the sight of Darwell's homely, expressive face and plump, (grand)motherly form was always welcome, even in such distinctly "B" efforts as *The Great Gildersleeve* and others of that ilk. If she was only to have one great part, it was a perfect one.

REVIEWS

Grapes of Wrath: Jane Darwell provides the family with strength and leadership in the mother part. (One of the most affecting scenes of the film was one without dialogue. It is where Ma Joad goes through her box of mementos and realizes the lifetime of memories she is leaving behind.) *Variety* 1/31/40.

Davenport, Dorothy (also known as Mrs. Wallace Reid), Boston, Massachusetts, 1895–1977

Silent: From about 1909 to 1917, Dorothy Davenport, daughter of character actor Harry Davenport, appeared in many films. Some were at Universal with her husband, the popular star Wallace Reid. Her features began about 1915 with such titles as *Mr. Grex of Monte Carlo, Barriers of Society, The Way of the World* and *The Scarlet Crystal.* After 1917, her on-camera appearances became rare and she made very few films during the 1920s.

After Reid's death from drug-related causes, Davenport, under the name of Mrs. Wallace Reid, produced and appeared in *Human Wreckage* (1923), a cautionary film about drug abuse. Other films included *The Fighting Chance, Every Woman's Problem, Broken Laws, The Red Kimono* and *The Satin Woman.* In the latter '20s she founded her own company to produce and direct films. Last silent: *Hellship Bronson* (1928).

Sound: The sound era saw Davenport acting in apparently only one film, 1933's *Man Hunt.* However, she remained active producing, directing and writing screenplays under the name of Dorothy Reid until about 1968.

REVIEWS

Man Hunt: Mrs. Wallace Reid makes a rather youthful mother. *Variety* 5/9/33.

Davidson, Max, Berlin, Germany, 1875/79–1950

Silent: After stage experience, Max Davidson began appearing in pictures about 1913 as a "Jewish" comedian and eventually worked at such studios as Biograph, Reliance-Majestic and Fine Arts. His work was confined mostly to short comedies, the best-known being the "Izzy" series, but he also played character roles in features, both comedy and drama.

Among Davidson's early full-length films, beginning in 1916, were *Mr. Goode, the Samaritan, The Hun Within, Intolerance, A Daughter of the Poor* and *The Hoodlum.* He continued appearances in both two-reelers (e.g., *Hats Off, The Call of the Cuckoo*) and features throughout the '20s. Among the latter were *The Idle Rich, The Extra Girl, Hold Your Breath, Hogan's Alley, Justice of the Far North, The Johnstown Flood* and *Cheaters.*

In *Old Clothes* and *The Rag Man* (both 1925), Davidson was co-starred with popular child star Jackie Coogan. His stereotypical "Hebrew" humor, with its attendant exaggerated gestures like beard-stroking, would not be politically correct now but he was a talented comic actor. Last silent feature: *Pleasure Before Business* (1927).

Sound: Davidson made his feature sound debut in 1929's *So This is College*. His accent was no problem but most of his appearances in full-length talkies were bit roles (e.g., he was last in the cast list as Old Man in *The Great Commandment*). He also continued making comedy shorts such as *The Shrimp*, *Oh! Oh! Cleopatra*, *Southern Exposure* and *No Feeling*.

Davidson's films included *Daring Danger*, *The Cohens and the Kellys in Trouble*, *The Cat and the Fiddle*, *Princess O'Hara*, *Union Pacific*, *Rogue of the Range*, *Kitty Foyle* and *The Mortal Storm*. His last movies came in the early 1940s, *Reap the Wild Wind* (1942) being one. In the 1960s, a clip from a two-reeler in which he was shown nude in a collapsing bathtub was included in the comedy compilation *Laurel and Hardy's Laughing '20s*.

Davidson, William B., Dobbs Ferry, New York, 1888–1947

Silent: William B. Davidson went from the stage to the screen about 1914 or '15 for Vitagraph and Metro. Although he played an occasional lead (*Her Second Husband*, *The Price of Malice*), he was mostly used in supporting roles. Among his pictures in the 'teens were *Thou Art the Man*, *The White Raven*, *The Whirlpool* and a couple with vamp star Theda Bara, *Lure of Ambition* and *La Belle Russe*.

Davidson was seen somewhat less during the 1920s but continued as a solid supporting actor in films like *Women and Gold*, *Conceit*, *Recompense*, *A Gentleman of Paris*, *The Gaucho* and *The Storm Daughter*. He played both villains and authority figures. Last silent: *Good Morning, Judge* (1928).

Sound: Sound seems to have given William B. Davidson a boost. The part-talker *The Carnation Kid* (1929) was his introduction to sound and all his films that year had some sound, including *Queen of the Night Clubs*, *Painted Faces* and *Woman Trap*. From that point on he was a dependable character man in as many as 15 movies a year, including some "B" westerns, and he was active to the year of his demise.

Davidson's films of the '30s included the Vitaphone short *Letters* and the features *Hell's Angels*, *The Silver Horde*, *Graft*, *The Animal Kingdom*, *I'm No Angel*, *Midnight Alibi*, *In Caliente*, *The Singing Kid*, *Coconut Grove* and *Each Dawn I Die*. The next

decade saw him in *Lillian Russell*, *Hold That Ghost*, *Saratoga Trunk*, *The Farmer's Daughter*, *My Little Chickadee* and *Tennesee Johnson*.

Davies, Marion (Marion Douras), Brooklyn, New York, 1897–1961

Filmography: *Films in Review* (July 1972); List of films in *Silent Film* (Summer 1970), *Film Dope* (Apr. 1976), *Classic Images* (Dec. 1982)

Silent: Starting out in Broadway musicals at a young age, Marion Davies came into the sphere of newspaper baron William Randolph Hearst, who took both her professional and personal life into his hands. Along the lines of Svengali — although she presumably was a willing pupil — he set out to make her an actress and star.

Davies made her first unheralded film appearance in *Runaway Romany* in 1918. Generally her films until 1922 were failures but she and her stories gradually improved. Among the more successful of her earlier pictures were *When Knighthood Was in Flower* and *Little Old New York*. They were made for Hearst's Cosmopolitan company, which eventually was affiliated with MGM.

The best of Davies's 28 silents were probably those where she could use her talent for comedy, especially the ones directed by King Vidor, e.g., *The Patsy* and *Show People*. Her other silents included *April Folly*, *Enchantment*, *Janice Meredith*, *Adam and Eva*, *Beverly of Graustark*, *Tillie the Toiler* and *The Fair Coed*. Last silent: *The Cardboard Lover* (1928).

Sound: The World War One story *Marianne* (1929) was Davies's first talkie starring role. It was a romantic comedy-drama with music in which she essayed a French accent throughout. Originally completed as a silent, it had been remade as a talkie with a substantially different cast. She had previously appeared as one of MGM's stable of stars in *The Hollywood Revue of 1929*, singing and winsomely tap dancing the song "Tommy Atkins" with a line of very tall male dancers.

Marion Davies remained at MGM until 1935 when she and/or Hearst became angered that she was not getting the roles she wanted. He took his company to Warner Bros. and it was there that her last poorly-received films were made.

Others of Davies's 14 talkies included *Not So Dumb*, *Polly of the Circus*, *Going Hollywood* with Bing Crosby, *Operator 13* with Gary Cooper, *Cain and Mabel* co-starring Clark Gable, *Hearts Divided*, *Peg o' My Heart* (considered by some to be her best talkie) and 1937's *Ever Since Eve*, her last.

Comments: At times during her film career, Davies successfully used her modest talent for comedy and could be an endearing performer. Much of the time she was enveloped in period costumes in over-produced and under-seen adventure-comedy-dramas ill-suited to her. As a result, many of her films were panned by the critics, (always excepting the Hearst papers of course).

In private life, Davies had a stammer which was not noticeable on-screen and her light speaking voice was well-suited to roles (or perhaps vice versa) which called for brittle and often wise-cracking dialogue. If her voice was not the problem, then certainly her (or Hearst's) choice of roles was.

Davies was in her mid– and late 30s in the 1930s but she was still being cast as an ingenue. She also seemed to have a penchant for playing "ugly duckling" parts, perhaps because she enjoyed the inevitable beautification which followed. Her co-stars, including such rising leading men as Gary Cooper, Bing Crosby, Robert Montgomery, Clark Gable and Dick Powell, were invariably her junior.

Apparently Davies's ideas of her talent came to match those of her lover's because she decided she wanted to play the leading roles in such films as *The Barretts of Wimpole Street* and *Marie Antoinette*. These roles were certainly unsuitable for her — and perhaps they were also for Norma Shearer, who actually did play them.

Before Davies got to think of herself as a grande dame, she displayed a self-deprecating streak that made audiences truly like her. By all accounts she was a beloved, generous and kind person in her private life. Unquestionably the initiation of her screen career was due to Hearst, as was her affiliation with the most prestigious studios. Without him, she would not have had Hearst Castle as her playground nor the 110-room Santa Monica beach house and assorted other playthings.

But that liaison tends to undervalue her. When she was allowed to reveal her naturally playful personality, Davies showed she more was than Trilby. A handful of her silent films were worthy and she deserves some credit for that.

REVIEWS

Marianne: Marion Davies mimics Maurice Chevalier. She has done an excellent job, handling her lines and herself with relish and ability and she also has overcome her slight stutter. *Variety* 10/23/29, *Harrison's Reports* 10/29/29.

The Bachelor Father: Davies ought to make it her first rule never to play anything but roles like this. She provides a note of sincerity that often has been missing from her work. Her acting is artistic. *Variety* 2/4/31, *Harrison's Reports* 2/7/31.

Five and Ten: This part fits right within Davies's range and she does well. *Variety* 7/14/31.

Blondie of the Follies: It is too bad that this popular actress should have given so poor a story. As usual Miss Davies is best in her few comedy chances but on the whole this is under par for her. (Although contemporary reviews would never dare mention it, this tale of a kept woman and a millionaire must have had a special resonance for Davies.) *Harrison's Reports* 9/10/32, *Variety* 9/13/32.

Peg o' My Heart: Essentially a monologue, it leaves Davies with the entire burden. She sings, dances, clowns and cries, with a brogue always present. The star passes up nothing, making it a field day for herself. *Variety* 5/23/33, *Harrison's Reports* 5/27/33.

Going Hollywood: Davies doesn't really fit in in the posh girl's school setting provided. She dances, which surprises some in the audience, and does the best she can with a weak story. *Variety* 12/16/33, *Harrison's Reviews* 1/6/34.

Operator 13: Marion Davies acts the part with artistry but it was poor judgment to make her impersonate a mulatto. *Harrison's Reports* 6/30/34.

Page Miss Glory: There was no unanimity among reviews. One said that despite a lavish production, Davies was miscast and forced to behave in a manner unsuited to her. Another stated that she dominated the picture and did well by her comedy opportunities in playing a chambermaid who is beautified to win a contest. *Harrison's Reports* 8/24/35, *Variety* 9/4/35.

Ever Since Eve: Davies is in a lighter ingenue role than those she has handled of late. There is nothing the actors can do to overcome the plot defect; they are placed in ridiculous situations.

(The 40-year-old Davies played a secretary who was so beautiful that she actually had to fight off her bosses' advances. She finally donned a disguise, including black wig and glasses, to make herself appear homely. It was plotlines like this that ended her career.) *Variety* 6/30/37, *Harrison's Reports* 7/10/37.

Day, Alice, Pueblo, Colorado, 1905–

Silent: Coming to films about 1923 (somewhat earlier than her younger sister Marceline), Alice Day was groomed by Mack Sennett to be his major female star. She appeared in two-reelers with Harry Langdon and former matinée idol Ralph Graves and also had her own series (*Tee for Two, Cold Turkey, Love and Kisses*, etc.).

Day's features included *The Temple of Venus, Secrets* (in which she played Norma Talmadge's daughter), *His New York Wife, The Gorilla* and *See You in Jail*. Last silents: *Phyllis of the Follies* and *The Way of the Strong*, released about the same time in 1928.

Sound: All eight of Day's 1929 films were talkies or part-sound. The first was *Red Hot Speed*; the others included *Little Johnny Jones, Times Square, Drag, Is Everybody Happy?* and *The Show of Shows*, in which she participated in the musical number "Meet My Sister" with Marceline Day.

Day had a full slate of films through 1930 and in some of them she received top billing, *Ladies in Love* and *Lady from Nowhere* being two. Her career clearly was on the wane, however. "B" westerns and melodramas for Poverty Row outfits seemed to be all that the future offered for the once-promising actress.

Alice Day appeared in only one picture in 1931 and three in her final on-screen year, 1932. Among her films were *Viennese Nights, Hot Curves, The Melody Man*, and *Gold*, a Jack Hoxie cheapie which was her last.

REVIEWS

Times Square: Alice Day is the heroine in this film with very minimal spoken dialogue. *Harrison's Reports* 6/15/29.

Drag: Day is sufficiently attractive and unsympathetic to make the character natural. In fact, she performs with exasperating perfection as the annoying and wishy-washy young dumb Dora. *New York Times* 6/21/29, *Variety* 6/26/29.

Is Everybody Happy?: Alice Day, as the sweet leading lady, has little to do and registers likewise. *Variety* 11/6/29.

Ladies in Love: Alice Day plays a radio favorite and sings the tuneful theme song. *Variety* 6/18/30.

Gold: Day almost overcomes a poorly written part. *Variety* 10/11/32.

Day, Marceline, Colorado Springs, Colorado, 1907/08–

Filmography: List of films in *Sweethearts of the Sage*

Silent: Pretty Marceline Day came to films in 1925, a couple of years after older sister Alice Day, and she briefly replaced Alice as Harry Langdon's leading lady at Sennett. For a time, Sennett publicity claimed that the girls were actually twins.

A busy actress, Day routinely appeared in at least six films a year, many for MGM. Her pictures included *The Taming of the West, College Days, That Model from Paris, Restless Youth* and *Fools of Fashion*.

Day also appeared in such major productions as *The Beloved Rogue* (with John Barrymore), *The Cameraman* (with Buster Keaton), *London After Midnight* (with Lon Chaney) and *Rookies* and *Detectives* (with the popular comedy team of Arthur and Dane). Last silent: *The One Woman*

Idea (1929), with synchronized music, made after her first part-talkie.

Sound: The first of Day's sound films was the part-talkie *The Jazz Age* (1929). Others that year were *The Show of Shows* (in which she joined Alice in a portion of the "Meet My Sister" number) and *The Wild Party*, Clara Bow's talkie bow. Before too long she was being cast in cheapie melodramas and westerns which did little to advance her career.

Among Day's other pictures through 1933 were *Paradise Island, The Pocatello Kid, The Fighting Fool, By Appointment Only* and *Via Pony Express*. She was seen one final time in 1937's *Damaged Lives*, a film dealing with syphilis and sponsored by the Canadian Social Health Council.

REVIEWS

The Jazz Age: Day is a peppy heroine in a film with only 1% spoken dialogue. *Harrison's Reports* 1/19/29.

Sunny Skies: Marceline Day doesn't fit the co-ed role very well, being too demure in appearance and manner. She is permitted to look beautiful and do no acting. *Variety* 5/21/30, *Harrison's Reports* 5/24/30.

Arm of the Law: Day has a trifling role, apparently to get another name for the film's advertising. *Variety* 7/5/32.

The Fighting Parson: Little in this Hoot Gibson western is contributed by Marceline Day, who doesn't get a chance to shine. *Variety* 8/8/33.

Day, Shannon (Sylvia Day), New York, New York, 1896–1977

Silent: Pretty Follies girl Shannon Day made her screen debut in a supporting role in 1920's *The Man Who Had Everything*. Through 1926 she was in a succession of films, the high point being her nine appearances in 1922. Almost all of her roles were supporting ones.

Rare quickie leads came in such films as *The Gypsy Romance* and *Silent Pal*. Among Day's other motion pictures were *Forbidden Fruit, Fools First, Manslaughter, All the Brothers Were Valiant, Breed of the Sea* and *So This Is Marriage*. Last silent: *Stranded* (1927).

Sound: As far as is known, Shannon Day made only three sound films. In the first, *Worldly Goods* in 1930, she played a chorus girl. Her others were *Big Town* (1932), in which she had a bit as a telephone operator, and lastly *Hotel Variety* in 1933.

Dean, Priscilla (Priscilla Fitzgerald?), New York, New York, 1896–1987

Filmography: *Films in Review* (Aug.-Sept. 1984)

Silent: Between 1911 and 1916, Priscilla Dean alternated theater roles with appearances as an extra for pioneering studios like Biograph, Edison, World and Pathe. In 1917 she began getting featured parts and, after signing with Universal, she became a star. Her first important roles were with director Tod Browning in a series of melodramas with titles like *Which Woman?*, *The Silk Lined Burglar* and *The Wicked Darling*.

Dean's major stardom began with such popular films as *The Virgin of Stamboul*, *Outside the Law* and *Reputation*, made in 1920 and '21. *Under Two Flags* (1922) was also very well received. Many of the best films were directed by Tod Browning. In light of her success, the decision to leave Universal in 1924 to work for Producers' Distributing Corporation proved to be unfortunate.

The motion pictures Dean made for her new company were routine and her star declined precipitously. In all she made about 80 silent films, not counting her unbilled appearances. Other features included *Wild Honey*, *The Gray Ghost*, *The Storm Daughter*, *West of Broadway*, *Forbidden Waters*, *Drifting* and *The Siren of Seville*. Last silent feature: *Birds of Prey* (1927); last silent appearance: *Slipping Wives*, (1927)a two-reel Laurel and Hardy comedy.

Sound: Dean returned in 1932 for three talkies. The films were all quickies and she did not have major roles in any of them. They were *Behind Stone Walls*, *Law of the Sea* and *Klondike*.

Comments: The title of Priscilla Dean's final silent, *Slipping Wives*, unfortunately mirrored her own, very much slipping career. It was not a fitting climax for a performer who had been extremely popular and who was still very talented. She was an unusually intelligent-looking actress and her persona, especially in the period from 1920–23, was that of a self-sufficient and capable woman.

Dean could "blaze" from the screen like no other actress of the time but her return in 1932 did her reputation no credit. All three films were poor melodramas made for the Poverty Row studios Mayfair and Monogram. In them, her former fire was muted beyond recognition.

Reviews

Behind Stone Walls: Priscilla Dean overplays, apparently by direction. *Variety* 4/19/32.

DeBrulier, Nigel, Bristol, England,
1878–1948

Silent: After appearing in stock, Nigel DeBrulier may have made his film bow as early as 1909 for Selig. By 1914 he was making features, the earliest of which included *The Pursuit of the Phantom*, *The Spanish Jade* and *The Dumb Girl of Portici*. He played mostly in support but had occasional leads.

Among DeBrulier's other films of the teens were *The Romance of Tarzan*, *The Dwelling Place of Light*, *Purity* and the interestingly titled *Me und Gott*. He was also in the serial *The Mystery of 13*. In the 1920s, the hatchet-faced actor became a favorite player of Douglas Fairbanks who used him in *The Three Musketeers* and *The Gaucho*.

DeBrulier also was cast in such prestigious films as *Ben-Hur*, *The Four Horsemen of the Apocalypse*, *Salome*, *Wings* and *Don Juan* as well as more mundane efforts like *His Pajama Girl*, *Mademoiselle Midnight* and *Soft Cushions*. He often played clerical figures. Last silent: *Me, Gangster* (1928), with synchronized music.

Sound: The 1928 part-talkie *Noah's Ark* followed soon thereafter as DeBrulier's first film with sound. All his 1929 releases had some sound as well, although Fairbanks's *The Iron Mask* had little audible speech. In it DeBrulier was the shrewd Cardinal Richelieu, a role he had also played in *The Three Musketeers*. Others that year were *Thru Different Eyes* and *The Wheel of Life*.

DeBrulier's pleasant English accent allowed him to conquer talkies without problems and he went on to make many pictures in the '30s, although he was busier in the last part of the decade. His films included *Moby Dick*, *Son of India*, *I'm No Angel*, *Rasputin and the Empress*, *Viva Villa!*, *The Garden of Allah* and *San Francisco*.

Also among DeBrulier's films were *The Three Musketeers* and *The Man in the Iron Mask*, remakes of two of the Fairbanks efforts. In them he continued his mini-industry of portraying Richelieu. He was seen in the serials *Zorro Rides Again*, *The Adventures of Smilin' Jack* and most memorably *Adventures of Captain Marvel*. In that acclaimed chapterplay DeBrulier played (and looked like) the ancient seer who gives Billy Batson (Frank Coghlan, Jr.) the secret of changing into the superhero. Otherwise he made but a few films during the early 1940s, including *For Beauty's Sake*, *Tonight We Raid Calais* and *One Million B.C.*, before he left the screen, distinguished and white-haired, about 1943.

DeGrasse, Sam, Bathurst, New Brunswick,
Canada, 1875–1953

Silent: Eventually to be known as one of the silents' most hissable villains, Sam DeGrasse entered films about 1912 and appeared in one- and two-reelers until *Birth of a Nation*. He frequently was seen as Douglas Fairbanks's nemesis and also was in many westerns and melodramas. He received top billing in Erich von Stroheim's first directorial effort *Blind Husbands* (1919).

DeGrasse's other films included *Anything Once, The Scarlet Car, Wild and Woolly, Smashing Through, The Skywayman, Robin Hood* (1923 version), *The Spoilers* (1923 version), *The Black Pirate, The King of Kings* and *The Racket*. Last silent: *Silks and Saddles* (1929).

Sound: DeGrasse made only two talkies, *Wall Street* (1929) and the musical *Captain of the Guard* (1930). In the latter he continued his evil ways and met the fate he had so often, dying on-screen. His retirement was most probably voluntary because his powers to portray villainy, at age 55, seemed undiminished.

REVIEWS

Wall Street: Sam DeGrasse turns in a good performance. *Variety* 11/7/29.

Captain of the Guard: One of the only performances of any distinction is Sam DeGrasse's villain. It's a compliment when his death brings forth applause. *Variety* 4/2/30.

De Lacey, Philippe (also De Lacy), France, 1917–

Silent: A favorite child actor for most of the 1920s, curly-haired Philippe De Lacey was a French war orphan who began his film career in small roles in *Without Benefit of Clergy* (1921) and 1922's *A Doll's House*. Frequently playing the leading man of the film when he was a boy, he went on to appear in such motion pictures as *Wasted Lives, Don Juan, Faithful Wives, The Student Prince, Beau Geste* and *Peter Pan*.

De Lacey was the brother of Mary Pickford in *Rosita* (1924) while in *Love* (1927), a version of *Anna Karenina*, he played the beloved son of heroine Greta Garbo. In *The Royal Rider* (1929), a strange combination of Ruritanian romance and western starring Ken Maynard, he was a boy king. Last silent: *The Four Feathers* (1929), with synchronized music and sound effects.

Sound: De Lacey's on-camera career did not long survive the advent of sound and his approaching metamorphosis from child to teenager. Among his 1929 films with some talking were *Four Devils, General Crack, The Marriage Playground* and *The Redeeming Sin*.

Like many child actors of his day, young Master de Lacey was quite adept at crying scenes. His two 1930 movies, *Sarah and Son* and *One Romantic Night*, were the last in which he had the opportunity to show his budding (and bawling) talents.

De Lacey was by no means finished with Hollywood, however. He eventually became an assistant producer and in the 1950s directed a Cinerama feature before becoming an executive in advertising and then in television.

REVIEWS

General Crack: The role John Barrymore plays is first introduced as a boy, played by Philippe De Lacey. *Harrison's Reports* 12/14/29.

The Marriage Playground: De Lacey does intelligent acting as the oldest boy. *New York Times* 12/14/29.

Sarah and Son: Young Philippe de Lacey appears during the most important stages of this chronicle. He is well suited to the role, particularly in the last part. *New York Times* 3/13/30, *Variety* 3/19/30.

De La Motte, Marguerite, Duluth, Minnesota, 1902/04–1950

Silent: Marguerite De La Motte was in films by 1918; her earlier pictures included *Arizona, For a Woman's Honor* and *A Sage Brush Hamlet*. She then was selected by Douglas Fairbanks as his leading lady in the early 1920s, and these remain her most memorable films: the swashbucklers *The Mark of Zorro* and *The Three Musketeers*, and his last silent comedy *The Nut*.

Among De La Motte's other pictures in her busiest period from 1920–27 were *The Jilt, Scars of Jealousy, Behold This Woman, Children of the Whirlwind, Fifth Avenue* and *Ragtime*. Last silent: *Montmartre Rose* (1929).

Sound: The 1929 part-talkie *The Iron Mask*, again with Fairbanks, was De La Motte's first. She was never again to appear in any film as important. Her first full talkie was a 1930 western *Shadow Ranch* and there were small roles in *A Woman's Man* (1934) and *Reg'lar Fellers* in 1942. There may have also been another brief appearance or two.

REVIEWS

Shadow Ranch: Marguerite De La Motte is the heroine of this western drama. *Harrison's Reports* 9/27/30.

Del Rio, Dolores (Dolores Martinez Asunsolo Lopez Negrette), Durango, Mexico, 1904/05–1983

Filmography: Films in Review (May 1967)

Silent: The Mexican society matron who was to become Dolores Del Rio had her first bit roles in *Joanna* (1925) and *High Steppers*. Her initial lead was in *Pals First* in 1926 but it was not until her fifth film, *What Price Glory?*, that she was really noticed. (Her character Charmaine was the subject of a popular song.)

Del Rio's tenth film, in which she played the tragic Helen Hunt Jackson heroine *Ramona* (1928), made her a star. Others of her 13 silents were *The Loves of Carmen, The Trail of '98* and *The Red Dance*.

Last silent: *Revenge* (1928), with synchronized music score and sound effects.

Sound: Dolores Del Rio showed she could speak English readily enough and even sing a little in her first part-talkie *Evangeline* (1929). It was followed by her first full sound feature, the melodramatic *The Bad One* in 1930. The lavish and lush South Sea melodrama *Bird of Paradise* was probably the talkie which most typified the exotic "Dolores Del Rio" persona.

Resuscitating a career that was faltering somewhat by this time, Del Rio went into musicals at RKO and had a surprise hit with *Flying Down to Rio*, in which she danced a brief tango with Fred Astaire. *Wonder Bar* with Al Jolson and *In Caliente* were other musicals of the mid-'30s.

Del Rio's career respite was only temporary. She made a film in England in 1936 and only five American films from 1937 to '42. The last of these was the Orson Welles–directed *Journey into Fear*. She returned for one final picture that decade, *The Fugitive* (1947). Other films included *Lancer Spy*, *Girl of the Rio*, *Madame Du Barry*, *I Live for Love*, *The Devil's Playground* and *Man from Dakota*.

In 1943 Del Rio returned to Mexico where, with *Flor Silvestre* and *Maria Candelaria*, she began a film career which made her the top female star of the Mexican cinema. She remained an important figure there for over two decades, winning four Arieles (the equivalent of the Academy Award).

Del Rio also made a couple of films in Spain. She came back to the U.S. in 1960 to play Elvis Presley's mother in the western *Flaming Star*. A few others followed; *Cheyenne Autumn* (1964) was one and *The Children of Sanchez* (1977), her last.

Comments: Dolores Del Rio was undeniably a dark and exotic (by American standards) beauty. This restricted her roles as much as or more than her acceptable voice with its agreeable accent. More than anything else, it was probably the limited acting ability she displayed in most of her American talkies which caused her career to falter.

Many of Del Rio's roles were in programmers and her acting rarely rose above them. When she appeared in successful films like *Flying Down to Rio* she was usually cast as pretty window-dressing. More charismatic performers, in this case Fred Astaire and Ginger Rogers, generally overshadowed her.

Perhaps Del Rio was simply not inspired by her roles, or perhaps with maturity her acting prowess also matured. She amply demonstrated her fine dramatic ability in Mexican cinema and her face also withstood the years well. Even in advanced age it retained a spiritual beauty that greatly enhanced her later roles.

REVIEWS

The Bad One: The "Bad One" is just that for Dolores Del Rio. She is miscast; she poses and is artificial. *Variety* 6/18/30.

Bird of Paradise: Its greatest asset is the truly fine performance of Dolores Del Rio. It is a role made to order for this electric young Mexican and it will go down among the best things she has ever done. Her acting is effective and sensitive. *Variety* 9/13/32, *Harrison's Reports* 9/17/32.

Flying Down to Rio: Del Rio, as a South American belle, looks well but seems cast just for her looks. *Variety* 12/26/33.

Madame DuBarry: Dolores Del Rio is unsympathetic. As an impetuous and frivolous woman of the streets she is rarely believable and is eclipsed by her co-stars. *Harrison's Reports* 6/30/34, *Variety* 10/30/34.

I Live for Love: As a temperamental actress, Del Rio gives a nice performance and has been well photographed. *Variety* 10/23/35.

The Man from Dakota: This marks Del Rio's first screen appearance in over two years and it's a not too auspicious re-entry. She is seen wallowing through the streams and woods of Virginia in tattered dress and dull expression. *Variety* 1/21/40.

The Fugitive: Del Rio's acting is of the highest order as a Mary Magdalen. *Harrison's Reports* 11/8/47.

Flaming Star: Dolores Del Rio remains durably lovely and ever feminine. She brings dignity and delicacy to the role of a full-blooded Indian mother. *Variety* 12/21/60.

Demarest, William, St. Paul, Minnesota, 1892–1983

Silent: After a varied career that included carnivals, stage acting, vaudeville and even prizefighting, William Demarest made almost 20 films in two years. There were 13 in 1927 alone, his very first year before the cameras; his maiden picture was *Finger Prints*.

Demarest's films included *The Bush Leaguer*, *Don't Tell the Wife*, *Matinee Ladies*, *The Gay Old Bird*, *The Butter and Egg Man*, *Five and Ten Cent Annie* and *The Escape*. Last silent: *The Crash* (1928), made after his first part-talkie.

Sound: The part-talkie in which Demarest appeared, but was not heard, was none other than *The Jazz Singer* (1927). However, he *was* heard in two Vitaphone shorts that year: *When the Wife's Away* and *The Night Court*. He also made the early talking shorts *A Night at Coffee Dan's* and *Papa's Vacation* (Vitaphone, 1928).

After that early start in talkies, Demarest did not make another feature until 1934 when he began his screen career in earnest, ultimately appearing in nearly 100 films. Many of the best were directed by Preston Sturges: *The Lady Eve, Sullivan's Travels, The Miracle of Morgan's Creek* (as the gruff Officer Kockenlocker), *Hail the Conquering Hero, The Great McGinty* and *Christmas in July.*

Among Demarest's other pictures were *Rebecca of Sunnybrook Farm, Charlie Chan at the Opera, Mr. Smith Goes to Washington, It's a Mad Mad Mad Mad World* and *That Darn Cat.* He was nominated for a Best Supporting Actor Academy Award for *The Jolson Story* (1946).

Demarest was less busy on the screen during the 1950s and afterward; his last film came in the 1970s following a long hiatus. He made some TV appearances and in the 1960s he played crusty but kindly Uncle Charlie in the popular sitcom *My Three Sons,* for which he was Emmy-nominated.

Comments: William Demarest in the silents could express but a small part of his screen persona; he needed sound to reach his apex as a character actor. The audience had to hear his very colorful voice, part-sneer, part-growl and part-roar, all coming through clenched jaws. Although a native Midwesterner, his enunciation had more than a little of the New York street tough about it.

Tough was what Demarest was born to play, but he sometimes could be kindly (and sometimes dumb) in his roles as sergeants, policemen and others in petty authority. His deadpan, weathered face could only belong to someone named "Lefty," "Mugsy" and others of that ilk. Amidst the rich variety of character men in the 1930s and '40s, he was quite unique.

REVIEWS

The Great McGinty: Demarest grabs attention as a political stooge. His performance is a gem. *Variety* 7/24/40, *New York Times* 8/15/40.

The Far Horizons: Demarest, as a flinty sergeant, is, as usual, excellent. *New York Times* 5/21/55.

Denny, Reginald (Reginald Daymore?),

Richmond, England, 1891–1967

Filmography: Classic Images (Dec. 1990); List of films in *Eighty Silent Film Stars*

Silent: Reginald Denny made his stage debut as a child in England and he performed on the American stage in the 'teens. His Hollywood film career began in supporting parts in 1919 with *Bringing Up Betty* and *The Oakdale Affair,* but before long he was receiving leading roles.

Denny appeared in about 25 two-reelers, nearly all of which were in the popular "Leather Pushers" boxing series from 1922 to '24. (His publicity claimed he actually had been a boxer for a brief time.) Among his other films were *Disraeli* (1921 version), *Sherlock Holmes, The Thrill Chaser, Oh, Doctor!, Fast and Furious, What Happened to Jones* and *I'll Show You the Town.*

Denny attained the height of his success at Universal in mid-decade playing in comedy-adventure films like *California Straight Ahead* and *Skinner's Dress Suit.* He made about 50 silents altogether, many with Laura La Plante. Last silent: *Clear the Deck* (1929), made after his first part-talkie.

Sound: Red Hot Speed, a 1929 part-talkie, was Denny's sound bow. Another, *His Lucky Day,* followed before he made his first full talkie *One Hysterical Night* later the same year. He went on to appear in about 80 talkies, mostly in support, although he maintained his leading man status until he left Universal in 1930.

Denny worked steadily through 1942. There were fewer appearances thereafter (except for 1947, a boom year for him) and he was seen sporadically until 1957, with a few more in the '60s (e.g., *Assault on a Queen* and *Batman* [his last]).

Other Denny films included *Rebecca, Mr. Blandings Builds His Dream House, Madam Satan, Kiki, The Lost Patrol, The Little Minister, Anna Karenina, Romeo and Juliet,* the "Bulldog Drummond" series, *The Macomber Affair* and *No More Ladies.* He also resumed some stage roles, the last in 1961.

Comments: Reginald Denny was born in the same year and in the same town as Ronald Colman but their careers took very different turns. Denny's major success came as a supposedly all-American boy in the silents when he was very popular in romantic action-comedies. This was no longer possible with the onset of sound. His beautifully modulated but very "Briddish" voice took him along a new path.

Denny's starring career came to a virtual end but he proved to be a worthy character actor and best friend of the hero-type for many years thereafter. If some of his roles were not of the highest caliber (the foolish and foppish Algy in the "Bulldog Drummond" pictures, for instance), many were of high quality. He also could essay an occasional villain convincingly, as in *Sherlock Holmes and the Voice of Terror.*

REVIEWS

What a Man: Universal put Denny into comedies when romantic, and even dramatic, roles fitted him far better, as this picture proves. He has never appeared to better advantage. His slight English accent and his good delivery make his talking pleasant. *Harrison's Reports* 4/5/30.

Of Human Bondage: Denny gets over a couple of lusty innings as a male on the hunt. *Variety* 7/3/34.

The Preview Murder Mystery: In his top-billed role, Denny makes his points smartly and makes every scene count. *Variety* 3/25/36.

Bulldog Drummond in Africa: Reginald Denny performs admirably. *Variety* 8/31/38.

International Squadron: Denny provides excellent support for Ronald Reagan. *Variety* 8/13/41.

The World for Ransom: Denny is acceptable in doing what is required of him. *Variety* 2/3/54.

Dent, Vernon, San Jose, California,
1895–1963

Silent: After working in cabaret and vaudeville, Vernon Dent starred in his own series of short screen comedies and then was transformed into a comic villain by Mack Sennett. He also appeared in two-reelers for studios like Mermaid and Educational.

Dent also was seen frequently as Harry Langdon's nemesis. Among his few features from 1921 were *Hail the Woman*, *The Extra Girl* (with Mabel Normand), *Soul of the Beast* and *His First Flame*. Last silent feature: *Golf Widows* (1928).

Sound: Dent made scores of shorts during the talkie era, working for Columbia for 17 years as a frequent comic foil for "The Three Stooges" and others. If he was not always an outright villain he generally was a ticked-off policeman or other petty authority figure. As far as his own "figure" was concerned, it grew plumper with the years.

In the 1930s, Dent also was appearing in small roles in many features including *Dragnet Patrol*, *Million Dollar Legs*, *Manhattan Melodrama*, *San Francisco*, *The Awful Truth* and *Mr. Smith Goes to Washington*. In the 1939 melodrama *Beasts of Berlin*, also known as *Hitler — Beast of Berlin*, he was just below the up-and-coming Alan Ladd in the cast list.

Dent continued to be seen in comedy shorts of the '40s but in fewer full-length pictures. Among them were *San Antonio*, *Mrs. Parkington*, *Rockin' in the Rockies*, *Wild Harvest*, *She Gets Her Man* and *It Had to Be You*.

There were more shorts for Dent until the mid–1950s and he was glimpsed in two silent comedy compilations of the early 1960s as well. Apart from his talents as a second banana, he was an accomplished songwriter and screenwriter.

Desmond, William, Dublin, Ireland,
1878–1949

Filmography: List of films in *Classic Images* (Dec. 1988); *Eighty Silent Film Stars*

Silent: Among William Desmond's first films in 1915 were *The Majesty of the Law* and *Peer Gynt*. He was best-known for his 12 serials, including *The Riddle Rider*, *The Return of the Riddle Rider*, *Perils of the Yukon*, *The Beast of Paradise*, *The Ace of Spades*, *Strings of Steel*, *The Winking Idol* and *The Vanishing Rider*.

During the first years of his career, Desmond appeared in comedy-melodramas and westerns for Triangle, Mutual and Pathe but his major fame came during his Universal years. His features, in which he was most active before 1920, included *Deuce Duncan*, *Twin Beds*, *Peggy*, *The Parish Priest*, *Big Timber*, *The Extra Girl* and *Tongues of Scandal*. Last silent: *The Devil's Trademark* (1928).

Sound: *No Defense*, a 1929 part-talkie, was Desmond's sound debut. He made only four films from 1929 to 1932 but from 1933 to '37 he was active in small roles. He returned in 1940 for additional appearances, his last being the Abbott and Costello film *The Naughty Nineties* (1945).

Other Desmond films included *Laughing at Life*, *The Frisco Kid*, *Born to Battle*, *Young Bill Hickok*, *Raiders of the West*, *Beyond the Pecos* and *Phantom of the Opera* (1943 version). He also continued serial appearances in *The Lightning Warrior*, *Heroes of the West*, *The Last Frontier*, *Gordon of Ghost City* and *The Perils of Pauline* (the mid–1930s version).

REVIEWS

No Defense: William Desmond does some good work. *Harrison's Reports* 7/6/29.

It's a Date: A large group of old-time film stars and favorites are paraded briefly before the camera, including William Desmond. *Variety* 10/16/40.

Devore, Dorothy (Alma Williams), Fort Worth, Texas, 1898–1976

Silent: Dorothy Devore was a nightclub and vaudeville performer when she made her picture debut in two-reel Christie comedies. She proved to be a vivacious and popular actress and she signed a long-term contract with Warner Bros. to make features, the first of which was 1920's *Forty-Five Minutes from Broadway*.

Devore's other pictures in the 1920s, in which she was usually top-billed or had the female lead, included *Hold Your Breath*, *The Narrow Street*, *The Magnificent Brute*, *Three Weeks in Paris*, *Fighting the Flames*, *The Wrong Mr. Wright* and *His Majesty Bunker Bean*.

Devore's feature career waned after 1927, a victim, she claimed, of conflict with the Warners. She returned to two-reelers, this time for Educational from 1927 to '29 and became one of the highest-paid actresses in films at an astonishing $5,000 per week. One of her last short comedies was 1929's

Auntie's Mistake. Last silent feature: *No Babies Wanted* (1928).

Sound: Devore apparently was seen in only a very few talkies, the first of which, *Take the Heir*, was a 1930 part-talkie in which she co-starred. Only one other is known, 1939's *Miracle on Main Street*, in which she played the "Woman in the Church." There may have been other unbilled bit parts.

Dillon, John Webb, England, 1877–1949

Silent: John Webb Dillon came from the stage to appear in the cinema. *Sins of the Parents* and *Three Weeks* were among his earliest films in 1914. A couple of years later he appeared with Theda Bara in several beginning with *Romeo and Juliet* (1916) and going on to *The Darling of Paris*, *Heart and Soul* and *The Tiger Woman*. Among his studios were Fox, Hodkinson, Rolfe, Associated Exhibitors, Pathe, American, FBO, Paramount, First National and Warner Bros.

Dillon was a supporting actor throughout his career and did not appear in a large number of films. Among them were such 1920s motion pictures as *The Law of the Yukon*, *Jane Eyre*, *Rip Roarin' Roberts*, *The Air Mail*, *The Vanishing American*, *A Bowery Cinderella* and *The Exiles*. He also appeared in the serials *Trailed by Three*, *Speed*, *House Without a Key*, *Snowed In* and *The Black Book*. Last silent: *Dry Martini* (1928), with synchronized music.

Sound: One of the first sound westerns, *In Old Arizona* (1929), was Dillon's first talkie. *Girl of the Port* followed in 1930 and then there was a batch more beginning in 1932. They included *Sally of the Subway*, *Blood Money*, *Carolina*, *Life Begins at 40*, *Love Begins at Twenty*, *Sergeant Madden* and *Young Tom Edison*. Following several 1940 movies, he apparently made only one more: *The Secret Heart* in 1946.

Dix, Richard (Ernest Brimmer), St. Paul, Minnesota, 1894–1949

Filmography: *Films in Review* (Oct. 1966); *Classic Images* (Apr. 1989); Academy of Motion Picture Arts and Sciences; List of films in *Eighty Silent Film Stars*

Silent: Stage-trained Richard Dix's first leading role came in 1921's *Not Guilty*, a First National production in which he played twin brothers. His first few films were made for Goldwyn; in 1923 he signed a contract with Paramount as the replacement for their fallen star Wallace Reid.

Dix's first major role was in *The Sin Flood* (1922) but after the English-made *The Christian* in 1923 he could be called a star. Of his almost 50 silent films, few besides the first version of *The Ten Commandments* (1923) are remembered today.

Among Dix's more prestigious pictures were *Icebound*, *Manhattan* and *The Vanishing American*. He was a versatile leading man, dubbed "The Jaw" for his masculine, rugged cognomien, and he made films in a variety of genres, including comedy. Last silent: *The Redskin* (1929), in which he played one of his Native American roles.

Sound: The first of Dix's more than 50 talkies was the routine 1929 Paramount programmer *Nothing but the Truth*. This was followed by two others—*The Love Doctor* and *The Wheel of Life*—which apparently convinced him that Paramount was not ready to cast him in a major talkie.

After signing with RKO, Dix's first role there was in the popular *Seven Keys to Baldpate*. It proved to be a shrewd choice well-fitted to his strengths. Based on the George M. Cohan comedy-melodrama, it had been filmed at least twice before.

Dix's greatest sound hit was *Cimarron* (1931), based on Edna Ferber's novel, an epic story which began with the Oklahoma land rush of 1889. He seemed born for the role of Yancey Cravat, and RKO presumably acquired the novel specifically for him. Although he never topped it it, established his persona as a rugged individualist.

For that performance, Dix was nominated for his only Best Actor Academy Award, but lost to Lionel Barrymore for *A Free Soul*. The film proved to be a popular epic against which future epics would be measured.

Although there would be a few high points in his '30s career including the popular *The Lost Squadron*, Dix mainly was cast in a series of melodramas like *Hell's Highway*, *The Ace of Aces* and *The Devil's Playground*. There were also routine westerns like *The Arizonian* and *West of the Pecos*.

Nineteen thirty-nine's *Man of Conquest*, in which Dix played Sam Houston, another part he seemed made for, proved to be somewhat of a career reviver. It led to his starring roles in some well-produced "A" westerns of the early 1940s.

These films, which included *Cherokee Strip*, *Badlands of Dakota*, *Tombstone, The Town too Tough to Die*, *American Empire*, *Buckskin Frontier* and *The Kansan*, were produced by Paramount, United Artists and Universal. They were sufficiently popular and were followed by Dix's offbeat casting as a murderous ship's captain in Val Lewton's melodrama *The Ghost Ship*, Dix's last RKO film.

Dix's final seven films in 1944–47, all for Columbia, were part of "The Whistler" series, based on a popular radio show. Although they were low-budget melodramas, some were well made and they were generally well-received. His final film was *The Thirteenth Hour*.

Comments: Although neither the handsomest of

leading men nor the best actor, Richard Dix undeniably had a screen presence despite his stolidity. (One writer called most of his talkie performances "stiff and stodgy.") Exuding masculinity, he could believably portray pilots and other macho types but could play villains as well, his role in *The Ghost Ship* being an exemplar.

Dix was also at home with morally ambiguous characters, continuing the good-bad man tradition along the lines of William S. Hart. More than most leading men, he was allowed to die at the end of many of his films.

Dix perhaps always played "Richard Dix," an actor of some — though not great — range, and it took a top-drawer director like William Wellman (who directed him in *The Conquerors* and *Stingaree*) to bring out the best in him. Although his range did not seem to extend very readily to sound comedy, he had made silent comedies, even farces, and his earliest talkies were comedies.

Dix's voice undoubtedly was an asset, deep and well-fitting to his persona, albeit occasionally somewhat "thick." His slightly battered face could believably be that of a hero or an anti-hero. He was a leading man throughout his entire talkie career and this was possibly a mixed blessing. As a hero, Dix's roles could only become less and less rewarding as he aged. Perhaps essaying smaller character parts would have allowed him roles in better films, but he did not take that path. Nevertheless, it was a most respectable career and his would have to be counted as one of the success stories of the transition to talkies.

Reviews

Nothing but the Truth: Dix is quite at home while speaking his lines and he is set for talkers, at least for the light comedy type. As much scared by the microphone as any film star, Dix has waged a winning battle against the invader. *New York Times* 4/22/29, *Variety* 4/24/29.

The Wheel of Life: Although Dix has an ingratiating presence, he is rather out of his element. That might be dismissed if he were more capable in handling his lines. But there is little spontaneity in his dialogue. *New York Times* 6/24/29, *Variety* 6/26/29.

Seven Keys to Baldpate: Dix gives an agile and pleasing performance as the hero. *New York Times* 12/26/29, *Harrison's Reports* 1/4/30.

Cimarron: Dix is surprisingly excellent, even magnificent. It is so easily his best performance that everything else he has done seems preparation for this triumph. The complex character is the most difficult he has ever undertaken, and could easily have become a bombastic in hands less adept.

The actor's humor and charm, his good nature and manliness, succeed in making the character understandable and sympathetic. *New York Times* 1/27/31, *Variety* 1/28/31, *Harrison's Reports* 2/7/31, *Picture Play*, 1931.

The Lost Squadron: A story about aviators in which Dix gives a forceful performance. (He played a stunt flyer and many flying sequences were featured. It benefited from the interplay between the phlegmatic Dix and scenery-chewing Erich von Stroheim in one of his signature roles as a nasty and murderous movie director.) *New York Times* 3/1/32.

The Conquerors: Dix seems to be hampered by the material that attempts to recreate the *Cimarron* magic. He does not give as convincing a performance as he usually does in a role that gives him small opportunity for the colorful heroics he thrives upon. *Harrison's Reports* 11/9/32, *Variety* 11/22/32.

The Great Jasper: Dix, who has been called on in his career to play many adventurous roles, tops everything he has done and tries hard to cope with the peculiarities of his role. *New York Times* 2/17/33.

Blind Alibi: It offers little more than the spectacle of Dix in another of his heroic quests but he is particularly likable in the leading role. Throughout much of it he has to feign blindness. *New York Times* 5/20/38, *Harrison's Reports* 5/21/38.

Man of Conquest: Richard Dix is impressive as Sam Houston without lapsing into exaggerated heroics. It is a full-bodied portrait, earthy, human and virile and acted with great skill. *Variety* 4/12/39, *New York Times* 4/28/39, *Harrison's Reports* 4/29/39.

American Empire: Richard Dix's stern visage stands out like something carved by Gutzon Borglum on Mount Rushmore. *New York Times* 1/14/43.

The Whistler: A new type of gangster-killer melodrama in which Richard Dix does well enough. *Variety* 5/3/44.

Dove, Billie (Lillian Bohny or Bohney), New York, New York, 1901/04–1998

Filmography: Films in Review (Apr. 1979)

Silent: Billie Dove was an extra in the studios at Fort Lee, New Jersey, before her first more sizable film role in *Get-Rich-Quick Wallingford* (1921). She was noticed even more in her supporting role in *Polly of the Follies* (1922). This was the real beginning of a 35-plus film silent career, much of it with First National.

Among Dove's roles were those in *All the Brothers Were Valiant*, *The Air Mail*, *Wild Horse Mesa*, *The Marriage Clause* and *The Roughneck*. She appeared in several westerns, one of which was the early Technicolor film *Wanderer of the Wasteland*. Doug Fairbanks's *The Black Pirate* also showed her in color to great advantage. Last silent: *Adoration* (1928), with synchronized music and sound effects.

Sound: Dove made her sound debut in the part-talkie *Careers* in 1929; all her films of that year were talkies. Other films in which she appeared were *The Notorious Affair*, *One Night at Susie's*, *Her Private Life* and *Sweethearts and Wives*.

Two of her last movies were produced by Howard Hughes, *The Age for Love* (1931) and *Cock of the Air* (1932). Her very last picture was that year's *Blondie of the Follies*, in which she supported Marion Davies.

Comments: Billie Dove had been a Follies girl and was undeniably one of the most beautiful actresses ever to appear in films. Many of her plots harked back to her own Follies background; besides those films mentioned above, there were *An Affair of the Follies* and *The Heart of a Follies Girl*.

But could she act? The answer was a qualified "yes" in silents (e.g., *The Sensation Seekers*) but Dove's talkie appearances were not strong. Her voice was satisfactory but her acting was barely so and the films were usually weak romantic melodramas. Howard Hughes (Dove's love interest at the time) tried to boost her career with two films that instead caused her career to come to a virtual end.

Reviews

Careers: This is Billie Dove's first appearance in a talker and the microphone holds no fears as far as she is concerned. *Variety* 6/12/29, *Harrison's Reports* 6/22/29.

Her Private Life: Whatever entertaining values it has, have been imparted to it by the good acting of Miss Dove. *Harrison's Reports* 11/30/29.

A Notorious Affair: Billie Dove plots hardly vary the traditional .005 of an inch. This one is too careless to be accepted even by admirers of Miss Dove even though her acting is good. And she is a beautiful woman. *Variety* 4/30/30, *Harrison's Reports* 5/3/30.

Sweethearts and Wives: Dove carries the picture and gives it what small entertainment value it has. The progress of this engaging actress has been severely hampered with poor scenarios and hurried product. *Variety* 7/2/30.

The Lady Who Dared: Instead of reviving Billie Dove's career, poor lighting shows her to disadvantage and her performance is limp and lifeless. *Variety* 6/9/31, *Harrison's Reports* 6/13/31.

The Age for Love: Everybody makes mistakes and this is one by Howard Hughes. Billie Dove,

noted for her beauty in the silent picture days, is minus much of that attractiveness and her acting is taut and mechanical. *Variety* 11/17/31, *Harrison's Reports* 11/21/31.

Cock of the Air: It drags out so that at times it appears the stars, in making it, were anything but inspired. *Variety* 1/26/32.

Blondie of the Follies: Her rather unsympathetic role is a departure for Miss Dove but she makes the transition without effort and turns in a good performance. *Harrison's Reports* 9/10/32, *Variety* 9/13/32.

Dresser, Louise (Louise Kerlin), Evansville, Indiana, 1878/82–1965

Silent: Nineteen twenty-two was the year Louise Dresser made her film debut after a singing career in vaudeville and in the theater. Her earlier films included *The Glory of Clementina*, *Prodigal Daughters* and *Cheap Kisses*. She was a supporting actress until the title role in *The Goose Woman* (1925) made her a minor star. That same year, she also had a showy role as the Empress of Russia in Valentino's *The Eagle*.

Among Dresser's films were *Ruggles of Red Gap* (1923 version), *Broken Hearts of Hollywood*, *Mr. Wu*, *Fifth Avenue*, *The Garden of Eden*, *White Flannels*, *The Next Corner*, *Enticement* and *Padlocked*. Although she was top-billed in a few films and was usually high up in cast lists, she basically remained a character actress. Last silent: *A Ship Comes In* (1928).

Sound: Dresser appeared in three part-talkies in a row, two in 1928 and one in '29. The first, *The Air Circus*, in which she had top billing, was followed by *Mother Knows Best* in which she played the title role. After 1929's *Not Quite Decent* (top-billed), she made her all-talkie debut in *The Madonna of Avenue A*.

In the '30s, Dresser's appearances were relatively few, although she made several films with Will Rogers, sometimes as his wife and at least once as his sister. These, now probably her best-known pictures, included *Doctor Bull*, *The County Chairman*, *David Harum*, *Lightnin'* and *State Fair*. Among her other films were *Mammy* (the mother of Al Jolson), *This Mad World*, *Caught*, *The Cradle Song*, *The World Moves On* and her last in 1937, *Maid of Salem*.

Comments: Louise Dresser received her stage name in a rather unusual way. Songwriter Paul Dresser, brother of novelist Theodore Dreiser, heard her sing one of his songs and befriended her. He then claimed she was his younger sister in order to further her career.

Because she was middle-aged at the time of her

screen debut, Louise Dresser inevitably was cast in mother roles, sometimes sweet and sometimes not. Her performances could have a hard edge to them which was perfect for roles such as wily Catherine the Great in *The Eagle* and Will Rogers's nagging wife, a somewhat thankless characterization she shared with Irene Rich.

Dresser's career decline was steep in the 1930s. Although she came from the stage, her speaking voice was somewhat flat, redolent of her native Midwest. It is not likely, however, that this was much of a determining factor. Her time had simply passed.

REVIEWS

Mother Knows Best: Dresser's speaking voice will never get her anywhere in the talkies unless they can improve it, or if her acting skills make her presence necessary. *Variety* 9/19/28.

Not Quite Decent: As the mother, Louise Dresser injects human interest and good acting into her role. Her performance magnifies the threadbare story. *Variety* 5/8/29, *Harrison's Reports* 5/11/29.

Mammy: Dresser is always great, and she doesn't have to play mother roles either. *Variety* 4/2/30.

Song of the Eagle: Louise Dresser speaks with an accent and builds up intense sympathetic interest. *Variety* 5/2/33.

Dressler, Marie (Leila Koerber), Cobourg, Ontario, 1869–1934

Filmography: *Classic Film Collector* (Summer 1972), including a stageography of U.S. and U.K. stage appearances; *Focus on Film* (Spring 1976)

Silent: Although Marie Dressler was one of the country's major film stars during the last few years of her life, she was primarily a theater performer for most of her career. From 1886's *Under Two Flags* to 1923 she appeared in musicals and comedies, becoming a star with *The Lady Slavey* in 1896.

Dressler also was in *The Mikado* and played Mrs. Malaprop in *The Rivals*; one of her biggest hits, *Tillie's Nightmare*, was the vehicle for her first film, *Tillie's Punctured Romance* (1914). Although she was the nominal star, it was also the first full-length film of both Charlie Chaplin and Mabel Normand.

Dressler followed the first "Tillie" film with *Tillie's Tomato Surprise* and *Tillie Wakes Up*. She also appeared in a few others in the 'teens, including *The Scrub Lady*. Nearly ten years passed before she returned for supporting roles in *The Joy Girl* and *Breakfast at Sunrise* (1927). During that time she may have made some one- or two-reelers in Europe.

Dressler was top-billed in her first MGM film, 1927's *The Callahans and the Murphys*, her first

teaming with raucous comedienne Polly Moran. The picture was prematurely withdrawn because of opposition from the Irish community to its stereotyped portrayals. Others included *Bringing Up Father*, in which she again appeared with Moran, and *The Patsy*. Last silent: *The Divine Lady* (1929), technically a silent though it contained singing sequences.

Sound: Dressler's first features in 1929 were *The Vagabond Lover*, Rudy Vallee's ill-starred screen debut, and *The Hollywood Revue of 1929* in which she sang several times and otherwise cavorted. She also rejoined Polly Moran in the short *Dangerous Females*.

Nineteen thirty proved to be Dressler's breakthrough year. Not only did she appear in seven films, including *Chasing Rainbows*, and *Let Us Be Gay*, but she gave Greta Garbo a run for her money in the latter's sound debut *Anna Christie*. Most importantly, she won the Academy Award for Best Actress in *Min and Bill* with Wallace Beery, thus establishing herself as a top star.

Despite the honor she had attained, not all of Dressler's remaining films were of the highest quality, certainly not her 1930–32 reteamings with Moran in *Caught Short*, *Reducing*, *Politics* and *Prosperity*. These featured much bickering and physical humor, with the short, feisty Moran usually getting the worst of the exchanges.

There were also the prestigious *Emma*, *Tugboat Annie* and *Dinner at Eight*, an all-star ensemble film that provided Dressler with one of her best roles as the wise old actress and the memorable tag line as well. From 1932 to the time of her death she was Number One at the box office. Her last film was *Christopher Bean* (1933).

Comments: Marie Dressler proved that nonyoung, non-pretty and non-thin actresses could reach the very pinnacle of their profession. It has rarely been true since so perhaps she was the exception that proved the rule. The root of her great popularity, besides her endearing personality, seemed to be her convincing portrayal of ordinary people with rough edges but proverbial hearts of gold.

Despite her characters' crustiness, Dressler projected decency and sweetness of character. Perhaps it was just acting but audiences seemed to believe it was true of the real person. Given the rocky life's experiences that shaped her, she was no doubt genuinely empathetic to those less fortunate.

Dressler's distinguished stage career had begun to languish when she reached the age of 50 or so. She had been so down-and-out at one point that she considered, or so the story goes, a job as a housekeeper. Rescued at the proverbial last minute, she showed what a trouper she really was. She also became a favorite of the society crowd.

Although possessing talent and a voice which perfectly suited her screen image, Dressler could be, figuratively speaking, larger than life on the screen. She had a tendency to mug, which it took a strong director to curtail. She also could and did steal scenes right and left, although in co-star Wallace Beery she met her match, as she did with Chaplin in her first film.

She was well beloved by her peers. On giving Marie Dressler her Academy Award, Norma Shearer called her "the grandest trouper of them all, the grand old war-horse of the screen." Despite a possible unfortunate choice of words in calling the portly Dressler a "war-horse," it summed up the feelings of the film community. On her death, Harold Lloyd said of her: "She was the greatest comedienne of this generation. She made age a beautiful thing on the screen. Her artistry will be her monument."

REVIEWS

The Vagabond Lover: Marie Dressler is the heart of this picture. The veteran comedienne is all over the screen. She keeps the audience roaring. It is doubtful if she has ever appeared to better advantage. *Variety* 12/4/29, *Harrison's Reports* 12/7/29.

Anna Christie: Dressler overacts occasionally but most of her performance is exceptionally clever. It is far and away her outstanding film characterization. She steps out of her usual slapstick and performs with an affecting and genuine pathos, accomplishing the unusual feat of drawing applause at the finish of a scene. (As "Marthy" she was but one of the experienced character actors with which MGM surrounded Garbo in her long-awaited sound debut ["Garbo Talks!"].) *New York Times* 3/15/30, *Variety* 3/19/30.

Min and Bill: No other actress anywhere could have played Dressler's role convincingly. She is excellent. *Variety* 11/26/30, *Harrison's Reports* 11/29/30.

Politics: When Marie Dressler and Polly Moran get together there usually is lots of laughter and this is no exception to the rule. *Harrison's Reports* 8/8/31.

Tugboat Annie: The combination of Marie Dressler and Wallace Beery is almost enough to assure entertainment even with a mediocre story. Both players are excellent; they provide the audience with many laughs and tears. *Variety* 8/15/33, *Harrison's Reports* 8/19/33.

Dinner at Eight: Although this is an atypical role for Dressler she handles the assignment with poise and aplomb that would be hard to match. This veteran trouper would probably do a trapeze act if called upon. *Variety* 8/29/33, *Harrison's Reports* 9/22/33.

Christopher Bean: Marie Dressler is tremendously popular, but this is not one of her outstanding roles. *Variety* 11/28/33.

Du Brey, Claire (also DuBrey, DuBray, Dubrey; Clara?), Bonner's Ferry, Idaho, 1892/93–1993

Silent: As the story goes, Claire Du Brey was a young New York matron when she answered a call for "society" types to appear in Thomas Ince productions. She was cast in dramas but also found herself in westerns, including a series of two-reelers with Harry Carey. Eventually, because she was tall and dark, she played "vamp" roles.

Nineteen seventeen to 1922 were Du Brey's busiest years on the screen in supporting roles and second leads and she sometimes made ten films in a year. Among her pictures during that period were *The Piper's Price, Triumph, Madame Spy, Up Romance Road, The Spite Bride, Life's Twist, My Lady's Latchkey* and *When Love Comes.*

From 1923 Du Brey appeared in only ten more silents, including the popular *Ponjola, The Sea Hawk* and *The Voice from the Minaret.* Some others were *Drusilla with a Million, Miss Nobody* and *Infatuation.* By this time she was well down in the cast lists. Last silent: *Two Sisters* (1929), with synchronized music.

Sound: Du Brey's first talkie was 1930's *For the Love o'Lil,* in which she played a small part. This set the pattern for the remainder of her talkie career, which extended well into the 1950s and perhaps beyond.

Rather acerbic-looking by the 1930s, Du Brey appeared as a bit and supporting player from 1933 (e.g., the duenna in Gene Autry's *South of the Border;* a red herring murder suspect in *Abbott and Costello Meet the Killer, Boris Karloff*).

Among Du Brey's other numerous films were *Shadows of Sing Sing, Jane Eyre, Ramona, Five of a Kind, Jesse James, Four Wives* and *The Shop Around the Corner.*

Dunn, Josephine (Mary J. Dunn), New York, New York, 1906–1983

Silent: Blonde and beautiful Josephine Dunn was given a contract after "graduation" from the Paramount School of Acting. An alumna of Broadway musicals, she made her film debut in *Fascinating Youth* (1926). Her other silents included *Swim, Girl, Swim, She's a Sheik, We Americans, Excess Baggage, Fireman, Save My Child* and *The Sorrows of Satan.* Last silent: *Our Modern Maidens* (1929), with synchronized music and sound effects, made after her first talkie.

Sound: Of the ten films Dunn made in 1929, the year she was named a Wampas Baby Star, about half were sound. They included *Melody Lane*, *Red Hot Rhythm* and *Big Time*. Her first talkie had been Al Jolson's phenomenally successful *The Singing Fool* in 1928.

Among Dunn's other films were *Safety in Numbers*, *Madonna of the Streets*, *Big City Blues*, *One Hour with You* and *Between Fighting Men*. She made only one film each in 1933 and '34 and then returned for a small role in the pseudo-documentary *The Birth of a Baby* (1938). In the meantime she had gone back to the stage.

Comments: Josephine Dunn could portray iciness well and she was typecast in that mode, most memorably as the uncaring wife of Al Jolson in *The Singing Fool*. As her sound career went on, she was given some sizable roles in poor films and small roles in better ones (e.g., Lubitsch's *One Hour with You*, in which she was nearly invisible).

When Dunn played the occasional heroine in a "B" quickie, she was generally thought to be unconvincing. This was no way to sustain a career and Broadway was where she returned to have one.

REVIEWS

The Singing Fool: Josephine Dunn doesn't talk so well and she looked pretty steely-hearted, even for a blonde. *Variety* 9/26/28, *Harrison's Reports* 10/13/28.

Air Police: Dunn is the heroine but she is not much seen and she appears to be miscast. *Variety* 4/29/31.

Two Kinds of Women: Josephine Dunn is amusing as the harmless paramour of a racketeer. *New York Times* 1/16/32.

Murder at Dawn: Dunn is out of her element as the heroine. *Variety* 4/5/32.

Big City Blues: The cast is full of standard film names and most of them are confined to brief bits, an example is the established ingenue Josephine Dunn. She does nothing but act stewed and pose on a couch. *Variety* 9/13/32.

Durfee, Minta, Los Angeles, California,
1897–1975

Silent: Beginning as a showgirl, red-haired Minta Durfee was the wife of popular Roscoe "Fatty" Arbuckle. The comic actress appeared with her husband and with Charlie Chaplin in many of their earliest Sennett one-reelers including the latter's first, *Making a Living* (1914), and *Caught in a Cabaret*, *His New Profession* and *The New Janitor*, among others.

Between 1913 and 1917, Durfee made hundreds of one- and two-reelers or; among them appearances with the Keystone Kops and Weber and Fields. She is credited by some as being the first person to take a pie in the face on-screen, although this is probably unprovable.

Durfee apparently was in only two silent features, the first being the first version of *Tillie's Punctured Romance* (1914). Last silent feature: *Mickey*, released in 1918 but completed much earlier.

Sound: Durfee returned to play numerous small and bit roles, off and on, from the early 1940s in films that included *The Man with Nine Lives* and *Rollin' Home to Texas*. Among her later efforts were *Funny Girl*, *Way ... Way Out*, *Hello Dolly*, *They Shoot Horses Don't They?*, *The Unsinkable Molly Brown*, *The Fortune Cookie* and *The Odd Couple*.

Durfee was also seen much on television. Although she and Arbuckle had separated at the time of his sex scandal in the early '20s, she spent much of her later life in a single-minded quest to prove his innocence.

Dwan, Dorothy (Dorothy Smith?),
1907–1970

Filmography: List of films in *Sweethearts of the Sage*

Silent: After her 1922 debut in *The Silent Vow*, Dorothy Dwan made over 25 films, a few of them with (and by) her husband, comedian Larry Semon; these included *The Perfect Clown*, *The Wizard of Oz* and *Spuds*. The major part of her career was spent in westerns in support of such stars as Tom Mix and Ken Maynard. She was also one of Rin Tin Tin's "leading ladies."

There were also roles in melodramas like *Sinners in Silk* and *Perils of the Coast Guard* as well as other films like *McFadden's Flats* and *Obey Your Husband*. All of Dwan's 1929 films were silents. Last silent: *The Peacock Fan* (1929).

Sound: Dorothy Dwan appeared in but a single talkie, *The Fighting Legion*, a Ken Maynard western for Universal.

REVIEWS

The Fighting Legion: Dorothy Dwan is the heroine of this thrilling western. *Harrison's Reports* 4/5/30.

Eddy, Helen Jerome, New York, New York,
1897–1990

Silent: Plain-faced Helen Jerome Eddy played generally high-class ladies in film from 1915's *The Gentleman from Indiana* through the remainder of the silent era. Along with occasional leads and co-starring stints she alternated supporting roles, sometimes small ones. Among her early films were *The Code of Marcia Gray, Redeeming Love, The Fair Barbarian, Rebecca of Sunnybrook Farm* and *Breakers Ahead.*

In the 1920s, Eddy was usually near the top of cast lists providing solid support to such films as *The Fire Patrol, The Other Woman, To the Ladies, The Dark Angel, Camille* and *13 Washington Square.* Last silents: *Blue Skies*, with synchronized music and sound effects, and *The Divine Lady*, technically a silent but with singing sequences, released about the same time in 1929.

Sound: In the talkies, many of Eddy's parts were small but she remained a reliable character actress in films like *Midstream*, her first part-talkie in 1929, *War Nurse, Mata Hari, No Greater Love* and *The Bitter Tea of General Yen*, in which she had virtually a single scene as matron in a Chinese orphan asylum.

Eddy also appeared in the 1930 Vitaphone shorts *Christmas Knight* and *Niagara Falls*. Among her other features through 1940, apparently the last year she appeared before the camera, were *Riptide, The Garden of Allah, City Streets, Mr. Smith Goes to Washington* and, possibly her final one, *Strike Up the Band.*

Reviews

Midstream: Eddy is worthy of favorable mention for the manner in which she plays a minor role. *Variety* 9/18/29.

War Nurse: Helen Jerome Eddy stands out above the other women. *Variety* 10/29/30.

Edeson, Robert, New Orleans, Louisiana, 1868–1931

Silent: A veteran of the theater, Robert Edeson appeared in over 100 features and two-reelers beginning about 1914. Among his first were *The Call of the North* and *Where the Trail Divides*. He was the hero of action melodramas before assuming character roles in the 1920s, including several in the DeMille films *The Ten Commandments, Feet of Clay, The King of Kings* and *The Golden Bed.*

Among Edeson's other films were *Eyes of Youth, The Spoilers* (1923 version), *The Danger Signal, Eve's Leaves* and *Keep Smiling*. Last silent: *George Washington Cohen* (1928), made after his first talkie.

Sound: Edeson's first sound film was the part-talkie *The Little Wildcat* (1928). All of his 1929 films were talkies, among them *Little Johnny Jones, Dynamite* and *Marianne*, Marion Davies's first essay into sound. He continued on in supporting roles, sometimes small, until the time of his death.

Also among Edeson's films were *Cameo Kirby* (1930 version), *A Devil with Women, The Way of All Men, The Doctor's Secret* (title role), *Dynamite, Pardon My Gun, Big Money* and *Aloha*, his ironically-titled swan song.

Reviews

The Doctor's Secret: Robert Edeson takes full advantage of his part and is a splendid choice for this role. He is always thinking of his role and what's being said by the other players. *New York Times* 2/4/29, *Variety* 2/6/29, *Harrison's Reports* 2/9/29.

Danger Lights: Well acted by Robert Edeson. *Harrison's Reports* 9/13/30.

Edwards, Neely (Cornelius Limbach), Delphi, Ohio, 1875/89–1957

Silent: Before his film bow, Neely Edwards had a varied career in vaudeville, burlesque and other stage pursuits. With his partner Ed Flanagan he developed the "Hall Room Boys" act which they brought to the two-reelers in 1919. He remained with the series until 1921 (all told there were almost 80 entries to 1923) and also began his feature career in 1920's *You Never Can Tell.*

Mustachioed with slicked-back hair, Edwards played some solid supporting roles in a relatively few full-length pictures in the 1920s, among them *Brewster's Millions* (one of Fatty Arbuckle's few released features), *The Green Temptation, I'll Show You the Town, Footloose Widows* and *The Princess on Broadway*. Last silent: *Excess Baggage* (1928), with synchronized music and sound effects.

Sound: The 1928 Vitaphone short *Hollywood Bound* may have marked Neely Edwards's sound debut. Nineteen twenty-nine's *Show Boat*, a part-talker, was his feature sound bow but he may not have appeared in the talking portion. Others that year were both fully sound: *Gold Diggers of Broadway* and *Dynamite.*

Edwards's sole full-length 1930 movie was *Scarlet Pages*, and that year he was in the Vitaphone short *Her Relatives*. The size of his feature parts was beginning to diminish by this time and in the '30s he was seen in relatively few, including *Okay America, Diplomaniacs, Gold Diggers of 1933, Broadway Melody of 1936, Sutter's Gold* and *Mr. Moto in Danger Island.*

There were very scattered appearances in the following decade for Neely Edwards, among them *Sin Town, Strictly in the Groove* and *George White's Scandals*. He found his true *métier* appearing for almost 30 years in the long-running Los Angeles stage production of the old-time melodrama *The Drunkard.*

Eilers, Sally (Dorothea S. Eilers), New York, New York, 1908–1978

Filmography: *Hollywood Players: The Thirties*; List of films in *Sweethearts of the Sage*; Academy of Motion Picture Arts and Sciences

Silent: Nineteen twenty-eight Wampas Baby Star Sally Eilers made her debut in Pathe shorts and small roles about 1927; her earliest features were *Slightly Used*, *Sunrise* and *Dry Martini*. She was Mack Sennett's last major female star and her first lead came in his *The Good-bye Kiss* in 1928. Last silent: *Trial Marriage* (1929), with synchronized music and sound effects.

Sound: The first of Eilers's sound films was *Broadway Babies* in 1929. Other pictures that year were *The Show of Shows*, *Sailor's Holiday* and Hoot Gibson's first talkie *The Long, Long Trail*. She continued to be a dependable lead in second features for Fox and Universal, frequently teamed with James Dunn, and an occasional lead and supporting player in major films throughout the '30s.

In later years Eilers was seen in supporting roles in a very few films until her last, *Stage to Tucson*, in 1951. She is probably best remembered for 1931's popular *Bad Girl*, but little she did subsequently lived up to that promise.

Other Eilers films included *Roaring Ranch*, *Quick Millions*, *State Fair*, *Carnival*, *Remember Last Night?*, *Florida Special*, *Strike Me Pink*, *Condemned Women*, *They Made Her a Spy*, *Central Airport*, *Strange Illusion* and *Coroner Creek*.

REVIEWS

Broadway Babies: Sally Eilers handles well the little she has to do. *Variety* 6/26/29.

Dough Boys: Eilers looks good and acts sweetly. *Variety* 9/24/30.

Bad Girl: Eilers's performance will surprise the film industry by its workmanship. She makes the central character ring true and look good. *Variety* 8/18/31.

Central Airport: Eilers acts quite well in a tough part but her voice is somewhat husky. *New York Times* 5/4/33, *Variety* 5/9/33.

Alias Mary Dow: Sally Eilers, whether directed to do it or not, arouses less sympathetic interest than her part may have intended. She is a bit too much the street tough and never gives an outstanding performance. *Variety* 7/3/35.

Coroner Creek: Sally Eilers does well by a character that is not too clearly defined. *Variety* 6/9/48.

Elliott, Gordon ("Wild Bill"; Gordon Nance) Pattonsburg, Missouri, 1902/03–1965

Filmography: List of films in *Films in Review* (June-July 1969), added films (Aug.-Sept. 1969)

Silent: An extra and bit player from about 1925, Gordon Elliott began receiving billing in 1927 in supporting roles and second leads. Among his films were *The Plastic Age*, *Napoleon, Jr.*, *Arizona Wildcat*, *The Private Life of Helen of Troy* and *Beyond London Lights*. Last silent: *Restless Youth* (1928).

Sound: The 1929 musical *Broadway Scandals* was Elliott's first; he was way down the cast list. He continued to play supporting roles through most of the 1930s in such films as *Crooner*, *The Case of the Howling Dog*, *Bullets or Ballots*, *Wonder Bar*, *The Case of the Velvet Claws* and *Wife, Doctor and Nurse*.

Elliott apparently also appeared as a dance extra during his stint at Warner Bros. in the mid-'30s and in an occasional western, sometimes as a villain. His luck — and his Christian name — changed in 1938 with his leading role in the serial *The Great Adventures of Wild Bill Hickok*. Its popularity led him to adopt the sobriquet as his own and it also led to a starring western series, the first of which was *In Early Arizona* the same year.

Elliott's western career flourished as he teamed with Tex Ritter in a series in 1941–42 and then he became a Columbia star with *Calling Wild Bill Elliott* in 1943. Other serials included *Overland with Kit Carson* and *Valley of Vanishing Men*.

Possibly the role with which "Wild Bill" Elliott became most identified was that of Red Ryder, whom he first played in *Tucson Raiders* (1944), the first of more than 15 Ryder films. His co-star, as Little Beaver, was the former "Our Gang" kid Bobby Blake (real name: Michael "Mickey" Gubitosi), later film and TV star Robert Blake.

Elliott made the first of his "A" westerns, *In Old Sacramento*, in 1946. It was about this time that "Wild Bill" became William, the name he used for the decade remaining in his career. In 1951, toward the end of the era of "B" westerns, he went to Monogram where his pictures predictably became more cheaply produced.

Eventually Elliott signed with Allied Artists for his last films, a series of hard-boiled detective melodramas beginning with *Dial Red O*. His final effort was 1957's *Footsteps in the Night*.

Comments: Gordon Elliott was your basic slicked-back hair, pretty-boy actor for much of his early career, and that career was not highly successful in terms of leading roles. His voice was an authoritative baritone, and as he aged during the course of his western career his face hardened interestingly. This finally made his roles more convincing.

Elliott downplayed the singing cowboy slickness then popular in the western films of Roy Rogers and Gene Autry to return to the more "realistic" heroes of the early silents. He was sometimes compared to William S. Hart in the relative grittiness of his pictures. It is likely that his career was extended because of it.

REVIEWS

Taming of the West: Elliott plays a type likely to become quite popular. He's more along the line of William S. Hart and somewhat of a slugger. *Variety* 10/11/39.

In Old Sacramento: Elliott makes his bow as a more substantial romantic figure. He is physically perfect, being tall and lean with a strong chin and voice of deep masculine timbre. His acting is a bit uncertain, with stiffness visible in some spots. *Variety* 5/1/46.

Waco: Elliott paces himself excellently and shows up well. *Variety* 2/27/52.

Calling Homicide: The name of Bill Elliott will carry it through as a follow-up to past entries with the same character. He shows to good advantage. *Variety* 10/17/56.

Ellis, Robert, Brooklyn, New York, 1892–1935

Silent: As well as being a popular matinee idol, Robert Ellis was also a director but that was to come a bit later. He came to the cinema about 1917, following a stage career, and appeared for MGM and other studios.

Among Ellis's films were *Brown of Harvard* (1917 version), *The Lifted Veil, A Fool and His Money, A Tailor Made Man, Mark of the Beast, Lady Robinhood, The Girl from Montmartre* and *Speed.* Last silent: *Restless Youth* (1928).

Sound: Ellis's premiere part-talkie was *Varsity* (1928). All of his 1929 pictures were full or part-talkies, including *Broadway, Tonight at Twelve, The Love Trap* and *Night Parade.* His sound career began with leads but he soon found himself playing supporting roles to the time of his death.

Among Ellis's generally unworthy films were *Undertow, Aloha, The Fighting Sheriff, Daring Danger, The Constant Woman, Thrill Hunter, Kid Millions* and *Hard Rock Harrigan.*

NOTE: Ellis's credits often contain those of a screenwriter of the same name (also known as Robert Reel Ellis) but they are two different people.

REVIEWS

Broadway: Robert Ellis as the bootlegger heavy supplies realism and is good in his part. *Variety* 5/29/29, *Harrison's Reports* 6/8/29.

The Night Parade: Ellis, as the villain in a minor role, rounds out a good cast. *Variety* 11/13/29, *Harrison's Reports* 11/16/29.

What Men Want: Robert Ellis's acting is artistic. *Harrison's Reports* 8/23/30.

Evans, Madge (Margherita Evans), New York, New York, 1909–1981

Filmography: Film Fan Monthly (Dec. 1972-Jan. 1973)

Silent: Prior to her film debut at World, Madge Evans was a child model and actress dubbed "The Loveliest Baby in America." She went on to make over 35 silent films in the East from 1915–19 including *Zaza, Husband and Wife, Sudden Riches, Maternity, The Gates of Gladness* and *The Love Net.*

Barely into her teen years, Evans went to California in 1921 and 1922 for two pictures shot in the experimental Prizma color process and then made two more films in 1923 and '24. Last silent: *Classmates* (1924).

Sound: Madge Evans's introduction to sound were several Vitaphone shorts, among which were *Many Happy Returns, The Riding Master, Envy* and *The Bard of Broadway.* After being signed by MGM, she made her sound feature debut in *Son of India* (1931).

Among Evans's better-known films were *Dinner at Eight* and *David Copperfield.* Others of her almost 40 talkies were *Guilty Hands, The Greeks Had a Word for Them, Hallelujah, I'm a Bum!, Moonlight Murder* and *Sinners in Paradise.* Her final film was 1938's *Army Girl.*

Comments: Madge Evans retained her serene beauty as an adult and her stage-trained voice was certainly an advantage. In MGM films she generally provided pretty window dressing and usually was given smaller roles in major films. Most of her leads came on loan-out to other studios.

Despite her obvious assets, Evans did not provide a strong screen presence in talkies and eventually her career dwindled into "B" films. She returned to the theater which undoubtedly appreciated her talents more and in which she could showcase aspects of her personality that the studios did not allow her to show.

REVIEWS

Son of India: The feminine lead is played in a passable manner by Madge Evans, who is sweet in a frail blonde way and who in her lightheadedness seemed shallow. *Variety* 7/28/31.

Huddle: Evans has a fairly easy time of it in pursuing Ramon Novarro through the story. *Variety* 6/21/32.

Hallelujah, I'm a Bum!: Evans, as the sincere and saccharine leading lady to Al Jolson, was well suited to that role. *Variety* 2/14/33.

Dinner at Eight: Madge Evans gives her role a perfunctory reading. *Variety* 8/29/33.

Calm Yourself: Evans is more animated than is customary. *Variety* 7/31/35.

Espionage: Madge Evans gives a good performance and does all she can to make the picture entertaining. *Harrison's Reports* 3/20/37.

Eyton, Bessie (Bessie Harrison), Santa Barbara, California, 1890–?

Filmography: List of films in *Sweethearts of the Sage*

Silent: Often teamed with Tom Santschi, Bessie Eyton was a star from about 1911 with Selig. One of her best-known films was *The Spoilers* (1914); others included *The Fifth Man, Playing with Fire, The Fork in the Road, The Smoldering Spark, Twisted Trails* and *Who Shall Take My Life?*

Eyton's career declined in the late teens and she appeared in only a few afterwards, including 1924's *Cheap Kisses.* Last silent: *The Girl of Gold* (1925) is the final silent in which Eyton was billed. She may have appeared in others in bit or extra roles.

Sound: It is fairly well accepted that Eyton did appear in some sound films but her work consisted of bits and extra work, and the specific films are not known with complete certainty.

Comments: Although the red-haired Eyton was a minor star in silents, her appearances could not compete with a real-life mystery; i.e., her complete *disappearance* after 1935. For film fans it is the most intriguing facet of her life.

Eyton apparently left home after an argument and was never heard of again by her family. Nor were those film buffs who are often successful in tracking down errant celebrities, and eager to track down obscure ones like Bessie Eyton, able to do so.

Fairbanks, Douglas (Douglas Ulman), Denver, Colorado, 1883–1939

Filmography: *8mm Collector* (Fall-Winter 1965); *Classic Film Collector* (Summer 1967); *Focus on Film* (Winter 1970); *Films and Filming* (May 1973); *Films in Review* (May 1976); List of films in *Film Dope* (Sept. 1978)

Silent: A successful stage star, Douglas Fairbanks was offered a large sum of money to appear in films the first of which was *The Lamb* (1915) for Triangle. He made numerous comedy-adventures in which he generally portrayed brash young men successfully overcoming adversity. Many of his pictures also showcased his athletic prowess.

Fairbanks founded his own film company in 1917 and continued to turn out successful films like *Reggie Mixes In, Manhattan Madness, The Matrimaniac, He Comes Up Smiling, Mr. Fix-It, Wild and Woolly* and *Say, Young Fellow!.* He also appeared in a few 1918 split-reelers made for the purpose of selling war bonds.

Later Fairbanks comedies like *The Mollycoddle* and *When the Clouds Roll By* might be termed transitional in that they had grown more lavish and contained considerable acrobatics. They foreshadowed the first of his big-scale, big-budget films, *The Mark of Zorro* (1920).

One more of the small comedies, *The Nut*, was made after it but from then on Fairbanks was seen in only seven films through 1929, all swashbucklers. They included *The Three Musketeers, Robin Hood, The Thief of Bagdad, Don Q, Son of Zorro* and *The Black Pirate.* His acrobatic derring-do in these pictures made him one of the most celebrated men in the entire world.

The famous Doug Fairbanks acrobatics were carefully planned to the last detail for the actor, who was not very tall. The tables and other furniture over which he so easily jumped were scaled to the exact size needed to make his movements look effortless. Some of his leaps were filmed in slow motion to accentuate his movements.

Trampolines aided Fairbanks's heroics as well as camouflaged handholds constructed in walls. Doubles were used as needed although this was kept hidden. One of his most memorable, albeit carefully staged, stunts was the descent down a huge ship sail on the point of a dagger in *The Black Pirate.* Last starring silent: *The Gaucho* (1928); his last actual silent film appearance was the briefest of cameos in *Show People* (1928).

Sound: *The Iron Mask* (1929) was primarily a silent film but it had at least one talking sequence along with its synchronized music and sound effects. Fairbanks's first full-talkie was *The Taming of the Shrew* co-starring his wife Mary Pickford. It was not a happy experience for either of them and probably set the filming of Shakespeare back a few years. Its celebrated and presumptuous credit "By William Shakespeare, with additional dialogue by Sam Taylor" is still being quoted more than 65 years later.

Although his voice was perfectly acceptable, talkies did not seem to be the aging Fairbanks's medium. He made only a few more pictures. Two of them, *Mr. Robinson Crusoe* and *Around the World in Eighty Minutes*, were as much travelogue as drama, especially the latter. The others were *Reaching for the Moon*, probably his best talkie, in 1931 and his last, the English-made and poorly-received *The Private Life of Don Juan* (1934).

Comments: The story goes that when Douglas Fairbanks was offered his Triangle Film contract, he was reminded that he would be making over $100,000 a year. He is supposed to have said, "I know, but the *movies.*" It is obvious that somewhere along the way he came to terms with them, and they enabled him to become a worldwide icon along with Mary Pickford.

Fairbanks's pre–1920 persona was the "all–American boy," despite the fact that he was 31 when he began. His characters succeeded by sheer American luck-and-pluck. He even wrote — or more likely had ghost-written for him — a column and several books on the same theme which were possibly some of the earliest examples of pop psychology.

Fairbanks's elaborately produced 1920s films were basically glossy extensions of the same theme, albeit his portrayals were generally not of Americans. In reality, of course, Fairbanks was the "King" to Mary Pickford's "Queen" of Hollywood society. His natural inclinations were snobbish and geared toward the rich and preferably aristocratic.

Also a shrewd businessman, Fairbanks was one of the founders of United Artists along with Pickford, D. W. Griffith and his great and good friend Charlie Chaplin. Attention to the bottom line was not the only difference between his off- and on-screen personas. In public always exuberant and cheerful, in private he could be moody, suspicious and insecure.

His true personality was not known to the legions of Doug Fairbanks fans. As long as he continued to display that inimitable panache on the screen, they flocked to his offerings. That came to an end with the talkies, but perhaps the new technology only hastened the decline that had already begun.

Fairbanks was aging and tiring even though he made a public show of maintaining his physical fitness. The social upheavals of the 1930s probably would have made his style of film less popular anyway. Although his theater-trained voice was more than adequate, his talkies simply lack the fire of his silents. In other words, he could talk but did not particularly want to. His usual ebullience seems forced and dispirited.

Truth to tell, his last few sound films were unworthy and lazily made. The fun seems to have gone out of filmmaking for him and the heart may have gone out of him as well. His marriage to "America's Sweetheart" also had turned unhappy. There was strife when he and Pickford made *The Taming of the Shrew*, although accounts of it have been reported largely through her eyes.

His wife's storied perfectionism apparently annoyed Fairbanks and he was sulky and difficult on the set, refusing to do retakes, for instance. Nevertheless, he came out of that experience with more credit than she, her performance generally being less well thought of.

When all is said and done, Douglas Fairbanks was a superstar and is one of the cinema's most enduring legends. He brought undeniable charisma and charm to the screen throughout most of his career. There have been many imitators in the years that followed but never any real equals. Surely the vision of his confidently mischievous smile flashing in that swarthily handsome, mustachioed face is one of the lasting images of silent films.

REVIEWS

The Taming of the Shrew: It's worth the price of admission to see Mary Pickford and Douglas Fairbanks do this kind of stuff. *Variety* 12/4/29, *Harrison's Reports* 12/7/29.

Reaching for the Moon: This is not a typical Fairbanks yarn. He looks to be in splendid shape and he doesn't have to fear a microphone. If given a suitable script he can continue to be a box office factor. *Variety* 1/7/31, *Harrison's Reports* 1/10/31.

Around the World in Eighty Minutes: It has only the face and voice of Douglas Fairbanks running through it to lend distinction. He enlivens much of the drab footage with his acrobatics. *Variety* 11/24/31, *Harrison's Reports* 11/28/31.

Mr. Robinson Crusoe: The talk sustaining the action is practically a 70-minute monologue by Fairbanks. Although his style is breezy and his chatter satisfying, there is too much dependence on unsuitable gags. To a certain degree it is amusing to watch him. *Variety* 9/27/32, *Harrison's Reports* 10/1/32.

The Private Life of Don Juan: The story is inane, parts of it are exceedingly vulgar and Fairbanks's acting is uninspired. (A presumed satire of a middle-aged man's desire to reclaim his youth by conquering young women. Perhaps an unconscious farewell to Fairbanks's own long-gone youth?) *Harrison's Reports* 11/24/34.

Fairbanks, Douglas, Jr. (Douglas Ulman, Jr.), New York, New York, 1909–

Filmography: List of films in *Film Dope* (Sept. 1978); *Films and Filming* (Sept. 1976, Jan. 1985)

Silent: Douglas Fairbanks, Jr., was top-billed in his very first film, 1923's *Stephen Steps Out*, but it was not a success. His next pictures came in 1925; among them were *Wild Horse Mesa* and *The Air Mail*. That year's major hit *Stella Dallas* was probably his best silent film although his role was not a large one.

Fairbanks remained busy through the rest of the silent era, often portraying callow playboys in generally lesser films like *Broken Hearts of Hollywood*, *A Texas Steer*, *Padlocked*, *Women Love Diamonds* and *Is Zat So?* Last silent: *Our Modern Maidens* (1929), with synchronized music and sound effects, made after his first talkies.

Sound: Fairbanks came into his own as a youthful leading man in 1929. His maiden part-talkie had been *The Barker* (1928) and all his subsequent films but one had some dialogue. Nineteen thirty's *The Dawn Patrol* was his best movie to that point.

The remainder of the 1930s saw Fairbanks in such worthy efforts as *The Prisoner of Zenda* (his first swashbuckler and a villain role), *Gunga Din*, *Morning Glory*, *Little Caesar* and *Catherine the Great*, for which he received an Academy Award nomination. He was teamed with Loretta Young on several occasions.

In the early '30s Fairbanks, Jr., made a couple of films in France and then from 1934 to '36 he appeared in a few English movies. In the latter part of the decade he essayed some rare comedy roles in *The Joy of Living*, *Having Wonderful Time* and *The Rage of Paris*.

Fairbanks's first starring swashbuckler *The Corsican Brothers* came in 1941. He made a few other pictures in the early '40s before his entry into distinguished military service for the next several years. When he returned to films in 1947, he began to appear more frequently in his father's kind of roles as *Sinbad the Sailor*, *The Exile* and *The Fighting O'Flynn*. His American screen career had begun to wind down when he resettled in the United Kingdom to make his last feature film appearances for over two decades in *State Secret* and *Mr. Drake's Duck*.

Fairbanks was seen in some film shorts of the 1950s and he produced some films as well. His last small screen role to date was in *Ghost Story* (1981). He was active on television in the '50s with his series *Douglas Fairbanks Presents* and other television shows and he has also appeared on the stage.

Comments: It can reasonably be said that Douglas Fairbanks, Jr.'s, screen career began as an exploitation of his famous name. As time went on, he proved himself a competent if not great actor in various genres and what he may have lacked in charisma he made up for in style and looks.

Although some of Fairbanks's earlier roles cast him as a "pretty boy" shallow youth, in his few unsympathetic roles — Rupert of Hentzau in *The Prisoner of Zenda*, for instance — he portrayed bad or at least morally ambivalent men with some panache.

No doubt in his own mind Doug Fairbanks's greatest on-screen challenge was to avoid comparison with his legendary father. He successfully eschewed such heroics for the first 15 years or so of his career. After "Senior's" 1939 death he did play similar roles a few times and, ironically, it is for those handful of roles he is probably now best-remembered.

REVIEWS

The Jazz Age: In this tale of the wild younger generation, Douglas Fairbanks, Jr., is well cast. *Harrison's Reports* 1/19/29, *Variety* 4/17/29.

Little Caesar: Fairbanks is splendid as the gunman's (Edward G. Robinson in his famous role as Rico) friend. *Variety* 1/14/31.

Scarlet Dawn: Fairbanks makes a dashing young officer and a fairly convincing lover, but he gets lost in the final stretches. It will add little, if anything, to his reputation. *Variety* 11/8/32.

Success at Any Price: Although Douglas Fairbanks, Jr., is in some ways a sympathetic character, his actions are so ruthless and brutal that he is at times repulsive. He never recovers. Somebody more matured in the his role would have made it a little more believable. *Harrison's Reports* 3/24/34, *Variety* 5/8/34.

Jump for Glory: Fairbanks, Jr., turns in a splendid characterization. *Variety* 3/24/37.

Gunga Din: Fairbanks sets his character definitely and maintains it right to the final fadeout. *Variety* 1/25/39.

Sinbad the Sailor: Fairbanks matches the do-and-dare antics of his late father and he measures up to the flamboyance required. *Variety* 1/15/47.

State Secret: For Fairbanks the role of the American doctor is a natural. This is an adventurous part and he plays it in a lively, intelligent fashion, scoring strongly with a subtle wit and an unfailing sense of humor. *Variety* 4/26/50.

Faire, Virginia Brown (sometimes
Browne; Virginia LaBuna), Brooklyn, New York, 1904–1980

Filmography: *Classic Images* (Apr. 1987); List of films in *Sweethearts of the Sage*

Silent: After playing bit roles in the East, Virginia Brown Faire won the 1919 Motion Picture Classic Fame and Fortune contest and came to Hollywood. Her first film was *Runnin' Straight* (1920) and she had a solid, if largely uninspiring, career the remainder of the decade.

Brown appeared in many westerns and two Rin Tin Tin films (*Tracked by the Police* and *A Race for Life*), as well as more prestigious ones like *Peter Pan* (as Tinkerbell) and Greta Garbo's *The Temptress*. Other films included *The Cricket on the Hearth*, *Friendly Enemies*, *White Flannels*, *The Calgary Stampede* and *The House of Shame*. Last silent: *The Body Punch* (1929).

Sound: All of Faire's 1929 films were silent except for *The Donovan Affair*, her first talkie. She continued making films (many of them westerns) until 1935 when her final effort *Tracy Rides* was released.

Her films included *The Lonesome Trail, Murder on the Roof, Breed of the West, The Secret Menace, The Lone Trail, The Rainbow Riders* and *West of the Divide.*

Faire's output also included the serial *The Sign of the Wolf* (1930). Her oater co-stars included John Wayne, Buck Jones and Hoot Gibson and among the studios for which she worked were Pathe, Fox, Rayart, Warner Bros., Universal, Columbia, Metropolitan and Reliable.

REVIEWS

Murder on the Roof: A pretty good double murder mystery in which Virginia Brown Faire is the girl who discovers the first murder. *Harrison's Reports* 2/1/30.

Farnum, Franklyn (also Franklin; William Smith), Boston, Massachusetts, 1876/83–1961

Filmography: Academy of Motion Picture Arts and Sciences; List of films in *Eighty Silent Film Stars*

Silent: After a career as a singer in vaudeville and musical comedy, Franklyn Farnum signed with Universal and appeared in the first of his several hundred films, 1916's *Love Never Dies.* In making his movies in various genres (increasingly westerns in the 1920s), he worked for a large number of studios including Selig, Metro, Bluebird, Lasky, Mutual and Triangle. He also made many of his later westerns for low-rent Independent Pictures.

Among Farnum's features were *The Car of Chance, Fast Company, Go Get 'Em Garringer, Vengeance and the Girl, The Fighting Stranger, Gold Grabbers, It Happened Out West* and *The Bandit Tamer.* He appeared in at least two serials, *The Vanishing Trail* in 1920 and *Battling Brewster* (1924). Last silents: *Double-Barreled Justice* and *Two Gun Sap,* released about the same time in 1925.

Sound: When Farnum returned in 1930 for *Beyond the Rio Grande,* it was as a second lead. Most of the roles he had in talkies were small and he played many a tiny bit part, but he was on-screen as late as 1960. Among his films were *Beyond the Law, Saddle Leather Law, Hell's Valley, The Silver Bullet, Honor of the Press, Hop-Along Cassidy, The Preview Murder Mystery* and *Hollywood Cavalcade.*

As well as numerous "B" films, Farnum could be seen (briefly) in such prestige productions as *The Plainsman, Stagecoach, North West Mounted Police* and *Sunset Blvd.* His later films included *Ten Wanted Men, The Buccaneer, King Creole* and *Rock-a-Bye Baby. Ice Palace* in 1960 is believed to have been his final picture. He also appeared in the serials *Deadwood Dick, Custer's Last Stand* and *The Clutching Hand* in the 1930s.

Comments: Although Farnum was not in any way related to the popular screen brothers William and Dustin, he was of the same burly physical type (more so as time went on) and he generally made the same sort of films. It would be disingenuous, therefore, to suppose his assumed name was not an attempt to cash in on their stardom.

Farnum, William, Boston, Massachusetts, 1876–1953

Filmography: Films in Review (Nov. 1983); List of films in *Eighty Silent Film Stars*

Silent: After much theatrical experience, William Farnum began at the top for Selig in *The Spoilers* (1914), a film legend because of its realistically brutal fistfight. By 1915 he was one of the most popular and highest-paid actors in pictures. Subsequently he moved to Paramount and thence to Fox.

Among Farnum's 50 or so films were such literary adaptations as *A Tale of Two Cities* and *Les Misérables,* as well as the popular *If I Were King* (1920). Others, many with frequent co-stars Louise Lovely and Jewel Carmen, included *Samson, The Conqueror, The Rainbow Trail, The Orphan, Drag Harlan, Shackles of Gold* and *Riders of the Purple Sage* (1918 version).

After Farnum sustained what proved to be a serious and long-lasting injury on a film set, and a subsequent illness, he temporarily departed the cinema. The career of his brother Dustin Farnum (1874–1929) was also declining at this time. Last silent: *The Man Who Stands Alone* (1924).

Sound: Farnum returned to the screen to play about 65 character roles, the first of which was in *DuBarry, Woman of Passion* (1930) as Louis XV. Until 1952 he appeared in films like *A Connecticut Yankee, Hangmen Also Die!, Cleopatra* (1934 version), *The Scarlet Letter, A Woman's Face, The Perils of Pauline* (1947 version), *Cheers for Miss Bishop* and *Samson and Delilah.*

The Abbott and Costello version of *Jack and the Beanstalk* was Farnum's last feature. He was also in some shorts in the early '30s, in numerous westerns and serials including *The Clutching Hand, Undersea Kingdom, The Lone Ranger* and *Adventures of Red Ryder.*

Comments: Although William Farnum left silent films near the top, he noticeably was getting too old to continue in leading man roles. Unlike some of his contemporaries, however, sound actually came to his rescue. With his theater-trained plummy voice and silver hair, he was a natural for sound character roles.

Despite Farnum's age at the time the movies

entered the sound era, his fisticuffs in *The Spoilers* seemed to have made a lasting mark. Even in advanced middle age, many of his roles called for vigorous and brutal fighting. It can be assumed that the use of doubles on these occasions was common.

REVIEWS

DuBarry, Woman of Passion: William Farnum's performance is not impressive but often his opportunity to shine is eclipsed by the lines he is called upon to speak. *New York Times* 11/3/30.

The Painted Desert: Farnum's presence, with gray hair, should attract some old-timers. *Variety* 3/18/31.

Between Men: The fisticuffs are worth seeing with veteran William Farnum putting up a good contest. *Variety* 1/29/36.

Farrell, Charles, Onset Bay, Massachusetts, 1900/01–1990

Filmography: *Films in Review* (Oct. 1976); List of films in *Film Dope* (Sept. 1978)

Silent: After extra work in numerous films, Charles Farrell's first lead was in *Wings of Youth* (1925). He appeared in routine programmers for Fox until *Old Ironsides* (1926) and 1927's *The Rough Riders* brought him some notice. Major stardom came in that year's great success *Seventh Heaven*, his first teaming with Janet Gaynor and the start of the late '20s greatest romantic team.

Others of Farrell's dozen or so silents, apart from extra appearances, included *A Trip to Chinatown*, *Fazil*, *The Love Hour* and *Sandy*. Last silent: *The Red Dance* (1928), with synchronized music and sound effects.

Sound: Farrell made his sound debut in the part-talkie *Street Angel* (1928), another successful pairing with Gaynor. This was followed by *The River*, and in 1929 *Lucky Star*, also a part-talkie, marked yet another Farrell-Gaynor film. His first full-sound film was *Happy Days* (1929), in which he played a cameo role.

That year the Gaynor-Farrell musical *Sunny Side Up*, in which the title song and "If I Had a Talking Picture of You" were featured, proved a major success and impelled further popular pairings, including musicals. They included *Delicious*, *The Man Who Came Back*, *High Society Blues*, *Merely Mary Ann*, *Tess of the Storm Country* and their final one together, *Change of Heart* in 1934.

Farrell left Fox and made films for other studios (Columbia, Paramount, First National, Universal) as well as in Europe in 1936–37. Later in the decade he was seen with Shirley Temple in *Just Around the Corner* and he also appeared in *Tail Spin* (1939). The last of his approximately 30 talkies was in 1941's *The Deadly Game*.

Other Farrell films included *Liliom*, *The Princess and the Plumber*, *Aggie Appleby, Maker of Men* and *The Big Shakedown*. About ten years after his screen career ended he came back to enjoy some popularity as the title character's father in the TV sitcom *My Little Margie*. He had retained much of his good looks in the interim. In another series he portrayed "himself" as the owner of the famous Palm Springs Racquet Club, which of course he was.

Comments: Handsome Charles Farrell made more talkies than silents but was probably a bigger romantic star in the earlier medium. Although his speaking voice improved as he went on, it was somewhat high in pitch and it retained marked vestiges of a New England accent. The very popular *Sunny Side Up* revealed a strong need for him to work on his voice and undoubtedly he took lessons that helped.

Although Farrell was in a few popular films on his own, it was his teaming with pert Janet Gaynor that brought him his greatest success. Fox apparently thought she was carrying the team; as the early '30s wore on, his star seemed to decline as hers rose. (She was very possibly a better actress than he was an actor.)

It may be that the teaming ultimately hurt Farrell's career more than it initially helped it. The public certainly did not seem to favor him when he did not appear with his frequent co-star. In any case, he was a fairly uncharismatic actor and the fact is that his somewhat prissy voice and touch of effeminacy did not really match his rugged romantic image.

REVIEWS

Sunny Side Up: Charles Farrell is pleasing as the rich hero and has an easy part and a pleasing, though weak, voice. *Variety* 10/9/29, *Harrison's Reports* 10/19/29.

Liliom: Reviewers differed, with one believing that Farrell did good work and another stating that he was miscast. The latter said that he had neither the voice nor the appearance for the title role and that it was far beyond the depth of Farrell's dramatic ability. The female lead's deep contralto voice made him appear almost insipid and self-conscious and he was over-gentle as well. *Harrison's Reports* 10/4/30, *Variety* 10/8/30.

Delicious: The strength of this film is in its co-stars Gaynor and Farrell. They are still in the flop-proof class. *Variety* 12/19/31.

Wild Girl: Charles Farrell is fair in this second-rate film. *Harrison's Reports* 11/5/32.

Fighting Youth: Farrell, who stars, remains an okay juvenile. (At 35 he was playing a rather unlikely football hero.) *Variety* 11/6/35.

Tess of the Storm Country: One review thought that Gaynor-Farrell fans would be disappointed because Farrell had slightly more than a bit part. Another said that the love affair between the hero and heroine was charming. *Variety* 11/22/32, *Harrison's Reports* 11/26/32.

Tailspin (or Tail Spin): Charles Farrell plays an expert mechanic. *Harrison's Reports* 2/11/39.

The Deadly Game: Farrell is a government agent. *Harrison's Reports* 8/16/41.

Fawcett, George, Fairfax County, Virginia,
1860/63–1939

Silent: A stage actor since 1886, George Fawcett found a solid niche in the cinema from about 1914 or '15, appearing in over 100 films and directing some in the late 'teens as well. While he had some early leads (*The Frame-Up*, *The Majesty of the Law*), he was generally seen in support portraying men of authority such as judges, politicos, military men and innumerable fathers.

In 1920, Fawcett was dubbed "The Grand *Young* Man of the Screen." He may have appeared in more D. W. Griffith films than any other actor; these included *Intolerance*, *Scarlet Days* and *True Heart Susie*. Among his other films were *Salomy Jane*, *The Flaming Frontier*, *The Valley of the Giants* and *Love*. He was very busy during the '20s, often making more than ten pictures a year.

In one of his last silents, Erich von Stroheim's *The Wedding March* (1928), Fawcett was again top-billed. Among the studios for which he worked were Paramount, Morosco, Ince, Universal, Selig, Fine Arts, Selznick, Artcraft and First National. Last silent: *Prince of Hearts* (1929?), made after his first talkies. (This film is *believed* to have been a silent.)

Sound: Fawcett leapt the sound barrier with no problem. He made a part-talkie, *The Little Wildcat*, in 1928 and most of his 12 1929 films were all or part-talking as well. They included *Hot for Paris*, *Innocents of Paris*, *Lady of the Pavements*, *Fancy Baggage* and *His Captive Woman*.

Nineteen thirty saw Fawcett in seven films but his career, possibly because of ill health, was drawing to a close. It was his penultimate year on the screen. Some of his other films were *Hello Sister*, *The Bad One*, *Men Are Like That* and his final three in 1931: *Drums of Jeopardy*, *Women of Experience* and *Personal Maid*.

REVIEWS

Hearts in Exile: Although most talkies he has appeared in have not brought out his voice clearly, George Fawcett's voice here is always distinct and audible. *Variety* 12/4/29.

Hello Sister: The cast fits, notably George Fawcett. For the brief interval he is visible he takes a grand bow. *Variety* 3/5/30.

Personal Maid: Wise exhibitors will play up the Mary Boland–George Fawcett combination. *Variety* 9/8/31.

Fazenda, Louise, Lafayette, Indiana,
1889/96–1962

Silent: Louise Fazenda began her film career about 1915 as an extra and stuntwoman. Graduating to Sennett's fun factory, she appeared in such films as *A Gay Old Knight* (possibly her first sizable role), *Her Fame*, *The Main Lady* and *Are Waitresses Safe?* She was starred in the 1920 feature *Down on the Farm*, where she displayed the gingham dress and spitcurls for which she became known.

Fazenda was with Sennett for about five years and eventually worked in numerous films at almost all the Hollywood studios in both leads and supporting roles. Other silents included *Quincy Adams Sawyer*, *The Gold Diggers*, *The Cradle Snatchers*, *The Bat*, *This Woman*, *The Old Soak*, *Babe Comes Home* and *Declassee*. Last silent: *Riley the Cop* (1928), with synchronized sound effects and music, made after her talkie debut.

Sound: Fazenda was seen in Warner Bros.' second all-talking Vitaphone feature *The Terror* and the part-talkie *Noah's Ark*, both made in 1928. All her 1929 efforts were either full sound or part-talkies and her busy career continued without let-up well into the sound period. Among Fazenda's films were several early musicals like *The Show of Shows*, *The Desert Song* (in which she sang), *Bride of the Regiment* and *No No Nanette*. Others included *High Society Blues*, *Leathernecking*, *Blue Blazes*, *Racing Youth* and *Swing Your Lady* with Humphrey Bogart. (It is considered one of his very worst movies.) Her last was *The Old Maid* (1939).

Comments: The Judy Canova of her day, at least for a part of the 1920s, Louise Fazenda's early persona was that of the bucolic and rowdy country girl. As the decade went on, her range broadened and she appeared in leading and character roles in various types of films, many of them comedies or comedy-melodramas.

Although in private life Fazenda was a cultured and not unattractive woman, studio publicity generally centered around her supposedly homely appearance. This may well have galled her but she had a successful career, helped not a little by her well-modulated voice. The end of her career presumably came at her own behest; she undoubtedly could have continued on as a highly regarded character actress.

Reviews

The Terror: Louise Fazenda provides a few laughs with a weird giggle resembling the whinny of a horse. She plays the part of a mad spiritualist and contributes considerable comedy with her fine acting. *Variety* 8/22/28, *Harrison's Reports* 8/25/28.

Loose Ankles: Louise Fazenda wrestles with her companion all over the floor. The sterling comedienne furnishes most of the comedy. *Harrison's Reports* 3/12/30.

Misbehaving Ladies: Fazenda is true to life in her role. *Harrison's Reports* 4/18/31.

Racing Youth: The most effective part is the comedy, with Louise Fazenda scoring nicely. *Variety* 4/19/32.

Swing Your Lady: Fazenda makes a particularly effective choice as the mountaineer Amazon. (In this farrago about wrestling and hillbillies, she played a lady blacksmith, with Humphrey Bogart as a wrestling promoter.) *Variety* 1/26/38.

The Old Maid: Fazenda stands out as the family maid. *Variety* 8/2/39.

Feld, Fritz, Berlin, Germany, 1900–1993

Silent: Before emigrating to America in 1923, Fritz Feld worked with famous theater impresario Max Reinhardt, whom he also later assisted in Hollywood. He had been in a couple of German films, *The Golem* being one, before his American debut.

Feld appeared in such late '20s dramatic features as *Blindfold*, *A Ship Comes In* and *The Last Command*. Because he often claimed to have been in some thirty silents, it is most probable that he had unbilled bits. Last known silent: *Black Magic* (1929), with synchronized music and sound effects.

Sound: *Broadway* (1929) was the first sound film of the man who was later to be known as much for a sound effect as for his other considerable talents. His other 1929 talkie was *One Hysterical Night*. He apparently did not make another until 1936's *Easy to Take*; in the interim he did some directing. Radio was another of his successful media.

Many of Feld's numerous talkie roles were memorable cameos as officious waiters, hairdressers, butlers, minor functionaries and even crooks. His films, in which he was still appearing in the 1980s, included *I Met Him in Paris*, *Tovarich*, *Bringing Up Baby*, *Idiot's Delight*, *Little Old New York*, *Julia Misbehaves*, *The Errand Boy* and *Hello Dolly!*

One of Feld's fondly remembered but atypical latter-day roles came as the scruffy owner of the Albanian restaurant in *Barefoot in the Park* (1966). His last movie appearance was apparently in *Homer and Eddie* in 1989, and he also frequently was seen on television, including commercials.

Comments: Fritz Feld was but one of the innumerable character men whose brief appearances were frequently the most memorable thing about '30s and '40s films. Perhaps if it were not for his longevity, he would not stand out above the veritable crowd of such colorful and indispensable players. But Feld remained very much on the scene until he was nearly 90, and he was much loved in the industry.

The clipped tones of Feld's German-accented voice perfectly fit his on-screen well-groomed, fastidious physical presence. His screen characters oozed superiority and it did not matter a jot if you thought he was officious or, even worse, unimportant. He had better things to do than to please you.

Feld's turns invariably were the highlight of many a picture. The shtick for which he was famous was the "pop," a sound made by slapping the palm of his hand quickly against his open mouth. He claimed it was a spontaneous invention during filming and was meant to simulate a champagne cork popping. Whatever its genesis, it was certainly one of the most imitated of filmdom trademarks. He was married to actress Virginia Christine, who died in 1996.

Reviews

Knickerbocker Holiday: Fritz Feld turns in a workmanlike characterization. *Variety* 3/1/44.

Captain Tugboat Annie: The best humor is found in the brief sequences of Fritz Feld as the eccentric symphony conductor. *Variety* 3/6/46.

Barefoot in the Park: Feld is fine in a brief scene. *Variety* 5/24/67.

Fellowes, Rockliffe (also Rockcliffe),
Ottawa, Canada, 1885–1950

Silent: From 1915's *Regeneration*, popular star Rockliffe Fellowes worked for at least 14 studios in making films like *The Panther Woman*, *Yes or No*, *The Stranger's Banquet*, *The Garden of Weeds*, *Declassee*, *The Road to Glory* and *The Taxi Dancer*. Last silent: *The Crystal Cup* (1927).

Sound: Fellowes's sound career was slow to take off. He made only one film each in 1929 and '30, the first being the part-talkie *The Charlatan*. The other was *Outside the Law*.

Fellowes found his stride in 1931, and until 1934 he was seen in about a dozen pictures including *Monkey Business* with the Marx Brothers, *Lawyer Man*, *The All American*, *Rusty Rides Alone* and his last, *Back Page*.

Reviews

The Vice Squad: Fellowes has one of the few 100% parts seen lately as the vice squad head. He's without a kind moment in the whole picture. *Variety* 6/9/31.

Monkey Business: The usual Marx madhouse, with Rockliffe Fellowes, who hasn't been around for some time, as a well-dressed gangster. *Variety* 10/13/31.

Huddle: Fellowes is natural as the heroine's father. *New York Times* 6/17/32.

Ferguson, Elsie, New York, New York,
1883–1961

Filmography: *Films in Review* (Nov. 1964)

Silent: Already an acclaimed stage star when she signed with Paramount-Artcraft, Elsie Ferguson appeared in 22 films from 1917 to 1922. She returned for one more in 1925. Her first role was in *Barbary Sheep*.

Other Ferguson pictures, many directed by Maurice Tourneur, included *The Song of Songs*, *The Danger Mark*, *His Parisian Wife*, *A Society Exile*, *The Counterfeit* and *Sacred and Profane Love*. Last silent: *The Unknown Lover* (1925).

Sound: An adaptation of the Broadway play of the same name, *Scarlet Pages* was a courtroom melodrama of 1930. It proved to be Ferguson's sole talkie; in it she played an attorney.

Comments: Elsie Ferguson carried her stage success to her films. She was a major star in the movies, although by the time of her last films she was probably waning somewhat in popularity. Her 1925 effort appears to have been little seen.

It was obviously not her voice that kept Ferguson from making additional talkies. More likely it was age — she was not far from 50 — and the fact that the relentless eye of the camera only emphasized it. Mother roles apparently had little allure for her; she returned to the theater.

REVIEWS

Scarlet Pages: Ferguson does very well as the modern Portia but her voice, probably because of faulty recording, came through poorly. Nevertheless it contains another of her capital emotional performances. Her persuasive playing does a great deal for it and she makes it genuinely affecting. *Harrison's Reports* 11/22/30, *New York Times* 12/6/30, *Variety* 12/10/30.

Ferguson, Helen, Decatur, Illinois,
1901–1977

Filmography: List of films in *Sweethearts of the Sage*

Silent: In a career that lasted from 1917 to the end of the silent era (although it was waning by the latter '20s), Helen Ferguson was often seen in adventure-melodramas. They had titles like *Shod*

with Fire, *The Call of the North*, *Straight from the Shoulder*, *Rough Shod*, *Double Dealing*, *Racing Luck* and *Spook Ranch*.

Ferguson also appeared in such straight dramas as *Miss Lulu Bett* and *The Famous Mrs. Fair*, as well as the serials *Casey of the Coast Guard* and *Fire Fighters*. She was named a Wampas Baby Star in 1922. Last silent: *Jaws of Steel* (1927), a Rin-Tin-Tin starrer.

Sound: Ferguson was seen in only two talkie features. She had the female lead opposite Henry B. Walthall in *In Old California* (1929). That same year she appeared in the Vitaphone short *Finders Keepers*.

The other full-length Ferguson movie was the 1930 melodrama *Scarlet Pages*, in which *Elsie* Ferguson was starred and in which Helen was last-billed as a secretary. She later became a respected Hollywood publicity agent.

Fetchit, Stepin (Lincoln Perry), Key West,
Florida, 1892–1985

Filmography: *Hollywood Players: The Thirties*.

Silent: Stepin Fetchit performed in a plantation show, the African-American equivalent of a minstrel show. As the story goes, he borrowed his stage name from a race horse. He made the first of about six silent films, *In Old Kentucky*, in 1927. His roles were generally quite small — "Porter," "Janitor," "Negro man" — with the exception of his last, *Hearts in Dixie* (1929)

In it Fetchit had a second lead which established his often controversial on-screen persona. Other films were *The Devil's Skipper*, *Nameless Men*, *The Tragedy of Youth* and *The Kid's Clever*.

Sound: Fetchit was seen in eight films in 1929, all but two part- or all-talking. The first was *The Ghost Talks*, followed by *Big Time*, *Show Boat*, *Fox Movietone Follies* and *Salute* among others. In some his roles continued to be small but he was beginning to obtain better parts.

Best-remembered for the pictures he made with Will Rogers in the mid–'30s, especially *Judge Priest*, Fetchit remained active on screen through most of the decade. His films included *Cameo Kirby*, *Carolina*, *David Harum*, *The County Chairman*, *Stand Up and Cheer*, *Steamboat 'Round the Bend*, *Charlie Chan in Egypt* and *Zenobia*.

By the 1940s, Fetchit's mainstream Hollywood career had faltered but he appeared in films like *Miracle in Harlem* and *Big Timers* that were made specifically for African-American audiences. In the early '50s he returned for roles in *Bend of the River* and *The Sun Shines Bright*, a remake of *Judge Priest* by the same director, John Ford.

The latter was Fetchit's last picture until cameo

roles twenty years later in *Amazing Grace* (1974) and *Won Ton Ton, the Dog That Saved Hollywood* (1976). In the former film his character's name was Uncle Lincoln, no doubt a fondly meant allusion to his real Christian name. Old age found him still making personal appearances in rather seedy second-rate night clubs.

Comments: Stepin Fetchit's performing persona was apparently set early in his career as one of "The Two Dancing Crows, Skeeter and Rastus." This extreme characterization of a lazy, sly and molasses-speeched "Negro" was one which was to bring him great wealth and, ultimately, the scorn of many of his fellow African-Americans and also of some film historians.

Had Fetchit only been seen in silent films, his stereotyped portrayal perhaps would have been less offensive to many. The addition of the exaggeratedly drawling voice only emphasized the caricature, although he claimed the extreme stereotypes were developed by his imitators and not him. While it is true that some African-American character actors who followed him, like Willie Best (Sleep-N-Eat), did adopt a similar persona, it would have been hard to be *more* extreme than Fetchit was.

Fetchit's sound roles were generally larger than his silent ones but his lowly on-screen station in life, usually that of a handyman or servant, remained the same. Character names like Sassafrass and Snowflake were common. White audiences eventually tired of him and he did not find a sympathetic hearing among his own race.

In 1970, after the TV series *Of Black America* was aired, Fetchit sued for $3,000,000 claiming he was defamed. He perhaps justifiably objected to the description of his movie persona as a "lazy, stupid, crap shooting, chicken stealing idiot."

Fetchit and some others have made the case that in his caricature he actually was mocking and satirizing the white man's view of the black man and thus revealing their prejudices. If so, Hollywood and white audiences did not seem to perceive his intentions; he was considered an accurate reflection of his race.

It is also fair to say that in those less enlightened times, mocking ethnic humor was much more acceptable. Asians were considered inscrutable, Latinos lazy, Jews crafty, Italians voluble, the Irish inebriates and so on. Those attempting to fight such stereotypes probably would have found themselves unemployed.

Fetchit professed to believe that his pioneering success made it easier for those African-American actors who followed him. "I wiped away the image of rapist from the Negro and made him a household word," he contended. He certainly did attain great financial rewards and was unafraid to flaunt his wealth. His high living was notable in an age of Hollywood excess.

It is surely possible that in Stepin Fetchit's mind he was an artist who was simply creating a character and indeed he could be considered just another "eccentric" character actor like many of his white contemporaries. In his best films, those with Will Rogers, he revealed hints of a more complex persona. Perhaps a re-evaluation is in order. There certainly are those who consider him to have been a fine and undervalued actor.

REVIEWS

The Ghost Talks: Especially good was the negro dialect talk of Stepin Fetchit who supplies the low comedy. The best gag had to do with the colored comic being chased from the haunted house by a dog. *Variety* 2/27/29.

Cameo Kirby: A comedy ditty is ruined on unintelligible delivery by the colored comic Stepin Fetchit. *Variety* 2/12/30.

Neck and Neck: Fetchit's garbled talking is still so much incoherent mumbling. *Variety* 11/17/31.

Judge Priest: Most of the comedy is contributed by Will Rogers and Stepin Fetchit, a natural foil to the Rogers character. *Variety* 10/16/34.

The County Chairman: Stepin Fetchit is again prominent as the slew-footed, dull-witted comedy relief. *Variety* 1/22/35.

Zenobia: Fetchit squeezes in several laughs with his lazy dialogue. *Variety* 3/15/39.

The Sun Shines Bright: Fetchit's extremely languid comedy furnishes a chuckle here and there. *Variety* 5/6/53.

Fields, W. C. (William Claude Dukenfield),
Philadelphia, Pennsylvania, 1879/80–1946

Filmography: List of films in *Film Dope* (Sept. 1978)

Silent: It was as a juggler, possibly the greatest of all time, that W. C. Fields first garnered international fame. After touring for many years, he headlined as a juggler in the Ziegfeld Follies from the mid-'teens to the early '20s, eventually accompanying his act with comic patter.

Fields's first celluloid appearance was the 1915 short *The Pool Shark*, based on his stage routine. He was not to return to the screen until 1924's *Janice Meredith* as a British sergeant. In the meantime, he had gained Broadway renown as Eustace McGargle in the musical *Poppy*, a role he first reprised in the D. W. Griffith–directed *Sally of the Sawdust* (1925).

Fields's other silents were *The Potters, It's the Old Army Game,* "*That Royle Girl,*" *So's Your Old Man, Running Wild, Two Flaming Youths* and the remake of *Tillie's Punctured Romance.* Last silent: *Fools for Luck* (1928).

Sound: Considering that Fields was to become one of the best-known comic actors in talkies his debut in the short *The Golf Specialist* in 1930 was not greatly auspicious. But it was sporadically amusing, and that inimitable voice came through with all its venom intact.

Although it was little more than a filmed stage skit, the short did foreshadow the major themes of Fields's features: his dexterity with various inanimate objects and the problematic relationship with children, women and other malevolents (which included most of the rest of humanity).

Fields's first sound feature (and Marilyn Miller's last) was the poorly received *Her Majesty Love* (1931). He made most of the '30s films that followed at Paramount and wrote many of them himself under various *outré* pseudonyms.

The 1932 oddity *Million Dollar Legs* gave a hint of the Fields screen magic even though he remained one of an ensemble as he was to do in his next few films (*If I Had a Million, International House, Alice in Wonderland, Six of a Kind*).

Fields was seen to better advantage in four shorts he made because they *were* pure Fields. *The Dentist* came in 1932 and there were three in the next year for Sennett: *The Barbershop, The Fatal Glass of Beer* ("And it's not a fit night out for man nor beast!") and *The Pharmacist.*

Nineteen thirty-three's *Tillie and Gus* was the first feature in which Fields had the undisputed lead. It was followed by such films as *The Old Fashioned Way,* the classic *It's a Gift,* as the put-upon Harold Bissonette ("pronounced Bissonay"), *The Man on the Flying Trapeze* and *Poppy,* the second film version of his stage play.

Perhaps Fields's most famous film role is that of Mr. Wilkins Micawber in MGM's ensemble production of *David Copperfield* (1935). It is generally believed that he was true to the Dickens character and he mostly sublimated his various scene-stealing mannerisms. In that year he also had an uneasy teaming with Bing Crosby in *Mississippi.*

As ill health began to dog him in the late 1930s, Fields turned increasingly to radio where his ongoing "feud" with Edgar Bergen's creation, the woodenheaded Charlie McCarthy, made him even more popular. Their repartee has been frequently quoted (Fields: "Your father was a gatelegged table"; McCarthy: "If my father was a table, your father was under it!"). Naturally, the comic's penchant for the pleasures of the grape did not go unremarked.

The success of this odd-couple teaming led directly to Fields's comeback film, and first for Universal, *You Can't Cheat an Honest Man* (1939), co-starring the ventriloquist and his dummy. It proved to be a high-grosser and was followed the next year by Fields's co-starring stint with the redoubtable but slipping Mae West in *My Little Chickadee.*

Nineteen forty's *The Bank Dick* is considered to be the second great W. C. Fields film, *It's a Gift* being the other. His blowhard would-be film director and bank guard Egbert Souse ("accent grave on the E") is one of cinema's finest comedy inventions.

There was only one starring Fields feature to follow, the bizarre *Never Give a Sucker an Even Break.* After 1941, Fields's only appearances were cameo roles in *Follow the Boys, Song of the Open Road* and, lastly, *Sensations of 1945.* His segment in the omnibus *Tales of Manhattan* (1942) was deleted from the release print.

Comments: Possessor of one of the most unique and imitated voices in show business, W. C. Fields was a natural for the talkies. His persona, no doubt partly based on and exaggerated from his real life personality, was also unique: eternal suspiciousness, hostility (covert, when not sneakily overt) and cowardice combined with unconvincing braggadocio.

Unfortunately, even with those beady blue eyes constantly on the defensive, the celluloid Fields was usually defeated by a combination of scheming and/or nagging women, whining adult offspring or, worst of all, small children or animals. He was dubbed a "grognosed platypus" and "Sir Toby Belch cruelly misplaced in the Prohibition era."

The incomparable Fields voice, often raised in protest against his unfair lot in life, was part snarl, part whine, part purr and part indescribable. When comparisons were attempted, they were to such unpleasant objects as a rusty lavatory chain and crushed glass. His gestures, as futile as were the rest of his defense mechanisms, completed the unhappy picture.

Some parts of Fields's films made little sense. The plots could be minimal or nonlinear and seemed as if they had been written hastily on the backs of old envelopes—which they often had been. The responsibility for such farragoes fell on screenwriters like Charles Bogle, Otis Criblecoblis and Mahatma Kane Jeeves who were, of course, all Fields alter egos.

This may explain why, with very few exceptions, the non-ensemble W. C. Fields films were all about him. Other characters existed merely to bounce jibes off of. Although he occasionally had co-stars who could give him a run for his tightly clutched money, for instance Alison Skipworth and of course McCarthy and West, they were usually nondescript.

For reasons which can be endlessly speculated upon, including his upbringing, Fields's gifts sprang from a deeply troubled and self-destructive man. He was definitely an alcoholic, possibly a misanthrope and clearly a neurotic. His talents were all the more unique for their source. One of his greatest gifts was realizing he was a much funnier "reactor" than he was an "actor." The cinema will never see his like again.

REVIEWS

Her Majesty Love: They couldn't quite submerge the natural comedy knack of W. C. Fields as a futile old man. He plays a Micawber-like character who would have been somebody in better circumstances. He is the only one in the cast who provides some real laughs, becoming drunk, juggling dishes and throwing French pastry around. *Variety* 12/1/31, *Harrison's Reports* 12/5/31.

Tillie and Gus: It consists of some of Fields's old vaudeville gags. He is his usual self but is handicapped by the material. *Variety* 11/14/33.

It's a Gift: Those who appreciate the W. C. Fields type of comedy will be entertained. Fields is at no time off the screen and he provokes comedy from the very beginning. It is practically a Fields monologue. *Harrison's Reports* 12/8/34, *Variety* 1/8/35.

David Copperfield: Mr. Micawber lives again in W. C. Fields who only once yields to his penchant for horseplay. In the main he makes Micawber as real as David and he gets entirely away from his usual line. *Variety* 1/22/35.

Mississippi: Fields works hard throughout the film and saves it, giving it whatever entertainment value it has. *Variety* 4/24/35.

You Can't Cheat an Honest Man: Fields's gags are of the hit-and-run variety. There are some new ones but they are mostly the familiar routines the comic has paraded many times on the screen. *Variety* 2/22/39.

The Bank Dick: A showcase for Fields's individualistic talents in both pantomime and buffoonery. Several times he reaches into satirical pantomime reminiscent of Charlie Chaplin's best efforts during his Mutual and Essanay days. *Variety* 12/4/40.

Never Give a Sucker an Even Break: Fields is himself throughout. He wrote it himself and knows how to handle the assignment. It is studded with Fieldsian satire and cracks. *Variety* 10/8/41.

Finch, Flora, London, England, 1869–1940

Silent: After stage experience, Flora Finch entered the cinema about 1907 and appeared for Biograph in the "Jones" pictures. Her subsequent fame derived from her teaming with the cherubic, greatly popular comedian John Bunny in a long series of eagerly awaited films (estimated at 250 to 300) from 1910 to 1915.

Called "Bunnygrams" or "Bunnyfinches," the one-reel comedies included *A Cure for Pokeritis*, *The New Stenographer*, *The Subduing of Mrs. Nag* and *Love's Old Dream*. Much of the humor sprang from the contrast between the rotund Bunny's easy-going character and the extremely angular Finch's acerbic one. In 1917, a couple of years after Bunny died, she formed her own company to make solo comedies but they were not too successful.

Finch began appearing in top supporting roles in features as early as 1915 with *How Cissy Made Good*, in which she played "herself." Other early roles came in *Prudence the Pirate*, *The Great Adventure* and *Oh, Boy!* The feature films continued throughout the silent era and included such major ones as *When Knighthood Was in Flower*, *Monsieur Beaucaire*, *The Cat and the Canary* (the perpetually frightened Aunt Susan) and *Quality Street*. Among her others were *Luck*, *Fifth Avenue*, *The Brown Derby* and *The Live Wire*. Last silent: *The Faker* (1929).

Sound: Finch's first sound effort was the part-talkie *Come Across* in 1929; *Sweet Kitty Bellairs* was her only 1930 feature. Further appearances were widely scattered through the decade and eventually, along with many other old-timers who had fallen on hard days, she was made a member of the MGM "stock company" and she did bits and extra work.

Among Finch's few features, in which she was generally cast for her physical attributes, if on-screen long enough to be seen at all, were *The Painted Veil*, *The Scarlet Letter*, *Show Boat*, *Way Out West*, *When Love Is Young* and *The Women*.

Finlayson, James, Falkirk, Scotland, 1887–1953

Silent: Bald and bandy-legged, Jimmy Finlayson may or may not have been a Keystone Kop but he definitely was a colorful presence in hundreds of one- and two-reelers from the mid-'teens. His trademark was a squinty-eyed double-take which he repeated endlessly in Sennett and Roach pictures after coming from the stage.

In 1920, Finlayson began feature work in *Down on the Farm* and *Married Life*. Other early '20s full-length films were *Home Talent*, *A Small Town Idol*, *The Crossroads of New York* and *Hollywood*. Most of his effort during that decade was in two-reelers, including those of Laurel and Hardy, but in 1927 he returned in such features as *No Man's Law*, *Bachelor's Paradise*, *Ladies Night in a Turkish Bath* and *Lady Be Good*. Last silent feature: *Show Girl* (1928), with synchronized sound effects and music.

Sound: Continuing to work for Hal Roach in short comedies, Finlayson also appeared in the 1929 part- and all-talkies *Hard to Get*, *Two Weeks Off* and *Wall Street*. In the 1930s, he was seen in both comedies and dramas like *The Dawn Patrol*, *Thunder Below* and *The Great Victor Herbert*. Most of his feature roles were in Laurel and Hardy films that included *Bonnie Scotland*, *Our Relations*, *The Devil's Brother*, *The Bohemian Girl*, *The Flying Deuces* and, most notably, *Way Out West*.

"Fin" also returned to the U.K. for some movie work and continued in American pictures into the 1940s, although more sporadically. He was again with Laurel and Hardy in small parts in *Saps at Sea* and *A Chump at Oxford*, and appeared later in *Yanks Ahoy*, *The Perils of Pauline* and *Grand Canyon Trail*.

Finlayson's final picture was apparently 1951's *Royal Wedding* in which he played a cabby. In the 1960s, he was reintroduced to audiences in several silent comedy compilations, including *When Comedy Was King*.

Comments: Because he was an eccentric-type character actor, Jimmy Finlayson's rich Scots burr could only enhance his value in the talkies. His waggling mustache and ice-blue eyes added to his generally unsympathetic characterizations, often as a landlord, military noncom or other pettily officious denizen. All this and the famous "Fin" leer combined to make him one of the more memorable comedy stooges of the movies.

Reviews

Hard to Get: James Finlayson plays little more than a bit part and gets a modicum of laughs. The funniest thing is his juggling with a four inch collar. *Variety* 10/2/29.

Bonnie Scotland: Good comic support for Laurel and Hardy comes from James Finlayson as a Scottish sergeant. *Variety* 8/28/35.

Saps at Sea: The film includes some old-timers, among them James Finlayson. (He plays the non-plussed doctor who advises Laurel and Hardy to take a sea voyage for Ollie's health [he has "Horno-mania"], with very dubious results.) *Variety* 5/1/40.

Flowers, Bess, Sherman, Texas,
1898/1900–1984

Filmography: Incomplete list of films in *Films in Review* (June-July 1984), added films (Jan. 1985, Nov. 1985)

Silent: Dubbed "The Queen of the Hollywood Extras," Bess Flowers did not always receive billing but was a fixture in hundreds of films. She was a tall brunette (later to be distinguished gray) who frequently played society matrons in fashionable clothes.

Among her credited films from 1923 were *Hollywood*, *The Silent Partner*, *Irene*, *Glenister of the Mounted*, *Laddie* and *Lone Hand Saunders*. In the latter three she had the leading female role but was usually to be found down the cast list. She was also in two-reeler comedies. Last credited silent feature: *Linda* (1929), with synchronized music and sound effects, made after her first talkie.

Sound: *The Ghost Talks* (1929) was Bess Flowers's first credited talkie feature. She had made her sound debut in the 1928 short *Ladies Man*. Others of her multitudinous but brief (and usually wordless) appearances came in *All About Eve*, *The Awful Truth*, *The Bad and the Beautiful*, *Double Indemnity*, *Gilda*, *The Greatest Show on Earth*, *Rear Window* and *Ninotchka*.

Flowers's final appearances were in the 1960s, *Good Neighbor Sam* (1964) probably being the last. She also made some comedy shorts with The Three Stooges and others and appeared on TV.

Comments: Her regal height undoubtedly kept Bess Flowers from more leading lady roles but also probably lengthened her career as a character actress. She also had a natural dignity and carriage that made her stand out from the crowd. Her slight Texas drawl would not have been too much of a factor in a successful talkie career.

Flowers's name (memorable in itself) lives on because her brief appearances sometimes came at opportune times in major films; for instance, she was the one who congratulated the title character in *All About Eve* on winning the Sarah Siddons award. But mainly it is because somewhere along the way she became a film buffs' icon.

Forbes, Ralph (Ralph Taylor), London,
England, 1902/05–1951

Silent: Handsome Ralph Forbes had already appeared in the English cinema from 1921 before he made his U.S. debut in the popular *Beau Geste* (as John Geste) in 1926. He became a leading man in such films as *The Enemy*, *Mr. Wu*, *The Actress*, *Restless Youth* and *The Masks of the Devil*. Last silent: *The Trail of '98* (1929), with synchronized sound effects and music.

Sound: The talkies revealed Ralph Forbes's cultured British accent. Although this certainly did not finish his career, it restricted him and he eventually found himself in supporting roles. He did make some prestigious films that included *The Barretts of Wimpole Street*, *Twentieth Century*, *Mary of Scotland, Stage Door, Romeo and Juliet* and *Kidnapped.*

Forbes also appeared in his share of quickies like *Inside the Lines, Calling Philo Vance* and *Her Wedding Night.* He also reprised his silent role as John Geste in the talkie *Beau Ideal.* His last was 1944's *Frenchman's Creek.*

Reviews

Mamba: Ralph Forbes is the hero. He plays the German officer rather well but wears a monocle. *Harrison's Reports* 3/15/30, *Variety* 3/19/30.

Inside the Lines: Forbes is an officer in the English army's secret service. He plays the role casually. *Variety* 7/9/30.

Beau Ideal: Forbes's accent is somewhat provoking for male movie customers but he records clearly and offers a good acting attempt. *Variety* 1/21/31.

Age of Indiscretion: In this film wealthy Ralph Forbes is dominated by his mother. *Harrison's Reports* 5/25/35.

Frenchman's Creek: Forbes is too much the dolt as the foppish husband. *Variety* 9/20/44, *Harrison's Reports* 9/23/44.

Ford, Francis (Francis Feeney), Portland,
Maine, 1881/82–1953

Filmography: Academy of Motion Picture Arts and Sciences; List of films in *Eighty Silent Film Stars*

Silent: After brief stage experience, Francis Ford, older brother of famed director John Ford, joined the Centaur film company in 1908. He was an actor and director at several early studios including Bison 101 (run by Thomas Ince), Edison and the Star Film Company, an affiliate of Méliès.

Among Ford's earliest acting chores was a series of New Jersey–made westerns. He had his own unit at Bison, the Broncho Motion Picture Company; however, there was a falling out with Ince because the latter apparently took credit for much of his director's work. From 1913 to '16 he was at Universal where he appeared in features like *From Rail-Splitter to President* in which he portrayed Abraham Lincoln, as he did in several others of his films.

Ford's greatest on-camera fame came from the serials he co-starred and co-directed with Grace Cunard. *Lucille Love — Girl of Mystery* (1914) was enormously successful as was *The Broken Coin* (1915) and (*The Adventures of*) *Peg o' the Ring* in 1916. He also appeared with Cunard in crime dramas, including the "My Lady Raffles" series. Many of his films also had occult themes.

Ford left Universal to found Fordart Films but soon abandoned the company to direct and star in

the serials *The Silent Mystery* and *The Mystery of 13.* His acting career waned in the '20s and he directed serials and westerns for much of the decade.

Ford did continue to perform occasionally in such films as *Action, Mine to Keep, The Village Blacksmith, Hearts of Oak, The Taming of the West, Uncle Tom's Cabin, Soft Shoes* and *Sisters of Eve.* His last directorial stint was *Call of the Heart*, a 1928 picture with a canine hero. Last silent: *The Lariat Kid* (1929).

Sound: The Black Watch (1929) was Ford's introduction to sound. It was the first of numerous character roles in sound films, many of them directed by his brother. His frequent persona was that of a coonskin-capped (and frequently drunk) old "coot" in dozens of westerns. He also played villains.

Ford's other films included *Judge Priest* (a well-received performance), *The Ox-Bow Incident, Stagecoach, The Quiet Man, Drums Along the Mohawk, My Darling Clementine, Tobacco Road, Wagon Master, The Loves of Edgar Allan Poe* and *The Prisoner of Shark Island.*

Among Ford's many serial appearances were *Gordon of Ghost City, The Indians Are Coming, Battling with Buffalo Bill, Heroes of the West, The Lost Special* and *Clancy of the Mounted.* One of the last of his 350 roles was in his brother's *The Sun Shines Bright* in the year of his death.

Reviews

Steamboat Round the Bend: Francis Ford shows up importantly on the comedy end. *Variety* 5/25/35.

The Timber Trail: Ford makes a hissable heavy. *Variety* 6/30/48.

Ford, Harrison, Kansas City, Missouri,
1884/94–1957

Silent: The "original" Harrison Ford was a matinee idol and light comedian of the teens and '20s. After theater experience, he entered films in 1915 with *Excuse Me* and ultimately co-starred with most of the leading actresses of the day including the Talmadge sisters, Gloria Swanson, Marion Davies and Clara Bow.

Ford's more than 45 silents were made for almost every studio extant and in most genres. Among his films were *A Roadside Impresario, A Pair of Silk Stockings, The Veiled Adventure, The Third Kiss, The Marriage Whirl, Such a Little Pirate* and *Zander the Great.* Last silent: *Three Week-Ends* (1928).

Sound: It is probable that Harrison Ford made his sound debut in the 1929 Vitaphone short *The Flattering Word.* His only other known talkie appearance was 1932's comedy *Love in High Gear.* It was a quickie and apparently was not much seen or reviewed.

Foxe, Earle, Oxford, Ohio, 1888/91–1973

Silent: A 6' 2" stage actor who first appeared in films at New York's Kalem studio, Earle Foxe played leading roles in the 'teens with actresses like the Talmadge sisters and Mabel Normand. Among his early films for such studios as Goldwyn, Lasky, Select and Mutual were *Ashes of Embers, Panthea, The Love Mask* and *The Studio Girl*.

In the '20s, Foxe continued to play leads in movies that included *The Man She Brought Back, Vanity Fair* and *Fashion Row*, while also assuming some villain roles which he played quite believably. Among his other films of that decade were *Innocence, Wages for Wives, Oh, You Tony!, Ladies Must Dress, Sailor's Wives* and *The Black Panther's Cub*. Last silent: *Black Magic* (1929), with synchronized music and sound effects, made after his first talkies.

Sound: The Ghost Talks (1929) was Foxe's first all-talkie although most of his 1929 films were silent. He had appeared in the part-talker *The River Pirate* the previous year. From 1930 to '37 he played supporting roles, many unsympathetic, in numerous pictures which included *Transatlantic, Scarlet Dawn, Blondie Johnson, Bright Eyes, The Informer, Mary of Scotland* and *We're on the Jury*.

Foxe returned in 1940 for one more, *Military Academy*, in which he played a major. This was an apropos role because he was a co-founder of the well-known Los Angeles military school for children of the stars, the Black-Foxe Academy.

REVIEWS

Good Intentions: Earle Foxe is a double-crossing lieutenant and he plays the role well. *Variety* 7/30/30.

Military Academy: Foxe is particularly good in his role. *Variety* 8/7/40.

Francis, Alec B., London, England, 1869–1934

Silent: From the stage and vaudeville to the cinema came Alec B. Francis, possibly as early as 1910. Among the studios for which he worked were Vitagraph, Goldwyn and World. His earliest starring one-reelers included *Vanity Fair* and *Robin Hood*.

From 1914, Francis was a leading man in such features as *The Pit, The Sins of Society, The Imposter, The Man of the Hour* and *The Heart of a Hero*. Sometime in the 'teens he also began to be seen in top supporting roles and he increasingly played men of religion, a characterization that was to become his specialty.

Among Francis's multitude of silent films were *Forget-Me-Not, The Crimson Gardenia, Earthbound, Charley's Aunt, Beau Brummell, Tramp, Tramp, Tramp, The Shepherd of the Hills* and *Camille*. To the end of the silent era he still played some leads and occasionally was even top-billed. Last silent: *The Companionate Marriage* (1928).

Sound: By now Francis had long since had the gray hair and open, kindly face which enabled him to convincingly play churchmen and other generally benevolent souls. His first part-talkie was one of the very earliest, Warner Bros.' *The Lion and the Mouse* (1928), and that year he also appeared in *The Terror*. He continued in harness right up to his death.

Among Francis's 1929 pictures were *Evidence, The Mississippi Gambler* and *The Sacred Flame*. From 1930 his films included *The Case of Sergeant Grischa, Outward Bound, Arrowsmith, Mata Hari, The Last Mile, Alice in Wonderland, Oliver Twist* and *The Cat's Paw*. He also made a couple of shorts.

REVIEWS

The Terror: Alec Francis plays with easy assurance. *Variety* 8/22/28.

Mississippi Gambler: Francis is in a role that suits him. *Variety* 10/30/29.

The Last Man: Alec B. Francis is remarkably able as the crooked ship owner. *Variety* 9/29/32.

Looking Forward: Mr. Francis contributes good work. *New York Times* 5/1/33.

Frazer, Robert, Worcester, Massachusetts, 1890/91—1944

Filmography: *Classic Images* (July 1986); List of films in *Eighty Silent Film Stars*

Silent: Robert Frazer made the first of his 60-plus silent films in the East about 1912. He had come from the stage and continued to intersperse theater appearances with film work until at least 1921. In his films he alternated between leads and supporting roles.

Frazer's motion pictures included *The Feast of Love, Her Code of Honor, Without Limit, The Bramble Bush, Partners of the Sunset, Men* and *Why Women Love*. Last silent: *The Woman I Love* (1929).

Sound: The 1929 part-talkie *Careers* was Frazer's first sound picture. His first all-talkie was that year's *The Drake Case*, followed by *Frozen Justice*. All told, he made over 100 sound films in which he was relegated mainly to supporting roles.

Among Frazer's movies were *Two Gun Caballero, White Zombie, Found Alive* (lead), *Ladies Crave Excitement, The Garden of Allah, One Man's Law* and *A Night for Crime*. His last feature was *Forty Thieves* in the year of his death. There were also such serials as *The Black Coin, The Clutching Hand* and *The Mystery Trooper*.

Reviews

The Drake Case: Several picture personalities of other days have returned to the screen. Most of them have been confined to independent films and freelance employment for quite a while. Among them is Robert Frazer whose voice registers well and he is convincing. *Variety* 9/18/29, *Harrison's Reports* 9/21/29.

White Zombie: Now and then a tendency to overplay jars slightly but the entire cast is well selected and the acting is of an even texture. Robert Frazer helps to maintain the atmosphere. *Variety* 8/2/32.

Frederick, Pauline (Pauline Beatrice or
Beatrice Pauline Libbey), Boston, Massachusetts, 1881/85–1938
Filmography: Films in Review (Feb. 1965)
Silent: "The Girl with the Topaz Eyes" was Pauline Frederick. A noted stage performer, she signed with Famous Players-Lasky in 1915 for *The Eternal City* and the films she made there were considered among the best of her silent career. After going over to Goldwyn, her pictures (except for 1920's *Madame X*) declined somewhat in quality and her later stay at Robertson-Cole saw yet a further decline.

Frederick also appeared for Warner Bros., Tiffany, Universal, FBO and Chadwick. Even though she continued to intersperse film and stage appearances, she still managed to make about 50 films. Among them were *Zaza, The Woman in the Case, Her Better Self, Fedora, Bonds of Love, Let No Man Put Asunder* and *Smouldering Fires.* Last silent: *The Nest* (1927).

Sound: Frederick's sound debut was in *On Trial* (1928), the fourth Warner Bros. all-talkie. Unfortunately the somewhat primitive sound equipment used on that film did not register her voice well. Other early talkies included *Evidence* and *The Sacred Flame.* She bore a strong resemblance to Joan Crawford and played her mother in *This Modern Age.*

Others of Frederick's more than 10 sound films were *The Phantom of Crestwood, Self-Defense, Social Register, My Marriage, Ramona* and *Wayward.* She brought her talents to a wide variety of fare, last appearing in the "B" series film *Thank You, Mr. Moto* (1937).

Comments: The perceived problem with Pauline Frederick's voice was of short duration and the stage veteran soon made it clear that she possessed a fine vocal instrument. She also made it clear that she was an accomplished scene-stealer as well.

The problem was to be that Frederick was hardly ever in a scene *worth* stealing. The quality of her

talkie roles was far from that of her early silent career when she was considered one of the premier dramatic screen actresses.

Reviews

On Trial: This proves that talkies can restore some silent performers to popularity, but the opposite is true of Pauline Frederick and faulty recording can hardly be blamed. She is so throaty and her talking efforts were so obvious that seldom more than muffled sounds came out of her mouth. She is far from meriting featured billing and her role is the least convincing in the cast. *Variety* 11/21/28, *Harrison's Reports* 11/24/28.

The Sacred Flame: There are good dramatic performances with Pauline Frederick's finished one. She plays a mother who poisons her own son. *Variety* 11/27/29.

This Modern Age: The most genuine thing about this is the resemblance between Joan Crawford and Frederick. The latter doesn't seem at home amid these silly melodramatics and attempts at comedy and has been over-directed in certain sequences. *Variety* 9/8/31.

My Marriage: Pauline Frederick gives a smart performance all the way, stealing the show from the others. *Variety* 2/26/36.

Friganza, Trixie (Brigid or Delia
O'Callaghan or O'Callahan), Lacygne, Kansas, 1871–1955
Silent: Known as "Broadway's Favorite Champagne Girl" in the 1890s and "The Grand Duchess of Comedy" (and in her later, plump years "The Perfect 46"), vaudeville and musical star Trixie Friganza entered films with top billing in 1923's *Mind Over Motor.*

Friganza played supporting roles in several more pictures over the next few years, including *Borrowed Finery, The Coming of Amos, The Road to Yesterday, Almost a Lady* and *Monte Carlo.* Last silents: *Thanks for the Buggy Ride* and *Gentlemen Prefer Blondes,* released about the same time in 1928.

Sound: Friganza's sound debut probably came with the Vitaphone short *My Bag of Trix* (1929). She made another, *Strong and Willing,* in 1930. In her first talkie feature she played Buster Keaton's prospective dragon of a mother-in-law in *Free and Easy* (1930).

The remainder of Friganza's talkies were scattered over the following ten years: *Myrt and Marge, The Wanderer of the Wasteland, Silks and Saddles, A Star Is Born* and, finally, *If I Had My Way* (1940). She also appeared in more shorts. Her career ultimately was cut short by an increasingly disabling arthritis.

Free and Easy: Trixie Friganza is the foil for Buster Keaton and a perfect choice for the part. *Variety* 4/23/30.

Myrt and Marge: Trixie Friganza is strictly synthetic as she is presented here. Her personality, customarily gay and infectious, is pseudo-jovial. *Variety* 1/23/34.

If I Had My Way: The floor show introduces several favorites of the old days, including Trixie Friganza. *Variety* 5/1/40.

Gallagher, Richard ("Skeets"), Terre Haute, Indiana, 1890/91–1955

Filmography: Hollywood Players: The Thirties

Silent: A popular figure in vaudeville and on the stage from about 1910, "Skeets" Gallagher made his screen bow in *The Daring Years* in 1923. It was not until four years later that he returned to the cinema and established himself as a reliable supporting actor in such films as *For the Love of Mike, The Potters, New York, Three-Ring Marriage* and *The Racket*. In 1928's *Alex the Great* he played the title role. Last silent: *Stocks and Blondes* (1928).

Sound: Although he had a voice that could seem somewhat high in pitch, sound made Gallagher a bigger name. He went on to appear in a long string of features, as well as some shorts, through the late '30s. In the early years of the decade there were several musicals, including *Paramount on Parade* (1930), in which he was one of the masters of ceremonies, and *Honey*.

Gallagher's '30s talkies included *Love Among the Millionaires, Possessed, Bird of Paradise, Alice in Wonderland, Riptide, Polo Joe* and *Idiot's Delight*. His roles declined substantially in the latter part of the decade and afterwards he was seen in only a few pictures.

Among "Skeets" Gallagher's 1940s pictures were *Citadel of Crime, Brother Orchid* and *The Duke of Chicago*. By the '50s he was virtually retired from the screen but he returned in '52 for a final role in *Three for Bedroom C*, Gloria Swanson's ill-advised follow-up to *Sunset Blvd.*

Close Harmony: Gallagher clicks on a comic display of egotism and fast chatter which keeps getting faster. (In this film, as in others, he was teamed with rising Paramount star Jack Oakie.) *Variety* 5/1/29.

Her Wedding Night: Skeets Gallagher does a capital job. *New York Times* 9/29/30.

The Road to Reno: Gallagher has the briefest role he has had as one of those Reno husbands. *Variety* 10/13/31.

The Perfect Clue: Gallagher tries hard to make a gumshoe role both mysterious and comical. *Variety* 3/17/37.

Garbo, Greta (Greta Gustafsson), Stockholm, Sweden, 1905–1990

Filmography: *Films in Review* (Dec. 1951, Nov. 1979); *Film Comment* (Summer 1970); *Screen Greats* (no. 8, 1972); *Focus on Film* (Summer 1973); List of films in *Film Dope* (Sept. 1979); *Hollywood Studio Magazine* (Nov. 1987); *Stars* (Sept. 1990)

Silent: Before becoming the preeminent actress in the American cinema, Greta Garbo had little professional training. After a bit of modeling, drama school and some minor stage work, she made her first brief film appearance in the Swedish comedy *Peter the Tramp* in 1922.

Garbo's first major role was in *The Atonement of Gosta Berling* and then she made the German film *The Joyless Street* (a.k.a. *The Street of Sorrow*). The story is that, while in Berlin, MGM chief Louis B. Mayer saw *Gosta Berling* and signed both her and mentor, director Mauritz Stiller.

Although it has usually been thought that MGM only wanted Stiller and had to take Garbo to get him, there may be some doubt about this. The pair arrived in America in 1925 and she made her American debut with Ricardo Cortez as her leading man in 1926's *The Torrent*. It would be the last time she was not top-billed.

It was in her third Hollywood film, *Flesh and the Devil* (1927), following *The Temptress*, that Garbo began displaying the screen allure that was to catapult her to the pinnacle of Hollywood stardom. With John Gilbert as her leading man for the first time, it made a sensation.

The romantic duo (off-screen for a while as well as on-) also appeared in *Love* (based on *Anna Karenina*) and *A Woman of Affairs*. Garbo's remaining silents were mediocre melodramas or domestic dramas in which she played a variation of the sophisticated "vamp." They included *The Mysterious Lady, The Divine Woman* (except for a few snippets, the only lost Greta Garbo film), *Wild Orchids* and *The Single Standard*. Last silent: *The Kiss* (1929), with synchronized music.

Sound: There was no star in Hollywood whose talkie debut was as eagerly awaited as that of Garbo. MGM was naturally anxious given their enormous investment in her career. With the punchy and ubiquitous catch-phrase "Garbo Talks!" ringing in everyone's ears, that debut came in the 1930 remake of *Anna Christie*.

To build the suspense, Garbo did not appear at all in the first reel. Her first words when she finally did come on the screen are probably the most famous of any star who made the transition. They were "Give me a whiskey, ginger ale on the side, and don't be stingy, baby."

With Garbo's not unpleasant Swedish accent it came out more like "viskey" but who cared? She could talk, and in a low, musical voice, too. She also "talked" in the Hollywood-made German-language version. *Anna Christie* and its follow-up *Romance* resulted in her first Academy Award nomination.

Garbo's voice was described as a "deep, husky and throaty contralto" which only enhanced her screen persona as a world-weary, slightly neurotic woman who had lived too much. Her talkies of the first half of the 1930s were by no means uniformly good and included insipid vehicles like *Mata Hari*, *Inspiration*, *As You Desire Me* and *The Painted Veil*.

There were much better ones like the all-star *Grand Hotel* in which Garbo somewhat improbably portrayed the fading ballerina. In *Queen Christina*, which reunited her with onetime lover John Gilbert, the close-up of her famously "blank" face in the last scene is one of the iconographic images of 1930s cinema.

In the six years remaining in Garbo's career after 1935, she made only five motion pictures beginning with the sound version of *Anna Karenina*. This was one of her best films and recouped the dip in her fortunes caused by the fevered melodrama *The Painted Veil*.

Garbo was now at her peak, following *Karenina* with the classic *Camille* (sometimes dubbed "Garbo *coughs*"). It is generally considered her best film and was the source of her third Academy Award nomination. Nineteen thirty-seven's *Conquest*, and the comedies *Ninotchka* ("Garbo laughs!") in 1939 and the poorly received *Two-Faced Woman* (1941), proved to be her last.

Garbo was far from being a natural comedienne, although *Ninotchka* won for her her last unsuccessful Oscar nod. Her performance was certainly good but her comedy came mainly from acting serious in funny situations rather than from any lightness of touch.

Garbo described her final film as her "grave." Of it a reviewer wrote, "Its embarrassing effect is not unlike seeing Sarah Bernhardt swatted with a bladder or seeing your mother drunk."

In the late 1940s, rumors abounded that Garbo finally would return to the screen. The most promising potential role seemed to be in *The Duchess of Langeais* for which color tests may actually have been shot. It did not eventuate but she was awarded a special Oscar in 1954 for her "unforgettable screen performances." Characteristically, she was not there to collect it.

Comments: The almost 50 years of semi-reclusiveness into which Greta Garbo retreated after 1941 only added to the larger-than-life image fostered during her career. Certainly no other star was the object of such frenzied interest and for so long a time. The sightings of her solitary New York rambles and the clandestine photographs were treasured like rare gems.

Overshadowing the millions of words about Garbo's aura of mystery is a deeper mystery: How did a rather dull Swedish peasant's daughter achieve such goddess-like status? Part of it was her own personality and life choices, part MGM's publicity mill and part the moviegoing public's penchant for investing stars with qualities they do not possess.

At the beginning of Garbo's tenure in Hollywood, MGM public relations people did not seem to know how to handle her. They began by publicizing her as a stereotypical athletic Swede. The photos of her self-consciously posing in track clothes reveal this idea's absurdity.

After the success of her first films, Garbo segued into a totally different image. Her screen persona and her natural, if not pathological, diffidence readily lent themselves to an air of mystery. She was even attributed with Sphinx-like qualities.

This image was of course closer to the real Greta Garbo. She was almost totally uncommunicative and insisted on closed sets. There seemed to be a very remote relationship between herself and most of the other stars in MGM's "heaven."

Garbo's real self was beside the point, however. In front of the camera she was transformed into someone totally apart; she and the camera had a love affair fed by her natural narcissism. Although her film type, the "vamp," had been seen many times before, she was clearly something new in the cinema, the first of the new brand of "sex" stars. It was said that many screen actresses who saw Garbo's first performances felt their own careers sinking into the West.

Garbo herself did not want to be just another vamp: "I do not want to be a silly temptress. I cannot see any sense in getting dressed up and doing nothing but tempting men in pictures." But MGM knew a moneymaking formula when they saw one. Some of her roles were better than others but they were variations on the same theme. Garbo's leading men were usually no match for her, with the exception of John Gilbert and (later) John Barrymore, Charles Boyer and Melvyn Douglas. Lewis Stone, who appeared with her in seven films, was older and gentlemanly and not to be considered in the same category as her other screen lovers.

Some of Garbo's co-stars were undeniably rather

callow and served basically as backdrops for her to emote off of. Among them were John Mack Brown, Ramon Novarro, Robert Montgomery, Conrad Nagel, Robert Taylor and the least known, Gavin Gordon. Clark Gable, who was just starting out, was at the time no match for her. Perhaps Herbert Marshall and her fellow Swede Nils Asther fought her to a draw.

Fortunately, Garbo's performances generally transcended the weak stories. Her gaze into the camera bespoke unplumbed depths; she could seemingly communicate the very souls of her characters through facial expressions and the use of her hands. She was a great screen actress despite certain mannerisms that recurred from picture to picture — throwing her head back to laugh, for instance.

Garbo could suffer beautifully and suffer she did, sometimes even finding regeneration. She also was one of the very few major stars who routinely could be allowed to get her comeuppance. Many of her films ended unhappily and in many she actually expired.

Garbo's characters were not temptresses of the Theda Bara mold by any means. Her actions sprung not from the evil inside her but from the angst. She genuinely could love the men she ruined and also exhibited mother love in several films. The sympathy of the audience generally was with her.

Finally, though, the sympathy and the interest of the audience waned. As Garbo had supplanted many a silent star, she was in turn supplanted. Although the studio did not officially drop her and she did not officially retire, her value to them was declining.

The onset of the Second World War blocked revenues from overseas markets which latterly had provided much of the profit for Garbo's films. Also, she was approaching "that certain age" when she could no longer play romantic roles convincingly and might not wish to be seen to grow older publicly. Probably as important from the studio's point of view, she was a high-priced and demanding commodity.

Retiring into wealthy professional inactivity with periodic whirls among the jet set, Greta Garbo retained the world's avid curiosity. This was a phenomenon that never would have existed had her career been allowed to sputter out. With probably little deliberation on her part, her fabled diffidence continued to feed into the unknowable quality of her screen persona.

This shy and severely limited woman would be forever invested as a cinema goddess. The final photos of her as an old and ill woman, with no trace of the "Divine Garbo" remaining, strangely did little to change that perception.

Reviews

Anna Christie: Its success is owed chiefly to the good acting of Greta Garbo. She speaks her lines with surprising clearness and with an imperceptible foreign accent. If she continues taking English lessons in a very short time she will be able to speak English flawlessly and without any accent whatever. Her acting reminds one of the acting of Jeanne Eagels. It is a part that exactly fits Garbo. "Garbo Talks" is beyond doubt an event of major box office significance. (Garbo is reputed to have thought this a bad film, and even walked out of a screening because she said real Swedes did not act that way.) *Variety* 3/19/30, *Harrison's Reports* 3/22/30.

Inspiration: Garbo never looked nor acted better. She plays it easily and convincingly, even contributing a sparkling brief bit of light comedy. *Variety* 2/11/31.

Mata Hari: Greta Garbo is sexy and hot in a less subtle way this time. *Variety* 1/5/32.

Grand Hotel: Reviews differed somewhat. One stated that Garbo gave the role of the dancer something of an artificial aura and was sometimes stagey. Another said her performance was most artistic and that in some scenes she was superb. *Variety* 4/19/32, *Harrison's Reports* 5/14/32.

As You Desire Me: It is Greta Garbo's acting, more than the story, that holds one's interest because she builds up so much sympathy for the character she portrays. Her performance is always absorbingly vivid and compelling in its appeal. *Variety* 6/7/32, *Harrison's Reports* 6/11/32.

Queen Christina: Garbo's performance too often keeps pace with the script's lethargy, but as often, and more, it is in keeping with the romantic highlights. Her regal impression is convincing. *Variety* 1/2/34.

Anna Karenina: Garbo has never had a part which suited her more comfortably. There is no flaw to be found in her current rendition as compared to 1927's *Love*. *Variety* 9/4/35.

Camille: Garbo has never done anything better. It is sure to go down among her best portraits. (Her performance is generally thought to be one of the greatest female tours de force in the history of the cinema. She captured every nuance of the Marguerite Gauthier character perfectly.) *Variety* 1/27/37.

Ninotchka: The star is excellent in her light role. *Variety* 10/11/39.

Two-Faced Woman: The experiment of converting Miss Garbo into a comedienne is not entirely successful but it is no fault of hers. There is no holding Garbo back when she finally steps down from the serious dramatic pedestal on which she has been perched. As a stunt the film is a triumph for Garbo and through all her acting as a siren she retains just the right amount of roguishness. *Variety* 10/22/41.

Garon, Pauline (Marie P. Garon), Montreal, Canada, 1900/04–1965

Silent: Pert blonde Pauline Garon made her debut in a small role in *A Manhattan Knight* (1920). She soon found herself cast as the archetypal flapper in saucy comedies but could also portray more conventional heroines.

Among Garon's films were DeMille's *Adam's Rib*, *The Painted Flapper*, *You Can't Fool Your Wife*, *Passionate Youth*, *Eager Lips*, *The Heart of Broadway* and *Naughty*. Last silent: *Must We Marry?* (1928).

Sound: A supporting role in 1929's *The Gamblers* was Garon's first essay into sound. Other early films were *The Show of Shows*, *In the Headlines* and the Vitaphone short *Letters*. Her talkie career was mediocre and she never again regained a vestige of her previous stardom, however minor. She also made French-language versions of Hollywood films (e.g., *The Merry Widow* and *Folies Bergère de Paris*).

Among Garon's films to the late 1930s were *The Thoroughbred*, *One Year Later*, *Lost in the Stratosphere*, *Easy Millions*, *King of Hockey* and *Bluebeard's Eighth Wife*, probably her last, in which she had a bit part. She was also seen, albeit briefly, in better films such as *Wonder Bar* and *Becky Sharp*.

REVIEWS

In the Headlines: Pauline Garon plays the hero's half-sister in this comedy-drama. *Harrison's Reports* 12/28/29.

Thoroughbred: Garon is the confederate of the crook. *Harrison's Reports* 9/6/30.

Easy Millions: The nominal lead is thrust into the background, which gives better chances to Pauline Garon. *Variety* 9/26/33.

Garvin, Anita, New York, New York, 1906–1994

Silent: Of all ex–Follies girl Anita Garvin's roles, her appearances in Laurel and Hardy two-reel comedies like *Their Purple Moment* and *Why Girls Love Sailors* are the most fondly remembered. A bit that involved her slipping on a pie in their classic *Battle of the Century* was memorialized in a compilation of silent comedy highlights.

Garvin also was seen in scores of other two-reelers and from 1926 she played supporting roles in a few features such as *Bertha the Sewing Machine Girl*, *The Valley of Hell*, *The Night Watch* and *The Play Girl*. Last silent feature: *Trent's Last Case* (1929), with synchronized sound effects and music.

Sound: Garvin continued appearing in comedy shorts for Hal Roach, working again with Laurel and Hardy as well as Our Gang, Charley Chase and Thelma Todd. She also had small parts in features like the 1929 part-talkies *The Charlatan* and *Modern Love* and her first all-talkie that year, *Red Hot Rhythm*.

Almost all of Garvin's sound films were two-reel shorts, with very brief roles in scattered Laurel and Hardy features like *Swiss Miss* and *A Chump at Oxford*. She retired in the early '40s having made an estimated 350 appearances.

Comments: Usually playing a hard-boiled type, narrow-eyed brunette Anita Garvin had the voice to match her persona. With its slight and not unpleasant New York accent and cutting edge, it well complemented her comically unsympathetic roles.

The revival and reassessment of the pictures of Laurel and Hardy and other comedians revealed to a new generation of moviegoers Garvin's considerable contributions. As an old woman, she was interviewed for television to elicit her memories about working with some of the greats and her own second-banana roles as well. She seemed to feel much satisfaction in knowing that she was newly appreciated.

Gaynor, Janet (Laura Gainer), Philadelphia, Pennsylvania, 1906–1984

Filmography: *Films in Review* (Oct. 1979); List of films in *Film Dope* (Dec. 1979)

Silent: After bit and extra appearances, red-haired Janet Gaynor played her first important role in *The Johnstown Flood* in 1926. This modest-enough beginning segued the following year into her enormous success in *Sunrise* and *Seventh Heaven*. For these two films and *Street Angel* she received the very first Academy Award for Best Actress.

The latter two motion pictures began Gaynor's popular teaming with Charles Farrell. Her few other silents like *The Blue Eagle*, *Two Girls Wanted*, *The Shamrock Handicap* and *The Midnight Kiss* were, by contrast, minor efforts. Last silent: *Christina* (1929), with synchronized sound effects and music, made after her first talkies.

Sound: *Street Angel* (1928) was the first of Janet Gaynor's part-talkies. The others in '29 were *Four Devils* and *Lucky Star*. Her cameo in *Happy Days* technically marked her first appearance in an all-sound film but the 1929 musical *Sunny Side Up*, with Farrell, was her first actual starring sound feature.

Among Gaynor's several talkies with Farrell were *Delicious, The Man Who Came Back, High Society Blues, Merely Mary Ann, Tess of the Storm Country* and *Change of Heart.* Among her other films were *Daddy Long Legs, State Fair, Servant's Entrance, One More Spring* and *Carolina.*

By 1936 Gaynor's starring career was clearly on the wane. It was actually announced that she would no longer be the sole star of Fox films, and *Ladies in Love* (1936) saw her in co-starring status.

Gaynor was rescued the following year with the major hit and enduring classic *A Star Is Born,* directed by George Cukor. She was nominated for an Academy Award. That success proved to be fleeting, however, and only two films followed. They were *Three Loves Has Nancy* and her final starring film, 1938's *The Young in Heart.*

Almost 20 years later, Gaynor returned for a final role, a supporting one, in *Bernardine* (1957). Late in life she made her Broadway debut in a musical version of the film *Harold and Maude.* She also was known for her painting skills.

Comments: Petite, almost elfin, Janet Gaynor rose to Fox superstardom in the late 1920s and early 1930s with her appealing, rather than traditionally pretty, looks. The popular musical *Sunny Side Up* was an auspicious start to her sound career but it revealed a voice needing further training.

Gaynor's voice recorded high and somewhat thin, as did that of her co-star Charles Farrell. Although it improved over the course of her films, it never became a commandingly used instrument. As for her acting, it at times relied too much on cute mannerisms.

Gaynor did render a fine performance in *A Star Is Born.* It showed that she could be a real actress. However, she was probably too old for the role of Esther Blodgett and she certainly was getting past the age where her established persona could long continue.

Reviews

Four Devils: Janet Gaynor's voice is a plaintive, childish voice, which, while it does not betray experience in speaking lines, is effective during some periods. She tends to recite lines rather than speak them but she touches a response with the audience. *New York Times* 6/18/29, *Variety* 6/19/29.

Sunny Side Up: The director has done so well by Gaynor that you even believe she has a voice. She has a sweet singing and talking voice in addition to her beauty and dramatic talent. *Variety* 10/9/29, *Harrison's Reports* 10/19/29.

Daddy Long Legs: Janet Gaynor, around whom the story centers, probably was never seen in better form. Her voice fitted everywhere. *Variety* 6/19/31.

Merely Mary Ann: Score another for the Gaynor-Farrell romantic partnership. The ingenue role is eminently suited to Miss Gaynor and she gets all there is out of it by her simple, artless method and her special knack in portraying the pathos of adolescence. *Variety* 9/15/31.

State Fair: Of chief interest is the debut of a new romantic team in Janet Gaynor and Lew Ayres. The combination should give Gaynor a fresh hold on her fans. *Variety* 1/31/33.

A Star Is Born: Gaynor gives to her role a characterization of sustained loveliness which will arouse generous sympathy. She is equally as good in the comedy passages and probably has not given a more satisfactory performance in her career. She will undoubtedly win back her fans and gain renewed popularity by her performance. *Variety* 4/28/37, *Harrison's Reports* 5/1/37.

George, Gladys (Gladys Clare), Patten, Maine, 1900/04–1954

Filmography: Film Fan Monthly (Mar. 1972)

Silent: After appearing in vaudeville (at the age of seven with "Little Gladys George and Company") in stock and on Broadway, Gladys George made the first of her seven silent films, *Red Hot Dollars,* in 1919. The others included *Below the Surface, Homespun Folks, The Woman in the Suitcase, Chickens* and *The Easy Road.*

George alternated between supporting and leading roles with stars such as Charles Ray, Thomas Meighan and Hobart Bosworth. It is likely she would have maintained a worthwhile career in silents were it not for an accident in which she was badly burned. Last silent: *The House That Jazz Built* (1921).

Sound: After spending the next dozen years back in the theater, George returned for the first of over 30 talkies in 1934's *Straight Is the Way.* She continued to appear on the stage as well, one of her '30s plays being the major success *Personal Appearance.*

It was her second film, the teary melodrama *Valiant Is the Word for Carrie* (1936), that established George as a credible film actress and brought her an Academy Award nomination (she lost to Luise Rainer). She was signed by MGM but then freelanced for most of her career, which lasted until 1953.

Among George's better-known pictures were *The Maltese Falcon,* in a small but juicy role, *The Best Years of Our Lives, The Roaring Twenties* and *The Way of All Flesh.* Others included *Marie Antoinette, They Gave Him a Gun, Christmas Holiday, Flamingo Road, Undercover Girl* and *He Ran All the Way.* Her last, after a hiatus, was *It Happens*

Every Thursday, in which she was way down in the cast list.

Comments: Gladys George portrayed world-weary characters most effectively. She certainly looked the part; there was something about her face that bespoke tragedy. Although she was a sensitive actress, she often was typecast as a stereotypical tough brassy blonde with a heart of gold.

George inevitably drifted into character roles in which she was often the best thing in an otherwise forgettable film. In truth, most of her films were unworthy of her.

REVIEWS

Valiant Is the Word for Carrie: This will certainly make Gladys George a popular screen actress, for her work is marvelous. She really is a find. This is her first [sic] picture and should lead her to box-office manna. (Perhaps one of the oddest tributes to this film was made by The Three Stooges, one of whose shorts was entitled *Violent Is the Word for Curly*.) *Harrison's Reports* 10/10/36, *Variety* 10/14/36.

Madame X: George's performance is effective, her makeup transitions are splendid and her characterization is faithful and moving. *Variety* 9/29/37.

A Child Is Born: The one character that should be hardest to take is the vaudeville performer, an assignment which Gladys George performs with all throttles open. *Variety* 1/17/41.

The Maltese Falcon: Advantageous support is provided by Gladys George who plays Iva Archer, the flirtatious wife of Sam Spade's murdered partner. *Variety* 10/1/41.

Undercover Girl: A polished job is done by Gladys George as a derelict. *Variety* 11/1/50.

Geraghty, Carmelita, Rushville, Indiana, 1901–1966

Filmography: List of films in *Sweethearts of the Sage*

Silent: Carmelita Geraghty's silents, from 1923, included the programmers *High Speed*, *The Mysterious Stranger*, *The Slaver*, *The Flying Mail* and *The Canyon of Light* as well as a few more prestigious ones like *Black Oxen* and *Venus of Venice*. She alternated between starring roles, second leads and supporting roles. Last silent: *Object — Alimony* (1928). This may have also been known as *Object–Matrimony*.

Sound: Geraghty's first talkie was *Paris Bound* (1929). All her other films that year, including *Mississippi Gambler* and *This Thing Called Love*, were sound, too. Among her later films were *Rogue of the Rio Grande*, *Texas Rangers*, *Millie* and *The Phantom of Santa Fe*, her last. She also was in the serial *The Jungle Mystery* and may also have appeared in at least one short.

REVIEWS

Men Without Law: An excellent western in which Carmelita Geraghty is the heroine. She plays opposite Buck Jones, with the romancing held down. *Harrison's Reports* 11/1/30, *Variety* 12/3/30.

Gibson, Helen (Rose H. Wenger), 1892/94–1977

Filmography: List of films in *Sweethearts of the Sage*

Silent: From 1912, for Kalem and other studios, Helen Gibson made numerous one- and two-reelers, most prominently those with a railroad theme. She replaced Helen Holmes in the long-running railroad serial *The Hazards of Helen*.

Gibson's starring career declined in the early 1920s and she later became a rider in Wild West shows. Among her features were *Loot*, *Fighting Mad*, *No Man's Woman*, *The Wolverine* and *Nine Points of the Law*. Last billed silent: *Thorobred* (1922). She appeared in later '20s films in small unbilled roles, stunt and extra work.

Sound: About 1932, Gibson returned for small roles and worked until the 1960s, so her career spanned more than 50 years. Among her films were numerous westerns including *The Way of the West*, *Cyclone of the Saddle*, *Danger Valley*, *Stagecoach*, and others such as *The Drunkard*, *Hollywood Story*, *Lady of Secrets* and *365 Nights in Hollywood*. Her last may have been *The Man Who Shot Liberty Valance*.

REVIEWS

Hollywood Story: As an added treat, four old-time stars including Helen Gibson appear briefly. *Harrison's Reports* 5/19/51.

Gibson, Hoot (Edmund Gibson), Tekamah, Nebraska, 1892–1962

Filmography: *Films in Review* (Oct. 1978), *Classic Images* (Apr. 1991); List of films in *Eighty Silent Film Stars*

Silent: A veteran of Wild West shows and winner of the title "World Championship Cowboy" in 1912, Hoot Gibson began dabbling in films about 1910. He appeared mostly in one-reelers until 1916 and then in two-reelers intermixed with a few features in which he played supporting roles.

Among Gibson's early longer films were *A Knight of the Range*, *Straight Shooting* and *Headin' South*. His major fame came in the 1920s at Universal, where he had his own production company for a time. Although most of his films were westerns, there were a few straight melodramas as well.

Gibson's pictures included *His Only Son*, *The Texas Sphinx*, *The Fighting Brothers*, *The Driftin' Kid*, *The Gentleman from America*, *Let 'Er Buck*, *The Wild West Show*, *The Thrill Chaser* and *Action* (1921), probably his first major feature.

Altogether, Gibson made about 170 silents and was seen in early serials like *The Voice on the Wire* and *The Hazards of Helen*, in which his wife Helen Gibson starred. He also appeared in some "specials" during the 1920s, the best of which may have been *The Flaming Frontier* (1926), the story of Custer at Little Big Horn. Last silent: *Points West* (1929).

Sound: With the coming of sound and his first talkies *The Long, Long Trail* and *Courtin' Wildcats* in 1929, Gibson's popularity slowly began to decline. He remained at Universal until 1931 and then worked steadily at independent studios until 1937, his last appearance being a supporting role in the serial *The Painted Stallion*. There were also a couple of films with Harry Carey, whom he had supported in the 'teens.

Gibson returned for 11 pictures in the Monogram "Trail Blazers" series in 1943–44. That was virtually the end of his 45 picture talkie career except for roles in 1946's *Flight to Nowhere*, *The Marshal's Daughter* (1953) and cameos in *The Horse Soldiers* (1959) and 1960's *Ocean's Eleven*.

Among Hoot Gibson's other films were *The Mounted Stranger*, *The Local Bad Man*, *Sunset Range*, *Swifty*, *Cavalcade of the West*, *Wild Horse Stampede* (the first of the Monogram series), *Blazing Guns* and *Outlaw Trail*. During his film hiatus in the late '30s, he toured with a circus.

Comments: Hoot Gibson was much loved by the juvenile trade for the comedy injected into his films. He was not a great one for physical action, generally overcoming his foes with wisecracks; however, he would fight if pressed. Ultimately the sameness of his persona contributed to his decline.

"Streamlined" is a term often applied to Gibson's films. The appurtenances of the Wild West vied with the modern conveniences of the day. He used motorcycles and planes, even a taxi, to pursue the villains. Unfortunately, when he returned in the '40s he was not in shape to pursue anyone. His aging was noticeable and it probably would have been better had he remained in dignified retirement.

Reviews

The Long, Long Trail: If Gibson can go on talking, with the same lucidity and ease of speech as in this one, he won't have to give up westerns. His

talking will likely prove a pleasant surprise to kids. *Variety* 11/6/29, *Harrison's Reports* 11/16/29.

The Hard Hombre: One of the best Hoot Gibson has made due mostly to the laughs. He plays for every ounce of fun in the character. *Variety* 9/29/31.

Dude Bandit: Hoot Gibson deftly handles his somewhat implausible changes from the dude to the bandit. *Variety* 6/27/33.

The Law Rides Again: Gibson now appears slightly overweight but he still makes a good western hero. *Variety* 8/11/43.

Gilbert, John (John Pringle), Logan, Utah, 1895/99–1936

Filmography: *Films in Review* (Oct. 1962); List of films in *Film Dope* (Dec. 1979).

Silent: Entering films about 1915 as an extra, John Gilbert had many supporting roles before he played his first lead in *Princess of the Dark* (1917). He was a player for Triangle and Fox, wrote scenarios and ultimately acted in about 70 silent films.

Gilbert was in many forgettable pictures before he became the fabled great lover of the 1920s and the only real rival to the more exotic Rudolph Valentino. His films included *The White Circle*, *While Paris Sleeps*, *Romance Ranch*, *Man, Woman and Sin*, *Heart o' the Hills*, *Bardelys the Magnificent* and *The Show*.

Gilbert went to MGM in 1924 for *His Hour* and there reached superstardom, particularly after *The Merry Widow* with Mae Murray and *The Big Parade*, both 1925. This pinnacle was further scaled in his co-starring films with Greta Garbo, the sizzling *Flesh and the Devil*, *Love* and *A Woman of Affairs*. Last silent: *Desert Nights* (1929), with synchronized music score and sound effects.

Sound: In his first talkie, Gilbert was one of the numerous MGM players showcased in *The Hollywood Revue of 1929*. He performed an abridged version of the balcony scene from *Romeo and Juliet* and traded nervous wisecracks with Norma Shearer and Lionel Barrymore.

Although *Redemption* was Gilbert's first completed starring talkie, it was deemed unreleasable and was then partly reshot and not released until 1930. The infamous Ruritanian melodrama *His Glorious Night* (1929), directed by Lionel Barrymore, thus became the first of his sound films to be screened.

Unfortunately, it was the vehicle that toppled the handsome Gilbert from the heights and thrust him into the stuff of legend. His performance, and more specifically his stilted elocution, gave rise to titters if not outright laughter from audiences.

What was intended to be fervent romancing became farce when Gilbert clutched the icy Catherine

Dale Owen to his bosom and theatrically declaimed, "I love you, I love you, I love you." This was of course the source of the satiric scene between Gene Kelly and Jean Hagen in the 1952 MGM musical *Singin' in the Rain.*

Gilbert had figuratively died but he refused to acknowledge it and stubbornly insisted upon making the films to which his contract committed him. Almost without exception they were unsuccessful, especially the now-released *Redemption.*

Gilbert's other talkies included *Way for a Sailor, The Phantom of Paris, Downstairs,* which he also wrote, *Fast Workers, West of Broadway* and his last, Columbia's *The Captain Hates the Sea* in 1934. His career was briefly resuscitated when Garbo requested him for 1933's *Queen Christina.* Although he was perfectly satisfactory in the role originally meant for Laurence Olivier, it was a case of too little too late.

Comments: John Gilbert's failure in talkies has attained mythic proportions and led to the widespread belief that this was the fate of all silent stars, especially the "lovers." Among the *cognoscenti,* his tragedy has been the subject of more speculation than that of anyone else who failed to cross the chasm to sound films.

Gilbert's is the ultimate cautionary tale — but of *what* exactly? While it is true that audiences responded by laughing at *His Glorious Night,* it was less the quality of his voice than the general "fruitiness" of the dialogue and Gilbert's perfervid delivery of it.

Rumors have been running rife ever since. The most prevalent is that Gilbert's career had been deliberately sabotaged by Louis B. Mayer working in tandem with the director Lionel Barrymore. The latter supposedly owed Mayer his undying allegiance, the possible reason being a drug dependency which Mayer helped to support and hush up.

Or was Gilbert's voice unsuitably high-pitched? Did he have the so-called "white voice"? The answer seems to be no. What does seem to be an incontrovertible fact is that he had been taking elocution lessons and rumor had it that not one but three teachers were working with him.

Gilbert's natural speaking voice, while not mellifluous, was a not-unpleasant light baritone. Whatever the reason for the failure of his first released sound film, his remaining ones, with the exception of *Queen Christina,* were certainly of poor quality. He may have been a fiery leading man in silents but he was an all too ordinary one in talkies.

Gilbert's was truly a tragic tale in that he was a decent man who seemed to have no idea about why he failed. He made matters worse by insisting that his contract be played out in light of the mediocre films he was assigned. His 1934 advertisement lamenting that MGM neither gave him work nor released him was the last link in a very sad chain of events.

REVIEWS

His Glorious Night: Reviewers did not fully agree. One said that Gilbert's voice was passably pleasant but not one rich in nuances. His performance was good but it would benefit by a little more wit. Other reviews were scathing, like the one that stated: A few more productions like this one and John Gilbert will be able to change places with comedian Harry Langdon. His prowess of lovemaking, which has usually held the working girls breathless, takes on a comedy aspect that gets them tittering at first and then laughing outright. The lines read far better than they sound from under the dainty Gilbertian mustache. The actors talk in a theatrical tone of voice. *New York Times* 10/5/29, *Variety* 10/9/29, *Harrison's Reports* 10/12/29.

Redemption: Unworthy of first-run theaters regardless of John Gilbert's presence. In fact, the more first runs this film plays the greater the injury which will be done to his stardom and he will be the chief sufferer. Although the producers of this picture attribute its poor quality to Gilbert's voice they are wrong. The fault is not in his voice, which is not bad, but in the poor quality of the screen story. The most melodious voice could not have made it more interesting because he is called upon to act as anything but a regular human being. *Variety* 5/7/30, *Harrison's Reports* 5/10/30.

Phantom of Paris: Gilbert is at his best yet in talkers but it isn't his presence that makes the picture. He is far more forceful than he has been since sound made him speak, his voice having been his greatest drawback at times. *Variety* 11/17/31.

Downstairs: John Gilbert, who used to be a scenario writer himself, must have known what he was doing when he didn't do right by himself with this script. Maybe he decided to finish his career by fashioning a story such as this, although he was quite effective in such dashing roguishly romantic moments as there are. The hero is a scoundrel from beginning to end and he does everything to alienate the audience's sympathy. *Variety* 10/11/32, *Harrison's Reports* 10/15/32.

Queen Christina: Jack Gilbert does one of his best chores since sound threw him for a loss. (He is especially convincing in his best sound work playing the Spanish ambassador with whom Garbo has a one-night affair.) *Variety* 1/2/34.

The Captain Hates the Sea: The acting is good.

(Gilbert played the not unlike him role of a constantly drinking writer. The film apparently tried to emulate *Grand Hotel* in its structure of several major stories occurring simultaneously). *Harrison's Reports* 12/2/34.

Gillingwater, Claude, Lauseanna, Missouri, 1870–1939

Silent: After extensive stage experience, Claude Gillingwater made his first feature about 1918. His motion pictures included Mary Pickford's *Little Lord Fauntleroy, Alice Adams* (1923 version), *Dulcy, Madonna of the Streets, Into Her Kingdom, Barbed Wire, The Gorilla, The Stranger's Banquet* and *Souls for Sale*. Last silent: *Oh, Kay!* (1928).

Sound: Gillingwater's first part-sound film was *Women They Talk About* (1928), and all his 1929 films contained some talking. The first two, *Stark Mad* and *Stolen Kisses*, also were part-sound; the rest were all-talking, among them *So Long Letty, Smiling Irish Eyes* and *The Great Divide*.

By this time, Gillingwater was a sour-faced and scrawny actor whose appearance and crotchety voice effectively matched the roles he often played: crusty curmudgeons with well-hidden soft hearts.

Among Gillingwater's films were *Before Midnight, You Can't Buy Everything, Broken Lives, In Love with Life, A Yank at Oxford, Mississippi* and *Poor Little Rich Girl*, with Shirley Temple. He also appeared in such prestigious pictures as *A Tale of Two Cities* and *The Prisoner of Shark Island*. His final effort was 1939's *Cafe Society*.

REVIEWS

Women They Talk About: Nothing saves it but Claude Gillingwater doing his well-known grouch and in rare form. The veteran of stage and screen will push this one through. It has just 14 minutes of dialogue and the audience only wants to hear the crabbing grandfather, Gillingwater. *Variety* 10/17/28.

Illicit: Support cast does standard work all the way. Among them Gillingwater is capable. *Variety* 1/21/31.

The Conquering Horde: The main comedy excellence is with Claude Gillingwater as the ranch foreman. *Variety* 4/1/31.

Cafe Society: Claude Gillingwater does an adept job as a foil and is a bit removed from his usual dour and dyspeptic roles. *Variety* 2/8/39.

Gilmore, Douglas (Harris Gilmore), Marion, Iowa, 1903–1950

Silent: *His Buddy's Wife* (1925) was theater-trained Douglas Gilmore's first screen appearance.

After being signed by MGM, his initial film there, in a supporting part, was the popular *Sally, Irene and Mary*. A leading role came in *Paris* (1926), one of several pictures with Joan Crawford.

Gilmore often portrayed cads in films that included *A Kiss in a Taxi, Object — Alimony, Love's Blindness* and *Rough House Rosie*. After his stay at MGM, he signed with Fox where he spent the remainder of his silent career. Last silent: *The One Woman Idea* (1929), with synchronized music score.

Sound: *Pleasure Crazed* (1929) marked Gilmore's sound debut; other 1929 talkies were *A Song of Kentucky* and *Married in Hollywood*. After his option was dropped by Fox, he ended his career freelancing for First National, Paramount and Vitaphone.

Other talkies included *The Big Party, Hell's Angels, The Naughty Flirt, Unfaithful* and *Desert Vengeance*. Gilmore's final feature was *The Girl Habit* (1931) followed by two shorts, the last of which was *My Bridge Experience* in 1933. His career was by no means over; he returned to the stage and was still active in the early days of television.

REVIEWS

A Song of Kentucky: Those in the cast who do good work include Douglas Gilmore. *Harrison's Reports* 12/18/29.

Gish, Dorothy, Masillon, Ohio, 1898–1968

Filmography: *Films in Review* (Aug.-Sept. 1968); List of films in *Film Dope* (Dec. 1979)

Silent: Before Dorothy Gish made her first starring feature-length film *Old Heidelberg* in 1915, she had already been in over 60 one- and two-reelers and a few other features. Her first screen appearance was for D. W. Griffith in *The Unseen Enemy* (1912), co-starring her older sister Lillian (with whom Dorothy had been in touring theater companies from childhood).

The devoted sisters were to make many films together, one of the most memorable being *Hearts of the World* in which Dorothy portrayed the Little Disturber. While Lillian specialized in drama, impish Dorothy was a talented comedienne who was called "The Female Chaplin."

After a well-received series of comedies including *I'll Get Him Yet, Remodeling Her Husband* (directed by Lillian) and *Nugget Nell*, Dorothy's screen appearances diminished in the '20s. She made some mediocre comedies and went to England for the last of her approximately 100 silents in 1926 and '27.

There were also some worthy films for Gish in the 1920s like *Romola* and D. W. Griffith's French revolution melodrama *Orphans of the Storm*, both co-starring her sister. Her other features included *The Bright Shawl, Nell Gwynn, The Country Flapper* and *Little Miss Rebellion*. Last American silent: *Clothes Make the Pirate* (1925).

Sound: Dorothy Gish's first talkie was *Wolves*, made in England in 1930. It had little or no release time in the United States. She apparently did not enjoy making that film nor the talkie medium itself, returning to the stage where she had become a highly regarded actress.

Gish was to make supporting appearances in character roles in only four sound films: *Our Hearts Were Young and Gay* (1944), *Centennial Summer* (1946), *The Whistle at Eaton Falls* (1951) and *The Cardinal* (1964).

Comments: Dorothy Gish has been unfairly neglected in recent years but there are other factors aside from the large shadow cast by her elder sister. Although versatile and quite capable of effective dramatic performances, she was primarily a comic actress. It seems that tragediennes generally get more respect.

Another factor is that many of the Gish films probably no longer exist for re-evaluation. Lastly, she showed no real interest in the talkies and her appearances in them were in minor, non-showy roles.

Dorothy Gish shone in those silent films where she could showcase her extroverted personality and the sense of fun that made her a natural for comedy. She also was a distinguished stage star who worked steadily in the theater throughout the 1930s and '40s. Her sound films, on the other hand, were undeniably a mediocre lot.

REVIEWS

Our Hearts Were Young and Gay: Dorothy Gish, making her film comeback, is okay. *Variety* 9/6/44.

Centennial Summer: Gish does well by the wife role. *Variety* 5/26/46.

The Whistle at Eaton Falls: Gish appears briefly as the widow. *Variety* 8/1/51.

The Cardinal: Dorothy Gish as the mother of the title character is natural. *Variety* 10/16/63.

Gish, Lillian, Springfield or Massillon, Ohio, 1893/99–1993

Filmography: Films in Review (Dec. 1962); *Films and Filming* (Nov. 1983); List of films in *Film Dope* (Dec. 1979)

Silent: The actress who would be called the greatest of all silent film actresses made her stage debut in stock at about the age of five. Along with her younger sister Dorothy she first appeared in pic-

tures under the aegis of D. W. Griffith in 1912's *The Unseen Enemy* and remained with him for the next ten years.

Gish made scores of one- and two-reelers, both in leading and supporting roles, including *Oil and Water, A Modest Hero, The Madonna of the Storm, Flirting with Fate* and *The Folly of Anne*. The first one apparently written specifically with her in mind was the two-reeler *The Mothering Heart* (1913). *Judith of Bethulia* was her first full-length picture.

In 1914, Lillian Gish began appearing in features such as *The Battle of the Sexes* and *Home Sweet Home*. The following year, after almost 50 motion pictures, she became a star (and Griffith a world-famous director) with *The Birth of a Nation*, in which she played Elsie Stoneman.

For the next few years Gish alternated between more two-reelers and minor features like *Diane of the Follies, An Innocent Magdalene* and *Sold for Marriage*. Of course there was also the epic *Intolerance* (1916) in which she was seen as the woman rocking the cradle to link the four interconnecting stories.

In 1918, Gish began a remarkable string of motion pictures, all directed by Griffith, which cemented her stardom. There were "small" pictures like *A Romance of Happy Valley, True Heart Susie* and *The Greatest Thing in Life* as well as the World War One epic *Hearts of the World*.

With 1919's *Broken Blossoms*, co-starring Richard Barthelmess and Donald Crisp, in which Gish convincingly portrayed a very young girl, she was recognized as a major world star. This was followed the next year by the enormously popular melodrama *Way Down East* and she also had her sole directing credit with *Remodeling Her Husband*, starring Dorothy Gish. *Orphans of the Storm* in 1921, again co-starring Dorothy, marked the end of the Griffith years.

In 1923 and '25, Lillian Gish partnered Ronald Colman in Inspiration Pictures' *The White Sister* and *Romola* before signing with MGM in 1926. There she appeared in five films the first of which was *La Bohème*; her co-star was the reigning matinee idol John Gilbert.

Other Gish pictures at MGM were *The Scarlet Letter, Annie Laurie* and *The Enemy*. Last silent: *The Wind* (1928), with synchronized sound effects, directed by the Swede Victor Sjostrom (Seastrom). This was definitely underappreciated at the time but is now considered an enduring silent classic.

Sound: After acting in the theater, Lillian Gish made her sound film debut in the creaky vehicle *One Romantic Night* in 1930. A version of the stage play *The Swan*, it was later remade for Grace Kelly.

Not particularly successful, it resulted in her concentrating on the stage for much of the next 20 years.

Gish's only other film of the decade was *His Double Life* in 1933. In the 1940s there were a few more, some quite trivial, beginning with *The Commandos Strike at Dawn* (1942). Others were *Top Man, Miss Susie Slagle's* (the title role) and *Portrait of Jennie*.

Gish's one major effort of the decade, and the one for which she received her only Academy Award nomination (for supporting actress), was David O. Selznick's perfervid 1946 western *Duel in the Sun*. She played Lionel Barrymore's wife; interestingly, she had played his daughter in the early silent days.

The following decade brought Gish what was probably her best talkie role in the Charles Laughton–directed *The Night of the Hunter* (1955). She played a stern yet loving woman who protected a houseful of children during the Depression and more especially two children against the menace of a crazed Robert Mitchum.

In *The Cobweb* the same year, Gish had a rare unsympathetic role. Other scattered films of the '50s and '60s included *Orders to Kill* (made in the U.K.), *The Comedians, The Unforgiven, Follow Me Boys!* and *Warning Shot*. More than ten years elapsed before her next film, the misfire Robert Altman comedy *A Wedding* (1978).

Hambone and Hillie and *Sweet Liberty* followed. Finally, 75 years after her very first movie, Lillian Gish co-starred in her last picture playing Bette Davis's *younger* sister (she actually was some 15 years Davis's *senior*) in 1987's *The Whales of August*. Her well-observed and dignified performance made it a most fitting departure.

Gish appeared in many Broadway productions, among them *Uncle Vanya, Hamlet* (as Ophelia to John Gielgud's Dane), *The Chalk Garden, Crime and Punishment* and *Life with Father*. In the 1930s she began appearing on the radio and in the '50s did a well-received live television version of *A Trip to Bountiful*. She continued to make sporadic appearances in that medium from the mid–'60s to the early 1980s.

Comments: Although Lillian Gish was in over 100 films, very few of them were made in the talkie era. Indeed, by the time she made her first sound film, her reputation had begun to suffer a bit. For one thing, her stay at MGM had not been propitious. Although *La Bohème* and possibly one or two other of her pictures were successful, the studio apparently had wanted an image change.

The story goes that Louis B. Mayer told Gish to "arrange a scandal" for herself; people were more interested in someone who fell off her pedestal.

Hers seemingly was too high for his tastes. Behind her back she was supposedly referred to as a "silly, sexless antique."

It is true that Gish's real-life persona (whether or not it reflected the real person is debatable) was that of an upright and virtuous woman. It was rather a dull one for Hollywood as was her usual screen persona as the fragile innocent. It was not in tune with the country's mood in the Jazz Age or the early days of the Depression.

Gish's first sound film showed her speaking voice to be adequate enough but her choice of vehicle, a talky and slow romantic melodrama, could have been better. Also, she was at that "certain age" for actresses, the late 30s. Her abilities were suited well enough to sound but her glory days really lay in the silent era. In that medium she excelled.

There were several factors that made Gish so perfect a silent film actress. In an age of overacting before the camera, she used small hand and body movements to express emotion. She was renowned for her variety of facial expressions and was quoted as saying, "Your face is all you have to play with."

Gish carved a certain niche beginning with her very first film as the heroine imperiled in pictures like *The Birth of a Nation, Way Down East, Orphans of the Storm* and *Hearts of the World*. Although many of her vehicles creaked from their own melodramatics, she was an exponent of realism on-screen.

The story of Lillian Gish starving herself and denying herself liquids while preparing for her role as the doomed heroine of *La Bohème* is well known. Her most discussed scene is probably that in *Broken Blossoms* where she reacted like a trapped animal to the certainty of her death at the hands of a brutish father.

Gish was one of the silent screen's greatest actresses because she was greatly talented but more than that she simply possessed whatever it was that the camera loved. She was certainly pretty enough but there were many prettier. There were also many with more personality — her sister Dorothy for one.

Lillian Gish had an ethereal screen presence described as being "behind a veil of silver chiffon." It was said that "her heroines perpetually hover in filtered half-lights … in the dusk-blues, the dawn-golds of medieval tapestries." What other screen star could be described that way?

REVIEWS

One Romantic Night: Gish is okay but her naturalness and simplicity are of little avail because everything is stupidly blunt except for the whimsical close-ups of Miss Gish. *Variety* 6/4/30.

His Double Life: Lillian Gish returns to the screen. She is an older, more cerebral actress who has been matured by the dramatic stage. *Variety* 12/19/33.

Duel in the Sun: Gish is the suffering mother, doing a quiet job until her death scene. *Variety* 1/1/47.

The Night of the Hunter: Lillian Gish shows great skill in a warm, sympathetic part. *Variety* 7/20/55.

The Unforgiven: Gish, a silent film favorite, is okay; however, she has a tendency to over-react emotionally. *Variety* 3/30/60.

Follow Me Boys!: One of the highlights is the appearance of Lillian Gish as a wealthy eccentric. She still possesses the delicate beauty, as remembered, and when she's on the scene she captures the full interest of the moment. *Variety* 10/12/66.

A Wedding: All the characters, except for Lillian Gish as the old money matriarch, are uninteresting and unsympathetic. *Variety* 10/6/78.

The Whales of August: Gish is still something of the silent screen innocent, but there's not a gesture or a line reading that doesn't reflect her nearly three-quarters of a century in front of a camera. Scenes are not purloined by others when she's on-screen. *New York Times* 10/17/87.

Gordon, Julia Swayne, New York, New York?, 1879?–1933

Silent: A pioneer leading lady of early silents, Julia Swayne Gordon was a Vitagraph player who began in one-reelers about 1906. She had appeared in stock and vaudeville previously. From 1914 she was in supporting roles in features such as *A Million Bid, The Battle Cry of Peace, My Lady's Slipper, Arsène Lupin, The Maelstrom* and *The Bramble Bush.*

In the 1920s, Gordon specialized in playing dowagers and other grandes dames in numerous motion pictures which included *Burn 'Em Up Barnes, Wildness of Youth, Lights of Old Broadway, It, The King of Kings, Scaramouche, Wings* and *Three Weekends.* Last silent: *The Viking* (1929), with synchronized music and sound effects, made after her first talkies.

Sound: Making the transition to sound with the 1929 part-talkie *The Younger Generation* (an early Frank Capra film), Gordon worked up to the time of her death in small roles as dignified matrons. Her other films included *Gold Diggers of Broadway, The Dude Wrangler, Captain Applejack, Secrets of the French Police, Hello, Everybody!* and her last, *Gold Diggers of 1933.*

REVIEWS

Hello, Everybody!: Julia Swayne Gordon's Park Avenue accent doesn't mix with her farmhouse mother role. *Variety* 1/31/33.

Gordon, Vera (Vera Nemirou), Russia, 1886/87–1948

Silent: One of the premier Jewish mamas of the silents was Vera Gordon. Best known for her continuing role in the "Cohens and the Kellys" series, she was already typecast in one of her earliest films, the popular *Humoresque* (1920). Occasionally top-billed, Gordon, a veteran of vaudeville and New York's Yiddish theater, was seen in such films as *Your Best Friend, Potash and Perlmutter* and its sequel, *Kosher Kitty Kelly, Private Izzy Murphy* and *Millionaires.*

Gordon's first appearance as Mrs. Cohen came in 1926's *The Cohens and the Kellys,* with Charlie Murray and George Sidney as the feuding protagonists. It proved to be so popular that several sequels ensued. The other silent entry in the series was *The Cohens and the Kellys in Paris.* Last silent: *Four Walls* (1928).

Sound: Not unexpectedly, Gordon's sound debut came in the 1929 part-talkie *The Cohens and Kellys in Atlantic City* and her next two films were also in the series (*...in Africa, ...in Scotland*). She did not appear in the final two series entries (*...in Hollywood, ...in Trouble*).

Gordon continued to make very sporadic appearances in the '30s, including *Fifty Million Frenchmen, When Strangers Meet, Michael O'Halloran* and *You and Me.* There was only a handful of films for her during the next decade as well.

In the 1940s, Gordon appeared in *The Living Ghost* and *The Big Street* (both 1942); her last film, *Abie's Irish Rose,* was in 1946. She was also briefly glimpsed as one of the celebrities working in the kitchen of the all-star *Stage Door Canteen* in 1943.

REVIEWS

The Cohens and Kellys in Atlantic City: Vera Gordon failed to achieve anything but negation in her dialogue opportunities. *Variety* 3/20/29.

The Cohens and the Kellys in Scotland: Gordon has been talking down to her parts lately, while waiting for another *Humoresque. Variety* 3/12/30.

You and Me: Vera Gordon is among the most prominent in support, and she is effective. *Variety* 6/8/38.

The Big Street: Gordon makes a minor, sympathetic bit stand out. *Variety* 8/5/42.

Abie's Irish Rose: Vera Gordon somehow manages a slightly more restrained performance but she is depicted as a narrow-minded nitwit. *Variety* 11/27/46.

Goudal, Jetta (Julie "Jetje" Goudeket), Amsterdam, The Netherlands, 1891–1985
Filmography: *Films in Review* (Oct. 1974)
Silent: Broadway player Jetta Goudal had an unbilled bit in her first film *Timothy's Quest*; her first credited role was in *The Bright Shawl* (1923). She ultimately became a popular, if exotic, leading woman in 16 films like *Open All Night, The Spaniard, Three Faces East, The Coming of Amos, The Forbidden Woman* and *Fighting Love*. Last silent: *The Cardboard Lover* (1928).
Sound: D. W. Griffith's *Lady of the Pavements* (1929), with talking and singing sequences, was Goudal's first sound film. She made only one other English-language talkie, an odd teaming between the exotic temptress and the homespun Will Rogers in *Business and Pleasure* (1932). There was also Hollywood's French-language version of *The Unholy Night*, called *Le Spectre Vert*, in 1930.
Comments: Jetta Goudal appeared for Paramount and DeMille's Producer's Distributing Company, where she gained an apparently wholly accurate reputation for being temperamental. She even sued DeMille over a contract disagreement.

In those days of obedient servitude to studio heads, feistiness was not appreciated as a virtue. Her battles certainly did not help her career and her not unpleasant accent was a perfect excuse, or perhaps a legitimate reason, not to employ her for talkies.

Goudal also was not inclined to be cooperative with the publicity flacks of the studio. Her famous remark that she was "born on the Moon 2,000 years ago" was colorful but perhaps not exactly what the studio wanted to convey to the public.

Indeed, Jetta Goudal wanted to convey as little of the truth as possible about her life. As later research revealed, her claimed 1898 birth in Versailles, France, turned out to be something far different.

REVIEWS

Lady of the Pavements: Goudal's quaint coiffure and tiny features are strikingly different. She takes the part of the Countess. *Variety* 3/13/29, *Harrison's Reports* 3/16/29.
Business and Pleasure: Jetta Goudal, with her slinky figure and clothes and her sinister foreign accent, makes an appropriate menace. At times it is extremely difficult to understand what she is saying. *Variety* 2/16/32, *Harrison's Reports* 2/30/32.

Gowland, Gibson (T. H. Gibson-Goland?), Spennymoor, England, 1872/77–1951
Silent: Now remembered for one towering achievement, the starring role of McTeague in Erich von Stroheim's legendary *Greed* (1925), Gibson Gowland began his American film career in the mid-'teens. He had previously acted in stock companies.

Among Gowland's early films, in which he played supporting roles, were *The Phantom Shotgun, Under Handicap, Breakers Ahead* and *Blind Husbands*, the first Stroheim-directed film. In the first years of the 1920s, his appearances were sparse.

From 1924 to '27 Gowland appeared in several films a year including *The Phantom of the Opera, Don Juan, Isle of Forgotten Women, The Land Beyond the Law* and *The Night of Love*. With the shining exception of *Greed*, he was almost always a supporting player. Last silent: *Rose-Marie* (1928).
Sound: The part-talkie *The Mysterious Island* (1929) was Gowland's first. His sound career was not notable, with such scattered films in the early '30s as *The Sea Bat, Hell Harbor, Land of Wanted Men* and *Doomed Battalion*. In these films he tended to repeat his McTeague characterization as a rough, even brutish man.

Gowland did have a fairly major role in the 1933 German production *SOS Iceberg* which starred the later-infamous actress and documentary maker Leni Riefenstahl. Perhaps hoping for a change of persona, he returned to England in mid-decade for more small roles (*The Private Life of Don Juan, The Mystery of the Mary Celeste, King of the Damned*).

Coming back to America in the early 1940s, Gowland ended his screen career with character bits. Among his later pictures were *Northwest Passage, Going My Way, The Picture of Dorian Gray* and *Kitty*. Long shorn of the permed blonde hair or wig so familiar from his one really significant role, he was doubtless unrecognized by filmgoers. He retired one last time to his native land.

REVIEWS

Hell Harbor: Gowland is adroit at these gutsy, uncouth fellows. His specialty leans to the muscular, hairy type of villainy with a tinge of the moron. *Variety* 4/9/30.
SOS Iceberg: Gowland gives a splendid performance as the maddened explorer. *New York Times* 9/25/33.

Graves, Ralph (Ralph Hosburgh?), Cleveland, Ohio, 1900–1977
Silent: After extra appearances, Ralph Graves had his first major role in 1918's *Sporting Life* and eventually became one of the silents' matinee idols. Among his roles were those in (minor) D. W. Griffith films like *Dream Street, Scarlet Days* and *The Greatest Question*.

Other Graves films included *Polly with a Past*,

Yolanda, Dust, The Extra Girl, Prodigal Daughters, Woman Power and the serial *The Fatal Warning*. Last silent: *The Eternal Woman* (1929).

Sound: After his first talkie *The College Coquette* (1929), Graves starred in a few others, including Frank Capra's *Flight* (1929). For a while he and Jack Holt were a popular Columbia team in several melodramas, many of them flying stories. He then became largely a supporting player and worked for Mack Sennett and also wrote and directed some films.

Graves appeared sporadically in the mid– to late '30s and made only a few the next decade, the last coming in 1949 (*Alimony*). Among his other talkies were *Hell's Island, Dirigible, Born to Be Bad, Ticket to a Crime, Double Exposure, Salvation Nell* and a serial, *The Black Coin*.

REVIEWS

Flight: Graves in the lead fits into this film like a rubber band. He will be given the best of it for his acting and it's an even bet that with his voice and presence he will rank among the leading draws of the screen within a year. He also wrote the story. *Variety 9/18/29, Harrison's Reports 9/21/29.*

Hell's Island: Graves gives the same sterling performance you can always depend on him to give. *Variety 7/23/30.*

Dirigible: Graves early in the film is light enough in his touches to give the zest the story needs. *Variety 4/8/31.*

A Dangerous Affair: Graves has been much better than he is in this effort. *Variety 12/1/31.*

Street of Missing Men: Graves, considerably heavier than in his starring days, is miscast. A former player of sympathetic roles, he is not altogether believable as a sinister film figure. *Variety 4/26/39.*

Gray, Gilda (Marianna Michalska), Krakow, Poland, 1897/99–1959

Silent: Blonde Gilda Gray had one big thing going for her and she parlayed it into a career in musical comedy and, briefly, films. She was the originator, or at least the popularizer, of the "Shimmy," a dance in which every part of her vibrated wildly from the shoulders on down. Supposedly a corruption of the word "chemise," it made her famous after she demonstrated it in the Follies and on Broadway.

Not surprisingly, Gray's first film role (a small one) was as a dancer in 1923's *Lawful Larceny*. She returned three years later as the star of *Aloma of the South Seas* and of the next year's *Cabaret*. Last American silent: *The Devil Dancer* (1927). Last silent: *Picadilly* (1929), made in the United Kingdom.

Sound: Gray's fame largely vanished along with the Jazz Age and she made but one talkie, the Jeanette MacDonald-Nelson Eddy operetta *Rose Marie* in 1936. She was billed last in the cast list as Belle. Apparently she also had a specialty in that year's *The Great Ziegfeld*, but was edited out.

Although Gray sporadically attempted to revive her career, she was largely unsuccessful. But she did make news in 1939 with her narrow escape on the last plane from Warsaw when the Nazis invaded. In the 1950s, long forgotten, the mistress of the Shimmy was the subject of a *This Is Your Life* television show.

REVIEWS

Rose Marie: Jeanette MacDonald's only moment of competition — and this was deliberately contrived — comes when Gilda Gray, who used to be great shakes in the old days, instructs her in the finer points of putting over a barroom ballad. It is one of the picture's most amusing moments. The strong supporting cast, notably Gray, are all bell ringers. *New York Times 2/1/36, Variety 2/5/36.*

Gray, Lawrence, San Francisco, California, 1898/1900–1970

Silent: After a stint in Broadway musicals, Lawrence Gray came to Hollywood in 1925. He partnered many of the leading actresses, including Marion Davies, Esther Ralston, Clara Bow and Colleen Moore, in such films as *The Coast of Folly, Oh, Kay!, The Patsy, Ankles Preferred, Diamond Handcuffs* and *The American Venus*. Last silent: *Trent's Last Case* (1929), with synchronized music and sound effects.

Sound: Gray's 1929 talkies included *Marianne*, his and Marion Davies's first, and *It's a Great Life*. He went on to appear in films until the mid–1930s, including a handful in which he sang. There were fewer parts after 1930 and they were in increasingly less prestigious films and then in support.

Gray's films included *Children of Pleasure, Going Wild, Spring Is Here, Golden Harvest, Timber War, Danger Ahead* and his final two in 1936, *A Face in the Fog* and *In Paris, AWOL*. After his film career ended, he served as the coordinator between the American and Mexican film industries for many years.

Comments: Lawrence Gray was one of those fairly bland 1920s leading men who could be depended upon not to overshadow the leading ladies who were the real stars. Conventionally handsome but able to portray ruggedness better than some of his contemporaries, he had a mildly successful career.

Gray's musical theater background stood him in

good stead in the first wave of sound musicals like *Spring Is Here, Sunny* and *The Florodora Girl* but when their popularity waned so did his. The quickie melodramas and comedies he then found himself in did little to sustain his career.

Marianne: Lawrence Gray is his usual serious-eyed, smiling self, bringing vast sincerity, a needed quality where horseplay is the main dish. He has a fair singing voice and renders several songs. *Variety* 10/23/29, *New York Times* 10/29/29.

Sunny: Gray managed to portray with pleasant sincerity the slightly feebleminded leading male character. *Variety* 12/31/30.

Going Wild: Lawrence Gray does better than he ever has in this comedy. *New York Times* 1/26/31.

Dizzy Dames: Gray plays a juvenile role, displaying a polite tenor for four songs. *Variety* 7/22/36.

Grey, Virginia, Los Angeles, California,
1917–

Filmography: List of films in *Sweethearts of the Sage*

Silent: A child of the "industry," Virginia Grey's parents were both employed in movies. She had her first screen role as Little Eva in the 1927 version of *Uncle Tom's Cabin*. The following year she was seen in *The Michigan Kid* and also could have made unbilled appearances in others. Last silent: *Heart to Heart* (1928).

Sound: Until the mid-'30s, Grey's roles were sporadic. Her first sound film was 1931's *Misbehaving Ladies*; in the next few years she was also seen in *The Firebird* and *Secrets*. In 1936 she began her adult career with supporting roles in numerous MGM films such as *The Great Ziegfeld, Another Thin Man, Rosalie, Test Pilot, The Shopworn Angel* and *Idiot's Delight*.

Possessed of a good voice and blonde prettiness, Grey gradually became a leading lady in "B" films, alternating with supporting roles, and was active throughout the 1940s. Her films included *The Captain Is a Lady, Blonde Inspiration, The Big Store, Grand Central Murder, Sweet Rosie O'Grady, Who Killed "Doc" Robbin?* (top-billed) and *Flame of the Barbary Coast*.

In the 1950s and '60s, Grey's roles again became largely supporting ones and her output decreased, although she was a favorite of producer Ross Hunter and was cast in many of his films. Among her latter efforts were *The Rose Tattoo, Back Street, Portrait in Black, Tammy Tell Me True* and, in 1970, *Airport*. She was later seen on TV, including the daytime soaps.

The Hardys Ride High: Grey is a flashy number and is just right for her showgirl assignment. *Variety* 4/19/39.

Swamp Fire: Virginia Grey is attractive and slinky enough as the predatory woman. *Variety* 5/15/46.

Griffith, Corinne (Corinne Griffin?),
Texarkana, Texas, 1898/1906–1979

Filmography: *Films in Review* (Nov. 1975)

Silent: After a career as a dancer, Corinne Griffith made her first film at Vitagraph as a replacement for their star Anita Stewart in 1916. She appeared in a long series of films, mostly romantic melodramas and comedies, but became a top star only in 1924 at First National. The serenely beautiful actress was dubbed "The Orchid Lady."

Among Griffith's films were *Black Oxen, Declassee, The Lady in Ermine, Lilies of the Field, The Garden of Eden* and *Syncopating Sue*. Last silent: *The Divine Lady* (1929), technically a silent although it contained singing sequences.

Sound: Two of Griffith's 1929 films were part-talkies: *Saturday's Children*, her biggest sound hit, and *Prisoners*. Other talkies were *Back Pay*, a remake of *Lilies of the Field* and her final released film for thirty years, *Lily Christine* (1932), made in England.

The failure of Griffith's talkies doomed any chance of a return to her former cinema glory. A 1957 film in which she played a role, *Stars in the Backyard*, was released in 1961 as *Paradise Alley*.

Comments: Corinne Griffith was an elegant actress whose cognomen "The Orchid Lady" fit her well. She was, however, not a *great* actress. Her vocal skills were not well-suited to sound films and she would have to be counted as among the more notable casualties of the talkies.

Griffith by no means limited herself to acting. In later life, the wealthy (from Beverly Hills real estate) and politically conservative actress was an outspoken and newsworthy opponent of the income tax as well as the author of several books on widely divergent topics.

Griffith's greatest post-film splash came in a divorce action against one of her several husbands. During the trial she made the absolutely startling claim that she was either the much younger sister or stand-in of the "real" Corinne Griffith, who was deceased. She was, therefore, much younger than the "real" star.

Although the case was officially settled by the testimony of other former silent film actresses who knew Griffith well, it made entertaining reading for many days and confirmed her reputation as an eccentric who was always good for a juicy news story.

REVIEWS

Saturday's Children: This reveals Corinne Griffith anew as an actress of persuasive beauty and captivating charm. Her performance is a great bit of high comedy but she discloses a speaking voice that escapes classification. It isn't a cultured voice or an elocutionist's voice, but it has a distinctly feminine quality that fits her personality. *Variety* 5/1/29, *Harrison's Reports* 5/4/29.

Prisoners: It is the poorest picture that has ever been released by First National with Griffith. There is not a spot where the emotions of the spectator are appealed to and the action is uninteresting and draggy. Griffith is the wistful-eyed waitress. *Harrison's Reports* 6/15/29, *Variety* 8/21/29.

Lilies of the Field: Reviews differed. One thought that Griffith did very good work but another said that she was probably the saddest person on the screen. Her voice was sad, her manner tear-drenched, her gestures were those of despair and her listless manner quite depressing even when feigning moments of happiness. The acting was smooth and satisfying with the exception of Corinne Griffith whose odd trick of speech will get a variety of reactions. To some, her talking is quite charming principally because of its variance from what passes on stage and screen for polite diction. *Harrison's Reports* 12/28/29, *New York Times* 2/22/30, *Variety* 2/26/30.

Back Pay: Corinne Griffith looks pretty in a role that no one could make thoroughly convincing and she never rates sympathy. *Variety* 6/4/30, *Harrison's Reports* 6/7/30.

Lily Christine: Of the film's redeeming attributes Griffith's appearance is the most important. She remains very lovely of face and figure, but not so her ability to handle dialogue. She has some way to go before the microphone ceases to be an impediment to her. Even her physical attractiveness cannot overcome the flatness of her voice and inept delivery. *Harrison's Reports* 9/17/32, *Variety* 9/20/32.

Griffith, Raymond, Boston, Massachusetts, 1890–1957

Filmography: List of films in *Film Dope* (Oct. 1980)

Silent: Raymond Griffith, the comic actor who later became known as a "Silk Hat Comedian," worked for various studios before going to Sennett in 1916 where he acted, wrote and directed. After playing minor roles for Universal in the early '20s, he began his years of stardom in 1925 with a series of smart comedies.

Griffith's films included *Rise and Shine, Paths to Paradise, Hands Up* (a Civil War story), *He's a Prince, Wet Paint* and *Fine Clothes.* Last silent: *Trent's Last Case* (1929), with synchronized sound effects and music.

Sound: Although this is disputed by some, Griffith reputedly could not speak above a whisper because of an old injury or perhaps overuse of his voice during a melodrama. Despite this, he left the performing side of the industry in a major film.

Griffith's sole sound film appearance was in *All Quiet on the Western Front* (1930). His small but memorable role was that of a dying French soldier in a foxhole. He later became a producer for Twentieth Century–Fox.

Comments: Raymond Griffith is today considered an underrated comic actor who has been belatedly recognized for the high quality of the films he made in the mid– and late 1920s. Many of those films are believed lost, a circumstance which makes it difficult to properly evaluate his work.

Griffith apparently honed his acting skills while traveling with a mime group all over Europe. He somewhat resembled French comedian Max Linder in his persona as a dapper gentlemen with elegant mustache.

REVIEWS

All Quiet on the Western Front: Raymond Griffith is the Frenchman who is stabbed and who dies in the trench. He didn't have to talk for he died as no one else has on-screen. After being bayoneted by the film's star Lew Ayres, Griffith's character groans all night long before his death. A more touchingly harrowing scene has seldom been seen on the screen. *Variety* 5/7/30.

Guinan, Texas (Mary Louise Guinan), Waco, Texas, 1884–1933

Filmography: *Texas Guinan* (biography); List of films in *Sweethearts of the Sage*

Silent: Long before she was queen of the speakeasies, and famous for her trademark greeting "Hello, sucker!," Texas Guinan was in Broadway musicals. She entered films in a Triangle drama, *The Fuel of Life* (1917), but soon found herself starring in westerns like *The Gun Woman* and *The She Wolf.* There was at least one other non-western, 1918's *The Love Brokers.*

In 1919, Guinan was cast in a series of about 25 two-reel westerns for Frohman and Reelcraft. These were released through 1920 and included *The Dangerous Little Devil, The Heart of Texas, Girl of the Rancho, My Lady Robin Hood* and *The Wild Cat.* Last silents: *I Am the Woman* and *The Stampede* released about the same time in 1921. She entered vaudeville and then found her real niche as a night club (i.e., speakeasy) hostess.

Sound: In recognition of her nationwide fame — or notoriety — as a symbol of Prohibition's failure, Texas Guinan pretty much played herself in *Queen of the Night Clubs* (1929). The character she portrayed was called Tex Malone. Later that year she appeared very briefly on-screen as "herself" in the Ziegfeld biopic *Glorifying the American Girl* (1929).

Guinan returned to the screen just once more. It was in a supporting role, again playing a night club owner and hostess named Tex, this time surnamed Kaley, in 1933's *Broadway Thru a Keyhole*. She was very shortly thereafter to die. A "Hollywoodized" biography, the Technicolor *Incendiary Blonde* (1945), starred Betty Hutton as Guinan.

Comments: Although Texas Guinan had been an actress, she perhaps was mainly famous for being famous. She did not really *do* anything but she was, nevertheless, a prominent symbol of the age in which she lived. At the height of her speakeasy fame, it was said that Mayor Jimmy Walker may have ruled New York City by day but that Texas Guinan ruled it by night.

REVIEWS

Queen of the Night Clubs: With Texas Guinan as the star, this talker is a natural. She hasn't much to do but does what she has pretty well. She's her natural self at all times and she knows how to control her tonsils. *Variety* 3/20/29.

Broadway Thru a Keyhole: Guinan plays herself but has not been favored with dialogue. *Variety* 11/7/33.

Gulliver, Dorothy, Salt Lake City, Utah, 1908/10–

Filmography: List of films in *Sweethearts of the Sage*

Silent: A Wampas Baby Star of 1928, Dorothy Gulliver earlier had won a beauty contest sponsored by Universal and was awarded a contract. She was placed in bit parts until being co-starred in *The Collegians* series which lasted from about 1926 to '29, and also was seen in many westerns like *The Rambling Ranger*, *One Glorious Scrap*, *Clearing the Trail* and *The Wild West Show*.

Among Gulliver's few non-westerns were *A Dog of the Regiment* (with Rin Tin Tin), *Good Morning, Judge* and *The Shield of Honor*. She also appeared in the serials *Strings of Steel* and *The Winking Idol*. Last silent: *Honeymoon Flats* or *Clearing the Trail*, released about the same time in 1928.

Sound: Gulliver's first sound film was *College Love* (1929) and her other pictures of that year, *Night Parade* and *Painted Faces*, were also talkies.

Among later sound films were a mix of westerns and action melodramas, including *The Fighting Marshal*, *In Old Cheyenne*, *Revenge at Monte Carlo*, *The Fighting Caballero*, *Honor of the Press* and *North of Shanghai*. One of her co-stars was Wild Bill Elliott.

Gulliver also appeared in such sound serials as *The Phantom of the West*, *The Galloping Ghost*, *The Shadow of the Eagle*, *Custer's Last Stand* and *The Last Frontier*. Her later roles were in support and she left the screen in the early 1940s. *Borrowed Heroes* may have been her last film.

Returning after 25 years to appear in support as a harridan in John Cassavetes's *Faces*, Dorothy Gulliver's performance was widely praised. In all, she made over 100 films, including shorts, and also played some TV roles.

REVIEWS

College Love: In this conglomeration of the "Collegian" series into a feature, Dorothy Gulliver is the heroine. *Variety* 8/7/29, *Harrison's Reports* 8/10/29.

Troopers Three: Gulliver supplies the heart interest. *New York Times* 2/17/30.

The Fighting Marshal: In this western with fast action and pretty tense suspense Dorothy Gulliver is the heroine. *Harrison's Reports* 1/9/32.

Hackett, Raymond, New York, New York, 1902/03–1958

Silent: A member of a prominent theatrical family, Raymond Hackett was a stage actor at a young age and also made his first films as a youth. In 1915 he appeared in *The Ringtailed Rhinoceros*. He made *Ginger* in 1919 and was back in 1922 for *The Country Flapper* and *The Cynic Effect*.

There were at least two more silents for Hackett, one of which was Gloria Swanson's *The Love of Sunya* in 1927. Last silent: *Faithless Lover* (also known as *The Pasteboard Lover*) (1928).

Sound: Whatever brief fame Raymond Hackett found in the cinema was in the early sound period. His first talkie was *The Trial of Mary Dugan*; others in '29 were *Madame X*, *The Girl in the Show* and *Footlights and Fools*. He had his busiest year in 1930 with seven films.

Hackett's film career flamed out rapidly and in 1931 he made only one. It was *Seed*, his last picture and one of Bette Davis's very first. Other of his films included *The Cat Creeps*, *Numbered Men*, *Our Blushing Brides* and *The Sea Wolf*.

Comments: Raymond Hackett was one of the handsomest of the early sound era's young actors and his performances had an air of sincerity. He was not a forceful film actor, however, and he was cast as the son or brother of the heroine in several films.

On other occasions Hackett was a rather callow leading man. He perhaps saw the handwriting on the wall — it was not propitious — and he returned to the stage, eventually becoming the husband of silent actress Blanche Sweet.

REVIEWS

Madame X: Raymond Hackett is the son. He showed little in the movie until the court scene and then he let loose. *Variety* 5/1/29, *Harrison's Reports* 5/11/29.

Footlights and Fools: Male lead Raymond Hackett as the gambling kid has a rather difficult assignment but he pulls it off neatly. *Variety* 11/13/29.

Not So Dumb: The cast is of uniform excellence, with Raymond Hackett getting featured billing. *Variety* 2/12/30.

Let Us Be Gay: For the secondary romantic lead Raymond Hackett was an excellent selection. *Variety* 7/16/30.

On Your Back: Hackett is the hero and he does well. *Harrison's Reports* 7/26/30.

Haines, William, Staunton, Virginia,

1900–1973

Filmography: *Filmograph* (nos. 3–4, 1973); *Films in Review* (Mar. 1984)

Silent: William Haines's film contract with Goldwyn came as a result of the New Faces contest. After a small role in *Brothers Under the Skin* (1922) and several more films, his first major part came in Mary Pickford's *Little Annie Rooney* in 1925.

That same year Haines signed with MGM and made his first appearance there in *Sally, Irene and Mary*. He came to specialize in playing athletes (*Slide, Kelly, Slide, Spring Fever, The Duke Steps Out*) or gauche characters who embarrassed themselves and frequently others.

Among Billy Haines's films were *Circe the Enchantress*, *West Point*, *Mike*, *Brown of Harvard*, with which he became a star in 1926, and *Tell It to the Marines*, generally thought to be his best. *The Duke Steps Out* was technically a silent but a radio broadcast was heard in it. Last silent: *Speedway* (1929), with synchronized music and sound effects, made after his first sound film.

Sound: *Alias Jimmy Valentine*, a 1929 part-talkie, was William Haines's initial sound film; *Navy Blues* was his first all-talking feature after his brief appearance in the all-star *The Hollywood Revue of 1929*. In it he had the dubiously funny job of ripping the buttons off the coat of master of ceremonies Jack Benny.

Haines became increasingly less popular in the talkies because of the sameness of his roles, and MGM dropped him in 1932. He made only two more films, both for Mascot, *Young and Beautiful* in 1934 and *The Marines Are Coming* the following year. Other films included *Way Out West, A Tailor-Made Man, The Fast Life, Remote Control* and *The Girl Said No*.

Comments: In silents, popular William Haines was the epitome of the all–American boy when he wasn't displaying his other, smart-alecky persona. In talkies, he was cast almost entirely in wisecracking roles in insignificant films and audiences tired of this.

Also, Haines's youthful good looks were not what they had been, nor was his somewhat broadening physique. His voice, while not bad, was not particularly good either and not quite suited to the scrappy athletic roles that he had played in the silents.

There is always the suspicion that Haines's homosexual lifestyle, well-known to Hollywood insiders, was the cause of MGM wanting to discard him. While it was unlikely, given the studios' protective public relations apparatus, that his predilection would have gotten out to a wider public, there was always that possibility.

There was also the very distinct possibility that MGM merely wanted to unload William Haines, a high-priced player who was no longer so popular. With charismatic upcoming stars like Clark Gable in the MGM stable, there was little incentive for keeping him on. But he proved not to need filmmaking for his livelihood; he became one of the country's premier interior decorators.

REVIEWS

Navy Blues: It will probably make money on the Haines name but doesn't deserve to. The main sufferer will probably be Haines who is overplaying for laughs playing a silly kid role. It won't further endear him to anyone. *Variety* 1/15/30.

Way Out West: Haines is in another mean role. There is audience satisfaction in seeing the smart-alecky Haines shorn of his usual aggressiveness. *Variety* 8/20/30.

Just a Gigolo: Haines, in a part true to his type, stands to benefit very little. He gives a more restrained performance than in any of his other pictures, yet he does not win the audience's sympathy. *Variety* 6/16/31, *Harrison's Reports* 6/20/31.

The Marines Are Coming: In his last film the reviews differed. One said that he was again seen as a wisecracking individual but was more sympathetic in this instance. Others were less generous, stating that his initial retirement was caused by the apathy of the public toward his smart-aleck roles. If he had learned his lesson it was not apparent because his character was still annoying and witless. *Harrison's Reports* 1/5/35, *New York Times* 2/23/35, *Variety* 2/27/35.

Hale, Alan (Rufus MacKahan or McKahn), Washington, D.C., 1892–1950

Filmography: *Classic Images* (Aug.-Sept. 1991); Academy of Motion Picture Arts and Sciences; List of films in *Eighty Silent Film Stars*

Silent: After much experience in vaudeville and on the stage, Alan Hale became a leading man in one- and two-reelers from about 1911 or '12. Early films included *His Inspiration, Jane Eyre, Martin Chuzzlewit, Pudd'nhead Wilson* and *The Purple Lady*. Increasingly, he went into features starting about 1916 and in the '20s became a much-sought-after supporting actor.

Among Hale's films in that decade were *The Four Horsemen of the Apocalypse, The Covered Wagon, Dick Turpin, Hollywood, Robin Hood, Skyscraper, Cameo Kirby, Black Oxen* and *Oh, Kay!* He worked for numerous studios including Reliance, Biograph, World, Metro and Fox. He also directed some films in the mid–1920s.

Topping off his 130 or so silents, Hale made a series of adventure-melodramas with William Boyd in the latter '20s. During that time he was often top- or second-billed, or almost always very high in the cast list. Last silent: *Power* (1928).

Sound: There were talking sequences in Hale's 1928 picture *The Spieler*. It was his first with sound, and was followed by the part-talkies *Sal of Singapore* and *The Leatherneck* in 1929. All his films that year had some talking, including *Red Hot Rhythm, Sailor's Holiday* and *The Sap*.

Although Hale continued to work steadily until his death, his career declined somewhat in the early 1930s. A brief but memorable scene in 1934's *It Happened One Night* proved to be what he needed to boost his fortunes, and his role in *Stella Dallas* re-established him as a bankable character actor.

Hale's 110 talkies included *The Sin of Madelon Claudet, The Lost Patrol, Susan Lenox: Her Fall and Rise, Of Human Bondage, Great Expectations, The Adventures of Robin Hood* (as Little John), *Dodge City, This Is the Army, Night and Day* and *The Inspector General*.

Alan Hale made a small cottage industry out of playing Little John, a role he had played in the 1922 Fairbanks version of *Robin Hood* as well as the Flynn version. He repeated it twice more in *The Bandit of Sherwood Forest* (1946) and *Rogues of Sherwood Forest* (1950), one of his last films.

Comments: Although not a major character *star* in the mold of, say, Wallace Beery, Alan Hale certainly was a major character actor. He somewhat resembled Beery in the type of roles he played, often being cast as a "good bad man" and he certainly could "roister" with the best of them.

Hale's signature role probably came in the 1938 version of *Robin Hood*. Like all his talkie roles it was immeasurably aided by his authoritative basso voice ideal for military men and other strong male figures. Although he was cast in a good many westerns and melodramas, he was also adept at comedy.

Hale was, quite simply, one of the most dependable and memorable character men produced by Hollywood. His son, Alan Hale, Jr., who somewhat resembled him, became well-known for his work as the Skipper on television's *Gilligan's Island*.

REVIEWS

The Sap: The film gets better when Alan Hale appears. *Harrison's Reports* 1/18/30, *Variety* 3/5/30.

The Lost Patrol: Fine performances by the entire cast, including Alan Hale. *Harrison's Reports* 2/17/34.

Stella Dallas: Hale makes a good deal out of his role and there are even a few good laughs cleverly put in for him. *Variety* 7/28/37.

Gentleman Jim: Those scenes that Jack Carson doesn't steal, Alan Hale does. *Variety* 11/4/42.

Hale, Creighton (Patrick Fitzgerald), Cork, Ireland, 1882–1965

Silent: Among Creighton Hale's earliest cinema efforts was the 1915 Pearl White serial *The Exploits of Elaine*. Nineteen fourteen seems to be the year he made his debut and he remained a popular leading man through the end of the silent days. His films included *A Fool There Was, Way Down East, Orphans of the Storm, The Marriage Circle, The Cat and the Canary* (as the frightened hero), *Seven Days, Oh, Baby!* and *Sisters of Eve*. Last silent: *House of Shame* (1928).

Sound: Hale made his sound debut in the part-talkie *Seven Footprints to Satan* (1929). His other film that year, and first all-talkie, was *The Great Divide*. Although his career soon evolved into supporting roles, shorts, and then bits, he continued to be active in films for two more decades.

Among Hale's pictures were *Holiday* (1930), *The Return of Doctor X, Crime By Night, The Perils of Pauline* (1947 version), *The Great Divide, One More Spring, Sangaree, Cowboy Quarterback* and *A Child Is Born*. He played "himself," i.e., a former silent star, in 1936's *Hollywood Boulevard*. By the time his career was over, he had bridged the gap from primitive silents to 3-D.

REVIEWS

The Perils of Pauline: Creighton Hale is among some of the early day names who again show their talent. *Variety* 5/28/47.

Hale, Georgia (Georgette Hale?), St. Joseph, Missouri , 1900/06–1985

Filmography: Charlie Chaplin: Intimate Close-Ups

Silent: It can be said without fear of contradiction that beauty contest winner Georgia Hale hit her screen pinnacle in 1925, a couple of years after she began appearing in films as an extra. Her two roles that year were in *The Gold Rush*, as the dance hall girl Georgia beloved by Charlie Chaplin, and in Josef von Sternberg's oddity *The Salvation Hunters*.

Perhaps Hale's other role of note was a supporting one in 1926's *The Great Gatsby*. Among her 13 silents, including several westerns, were *Man of the Forest, The Hills of Peril, Gypsy of the North, A Woman Against the World* and *The Rawhide Kid*. Last silent: *The Floating College* (1928).

Sound: As far as can be determined, Georgia Hale appeared in only one sound vehicle, the 1931 serial *The Lightning Warrior*. The male star was the canine wonder dog Rin Tin Tin. It was the last film for both.

Comments: Georgia Hale was a pretty actress with liquid dark eyes, but she was an untrained one. Apparently her only professional experience before she became an extra had been in a Chicago musical revue. Despite the fact her career was almost entirely undistinguished, she is one of the most recognized of the minor silent actresses because of the classic status of *The Gold Rush*.

Hale almost had another classic film to her credit. Charlie Chaplin became dissatisfied with the performance of Virginia Cherrill during the making of his 1931 release *City Lights*. Tests exist from 1929 with Hale in the role of the blind girl, but presumably too much footage had been shot with Cherrill and she remained in the final version.

Like many of his leading ladies, Georgia Hale was involved in Chaplin's personal life as well. She was on his payroll until 1953 and remained intensely devoted to him all her life, so much so that she never married. She wrote a memoir of their times together that was not published until 1995.

Hall, James (James Brown), Dallas, Texas, 1900–1940

Filmography: Films in Review (Jan. 1992)

Silent: Coming from a successful New York stage career, James Hall made his first picture for Paramount, *The Campus Flirt*, in 1926. He also had appeared in a 1923 film called *The Man Alone*. He made about 15 silents altogether.

Several of Hall's pictures were teamings with Bebe Daniels (*Swim, Girl, Swim, Señorita*) and he also was seen in *Hotel Imperial, Ritzy, The Fleet's In, Rolled Stockings* and John Ford's *Four Sons*, considered to be one of his best performances. Last silent: *The Case of Lena Smith* (1929).

Sound: The first talkie in which Hall appeared was 1929's *The Canary Murder Case*. Others he made that year included *Smiling Irish Eyes* and *The Saturday Night Kid*. The next year he played the "good" brother in his most famous film, *Hell's Angels*. Some other sound films were *This Is Heaven, Dangerous Nan McGrew, Maybe It's Love* and *Sporting Chance*.

After being released by Paramount in 1930, Hall made several pictures in 1931 freelancing for such studios as Warner Bros., Tiffany and Universal. The final one of his over 15 sound film roles came in 1932's *Manhattan Tower*.

Comments: James Hall's screen career was brief, less than 35 films in six or seven years, but it had been a promising one at the start. He could be a sensitive and winning actor in a good role, as he revealed in *Four Sons* and *Hell's Angels*, and he appeared with many leading actresses of the ilk of Pola Negri, Clara Bow and Vilma Banky, as well as Daniels, Colleen Moore.

As far as Hall's transition to the talkies goes, it was smooth enough and his voice well-suited to his persona. His private life was tempestuous, however, and his ego (and libido) apparently were his downfall. Paramount released him, as they had many others, for "temperament" and in his case there was some truth to the charge.

Hall partied hard and openly, eventually causing highly publicized problems with his wife. The adverse publicity led to the end of his film career. The end of his life was itself redolent of a movie melodrama. Alcoholic, all of his film earnings gone, he kept body and soul barely together by appearing as a master of ceremonies in third-rate New Jersey night spots.

REVIEWS

Smiling Irish Eyes: As the hero in Colleen Moore's first talkie, James Hall is somewhat of a fiddling fool but it is palpably faked. *Variety* 7/31/29.

Hell's Angels: Hall has the only role aimed for sympathy but he sparkles only occasionally. There's many a spot where he actually looks flabby. *Variety* 6/4/30.

Millie: There are a couple of juveniles, James

Hall and Robert Ames. Hall's performance bests Ames's because his personality seemed the more attractive. *Variety* 2/11/31.

The Sporting Chance: Hall gives fair support in a playboy role. *Variety* 12/1/31.

Hall, Thurston, Boston, Massachusetts,
1883–1958

Silent: A player on Broadway from 1901 and in vaudeville, Thurston Hall made his first one-reeler in 1915 and by 1917 was co-starring in features such as *Cleopatra* with Theda Bara. For the next few years he was busy on screen starring, and occasionally playing secondary roles, in films like *The Brazen Beauty, The Mating of Marcella, The Spitfire of Seville, The Weaker Vessel, Empty Arms* and *Mother Eternal.* Last silent: *Wildness of Youth* (1922).

Sound: After another dozen years on the stage, Hall came back to Hollywood to begin a long string of character roles which his commandingly deep voice and overbearing manner made memorable. He became the veritable King of Bluster.

From 1935 Hall's films included *Metropolitan, Theodora Goes Wild, The Great Lie, City for Conquest, Cover Girl, Mourning Becomes Electra, The Secret Life of Walter Mitty, Skirts Ahoy* and *Wilson.* In the 1950s he made fewer, *Affair in Reno* (1957) being one of his last.

Comments: Although an unmemorable silent leading man, Thurston Hall later ranked among the very best of character actors. He invariably played petty men of power and when there was a gray-haired, jowly politician or dictatorial company president on the scene it was, more often than not, he.

No one could "harumph" at and bully his unfortunate subordinates better than Hall. One of his signature roles was undoubtedly that of the demanding (and demeaning) pulp magazine publisher in *The Secret Life of Walter Mitty* with Danny Kaye. While his blowhard ways may have been hard on his subordinates, they were the delight of moviegoers.

Reviews

Parole Racket: Thurston Hall makes a lusty city editor. *Variety* 3/10/37.

Hamilton, Hale, Fort Madison, Iowa,
1880–1942

Silent: Stage star Hale Hamilton had his major screen popularity as a leading man before 1920. From 1918 his early films included *Five Thousand an Hour, After His Own Heart, Full of Pep* and *In*

His Brother's Place. During the '20s he appeared only sporadically in such efforts as *The Manicure Girl, The Great Gatsby, Summer Bachelor* and *Girl in the Rain.* Last silent: *The Telephone Girl* (1927).

Sound: Hamilton found a new lease on movie life in the talkies. From 1930 he provided distinguished support in numerous films through 1935 and then in a few more until 1940. They included *Common Clay, Paid, Beau Ideal, Murder at Midnight, Susan Lenox: Her Fall and Rise, Love Affair, Strange People* and *The Girl from Missouri.* His last films were *The Adventures of Marco Polo* and *Edison the Man.*

Reviews

Beau Ideal: Hale Hamilton, an excellent actor, is one of the offenders in the film. When he is shouting at the troops it sounds much like an announcer announcing the boxers' weights at Madison Square Garden. *New York Times* 1/19/31.

Reform Girl: The familiar faces in the cast don't hurt. Among them is Hale Hamilton, who is likable. *Harrison's Reports* 9/9/33, *Variety* 12/12/33.

Hamilton, Lloyd, Oakland, California,
1887/91–1935

Silent: Beginning about 1914, Lloyd Hamilton made his first films at Kalem after having honed his comedy skills in stock and burlesque. His greatest fame came as a member of the team of "Ham and Bud" with Albert (Bud) Duncan. The contrast between the hulking Hamilton (six feet plus) and the diminutive (4'11") Bud provided much of the mirth.

Hamilton made about 130 "Ham and Bud" comedies as well as one- and two-reelers for Lubin, Fox, Universal, Santa Paula, Sunshine, Educational and, in the mid–1920s, for his own production company. His persona was usually that of a bashful and blundering youth. For some while in that decade he made no films at all and he appeared in a very few features including *Hollywood* and *His Darker Self.* Last silent feature: *A Self-Made Failure* (1924), in which he had the lead.

Sound: Tanned Legs and *The Show of Shows,* released about the same time in late 1929, marked Hamilton's sound debut in full-length movies. In the latter he was featured in a couple of numbers, including one with Bea Lillie and Louise Fazenda.

Most of Hamilton's talkie career was spent in Sennett and Educational shorts with apparently only one other feature appearance to his credit, the disastrous Bea Lillie starrer *Are You There?* (1930).

Comments: As his extended turn in the all-star *The Show of Shows* revealed, Lloyd Hamilton was not well-suited to talkies. He had a major problem with slurring his speech, whether from an actual defect or lack of proper training. He found work in sound films but his best days were those he spent in silence.

Before his relatively early demise, in his personal life Hamilton had been somewhat of a hard luck case. He had some severe, even life-threatening, accidents and his domestic relations were stormy. The coming of sound was merely an additional blow.

REVIEWS

Are You There?: It's too bad that Fox could not have forgotten it forever. It is a ridiculous talker and worse than a quickie of any kind. (This is the film that caused Bea Lillie to happily desert the cinema for the more welcoming arms of the stage. It was shelved for an entire year before being thrown out to obscure theaters to play out its brief life. It obviously was no help in giving Hamilton a foothold in talking films.) *Variety* 7/14/31.

Hamilton, Mahlon, Baltimore, Maryland, 1883/85–1960

Silent: Stage star Mahlon Hamilton made his screen bow about 1914, perhaps in *Three Weeks*. Other early films were *The Eternal Question*, *The Soul of a Magdalen*, *Daddy-Long-Legs* (1919 version) and *Exile*. He partnered some of the screen's most popular actresses including Mary Pickford and Marion Davies.

By the 1920s Hamilton was alternating supporting and leading roles and by mid-decade his appearances were declining. He still continued to receive billing as a leading man late in the decade, albeit for small studios. Other films included *Ladies Must Live*, *A Fool There Was* (1922 version), *The Christian*, *Playthings of Desire*, *The Wheel* and *Her Indiscretions*. Last silent: *The Single Standard* (1929), with synchronized music and sound effects.

Sound: From 1929 to 1937 Mahlon Hamilton played supporting roles in an admixture of major films, westerns and melodramas. One of his first talkies was *Honky Tonk* in 1929; others included *Sporting Chance*, *Anna Karenina*, *Back Street*, *Mississippi*, *The Boss Rider of Gun Creek*, *Madame X* (1937 version) and *Code of Honor*.

REVIEWS

Honky Tonk: Hamilton is very good in the lead as the cabaret owner. *Variety* 6/12/29, *Harrison's Reports* 6/15/29.

Rich People: The acting is so good, including Mahlon Hamilton as the heroine's father. *Harrison's Reports* 1/18/30.

Boss Rider of Gun Creek: Mahlon Hamilton has a minor assignment in this Buck Jones western. *Variety* 12/16/36.

Hamilton, Neil (James N. Hamilton), Lynn, Massachusetts, 1899–1984

Filmography: *Films in Review* (Mar. 1982), with additions (June/July 1982)

Silent: After a modeling career and extra work, Neil Hamilton was selected in 1923 by D. W. Griffith for *The White Rose* and then *America* and *Isn't Life Wonderful?* He went on to Paramount as a romantic leading man, teaming with Bebe Daniels, Esther Ralston, Evelyn Brent and Jean Arthur (among others).

Hamilton's 30 or so films included *The Patriot*, *New Brooms*, *Desert Gold*, *The Great Gatsby*, *The Joy Girl* and *Men and Women*. Last silent: *Why Be Good?* (1929).

Sound: Aside from one silent, all Neil Hamilton's 1929 films were part- or full-talkies. The first was *A Dangerous Woman*. Among his early prestige talkies was *The Dawn Patrol* (1930 version), probably his best film role, although his acting was perhaps over-theatrical. In it he played the major who ultimately sickened at sending young aviators off to die in World War One.

Other notable Hamilton films were *The Wet Parade*, *The Animal Kingdom*, *What Price Hollywood?* and *One Sunday Afternoon*. By the mid-'30s his career was beginning to decline but he worked steadily in films including shorts, until about 1945. Some of his roles were supporting ones, sometimes as villains (as in the serial *King of the Texas Rangers*). His various studios included Fox, Columbia, First National, RKO, Warner Bros., Majestic, Republic and Universal.

Hamilton returned to movies in 1964 with *Good Neighbor Sam*. In 1966 he joined the cast of the popular *Batman* TV program as Commissioner Gordon and also appeared in the film version of that series. By the time he left the screen, he counted among his 65 talkies *Ladies Must Play*, *The Great Lover*, *The World Gone Mad*, *Honeymoon Limited*, *Queen of the Mob*, *Why Strangers Marry* and his last, *Which Way to the Front?* (1970). He also made many stage appearances.

Comments: Neil Hamilton was certainly a "pretty face" and, though an average actor at best, his baritone voice was well-suited to talkies despite a noticeable New England accent. He continued his career without letup after sound arrived, no doubt assisted by the fact that he was the bland, non-threatening type of leading man whom strong actresses liked.

Hamilton eventually partnered Joan Crawford, Norma Shearer, Irene Dunne, Helen Hayes and

Myrna Loy among others. He himself said that the end of his starring career affected him greatly but he indomitably pressed on through career heights and depths. If his 1960s "15 minutes of fame" was due to a campy role on a campy program, he at least had become a well-known figure again.

Darkened Rooms: It is difficult to accept Hamilton as the pseudo-hypnotist and clairvoyant due to his boyish appearance. *Variety* 12/18/29.

Ex-Flame: Hamilton was starred for some reason and he plays the English lord mechanically. *Variety* 1/28/31.

The Wet Parade: Excellent performances are given by the stars, assisted by Neil Hamilton. *Harrison's Reports* 4/30/32.

Batman: The acting is uniformly, impressively improbable. Neil Hamilton repeats his teleseries role. *Variety* 7/20/66.

Hampton, Hope, Philadelphia, Pennsylvania or Houston, Texas, 1898/1900–1982

Silent: After winning a beauty contest and doing some extra work, Hope Hampton began a starring career in motion pictures that was entirely impelled by one man, wealthy Jules Brulatour, whom she later married. He formed Hope Hampton Productions and single-mindedly set out to make her a star. Her first picture was 1920's *A Modern Salome;* over a dozen more followed.

Hampton's films, released through Fox, First National, Paramount and Metro, included *The Bait, Does It Pay?, The Gold Diggers, The Price of a Party, Lover's Island* and *Lawful Larceny.* There apparently was also a short made in early Technicolor called *Marionettes.* When her screen career was over, she became an opera singer. Last silent: *The Unfair Sex* (1926).

Sound: Hampton's singing voice was first heard on-screen in the Vitaphone short *Hope Hampton in the Fourth Act of Manon* (1929). She did not appear in another talkie until 1938's *The Road to Reno,* a musical melange with Randolph Scott. After that there were musical stage revues and only one more brief film role: She played "herself" in the 1961 teen movie *Hey, Let's Twist.*

Comments: Called the "Duchess of Park Avenue" for the socialite's life she led, courtesy of Brulatour's money, Hope Hampton was a fixture in her expensive clothes, furs and jewels at every opening in New York. She prided herself, perhaps mistakenly, on her eternal youthfulness and was a particular fan of the dance "The Twist," hence her final film role.

It is tempting to see in Hampton the real prototype for *Citizen Kane's* Susan Alexander. Actually, her career seemed much more similar to Alexander's than the person that character was presumably based on, William Randolph Hearst's mistress Marion Davies. In any case, there was something rather pitiable in two careers so publicly bought and paid for by besotted lovers.

The Road to Reno: Reviewers differed regarding Hampton's return to the screen. One stated there was not much hope of her becoming popular but another thought that she was very attractive and retained her highly appealing voice which was dulcet and impressive. Her singing technique was flawless. *Harrison's Reports* 9/17/38, *Variety* 10/5/38.

Hansen, Juanita, Des Moines, Iowa, 1895/97–1961

Silent: Tall, blonde Juanita Hansen worked in Mack Sennett comedies, perhaps as one of his bathing beauties. She also co-starred with Tom Mix and William S. Hart but it was for her serial appearances that she became famous. They included *Secret of the Submarine, The Yellow Arm, The Lost City, The Brass Bullet* and *The Phantom Foe.*

Hansen's features, in which she appeared from 1914 to '23, included *The Patchwork Girl of Oz, The Mediator, Glory, The Sea Flower, Lombardi Ltd.* and *The Broadway Madonna.* Her starring career was prematurely ended after an accident in which she was burned. Last silent: *Girl from the West* (1923).

Sound: The 1933 film *Sensation Hunters* was the only 1930s film Hansen is known to have appeared in although she also may have done some unbilled bits. After she left the screen, she worked for a circus. In the late '30s she co-wrote a book dealing with drug abuse, a demon against which she had struggled for a long time.

Sensation Hunters: An occasional boost is provided by the veteran Juanita Hansen, as the owner of the resort, who contributes a number of good bits. *Variety* 1/9/34.

Hardy, Oliver *see* Laurel, Stan, and Oliver Hardy

Hare, Lumsden (Francis L. Hare), Tipperary, Ireland, 1874–1964

Silent: After a theater career, both as actor and director, that began in England in the 1890s and in the U.S. about 1905, Lumsden Hare eventually came to the screen in 1916 playing leads in such films as *Arms and the Woman, Love's Crucible, Envy* and *The Test*.

After 1920 Hare's roles were sparse, no doubt due to his stage career, and he was seen in only a film a year until 1925. By that time his roles had become supporting ones and he did not return to the screen until the last year of the decade.

Among Hare's motion pictures were *The Education of Elizabeth, Sherlock Holmes, The Frisky Mrs. Johnson, On the Banks of the Wabash* and *Second Youth*. Last silent: *Girls Gone Wild* (1929), with synchronized sound effects and music.

Sound: Soon after the introduction of sound, the distinguished-looking Hare began playing the type of role with which he became identified, a pillar of the British Empire, usually a military officer or other authority figure. His 1929 sound films included *The Black Watch* and *The Sky Hawk* and the next year he was seen in *Scotland Yard* and *So This Is London*.

Hare continued as a well-respected character actor through the early 1960s. In the '30s he appeared in such prestigious films as *Arrowsmith, Svengali, The House of Rothschild, Clive of India, The Lives of a Bengal Lancer, Lloyds of London* and *Gunga Din*.

The 1940s saw Hare in *Rebecca, Sister Kenny, Dr. Jekyll and Mr. Hyde* and *The Paradine Case*, among many others. His output of films slowed during the 1950s and they were not of the quality they had been, although certainly he had always made his share of "B" movies, and also shorts.

Among Hare's later motion pictures were *David and Bathsheba, Julius Caesar* and *My Cousin Rachel*. By 1959 he was near the end of a worthy career even if the final films were not. They were *Count Your Blessings, The Oregon Trail* and *The Four Skulls of Johnathan Drake*.

REVIEWS

So This Is London: An appreciable share of the comedy is contributed by Lumsden Hare who impersonates a phlegmatic, heavily mustached Lord. The picture closes with Will Rogers and Hare singing "My Country 'Tis of Thee" and "God Save the King." *Variety* 5/28/30, *Harrison's Reports* 5/31/30.

Harlan, Kenneth, Boston, Massachusetts, 1895/98–1967

Filmography: *Classic Images* (Aug.-Sept. 1990); List of films in *Eighty Silent Film Stars*

Silent: Kenneth Harlan was a square-chinned matinee idol whose career began about 1917, possibly with *The Wife He Bought*. He worked at many studios during the course of his silent stardom, including Universal, Triangle, Metro, Goldwyn and Preferred.

Among Harlan's leading ladies were the Talmadge sisters, Mary Pickford, Pola Negri, Clara Bow and Bebe Daniels. His films included *The Wine Girl, Dollars and Sense, The Girl Who Came Back, Soiled, Polly of the Follies, Cheating Cheaters, Twinkletoes* and *The Virginian* (1923 version).

By the end of the decade, Harlan was making fewer films — he made over 80 silents — and he had slipped into supporting roles in major films and leads for smaller companies. Last silent: *Man, Woman and Wife* (1929), with synchronized music and sound effects.

Sound: Although Harlan's voice proved to be perfectly satisfactory, his first talkies, *Paradise Island* and *Under Montana Skies*, were not made until 1930 for Tiffany. By the time his career ended in the 1940s, he had made 70 or more sound films, in most of which he was a character player.

Among Harlan's pictures were *Wanderer of the Wasteland, Air Police, Women Men Marry, Held for Ransom, You Can't Beat the Law* and *The Underdog*. When he was noticed at all in his later roles, many in westerns and other quickies, reviewers invariably referred to him as a former silent star.

Harlan also made shorts and was seen in such serials as *Danger Island, Shadow of the Eagle, The Mysterious Pilot, The Masked Marvel* and *Dick Tracy's G-Men*. He made films for studios both big and small, including Grand National, Universal, Warner Bros., Republic, Columbia and Monogram.

REVIEWS

Under Montana Skies: An always winning and sure-shooting hero is Kenneth Harlan. It's his first western in some time. *Harrison's Reports* 9/6/30, *Variety* 10/22/30.

Public Enemy's Wife: Harlan does well in a minor assignment as a G-man. *Variety* 7/15/36.

Law of the Texan: Kenneth Harlan, in one of the biggest parts he's had in years, is a suitably slick villain. *Variety* 10/26/38.

Range War: Kenneth Harlan, an old-timer, has a bit part as a banker. *Variety* 8/30/39.

Desperate Cargo: Harlan, a former silent star, contibutes an important secondary role with polish. *Variety* 10/8/41.

The Law Rides Again: Kenneth Harlan, a veteran of silent films, does all right as a crooked Indian agent. *Variety* 8/11/43.

Harlan, Otis, Zanesville, Ohio, 1864/65–1940

Silent: A stage veteran from the 1880s to 1914, Otis Harlan was top-billed in the 1915 feature *A Black Sheep* and then apparently did not make another until 1920's *The Romance Promoters.* Throughout the remainder of the decade he appeared in films in various genres as a character actor, with a specialty in portraying elderly men.

Among Harlan's numerous pictures, sometimes as many as ten a year, were *The Girl in the Taxi, Two Kinds of Women, Captain Blood, Abraham Lincoln, The Perfect Clown, The Prince of Pilsen* and *The Student Prince.* He often played very small roles. Last silent: *Clear the Decks* (1929).

Sound: Of Harlan's eight films in 1929, six had some or full sound. They included *Broadway, The Mississippi Gambler, Show Boat* and *His Lucky Day.* He continued in films until 1938, capping his career as the voice of the dwarf Happy in *Snow White and the Seven Dwarfs.*

Others of Harlan's 1930s motion pictures, including many "B" westerns, were *The King of Jazz, Aloha, Riders of Death Valley, A Midsummer Night's Dream, The Telegraph Trail, Music in the Air, Diamond Jim, Western Gold, Can This Be Dixie?* and *The Texans.* He was the uncle of the matinee idol and character actor Kenneth Harlan.

REVIEWS

Barnum Was Right: Otis Harlan plays an Englishman, and as usual he speaks in an exaggerated English accent. *Variety* 10/30/29.

Dames Ahoy: Harlan, as an unwilling husband, is pretty good. *Harrison's Reports* 4/5/30.

Harris, Mildred (also known as Mildred Harris Chaplin), Cheyenne, Wyoming, 1901–1944

Silent: Mildred Harris was a pretty child actress who began her film career at the age of ten for Thomas Ince. She also worked at such studios as Vitagraph, Oz, Majestic, Reliance and Fine Arts. Among her very early films were several 1914 "Wizard of Oz" adventures, *The Warrens of Virginia, Hoodoo Ann, A Love Sublime* and *Intolerance,* in which she had a bit.

Harris's career prospered in leads and supporting roles throughout the '20s. She had been Charles Chaplin's first wife and it reasonably could be said that her liaison with him had had a salutary effect on that career. Her films included *A Prince There Was, By Divine Right, Frivolous Sal, The Cruise of the Jasper B, Husband Hunters* and *Lingerie.* Last silent: *Power of the Press* (1928), made after her initial talkie.

Sound: Harris's first talkie was *Melody of Love* (1928), in which she played the female lead opposite Walter Pidgeon. Her other early talkies generally found her in supporting roles and then she descended into bit parts.

Harris's pictures included *Side Street, Sea Fury, The Melody Man, No, No Nanette, Lady Tubbs* and *Never Too Late.* She may also have had bits in a few features of the early 1940s as well. She also was seen in shorts, including at least one Three Stooges comedy.

REVIEWS

Melody of Love: Harris comes from vaudeville and the stage, but her talking sequences do not register. She clicks, as far as sound is concerned, only in her song interpolations. As a French girl in a blonde wig, she is demure and sympathetic, and aside from a little over-acting, is acceptable. *Variety* 10/17/28, *Harrison's Reports* 11/10/28.

Harron, John (Johnny or Johnnie), New York, New York, 1903–1939

Silent: In what may have been his first film, John Harron had a cameo in his older brother Robert Harron's *Hearts of the World* in 1918. He was back in 1921 with supporting roles in *The Grim Comedian* and *Through the Back Door* and eventually progressed to romantic leads.

Harron's films included *Penrod, My Wife and I, Bride of the Storm, Hell-Bent fer Heaven, Silk Stockings* and *Their Hour.* Last silent: *Green Grass Widows* (1928).

Sound: The very popular *Street Girl* (1929) was Harron's first sound film. He continued in leading roles through 1934 although they became largely limited to quickies. Probably his best-known film to modern audiences is the minor horror classic *White Zombie* (1932).

Among Harron's others were *Big Boy, The Easiest Way, The Czar of Broadway, Beauty Parlor, Midnight Warning* and *Stolen Sweets.* From 1937 to the time of his death he appeared in numerous bit parts, several being released in 1940 after his death.

REVIEWS

Street Girl: The fine acting of John Harron makes the character a sympathetic young man. *Harrison's Reports* 8/10/29.

The Czar of Broadway: Harron plays the reporter like a Dick Merrill college hero. *Variety* 7/2/30.

White Zombie: All the actors have strange lines to say but those given to Harron seem to be the most fantastic. He helps to maintain the atmosphere. *New York Times* 7/29/32, *Variety* 8/2/32.

Hart, William S(urrey), Newburgh, New York, 1864/70–1946 (A Special Mention)

Athough William S. Hart made no feature length or other films after 1925's *Tumbleweeds,* his voice was heard on-screen in 1939 when he filmed a moving introduction for the re-release of that film about the Oklahoma land rush.

The quality of Hart's sonorous stage-trained — and perhaps also stagey — voice gave an indication of how talkies would have been enriched had he chosen to pursue a career as a character actor.

Unashamedly playing for pathos, Hart reminisced about the "old days" of making western movies and about his beloved pinto pony Fritz. It was a most fitting and unabashedly sentimental coda to his distinguished film career.

Hatton, Raymond, Red Oak, Iowa, 1887–1971

Filmography: *Classic Images* (Jan.-Mar. 1989); List of films in *Eighty Silent Film Stars*

Silent: Stock and vaudeville were in Raymond Hatton's resume when he began in films about 1911 or '12. After stints at Biograph, Sennett and Kalem, he joined the Lasky Film Corporation where he made at least 20 films with Cecil B. DeMille. One of these was the major hit *The Whispering Chorus* (1918), in which he was starred.

Hatton played supporting roles in most of his pictures which included *The Little American, Joan the Woman, The Hunchback of Notre Dame, The Devil's Cargo, The Affairs of Anatol, The Poor Boob, Kindling, Silence* and *Lord Jim*.

The height of Hatton's career was the initially popular eight comedies in which he co-starred with Wallace Beery in the latter 1920s. Among them were *We're in the Navy Now, Now We're in the Air, Partners in Crime* and *Fireman, Save My Child*. In retrospect it can be seen that these films led to Beery's temporary decline as a character star and Hatton's permanent one. Last silent: *Trent's Last Case* (1929), with synchronized sound effects and music.

Sound: *The Office Scandal*, a 1929 part-talkie, was Hatton's first. His first all-talking feature was *The Mighty* the same year, and he also appeared in some shorts. With the coming of sound he became primarily a character actor and it was not long before he found himself in westerns, a genre he was seldom to leave for the remainder of his career.

Hatton became one of the best known of the "old coot" western sidekicks in numerous "B" westerns with a variety of sagebrush stars including Roy Rogers, Buck Jones, Johnny Mack Brown and Tim McCoy. He was not above indulging in the inanities of such sidekicks, which one film writer has referred to as "scriptless, witless knockabout."

In a career which stretched almost without interruption to 1957, Hatton's hundreds of films included *Road to Paradise, Malay Nights, Arrowsmith, Fifteen Wives, Wagon Wheels, Steamboat 'Round the Bend, Fury, Marked Woman, Love Finds Andy Hardy, Reap the Wild Wind, The Fighting Ranger, Rhythm Round-Up* and *The Sheriff of Medicine Bow*.

Hatton's westerns included the popular "Rough Riders" and "Three Mesquiteers" series and he also appeared in several serials, among them *The Three Musketeers, The White Eagle, Undersea Kingdom, Jungle Jim* and *The Vigilantes Are Coming*. Although his career had pretty much ended by the late 1950s, he returned for a few roles in the mid–'60s: *The Quick Gun, Requiem for a Gunfighter* and *In Cold Blood* (1967), his last.

REVIEWS

The Mighty: Raymond Hatton contributes some excellent comedy and he gets a deserved niche in the film for himself. *Variety* 1/1/30.

Law and Order: Hatton does his usual act again. *Variety* 3/1/32.

Public Wedding: Raymond Hatton is seen briefly but never has a chance. *Variety* 9/15/37.

Gun Man from Bodie: Hatton's reading of his alleged comedy lines is as pathetic as the lines themselves. *Variety* 10/29/41.

Border Bandits: Raymond Hatton tries hard to inject some vim into the production. *Variety* 4/3/46.

Haver, Phyllis (Phyllis O'Haver), Douglas, Kansas, 1899–1960

Filmography: *Focus on Film* (Autumn 1974)

Silent: Of the Mack Sennett bathing beauties, Phyllis Haver was one of the most famous, and Sennett considered the statuesque actress to be the archetypal "Beauty." She apparently had started out playing the piano as an accompaniment to silent films and ascended from there.

Haver appeared in numerous Sennett one- and two-reelers from about 1917 until 1922, and also had supporting roles in a few features like *A Small Town Idol*. After she left the "Fun Factory," her dramatic role in the popular *The Christian* (1923) began a new career in features.

Haver most often appeared in support or second leads, generally as the "bad" girl or "other woman." Even when she had leads, as in *Chicago*, her moral character was usually questionable.

Among Haver's numerous 1920s features in various genres were *Hard Boiled, The Snob, Three Bad Men, Fig Leaves, The Nervous Wreck, Up in Mabel's Room* and *So Big*. Last silent: *Thunder* (1929), with synchronized music and sound effects. This was also her last film, made after her part-talkies.

Sound: Haver's career ended in mid–1929. She had made three part-talkies: *The Office Scandal, Sal of Singapore* and *The Shady Lady*. She was top-billed in each of these and continued to display the tough lady persona with which she had become so identified.

REVIEWS

Sal of Singapore: Haver does some good work and it speaks well for her that she can arouse sympathy despite a role that is thick with riverfront veneer. However, the spoken parts are not especially good; the lines and pauses give these episodes a staccato character. *Variety* 1/20/29, *New York Times* 1/29/29.

The Shady Lady: Haver does good work as the supposed shady lady but the way the dialogue sounds, and the actors look, while speaking the out-of-kilter dialogue suggests the film might have been better in complete silence. *Harrison's Reports* 1/12/29, *Variety* 3/27/29.

Hawley, Wanda (also known as Wanda

Petit; also Wanda Pittack?), Scranton, Pennsylvania, 1895/97–1963

Filmography: List of films in *Sweethearts of the Sage*

Silent: In the decade from 1917 to 1926, Wanda Hawley was a popular leading actress, often in vamp roles. She was a DeMille favorite for a while and appeared in his *Affairs of Anatol, For Better, For Worse* and *Old Wives for New*. Her career was on the decline by the time the silent era ended.

Other Hawley films included *The Border Wireless, Double Speed, The Love Charm, A Kiss in Time, Too Much Wife, The Young Rajah* (with Rudolph Valentino), *The Unnamed Woman* and *Whom Shall I Marry*. Last silents: *Eyes of the Totem* and *Pirates of the Sky*, released about the same time in 1927.

Sound: As far as is known, Wanda Hawley appeared in only two talkies, *Trails of the Golden West* and *The Pueblo Terror*. Both cheapie westerns were made in 1931 and in both of them she was the female lead.

Hayakawa, Sessue (Kintaro Hayakawa),

Chiba, Japan, 1886/90–1973

Filmography: *Films in Review* (Apr. 1976), with additions (Nov. 1976)

Silent: Nineteen thirteen's *The Wrath of the Gods* was Sessue Hayakawa's first film. His second, *The Typhoon* (1913), was based on a play in which he had appeared. It was a hit and launched him on an almost 10-year and 50-film starring career. He often co-starred with his wife Tsuru Aoki.

After some two-reelers, Hayakawa appeared in Cecil DeMille's sensational *The Cheat* (1915) and, unexpectedly, he became a matinee idol with his own production company. His co-star, the ever smooth-faced Fannie Ward, also benefited greatly.

By 1922, Hayakawa's American career was declining and he left to make films in England and France. His domestically released films included *After Five, The Vigil, The Jaguar's Claws, The White Man's Law, The Man Beneath, The Devil's Claim* and *The Swamp*. Last U.S. silent: *The Vermilion Pencil* (1922); last English silent: *Sen Yan's Devotion* (1924).

Sound: A Vitaphone short entitled (*Sessue Hayakawa in*) *The Man Who Laughed Last* was his first sound endeavor. Hayakawa's first feature came with *Daughter of the Dragon* (1931). It was not successful enough to sustain an American talkie career and he made no more U.S. films until the end of the 1940s. He did make films in France and Japan in the interim.

Tokyo Joe (1949) marked Hayakawa's return to the American cinema. Other appearances were in *Three Came Home* (1950) and *House of Bamboo* (1955) before his sensational success playing the Japanese prisoner-of-war camp commandant in *The Bridge on the River Kwai* (1957). For this epic David Lean film, he received an Academy Award nomination.

This notable motion picture was followed by the Jerry Lewis comedy *The Geisha Boy* and Audrey Hepburn's *Green Mansions* in the late 1950s. *Hell to Eternity* and *Swiss Family Robinson* came in 1960. His last film, *The Big Wave* (1962), was made in Japan. He was also seen on television.

Comments: Those who know Sessue Hayakawa solely through his powerful role as the elderly and cruel prison camp commandant of *The Bridge on the River Kwai* might well be surprised at his considerable silent film fame. He was undoubtedly the most famous Asian in silent films.

Most "Oriental" performers played villains when they could find a role at all. Much of the time, Asian roles were taken by white actors as indeed were many roles for African-Americans. The handsome Hayakawa most often portrayed the hero and was a true matinee idol. His reign lasted until Valentino replaced him.

Hayakawa was not solely a novelty but a good actor whose naturalistic style enhanced his films. However, his heavy accent and age made it unlikely he would ever be a romantic lead in talkies. Although sadly underutilized in that medium, he did continue to contribute outstanding performances when given his chance. He invested his silent heroes and talkie character parts alike with a complexity that was a credit to his talent.

REVIEWS

Daughter of the Dragon: Sessue Hayakawa is making a comeback in this Fu Manchu picture in which he plays a Chinese detective. White actors impersonating Orientals seem more like the Chinese type than he does. He never gives the role plausibility. *Variety* 8/25/31.

Tokyo Joe: Hayakawa's Japanese heavy is suave, and underplayed to point up the menace. *Variety* 10/12/49.

Three Came Home: Particularly noteworthy is the outstanding work of Sessue Hayakawa as a stern but humane Japanese colonel. He plays a particularly complex character and his acting is tops, coming close to outright larceny of every scene in which he appears. *Harrison's Reports* 2/11/50, *Variety* 2/15/50.

House of Bamboo: Hayakawa plays his role with a welcome relief from flamboyance. *Variety* 7/6/55.

The Bridge on the River Kwai: Once a star in American silents, Hayakawa is solidly impressive as the Japanese officer. He turns in a fine acting job. *Variety* 11/20/57, *Harrison's Reports* 11/23/57.

Hell to Eternity: Hayakawa is very convincing in an important role as a Japanese general. He is making a virtual career of his *Kwai*-type casting. *Variety* 8/3/60, *Harrison's Reports* 8/13/60.

Henderson, Del (also Dell; George D. Henderson), St. Thomas, Ontario, 1877/83–1956

Filmography: Academy of Motion Picture Arts and Sciences (silents only, including films directed)

Silent: Coming from the theater, Del Henderson acted for D. W. Griffith from 1908 in such early one-reelers as *Lines of White on a Sullen Sea*, *The Tenderfoot's Triumph*, *The Two Paths*, *The Lonedale Operator* and *Enoch Arden*. From 1912 to 1926 he directed over 300 films, mostly one- and two-reelers, for Griffith, Sennett, Famous Players-Lasky and American.

As a character actor, Henderson returned to the business end of the camera with *The Clinging Vine* in 1926 and was thereafter seen in such films as *Getting Gertie's Garter*, *The Crowd*, *The Patsy*, *Three-Ring Marriage*, *Show People* and *The Power of the Press*. Last silent: *Riley the Cop* (1928), with synchronized music and sound effects.

Sound: Henderson began his talkie career in 1929 comedy shorts in which he appeared until 1935 with such stars as Laurel and Hardy, the Three Stooges, Charley Chase and Thelma Todd. His feature bow came with 1930's *Hit the Deck*, followed by *Sins of the Children*.

Henderson was active through the 1930s in numerous films like *The Easiest Way*, *Lone Cowboy*, *Bolero*, *Diamond Jim*, *Ruggles of Red Gap*, *Poppy* and *Love Affair*. In the '40s he appeared less frequently. Among Henderson's pictures in his final decade of work were *Abe Lincoln in Illinois*, *The Major and*

the Minor, Wilson, Du Barry Was a Lady, State of the Union and Neptune's Daughter (1949), possibly his last film. He also appeared in a snippet of a silent comedy in the 1965 documentary *Laurel and Hardy's Laughing 20s*.

Herbert, Holmes (Edward Sanger?), Dublin, Ireland or Mansfield, England, 1878/83–1956

Silent: Holmes Herbert was a stage actor in England before arriving in America in 1912 as a star on Broadway. Although *The Man Without a Country* (1917) was his first major film, he had essayed leads in at least two films prior to that, 1915's *His Wife* and *Her Life and His* in 1917. In many of his earlier films he was billed as H. E. Herbert.

Herbert continued with a long string of roles throughout the silent era, including *Other Men's Wives*, *My Lady's Garter*, *Evidence*, *Toilers of the Sea*, *Sinners in Heaven*, *The Wanderer*, *One Increasing Purpose*, *Gentlemen Prefer Blondes* and *Through the Breakers*.

During the decade of the 1920s, Herbert alternated between leads and top supporting roles. Last silent: Greta Garbo's *The Kiss* (1929), with synchronized music, made after his first talkies.

Sound: Two early sound films, *The Terror* and *On Trial*, both released in 1928, served as showcases for Herbert's smooth voice and pleasant accent. In the latter he played the victim whose murder precipitates the trial. All but one of his 1929 films were at least part-talking and in *The Charlatan* he was top-billed.

Well-launched on a career as a distinguished character actor, among Herbert's motion pictures in the 1930s were *Dr. Jekyll and Mr. Hyde*, *The Invisible Man*, *The House of Rothschild*, *Lloyds of London* and *Juarez*. He frequently played figures of authority.

In the following decade Herbert's pictures included *This Above All*, *Our Hearts Were Young and Gay*, *Singapore* and *Johnny Belinda*. In 1950 he celebrated his sixtieth year in show business. His film career came to an end shortly thereafter in such films as *David and Bathsheba* and *The Brigand* in 1952.

REVIEWS

The Terror: Holmes Herbert, with considerable legitimate stage experience, performs with easy assurance. *Variety* 8/22/28.

The Thirteenth Chair: The leading man is adequate, as is Holmes Herbert. *Harrison's Reports* 12/21/29.

Ship from Shanghai: Herbert fills a small part as the owner of the ship. *Variety* 4/30/30.

The Curtain Falls: Creditable work is turned in by Holmes Herbert. *Variety* 5/22/35.

Hersholt, Jean, Copenhagen, Denmark,
1886–1956

Filmography: Classic Images (Mar. 1991); List of films in *Eighty Silent Film Stars*

Silent: After stage and cinema experience in his native country, Jean Hersholt's first American film came about 1915. One of his earliest known appearances was in William S. Hart's *Hell's Hinges* (1916). He later claimed that he had appeared in 100 films his first year but this is not possible to authenticate. If true, most of his appearances were undoubtedly as an extra.

During the course of Hersholt's known 80-plus silent films, he worked for studios such as Kaybee, Triangle, Imp, First National, FBO and MGM. His films, in all genres, included *The Aryan, The Greater Law, The Man of the Forest, Jazzmania, The Secret Hour, My Old Dutch, Red Lights* and *Fifth Avenue Models.* Among his best-known were *Greed* (Marcus the villain), *So Big* and *Stella Dallas.* Last silent: *Jazz Mad* (1928).

Sound: Give and Take, Hersholt's final 1928 film, and all his 1929 efforts were part-talkies, including *Abie's Irish Rose* and *The Younger Generation.* He went on to appear in numerous sound films through the early '40s. Among these were two brief series in which he played kindly doctors: Dr. Dafoe, of Dionne Quintuplets fame, and Dr. Christian, based on his popular radio series. The former series consisted of *The Country Doctor, Reunion* and *Five of a Kind;* the latter included *Meet Dr. Christian, Remedy for Riches* and *They Meet Again.*

Hersholt's other films included *Christopher Bean, Seventh Heaven* (1937 version), *Happy Landing, Alexander's Ragtime Band, Grand Hotel, Mark of the Vampire* and *Men in White.* He made only three more appearances after the "Dr. Christian" series ended in 1941: a cameo in *Stage Door Canteen, Dancing in the Dark* and his only '50s film, *Run For Cover* (1955). By that time he had made almost 60 talkies.

Comments: Pipe-smoking Jean Hersholt looked like everyone's favorite uncle and this was put to effective use in his many "genial" roles, notably as Dr. Christian. But he was a formidable villain as well in many silents and talkies, *Tess of the Storm Country* (1922 version), *Greed* and *Mark of the Vampire* perhaps being the best-known to modern audiences.

Hersholt's soft and pleasing Danish accent seemed to be no impediment to his continuing career in the sound era except for the obvious fact that he could not play an American. No doubt it had some small effect on his starring career but, given his age when talkies arrived, character parts were all he could reasonably expect.

Hersholt had begun his film career in Denmark and always remained closely tied to his native country. During World War Two he was an influential voice for aid and comfort to the Danes. It may have been the time involved in these efforts, rather than lack of studio interest in him, which caused his picture career to virtually end at that time. Another of his favored avocations was as a noted collector and translator of Hans Christian Andersen works.

Although many of Hersholt's films were classics, he is probably remembered more for his efforts on behalf of the Hollywood community. He was instrumental in the establishment of the Motion Picture Home and he headed the Academy of Motion Picture Arts and Sciences. For these services he received two special Academy Awards and the Academy named the Jean Hersholt Humanitarian Award for him.

REVIEWS

The Younger Generation: The acting is good, particularly that of the old reliable actor Jean Hersholt; he awakens warm sympathy. *Harrison's Reports* 3/16/29.

Mamba: The acting is good in this color production but that of top-billed Jean Hersholt is superb and towers above that of all the others. It is impressive even though it is a villainous part. *Harrison's Reports* 3/15/30, *Variety* 3/19/30.

Flesh: A supporting role is handled with notable finesse by Jean Hersholt who plays in Dutch dialect. *Variety* 12/13/32.

The Song of the Eagle: Hersholt, playing the proud old German, makes much of the role. *Variety* 5/32/33.

The Country Doctor: Hersholt's impersonation is an excellent job of convincing acting. He looks the part and he acts it with sensitive and intelligent understanding. *Variety* 3/18/36.

Run for Cover: Hersholt's scenes show up excellently. *Variety* 3/23/55.

Heyes, Herbert, Vader, Washington,
1889/90–1958

Silent: A distinguished star of the theater, Herbert Heyes came to Hollywood as a co-star of screen "vamp" Theda Bara in several films from 1916 to '18 including *The Vixen, Under Two Flags, The Tiger Woman, Salome* and *The Darling of Paris.*

Among Heyes's other pictures to 1921, when the busiest period of his silent career concluded, were

The Slave, The Heart of Rachel, The Land of Jazz, Ever Since Eve and *The Queen of Sheba.* Last silent: *It Is the Law* (1924).

Sound: Heyes seemed to find the theater more fulfilling than the cinema and he did not return to films for almost 20 years. In the 1940s he became a well-regarded character actor in such motion pictures as *Tennessee Johnson, The Fighting Seabees, Wilson* and *Miracle on 34th Street.* There were also a few westerns and "B" pictures like *Campus Rhythm.*

In the '50s Heyes appeared in several prestigious films including *A Place in the Sun* (as Eastman, the industrialist, uncle of Montgomery Clift's character), *The Court-Martial of Billy Mitchell, Love Is a Many-Splendored Thing* and *The Ten Commandments,* which may have been his last. He also was seen in *The Seven Little Foys* and *Sincerely Yours* and was active on the radio and in television.

REVIEWS

Teen Age: Herbert Heyes, as the District Attorney, has the embarrassing task of occasionally directing his remarks at the theater audience. *Variety* 6/21/44.

Park Row: Heyes, as an old, cynical and wise reporter who writes his own obituary, is gentle and genuine. *New York Times* 12/22/52.

Sincerely Yours: Seen to advantage is Herbert Heyes. *Variety* 11/2/55.

Hines, John (Johnny), Golden, Colorado, 1895/97–1970

Filmography: Classic Images (July 1987); List of films in *Eighty Silent Film Stars*

Silent: Following stage experience from the time he was a youth, Johnny Hines was first seen on-screen in *Man of the Hour* in 1914. He was in numerous films during the 'teens but it was his popularity in the "Torchy" series of two-reelers (1920–22) which led to important features.

These action-filled films established Hines's persona as a brash and breezy young man who generally won out over adversity. They included *Burn 'Em Up Barnes, Sure Fire Flint, Luck, The Speed Spook, The Crackerjack* and *The Live Wire.* Last silent: *The Wright Idea* (1928).

Sound: Hines apparently had his sound debut in the short *Johnny's Week End* (1930). He made several supporting appearances up to 1938 in such films as *Only Eight Hours, Runaround, The Girl in 419, Her Bodyguard, Society Doctor* and his last feature, *Too Hot to Handle.* He also appeared in a few shorts in the early '40s, and then he went on to direct some Pete Smith shorts.

Comments: Johnny Hines was very popular during most of the 1920s but that popularity already had begun to wane by the end of the decade. His signature persona seemed to belong to the more optimistic, anything-is-possible beliefs of the early and mid-part of the '20s. It was not so much in synch with the more pessimistic winds that heralded the Depression.

Hines's deep voice exactly fit the roles he played in the talkies (the fast-talking, wisecracking sidekick), and he was quite suitable for sound. It is somewhat of a mystery that he did not make more sound films but those he did make were certainly aided by his enjoyable performances.

REVIEWS

The Runaround: Johnny Hines plays one of the ring leaders and he endeavors to add to the none-too-effective fun. *Harrison's Reports* 6/27/31, *New York Times* 8/10/31.

Whistling in the Dark: Nobody else of distinction is in the all-around good supporting cast excepting Johnny Hines as an imported gangster from Chicago. *Variety* 1/31/33.

Holmes, Helen, Chicago, Illinois, 1892–1950

Filmography: List of films in *Sweethearts of the Sage*

Silent: Helen Holmes was the original title character in the 119-episode railroad series *The Hazards of Helen* (1914–16), before being replaced by Helen Gibson sometime during its run. She had begun her career with Keystone (her first film may have starred Mabel Normand) and she was also a scenario writer for Kalem, the studio which produced *Hazards.*

Holmes left Kalem about 1916 to join Mutual-Signal. In time she made numerous westerns for Universal and appeared in several serials, among them *The Girl and the Game, A Lass of the Lumberlands, The Tiger Band, The Railroad Raiders, The Fatal Fortune* and *The Riddle Rider,* her last, in 1924. At one time she had her own production company.

Holmes's features, many with a railroad theme, included *The Runaway Freight, A Man's Soul, The Flying Switch, The Demon of the Rails, Stormy Seas* and *Barriers of the Law.* Last silent: *Peril of the Rail* (1926).

Sound: Helen Holmes's career had faltered in the late 1920s and when sound arrived she was reduced to bit roles and work as an extra. Among the films in which she appeared were *The Spoilers* (1930 version), *The Californian, Dude Cowboy* and *Tail Spin.* Her last film may have been *Beyond the Law* in 1938 or she may have continued on in unbilled roles for some time longer.

Holmes, Stuart (Joseph Liebschen and other variations of the surname), Chicago, Illinois or Schweidnitz, Germany, 1882–1971

Silent: Stuart Holmes may have begun his lengthy career with Edison. He was almost certainly in films by 1909 with Selig in Chicago. Although he specialized in playing mustachioed villains, he was at home in many types of roles and appeared in hundreds of movies over more than 50 years.

Holmes was in Fox's first big hit *Life's Shop Window* in 1914 and one of his frequent Fox co-stars was Theda Bara in films like *East Lynne, The Galley Slave, The Kreutzer Sonata* and *Her Double Life*.

Holmes also appeared in such films as *The Four Horsemen of the Apocalypse, The Prisoner of Zenda, Tess of the D'Urbervilles, The Scarlet Letter* (1917 version), *The Derelict, Broken Hearts of Hollywood* and *The Scarlet Lady*. Last silent: *The Heroic Lover* (1929), with synchronized sound effects and music.

Sound: Holmes's sound career got off to a rather slow start. He did not make his talkie debut until the 1930 operetta *The Captain of the Guard*, in which he played King Louis XVI. It was his only appearance that year but he made up for it by numerous appearances during the remainder of the decade.

Holmes continued, albeit somewhat less actively and in smaller roles, right up to the 1960s. His later films included *Gypsy, Two Weeks in Another Town* and *A Majority of One*. Some of his others were *Belle of the Nineties, Hearts Divided, Melody for Two, The Sisters, Dark Victory* and *They Made Me a Criminal*.

Holmes, Taylor, Newark, New Jersey, 1878/79–1959

Silent: Before he entered films, Taylor Holmes had a most varied career on the stage, in vaudeville and even in the English music halls. Beginning about 1917 he brought his matinee idol good looks to the cinema for starring roles in such films as *Fools for Luck, Ruggles of Red Gap, Two-Bit Seats, The Very Idea, Nothing but the Truth* and *Upside Down*. He ultimately had his own production company.

After he decided to concentrate on the theater at the beginning of the 1920s, Holmes's subsequent film roles were sporadic and were in support, some of them quite small. They included *$20 a Week, Borrowed Finery, Her Market Value* and *The Verdict*. Last silent: *One Hour of Love* (1927).

Sound: From 1932 to '36, Holmes returned for a few talkies beginning with *It Happened in Paris*. Others were *Before Morning, The Crime of Dr.*

Forbes, The First Baby and *Make Way for a Lady*. In 1947, now gray-haired and distinguished-looking, he came back to the screen for a series of character parts.

Some of Holmes's later roles were as rather sleazy (though always well-groomed) and villainous types. Among his '40s films were *Kiss of Death, Boomerang, Joan of Arc* and *Nightmare Alley*, in which his role of the wealthy Ezra Grindle won him plaudits.

Holmes's 1950s pictures were of generally modest quality but he was active up to a time shortly before his death in films like *Copper Canyon, Rhubarb, Gentlemen Prefer Blondes, Hell's Outpost, The Peacemaker* and *Wink of an Eye*, which may have been his last, in 1958. He also acted on television. His son Phillips Holmes was a popular actor of the 1930s.

REVIEWS

Kiss of Death: Holmes earns a big hand as a shyster lawyer in league with a band of crooks. *Variety* 8/13/47.

Act of Violence: Taylor Holmes makes a strong impression as a ghoulish underworld character. *Variety* 12/22/48.

Holt, Jack (Charles J. Holt), the Bronx, New York or Winchester, Virginia, 1888–1951

Filmography: *Classic Images* (Mar. 1981)

Silent: Jack Holt's first-known credit was in *A Cigarette — That's All* in 1915 but he may have been an extra as early as 1912. He became a leading man in the serial *Liberty* in 1916 and a Paramount stalwart the next year, eventually appearing as the hero in numerous Zane Grey westerns.

Among Holt's many films were *The Little American, Wanderer of the Wasteland, The Woman Thou Gavest Me, Eve's Secret, The Warning, The Man Unconquerable* and *The Smart Set*. Last silent: *Sunset Pass* (1929).

Sound: The successful *The Donovan Affair* (1929) was Holt's first talkie. His others that year were *Flight* and the part-talkie *Father and Son*. He soon left Paramount for Columbia where, between 1930 and 1941, he starred in a lengthy series of action-adventure tales. In many of his early sound films he was teamed with former matinee idol Ralph Graves.

Holt's films included *Hell's Island, Dirigible, The Littlest Rebel, The Cat Woman, San Francisco, The Woman I Stole* and *Reformatory*. His last Columbia film was the serial *Holt of the Secret Service* (1941). In some of his later prewar movies he had top supporting roles.

In spite of his age, Holt went into the service

during World War Two and did not return to the screen until 1945. He then appeared in a string of about 15 or so films until his last appearance in *Across the Wide Missouri* (1951). His children Tim and Jennifer were also movie actors.

Comments: Although he was not considered a highly talented actor, nor was he conventionally handsome, mustachioed Jack Holt obviously had some quality that sustained a 35-year career. His voice was fine and he could play a rugged hero with ease, as he did in his numerous westerns, and also a villain if it came to that. Basically, he was a gentleman and it showed on the screen.

REVIEWS

The Donovan Affair: Holt gets top billing as the inspector and does some good acting. *Variety* 5/1/29.

The Best Man Wins: A sea-diving melodrama which is similar to those Columbia used to produce with Jack Holt several years ago. *Harrison's Reports* 1/12/35.

Trouble in Morocco: Holt is in the Foreign Legion. His casting is a happy choice despite the unbelievable claptrap with which he is surrounded. He contributes a nicely paced job. *Variety* 3/16/37, *Harrison's Reports* 3/27/37.

King of the Bullwhip: Holt is adequate in responding to the light demands of the script. *Variety* 12/13/50.

Hopper, Hedda (Elda Furry), Hollidays-
burg, Pennsylvania, 1885/90–1966

Silent: Before she became a movie player and well before she became a columnist, Hedda Hopper was a chorus girl and musical comedy performer in stock. Her husband, with whom she came to Hollywood, was Broadway star DeWolf Hopper, long famed for his "Casey at the Bat" recitation. (Interestingly, the names of his previous wives had been Ella, Ida, Edna and Nella.)

Hopper's first film, made under her real name, was 1916's *Battle of Hearts* in which she co-starred with William Farnum. Other early films included *Seven Keys to Baldpate, Virtuous Wives, Sadie Love* and *The New York Idea*. Although she played a few leads, her roles increasingly became supporting ones.

Hopper played character roles, many of them mothers, in a great number of films of the 1920s including *Sherlock Holmes, Reno, Sinners in Silk, Zander the Great, Don Juan, Wings, Adam and Evil, Harold Teen* and *Undressed.* Last silent: *Girls Gone Wild* (1929), with synchronized sound effects and music.

Sound: The coming of the talkies revealed Hedda Hopper to have a voice that was suitable for sound, although somewhat affected with its mid–Atlantic, pseudo–English accent which loudly bespoke elocution lessons. But it fit very well the society women she often played, as did her cool elegance.

Among Hopper's early talkies were the ill-fated *His Glorious Night, The Last of Mrs. Cheyney, A Song of Kentucky* and *Half Marriage*. The 1930s were her prime decade in talkies, albeit sometimes in small parts, with films like *Alice Adams, As You Desire Me, Pilgrimage,* and *The Women*.

By the early 1940s, Hopper's on-screen career was fast fading but she already had begun writing a fashion column. This evolved into the gossip column that was to bring her far greater fame and power than her acting career ever did.

There were a few films left for Hopper in the '40s such as *Cross-Country Romance, Queen of the Mob, I Wanted Wings* and *Reap the Wild Wind*, and she played "herself" in *Breakfast in Hollywood* and *Sunset Blvd.*, among others.

In the early 1940s, Hopper made a series of shorts with the same title that she used for her columns (*Hedda Hopper's Hollywood*), and she had been heard on the radio since 1939. In the 1960s she played cameo roles in *Pepe, The Patsy* and *The Oscar*, made the year of her death.

Comments: Tall and stately, Hedda Hopper was not considered more than a journeyman actress but she definitely looked, as well as sounded like, the uppercrust lady she most certainly had not been born. This no doubt lent cachet to her efforts to eventually topple her hated rival Louella Parsons from the pinnacle of Hollywood gossip columnists.

Of course, "gossip" was a mild word for what Hopper dispensed. She became powerful, feared and was more than occasionally vindictive. A negative word from her could be sufficient to end all but the most secure careers. In the late '40s and '50s, she grew increasingly more political (i.e., conservative, even reactionary).

Hopper wholeheartedly embraced the anti–Communist campaigns of that era and her often-misplaced zeal possibly led to the blacklisting of many actors. By the latter 1950s her sway had lessened, as the kick to her rear end delivered by Joseph Cotten and the receipt of a live skunk from Joan Bennett demonstrated.

Hopper did have her good side as well. She was said to be loyal and charitable to such friends as she still had and she possibly may have even had her moments of self-deprecation. For one thing, she could poke fun at her passion (possibly publicity-driven) for hats that frequently defied description.

Let Us Be Gay: Hedda Hopper, as an elegant poseur, had one of her finest opportunities in several seasons. *Variety* 7/16/30.

The Unwritten Law: The top performance is turned in by Hedda Hopper. She has forsaken her usual sophisticated comedy roles for some heavy and dramatic acting. She's better than her part. *Variety* 12/20/32.

Bunker Bean: Hopper is not quite as strong as usual. *Variety* 7/1/36.

Reap the Wild Wind: Hedda Hopper has a bit part. *Variety* 3/25/42.

Horton, Edward Everett, Brooklyn, New York, 1886–1970

Filmography: Focus on Film (Jan.-Feb. 1970)

Silent: Following a varied career in stock and on Broadway, primarily in musical comedies, Edward Everett Horton had his screen bow in 1922's *Too Much Business.* He was billed as Edward Horton, as he was in several of his early films.

Horton was top-billed in many of his pictures and was high in the cast list of the rest. They included *Ruggles of Red Gap* (title role), *To the Ladies, The Man Who Fights Alone, La Bohème, Poker Faces, The Ladder Jinx* and *The Whole Town's Talking.* Last silent: *Taxi! Taxi!* (1927).

Sound: One of the very earliest Vitaphone all-talkies, *The Terror* (1928), had Horton in a key role as the seemingly befuddled hero. It was his only feature film that year but he also was seen in the Vitaphone short *Miss Information.*

All Horton's 1929 films were sound and he was starred in three: *The Sap, The Aviator* and *The Hottentot*; the other was *Sonny Boy.* He also appeared in some shorts that year. The 1930s marked Horton's apex on the screen although he continued on well into the latter '40s.

From 1933 to '38 Horton made some films in England as well. Among his talkies were *The Gay Divorcee, Top Hat, The Front Page, Trouble in Paradise, The Merry Widow, Lost Horizon, Here Comes Mr. Jordan, Summer Storm* and *Cinderella Jones.*

By the 1950s Horton was spending more time with his perennial starring vehicle, the lightweight stage comedy-farce *Springtime for Henry* in which he had been touring since 1932. He had had a radio show in the mid–'40s and later was to appear on TV, notably in the western series *F Troop* as the Native-American medicine man Roaring Chicken.

From 1947 to 1971 Edward Horton was seen in minor parts in only a small number of films including *Sex and the Single Girl, The Perils of Pauline* and *It's a Mad Mad Mad Mad World.* In his final picture, 1971's *Cold Turkey,* he played a key role but did not speak on-screen.

Comments: Although Edward Everett Horton was successful in the silents, he was convinced it was not his medium. He felt he did not fit into the mold of physical comedy in which so many of the leading comic actors excelled. He was more of a character comedian; unless he could use his voice, his persona was incomplete.

A versatile actor, Horton could play serious parts but he was generally typecast as somewhat silly and prissy. At the height of his fame he played to this type in two classic RKO films with Fred Astaire and Ginger Rogers, *The Gay Divorcee* and *Top Hat.*

Horton showed what he could do in one of his favorite roles, that of a Russian aristocrat in *Summer Storm,* but these parts were not offered frequently. Perhaps one reason for his continued touring was a desire to get away from stereotyped characterizations.

The Terror: Horton handles light comedy with good results and, in the leading role, establishes himself as a valuable player for talkies. *Variety* 8/22/28.

The Sap: Most of the comedy is caused by Horton's excellent acting and his expressive voice. It will do well where he is known because he dominates the picture. *Harrison's Reports* 1/18/30, *Variety* 3/5/30.

Holiday: Edward Everett Horton carries the comedy. *Variety* 7/9/30.

A Bedtime Story: The comedy is placed in Horton's capable hands as the foil for Maurice Chevalier. He plays a servant and will provoke hearty laughter. *Variety* 4/25/33, *Harrison's Reports* 4/29/33.

The Gay Divorcee: Edward Everett Horton contributes to the gaiety. *Harrison's Reports* 10/13/34.

The Singing Kid: Horton works hard for laughs but doesn't get many because of the poor material. *Variety* 4/8/36.

Springtime in the Rockies: Horton prominently displays his particular brand of comedy. *Variety* 9/23/42.

Summer Storm: Edward Everett Horton is a flustery and decadent land-owning aristocrat. *Variety* 5/24/44.

Cold Turkey: Horton does effectively without dialogue. *Variety* 2/3/71.

Howes, Reed, Ogden, Utah or Washington, D.C., 1900–1964

Silent: Beginning in 1923, former Arrow Collar Man Reed Howes began a popular string of adventure-melodramas called the Rayart-Reed Howes series. Included were indicative titles like *High Speed Lee, Geared to Go, Courageous Fool, The Snob Buster, The Gentle Cyclone* and *Romantic Rogue.* By the end of the decade he was appearing in supporting as well as starring roles. Last silent: *Fashion Madness* (1928), made after his first talkie.

Sound: Howes began the talkie era as he had finished the silent era, in a mixture of leads and supporting roles. The very popular Al Jolson vehicle *The Singing Fool* (1928) was Howes's first part-talkie. He appeared in two 1929 part-talkies (*Come Across* and *Stolen Kisses*) and then made a single 1930 film, *Clancy in Wall Street.*

The remainder of Howes's lengthy career was mainly in character roles, often as a bad guy in westerns, and in stunt work. He was still to be seen in bit roles as late as the early 1960s. His films included *Sheer Luck, Hell Divers, Flight to Fame, Roll Wagons Roll, Under Arizona Skies* and *The Stranger Wore a Gun.*

Reed Howes was also a staple in such serials as *Terry of the Times, Queen of the Jungle* (lead), *The Clutching Hand, Buck Rogers, Custer's Last Stand* and *Dick Tracy Returns.*

REVIEWS

Come Across: In this picture, with very little talk to entitle it to be classed even as a part-talkie, Reed Howes is the hero. *Harrison's Reports* 7/27/29.

Anybody's Blonde: Howes has the physique to uphold his characterization as the Irish fighting near-champ. He isn't so effective with some of his lines but that may be because he lacks stage experience. *Variety* 11/24/31.

The Gorilla Ship: Reed Howes and his co-star don't seem to know why they are supposed to be in love. *Variety* 8/2/32.

Hoxie, Jack (Hartford Hoxie), Oklahoma, 1885/95–1965

Filmography: Classic Images (Aug. 1982, Aug. 1989); List of films in *Eighty Silent Film Stars*

Silent: Jack Hoxie may have appeared on-screen as early as 1912 when the Wild West show of which he was a part was used in a film. As Hart Hoxie he did extra work and had roles in Kalem two-reelers in 1913 and '14. His features, starting in 1915, included *The Scarlet Sin, The Dumb Girl of Portici, Jack and Jill* and *Nan of Music Mountain.*

Hoxie also appeared in some chapters of the long-running serial *The Hazards of Helen.* A supporting role in William S. Hart's *Blue Blazes Rawden* (1918) brought him some notice and the serials *Lightning Bryce* (1919) and *Thunderbolt Jack* (1920) finally established him as a leading man.

Hoxie became a Universal star and one of their top moneymakers in the '20s, particularly after *Don Quickshot of the Rio Grande* in 1923. Among his other films were *Cyclone Bliss, Dead or Alive, The Man from Nowhere, Cupid's Brand, The Red Warning, The White Outlaw* and *Grinning Guns.*

One of Hoxie's major roles was as Buffalo Bill Cody in the 1926 "special" *The Last Frontier.* After his release by Universal his screen career, which had encompassed about 120 films, came to a virtual standstill. Last silent feature: *The Fighting Three* (1927). Last silent: *Heroes of the Wild,* a 1927 serial.

Sound: Hoxie returned in 1932 and '33 for a series of six cheaply made westerns for Majestic. They were *Gold, Outlaw Justice, Law and Lawless, Via Pony Express, Gun Law* and *Trouble Shooters.* Among his leading ladies were the Day sisters, Alice and Marceline, finishing out their once-promising careers in quickies.

Hoxie was not well-suited to the demands of sound and thereafter made no further films. For a while he toured with the Jack Hoxie Circus and then he went into retirement. His brother Al Hoxie was also a western star whose career did not outlast silents.

REVIEWS

Gold: Hoxie's horse comes in for a share of the credit. Hoxie keeps the sympathy of the spectator well. *Variety* 10/11/32.

Outlaw Justice: A Jack Hoxie story with plenty of action but it includes some fist fights which are not altogether convincing. *Variety* 2/28/33.

Via Pony Express: Hoxie contributes good bits but the acting ability is low. *Variety* 5/9/33.

Hughes, Gareth, Llanelly, Wales, 1894–1965

Silent: After stage experience, Gareth Hughes got his start in America about 1918 playing youthful innocents in such films as *Every Mother's Son, Mrs. Wiggs of the Cabbage Patch* and *The Eternal Mother.* He became a popular leading man and a star with 1921's *Sentimental Tommy.*

By the end of the decade Hughes's popularity had waned seriously. Among his other films were *The Christian, Shadows of Paris, The Whirlwind of Youth, Top Sergeant Mulligan* and *Heroes in Blue.* Last silent: *Silent Sentinel* (1929), in which a dog, Champion, was top-billed.

Sound: The talkies pretty well spelled *finis* for Gareth Hughes. His first sound effort was *Broken Hearted,* a 1929 part-talkie, and he was to make only two others: *Mr. Antonio* the same year, and 1931's *Scareheads.*

Hughes eventually gave up show business and as Brother David became a missionary to the Indians of the Southwest.

Mr. Antonio: Gareth Hughes, as the mind-wandering attaché, plays a stupid role intelligently and succeeds in getting whatever laughs the audience could find. *Variety* 12/11/29, *Harrison's Reports* 12/14/29.

Scareheads: The acting is of low caliber and there is much miscasting. *Variety* 10/27/31.

Hughes, Lloyd, Bisbee, Arizona,
1896/99–1958

Filmography: Films in Review (Jan. 1979); *Classic Images* (Feb. 1989)

Silent: After working as an extra, Lloyd Hughes's first-known featured role was in *Impossible Susan* (1918). His starring role later that year in *The Turn in the Road* began a string of more than 55 silents in which he generally appeared as leading man. His first films were made for Ince and he was apparently thought of as a Charles Ray–type of all–American boy — but with slicked-back hair.

Among Hughes's better-remembered silents were the 1922 remake of *Tess of the Storm Country* with Mary Pickford, the science fiction thriller *The Lost World, Declassee* and *Ella Cinders* with Colleen Moore. He made a total of five films with Moore and teamed eight times with Mary Astor beginning in 1925.

The apex of Hughes's silent career probably was the mid–1920s which were spent working at First National. His first film there was *The Sea Hawk* in which he played a rare villainous role. Last silent: *Where East Is East* (1929), also one of Lon Chaney's final silents.

Sound: Hughes's first talkie was the melodrama *Acquitted* in 1929. This was followed by about 30 more, including one of his best-known, the part-talkie *The Mysterious Island* co-starring Lionel Barrymore. Nineteen thirty was the last year in which Hughes consistently appeared in major studio films.

Among Hughes's efforts of that year were *Big Boy,* an Al Jolson starrer, *Love Comes Along* with Bebe Daniels, *The Runaway Bride,* his last film with Mary Astor, and *Moby Dick* with John Barrymore. The following year saw his decline into "B" programmers for various low-rent studios like Monogram and several other "indies."

Hughes generally remained a leading man in melodramas and comedies but also had supporting roles, sometimes small ones. Among his efforts in the early '30s were *Drums of Jeopardy, Ships of Hate, Air Eagles* and *Heart Punch.* His later films included *Reckless Roads, Skybound, Kelly of the Secret Service* and *Numbered Woman.* The end of the 1930s saw his output dwindling and his last film, 1940's *Vengeance of the Deep,* was made in Australia.

Comments: Lloyd Hughes was an exceptionally handsome journeyman actor who was undoubtedly valued as a non-threatening leading man to some powerful silent screen actresses. It was often stated that his chief ability was that of showing sincerity on the screen. Occasionally he could turn in competent performances in melodramas such as *Scars of Jealousy* and *The Lost World.*

In talkies, Hughes had little screen presence. His voice, although passable, did nothing to compensate for his lack of on-screen charisma. His face had been his fortune and he was already past his first youth. The fact that he often was not mentioned, or was merely named, in reviews of films in which he was the male lead seems a telling point.

In films with strong leading ladies and/or interesting villains, the notices went to them. Hughes's frequent teaming with Mary Astor, meant to establish them as a romantic team in the Charles Farrell-Janet Gaynor mode, did not create much on-screen chemistry.

In her frank autobiography, Astor said that she and Hughes "were the most unsexy pair ever to appear on the silver screen ... Lloyd was a nice guy who should never have been an actor and who knew it." Hughes's declining fortunes in talkies seems to bear out her typically blunt assessment.

Acquitted: The story resembles a sailor's knot and it trips whatever opportunity Lloyd Hughes has. *Variety* 12/11/29.

The Mysterious Island: Lloyd Hughes, as the hero, and his co-star supply an attractive background. *Variety* 12/25/29, *Harrison's Reports* 12/28/29.

Love Comes Along: Reviews differed. One thought that Hughes was miscast as a rollicking seaman; his assumed braggadocio made his part far too obvious. Another thought he did well. *New York Times* 2/1/30, *Variety* 2/5/30.

Heart Punch: Hughes makes a likable boxer. *Variety* 12/13/32.

Society Fever: A light comedy with no outstanding names. There are stilted and weak performances but Lloyd Hughes works like a real trouper. *Variety* 11/27/35.

Clipped Wings: In no way does any of the cast offset the story handicaps. *Variety* 5/4/38.

Hulette, Gladys, Arcade, New York,
1896–1991

Silent: A youthful leading lady for such studios as Thanhouser, Edison and Vitagraph, Gladys Hulette made over 130 films, mostly one- and two-reelers beginning in 1909. She had been an even younger stage actress. Her first feature *Eugene Aram* was made about 1915; other early films included *Prudence the Pirate, The Shine Girl, The Candy Girl* and *Miss Nobody.*

Hulette continued on through the end of the silent era and appeared in two classics, *Tol'able David* (1921) and John Ford's *The Iron Horse* in 1924. Among her other films were *How Women Love, Whispering Palms, The Ridin' Kid from Powder River, The Mystic* and *A Bowery Cinderella.* Last silent: *Life's Crossroads* (1928), in which she received top billing.

Sound: Hulette's sound film appearances were few and in small roles. The first-known one was *Her Resale Value* in 1933 followed by *The Girl from Missouri* and *One Hour Late* the next year. She may also have appeared in *Fugitive Lovers* in 1933 but this is not certain. It is possible that she had other uncredited bits as well.

Hull, Henry, Louisville, Kentucky, 1890–1977

Filmography: List of films *Classic Images* (July 1990)

Silent: Primarily a stage actor from 1910, Henry Hull made many films but was best known for his role as Jeeter Lester in the long-running (3,000+ performances) *Tobacco Road.* He made a handful of silents in the 'teens beginning with *The Man Who Came Back* (1916) and including *The Family Honor, Rasputin, the Black Monk* and *The Volunteer.*

Hull returned as the hero in D. W. Griffith's mystery melodrama *One Exciting Night* in 1922. Other pictures, in which he played both leads and supporting roles, included *A Bride for a Knight, The Last Moment, For Woman's Favor, The Hoosier Schoolmaster, Roulette* and *Wasted Lives.* Last silent: *The Wrongdoers* (1925).

Sound: Hull's distinctive deep and growly voice was first heard in 1934's *Midnight.* One of his best-known roles soon followed: *Werewolf of London* (1935). It was the first film of that subgenre and he gave a fine, anguished performance in the title role. Among his other notable sound films was Alfred Hitchcock's *Lifeboat* (1944), in which he had one of his best talkie roles as the millionaire proto-fascist Ritt Rittenhouse.

Hull also appeared in *Mourning Becomes Electra, The Great Waltz, Great Expectations* (1934 version), *Yellow Jack, My Son, My Son, The Great Gatsby* (1949 version) and *High Sierra.* He continued to alternate theater and cinema for much of his career and also was seen on television. His last three films were scattered in the 1960s, the final one being 1966's *The Chase.*

Comments: Henry Hull was apparently a driven perfectionist who was not always very popular with his co-workers because he gave and expected the best. He was certainly an actor who made a strong impression on audiences, both stage and screen, with his authoritative voice and stern visage. Had he chosen to appear more in film, he would no doubt have left some really memorable work behind him. He was the brother-in-law of character actress Josephine Hull.

REVIEWS

Great Expectations: Hull, in the role of the convict, is magnificent; when he is on the screen he makes the story seem real. His is by far the standout performance; in his characterization he has woven a keen understanding of the author's creation. *Harrison's Reports* 10/27/34, *Variety* 1/19/35.

The Werewolf of London: Hull, as the werewolf, is required to do too many fantastic things for any actor's own good, yet he surmounts most of the handicaps with a sterling performance. Hollywood certainly can use another Lon Chaney, and here is one right in its lap. *Variety* 5/15/35.

Lifeboat: Henry Hull as the millionaire delivers an excellent characterization. *Variety* 1/12/44.

Hurst, Brandon, London, England, 1865–1947

Silent: A stage actor with the distinction of playing the original Charley in the farce *Charley's Aunt*, Brandon Hurst essayed an early film role in 1915's *Via Wireless.* His 1920 role in the John Barrymore version of *Dr. Jekyll and Mr. Hyde* foreshadowed his propensity for appearing in horror films, or at least pictures with a touch of the bizarre.

The Hunchback of Notre Dame (1923) established Hurst as a villain but he went on to play various types of roles in silent movies that included *Cytherea, He Who Gets Slapped, The Thief of Bagdad, The Grand Duchess and the Waiter, The King of Kings, Love, Seventh Heaven* and *The News Parade.* Last silent: *The Voice of the Storm* (1929).

Sound: Brandon Hurst's accent did not slow him down and he went easily into such 1929 talkies as *The Greene Murder Case, Interference, Her Private Life* and *The Wolf of Wall Street.* In the '30s he was seen in many, including *A Connecticut Yankee, The House of Rothschild, A Tale of Two Cities, The Charge of the Light Brigade* and *Suez.*

In line with his seeming *métier*, Hurst also appeared in such horror films as *Murders in the Rue Morgue, White Zombie* and *House of Frankenstein,* among others. He also appeared in non-horrific features like *The Blue Bird, Charley's Aunt, Tennessee Johnson, Road to Utopia* (and *...Rio*), *The Corn Is Green* and, the year of his death, *My Wild Irish Rose.*

Hurst, Paul, Traver, California, 1888–1953

Filmography: List of films in *Films in Review* (Dec. 1967)

Silent: The man who was to become a memorable screen villain went on the stage about 1907 and joined Kalem some five or six years later. For that studio and Signal, Paul Hurst appeared in such 'teens films as *The Stolen Invention*, *The Rajah's Vow*, *The Man in Irons*, *The Pitfall* and the "Stingaree" series.

Hurst directed serials as well; *The Hazards of Helen*, *Lightning Bryce* and *The Tiger's Trail* were some with which he was involved. He spent the first half of the 1920s directing and sometimes writing numerous westerns and melodramas, then brought his beetle brow and nasty leer back in front of the cameras in 1927.

Thereafter, Hurst was rarely out of view again. Among his films were *Buttons*, *Red Raiders*, *The Valley of the Giants*, *The Man from Hardpan* and *The Cossacks*. Last silent: *The California Mail* (1929).

Sound: About half of Hurst's 1929 pictures were sound. They included *His Last Command*, *The Racketeer*, *Oh, Yeah!* and his first talkie, *Sailor's Holiday*. He was ensconced as a character actor, both villainous and comic, until the time of his death.

Hurst appeared in such films as *My Pal the King*, *Mississippi*, *Edison the Man*, *Tugboat Annie Sails Again*, *Night in New Orleans*, *Dakota*, *Yellow Sky*, *The Old Frontier*, *Big Jim McLain* and his last, 1953's *The Sun Shines Bright*.

One of Hurst's more memorable roles was that of the Captain in *Island of Lost Souls*. Undoubtedly, though, *Gone with the Wind* brought his best-remembered role, brief though it was. He was the Yankee deserter and would-be looter who was shot in the face on the stairs of Tara by Scarlett O'Hara.

Reviews

The Single Sin: Paul Hurst's effort at comedy is rather painful. *New York Times* 3/17/31.

My Pal the King: Hurst contributes bits of dry humor. *New York Times* 10/3/32.

The Big Race: The trainer, a fine comedy type, is played by Paul Hurst. He stands out brightly among those in the cast. *Variety* 3/6/34.

Hyams, Leila, New York, New York, 1905–1977

Silent: From a family of vaudevillians and one of the most fetching of the late 1920s ingenues, blonde Leila Hyams made her first film, *Sandra*, in 1924. Dubbed "The Golden Girl," she had a moderately successful career for the next dozen years or so. Her silent films included *Summer Bachelors*, *White Pants Willie*, *The Branded Sombrero*, *Honor Bound* and *The Brute*. Last silents: *Spite Marriage* and *The Far Call*, the latter with synchronized music and sound effects, released about the same time in 1929.

Sound: The quality of Hyams's sound films, many for MGM, generally was a cut above those of the silent era. Her initial part- and all-talking films in 1929 were *Alias Jimmy Valentine*, *The Idle Rich*, *Masquerade* and *Wonder of Women*. In 1930 alone she appeared in ten pictures.

Hyams was a frequent co-star of John Gilbert, albeit that meant sharing the poor vehicles into which he was now being placed. Her most notable 1930s films were probably *Island of Lost Souls*, *Freaks* and *Ruggles of Red Gap*, in which she played a small role.

Other Hyams motion pictures included *Gentleman's Fate*, *The Phantom of Paris* and *Way for a Sailor* (all with Gilbert), *$1000 a Touchdown*, *The Big Broadcast* (Bing Crosby's first feature), *Sing, Sinner, Sing* and her last, *Yellow Dust* (1936). There was also at least one later short.

Reviews

Jimmy Valentine: This is Leila Hyams' first important talker and she does herself credit. Her girlish charm suits the role perfectly. *Variety* 11/21/28.

The Thirteenth Chair: Hyams is charming as the medium's beautiful daughter. She looked and read lines prettily and otherwise carried her role through nicely. *Harrison's Reports* 12/21/29, *Variety* 1/22/30.

Men Call It Love: As the wife, Leila Hyams gets the opportunity in the picture and is likable and pretty. *Harrison's Reports* 4/11/31, *Variety* 6/23/31.

Yellow Dust: Leila Hyams, the heroine, contributes a couple of so-so songs and gives a good performance. *Variety* 2/26/36, *Harrison's Reports* 2/29/36.

Janis, Elsie (Elsie Bierbower), Columbus, Ohio, 1889–1956

Silent: One of the most popular entertainers of her day, especially at the time of World War One, was Elsie Janis. She was on the stage as a child in vaudeville and stock and made her mark as an impersonator of other celebrities of the day in the show *When We Were Forty-One*.

Besides displaying her talents on the Broadway stage, Janis became world famous as "The Sweetheart of the A.E.F." (Allied Expeditionary Forces) when touring the French front during the Great War. The popular revue *Elsie Janis and Her Gang* followed.

Janis also made sporadic film appearances from 1915 when she starred in pictures such as *Betty in Search of a Thrill*, *The Caprices of Kitty* and *Nearly a Lady*. She returned for a couple more in 1919, one being *The Imp*. She also did work on the story of *Oh, Kay!* in 1928. Last silent: *A Regular Girl* (1919).

Sound: Janis worked as a screenwriter in the early '30s for Paramount and co-wrote several film songs throughout the decade. She also was credited as the "supervisor" of the all-singing, all-dancing *Paramount on Parade* in 1930.

Janis's sparse on-screen career in the talkies began with one of the earliest Vitaphone shorts in 1926 in which she performed some of her famous World War One songs. Her appearances thereafter were limited to Warner Bros. shorts in the 1930s and a single role in a feature: 1940's *Women in War*, in which she received top billing.

Janis entertained troops during the Second World War as well and in that capacity was occasionally seen in such short subjects as *Hedda Hopper's Hollywood* and other newsreel-like films.

REVIEWS

Women in War: Reviews differed. One recognized that the importance of the picture was the screen return of Elsie Janis after a lapse of many years. It said that she turned in a most persuasive performance as the matron of a British nursing unit. Another stated that even the return of Janis, the memorable "Sweetheart of the A.E.F." to the screen, was of little advantage even though she played with taut reserve. *Variety* 5/29/40, *New York Times* 5/30/40.

Jessel, George, New York, New York,
1898–1981

Silent: In vaudeville by the age of 10 or so, George (then known as Georgie) Jessel eventually became part of the Gus Edwards "School Days" troupe which also included Eddie Cantor and "Cuddles" (Lila) Lee. He turned successfully to vaudeville as an adult too, touring both the U.S. and the United Kingdom, and in 1919 he made a feature appearance in *The Other Man's Wife*.

Jessel's film debut apparently had been made in the early 'teens two-reeler *The Widow at the Races*. The Broadway stage was really his *métier* and he scored a major success in the original stage play of *The Jazz Singer* which ran for a year and a half. A few films followed: *Private Izzy Murphy*, *Ginsberg the Great* and *Sailor Izzy Murphy*. Last silent: *George Washington Cohen* (1928).

Sound: Jessel appeared in one of the very earliest Vitaphone shorts in 1926, in which he performed a comedy routine. This was followed by two more the next year in which he did other well-worn comedy skits.

Jessel played a character named George Jessel in his first sound film, the possibly autobiographical 1929 part-talkie *Lucky Boy*. In it he sang his signature song "My Mother's Eyes" not once, not twice, but four times. His first all-sound film that year was *Love, Live and Laugh*, in which his character was Italian.

Jessel played "himself" in a cameo role in 1930's *Happy Days* and then further appearances on the screen were rare. He did his famous "Hello, Mama" telephone routine in *Stage Door Canteen* (1943) and was basically "himself" in the next year's *Four Jills in a Jeep*.

In the '60s Jessel was seen in *The Busy Body* (as Mr. Fessel) and the X-rated *Can Hieronymus Merkin Ever Forget Mercy Humppe and Find True Happiness?*; in 1970 he was one of a cast of old-timers in the largely unseen *The Phynx*. That year he was given a special Oscar, the Jean Hersholt Award for Humanitarianism, for his fund-raising and personal appearances on behalf of worthy causes.

Jessel continued to headline in vaudeville and was heard on the radio. In the 1940s he became a producer at Twentieth Century–Fox with such movies as *The Dolly Sisters*, *Tonight We Sing*, *Leave Her to Heaven* and *When My Baby Smiles at Me* to his credit. There were almost 25 altogether. In later years his greatest renown came from his abilities as a public speaker, dubbed "The Toastmaster General," and from TV appearances.

Comments: George Jessel was, of course, more famous for the movie role he did not get than any he actually played. He was the natural front runner to reprise his stage role in *The Jazz Singer* but as film history records, he lost out to Al Jolson. Money apparently was the reason and it was to rankle him for his entire life. Also rankling were those who inevitably compared him to Jolson, his generation's greatest showman.

As an actor, Jessel could be termed somewhat hammy (or schmaltzy), with a plummy voice that no doubt stood him in good stead in his later speechmaking years. He was, in a sense, larger than life on the screen and always played a version of Georgie Jessel, with the mannerisms that encompassed. Although he was a likable film performer, live appearances were really his forte.

Referring to Jessel's penchant for speechmaking, Will Rogers once tellingly joked, "Every time Jessel sees half a grapefruit he automatically rises and says: 'Ladies and gentlemen, we have with us tonight...'" But had he chosen, later in life, to do character roles, he might have effectively chewed some scenery.

REVIEWS

Lucky Boy: There was a range of opinions. One review said that Jessel could sing and was a finished actor. He had personality and was natural, whether acting, singing or talking. He was a showman besides being a splendid actor and having great promise. Another review said that he lacked warmth compared to Al Jolson who was able to express depths of emotion. Jessel lacked that power and was too inflexible. (Comparisons to Al Jolson were natural and Jessel was not found wanting by some reviewers. Comparisons were even more inevitable because the theme of this film and *The Jazz Singer* were not dissimilar.) *Variety* 1/9/29, *Harrison's Reports* 1/12/29.

Love, Live and Laugh: The film has a highly artificial atmosphere, dominated by Jessel. There is not a person in the cast who can handle the Italian dialect. Only once in a while does Jessel remember he's an accordion player. He is too cold for the part of the hero; in situations where he is required to show deep emotions he is like an icicle. *Variety* 11/6/29, *Harrison's Reports* 11/9/29.

Johnson, Noble, Colorado Springs, Colorado, or Marshall, Missouri, 1881–1978

Filmography: Partial list of films in *Classic Images* (Apr. 1989)

Silent: Among Noble Johnson's first-known films was 1909's *Eagle's Nest*, a Lubin production. It is believed that his primary task was handling horses for Lubin and that he did not begin his major acting career until as late as 1914. He played mostly white, Native American and even Asian roles but he actually was an African-American.

In 1916 Johnson and his brother founded what was apparently the first black film company, the Lincoln Motion Picture Company. He appeared in the first few productions which included *The Realization of a Negro's Ambition* and *Trooper of Company K*. He became a Universal player for much of his career and appeared in villain roles in serials like *The Red Glove*, *The Midnight Man* and *Daredevil Jack*.

Among Johnson's features were *The Indian's Lament*, *Hero of the Hour*, *The Yellow Cameo*, *The Thief of Bagdad*, *Law of the Snow Country*, *The King of Kings*, *The Black Ace* and *The Dancers*. Last silent: *The Four Feathers* (1929), with synchronized music and sound effects, made after his first talkie.

Sound: Two part-talkies marked Johnson's introduction to sound, the first being *Noah's Ark* (1928) followed by *Sal of Singapore* the next year. His first all-talking picture was *The Mysterious Dr. Fu Manchu* (1929). In 1933 he appeared in what is probably his best-remembered role, the native chief in *King Kong*, for which his skin color was considerably darkened. He reprised the role in the same-year sequel *The Son of Kong*.

Johnson's other talkies included *Moby Dick* (1930 version), *The Mummy*, *Murders in the Rue Morgue*, *North West Mounted Police*, *The Lives of a Bengal Lancer*, *The Ghost Breakers* (as a zombie) and John Ford's *She Wore a Yellow Ribbon* and *Fort Apache*. His last may have been Roy Rogers's *North of the Great Divide* in 1950.

Comments: Noble Johnson was a powerful (6'2") and handsome man who, in a later day, might have played leads in mainstream films. His misfortune was to come along at a time when even small African-American roles were frequently played by white actors in blackface. Ironically, he was of light skin and as was the custom then he frequently donned blackface himself. He is thought to have appeared in over 150 films.

Johnson's whole career may have been an exercise in frustration, even though he was possibly the best-known African-American film actor until Stepin Fetchit came along. The pioneering film company which he co-founded was out of existence by the early 1920s, possibly at Universal's behest, and his roles in talkies were generally small. When he left Hollywood he disappeared completely, and he was thought to be deceased many years before his actual death.

REVIEWS

Safe in Hell: Noble Johnson is called upon mainly to express lust in various ways. *Variety* 12/22/31.

King Kong: Noble Johnson adds to the interest of this weird tale. *New York Times* 3/3/33.

North of the Great Divide: Johnson plays one of the principal Indian characters. *Variety* 10/31/51.

Johnston, Julanne (also Julianne), Indianapolis, Indiana, 1900/06–1988

Silent: Julanne Johnston lives on in cinema memory for her role as Douglas Fairbanks's beloved Princess in *The Thief of Bagdad* (1924), and for little else. She had occasional leads but much of her career, which began in 1919, was in support. Her other films included *Fickle Women*, *Madness of Youth*, *Big Pal*, *Twinkletoes*, *The Whip Woman* and *Oh, Kay!* Last silent: *Synthetic Sin* (1929), with synchronized music score.

Sound: All but one of Johnston's 1929 pictures had some talking sequences. They included *The Show of Shows*, *Prisoners*, *The Younger Generation* and *General Crack*. The coming of sound brought a virtual end to her career; her first roles were supporting ones and after 1930 they were bits.

The 1930 picture *Strictly Modern* brought Johnston her last real opportunity. Through 1934, probably the last year on-screen, some of her other films were *Golden Dawn*, *Madam Satan*, *Cleopatra*, *Stepping Sisters*, *Morning Glory* and *The Scarlet Empress*.

REVIEWS

General Crack: Julanne Johnston is in only a scene or two. *Variety* 12/11/29.

Strictly Modern: Johnston's performance and that of the female lead are the picture's best assets. *Variety* 5/7/30, *Harrison's Reports* 5/10/30.

Jones, Buck (Charles Gebhardt, Gebhart or Gebhard), Vincennes, Indiana, 1889/91–1942

Filmography: List of films in *Films in Review* (Mar. 1960); *Film Dope* (Dec. 1983)

Silent: Buck Jones came out of ranching and Wild West shows to become an extra at Universal and Selig, and a double for such cowboy stars as William S. Hart and Tom Mix. He was ultimately built up by the Fox studio as a potential rival to the temperamental Mix to keep the latter in line.

Before getting a starring Fox contract and a new name, Jones had small roles in several 1918 and '19 films including *The Speed Maniac*, *Western Blood* and *Riders of the Purple Sage*. His first major role came in 1920's *The Last Straw*.

Jones spent 11 years at Fox and starred in numerous popular films, some of which he wrote and directed. Among them were *Just Pals*, *The Big Punch*, *The Man Who Played Square*, *30 Below Zero*, *Hills of Peril*, *Hell's Hole*, *Western Luck* and *Pardon My Nerve!* Many of his pictures were made under the aegis of his own production company. Last silent: *The Big Hop* (1928), with synchronized sound effects.

Sound: Jones appeared in no films for almost two years. He had left Fox, voluntarily or otherwise, after a falling out and had then toured in his own Wild West company. It did not prove successful and he was back in films by 1930. His first talkie was *The Lone Rider*; other early efforts were *The Dawn Trail* and *Shadow Ranch*.

A Columbia contract was proffered to Buck Jones in the early '30s and he made many of his pictures there, including several non-western action melodramas. The oaters he made for that studio are considered to be among his best. Considerably later he went to Monogram for the "Rough Riders" series with Raymond Hatton and Tim McCoy.

Jones also appeared in serials like the popular *Gordon of Ghost City*, *The Red Rider*, *Riders of Death Valley*, *The Phantom Rider*, *White Eagle* and *The Roaring West*. Other films included *Men Without Law*, *Child of Manhattan*, *The Cowboy and the Kid* and *The Overland Express*. He was the number one western moneymaker in 1936 and was among the top ten western stars from 1937 to '39. In the latter part of the decade, he had a radio show called *Hoof Beats*.

Jones's career waned in the late 1930s and he even played the villain in 1940's *Wagons Westward*, much to the chagrin of his fans. He completed his last pictures *Down Texas Way* and the highly regarded *Dawn on the Great Divide* in 1942. That year he was among the victims of a disastrous Boston night club fire. Truth followed fiction; he was killed while heroically trying to rescue others.

Comments: Square-jawed and ruggedly handsome, Buck Jones was a cowboy star in the gritty "realistic" tradition. His baritone speaking voice was fine but he was not one for warbling around the campfire. When the slickly made singing westerns became ascendant in the mid–'30s, his style of cowboy hero was less popular and his career suffered accordingly.

Jones had also begun showing his age by that time and was not as convincing in scenes requiring hard riding and fistfights. His place among the best of the "B" western stars is assured even though his brave death came at a time when his career would inevitably have been coming to its conclusion.

REVIEWS

Shadow Ranch: As the hero Buck Jones does very good work. *Harrison's Reports* 9/27/30.

High Speed: The thrilling film gives Jones the chance to shine in a policeman's uniform. *Variety* 4/12/32, *Harrison's Reports* 4/16/32.

Man Trailer: The story is mostly he-man stuff with Jones easily holding his own. *Variety* 5/29/34.

The Cowboy and the Kid: Buck Jones should stick to his boots and saddle. This presents him at his worst because he has far too much to say and his attempts at sentiment are pretty sad. *Variety* 7/29/36.

Empty Saddles: Buck Jones continues to be ambitious and his western epics continue to suffer. The picture strives for originality, quaint touches and new twists but not one of them clicks. Jones does appear as rugged and athletic-looking as ever. (The leading lady was Louise Brooks in her penultimate film.) *Variety* 2/3/37.

Headin' East: This is one of the best pictures ever made by Buck Jones. Up to now the Columbia series has been his best in a long time. *Variety* 12/29/37.

Wagons Westward: After all these years on the

right side of the law it's a little incomprehensible (especially for the youngsters who have long accepted him as a hero) for Buck Jones to step into a villain part that has no element of sympathy. Actually he has little to do. *Variety* 6/26/40 (first review), *Variety* 7/24/40 (second review).

Joy, Leatrice (Leatrice J. Zeidler), New Orleans, Louisiana, 1892/96–1985

Filmography: *Films in Review* (Apr. 1977)

Silent: Because she was to be so identified with playing sophisticated heroines, it is perhaps a bit surprising that Leatrice Joy had her first leading roles co-starring with knockabout Chaplin imitator Billy West. Earlier she had been an extra at the Fort Lee, New Jersey, studios.

After a few features such as *A Girl's Folly*, *Wedlock* and *The Man Hunter*, Joy signed with Goldwyn in 1921 to star in films like *Bunty Pulls the Strings* and *The Night Rose*. It was her work for Cecil DeMille, beginning in 1922, in *Manslaughter*, *The Ten Commandments* and other films which made her a major star.

Among Joy's 40 silent films were *Java Head*, *You Can't Fool your Wife*, *The Marriage Cheat*, *The Dressmaker from Paris*, *Eve's Leaves*, *For Alimony Only*, and *Man-Made Woman*. Last silent: *Strong Boy* (1929), with synchronized music and sound effects.

Sound: *The Bellamy Trial*, a 1929 part-talkie, was Joy's first sound film; *A Most Immoral Lady* (1929) and *The Love Trader* (1930) followed. She was then off-screen until the end of the decade when she played a supporting role in the Deanna Durbin starrer *First Love*.

Except for an appearance in *The Old Swimmin' Hole* (1940), Joy made no more films until 1949's *Red Stallion in the Rockies* and *Air Hostess*. Her final role was in *Love Nest* (1951), which contained one of Marilyn Monroe's first important roles.

Comments: With her closely cropped hair and sometimes mannish attire, Leatrice Joy created a special niche for herself in 1920s romantic comedy and melodrama. Her image was somewhat shattered by sound which revealed a heavy Southern accent that she apparently could not, or chose not to, overcome.

Joy's final starring role in 1930 was for an independent studio. A declining career in quickies might have been what she had to look forward to and she apparently decided this was not the future she wanted. She did keep active in some later stage roles. As an old woman being interviewed for a TV series about Hollywood she revealed a keen sense of humor.

REVIEWS

The Bellamy Trial: Leatrice Joy has a rather good voice for films. *Variety* 1/30/29, *Harrison's Reports* 2/2/29.

A Most Immoral Lady: Joy gives as good a performance as possible but she taxes the audience with a singing voice that would only pass as sweet parlor singing if heard once or twice. *Variety* 10/23/29, *Harrison's Reports* 10/26/29.

The Love Trader: Leatrice Joy is the heroine and she does justice to her part, but her part doesn't do justice to her. *Harrison's Reports* 11/1/30, *Variety* 11/26/30.

First Love: A former star of silent pictures is prominent in support. Leatrice Joy returns after long absence as the socialite aunt who is flighty and scatterbrained. *Variety* 11/8/39, *Harrison's Reports* 11/18/39.

Air Hostess: Leatrice Joy runs a school for air hostesses. *Harrison's Reports* 7/9/49.

Joyce, Alice, Kansas City, Missouri, 1889/90–1955

Filmography: *Films in Review* (Dec. 1976)

Silent: Beautiful Alice Joyce went from modeling to stardom at Kalem perhaps as early as 1911. After numerous films, she joined Vitagraph late in 1916 to make *Whom the Gods Destroy* and had a major hit with 1917's *Within the Law*. Later films included *The Young Millionaire*, *The Cabaret Dancer*, *Dollars and the Woman*, *White Man*, *Mannequin* and *Dancing Mothers*.

Joyce was off-screen in the early 1920s, after which she began to freelance. Her first film was *The Green Goddess* with George Arliss. Although her output lessened overall in that decade, she appeared in prestigious films like *Stella Dallas*, *Sorrell and Son* and *Beau Geste*. She also made films in England. Last silent: *13 Washington Square* (1928).

Sound: Joyce appeared in four sound films, the first of which was *The Squall* (1929). It co-starred an up-and-coming Myrna Loy and Loretta Young. The indifferent reviews of Joyce's performance foretold a quick end to her motion picture career.

A trio of 1930 films remained for Joyce. They were a remake of *The Green Goddess*, again starring George Arliss, *Song o' My Heart*, which showcased Irish tenor John McCormack, and *He Knew Women*, her last.

Comments: Tall and serene-looking Alice Joyce was, at the height of her fame in the 'teens, known as "The Madonna of the Screen." She was a major star in early silents, specializing in innocent women wronged. Although in the latter silent period she was not quite the star she had been, she nevertheless continued to appear in respectable films, often in mother roles.

Talkies were another matter. Her voice was low and pleasant but her acting style apparently was not well-geared to the requirements of sound film. After appearing in about 150 silents, it took only four pictures to demonstrate that Alice Joyce could not survive sound.

REVIEWS

The Squall: Reviewers disagreed, but most were critical of Alice Joyce. A couple said that she was usually charming on the screen but in this film showed little or no aptitude as an actress for dialogue pictures. Had there not been close-ups of her during her talking moments, her role would have been more meritorious. Her endeavor to articulate within a few feet of the camera, coupled with a voice of monotone register, made her seem conscious of the microphone. Another thought that Joyce rose to heights of acting she had not reached before. *New York Times* 5/10/29, *Variety* 5/15/29, *Harrison's Reports* 5/18/29.

The Green Goddess: This does not appeal to the rank and file of picturegoers because the average American does not relish seeing an Oriental (George Arliss) trying to win over a white woman (Alice Joyce). *Harrison's Reports* 2/22/30.

Song o' My Heart: Joyce is always easy to gaze upon though she is a pathetic figure as the destitute mother. *Variety* 3/19/30, *Harrison's Reviews* 3/22/30.

He Knew Women: It is enjoyable to watch the players act; they seem as if they were flesh and blood and perform their parts artistically. Alice Joyce plays a wealthy widow. *Harrison's Reports* 4/26/30.

Karloff, Boris (William Henry Pratt), London, England, 1887–1969

Filmography: *Films in Review* (Aug.-Sept. 1964), update (Nov. 1970); *American Classic Screen* (Mar.-Apr. 1983); List of films in *Classic Images* (Summer-Fall 1969); *Film Dope* (Mar. 1984); *Cinema* (Beverly Hills) (v. 5, no. 1)

Silent: After some years in theater stock companies, Boris Karloff came to the cinema as an extra in 1919. He soon began to receive larger roles, his first sizable one being in 1920's *The Deadlier Sex*. With rare exceptions he was a supporting player throughout the silent era in about 40 movies.

Karloff's showiest role in the 1920s was as the Caligari-like mesmerist in the 1926 melodrama *The Bells*. Sometimes he appeared high in cast lists, at other times his appearances were brief indeed. Because of his naturally swarthy complexion and dark eyes he frequently was seen in "exotic" roles.

Karloff's films included *The Cave Girl*, *Omar the Tentmaker*, *Parisian Nights*, *Old Ironsides*, *The Princess from Hoboken*, *Dynamite Dan*, *The Little Wild Girl* and *The Meddlin' Stranger*. He also appeared in the serials *The Hope Diamond Mystery*, *Vultures of the Sea* and *The Fatal Warning*. Last silent: *Phantom of the North* (1929).

Sound: Of Karloff's six 1929 films, only two were sound, *Behind That Curtain* and *The Unholy Night*. In both of them he had small red-herring roles as sinister Arabs so it was not until the next year that his distinctive voice was heard at length from the screen. In '29 he also appeared in the serial *King of the Kongo*, released in both silent and sound versions.

Karloff's 1930 films *The Sea Bat* and *The Utah Kid* continued his string of unprepossessing roles but that was to change dramatically in the following year. He made a dozen films in 1931 including fluff such as *Cracked Nuts* and *I Like Your Nerve*, but he also had strong roles in *The Criminal Code* (based on an earlier stage performance) and *Graft*.

It may have been his appearance in those latter pictures which led to Karloff's selection as the Monster in *Frankenstein* although he was by no means the first choice. That honor was undoubtedly Bela Lugosi's, who rejected it. The film, in which his billing at the beginning was literally a question mark, was a smash success and his career was made.

Subsequently billed by Universal in a few films only as "Karloff," he went on to make many more horror films as well as those in other genres. As time went on, he became increasingly relegated to cheaply made second features. Among his '30s films were two sequels to his Monster role: *Bride of Frankenstein* (1935) and *Son of Frankenstein* (1939), both eminently respectable follow-ups. *Bride* is considered to be one of the very best of its type.

Some non-horrific Boris Karloff motion pictures of the '30s were *Scarface*, *Donovan's Kid*, *The House of Rothschild*, *Charlie Chan at the Opera*, *Five Star Final* and *The Lost Patrol*, in which he believably played a mad religious fanatic. In the horror genre there were several standouts including *The Mummy* (the first film in which he received star billing), *The Mask of Fu Manchu*, *The Black Cat*, *The Raven* and *The Invisible Ray*. In some of these he teamed with Bela Lugosi. From 1938 to '40 he appeared as the Chinese detective Mr. Wong in a low-rent Monogram series.

The '30s also brought the beginning of a cycle of "mad scientist" roles to Karloff. In this category were *The Man with Nine Lives*, *Before I Hang* and *The Man They Could Not Hang*. He also made several films in his native England beginning with *The Ghoul* (1933) and in that decade appeared in his final serial, *King of the Wild*.

Boris Karloff's roles in the 1940s were generally inferior to his previous efforts and later in the decade they tended toward parody of his persona. Among his better-regarded efforts were *The Climax* (an obvious knock-off of *Phantom of the Opera*) and a trio of Val Lewton productions (*The Body Snatcher*, *Bedlam* and *Isle of the Dead*). He also essayed some comedy roles including those in *You'll Find Out*, *The Boogie Man Will Get You*, *The Secret Life of Walter Mitty* and *Abbott and Costello Meet the Killer, Boris Karloff*.

The 1950s saw Karloff cast mostly in poor films, a situation that prevailed until the end of his career with few exceptions. Such titles as *Abbott and Costello Meet Dr. Jekyll and Mr. Hyde*, *The Black Castle*, *Voodoo Island* and *The Hindu* illustrate the quality of that decade's offerings.

The 1960s were even less promising. *Curse of the Crimson Altar*, *The Ghost in the Invisible Bikini*, *The Snake People*, and *Cauldron of Blood* were among Boris Karloff's later pictures. Happily, one of the last of his 90 talkies, Peter Bogdanovich's *Targets* (1968), proved a very fitting almost-farewell to the screen. In it he played Byron Orlock, a retired horror film actor, who helps to capture a murderous sniper. A clip from *The Criminal Code* was shown in the film.

By the time of Karloff's death he had worked for almost all the major studios: MGM, Columbia, United Artists, RKO, Fox, Warner Bros., Paramount and, of course, Universal, the scene of his greatest triumphs. In latter years American-International, the schlock company, featured him extensively.

Karloff's major acting opportunities during the last 25 years or so of his life proved to be in the media of stage and television. He made his Broadway debut in 1941's long-running comedy *Arsenic and Old Lace* and was consequently out of films for about two years. He also had distinguished roles in *The Lark* and *Peter Pan*.

Karloff's hosting of the television series *Thriller* often provided memorable chills and he also played the lead in the English series *Colonel March of Scotland Yard*. He was much heard on radio and made recordings, especially those for children. For many of them he *was The Grinch Who Stole Christmas* (he supplied the voice of this cartoon character in one of his most popular TV programs).

Comments: Black-eyed and beetle-browed with pronounced bowed legs, Boris Karloff was an unlikely candidate for stardom. In the silents he portrayed western baddies, Indians and villains of all kinds and he seemed to be headed for more of the same in talkies, with possibly the addition of gangster roles to his repertoire.

Perhaps, after all, Karloff attained stardom in the only way he could — behind a great amount of makeup. It was not so much the frightening aspect of Frankenstein's Monster but its humanity that made Karloff a star. It proved there was a sensitive actor behind the grotesque exterior, something he was able to show in many of his better roles.

What Karloff certainly was able to reveal in talkies was the power of understated menace, helped immeasurably by his delightfully inimitable voice with its pronounced lisp and careful British enunciation. It enhanced many an otherwise mundane part. He also revealed a talent for tongue-in-cheek humor.

Unfortunately Karloff was a prime example of the cliché that one should quit while he is ahead. The execrable later films, presumably made for the money or perhaps just to keep working, tarnished but fortunately did not destroy his reputation. That deserves to be among the highest for he helped create one of Hollywood's most popular genres.

REVIEWS

Frankenstein: Karloff makes a memorable figure of the bizarre Monster, with its indescribably horrifying face of demoniacal calm. He gives a remarkable performance.

(Karloff's ability to show the emotions of the Monster was even more remarkable considering the 60 pounds of clothing he had to lug around; the shoes alone weighing 18 pounds apiece. His Jack Pierce–designed makeup took almost seven hours a day to apply and remove.) *Variety* 12/8/31, *Harrison's Reports* 12/12/31.

The Bride of Frankenstein: Karloff is at top form as the Monster, using the same bizarre makeup as in the first film. He manages to invest the character with some subtleties of emotion that are surprisingly real and touching.

(This was one sequel superior to its original. The Monster's limited speech ability, which he was given for this picture only, added to the emotions Karloff so well portrayed.) *Variety* 5/15/35.

Night Key: Karloff is realistic as the inventor. *Variety* 4/21/37.

Before I Hang: There's not much room in the film for anyone but Karloff who wanders about amidst an array of bubbling gadgets. *Variety* 10/2/40.

The Climax: Karloff excellently handles the role of the maniacal physician.

(This Universal Technicolor film was probably Karloff's first in color.) *Variety* 9/27/44.

The Body Snatcher: Karloff performs his sadistic role in characteristic style. *Variety* 2/21/45.

The Strange Door: Karloff competently portrays the loyal servant. *Variety* 10/31/51.

Karns, Roscoe, San Bernardino, California, 1893–1970

Silent: The quintessential fast-talking wise-cracker of 1930s films, Roscoe Karns had to settle for pantomiming at the start of his film career which came in 1919 with *Poor Relations.* He had also performed in stock and on Broadway. His first picture was followed the next year by *The Family Honor* and *The Life of the Party,* and several more through 1927 such as *The Man Tamer, The Trouper, The Foolish Virgin, The Overland Limited* and *Ten Modern Commandments.*

Although Karns played the lead in 1921's *Too Much Married,* nearly all his roles were to be supporting ones. He alternated picture and stage roles until 1928 when he returned to films full-bore, making 11 that year alone, including *Jazz Mad, Beau Sabreur, The Vanishing Pioneer* and *Win That Girl.* Last silent: *Object — Alimony* (also known as *Object — Matrimony*) (1928), made after his first part-talkie.

Sound: That first part-talkie was *The Jazz Singer* (1927), although Karns's distinctive voice was not heard. Two part-talkies, *Beggars of Life* and *The Shopworn Angel,* followed in 1928. His 1929 films *New York Nights* and *This Thing Called Love* began a long string of comedies and melodramas in which frequently he was typecast as a newspaperman.

This came about largely as a result of Karns's success playing Hildy in the West Coast version of *The Front Page.* After receiving a Paramount contract in 1932, he became a top character actor and occasional lead in films such as *Alice in Wonderland, It Happened One Night, Twentieth Century, Cain and Mabel, Thanks for the Memory* and *Clarence.*

Karns also was a key cast member, top-billed as Joe Higgins, in the "Higgins Family" series. In the '40s he was somewhat less visible but appeared in some worthwhile films like *His Girl Friday, Woman of the Year, Old Acquaintance, They Drive by Night* and *It's a Wonderful Life,* among others.

Karns became active on television in the late 1940s, starring for five years in the live drama *Rocky King, Detective.* Later he was a regular on the *Hennesey* show. After a decade's absence he returned to the screen in the late '50s for a role in *Onionhead* and subsequently in *Man's Favorite Sport?,* his last, in 1964.

Comments: Roscoe Karns was a colorful character actor whose deep, somewhat gravelly voice and beetle-browed mien made his performances stand out in any film in which he appeared. He was Hollywood's stereotypical idea of a newspaperman: smart-alecky and motor-mouthed, with an ever-ready wisecrack at his command. Although California-bred, he always seemed to have just come off the streets of Brooklyn. He indisputably was one of the panoply of memorable character people who could hold their own against any mere star.

REVIEWS

Little Accident: Karns acts so over-zealous that he is never funny. *Variety* 8/56/30.

Clarence: As the hero, Roscoe Karns is merely a capable bit player staggering under too heavy a load of acting. (In an interesting bit of casting, Karns inherited a role played on the stage by Alfred Lunt.) *Variety* 3/10/37.

Keaton, Buster (Joseph Keaton, Jr.), Piqua, Kansas, 1895–1966

Filmography: Film Dope (Mar. 1984); *Buster Keaton: Cut to the Chase*

Silent: From the time he was a very small boy, Buster Keaton had appeared in his family's knock-about vaudeville act. Much of it consisted of his being hurled at pieces of scenery and even offstage and seemingly emerging unhurt. He departed the act about 1917 and headed for Broadway where he had secured a role in *The Passing Show.*

After a chance meeting with popular comedian Roscoe "Fatty" Arbuckle, that opportunity went by the boards. Instead Keaton made his screen debut in a small role in the Arbuckle two-reeler *The Butcher Boy.* He then apprenticed with Arbuckle for a couple of years, appearing in many of his Comique films.

Although their relationship was a close one, Keaton's preferred style of comedy was different from that of the rotund slapsticker. Under the aegis of Joe Schenck, who financed a production company for him, he struck out on his own.

In 1920 Keaton made *The High Sign,* the first of his 19 two-reelers, many of them now considered minor classics. He also starred that year in his first feature, *The Saphead,* a remake of Douglas Fairbanks's *The Lamb,* and apparently as a gag played an unbilled bit as an Indian in Arbuckle's first feature *The Round-Up.*

In 1921 and '22 Keaton continued making two-reelers like *Balloonatics, The Playhouse, The Paleface, The Goat, Cops* and *The Boat.* Other features followed from 1923: *The Three Ages, Our Hospitality* (co-starring his wife Natalie Talmadge), *The Navigator, Sherlock, Jr., Go West, Seven Chances, Battling Butler, College* and *The General,* his now-acknowledged 1927 masterwork.

Steamboat Bill, Jr. (1928) proved to be Keaton's final independent film. In 1928 he reluctantly signed with MGM when his now brother-in-law Joseph Schenck dissolved the production company through which he had released his pictures for almost a decade. His last films had lost money, especially *The General*, which incurred major production costs.

Keaton's first MGM film *The Cameraman* was a substantial success and is considered equal to his independent efforts. Soon thereafter the end of his independence led to a career decline, at first slow, then rapid, from which he never recovered. Last silent: *Spite Marriage* (1929), with synchronized music.

Sound: Keaton made his first appearance in a sound film in MGM's all-star extravaganza *The Hollywood Revue of 1929* but did not speak in his one comedy routine, an ersatz ballet in drag as a harem girl. He also reprised the song "Singin' in the Rain" with the other stars of the picture.

Keaton's surprisingly deep voice was first heard in 1930's *Free and Easy* (he sang the title song) and subsequently in the World War One themed *Dough Boys*. In both films his character was called Elmer, a name that was to persist throughout the rest of his starring feature career.

Although he was still top-billed, Keaton's 1931 films *Sidewalks of New York* and *Parlor, Bedroom and Bath* downgraded him to an ordinary comic actor, one among many others. The final blow came the next year when he was teamed with the irrepressible Jimmy Durante, a pairing that just about reduced his "Elmer" character to a straight man.

After three with the "Schnozzola" (*The Passionate Plumber*, *Speak Easily*, considered by some his best sound comedy, and *What — No Beer?*), Keaton was fired by MGM in 1933. In the mid–'30s he finished out his starring feature career in the French film *Le Roi des Champs Elysées* (*The King of the Champs Elysées*) and *The Invader*, known in America as *An Old Spanish Custom*. He spent the rest of the decade and the early '40s in Educational and then Columbia comedy shorts. A very few were fair but most were poor and certainly not up to his talents. He was said to have "phoned in" his performance in the later ones. They included *Palooka from Paducah*, *Grand Slam Opera*, one of Keaton's best-regarded shorts, *Love Nest on Wheels*, *Nothing but Pleasure* and *Pest from the West*, a remake of his British feature *The Invader*.

By the end of the '30s Keaton had begun getting occasional supporting roles in films like *Hollywood Cavalcade*. In the 1940s he had a few small roles and also was a gag man for such popular comics as Lou Costello and Red Skelton. His picture appearances included *L'il Abner*, *New Moon*, *The Villain Still Pursued Her*, *San Diego, I Love You* and *Sunset Blvd.*, as one of the "waxworks." He had two words in a single scene.

The following decade finally brought the beginnings of a Buster Keaton renaissance. In the remaining 15 years of his life he appeared much on television, including commercials, was on the stage and headlined at the Cirque Medrano in Paris. He also continued small roles in pictures like *Limelight*, in which he did a musical act with Charles Chaplin, *Around the World in 80 Days*, *It's a Mad Mad Mad Mad World*, a few of the popular AIP Beach musicals, *A Funny Thing Happened on the Way to the Forum* and the short *The Railrodder*.

The Buster Keaton Story, a 1957 film biography starring Donald O'Connor, was produced but most agreed it was not an accurate reflection of the man or his life. This misfire was more than adequately compensated for when, in 1959, his contributions were finally recognized by the film community with a special Oscar.

The importance of the 1960s to Keaton was not his new film roles but the growing recognition of the classic quality of those films he had made in his prime. There were film festivals devoted to him and he was a popular interviewee and the subject of many articles. At the time of his death, he surely could take satisfaction in his triumphant rediscovery.

Comments: Considered to be one of the three greatest silent comic actors, along with Charles Chaplin and Harold Lloyd — and possibly Harry Langdon as, briefly, the fourth — Buster Keaton was certainly not aided by the coming of sound. Although his voice did not destroy him, it most certainly did not help him recover from the alcoholic decline in which he found himself.

Although it was fine as a normal speaking voice, Keaton's did not really match the characters he played in the talkies. Like the other silent comedians, he fared better without the necessity of speaking dialogue. It brought an unwelcome dose of reality into his comic world and he simply could never be the same.

Widely identified by the sobriquet of "Stone Face," Keaton never smiled in his starring films and over the years there has been much (pseudo)-psychological analysis as to the reason(s) for this. Never one to admit there was a psychological subtext to his films, he would have been highly amused at the speculation. The same also applies to analyses of other aspects of his *oeuvre*.

For instance, some of Keaton's 1920s shorts are said to contain strains of surrealism, especially when they involved the battle of Man vs. Machine. Even streaks of a ghoulish fatalism have been detected. It naturally is tempting to want to relate that to his own outlook but again he would probably maintain that he just made films for fun.

The truth is that much of Keaton's life from his abused childhood on was desperately unhappy, including two of his marriages and of course the sadly aborted career. He was a marginally literate, seriously ill alcoholic and was subject to moodiness and occasional violence. His worldview must have been at least an unconscious factor in his films but he certainly did not talk about it either in interviews or his supposed autobiography.

As has been presciently pointed out, being stonefaced did not mean Keaton expressed no emotions. He was smitten with love in many of his pictures and if his face did not show his amorous longings, his body certainly did and in numerous ways.

A mark of most of Keaton's independent features were their tight structures and well-made plots. They seemed to have a recurrent theme: An ordinary man is placed in extreme circumstances, overcomes them, and grows in so doing. Because he had almost complete control over every facet of making his pictures, he could well be called an "auteur" in the era before that word was used. His films often had credited directors but he certainly was responsible for much of the direction as well as the gags and storyline.

Keaton apparently had a keen grasp of and liking for America's pastoral past, and such films as *Our Hospitality*, *The General* and *Steamboat Bill, Jr.* have carefully drawn and seemingly accurate historical backgrounds. Technically, he went to great lengths for interesting framing of shots and long shots that showed all the action within the frame. He is reputed to have done most of his own stunts and his method of filming, with minimal cuts, reveals this.

More than most of the comic actors of his day, Keaton seemed to have a well-developed vision when he began making his own pictures. While others at the beginning of their careers tended to imitate those who had gone before, often Charlie Chaplin, he started with a more personal vision. His progress as a mature artist was stifled when he lost his own production company.

The question of why Keaton allowed himself to be subsumed into MGM when he was progressing so well creatively is answered by the old "bottom line." He was no businessman and he spent freely on his films. Schenck saw no incentive in continuing with an independent production unit. Later generations may look upon *The General* and *Steamboat Bill, Jr.* as undying classics but at the time they lost money.

Keaton needed freedom to create films according to his own vision and that kind of independence neither MGM, nor any other studio for that matter, tolerated. Everything at MGM was tightly controlled and he was a comic no better than many others in their estimation. Two comics were better than one in their eyes, hence his ill-advised teaming with Durante.

The fact that his inferior talkies made money, some quite a bit, clinched the studio's belief that they knew what was best for Keaton. Even though he was one of the highest-paid performers at MGM, he could not accept his fate. Battling Louis B. Mayer proved to be fruitless, if momentarily satisfying, and he fell that long, long way from the pinnacle to the hardest of hard times. It is small wonder that Keaton retained his "great stone face" for the rest of his career.

That face may have seemed immobile, but glowing descriptions of it abound. Critic James Agee said "Keaton's face ranked almost with Lincoln's as an early American archetype; it was haunting, handsome, almost beautiful, yet it was irreducibly funny." Another described it as "the great blank page on which he could write every process of thought." For almost ten glorious years that face made millions laugh.

REVIEWS

Free and Easy: Keaton reads his lines and can handle the dialog well. He comes back into his own again and does gags that are thoroughly amusing. *Variety* 4/23/30, *Harrison's Reports* 4/26/30.

Dough Boys: Keaton makes a successful comeback. It is somewhat surprising to hear his deep voice when a kind of soprano is the usual pitch for his type of comic. He uses his voice intelligently, adapting it to his style. There is nothing changed from his established characterization of silent films, except for the voice. *Variety* 9/24/30, *Harrison's Reports* 9/27/30.

Parlor, Bedroom and Bath: In those locales where Keaton may be slipping, if that's anywhere, a strong second feature will be needed. He goes through his familiar paces in an even manner. *Variety* 4/8/31, *Harrison's Reports* 4/4/31.

Sidewalks of New York: In Buster Keaton's heyday this film would have been only a little below first rate. Today it is very outdated. His performance is formulaic throughout. *Variety* 11/17/31.

The Passionate Plumber: Reviewers differed on whether Keaton or Durante dominated. One said that more care should have been used to keep things interesting while Durante was not in the scene because the highlights occurred when he was on. Another said that most of the comedy was caused by Keaton. *Variety* 3/15/32, *Harrison's Reports* 3/19/32.

Speak Easily: Keaton, as the college professor, is much more satisfying than he has been in his last several films. Perhaps for the first time in talkies he really finds his old stride but this is not due to any change in voice or manner of speech. He is chiefly effective when taking pratfalls. *Variety* 8/23/32, *Harrison's Reports* 8/27/32.

What! No Beer?: Jimmy Durante dominates almost every scene and Keaton's quiet dead-panning is almost eclipsed as a result. It's not so much that Keaton plays straight man to Durante, as that the script more or less favors the latter. *Variety* 2/14/33.

Pajama Party: Buster Keaton, playing the Indian Chief Rotten Eagle, socks over his role. *Variety* 11/18/64.

A Funny Thing Happened on the Way to the Forum: The late Buster Keaton's dead-pan trot about the Seven Hills of Rome brings back nostalgia for the master of the silent days. *Variety* 9/28/66.

Keith, Donald (Francis Feeney), Boston,
Massachusetts, 1903–

Silent: Among the group of bland leading men with slicked-back hair who co-starred with the major silent actresses of the 1920s was "pretty boy" Donald Keith. He had begun his feature career as a teenager in 1918 under his real name in *Berlin via America*. Another early effort was *Little Miss Hawkshaw*, and later there were *K — the Unknown* and *Secrets*.

Under his new name, Keith began appearing in features in 1925 (one of his frequent leading ladies being Clara Bow) after working in Christie comedies. Among his mid–'20s films were *My Lady of Whims*, *The Plastic Age*, *Parisian Love* and *Dancing Mothers*. Filling both leading and supporting roles, many at Paramount, Keith continued on through the silent era in generally second-rate films, with an occasional better one like Emil Jannings's *The Way of All Flesh*.

Other of Keith's motion pictures included *Collegiate*, *Broadway Madness*, *The Whirlwind of Youth* and *Bare Knees*. Last silents: *The Phantom of the North* and *Just Off Broadway*, released about the same time in 1929, made after his first part-talkies.

Sound: Should a Girl Marry? (1928) was Keith's first part-talkie; 1929's *The Lone Wolf's Daughter* was his next. Released by Paramount, he appeared in support in several low-budget quickies, includ-

ing westerns, from 1931 until the mid–1930s. Among these were *Branded Men*, *First Aid*, *Midnight Lady*, *The Big Bluff*, *Twisted Rails* and *Arm of the Law*.

Apparently Keith made a "comeback" of sorts in the 1950s with small roles in *The Human Beast* and *It Should Happen to You*. There also may have been some others.

Reviews

The Lone Wolf's Daughter: The sound quality is so poor that it is unintelligible, as if the characters talked through their noses while their mouths and noses were gagged. *Harrison's Reports* 3/9/29.

Should a Girl Marry?: The acting is good. The hero, played by Keith, is step-son of the villain. *Harrison's Reports* 9/14/29.

Keith, Ian (Keith M. Ross), Boston, Massachusetts, 1899–1961

Filmography: Classic Images (July 1991)

Silent: After his debut in 1924's *Christine of the Hungry Heart*, prominent stage actor Ian Keith worked at First National, Paramount, Fox and Columbia. Among his co-stars were Gloria Swanson and Corinne Griffith.

Keith's films included *Manhandled*, *Her Love Story*, *Two Arabian Nights*, *The Love of Sunya*, *Street of Illusion* and *The Greater Glory*. Last silent: *The Divine Lady* (1929), technically a silent although it contained singing sequences.

Sound: Nineteen twenty-nine's *Prisoners*, a part-talkie, was Ian Keith's first venture into sound. That year's *Light Fingers* was wholly sound and it was followed by *The Great Divide*. He had fewer leading roles in the sound era but continued to be active into the '50s, although decreasingly so, and he had some periods off-screen, including the years 1949 to '53.

Keith's films ranged from prestigious to quickie. Among his "B" efforts were *The Sundown Kid*, *I Escaped from the Gestapo*, *The Chinese Cat*, *She Gets Her Man* and *It Came from Beneath the Sea*. His classier productions for such studios as MGM, Paramount, Warner Bros. and Twentieth Century–Fox included *Abraham Lincoln*, *Queen Christina*, *Cleopatra* (1934 version), *The Sign of the Cross* and *Forever Amber*.

His portrayal of the alcoholic in 1947's *Nightmare Alley* was judged to be among Ian Keith's best efforts. He also appeared in numerous westerns and melodramas for Poverty Row outfits like Republic, Monogram and PRC but he went out in style. His last role was that of the Pharaoh in the 1956 remake of *The Ten Commandments*.

Comments: Ian Keith had a matinee idol's looks, talent and a voice well-suited for talkies. He also continued to make stage and radio appearances while making films. His picture career, largely limited to supporting roles in talkies, undoubtedly could have been greater but alcohol was a problem and it (and possibly other vices) kept getting him into difficulties.

Keith had numerous well-publicized marital problems and made at least one apparent suicide attempt. In a notorious 1953 incident he was disciplined by his union (AFTRA) after becoming rowdy while actually broadcasting on the air. His was indeed a talent ill-used.

REVIEWS

Light Fingers: Ian Keith's stage training brings results with an easy delivery. He is a handsome crook-hero. *Variety* 8/21/29, *Harrison's Reports* 8/24/29.

A Tailor Made Man: Keith performs competently and contributes small but good histrionic highlights. *New York Times* 4/25/31, *Variety* 4/29/31.

The Preview Murder Mystery: Keith renders a theatric impersonation of what people probably imagine a director ought to look and act like. *New York times* 3/21/36.

Nightmare Alley: Ian Keith plays a hopeless alcoholic, ending up as a carnival sideshow "geek" and he is outstanding. *Harrison's Reports* 10/11/47, *Variety* 10/15/47.

Kelly, Paul, Brooklyn, New York, 1899–1956

Filmography: Hollywood Players: The Thirties

Silent: The man who was to become known as one of filmdom's tough guys began his career as a child on Broadway and in numerous Vitagraph one- and two-reelers, perhaps several hundred. He claimed to have been known as "The Vitagraph Boy." In the 'teens he graduated to leading roles in *Knights of the Square Table* and *Anne of Green Gables.*

In the early 1920s Kelly appeared in supporting roles in *Uncle Sam of Freedom Ridge, The Great Adventure* and *The Old Oaken Bucket.* He was off-screen for several years, undoubtedly appearing in some of his 75 stage plays, and returned in 1926 for secondary parts in *The New Klondike* and *Slide, Kelly, Slide.*

About this time, Kelly was convicted of accidentally killing his romantic rival in a fight and he was sentenced to a two-year prison term for manslaughter. Last silent: *Special Delivery* (1927).

Sound: Kelly overcame his rumored blacklisting by Hollywood for his offense and returned to the screen in 1932's *The Girl from Calgary.* This was the first in a lengthy series of pictures, until the time of his death, that resulted in his unofficial designation as the "King of the Bs."

Kelly also continued to play stage roles. Among his films of the 1930s were *Side Streets, Broadway Through a Keyhole, The President Vanishes, My Marriage* and *Navy Blue and Gold.* His roles had him on both sides of the law as hero and villain, detective and gangster. He carried leads in second features until fairly late in his career and did notable character parts in more prestigious films.

In the '40s Kelly was seen in *Mr. and Mrs. North, Tough as They Come, Flying Tigers, The Story of Dr. Wassell, The Cat Creeps* and *Guilty of Treason,* among others. He also made the serials *Gang Busters* and *The Secret Code.* His theater work culminated with his performance in the World War Two drama *Twelve O'Clock High* for which he received a 1948 Tony award.

Few of Kelly's later films would prove to match that career high point. They included *The Painted Hills, The High and the Mighty, Storm Center* and his last, released posthumously in 1957, *Bailout at 43,000.* He was also seen on television.

Comments: Perhaps it could be said that Paul Kelly's talents were largely wasted in Hollywood. He appeared in few outstanding films and he was typecast in tough guy roles that rarely allowed him to stretch his acting muscles. But he was suited to such roles because there undeniably was an element of danger about him that came across on the screen.

Even if Kelly had not lived his own unfortunate true life melodrama, his pugnacious Irish mug and in-your-face attitude probably would have resulted in much the same kind of roles. That he was capable of better was proven all too seldom — in Hollywood, at least.

REVIEWS

The Girl from Calgary: Paul Kelly does the best he can with the press agent assignment. *Variety* 11/22/32.

Public Hero No. 1: Kelly as the G-Man chief makes his contribution stand up. *Variety* 6/12/35.

Parole Racket: On Paul Kelly's capable shoulders falls the burden of the acting. He covers up the triteness of his role by a good performance. *Variety* 3/10/37, *Harrison's Reports* 3/13/37.

Six Thousand Enemies: Kelly is decidedly sympathetic as the prison doctor. *Variety* 5/31/39.

Flying Tigers: Kelly is barely adequate in this major assignment. *Variety* 9/23/42.

Kennedy, Edgar, Monterey, California, 1890–1948

Filmography: List of films *Film Fan Monthly* (Dec. 1967)

Silent: One of the most famous character comedians of the cinema was Edgar Kennedy, known for his patented "slow burn" and perennial irascibility. He joined Keystone in 1914 as a Keystone Kop, after vaudeville and musical comedy experience from age 11, and appeared with Charlie Chaplin in such films as *Caught in a Cabaret*, *The Star Boarder* and *Tillie's Punctured Romance*.

Kennedy may actually have made his first one-reeler as early as 1911. The rest of the 'teens was spent in one- and two-reelers in support of other comedians. He began freelancing in the early 1920s, mostly in two-reelers like the "Leather Pushers" series but with some appearances in feature-length comedies and melodramas.

Kennedy's features included *Skirts*, *The Battling Fool*, *The Golden Princess*, *Oh, What a Nurse!*, *My Old Dutch*, *The Chinese Parrot*, *Wet Paint* and *The Wrong Mr. Wright*. He also directed some comedy shorts, including those of Laurel and Hardy. Last silent: *Trent's Last Case* (1929), with synchronized music and sound effects.

Sound: Kennedy's first sound feature was the 1929 Will Rogers starrer *They Had to See Paris*. Most of his '30s work was in shorts for Hal Roach (including a few early "Our Gang" comedies), Pathe, Educational and RKO. He co-starred with professional screen drunk Arthur Housman in several and in 1931 began his long-running (18-year) series the "Average Citizen" in which he portrayed a man sorely beset by his wife and assorted mangy in-laws.

In full-length films Kennedy was seen frequently as a policeman, detective or other would-be authority figures. Among his features were *Duck Soup*, *Little Orphan Annie*, *Twentieth Century*, *Cowboy Millionaire*, *San Francisco*, *Snuffy Smith*, *Crazy House*, *Variety Time*, *Anchors Aweigh*, *The Sin of Harold Diddlebock* and *Air Raid Wardens*. His last (posthumous) appearance was in *My Dream Is Yours* (1949).

Comments: There were times when the sour face of Edgar Kennedy seemed omnipresent on-screen. In his 35 years or so in films he supposedly made about 200 shorts and 100 features, 80 of them sound. His "slow burn," featuring his hand drawn slowly down his face in exasperation, was generally to be seen at least once in every performance.

Kennedy was the screen's king of frustration. He could not win for losing and could do nothing more constructive than to express his befuddle-ment and anger at a world he could not control. His growly voice, spewing impatience, completed the effect.

REVIEWS

Scarlet River: Several of the situations are extremely mirth-provoking, such as the one in which Edgar Kennedy is a motion picture director. *Harrison's Reports* 3/4/33.

The Return of Jimmy Valentine: Edgar Kennedy provides comedy relief. He does his familiar irritated man routine but is favored here with an excellent foil, as well as by the smartest lines of the film. *Variety* 3/4/36.

The Quarterback: Kennedy supplies plenty of broad comedy. *Variety* 10/2/40.

Captain Tugboat Annie: The horseplay and comedy is handled by Edgar Kennedy. *Variety* 3/6/46.

Kennedy, Madge, Chicago, Illinois, 1891–1987

Filmography: *Films in Review* (Mar. 1984)

Silent: A leading stage comedienne from about 1910, Madge Kennedy was signed by Goldwyn and between 1917 and '21 appeared in more than 20 features, mostly marital farces. The first of these was *Baby Mine*. After her contract ended she returned to the theater (one major hit being *Poppy*), but she then made a half dozen or so additional pictures.

Other Kennedy films were *The Fair Pretender*, *Leave It to Susan*, *The Blooming Angel*, *Three Miles Out*, *The Truth*, *The Highest Bidder*, *Help Yourself* and *Lying Wives*. She wanted to play dramatic roles but when they were not forthcoming she once again returned to the theater. Last silent: *Oh, Baby!* (1926).

Sound: Madge Kennedy continued to star on stage in such vehicles as *Paris Bound* and *Private Lives* while also appearing in vaudeville in 1929. She ultimately returned to films as a character actress in 1952's *The Marrying Kind* and was seen in some 14 talkies.

Among Kennedy's sound pictures were *The Rains of Ranchipur*, *North by Northwest*, *They Shoot Horses Don't They?* (in a much praised role), *Lust for Life*, *The Catered Affair*, *Let's Make Love*, *The Day of the Locust* and, lastly, *The Marathon Man* in 1976. She also did television work and returned to Broadway for a final role in 1965.

REVIEWS

The Marrying Kind: The kindly judge is beautifully played by third-billed Madge Kennedy, a silent screen name. *Variety* 3/12/52.

Three Bad Sisters: Kennedy is the tippling, psycho aunt. *Variety* 1/11/56.

A Nice Little Bank That Should Be Robbed: Kennedy, once a leading lady of the silent screen, contributes a few moments of hilarity as the terrified employee. *New York Times* 12/11/58.

The Baby Maker: In key support is Madge Kennedy. *Variety* 9/30/70.

Kennedy, Tom, New York, New York, 1884/85–1965

Silent: The battered mug atop the 6'3" frame of Tom Kennedy was seen on screen as early as 1915 when he was supposedly one of the Keystone Kops. Besides numerous one- and two-reelers there were occasional full-length films in the 'teens like *Double Trouble* (with Douglas Fairbanks), *Mickey* (starring Mabel Normand) and *The Island of Intrigue.*

A boxer as well as an actor, Kennedy continued to participate in matches until the early 1920s, thereby further disarranging his already distinctive physiognomy. From 1920 he was a popular character player in features while still appearing in comedy shorts with the likes of Lupino Lane and Slim Summerville.

Among Kennedy's films were *Skirts, Our Leading Citizen, Scaramouche, Mantrap, Silver Valley, Tillie's Punctured Romance* (1928 version) and *The Better 'Ole.* He also drew favorable attention for his role in *Behind the Front.* Last silents: *Marked Money* and *Love Over Night,* released about the same time in 1928.

Sound: In the talkies, Kennedy revealed a perfect voice for the slow-witted policemen, bartenders and crooks he was usually called upon to play. He of course already had the perfect face and bulk as well. His first full-length part-talkie was 1929's *The Cohens and Kellys in Atlantic City* and other films that year included *Glad Rag Doll, Big News* and *The Shannons of Broadway.*

In the '30s Kennedy continued to appear in many shorts and countless features like *The Big House, Monkey Business, 42nd Street, The Devil Is Driving, She Done Him Wrong, Poppy, Slave Ship* and *Smart Blonde.* He was also a regular in the "Torchy Blane" series.

Kennedy was still seen in comedy shorts during the following decade and among his full-length pictures in the 1940s were *Curtain Call, The Kid from Brooklyn, They Live by Night, The Paleface* and *Dixie.*

His career wound down in the '50s but he could still be glimpsed in such films as *Border Rangers, Invasion U.S.A.* and *Some Like It Hot.* He was last seen providing his inimitable, colorful performance in 1963's *It's a Mad Mad Mad Mad World.*

REVIEWS

Forty Naughty Girls: Tom Kennedy did his usual routine as the stupid assistant to the police inspector. *Variety* 9/8/37.

Kent, Barbara (Barbara Klowtman), Gadsby, Alberta, 1906/09–

Silent: Barbara Kent's first film was the western *Prowlers of the Night* in 1926. The petite brunette's second, a definite step up, was the Garbo-Gilbert starrer *Flesh and the Devil.* Others included *The Drop Kick* (starring Richard Barthelmess), *No Man's Law, The Lone Eagle* and *That's My Daddy.* Last silent: *Modern Mothers* (1928).

Sound: After her first part-talkie, 1928's *Lonesome,* Kent made another, *Shakedown,* in 1929 and then was chosen as Harold Lloyd's leading lady for his first sound film *Welcome Danger.* She appeared with him again in the next year's *Feet First.*

Among Kent's other films were *Dumbbells in Ermine, Indiscreet* (as Gloria Swanson's sister), *Emma, Vanity Fair, Her Forgotten Past, Chinatown After Dark* and *Guard That Girl.* She appeared on-screen steadily until 1935, making seven pictures in 1932 alone, then returned in 1939 for a bit role in *Blondie Meets the Boss.* Her last may have been 1941's *Under Age.*

REVIEWS

Shakedown: Barbara Kent, as the heart interest, just looks nice and says little. *Variety* 4/10/29.

Welcome Danger: Kent is an attractive leading lady to Harold Lloyd. She photographs nicely and speaks distinctly. *Variety* 10/23/29, *Harrison's Reports* 10/26/29.

Grief Street: This picture brings up the question of why Barbara Kent isn't cast in better films. She has the personality, voice, figure and ability that could go somewhere with intelligent handling. *Variety* 10/13/31.

Kenyon, Doris (Margaret D. Kenyon), Syracuse, New York, 1897/98–1979

Filmography: Films in Review (Apr. 1980)

Silent: Doris Kenyon began with the World Film Corporation in 1916 making such motion pictures as *The Rack* and *The Pawn of Fate.* She also appeared in the 1917 serial *The Hidden Hand.*

Kenyon later became a popular First National star and co-starred several times with her husband-to-be Milton Sills. Among her films were *Monsieur Beaucaire* with Rudolph Valentino, *Twilight, Bright Lights of Broadway, I Want My Man, The Blonde Saint* and *Wild Honey.* Last silent: *The Hawk's Nest* (1928).

Sound: 1928's *The Home Towners* was Warner

Bros.' third all-talkie and Kenyon's first. It was followed by the Paramount hit *Interference* the same year. Her films included *Beau Bandit, Alexander Hamilton, Voltaire* (the latter two with George Arliss), *Counsellor-at-Law* with John Barrymore, *The Human Side* and *Girl's School*.

Possessed of a good singing voice, Kenyon interspersed stage roles and concertizing with her filmmaking. After her film career ended with 1939's *The Man in the Iron Mask*, she appeared on radio and then television.

Comments: Doris Kenyon was given the opportunity to display her singing voice in *Beau Bandit* and *Alexander Hamilton*, in which she warbled "Drink to Me Only with Thine Eyes." By the mid–1930s she was undeniably slipping, however. Her role in the prestigious *Counsellor-at-Law* was an unsympathetic one and her films after 1933 generally were minor efforts.

By the time of Kenyon's last role she was in small supporting parts. Nevertheless, considering that she had been in films since the mid-'teens, she would have to be counted as one of the successes of the transition.

REVIEWS

The Home Towners: Doris Kenyon is limited to carrying the story and playing it straight. She performs and screens well but her voice is a bit too high in pitch to sound natural. *Variety* 10/31/28.

Interference: Kenyon is handsomely unbelievable. *Variety* 11/21/28, *Harrison's Reports* 11/24/28.

Alexander Hamilton: Kenyon plays Betsy Hamilton with all the cloying sweetness of a Victorian wife. *Variety* 9/22/31.

Voltaire: Doris Kenyon gets a small opportunity as Madame Pompadour but makes the most of the part and her moments stand out. *Variety* 8/29/33.

Counsellor-at-Law: A featured player is the statuesque Doris Kenyon. It is a tough role for her but she gives it what the doctor ordered. *Variety* 12/12/33.

Whom the Gods Destroy: Doris Kenyon has a meaty part and she makes the most of it. *Variety* 7/17/34.

Kerry, Norman (Norman or Arnold Kaiser), Rochester, New York, 1889/95–1956

Filmography: *Classic Images* (Sept. 1987); List of films in *Eighty Silent Film Stars*

Silent: After his debut in 1915 (*Manhattan Madness* may have been his first film), Norman Kerry played supporting parts until about 1919 when his leading role in *Soldiers of Fortune* proved a success. Prior to that he had changed his surname in reaction to fierce anti–German feelings during the First World War.

In 1923 Kerry signed with Universal for whom he made such hits as *The Hunchback of Notre Dame, Merry-Go-Round* and *The Phantom of the Opera*. Others of his silent films were *Amarilly of Clothesline Alley, Getting Mary Married, Passion's Playground, Proxies, Annie Laurie, The Barrier* and the offbeat Lon Chaney thriller *The Unknown*.

Kerry portrayed both heroes and villains in his almost 60 silent films. Among his many important female co-stars were Mary Pickford, Lillian Gish, Mae Marsh, Marion Davies, Bebe Daniels, Joan Crawford and Corinne Griffith. Last silent: *The Prince of Hearts* (1929).

Sound: A supporting role in *Ex-Flame* (1930) was Kerry's first sound effort. He made only a few more, including small roles in *Bachelor Apartment* and *Air Eagles*, both 1931. Other known appearances were in *The Phantom of Santa Fe* (1936) and lastly *Tanks a Million* (1941).

Comments: Six-feet-two-inch Norman Kerry, with his signature waxed mustache, made a dashing figure on-screen and if his publicity was to be believed, off-screen as well. The story of his stowing away on an ocean liner to woo back his estranged wife was widely publicized. He later supposedly joined the Foreign Legion and returned to the U.S. only after France had been overrun by the Nazis.

Kerry certainly had a problem in the talkies. He did not have a good speaking voice for films; its timbre was poor and he tended to slur his words. Perhaps it could have been improved with training but he was no longer young enough for romantic leads and character roles may not have been the future he wanted.

REVIEWS

Bachelor Apartment: Kerry is photographed at bad angles and his lines are mostly silly. *Variety* 5/20/31.

Air Eagles: Norman Kerry, as the German, is handicapped by his voice. *Variety* 1/26/32.

King, Charles (also billed as Charles L. King and other variations), Hillsboro, Texas, 1895–1957

Filmography: List of films in *Classic Images* (July 1986)

Silent: Charles King was an extra in silents from about 1915, eventually winding up in comedy shorts of the '20s, among them the "Mike and Ike" series. He also made the first of many serials in *What Happened to Jane?* (1926).

King's features were relatively few in that decade and included *A Motion to Adjourn* (possibly his first), *Singing River, The Price of Youth, Merry-Go-Round,*

Hearts of the West, Range Courage and *Sisters of Eve.* Last silent: *Slim Fingers* (1929).

Sound: It was not until 1930 that audiences heard Charles King's menacing baritone in *Beyond the Law* and *Oklahoma Cyclone.* They were the first in a very long string of "B" westerns in which he played a "baddie," usually as a henchman to the mastermind of all the bad guys.

In hundreds of feature shorts and serials, King with his black mustache (he was nicknamed "Blackie") menaced nearly every sagebrush hero. Among his films were *Along the Sundown Trail, Bordertown Gunfighters, The Kid Ranger, The Pinto Bandit, The Texas Kid* and *Utah Trail.* He also appeared in non-westerns like *See Here, Private Hargrove, The Reckless Age* and *Headline Crashers.*

King's serials were legion: *The Painted Stallion, The Adventures of Rex and Rinty, Adventures of Sir Galahad, The Black Arrow, The Great Adventures of Captain Kidd, Ghost of Zorro, The Green Archer* and *Hurricane Express.* There were others as well, including what might have been his last on-screen appearance in *Bruce Gentry — Daredevil of the Skies* (1949).

NOTE: King's filmography is sometimes confused with, or even combined with, that of the stage singer Charles King (1894–1944), who appeared in early MGM musicals like *The Broadway Melody* and *Hollywood Revue of 1929.*

Comments: As the 1940s faded into the '50s, Charles King's bread-and-butter, the "B" western, headed towards oblivion, a victim of the inroads of television. As his opportunities were decreasing he had been noticeably *increasing,* i.e., putting on a considerable amount of weight. As a result, he became less convincing in those parts still available to him. By the end of his career he was literally a "heavy" and a somewhat immobile one at that.

REVIEWS

Outlaw Justice: Charles King makes good on the villain assignment. *Variety* 2/28/33.

Kingston, Natalie, Vallejo, California, 1904/05–1991

Silent: After a stint in Sennett two-reelers beginning in the mid-'20s, including many with Harry Langdon and Ben Turpin, statuesque Natalie Kingston began her feature career in 1926 with such films as Eddie Cantor's *Kid Boots* and *Don Juan's Three Nights.*

Other Kingston pictures were *Wet Paint, His First Flame, The Port of Missing Girls* and *Figures Don't Lie.* She also made a fetching Jane in the serials *Tarzan the Mighty* and *Tarzan the Tiger.* Last silent: *Painted Post* (1928), made after her first part-talkie.

Sound: Kingston's most memorable talkie was her first, the part-sound *Street Angel* (1928), starring the romantic team of Janet Gaynor and Charles Farrell. Her only leading roles came in 1930 in the western *Under Texas Skies* and *The Swellhead.*

In her other early sound pictures, *River of Romance* (1929) and *Her Wedding Night* (1930), Kingston was down in the cast list. She returned in 1933 for small roles or bits in *Forgotten, His Private Secretary* and *Only Yesterday.*

REVIEWS

Street Angel: Natalie Kingston in support as the streetwalker does very well. *Variety* 4/11/28, *Harrison's Reports* 4/21/28.

The Swell Head: A very good boxing story in which Natalie Kingston is the heroine. *Harrison's Reports* 4/12/30.

Kirkwood, James, Grand Rapids, Michigan, 1883–1963

Silent: Handsome stage star James Kirkwood was a Griffith lead in one- and two-reelers as early as 1909. His feature career as a matinee idol started in 1914 with such films as *Cinderella, Fanchon the Cricket, Mistress Nell* and *Home, Sweet Home.* He also directed some films in the mid-'teens.

Other earlier Kirkwood efforts included *Melissa of the Hills, Periwinkle, Marriage* and *The Branding Iron.* In the '20s he was somewhat less active but continued in starring roles to the end of the decade. Among his films were *Ebb Tide, Human Wreckage, Circe the Enchantress, Love's Whirlpool, Secrets of the Night* and *Million Dollar Mystery.* Last silent: *Someone to Love* (1928).

Sound: Kirkwood's first sound films were *The Time, the Place and the Girl* and *Hearts in Exile* in 1929. He continued to play leads for a couple of years but as he neared 50 his starring career was coming to an end. After 1934 he was not seen on-screen again until sporadic appearances in the 1940s and '50s.

Kirkwood appeared in some westerns (e.g., *The Last Posse, My Pal the King*) and in such films as *The Devil's Holiday, Young Sinners, Charlie Chan's Chance, Fancy Pants, Hired Wife, Madame Curie, Joan of Arc* and *Intruder in the Dust.* His last film was 1956's *The Search for Bridey Murphy.*

Comments: James Kirkwood undoubtedly was a major star in silent films and he co-starred with some of the most important female stars of the era, including Blanche Sweet, Mary Pickford and Lillian Gish. He was handsome and popular but was also fond of roistering, and his weakness for alcohol did neither his career nor his marriage to actress Lila Lee any good.

Although Kirkwood's stage-trained voice was very suited for talkies, a supporting career was all he could hope for and his sound career was not distinguished. His name did live on after him when his son and namesake became a praised novelist and playwright in the 1970s and '80s.

REVIEWS

The Time, the Place and the Girl: James Kirkwood, as a professor, has a nicely done light comedy part. *Variety* 7/10/29.

Hearts in Exile: Kirkwood, in spite of his pronounced English accent, cuts an impressive figure. *Variety* 12/4/29.

The Devil's Holiday: Kirkwood plays the hero's narrow-minded brother. *Harrison's Reports* 5/17/30.

Cheaters at Play: The only other cast member of prominence is James Kirkwood, as a detective. He registers mildly. *Variety* 3/1/32.

The Search for Bridey Murphy: Playing Bridey's husband is James Kirkwood. *Variety* 10/10/56.

Kohler, Fred (later Fred Kohler, Sr.),
Dubuque, Iowa, or Kansas City, Missouri, 1888/89–1938

Filmography: List of films in *Eighty Silent Film Stars*

Silent: Perhaps as early as 1911, after working in stock and vaudeville, Fred Kohler's menacing face first was seen on-screen. Sometimes (unfairly) called the ugliest man in films, he was certainly a screen villain to be reckoned with. To complete the effect, he was missing two fingers on one hand, although this was a fact usually concealed from the camera. Besides acting, he also directed some pictures in the 'teens.

Kohler's feature appearances began about 1919 in *Soldiers of Fortune*; others included *The Kentucky Colonel*, *Cyclone Bliss*, *The Scrapper*, *Anna Christie* (1923 version), *Shadows of the North*, *Abraham Lincoln*, *The Way of All Flesh*, *Underworld*, *The Ice Flood* and *Forgotten Faces*. Among the studios for which he appeared were Arrow, Pathe, Hodkinson, Associated and Universal. Last silent: *Stairs of Sand* (1929), made after his first part-talkie.

Sound: In late 1928, Kohler made his first appearance in a film with sound, the part-talkie *The Spieler*. Of his several 1929 films, the majority had at least some sound, including *Sal of Singapore*, *Say It with Songs*, *Thunderbolt*, *Broadway Babies* and *River of Romance*.

Kohler remained active to the time of his death in both westerns and non-westerns including shorts — although he is probably now best-known for his gangster roles and western villainy — at studios such as Fox, Paramount, Columbia, MGM,

Warner Bros., Republic and RKO. Among his films were *Mississippi*, *Marie Antoinette*, *The Buccaneer*, *Queen Christina*, *Call Her Savage*, *The Fiddlin' Buckaroo*, *Wilderness Mail*, *Goin' to Town*, *The Plainsman*, *Daughter of Shanghai* and *Billy the Kid Returns*. His last released film was *Boy Slaves* in 1939.

REVIEWS

The Spieler: A classy performance is given by Fred Kohler. His gorilla-like physical proportions fit the tough guy role perfectly. He is an all round so-and-so. *Variety* 2/27/29.

Broadway Babies: Kohler does great work as the gambler. *Harrison's Reports* 6/29/29.

Roadhouse Nights: Kohler is a blue-ribbon bad man; he manages to make a trite bootlegger and killer part pretty exciting. *Variety* 2/26/30.

The Man from Hell: Fred Kohler is sufficiently well able to keep the audience in their seats. *Variety* 10/2/34.

Hard Rock Harrigan: It's to the credit of the performance by Fred Kohler that this film holds up. *Variety* 7/31/35.

Kornman, Mary, Idaho Falls, Idaho,
1917–1973

Filmography: *Classic Images* (July 1986)

Silent: Blonde Mary Kornman almost toddled her way into films with a 1920 appearance in *Iron Heart*, about the same time that she started in vaudeville. From 1922 to '26 she was a winsome little girl in "Our Gang" comedies beginning with *Young Sherlocks*. There were apparently no further features. Last silent: *The Fourth Alarm* (1926), a two-reeler.

Sound: Kornman's talkie career began in 1930 with the "Boy Friends" series, the first possibly being *Doctor's Orders*. She appeared in many comedy shorts and also in features throughout the '30s such as *College Humor*, *Flying Down to Rio*, *Strictly Dynamite*, *The Desert Trail*, *Youth on Parole*, *Swing It, Professor*, *King of the Newsboys* and *I Am a Criminal*.

Kornman is probably best-known for her role in "Our Gang" shorts of the 1930s in which she had graduated from the ranks of the pupils to being the schoolteacher Miss Crabtree. She had what was probably her major (and the title) role in the mid–'30s serial *Queen of the Jungle*. After that she made only brief appearances in her movies, the final one, *On the Spot*, coming in 1940.

REVIEWS

The Desert Trail: Mary Kornman is featured in the cast, but has little to do. She's the little blonde from Our Gang and is pleasing enough. *Variety* 8/21/35.

On the Spot: Mary Kornman is high in the billing as the girl friend but she does not have very much to do. *Variety* 6/26/40.

Kortman, Robert (Bob), New York, New York, Bracketville, Texas, or Philadelphia, Pennsylvania, 1887–1967

Filmography: List of films in *Eighty Silent Film Stars*

Silent: Robert Kortman may have begun his connection with movies in the capacity of a horse trainer at Ince. From about 1911 he was seen in short comedies like *Ambrose's Rapid Rise* and *His Nasty Thought*, as well as dramas and westerns, including such William S. Hart films as *Hell's Hinges*, *The Narrow Trail* and *The Captive God*. His first feature credit may have been *Lieutenant Danny, U.S.A.* in 1916.

Other of Kortman's relatively few silent features were *Through the Wrong Door*, *Montana Bill*, *Arabian Love*, *All the Brothers Were Valiant*, *The Devil Horse*, *Blood Will Tell* and *Sunrise*. He also appeared in the serial *The Great Radium Mystery* in 1920. Last silent: *Fleetwing* (1928).

Sound: Kortman's narrow eyes and high cheekbones made him an arresting-looking villain. He was primarily associated with "B" westerns but also was a supporting player in dramas. Among his films were *Branded*, *Come On Tarzan*, *Island of Lost Souls*, *Sunset Pass*, *Spitfire*, *Hotel Imperial*, *When the Daltons Rode* and *Heroes of the Range*.

Kortman also made a formidable villain in sound serials like *Burn 'Em Up Barnes*, *Mystery Squadron*, Ken Maynard's *Mystery Mountain*, Tom Mix's *The Miracle Rider*, *The Vigilantes Are Coming* and *Secret Agent X-9*.

Kortman made films for numerous studios, both major and distinctly minor, including Metro, Fox, Paramount, Goldwyn, Universal, Gladstone, Pioneer and Rialto. His final film is believed to have been 1951's *Flaming Feather*.

Kosloff, Theodore, Moscow, Russia, 1882–1956

Silent: Ballet dancer Theodore Kosloff became a C. B. DeMille favorite, making his first appearance in that director's *The Woman God Forgot* (1916) and then in such films as *The Affairs of Anatol*, *Why Change Your Wife?*, *Adam's Rib*, *Fool's Paradise*, *The Golden Bed*, *Feet of Clay* and *Forbidden Fruit*. He also choreographed several films.

Kosloff was occasionally starred but more often played supporting, sometimes villainous and almost always "exotic" roles. Among his other pictures to the late '20s were *The Lane That Had No Turning*, *Hollywood*, *Children of Jazz*, *Triumph*, *New Lives for Old* and *The Little Adventuress*. Last silent: *Woman Wise* (1928).

Sound: As far as is known, Theodore Kosloff made only two sound appearances. They consisted of bits in DeMille's *Madam Satan* (1930) and in 1937's *Stage Door*. He returned to dancing, his first love, choreographing an occasional film and teaching ballet.

Lackteen, Frank, Asia Minor?, 1894–1968

Silent: Rarely has so menacing a face been seen on the screen as that of Frank Lackteen. Swarthy and hollow-cheeked, he was the perfect villain's henchman in numerous features and serials. Beginning at Vitagraph, he graduated to serials of the late 'teens and '20s, many with Walter Miller and Allene Ray, including *Sunken Silver*, *Hawk of the Hills* (in which he played the title character), *The Yellow Menace* and *The Avenging Arrow*.

Among Lackteen's features were *The Pony Express*, *Desert Gold*, *Unknown Frontier*, *The Virgin*, *The Warning* and *Prowlers of the Sea*. Last silent: *Court-Martial* (1928). The 1929 feature *Hawk of the Hills* was an abbreviated version of his earlier serial of the same name.

Sound: Talkies revealed that Frank Lackteen had a noticeable but undefinable accent which only enhanced his bona fides as an all-purpose bad man. In the 1930s he continued his appearances in serials including *Heroes of the West*, *Red Barry*, *The Jungle Mystery*, *The Perils of Pauline*, *The Mysterious Pilot* and *Tarzan the Fearless*.

There were also '30s features for Lackteen, among them the usual "B" material like *Law of the Tong*, *Escape from Devil's Island* and *I Cover the War*, but also occasional superior fare like *Anthony Adverse* and *Juarez*. In the next decade he was seen in the serials *Don Winslow of the Navy* and *The Desert Hawk* as well as such features as *The Sea Wolf*, *Moonlight and Cactus*, *Chetniks!* and *Singin' in the Corn*.

Lackteen also made some shorts, including at least one with The Three Stooges. By the 1950s he was seen less frequently but he still put in occasional appearances in films like *King of the Khyber Rifles*, *Flesh and the Spur* and *The Atomic Submarine*. In the 1960s he was way down in the cast lists of *Requiem for a Gunfighter* and *The Bounty Killer*, films which brought back to the screen for the last time many old-time stars and supporting players.

Reviews

Chetniks!: Splendidly acted by Frank Lackteen. *New York Times* 3/19/43.

Lake, Alice, Brooklyn, New York, 1896/98–1967

Silent: Tiny "Sweet Alice" Lake paid her dues in Sennett comedies before graduating to features, among the first of which was *Playing Dead* in 1915. Other early ones included *Blackie's Redemption*, *Lombardi, Ltd.* and *Love's Triumph*. In the '20s she became a leading lady for Metro and other studios.

Lake appeared in such films as *The Infamous Miss Revell*, *Hate*, *Broken Hearts of Broadway*, *The Virgin*, *The Overland Limited*, *The Wives of the Prophet* and *Women Men Like*. By the end of the decade she had been relegated to supporting roles. Last silent: *Circumstantial Evidence* (1929).

Sound: Lake's two 1929 talkies were *Twin Beds* and *Frozen Justice*. In both she was down in the cast list. She had small roles, declining to bits and then extra appearances in 1930s and early '40s films including *Wicked*, *Skyway*, *The Mighty Barnum*, *Broadway Bill*, *Wharf Angel* and *Death on the Diamond*.

REVIEWS

Wicked: Such former silent names as Mae Busch, Eileen Percy and Alice Lake are hidden beneath trick makeup. They are portrayed as bad moral examples in the prison scenes. *Variety* 9/22/31.

Lake, Arthur (Arthur Silverlake), Corbin, Kentucky, 1905–1987

Silent: It was in 1925 that Arthur Lake made his adult screen bow in *Where Was I?* He previously had been in the all-juvenile version of *Jack and the Beanstalk* in 1917. His fresh-faced youth was used to advantage in such films as *Skinner's Dress Suit*, *The Cradle Snatchers*, *The Irresistible Lover*, *The Count of Ten* and *Stop That Man*.

Lake also appeared in Universal's "Sweet Sixteen" comedies. Last silent: *Harold Teen* (1928), based upon the popular comic strip, in which he played the title role.

Sound: The part-talkie *The Air Circus* (1928) was Lake's sound debut. His high voice also was heard in such early talkies as *On with the Show*, *Tanned Legs* and *Dance Hall*. In the last two he was the male lead. Throughout the 1930s he continued to be seen in light fare like *Cheer Up and Smile*, *She's My Weakness*, *Indiscreet*, *Orchids to You*, *It's a Great Life!*, *23½ Hours Leave* and *Women Must Dress*.

Lake was also seen in such "B" melodramas as *The Silver Streak*, *I Cover Chinatown* and *Exiled to Shanghai*, with an occasional "A" picture like *Topper* (1937). In the latter film he had a small but showy role as an elevator "boy." That portrayal

may have contributed to his being cast as Dagwood Bumstead in the first *Blondie* film in 1938. Based on the Chic Young comic strip, it was a role he rarely strayed from for the next 12 years.

The title role of Lake's long-suffering wife was essayed by Penny Singleton, now blonde but formerly known in films as the brunette Dorothy McNulty. Among the 28 films in the "Blondie" series were *Blondie Takes a Vacation*, *...Has Servant Trouble*, *...Plays Cupid*, *...on a Budget*, *...Hits the Jackpot*, *...Goes Latin*, *Blondie's Big Deal* and *Life with Blondie*.

Lake also played in a small handful of other films during the '40s including *The Ghost That Walks Alone* and *16 Fathoms Deep*. *Beware of Blondie* was the last of the series in 1950 and his last film as well. He repeated the role on radio and with another actress playing his wife on television too. (There also was a very brief late '60s version in which he did not participate.) Finally, he was seen in the series *Meet the Family*. He had a professional reunion with Singleton in a 1970s dinner theater production.

Comments: Like many another actor trapped in a role with which he was totally identified, Arthur Lake no doubt found his alter ego Dagwood to be both a blessing and a curse. It is also undeniable that before he was cast as the simple but good-hearted Bumstead his career was definitely not prospering by the mid-'30s. Although others were considered for the part, including Frank Albertson, his marriage to Marion Davies's niece did not hurt his own chances.

Lake's voice was made for the talkies; it was like no other. High-pitched and whiny, it was much imitated, especially his hapless cry of "Oh, Blondieee!" Prominent bits from the comic strip, including his daily collisions with the postman and the famous, immense Dagwood sandwich, were also a continuing and endearing part of the series.

Post-career, Arthur Lake's name was of interest mainly because of continuing fascination with the W. R. Hearst-Marion Davies menage. His marriage to Patricia Van Cleve had supposedly been an arranged one. Rumors that Mrs. Lake was really the love child of Davies and Hearst provided titillating tittle-tattle never actually proved or disproved.

REVIEWS

The Air Circus: Lake is the comedian of the picture, and a very good one. He also stands out in his use of dialogue. *Variety* 9/5/28.

Indiscreet: Arthur Lake, as a love-sick kid, gets his points over well. *Variety* 5/13/31.

Blondie: Lake uses many of the mannerisms of the pen-and-ink Dagwood. His is an excellent recreation of the character. *Variety* 11/2/38.

Beware of Blondie: Lake is up to all the demands of the character he has played for so long. *Variety* 4/5/50.

Landis, Cullen, Nashville, Tennessee,
1895/98–1975

Filmography: Classic Images (Spring/Summer 1970)

Silent: Cullen Landis began his film career about 1916, his earliest-known film being *Joy and the Dragon* (billed as J. Cullen Landis). He appeared in the 1917 serial *Who Is Number One?* and was a stalwart in Christie comedies, making almost 50 by 1923.

Landis proved to be a popular player in almost 60 features, among them *The Fighting Coward, Youth to Youth, The Man Life Passed By, Soul of the Beast, Peacock Feathers, Jack of Hearts, Frenzied Flames* and *The Fog.* There also were two more serials: *On Guard* and *A Crimson Flash.* Last silent: *The Little Wild Girl* (1928), made after his first sound film.

Sound: Landis had the male lead in the first all-talking film, Warner Bros.' *Lights of New York* (1928), made with the Vitaphone process. He made only one other, the obscure quickie *The Convict's Code* in 1930. After his on-camera career ended, he became a well-known industrial filmmaker for automobile companies and a director of documentaries and TV programs.

Comments: Despite his short stature, Cullen Landis was a very popular star in silents, playing in various genres including many vigorous adventure melodramas. His disappearance after sound arrived was sudden. This may have been due to his own reluctance to tackle the new medium as to any lack of suitability, but the "honor" of appearing in the first all-talkie proved illusory and a bane to both its leading players.

Female lead Helene Costello had an equally steep plunge from her pinnacle of minor stardom. Neither she nor Landis recovered from the generally poor reception of the film. It was simply of low quality, both in the sound recording and the story itself. The fact that it was so highly publicized meant all eyes were upon it — and they did not like what they saw.

REVIEWS

Lights of New York: The reviewers disagreed on Cullen Landis's performance in this seminal film. One states that he would never make anyone believe his characterization, and that he seemed to talk with much effort. Another thought that he was surprisingly good in his handling of the dialogue. *Variety* 7/11/28, *Harrison's Reports* 7/14/28.

Lane, Lupino (Henry Lupino), London,
England, 1892–1959

Silent: Appearing on the British stage from the age of four and in British-made comedy shorts, diminutive Lupino Lane, a member of the famous Lupino theatrical family, brought his great acrobatic skills and likable personality to America in 1920. He appeared in Broadway musicals and subsequently the Ziegfeld Follies.

About 1923 Lane went to Hollywood to become a star for Educational Pictures and his two-reelers are considered to be probably the best that that company made. One of his specialties was spoofing prominent features of the day like *Ben-Hur.* He also was seen in a couple of features of his own, the first of which was *A Friendly Husband,* in which he starred. Last silent feature: *Isn't Life Wonderful?* (1924).

Sound: Naturally Lupino Lane had an English accent but it was a pleasant enough one that certainly would have enabled him to play character roles in American films. He ultimately decided, however, that his future lay back in his native country.

Lane only made a few talkies in the U.S., all musicals, beginning with *The Show of Shows* and *The Love Parade* in late 1929. Two followed in 1930: *Bride of the Regiment* and *Golden Dawn.* He also made the Technicolor Vitaphone short *Evolution of the Dance.*

Returning to England shortly thereafter, Lane starred in and directed several features and appeared on the stage as well. He was in the long-running musical comedy *Me and My Gal* that featured the enormously popular dance "The Lambeth Walk." He was a cousin of actress Ida Lupino.

REVIEWS

The Love Parade: Lane has a production number to himself, a tricky little tune that serves him well. The Lane and Lillian Roth combination provides what comedy isn't otherwise found. As a comedian Lane comes through. *Variety* 11/27/29.

Bride of the Regiment: Lupino Lane, as a ballet master, performs his comedy assignments exceedingly well. *Variety* 5/28/30.

Golden Dawn: There was some difference of opinion. One review said that the film was without comedy because Lupino Lane was expected to be funny but he wasn't. Another stated that the comedy provoked by Lupino Lane and some others did provide some comedy relief. *Variety* 7/30/30, *Harrison's Reports* 8/2/30.

Langdon, Harry, Council Bluffs, Iowa,
1884–1944

Filmography: Films in Review (Oct. 1967); List of films in *Film Dope* (Nov. 1985)

Silent: Harry Langdon came to films in 1923 after a lengthy and successful career in stock and vaudeville. In the latter, his act "Johnny's New Car" was a standard for over 20 years. For three years he worked at Mack Sennett's studio turning out two-reelers and honing his screen persona. It was not to be completely perfected until he began appearing in features at First National.

Langdon's 23 or so silent shorts included *Picking Peaches*, his first, *The Sea Squawk, Boobs in the Wood, Saturday Afternoon, The First Hundred Years* and *Feet of Mud*. It was with *The Luck of the Foolish* that he began to show something of his soon-to-be-famous characterization. Two of his frequent co-stars were Natalie Kingston and comic—and literal—heavy Vernon Dent.

Langdon gained much popularity with Sennett, especially in his later two-reelers, although that studio with its reliance on fast action and often mindless gags was not the ideal place for his style of comedy. By 1925 he was being called "The Maharajah of Mirth" and the comedy find of the decade. His first feature, *His First Flame*, was made for Sennett although it was released as a three-reel picture.

It was at this point that Frank Capra began to work on Langdon's films. In his first released feature, 1926's *Tramp, Tramp, Tramp*, the comedian found the formula for success. He perfected the childlike persona which he used most successfully in *The Strong Man* and *Long Pants* and increasingly less so in the films he personally directed including *The Chaser* and *Three's a Crowd*. Last silent: *Heart Trouble* (1928).

Sound: Langdon's first forays into sound were in a series of Hal Roach shorts in 1929 and '30. His first sound features *A Soldier's Plaything* and *See America Thirst* came in late 1930. He was off the screen for most of the next two years, returning for some Educational shorts in 1932 and then a role in Al Jolson's not-very-successful *Hallelujah, I'm a Bum* (1933).

Langdon signed with Columbia in 1934 for an additional series of shorts and continued to appear in scattered 1930s full-length films like *Atlantic Adventure, My Weakness* and *Zenobia*. In the latter, a Roach film, he co-starred with a temporarily Laurel-less Oliver Hardy. He was not seen on American screens from 1936 to '38 although he worked on screenplays and appeared in English films and directed one as well.

In the 1940s Langdon had leads (*Misbehaving Husbands, House of Errors*) and small roles in quickies as well as continuing his appearances in shorts, some with El Brendel. Other features included *All-American Co-ed, Double Trouble, Hot Rhythm, Block Busters* with the East Side Kids and his last, *Swingin' on a Rainbow*. He was still in harness when he was fatally stricken and some of his completed films were released posthumously.

Comments: Harry Langdon's rise and fall were rapid, particularly the latter, and unlike some of the other great silent comedians he did not live to see his reputation restored. That reputation was sullied by his last unsuccessful silents and by Frank Capra, who once served as his gag man and director.

Capra may have helped greatly to popularize Langdon but also was one cause of his ultimate failure. He publicly accused the comedian of being egotistical, impossible to work for and improperly insistent on being involved in every aspect of his films. He strongly implied that he was the sole cause of Langdon's success.

Of Langdon's almost 70 shorts and 25 or so features from 1923 to 1945, only a relative handful could be called more than routine. But he brought a unique persona to the screen that allowed him to stand out from every other cinema comic actor. It was what has been described as malevolent infantilism.

Langdon's character was almost babylike on the surface but was nonetheless possessed of great complexity. His clown-white face bespoke gullible innocence but when he finally caught up to what was going on, he could express many emotions.

He was a master of small gestures. Emotions were expressed almost imperceptibly with slow blinking or staring of the eyes and the slight movement of hands or feet. Also among Langdon's litany of gestures were the finger shake, the back and forth dance and the futile rubbing of the face.

Sound revealed that Langdon's voice fit his physical appearance satisfactorily but what voice could fit that fragile persona? It was yet another blow to his career. His genius, if genius it was, lay in his mimicry and the expressive use of his hands, not in his ability to tell a gag. He was made for silence.

The critic James Agee said of Langdon that he had "one queerly-toned unique little reed. But out of it he could get incredible melodies." He was not the kind of comedian who always made audiences roar with laughter but for all too brief a time he certainly had them in the palm of his hand.

REVIEWS

See America Thirst: More pantomime and less dialogue would better suit the Langdon characteristics of misty eyes and stark white face. It would have created some subtlety that's totally lacking. His voice is already known through his shorts. *Variety* 12/17/30.

A Soldier's Plaything: For those who like their comedy rowdy and sometimes bordering on vulgarity Langdon does good work. *Harrison's Reports* 1/3/31.

Hallelujah, I'm a Bum: Harry Langdon uses his familiar deadpan in a sort of technocratic role. *Variety* 2/14/33.

Atlantic Adventure: Langdon, as a news cameraman, provides laughs and is a splendid foil. *Variety* 1/4/35.

Misbehaving Husbands: About the only redeeming feature of this absurd comedy drama is Harry Langdon's sprightly comedy characterization. Hollywood will have to do better by him. He shows possibilities in moving away from his former pantomimic type of clowning, although he was not capably directed here.

(Langdon was teamed with former silent siren Betty Blythe in this marital comedy which was to be the first of a series. Its lack of success precluded further pairings.) *Variety* 1/15/41.

La Plante, Laura, (Laura La Plant?), St.
Louis, Missouri, 1903/04–1996

Filmography: Films in Review (Oct. 1980); *Classic Images* (Oct. 1982); List of films in *Sweethearts of the Sage*

Silent: Pert Laura La Plante began her career in Christie comedies in 1919 and also appeared in the serial *The Great Gamble*. Her first feature was 1920's *813*, in which she was way down in the cast list. She also supported western stars Hoot Gibson and Art Acord.

La Plante had her first important role in Charles Ray's *The Old Swimmin' Hole* in 1921. That same year she signed with Universal and continued appearing in one- and two-reelers such as the "Bringing Up Father" (Maggie and Jiggs) series. Named a Wampas Baby Star in 1923, her major breakthrough came in *Sporting Youth* the next year.

Other La Plante films were *Shootin' for Love*, *Burning Words*, *Finders Keepers*, *Butterfly*, *Smouldering Fires* and *Poker Faces*. Among her notable successes were *Skinner's Dress Suit* (in which she appeared with frequent co-star Reginald Denny) and *The Cat and the Canary*. She was also in the serials *Around the World in 18 Days* and *Perils of the Yukon*. Last silent: *Home James* (1928).

Sound: La Plante made about 20 talkies and part-talkies, most of them completed by the end of 1931. The first was *The Last Warning* in 1929; others that year were *Show Boat* and *Scandal*. Among her other sound films were the musicals *Captain of the Guard*

and *The King of Jazz*, and *Lonely Wives*, *Meet the Wife*, *Men Are Like That* and *God's Gift to Women*.

La Plante appeared in a couple of Masquer two-reelers (1931, 1933), and her last U.S. film in the '30s was the quickie Peerless melodrama *The Sea Ghost*. During 1933 to 1935, she made some films in England and then only two more American movies ensued: *Little Mr. Jim* (1946) and, ten years later, *Spring Reunion*. In the 1950s she made stage and television appearances as well.

Comments: With her signature close-cropped blonde hair, Laura La Plante was a popular star in the 1920s, probably Universal's biggest female star. The talkies were not kind to her, although her voice was adequate, and her roles quickly became secondary leads for smaller studios.

La Plante was all too soon another fallen silent star. Although she took advantage of English filmmakers' desire to cast American (ex-)stars in their mid–1930s pictures, it did nothing to resuscitate her career.

REVIEWS

Scandal: Reviewers differed slightly. One said that La Plante had a speaking voice which should improve. Another stated that she had a pleasing voice and was a good actress and an appealing heroine. *Variety* 4/24/29, *Harrison's Reports* 5/4/29.

Captain of the Guard: It never seemed as though Miss La Plante was doing her own singing. She is better as a comedienne than as a singing French girl. *New York Times* 3/29/30.

Lonely Wives: La Plante is only moderately interesting. *New York Times* 3/16/31.

God's Gift to Women: La Plante gets more out of the picture than the other players. She looks like the screen's flashiest blonde and acts well. *Variety* 4/22/31.

Meet the Wife: The film's outstanding assets are Laura La Plante's appearance and performance. She looks delectable and does exceedingly well as a mildly dumb blonde. The question is why she is cast in such as this. *Variety* 6/23/31.

Men Are Like That: La Plante is not convincing in the role. (Her co-star, a young actor named John Wayne, was also panned.) *New York Times* 8/17/31.

Little Mister Jim: Laura La Plante is adequate. *Variety* 6/5/46.

Spring Reunion: Laura La Plante, as the understanding mother, gets more out of her role than anyone else. *Variety* 3/13/57, *Harrison's Reports* 3/16/57.

La Rocque, Rod (Roderick or Rodrique La
Rocque), Chicago, Illinois, 1896/98–1969

Filmography: Films in Review (Aug.-Sept. 1977);

Classic Images (June 1987); List of films in *Eighty Silent Film Stars*

Silent: After working in the theater, Rod La Rocque became an extra at Essanay about 1914. He was a supporting player and second lead from 1917 to 1925 for Cecil B. DeMille and others in films such as *The Ten Commandments*, *Hidden Fires*, *Easy to Get*, *Feet of Clay* and *Jazzmania*.

La Rocque became a star in *The Coming of Amos* (1925). Appearances thereafter included *Braveheart*, *The Fighting Eagle*, *Captain Swagger*, *The Cruise of the Jasper B* and *Gigolo*. Last silent: *Our Modern Maidens* (1929), with synchronized music and sound effects, made after his first talkie.

Sound: Rod La Rocque's first sound vehicle was *The Man and the Moment* (1929), a Billie Dove starrer. Others that year were *The Delightful Rogue* and *The Locked Door*. He made a few in 1930, including *Beau Bandit* and *One Romantic Night* (Lillian Gish's first sound film), and then returned for one more major starring role in 1933's *SOS Iceberg* with German actress (and later filmmaker) Leni Riefenstahl.

From 1935 until his last film in 1941, Frank Capra's *Meet John Doe*, La Rocque appeared in numerous supporting roles, sometimes as a villain, and a very occasional lead in B efforts. These included *Hi Gaucho*, *Till We Meet Again*, *Beyond Tomorrow* and *The Preview Murder Mystery*.

Comments: Dark, suave Rod La Rocque labored long in the film vineyards before he attained stardom, but he could always be depended on to give a competent performance. At six-foot-three he literally stood out from most other actors as he supported (and towered above) such leading ladies as Mae Murray, Gloria Swanson, Jetta Goudal, Corinne Griffith, and Pola Negri.

La Rocque made the transition to sound with ease. His voice was a perfect match for his physical presence and he brought a certain easy and likable self-deprecation to even his villainous roles. His absence from talkies in the early 1930s was at least partly due to touring in a play with his wife, ex-silent star Vilma Banky.

REVIEWS

The Man and the Moment: Both leads give a worthwhile performance, especially Rod La Rocque. *Variety* 8/7/29.

The Locked Door: The trouble with it is that the leading man part played by Rod LaRocque, instead of being a hero, is a villain. *Harrison's Reports* 1/25/30.

Beau Bandit: La Rocque, as a suave and refined Latin-American bandit, gives one of the poorest reading of lines in his career. Probably his inabil-

ity to get the shading of the humor had a lot to do with the mild effect. *Harrison's Reports* 3/29/30, *Variety* 6/18/30.

One Romantic Night: La Rocque takes the part of the Prince. He plays with an overbearance that at times becomes insufferable. He is wooden. *Harrison's Reports* 5/3/30, *Variety* 6/4/30.

SOS Iceberg: Rod La Rocque is shunted into the background. *Variety* 9/26/33, *Harrison's Reports* 9/30/33.

Frisco Waterfront: Rod La Rocque gives an oftentimes slipshod characterization in an unsympathetic role. *Variety* 12/25/35.

Laurel, Stan (Arthur S. Jefferson), Ulverston, England, 1890–1965; and Oliver, Hardy, Harlem, Georgia, 1892–1957

Filmography: List of films in *Classic Images* (Feb. 1964); *E-Go Collectors Series* (Apr. 1976); *Film Dope* (Sept. 1981, Hardy alone; Nov. 1985, Laurel alone and Laurel and Hardy together).

Stan Laurel, Silent: Stan Laurel arrived in the United States as a member of Fred Karno's Pantomime Company troupe and understudy to Charlie Chaplin. He entered films about 1917 at Universal, perhaps in *Nuts in May*. After appearing in several more pictures in 1918, he played in vaudeville for almost two years.

In the 1920s, Laurel alternated between directing and on-camera appearances that were not too successful. He was still trying to find a comic style and often seemed content with imitating Chaplin. His most popular ventures were those in which he kidded popular films of the day.

Among Laurel's parodies were *Mud and Sand*, *The Soilers*, *When Knights Were Cold* and *Dr. Pyckle and Mr. Pride*. He was by no means the only comic to do this so even these sometimes amusing efforts were not all that original. Among Laurel's other pictures were *No Place Like Jail*, *Kill or Cure*, *Phoney Photos* and *West of Hot Dog*. He apparently did not have any solo feature roles during the silent era.

Stan Laurel, Sound: Stan Laurel founded his own production company which made some western movies in 1938 and '39. He apparently made no solo sound film appearances. In 1961 he was awarded a special Oscar which he was too ill to receive in person. It was accepted for him by Danny Kaye although Laurel had apparently wanted Jerry Lewis.

Oliver Hardy, Silent: After opening Milledgeville, Georgia's first movie theater, Oliver Hardy joined the Lubin studios in Florida. They had been looking for a Roscoe Arbuckle type; i.e., a "fat boy." He was made to imitate the enormously popular (and just plain enormous) Arbuckle, even to the latter's stomach-bouncing routine.

Hardy also performed other tasks at the studio, thereby grounding himself thoroughly in various aspects of filmmaking. (It was supposedly at Lubin he got the nickname "Babe.") He eventually joined Vitagraph, acting in and sometimes directing Larry Semon comedies in which he often was the "heavy."

Other studios for which Hardy worked were VIM and Chadwick. He frequently played the villain in Chaplin imitator Billy West's comedies and at one point in his career was teamed with skinny comic Billy Ray. This foreshadowed his far more successful teaming.

Some of Hardy's signature "shtick," including the delicate hand gestures, could be seen even in early films. Among his two-reel pictures were *Kidnapping the Kid, The Tramps, Babe's School Days, One Two Many, The Candy Kid, He Laughs Last, No Wedding Bells* and *Is Marriage the Bunk?* He continued making solo appearances as late as 1928.

"Babe" Hardy's features from 1922 included *Little Wildcat, One Stolen Night, The Girl in the Limousine, The Wizard of Oz, Stop, Look and Listen* and *The Gentle Cyclone.* Last silent feature: *No Man's Law* (1927).

Oliver Hardy, Sound: At a time when Laurel and Hardy were temporarily between Hal Roach contracts, Hardy was teamed with Harry Langdon, possibly in an effort to supplant Laurel. Their one film together was *Zenobia* in 1939. He also played character roles in two later features, John Wayne's *The Fighting Kentuckian* (1949) and Bing Crosby's *Riding High* (1950).

Laurel and Hardy, Silent: Although Stan Laurel and Oliver Hardy appeared in the same films several times, the first possibly being *Lucky Dog*, they did not do so as an official team. Laurel also directed Hardy at least twice, in *Madame Mystery* and *Yes, Yes, Nanette.*

Laurel and Hardy's intentional and, in retrospect inspired, teaming was engineered by Hal Roach in *Putting Pants on Philip* (1927). This came about (or so the story goes) when Hardy burned himself in a household accident and Laurel substituted for him in a film. Roach liked what he saw and told Laurel to write himself into Hardy's next film.

The "Boys" went on to make many two-reelers like *Leave 'Em Laughing, You're Darn Tootin', The Second Hundred Years, Liberty, Big Business, Double Whoopee, Two Tars* and *Wrong Again.* They did not appear in any silent features together.

Laurel and Hardy, Sound: Laurel and Hardy's first talkie was the appropriately named short *Unaccustomed as We Are* (1929). Their voices proved perfectly matched to their personas and sound seemed to make little difference in the way they worked. If anything, it enhanced their popularity. Hardy's very pleasant singing voice was heard several times in pictures thereafter.

Other Laurel and Hardy sound shorts, which they made until 1935, included *Angora Love, Below Zero, Hog Wild, Laughing Gravy, Any Old Port, The Music Box* (an Academy Award winner for Best Short Subject), *Twice Two, Dirty Work, Oliver the Eighth* and *Tit for Tat.* Their last was *Thicker Than Water.*

Some of the earlier shorts also were made in Spanish, German and Italian; the team read their lines phonetically from cue cards. In the mid-'40s they made a short film in color about the various uses of trees.

The first teaming of "The Boys" in a feature was in MGM's all-star *The Hollywood Revue of 1929*, in which they performed a magic sketch. This was followed by their use as comedy relief in 1930's *Rogue Song*, footage apparently added after the film had been completed.

Nineteen thirty-one's *Pardon Us* marked Laurel and Hardy's first starring feature. Although far from their best, it did showcase Hardy's tenor voice in the song "Lazy Moon." Besides appearing in their own features they made "guest" appearances in *Hollywood Party* and *Pick a Star.*

The first couple of the team's full-length films still had the feel of patched-together two-reelers. Their first fully coherent stories, *The Devil's Brother* (a.k.a. *Fra Diavolo*) and *Babes in Toyland* (a.k.a. *March of the Wooden Soldiers*) were based upon stage operettas.

With 1934's *Sons of the Desert*, now considered the team's best, they had their first feature which truly was an integrated whole. Among their other starring feature films in the 1930s, mainly for Hal Roach, were *Bonnie Scotland, Our Relations, Way Out West*, also considered one of their best films, *Block-Heads* and *Flying Deuces.*

Laurel and Hardy's last operetta *The Bohemian Girl* came in 1936. The musical melange *Swiss Miss* may have been an original story but it had an operetta feel to it. In it was the scene that critic James Agee found so hilarious: While moving a piano across a swaying wooden suspension bridge, they meet a gorilla coming in the other direction.

In 1940 the team made their last features for Hal Roach, *A Chump at Oxford* and *Saps at Sea.* The next year saw the beginning of their rapid decline after they signed with Fox and then MGM. Their first post–Roach picture was *Great Guns.* Others in the first half of that decade were *A-Haunting We Will Go, Air Raid Wardens* and *The Big Noise* (1944), considered their worst feature.

Laurel and Hardy's two 1943 efforts, *Jitterbugs* and *The Dancing Masters*, were probably their best post–Roach features, particularly the former. By 1945 their final American movies *Nothing but Trouble* and *The Bullfighters* had been completed.

Several years after a wildly successful tour of England, "The Boys" made one more ill-starred film known variously as *Atoll K, Utopia* and *Robinson Crusoeland* in 1950. It featured an international, and ill-matched, cast.

After their careers ended and they were virtually forgotten, clips from Laurel and Hardy pictures appeared in several compilations of silent comedies. They were even featured in cartoons and were also the subject of a *This Is Your Life* television program. A comeback of sorts was apparently planned when Hardy became too ill to consider working.

Comments: Although Stan Laurel and Oliver Hardy made numerous solo screen appearances before their teaming, it is barely conceivable to think of them as anything but a team. They were the beloved "Boys" and both of them contributed mightily to the success of their pictures.

Fortunately they had different comic strengths to contribute. Laurel's forte was more in reacting to others, perhaps a clue as to why he did not prove strong enough to carry his own films. As "Stan" he generally was passive but he could turn aggressive, and even violent, upon occasion.

"Ollie" Hardy thought himself to be the smart one and was usually the progenitor of their sometimes ill-considered ventures. Always confident, his poorly placed aplomb led often to disastrous results. Not for nothing was he called "sublimely incompetent."

There is no question that Laurel was the most important creator of their comic genius. He had a firm understanding of comedy even though he had not been too successful in his own career. For instance, he always insisted that their films be shot in sequence to preserve the build-up of the gags. His credo was "Never try to outsmart the audience."

What is the secret of Laurel and Hardy's enduring appeal? As one writer said, "In terms of sheer laugh content and brilliance of comic invention and construction, [they] take second place to no one.... Their humor is universal and timeless and ... their comedies seem even funnier as time goes on."

It is certainly true that most of Laurel and Hardy's pictures were funny, some less so and some hilariously so. But that is no guarantee of adulation 65 years later. There obviously is more. Their latter-day fans are so devoted they founded the Sons of the Desert, an international group devoted to perpetuating their memory.

Perhaps the major factor in the team's great appeal is their ability to gain the audience's empathy; they evoke warmth and sympathy. Their humor was not just wisecracks and one-liners. Unlike many another comedy duo, they genuinely seemed to like each other.

"The Boys" established familiar characters which were reinforced by identifiable physical actions: Hardy's tie twiddling, exaggerated courtliness and into-the-camera stare, Laurel's crying, their exasperated mutual shoving, etc.

There were also immediately identifiable catchlines like "Here's *another* nice mess you've gotten me into" and "Why don't you do something to *help* me?" The situations in which they found themselves had timeless appeal as well: poverty, marital strife, work problems, unrequited love.

The "Stan" and "Ollie" characters seemed to appeal to all age groups and across national boundaries as well; they were lionized more abroad than in their own country. Their tours in England were phenomenally successful and much later there was even a best-selling recording in the U.K. of songs from their films.

Laurel and Hardy also had a stock company of players who did their bits for the comedy. Among the more memorable were Mae Busch, Jimmy Finlayson, Thelma Todd, Charlie Hall, Anita Garvin and Edgar Kennedy.

Although Laurel played a large role in the production of their shorts, credit should also go to directors such as Leo McCarey who directed an important part of their *oeuvre* from 1927 to 1930.

In their comedies after 1940, Laurel was usually downgraded to a basically nitwit stooge. Because he had aged so noticeably, that persona was not very funny. Also, he was dispirited because the studios were no longer interested in his creative contributions to scripts. Hardy was perhaps less affected; he still apparently wanted to perform.

Laurel and Hardy are credited with having made 105 comedies as a team. Not all of them were good and some of them apparently no longer even exist. What does remain more than amply proves that the team was so much more than the sum of its parts. Separately, they were all right; together, they were magic!

LAUREL AND HARDY REVIEWS

Pardon Us: Reviewers differed slightly although all thought the storyline was deficient; that it was a two-reel idea on a six-reel frame. One said the film proves nothing for Laurel and Hardy; they need story strength. In shorts they are valuable property but one more feature like this may harm their standing in the two-reel field as well as wash them up as full-length prospects. Another reviewer thought they were personally excellent. *Variety* 8/25/31, *Harrison's Reports* 8/29/31.

Pack Up Your Troubles: Again reviews diverged. One opined that 70 minutes of slapstick was a tall order for Laurel and Hardy and they hardly filled it. Another said that although the gags were not new they are still comical because of the way Laurel and Hardy put them over. *Variety* 10/4/32, *Harrison's Reports* 10/15/32.

Sons of the Desert: Contemporaneous reviewers were not as enthusiastic about this picture as later generations were. One said the story was thin to the point of attenuation and that the stars were about as usual. Another admitted that Laurel and Hardy fans would be amused by this comedy; it is filled with funny gags. *Variety* 1/9/34, *Harrison's Reports* 1/13/34.

Way Out West: The picture just about extinguishes the good results achieved in their previous film *Our Relations*. It will be tough sledding for the audience. It follows closely the old methods used in their shorts; there's too much driving home of gags.

(Again such reviews show how reactions to films change over the years. This film is now considered one of their funniest features while the gimmicky *Our Relations* is not highly favored in their canon.) *Variety* 5/5/37.

Block-Heads: An awful letdown for them. Many two-reelers have been more justified in trying to bluff their way to feature length. It didn't have much in the way of dialogue for Laurel and Hardy; they seldom have much to say. *Variety* 8/31/38.

The Dancing Masters: The pair go through their usual slapdash stuff. Laurel is the simpleton, and Hardy the one who usually gets clipped by the former's nonsense. *Variety* 10/27/43.

Atoll K: An improper mix of fantasy, satire and slapstick. Old Laurel and Hardy routines seem to lack their previous zest. *Variety* 11/21/50.

OLIVER HARDY REVIEWS

Zenobia: Reviewers differed. One said that Hardy in a straight comedy role provided a minimum of slapstick antics and knockabout stunts. He demonstrated he could easily handle straight comedy. Another believed that Hardy was an excellent short subject comedian but was bad when put into a feature. When coupled with the elephant (Zenobia) it was unbearable.

(Although there may have been an intention to form a Hardy-Langdon team, their actual screen time together was brief and they struck no sparks.) *Variety* 3/15/39, *Harrison's Reports* 4/22/39.

La Verne, Lucille, Nashville or Memphis, Tennessee, 1872–1945

Silent: On the silent screen, Lucille La Verne is perhaps best remembered for her role as the mean crone Mother Frochard in D. W. Griffith's *Orphans of the Storm* (1921). In the theater since 1888, she was a distinguished actress with her own stock company and a memorable Broadway role in the long-running 1923 rural drama *Sun-Up*.

La Verne's first features were made in 1916 (*Sweet Kitty Bellairs*, *The Thousand Dollar Husband*) and she made a handful more over the years including *Polly of the Circus*, *The White Rose*, *Zaza*, *America* and the film version of *Sun-Up* in 1925. Last silent: *The Last Moment* (1928).

Sound: The talking picture revealed to movie audiences what theater audiences already knew: Lucille La Verne had a unique voice. Deep and hoarse, it gave her roles great distinctiveness and it was memorialized in her final film role as the voice of the wicked Queen in *Snow White and the Seven Dwarfs* (1937).

The La Verne voice also enabled her to actually play men's roles, such as her portrayal of Shylock in an English production of *The Merchant of Venice*. Legend has it that she approached D. W. Griffith with an offer to star in the *title role* of his 1930 production *Abraham Lincoln*. She did receive a part in the film but it was a bit, that of a midwife.

Other talkies in which La Verne appeared, usually in small parts, were *Sinner's Holiday*, *An American Tragedy*, *Little Caesar* (as the scuzzy Ma Magdalena), *Breach of Promise*, *Wild Horse Mesa*, *Pilgrimage* and *The Mighty Barnum*.

One of La Verne's last roles was an echo of the one she had played in *Orphans of the Storm*. It was as The Vengeance, another crone of the French Revolution, in *A Tale of Two Cities* (1935). After that she was not seen again on-screen but certainly was memorably heard in the Walt Disney classic.

REVIEWS

Sinner's Holiday: A truly fine performance by Lucille La Verne of the only sympathetic character in the picture.

(This was a story of carnival life in which La Verne played the mother of Jimmy Cagney in his first film.) *Variety* 10/15/30.

Alias the Doctor: La Verne is effective. *New York Times* 3/3/32.

Strange Adventure: La Verne goes overboard in one heavily dramatic scene. *Variety* 2/14/33.

School for Girls: The outstanding performance is that of Lucille La Verne as the cruel boss. She gives it a fine note of authority. *Variety* 2/20/35.

A Tale of Two Cities: LaVerne overplays her role. *Variety* 1/1/36.

Lawrence, Florence (Florence Bridge-
wood?), Hamilton, Ontario, 1886/90–1938
Filmography: Films in Review (Aug.-Sept. 1980)
Silent: Called "Baby Flo, the Child Wonder" as a child actress, Florence Lawrence was to be known worldwide as "The Biograph Girl." She may have been in films as early as 1907 for Edison and, besides Biograph, was starred at Victor, Lubin, Vitagraph and IMP, where she was dubbed "The Imp Girl."

Lawrence may have been D. W. Griffith's first star and ultimately made over 200 films, mostly one-reelers. For a time she had her own production company. Her early films included *In Swift Waters, The Salvation Army Lass, The Taming of Jane, Sisters* and *The Closed Door.*

Elusive Isabel (1916) for Bluebird apparently was Lawrence's only full-length feature of the 'teens. In the 1920s she had billing in three, including *The Unfoldment* (1922) and *The Satin Girl* (1923). Last known silent: *Gambling Wives* (1924). She may have appeared unbilled in later films of the '20s, possibly *The Johnstown Flood* and *The Greater Glory* (both 1926).

Sound: Lawrence had bits or small roles in the talkies *Hard Hombre, Sinners in the Sun* and *Secrets* (1933 version), in which she portrayed one of Mary Pickford's middle-aged children along with other old-timers. She may have had bits in other pictures as well and she worked as an extra up to the time of her death.

Comments: The story of Florence Lawrence is one of almost archetypal triumph and tragedy. She once had the renown of much of the world and then was cast into almost total oblivion. Among the first stars to be billed by name, she was the recipient of one of the earliest publicity campaigns. As part of this, fake news of her death in a street-car accident was put about. It was greeted with the appropriate hysteria.

Lawrence was burned in a filming accident in 1914 and was off the screen for a while. Even had this not occurred, others had already begun to take her place in the public's fancy. She was evidently not the best manager of her career, perhaps lacking the necessary business skills.

In the 1930s, she was signed as one of a "stock company" of silent players who had fallen on hard days. This basically translated into doing occasional extra work. Ultimately the gesture was not enough; she took her own life.

Lease, Rex, Central City, West Virginia,
1901–1966
Silent: An extra from about 1922, Rex Lease had his first featured role two years later in *A Woman Who Sinned* and his first starring role in 1927's *Clancy's Kosher Wedding.* He also appeared in several westerns.

Other Lease pictures were *The Last Alarm, Somebody's Mother, The College Hero, Law of the Range, Moulders of Men, Broadway Daddies, Speed Classic* and *Riders of the Dark.* Last silent: *Two Sisters* (1929), with synchronized music.

Sound: Rex Lease continued to be a popular and top-billed leading man for several years in talkies. His first, in 1929, was the part-sound *The Younger Generation* and he went on to appear in such films as *In Old Cheyenne, The Lone Trail, Wings of Adventure, The Utah Kid, Borrowed Wives, Sunny Skies, The Cannonball Rider, Frontier Gal, The Cowboy and the Señorita* and *The Ghost Rider.*

After a while Lease's career came to be primarily in westerns which he made for such companies as Tiffany, World Wide, Superior, Crescent and Columbia. One of his last starring roles was in the 1936 serial *Custer's Last Stand,* although he was occasionally top-lined thereafter.

Lease then became a dependable supporting player to such western stars as Roy Rogers, Gene Autry, Bob Steele, Rex Allen and Johnny Mack Brown. He was seen on-screen in small roles until the '50s, his last appearance possibly being in 1957's *A Hatful of Rain.* He also made shorts.

Among Lease's serial appearances were *Sign of the Wolf, The Clutching Hand, The Mysterious Pilot, The Lone Ranger Rides Again, Daredevils of the West, The Crimson Ghost* and *Perils of the Wilderness.*

REVIEWS

Troopers Three: Rex Lease undertakes the type of role popularized by William Haines, an aggressively impudent person. *New York Times* 2/17/30.

Is There Justice: The cast is capable, among them Rex Lease as the news reporter. *Variety* 7/22/31.

Inside Information: Lease walks through the lead but gives no punch to the poorly told story. *Variety* 1/8/35.

The Silver Trail: Lease is the least colorful of the cowboy actors. His acting is okay but his physique and getup don't mix well with the western milieu. *Variety* 1/5/38.

Lebedeff, Ivan, Uspoliai, Lithuania,
1894/99–1953
Silent: With his slightly Tatar looks, mustache

and slicked-back hair, Ivan Lebedeff made a perfect gigolo and all-around suave villain of various nationalities. This persona was aided by the mystery of his background; he claimed to come from a family that was close to the Czar of Russia.

What is certain is that Lebedeff appeared in German and French films before coming to the U.S. in the mid–'20s to appear in D. W. Griffith's *The Sorrows of Satan*. He made a handful of other silent films including *The Angel of Broadway, The Love of Sunya, The Forbidden Woman, Let 'Er Go Gallagher* and *Walking Back*. Last silent: *The One Woman Idea* (1929), with synchronized music, released after his first talkie.

Sound: All but one of Ivan Lebedeff's 1929 motion pictures were sound; among them were *Sin Town, Street Girl* and *They Had to See Paris*. He had an unmistakable accent but his career was not unduly affected because he had already been stereotyped in "exotic" roles.

During the 1930s Lebedeff continued playing such parts in films like *Midnight Mystery, The Gay Diplomat* (title role), *Bombshell, Moulin Rouge, China Seas, History Is Made at Night* and *You Can't Cheat an Honest Man*.

Lebedeff continued on-screen through the mid–'40s, with character roles in *Rhapsody in Blue, Passport to Alcatraz, The Shanghai Gesture, Foreign Agent* and *Mission to Moscow*. In the early '50s he scored a mini-comeback in *The Snows of Kilimanjaro, California Conquest* and *The War of the Worlds*.

REVIEWS

Street Girl: Ivan Lebedeff creditably impersonates Prince Nickolaus, playing the role with admirable restraint. *Variety* 8/7/29.

They Had to See Paris: Lebedeff contributes a good performance. *New York Times* 10/12/29.

The Cuckoos: The heavy is played by Ivan Lebedeff who starts the troubles. *Variety* 4/30/30.

Goin' to Town: Lebedeff is cast as an impossible gigolo. *Variety* 5/15/35.

Lee, Gwen (Gwendolyn; Gwendolyn Le Pinski or Lepinski), Hastings, Nebraska, 1904/05–1961

Silent: Tall, blonde and sharp-featured, Gwen Lee was a dependable MGM "other woman," occasional villainess and friend of the heroine during the last half of the 1920s. Her first films were *Pretty Ladies* and *His Secretary* in 1925.

Other Lee pictures included *Upstage, Diamond Handcuffs, Laugh, Clown, Laugh, Her Wild Oat, Adam and Evil* and *The Lone Wolf Returns*. She was named a Wampas Baby Star of 1928. Last silents:

Show Girl, with synchronized sound effects and music, and *The Baby Cyclone*, released about the same time in 1928.

Sound: A Lady of Chance, a 1928 part-talker, was Lee's introduction to sound. All her 1929 films were sound or part-sound as well; they included *The Hollywood Revue of 1929, Lucky Boy, The Man and the Moment* and *Untamed*.

Lee was released by MGM in 1930 and she freelanced for various studios, eventually winding up in small roles in quickies for Poverty Row studios, and in shorts. Among her films were *Our Blushing Brides, Paid, Alias Mary Smith, City Park, $20 a Week, Fury, My Dear Miss Aldrich* and *Mannequin*. Her last known film appearances were made in 1938.

Comments: Gwen Lee supported the top MGM actresses including Greta Garbo, Crawford and Shearer, and the likes of Colleen Moore when she (Lee) was on loanout. She was not conventionally pretty except for striking blue eyes, and her brassiness made her a convincing wisecracker (with the aid of titles in silents) or a downright "bad girl." She was perhaps somewhat comparable to Lilyan Tashman in the silents and Eve Arden in talkies.

Lee's height lent conviction to her usual sorts of roles but it worked against her ever becoming a leading lady. Her voice did fit her image perfectly and she continued appearing through much of the '30s although her roles in better films were minimal.

REVIEWS

A Lady of Chance: Gwen Lee is Norma Shearer's accomplice in the badger game. *Harrison's Reports* 1/19/29.

Untamed: Gwen Lee plays the hero's former sweetheart in Joan Crawford's maiden talkie. *Harrison's Reports* 12/7/29.

The Intruder: Lee is wasted in a poor assignment. *Variety* 4/25/33.

Lee, Lila (Augusta Appel), New York, New York, 1901/05–1973

Silent: Lila Lee, known as "Cuddles" in her early show business years, was in vaudeville with Gus Edwards. Her first films, made for Famous Players-Lasky, were *The Cruise of the Make-Believe* and *Such a Little Pirate* (1918). These were closely followed by her supporting role in DeMille's *Male and Female*.

Lee's 50 or so silents included *Crazy to Marry, Ebb Tide, Wandering Husbands, The Adorable Cheat, The Charm School, Rent Free* and *Is Matrimony a Failure?* Some of her billings, even after she became a Paramount star, were for supporting roles.

Teamed 11 times with leading man Thomas Meighan, Lee appeared opposite Wallace Reid as well. Her best-known silent role was undoubtedly as Valentino's naive young wife in *Blood and Sand*. Last silent: *The Black Pearl* (1928).

Sound: Lee was very busy at the dawn of the sound era appearing in nine films in 1929 alone, all of them in sound. Among these were *Queen of the Night Clubs*, *Live, Love and Laugh*, *Drag* and *The Argyle Case*.

Later Lee talkies included *Those Who Dance*, *Night of June 13*, *Lone Cowboy*, *The People's Enemy* and *A Nation Aflame* (1937), her last. Her appearance in the 1930 remake of *The Unholy Three*, starring Lon Chaney, may have been the highlight of her 35-plus film sound career.

Comments: Lila Lee was one of the prettiest of the second-string silent stars and an effective actress as well. Early in her career there was thought given to making her "another" Mary Pickford. Instead, she ended up in a series of generally undistinguished comedies and dramas.

As evidenced by the large number of films in which she appeared during 1929 and '30, Lee's voice and screen presence were deemed to be effective for talkies. It was said that her transition to the new medium was among the best of any silent actress and it was expected that she would be an important talkie star.

This did not happen for more than one reason. Lee was a good but not particularly charismatic actress and bouts of ill health (and possibly overindulgence in alcohol?) kept her off the screen for lengthy periods of time. Also she simply may have been overexposed in the earliest days of sound.

As the early '30s progressed, Lee tended to have leads in quickies made by such studios as Capital, World Wide, Allied and Chesterfield but her appearances in more prestigious films were usually in support (e.g. *The Ex-Mrs. Bradford*).

The last straw for Lila Lee's career may have been an incipient scandal concerning a suspicious death at an estate where she was staying, although she was not personally implicated. With all her undoubted disappointments, however, it reasonably could be said that Lee's talkie career was a modest success story.

Lee came back into public notice in a low-key way when the novel *There Must Be a Pony*, written by her son James Kirkwood, Jr., appeared. Supposedly based on his bittersweet relationship with his actor-parents, it did not reflect kindly on the now-deceased actress.

REVIEWS

Drag: Lila Lee will be on the "A" list after this picture gets around. Still youthful after 12 years in films, she is again on the upgrade with her best performance and biggest opportunity in years. She handles lines well and looks fine. *Variety* 6/26/29, *Harrison's Reports* 6/29/29.

Flight: Reviews did not agree on Lila Lee's performance. One said that her role was lightweight, with trite lines given to her. Another thought her work was excellent. *Variety* 9/18/29, *Harrison's Reports* 9/21/29.

Murder Will Out: Lee, in her small part, is a pleasing heroine but is not given the right opportunity. *Harrison's Reports* 4/12/30, *Variety* 5/7/30.

The Unholy Three: Lila Lee isn't nearly as convincing as Mae Busch was in the silent version. *Variety* 7/9/30.

Unholy Love: The leading actor has never turned in such a poor performance, and Lee is nearly as bad. *Variety* 8/30/32, *Harrison's Reports* 9/24/32.

Two Wise Maids: Lila Lee is featured but has only a bit. *Variety* 3/10/37.

Leiber, Fritz (also billed as Lieber), Chicago, Illinois, 1882/83–1949

Silent: With his distinctive Roman profile it is fitting that Fritz Leiber had his major silent film role as Caesar in the Theda Bara version of *Cleopatra* (1917). A renowned stage actor since 1902, with his own Shakespeare company, he had made his film debut as Mercutio in *Romeo and Juliet* (the Bushman-Bayne version) the previous year.

Leiber had the lead or top supporting roles in only six or so silent films, interspersing them with stage work. They included *The Primitive Call*, *If I Were King* and *The Song of the Soul*. Last silent: *The Queen of Sheba* (1921), in which he was the leading man as King Solomon.

Sound: In 1935 Fritz Leiber brought his resonant speaking voice back to the screen for the first of many distinguished supporting roles in *A Tale of Two Cities*. Other '30s roles were in *Anthony Adverse*, *The Story of Louis Pasteur*, *The Prince and the Pauper* and *The Hunchback of Notre Dame*.

In the following decade Leiber was seen in *The Sea Hawk*, *The Song of Bernadette*, *The Spanish Main*, *The Bells of San Angelo*, *Another Part of the Forest*, *Monsieur Verdoux* and his last, *Devil's Doorway* (1950).

REVIEWS

The Spanish Main: Fritz Leiber shows up well. *Variety* 10/3/45.

The Web: Leiber makes his short footage count. *Variety* 5/28/47.

Lewis, Mitchell, Syracuse, New York, 1880–1956

Silent: Tall and burly, Mitchell Lewis made his feature debut about 1916 in films like *The Flower of No Man's Land* and *The Come-Back.* He appeared steadily in leading and supporting roles, many times a "heavy," in numerous films right up to the dawn of sound. Among his early studios were Reliance and Thanhouser.

Other Lewis films included *The Mutiny of the Elsinore, The Marriage Chance, The Sea Wolf* (1926 version), *Ben-Hur, Rupert of Hentzau, Three Weeks, The Spoilers* (1923 version), *Old Ironsides, The Docks of New York* and *Beau Sabreur.* He also appeared in the serial *The Million Dollar Mystery.* Last silent: *Linda* (1929), with synchronized music and sound effects, made after his first part-talkie.

Sound: Lewis made his talkie debut in 1928's part-talkie *Tenderloin* and that year was also in the Vitaphone short *The Death Ship.* All but one of his '29 pictures had some sound sequences, including *One Stolen Night, The Bridge of San Luis Rey* and *Madame X.* His career continued without appreciable letup through the next 20 years, including appearances in shorts.

Lewis continued to portray villains frequently. Among his sound films were *Kongo, A Tale of Two Cities, Big City, Waikiki Wedding, Arsène Lupin Returns, Go West, Young Tom Edison, Courage of Lassie* and *All the Brothers Were Valiant,* which may have been his last in 1953.

REVIEWS

Tenderloin: Notable here is Mitchell Lewis who has the best voice. As the heavy he is always at home. *Variety* 3/21/28.

The Black Watch: Of comedy there is little or none, with Lewis handling the majority of a meager quantity. He could have stood more footage with his splendid voice and burly personality. *Variety* 5/15/29.

The Girl of the Port: Mitchell Lewis is the villain. *Harrison's Reports* 1/25/30.

Mysterious Mr. Moto: Lewis, too long absent from films, makes a minor part stand out. *Variety* 6/1/38.

Lewis, Ralph, Englewood, Evanston or Chicago, Illinois, 1872–1937

Silent: Memorable as Senator Austin Stoneman in *Birth of a Nation,* Ralph Lewis was a frequent D. W. Griffith character player who began his career about 1912, possibly at Reliance-Majestic. The first feature appearances came in 1914 in such pictures as *The Avenging Conscience, Home, Sweet Home* and *The Gangsters.* He had previously appeared on the stage.

Lewis was seen steadily throughout the silent era in films that included *Macbeth* (1916 version), *Fires of Youth, Outside the Law, Broad Daylight, Vengeance of the Deep, Dante's Inferno, Who Cares, The Lady from Hell* and *Casey Jones.* Last silent: *Crooks Can't Win* (1928).

Sound: Ralph Lewis's first part-sound film and his only one in 1929 was *The Girl in the Glass Cage.* In 1930 he again appeared for Griffith in that director's penultimate film and first talkie *Abraham Lincoln.* Until the time of his death he alternated between small roles in "A" films (*San Francisco, Diamond Jim, Maid of Salem, The Buccaneer*) and larger ones in quickies and westerns.

Among Lewis's other films were *The Fourth Alarm, American Madness, Riot Squad, Terror of the Plains, Outlaw Rule, Thanks a Million* and *Singing Outlaw.* He also appeared in the serial *The Lost City* (1934). His final films were posthumously released.

Lewis, Sheldon, Philadelphia, Pennslyvania, 1869–1958

Silent: After 30 years on-stage, Sheldon Lewis's feature career began about 1915 with such films as *The House of Fear* and *The Menace of the Mute.* In that year he also appeared in Pearl White's serial *The Exploits of Elaine.* His feature roles were relatively sparse until 1923 but from then to the end of the silent era he often made more than ten a year, frequently playing heavies.

Lewis's films included *Don Juan, Charity, Wolves of Kultur, Orphans of the Storm, The Dangerous Flirt, The Red Kimono, Burning Gold, The Sporting Chance* and *Silent Sanderson.* He continued his serial work in *The Iron Claw* and *Lightning Hutch.*

Last silent: *Black Magic* (1929), with synchronized music and sound effects, made after his first part-talkies. Sheldon Lewis's 1930 film *The Danger Man,* also a silent, was the feature version of his 1926 serial *Lightning Hutch* with added music and sound effects.

Sound: The late 1928 part-sound *The River Woman* was Lewis's first. It was followed by the part-talkie *Seven Footprints to Satan* (1929), his sole sound picture that year. Among his handful of others were *Firebrand Jordan, The Monster Walks, Gun Justice, Riders of the Rio* and *Tex Takes a Holiday.*

The Cattle Thief proved to be Sheldon Lewis's last picture; it was made after a three-year hiatus in 1936. The 1933 film *Missing Daughters* actually was a re-release, with an added talking sequence and sound effects, of his 1924 film by that name.

REVIEWS

The Monster Walks: Sheldon Lewis does not have enough to do as the heavy. *Variety* 5/31/32.

Lincoln, Caryl, Oakland, California, 1908–1983

Filmography: List of films in *Sweethearts of the Sage*

Silent: Wolf Fangs marked Caryl Lincoln's 1927 debut. In it she supported the dog star, Thunder, a Rin-Tin-Tin wannabe. Her other films were *A Girl in Every Port* (way down the cast list), *Hello Cheyenne* (as Tom Mix's leading lady) and *Wild West Romance.* Last silent: *Tracked* (1928), with Ranger, another canine leading "man."

Sound: Named a Wampas Baby Star of 1929, Lincoln made her sound bow as the heroine of 1930's *The Land of Missing Men,* also known as *The Port of Missing Men.* She was in about 15 films until 1934, alternating westerns with roles in quickie melodramas and an occasional "A" film. Her appearances in the latter (e.g., *Back Street, Okay America*) were bits.

Other pictures of Caryl Lincoln's included *The Man from New Mexico, Man of Action, Quick Trigger Lee, Charlie Chan's Courage, Elinor Norton, Thrill of Youth* and *The Cyclone Kid.* Among her talkie co-stars were Tom Tyler, Buck Jones and Tim McCoy.

REVIEWS

Land (Port) of Missing Men: Caryl Lincoln is featured on some of the billing but it is hard to know why. *Variety* 10/29/30.

Man from New Mexico: Caryl Lincoln, as the heroine, can act intelligently and she rides like a trouper. Western heroines who can do something besides looking foolish are pretty scarce these days, and Lincoln is welcome. *Variety* 8/30/32.

War of the Range: Lincoln is the inconspicuous love interest. *Variety* 12/12/33.

Lincoln, Elmo (Otto E. Linkenhelt), Rochester, Indiana, 1889–1952

Filmography: Classic Images (Fall 1974)

Silent: Burly Elmo Lincoln worked for American and other studios and could be spotted in D. W. Griffith films like *Judith of Bethulia, Birth of a Nation* and *Intolerance.* The role that brought him fame was that of Tarzan in *Tarzan of the Apes* and *The Romance of Tarzan* (1918).

Lincoln was also seen in the serials *The Flaming Disc, The Adventures of Tarzan, Elmo the Mighty* and *Elmo the Fearless.* His other films, in which he frequently played blacksmiths to showcase his physique, included *The Kaiser, the Beast of Berlin, Under Crimson Skies, Quincy Adams Sawyer, Fashion Row, All Around the Frying Pan* and *Rupert of Hentzau.*

As the '20s wore on, Lincoln's roles became sup-porting ones in fewer pictures. Last silent feature: *Whom Shall I Marry?* (1926). Last silent: *King of the Jungle,* a 1927 serial.

Sound: Elmo Lincoln returned to films about 1938 or '39 and was seen in bit roles in several, among them *Colorado Sunset, Joan of Arc, The Man Who Walked Alone, Badmen's Territory, Albuquerque* and *Tarzan's Magic Fountain,* in which he did not play the lead role.

In later years, Lincoln joined the circus where he was displayed as the "Original Tarzan." He remained active as an extra or bit player nearly until the time of his death.

Littlefield, Lucien, San Antonio, Texas, 1895/96–1960

Silent: From the time of his first features about 1913 or '14, Lucien Littlefield was a renowned master of makeup. He frequently portrayed much older men and made a specialty of "old coot" characterizations. Some of his early pictures were *The Ghost Breaker* (he played a judge at age 19), *To Have and to Hold, The Golden Fetter* and *The Warrens of Virginia.*

Littlefield made numerous films throughout the 1920s, sometimes appearing in as many as ten a year, albeit frequently in small roles. They included westerns, comedies, dramas and melodramas, among them *The Sheik, Manslaughter, The French Doll, Babbitt, Charley's Aunt* (1925 version), *Tumbleweeds, The Torrent* and *Uncle Tom's Cabin.*

In the 1927 classic mystery-melodrama *The Cat and the Canary,* Littlefield was eerily made up to resemble Dr. Caligari from the famous German expressionistic film. Last silent: *Clear the Decks* (1929), made after his first part-talkie.

Sound: Sound did nothing to slow Littlefield. His output was prodigious and by the time he was through he had appeared in hundreds of films. He made nine feature films in 1929 alone, all but one with some talking, including *Dark Streets, Drag, Saturday's Children, Seven Keys to Baldpate* and *The Great Divide.*

Littlefield also made several Vitaphone shorts portraying the head of the Potter Family. Others of his films were *No No Nanette, It Pays to Advertise, If I Had a Million, I Dream Too Much, Whistling in Dixie* and *Casanova's Big Night.*

Littlefield was also to be seen in such major opuses as *Ruggles of Red Gap, The Bitter Tea of General Yen, Rose-Marie, Alice in Wonderland* and *The Little Foxes.* His last may have been 1958's *Wink of an Eye* where he was credited just as "Old Man."

REVIEWS

Making the Grade: Lucien Littlefield does a little of the talking as the hero's companion and employee. He has a good voice and adds to the comedy. *Harrison's Reports* 4/27/29, *Variety* 5/8/29.

Livingston, Margaret (Marguerite Livingston?), Salt Lake City, Utah, 1896/1900–1985

Silent: Red-haired "vamp"-to-be Margaret Livingston played small parts from 1916 (*Alimony, Haunting Shadows*) and appeared in serials before signing with Ince. Her roles continued to be mostly supporting ones until 1924 when *The Chorus Lady* gave her a solid lead.

Livingston's other films included *Lying Lips, Colorado Pluck, Love's Whirlpool, Havoc, The Mad Hour, Married Alive* and *Say It with Sables*. In what is regarded as her best film, *Sunrise* (1927), she portrayed the woman from the city who seduces the hero. Last silents: *The Apache* and *His Private Life*, released at about the same time in 1928.

Sound: Beware of Bachelors was the 1928 part-talkie that introduced Livingston in talkies. All nine of her 1929 films were sound or part-talkie. They included *The Bellamy Trial, Innocents of Paris* (with Maurice Chevalier), *Seven Keys to Baldpate* and *Tonight at Twelve*.

Livingston continued a hectic schedule of filmmaking through 1931 and then she almost completely vanished from the screen. After single appearances in 1932 (a small role in Clara Bow's *Call Her Savage*) and 1934's *Social Register*, she was seen no more. Among her other films were *The Office Scandal, Murder on the Roof, What a Widow!* and *Smart Money*.

Comments: Although she was undoubtedly attractive enough, Margaret Livingston was not conventionally pretty. There certainly was something about her which typed her as a "vamp"; perhaps her narrow, even leering, eyes. Or maybe she simply exuded on-screen sexuality. Whatever it was, she could claim jokingly that she murdered others and was murdered more often on-screen than almost any other actress.

Of course Livingston could, and did, portray "nice" girls as well. What is certain is that she made an easy transition to talkers and was as busy as any leading lady in the early days of sound. Her voice matched her persona and it was good enough to dub Louise Brooks in *The Canary Murder Case*.

Livingston claimed that she willingly gave up her career when she married orchestra leader Paul Whiteman. This may have been true or, because of her age and over-exposure, her popularity may have been waning anyway. In any case, public tastes were changing and her "vamp" character was now out of date.

REVIEWS

The Charlatan: The real crime is the removal of the lovely Margaret Livingston from the scene so early in the story. She is the film's most decorative player. Her death should be atoned for not by the screen culprit but by the director. *New York Times* 4/15/29.

Seven Keys to Baldpate: Margaret Livingston is attractive but her voice does not register particularly melodiously. *New York Times* 12/26/29.

Lloyd, Harold, Burchard, Nebraska, 1893–1971

Filmography: Harold Lloyd: The Shape of Laughter; Films in Review (Aug.-Sept. 1962); List of films in *Film Dope* (Sept. 1986); *Stars* (Dec. 1988)

Silent: The illustrious career of Harold Lloyd began with extra work about 1913, perhaps in Edison's *The Old Monk's Tale*. He befriended a fellow extra Hal Roach and the two soon joined forces to produce one-reel comedies.

Out of Lloyd's teaming with Roach came the "Willie Work" character which was soon succeeded by the more successful "Lonesome Luke" series co-starring Bebe Daniels. The series entries were initially one-reelers and then expanded to two reels by 1917.

Despite a different style of dress (tight clothes instead of loose-fitting ones), the Luke character was basically a Chaplin imitation and the ambitious Lloyd thought it a dead end. By 1918 he had discontinued it.

The so-called "Glasses" character, first seen in the 1917 one-reeler *Over the Fence*, came out of Lloyd's search for a new image. Although initially it was still played for knockabout comedy the characterization did evolve. With Mildred Davis as his new leading lady, he further developed it in two-reel Pathe comedies.

In 1920 disaster struck Harold Lloyd when a supposedly harmless prop bomb exploded, causing the thumb and forefinger of his right hand to be removed. His face and eyes also were extensively scarred but fortunately healed completely.

Fighting back after a long recuperation, Lloyd went to the three-reel format in *Never Weaken*. It was another of his so-called thrill-comedies following *Look Out Below* and *High and Dizzy*. He expanded his pictures to four reels with 1921's *A Sailor-Made Man*.

Lloyd's movies had now attained quasi-feature status, a transition completed with the next year's five-reelers. They were the popular *Grandma's Boy* and *Doctor Jack*. His previous doubts that audiences would accept the longer format were dispelled.

By now Lloyd had further refined his character into a never-say-die average all–American boy who with pluck overcame all obstacles. In the early years of the 1920s this had a strong resonance with audiences and he had started on his way to enormous popularity and wealth. His status was strongly confirmed with his best-remembered and almost iconographic film *Safety Last* (1923), the ultimate thrill-comedy.

A painstaking and fastidious filmmaker, Lloyd's output was carefully measured during his feature days and after 1924 he produced only a single film each year. By this time Jobyna Ralston was his leading lady, Mildred Davis having become Mrs. Lloyd in 1923.

Lloyd's other silent films were *Why Worry?*, *Hot Water*, *Girl Shy*, *The Freshman* (a hugely successful 1925 film), *For Heaven's Sake* and *The Kid Brother*, his first released through Paramount rather than Pathe. Last silent: *Speedy* (1928).

Sound: With the arrival of sound, Lloyd decided to reshoot his silent film *Welcome Danger* and it became his first talkie in 1929. Although financially successful, its uneasy melding of comedy and melodrama did not measure up to the achievements of his previous efforts. It is perhaps for that reason that he fell back on his formula thrill pictures for his next effort, 1930's *Feet First*.

With sound, Lloyd became an even more deliberate filmmaker. For the remainder of the decade there were only four more pictures at two-year intervals: *Movie Crazy*, probably his most successful talkie, *The Cat's Paw*, *The Milky Way* and *Professor Beware*. By the late 1930s his popularity was definitely slipping and he stopped making films, becoming for a short time an RKO producer.

Lloyd made an ill-advised comeback in Preston Sturges's *The Sin of Harold Diddlebock*, later known as *Mad Wednesday*, in 1947. The film began with the last reel of *The Freshman* but it soon flagged in inspiration and fell back on a very tired thrill-comedy finale. This was the last of perhaps 300 film appearances.

In recognition of his service to Hollywood, Lloyd received a 1952 special Oscar. He brought the silent comedy compilation film *Harold Lloyd's World of Comedy* to the screen in the 1960s and also worked on *Harold Lloyd's Funny Side of Life*, which had a limited distribution.

Comments: It is generally considered that Harold Lloyd's reputation has not endured as well as those of the other great silent comic actors Charles Chaplin and Buster Keaton. His comedy is now considered by some to have been too programmed and without real heart. Also his strive-and-succeed "rah rah" character seems less timeless than the others, more a reflection of an era when anything seemed possible.

Indeed, by the early 1930s Lloyd's screen persona was becoming out of place in disillusioned, Depression-ridden America. That persona did seem to mirror the "real" Harold Lloyd however. By ambition and shrewdness he had succeeded, probably beyond his wildest imaginings.

Lloyd undeniably had considerable comedy talents and they should not be minimized. He was an inventive if not always a totally original comedian. With his complete control over his later films, he well could be considered an "auteur," even though others may have nominally directed them.

Lloyd had definite theories about comedy, one of them being that it should stay away from plotlines that were "fantastic" (i.e., containing situations that could not possibly occur in real life). Perhaps his thrill-comedies stretched this credo somewhat but he made relatively few despite their disproportionate place in revivals of his films.

In the talkies, Lloyd's allure became more problematic. His voice, although fitting his "average" persona — and what name is more average than Harold — was flat, somewhat high and redolent of the Midwest prairies. It really seemed more suited to the Shriner he became than it was to an actor.

Consequently, Lloyd's performances in sound films could be rather colorless. His frenetic physical activity also was less suitable for talkies and indeed less suitable for a man his age. He was almost 40 and the glasses could no longer disguise the fact that he was aging.

Because Lloyd's persona was that of a *young* go-getter, maintaining his familiar characterization became an increasing problem. When he played the same character at the age of 45 in *Professor Beware*, it had become most unsuitable.

REVIEWS

Welcome Danger: Lloyd's voice is sometimes prone to weakness and even self-consciousness but it arises to the occasion and the audience will be likely to forget or overcome any disappointment over it. He does the best work of his career. *Variety* 10/23/29, *Harrison's Reports* 10/26/29.

Feet First: Full of Lloyd gags, stunts and tricks. It is not so easy for a comedy star like Lloyd, who does so much in every picture, to continually find funny ways to make people laugh. *Variety* 11/5/30.

Movie Crazy: Still of the familiar synthetic school of Lloyd's productions, but he not only circumvents any suspicion of sameness but develops along new lines.

(This film presented Lloyd with his most sophisticated interaction with a female co-star, in this case

LOGAN 186

Constance Cummings. She was a distinct change from the usual pretty but bland leading lady.) *Variety* 9/20/32.

The Cat's Paw: One of the best roles Lloyd has had since the story offers him a chance for straight acting instead of slapstick. It is the most adult comedy yet attempted by him and there's no denying its merit as a laugh entertainment. *Harrison's Reports* 7/21/34, *Variety* 8/21/34.

The Milky Way: Almost made to order for Lloyd and he plays it to the hilt. It is a milestone for the former silent screen favorite. With the advent of sound he didn't fare too well but this leaves little doubt. *Variety* 4/1/36.

Professor Beware: Lloyd's formula is to start running and keep going. It compares favorably with the best work he has done in sound pictures. *Variety* 7/13/38.

The Sin of Harold Diddlebock: Neither he nor his comedy has changed much, which should be enough for any audience. He handles his role in his usual funny fashion. *Variety* 2/19/47.

Logan, Jacqueline, Corsicana or San Antonio, Texas, 1901/04–1983

Silent: Follies girl Jacqueline Logan first appeared on-screen in *A Perfect Crime* (1921). Other films included *Molly O'*, *A Man Must Live*, *The Light That Failed*, *Tony Runs Wild*, *Broadway Daddies* and *Playing with Souls*.

It is undoubtedly for her role as Mary Magdalene in *The King of Kings* (1927) that Logan is best remembered today. Among her other DeMille films were *The Leopard Lady* and *Fool's Paradise*. Last silent: *The Faker* (1929), made after her first part talkie.

Sound: Nineteen twenty-nine was the last year of Logan's American film career. Besides her brief appearance in *The Show of Shows*, other roles that year were in the part-talkie *The Bachelor Girl* and the talkies *Stark Mad* and *General Crack*. Her role in the latter, John Barrymore's first starring sound feature, was small. She had made her talkie debut in 1928's part-sound *The River Woman*.

Logan did play the heroine in one of the earliest talking serials, *King of the Kongo*; it was also one of the last silent ones. In 1930 she went to England to appear in the short feature *Middle Watch* and then co-directed another film a couple of years later. This was apparently her screen swan song but she may have done some later work on stage.

Comments: Few silent actresses faded out as quickly as the beautiful red-haired Jacqueline Logan. A popular, if not a major, silent star, she sank almost without a trace at the dawn of sound. This obviously affected her greatly. Even in advanced age, she was still insisting that her voice had been perfectly fine for sound.

REVIEWS

Stark Mad: A good cast but Jacqueline Logan is a little nervous in reciting her lines. *Variety* 7/3/29.

The Bachelor Girl: Logan is a good heroine but the talk is mainly blah. She and her co-star are hardly a well matched pair but both make the most of a lightweight story. *Harrison's Reports* 7/24/29.

General Crack: Logan is in but a scene or two. *Variety* 12/11/29.

The Middle Watch: Jacqueline Logan runs around in pajamas. She is attractive and acts fairly well. *New York Times* 12/28/30.

Lombard, Carole (Jane Peters), Fort Wayne, Indiana, 1908–1942

Filmography: Films in Review (Feb. 1961); List of films in *Film Dope* (Feb. 1987)

Silent: Carole Lombard first had a tentative brush with the cinema in a bit part in 1921's *A Perfect Crime*. She returned to begin her career in earnest at Fox in *Hearts and Spurs*, *Durand of the Bad Lands* and *Marriage in Transit*, all 1925. A serious auto accident then sidelined her for the better part of a year, leaving her with a facial scar.

After her recovery, Lombard received a Sennett contract in 1927 and appeared in more than a dozen two-reelers. Among them were *The Girl from Everywhere*, *His Unlucky Night*, *The Swim Princess* and *The Girl from Nowhere*. Her other features, in which she played supporting roles, included *Divine Sinner* and *Power*. Last silent: *Me, Gangster* (1928), with synchronized music.

Sound: Nineteen twenty-eight's *Show Folks*, a part-sound picture, was Lombard's first. All her 1929 films were talkies, including *Ned McCobb's Daughter*, *Big News*, *High Voltage* and *The Racketeer*. In 1930 the spelling of her first name (which had been "Carol") was changed to "Carole" through an error in the billing on one of her films.

Although Lombard was now receiving leading roles, they were mostly very ordinary ingenues. Such films as *The Arizona Kid*, *It Pays to Advertise*, *No One Man*, *Up Pops the Devil*, *From Hell to Heaven* and *Virtue* had her career on a fast track to pretty much nowhere. During this period she also made *No Man of her Own*, her only film with husband-to-be Clark Gable.

It was 1934's *Twentieth Century*, a screwball comedy with John Barrymore, which first showed audiences the comedic heights Carole Lombard was capable of reaching. She then was cast in a series of comedies that showcased her effervescent personality, including *Hands Across the Table, The Princess Comes Across* and *Love Before Breakfast*.

After *My Man Godfrey* in 1936 and *Nothing Sacred* the next year, Lombard became a major Paramount star. The former film brought her an Academy Award nomination. Her films after 1937 were perhaps not as worthy; the remainder of her 35 or so talkies were a combination of comedies and dramas that did not always succeed.

Among them were *Swing High, Swing Low, In Name Only, Vigil in the Night, They Knew What They Wanted* and *Mr. and Mrs. Smith*, one of Alfred Hitchcock's few comedies. When Lombard was killed in a plane crash after appearing at a bond rally, she had one film still unreleased.

That film was the Ernst Lubitsch comedy *To Be or Not to Be* (1942), co-starring Jack Benny in his best screen work. Although its Nazi-kidding subject matter did not make it particularly successful at the time, it has proved to be at least a minor masterwork and a most worthy finale to Lombard's career.

Comments: Carole Lombard's mellifluous voice made her a cinch for the transition to talkies, but it was quite a while before she established a niche beyond that of traditional leading lady. When she did, it was one that very few or perhaps no other actresses occupied in the '30s.

Lombard's screen persona was a study in contrasts: sexy and beautiful but certainly no "bimbo," sometimes staid and sometimes charmingly hyperactive. She could be ladylike but also could roister with the best of them. On-screen she seemed to be the most approachable of the important cinema stars and was very possibly so in real life too. She could be very earthy and not for nothing was she dubbed "The Profane Angel."

Lombard's scar was disguised by makeup, camera angles and lighting. Even with it, she remained a real blonde beauty and the camera loved her bright blue eyes and high cheekbones. The fact that she did not allow the horrible accident to halt her career said much about her character.

A gutsy lady both on and off the screen, Lombard is one of the most enduring and fondly remembered comediennes of the cinema. In her last role she revealed a more mature acting style that undoubtedly would have put her in good stead throughout the rest of her starring career.

REVIEWS

The Racketeer: The performance of Carol Lombard in this routine bootlegger story is good. *Variety* 1/8/30.

Fast and Loose: Carol Lombard is a stage star [!] but she takes to screen acting like a duck to water. *Harrison's Reports* 11/22/30.

Up Pops the Devil: The shining light of this film is Carole Lombard whose sincerity of acting is surpassed only by her exquisite beauty. *New York Times* 5/16/31.

No Man of Her Own: The film gives Carole Lombard the advantage of getting a buildup as Clark Gable's leading lady. *Variety* 1/3/33.

Twentieth Century: Lombard manages to shine despite practically being reduced to stooging for John Barrymore. She looks very well, even when taking Barrymore's abuse. When she goes temperamental herself, she's permitted to go head-to-head with her co-star.

(Lombard's Lily Garland, *née* Mildred Plotka, was a wonderful comic creation, a right-on satire of the prima donna star.) *Variety* 5/8/34.

My Man Godfrey: William Powell and Carole Lombard are pleasantly teamed. She has played screwball dames before, but none so screwy as this one. Her role is the more difficult because it calls for high-pressure acting all the way. *Variety* 9/23/36.

Nothing Sacred: Lombard's stock will be helped by the picture. She wears clothes well but not enough attention perhaps has been paid her in that matter lately. *Variety* 12/1/37.

In Name Only: Lombard emerges as highly impressive. In this romantic drama she turns in a fine performance. *Variety* 8/9/39.

To Be or Not to Be: This represents an acting triumph for Lombard, who delivers an effortless and highly effective performance that provides a memorable finale for her brilliant screen career. *Variety* 2/18/42.

London, Babe (later Jean "Babe" London; Ruth Glover), Des Moines, Iowa, 1901–1980

Silent: A recruit from vaudeville, Babe London was the archetypal "fat girl" (250 pounds plus) of the silents in numerous two-reelers from 1918. She was at Vitagraph, then with Christie from 1920 as a featured and starring comedienne, and from 1925 at Educational.

Comic Lloyd Hamilton was a frequent London co-star; she also worked with Chaplin in *A Day's Pleasure* and with Buster Keaton as well. Her features from 1920 included *Merely Mary Ann, Golden Dreams, The Boob, Ain't Love Funny?, The Princess From Hoboken* and *All Aboard*. Last silent feature: *Tillie's Punctured Romance* (1928).

Sound: London returned to vaudeville, continued her work in shorts, including at least one of Laurel and Hardy's (*Our Wife*), and appeared in sporadic features from the 1940s. In the latter she appeared in the credits as Jean "Babe" London.

London's full-length films included *Dancing in the Dark, No Leave, No Love, The Other Love, The*

Paleface, Mother Didn't Tell Me, Sex Kittens Go to College, Single Room Furnished and *Dirty Dingus McGee.* Her last role was a brief appearance in *Kotch.*

Because she was typecast as a "chubby" (she was known as "Hollywood's Perfect 63," the reverse of 36), a substantial weight loss resulted in an almost total cessation of Babe London's career. She ultimately had to put much of her weight back on again in order to get some movie and television work.

Long, Walter, Milford, New Hampshire, 1879/84–1952

Silent: Craggy-faced Walter Long began his career on-screen perhaps as early as 1909 for Essanay after stock and vaudeville experience. He was a member of the D. W. Griffith company and had a notable role (in blackface) as the villainous Gus in *Birth of a Nation.* He also played a gangster in *Intolerance* and was again a bad guy (a brushcut Prussian this time) in Mary Pickford's *The Little American.*

Other Long pictures included *The Woman God Forgot, Joan the Woman, The Evil Eye, The Queen of the Sea, Moran of the Lady Letty, White Pants Willie, Blood and Sand, Shadows* and *Eve's Leaves.* Last silent: *Forbidden Grass* (1928).

Sound: Long's introduction to sound was in the part-talkie *Gang War* in 1928. He made his first full-sound film *The Black Watch* in the following year. This was closely followed by such pictures as *Beau Bandit, Conspiracy, Moby Dick* and *Pardon Us,* Laurel and Hardy's first starring talkie feature in 1931.

Long continued his malevolent ways in comedy (including shorts), melodrama, westerns and drama through the '30s and intermittently in the '40s as well. During part of that decade he returned to the stage. Most of his films were of the "B" variety but he was seen in such major productions as *Sutter's Gold* and *The Thin Man.*

Other Walter Long efforts included *The Maltese Falcon* (1931 version), *Call Her Savage, The Frisco Kid, Pick a Star, Bar 20 Justice, Flaming Lead, When the Daltons Rode* and *Wabash Avenue,* one of his last, in 1950.

Comments: His deep and growly voice perfectly matched Walter Long's persona and allowed him a satisfying career in talkies. He seemingly was partial to roles in which he could disguise himself and throughout his career played such varied ethnic types as Latins, half-castes and African-Americans.

Long was also good at authority figures like sea captains and, of course, he chewed his way through many a killer role. In all his parts, however, even the deepest-dyed villains, there must have been a trace of tongue-in-cheek. No one could look — or be — so totally, unredeemingly rotten.

REVIEWS

The Black Watch: Walter Long plays the menace Harrim Bey, and is permitted to overact. *Variety* 5/15/29.

Pardon Us: Long portrays a snarling prisoner. *New York Times* 8/22/31.

Love, Bessie (Juanita Horton), Midland, Texas, 1898–1986

Filmography: Films in Review (Feb. 1959); List of films in *Monthly Film Bulletin* (Feb. 1972), *Film Dope* (Feb. 1987)

Silent: One of the multitude of extras in *Intolerance,* Bessie Love went on to play supporting parts from about 1916 in Triangle films and then transferred to Vitagraph about 1918. She appeared with William S. Hart, Douglas Fairbanks and John Gilbert in some of their early roles. Because of her short stature, she easily portrayed very young girls.

Love was in the first "class" of Wampas Baby Stars (1922). During the course of her almost 70 silents she worked for several studios including, in the '20s, some Poverty Row outfits. Among her films were *Forget-Me-Not, The Aryan, Reggie Mixes In, The Lost World, Soul Fire, Lovey Mary* and *The Swamp.* Last silent: *Anybody Here Seen Kelly?* (1928).

Sound: Love's sound career began with the Vitaphone short *The Swell(ed) Head* in 1928. It was the resounding triumph of *The Broadway Melody* (1929), an archetypal MGM backstage musical with color sequences, that put her back on top, albeit briefly. It won the Academy Award for Best Picture.

Love's other films that year were *Hollywood Revue of 1929,* in which she had some major musical numbers, *The Girl in the Show* and *The Idle Rich.* She continued to appear in both musicals (*Chasing Rainbows, Good News*) and non-musicals (*Morals for Women, See America Thirst, Conspiracy*) into 1931.

It soon became apparent that Love's starring career was not being sustained and in the mid-'30s she moved to England. Her first British film was *Live Again,* made in 1936. For almost the next five decades she appeared in films, on television and on the stage in England.

Among Love's later film appearances were *Isadora, Sunday, Bloody Sunday* and *Touch and Go.* She also had character roles in such American-made pictures as *The Barefoot Contessa* and *No Highway in the Sky.* Her last film appearance was in 1983's *The Hunger.*

Comments: Few actresses had the roller coaster career that Bessie Love endured. Although she appeared in numerous silent movies, she was adjudged to be finished more than once and was bounced back and forth between major productions and quickies.

Although Love did not possess a really strong speaking voice and was not conventionally pretty, "The Little Brown Wren" (as she was dubbed earlier in her career) came back blonde and rejuvenated with *The Broadway Melody*. Her enhanced status was reflected in the considerable screen time she was given in *The Hollywood Revue of 1929*, more than some of the bigger MGM stars.

Poor vehicles soon put Bessie Love in a downward spin again. Her move to England was a brave career decision which paid off in more or less steady work until the 1980s. Latter-day roles included the musical stage version of *Gone with the Wind* (as Aunt Pittypat) and the popular TV mini-series *Edward and Mrs. Simpson*. (In the latter she uttered the witty line, referring to Wallis Simpson's cuckolded husband, about the "*unimportance* of being Ernest.")

Most people in the American audiences who saw her latter-day films probably never heard of Bessie Love. But they certainly noticed the spry little lady, elderly but still bearing traces of the cute little "wren" she once was, shining in her cameo roles.

REVIEWS

The Broadway Melody: Love is now the best leading lady in talkers. They call her a trouper in the picture and that's what she is. The film proves beyond the possibility of any doubt that she is an actress of the first rank. One may safely compare her to Fannie Brice. *Variety* 2/13/29, *Harrison's Reports* 2/16/29.

The Girl in the Show: They have not done well by Bessie Love. This film is just bad. *Variety* 10/9/29, *Harrison's Reports* 10/19/29.

Good News: Gus Shy and Bessie Love make a great comedy team. Love is an apt student of talkie roles. *Variety* 9/10/30, *Harrison's Reports* 9/13/30.

Morals for Women: Excellently played by a cast of sterling secondary film names, including Bessie Love as the somewhat soiled dove. *Variety* 11/17/31.

Isadora: Supporting players include Bessie Love, veteran film actress, who is back again as mother Duncan. *Variety* 12/25/68.

Love, Montague (sometimes Montagu),

Portsmouth, England, 1877/80–1943
Filmography: Classic Images (July-Aug. 1988); List of films in *Eighty Silent Film Stars*
Silent: Tall (6'2") Montague Love was first seen on-screen about 1914 with World Pictures. He came to films, after much theater experience, as a romantic leading man but made his mark playing dastardly villains in numerous silents like *Don Juan* and *Son of the Sheik*. He also continued working on the stage.

Love's films included *Yankee Pluck, Hands Up, The Hidden Scar, Rasputin, the Black Monk, Vengeance, The King of Kings* and *The Wind*. He worked at numerous studios big and small, among them Famous Players-Lasky, First National, Warner Bros., Tiffany, Cosmopolitan and Banner. Last silent: *The Divine Lady* (1929), technically a silent although it contained singing sequences.

Sound: Love went into talkies without missing a beat. He was seen in the Vitaphone short *Character Studies* in 1928 and 11 of his films were released in 1929, all but three talkies or part-talkies.

Among Love's early sound films were *The Mysterious Island, Bulldog Drummond* and *A Most Immoral Lady*. He remained busy in brief and large supporting roles until the time of his death in 1943. One of the final films he made in '43 (*Devotion*) was not released until three years after.

Among Love's over 70 sound films, many of them prestige productions, were *The Prince and the Pauper, The Life of Emile Zola, Tovarich, The Adventures of Robin Hood, Tennessee Johnson, Juarez, Parnell* and *Kidnapped*.

REVIEWS

Love Comes Along: Montague Love is the villain and does well. *Harrison's Reports* 12/21/29, *Variety* 2/5/30.

The White Angel: Love seems to be specializing in pompous British do-nothing officials. *Variety* 7/1/36.

Lowe, Edmund, San Jose, California,

1890/93–1971
Filmography: Classic Images (Nov.-Dec. 1985)
Silent: The Wild Olive (1915) was Edmund Lowe's first-known film. Other early efforts included *The Spreading Dawn, Vive La France!* and *Eyes of Youth*. His first major lead came in 1920's *Someone in the House*, and stardom arrived with *What Price Glory?* (1926), in which he co-starred memorably as Sgt. Quirt, with Victor McLaglen as Captain Flagg. It was a role he was to repeat in talkies.

Other Lowe silent films included *The White Flower, Is Zat So?, Happiness Ahead, The Devil, East Lynne* (1925 version), *Nellie, the Beautiful Cloak Model* and *One Increasing Purpose*. Last silent: *Outcast* (1928), with synchronized sound effects and music.

Sound: Lowe's first sound film was the part-talkie *Making the Grade* in 1929. He made numerous films that year including *In Old Arizona*, *The Painted Angel*, *Thru Different Eyes* and *The Cock-Eyed World*, which continued the characters introduced in *What Price Glory?* There were to be yet further appearances of his Sgt. Quirt role in *Women of All Nations* and *Hot Pepper*.

Lowe continued steadily in films until 1946, and then was little seen subsequently. Among his roles was that of detective Philo Vance. Other films included *Scotland Yard*, *Dinner at Eight*, *The Great Impersonation*, *Every Day's a Holiday*, *Dillinger* and *Her Bodyguard*.

Lowe's last appearance came, after a considerable hiatus, in George Cukor's *Heller in Pink Tights* (1960). He also worked on television during the 1950s in the *Front Page Detective* series.

Comments: Known as much for his sartorial splendor as for his acting (as was his onetime wife Lilyan Tashman), Edmund Lowe nonetheless had a long and worthwhile career. As amply proved by the great number of films he made in 1929 and thereafter, he could "talk" well.

Although mustachioed elegance was Lowe's stock-in-trade, his greatest fame came with his Sgt. Quirt roles (sans mustache) which were far from his established image. He had one of the longest careers of any silent leading man and worked for all the major studios and some of the minor ones as well. While not a great actor, he brought an undeniable flair to his roles.

REVIEWS

The Cock-Eyed World: Lowe is excellent and shares equally in the plaudits, although as the good-looking one of the rivals he gets less sympathy. *Variety* 8/7/29, *Harrison's Reports* 8/10/29.

The Painted Angel: Lowe is a sympathetic figure as the hero. *Harrison's Reports* 11/2/29.

The Garden Murder Case: Lowe makes an excellent detective of the sophisticated school. *Variety* 3/4/36.

Men Against the Sky: Lowe has a good role as the slick plane manufacturer. *Variety* 8/28/40.

Dillinger: The top-billed Lowe has a comparatively inconspicuous part as the gang chief whom Dillinger succeeds. *Variety* 3/14/45.

Heller in Pink Tights: A name which should help at the box-office is Edmund Lowe as a veteran character actor. *Harrison's Reports* 3/12/60.

Loy, Myrna (Myrna Williams), near Raidersburg, Montana, 1905–1993

Filmography: Films in Review (Feb. 1963)

Silent: A chorus girl and dancer in Los Angeles, Myrna Loy supposedly was discovered by none other than Rudolph Valentino after he saw her photograph. Although she played many bits in movies, including one in 1925's *Ben-Hur*, she did not receive screen credit until 1926, the year she got a five-year contract from Warner Bros. Her silent career was busy, if not notable, and she did attain top-billing in 1928's *Crimson City*.

Loy made about 25 generally undistinguished films, some of which were brief appearances. They included *The Girl from Chicago*, *The Caveman* (the first under her Warners contract), *Bitter Apples*, *Beware of Married Men*, *Ham and Eggs at the Front*, *If I Were Single* and *Turn Back the Hours*. There were a few better ones as well, notably *Don Juan*.

Loy was almost invariably seen in roles that highlighted her supposed exoticism. Presumably she looked like a half-caste or South Seas siren. In reality she was a freckle-faced redhead but photographed darker and usually was heavily made-up. Last silent: *Pay as You Enter* (1928), with synchronized music score and sound effects, made after her first part-talkie.

Sound: Although she did not actually speak in it, Loy's first part-sound film was *The Jazz Singer* (1927); she had a small part as a chorine. Other full- or part-sound films followed in 1928: *State Street Sadie*, *The Midnight Taxi* and *Noah's Ark*. All of her eight 1929 pictures had some talking in them as well.

By this time Loy was alternating between leads and supporting roles in such films as *The Desert Song*, *Evidence*, *The Black Watch*, *Hardboiled Rose* and *The Squall*. In the all-star melange *The Show of Shows* she did a couple of musical numbers, one, inevitably, as an exotic dancer in a color sequence.

Loy continued to appear in numerous films in the early '30s; *Arrowsmith* (1931) provided a strong role that brought her some notice. She went to MGM where ultimately she was to reach stardom. Her first film there was *Emma* and she finally portrayed her last "Oriental" temptress in 1932's *The Mask of Fu Manchu*.

Among Loy's notable motion pictures in the first part of the 1930s were *The Animal Kingdom*, *The Wet Parade*, *Manhattan Melodrama* (her first teaming with William Powell), *Love Me Tonight*, *Topaze* and *Men in White*. It was, however, in a relatively minor film, *The Thin Man* in 1934, that her stardom became assured.

Loy's chemistry with William Powell in that film proved to be cinema gold and they co-starred in many films thereafter including several "Thin Man" sequels to 1947. *Libeled Lady*, also starring Powell's heartthrob Jean Harlow, is usually considered their best pairing.

Although the number of Loy's films and perhaps their quality diminished in the latter part of the decade, she continued to be a popular leading lady in such pictures as *Parnell, Test Pilot, Too Hot to Handle, The Great Ziegfeld* and *Another Thin Man.*

In 1936 Loy was dubbed "Queen of the Movies" in an Ed Sullivan poll and number one at the box office by U.S. theater owners. Early in the next decade her output declined sharply. Between 1941 and '45 she was occupied with war work and her sole effort was *The Thin Man Goes Home* (1944). The smash success of Sam Goldwyn's *The Best Years of Our Lives* in 1946 made her again a name to be reckoned with.

The remainder of the decade saw Loy in a couple of popular films, *The Bachelor and the Bobby Soxer* and *Mr. Blandings Builds His Dream House,* but her film career was winding down. There were a few more in the 1950s, among them *Cheaper by the Dozen, Belles on Their Toes* and *The Ambassador's Daughter.*

Thereafter Loy was seen in character parts in a very small number of widely scattered pictures including *April Fools, From the Terrace* and *Airport 1975.* Her final screen appearance came in 1980's *Just Tell Me What You Want.* Much of her last three decades were devoted to work with UNESCO.

Loy also made occasional television appearances and her stage debut came in 1962, one of her roles being in *Barefoot in the Park.* A distinguished career was capped by the awarding of an honorary Oscar in 1991 which she was too ill to accept in person. Other tributes included honors given her by the Kennedy Center for the Performing Arts.

Comments: Few actresses have made such a seachange in their screen personas as did Myrna Loy. In the silents and early talkies her very stage name reflected the type of parts she was assigned. From an archetypal homewrecker she was metamorphosed into the archetypal perfect wife and mother.

Loy's voice was a mellifluous one so there was little doubt that she would transition to talkies, but with her typecasting there was some question as to how long her career might endure. She was nothing if not persistent; it took about 60 film appearances for her to attain real stardom, but she did it.

Myrna Loy worked with many of the cinema's great male stars but her teaming with Bill Powell in 13 films, including six "Thin Man" movies, proved enduringly popular. They both brought warmth, likeability and sophistication to their roles as well as talents for deft underplaying and wisecracking comedy.

Although Loy was unquestionably a good actress, she had a certain range within which she was most successful. Heavy dramatic roles were not her particular forte unless they could be successfully underplayed.

Stardom did not deter Myrna Loy from realizing a productive life off the screen. The concerns of the world were her concerns and she genuinely wanted to do something about them. Perhaps her life was all of a piece; her real humanity reflected itself in her performances and always made her an actress entirely worth watching.

Reviews

The Squall: Loy's character's overconfidence in her gypsy sex prowess is doubtless the fault of the script, nevertheless she acts with art and speaks her lines well. *Variety* 5/15/29, *Harrison's Reports* 5/18/29.

Emma: Loy decorates the picture with grace. *Variety* 2/9/32.

The Thin Man: It is a pleasure to watch the grand companionship between William Powell and Myrna Loy, both of whom give fine performances. The comedy as played by Loy carries the picture along and both shade their semi-comic roles beautifully. *Harrison's Reports* 6/23/34, *Variety* 7/3/34.

Test Pilot: Loy more than satisfactorily sustains her end with Clark Gable and Spencer Tracy. *Variety* 4/20/38.

Love Crazy: William Powell and Loy demonstrate their combined ability to provide utmost entertainment and take advantage of every opportunity to create a maximum of laughs. *Variety* 5/14/41.

Lucas, Wilfred (James Bruce), Ontario, Canada, 1871–1940

Silent: Beginning in 1908, when he appeared for Vitagraph, Wilfred Lucas was a leading man and supporting player in numerous films. He entered features about 1915 with *The Lily and the Rose* and *The Spanish Jade* and thence was seen steadily through 1925. He also directed some early pictures.

Others of Lucas's films were *A Love Sublime, The Hushed Hour, The Fighting Breed, Flesh and Blood, Jazzmania, Dorothy Vernon of Haddon Hall, Riders of the Purple Sage* and *Her Sacrifice.* He made a few in 1926 and '27 and then was not seen again for the rest of the decade. Last silent: *The Nest* (1927).

Sound: Lucas did not make his first sound film, *Hello Sister,* until 1930 but he made up for his tardy talkie debut by appearing in a vast number of films, sometimes 20 a year, until his death. His diction was clear and his voice proved to be fine. By the talkie years, he was gray-haired and distinguished and often played figures of authority.

Lucas's films, in which he sometimes just had bits, included *Madam Satan, Just Imagine, I Cover the Waterfront, Pardon Us, Cleopatra, Alibi Ike, Les*

Miserables, The Prisoner of Shark Island, Mary of Scotland, The Adventures of Robin Hood and *They Drive by Night*. His last film may have been *The Sea Wolf* (1941). He also made shorts.

Luden, Jack (Jacob Luden), Reading, Pennsylvania, 1902–1951

Silent: One of 14 "students" at the first Paramount Pictures School of Acting on Long Island, Jack Luden made his debut in their graduation film *Fascinating Youth* (1926). (Among his class *compères* were Buddy Rogers, Josephine Dunn and Thelma Todd.)

Luden soon became a promising leading man in films that included *The Jade Cup, Aflame in the Sky, Two Flaming Youths, Forgotten Faces, It's the Old Army Game* and *The Woman from Moscow*. He also appeared in the first of his westerns: *Under the Tonto Rim* and *Shootin' Irons*. Last silent: *Sins of the Fathers* (1928), with synchronized sound effects and music. It also contained a singing sequence.

Sound: All of Luden's 1929 films were talkies, including two with Clara Bow, *Dangerous Curves* and *The Wild Party*. Others that year were *Innocents of Paris* and *Why Bring That Up?* Unfortunately, he had a speech problem — a stammer — which could not be completely hidden from the microphone.

In 1930 Luden was in only a single film and then was off the screen until 1934's *I Believed in You*. In the interim his speech defect had been somewhat ameliorated, but when he returned he was relegated to small roles in a handful of films.

Luden had a brief revival of leading man status in several 1938 westerns for Larry Darmour (*Phantom Gold, Pioneer Trail, Stagecoach Days* and *Rolling Caravans*) before once again reverting to small parts. By the 1940s he was being seen in support of other western players.

Among Luden's other films were *King of the Royal Mounted, Susannah of the Mounties* and *Flight Command*. After being convicted of writing bad checks and drug-taking, he was sent to, and died at, San Quentin Prison.

REVIEWS

Rolling Caravans: Columbia's attempt to introduce another western name in Jack Luden has not amounted to much. He has been in films since 1925 although not too prominently. The lines written for him make him appear to be slightly dopey. (Luden is showcased as a versatile performer. Not only does he fight off the outlaws but he sings, plays an instrument, does ventriloquism and puts his dog through several tricks.) *Variety* 8/17/39.

Lugosi, Bela (also known as Arisztid Olt) (Bela Blasko), Lugos, Hungary, 1882–1956

Filmography: List of films in *Films in Review* (Oct. 1964); *Film Dope* (June 1987)

Silent: The man who was to become the embodiment of pure cinema evil first was one of Hungary's premier screen and stage matinee idols under the name of Arisztid Olt. Among the vehicles in which he starred were *Romeo and Juliet, Camille* and *Anna Karenina*. He also was seen in German films of the late 'teens and early '20s.

Despite the fact that he spoke the language very poorly in his early years in America and indeed for many years thereafter, Lugosi managed to win several roles on Broadway in which he spoke his lines phonetically. His major theater triumph, and the role with which he was forever after to be (over)identified, was 1927's *Dracula*.

Prior to that, Lugosi had made his U.S. screen debut in a leading role in 1923's *The Silent Command*. He made only a few other silent films: another lead in *The Rejected Woman* (1924), *Midnight Girl* (1925) and the short *Punchinello* in 1926. There is some question about his participation in two others, *Daughters Who Pay* (1925) and *How to Handle Women* (1928). If he appeared in the latter, it would have been his last silent.

Sound: Although he was still speaking lines phonetically, Lugosi made his sound bow in the 1929 part-talkie *Prisoners*. The all-sound *The Thirteenth Chair* came later that year. Nineteen thirty saw him in minor roles in minor pictures such as *Oh, for a Man!, Renegades* and *Wild Company*. He was, however, hovering on the threshold of fame.

That fame, and ultimate curse, came for Lugosi in the recreation of his most renowned stage role in Universal's *Dracula* ("Dracoola," as he pronounced it). (The part had been originally intended for Lon Chaney.) The 1930 film, static and stagey though it was, proved a huge success and launched him into stardom. He soon after was offered, and rejected, the Monster role in *Frankenstein* because the part had no actual dialogue.

Lugosi's time as a star proved to be short-lived. Leading roles quickly began alternating with supporting ones and decent films were too often lost amid cheap quickies. He was shown to advantage in such '30s pictures as *Murders in the Rue Morgue, White Zombie, The Raven, The Black Cat, The Invisible Ray* and *Son of Frankenstein* but also was seen in much trivia including *The Death Kiss, The Mysterious Mr. Wong* and *The Gorilla*.

Too often for a supposed star he was used in minor roles, sometimes as a "red herring" butler or other servant. He was actually a red herring vampire in MGM's *Mark of the Vampire* but at least that was a Grade A production. In *Island of Lost Souls* he was completely unrecognizable as the fur-covered Sayer of the Law.

In that decade Lugosi also made several serials, usually as the chief menace. They included *The Whispering Shadow*, *The Return of Chandu*, *SOS Coast Guard*, *Shadow of Chinatown* and *The Phantom Creeps*. He also played in occasional non-villainous parts, his Russian commissar in 1939's *Ninotchka* with Greta Garbo being one of his few comedies. (Its famous publicity campaign "Garbo Laughs!" perhaps also should have said "Lugosi Laughs!")

The 1940s saw Lugosi's stature permanently diminished. He finally did play Frankenstein's Monster in *Frankenstein Meets the Wolf Man* and was seen in such similar films as *The Wolf Man*, *The Ghost of Frankenstein*, *The Return of the Vampire* (in a Dracula-like role) and finally as Dracula himself for the last time in *Abbott and Costello Meet Frankenstein* (1948).

Most of Lugosi's 1940s pictures featured him as a vaguely "mad" scientist or general "baddie." Such films as *Spooks Run Wild*, *The Corpse Vanishes*, *The Devil Bat*, *Invisible Ghost*, *Night Monster*, *Return of the Ape Man* and *Zombies on Broadway* were typical. Of his very few worthwhile roles, 1945's *The Body Snatcher* was among the best.

The 1950s found Lugosi a mere shadow of himself and in evident physical decline from longtime drug addiction. His roles were parodies of his once-powerful persona: Ed Wood's *Glen or Glenda?* and *Bride of the Monster*, *Bela Lugosi Meets a Brooklyn Gorilla* (a.k.a. *The Boys from Brooklyn*), *Mother Riley Meets a Vampire*, and *The Black Sleep*. He also had the dubious privilege of being featured in what has been called the worst film ever made, Wood's *Plan 9 from Outer Space*. Almost 40 years after Lugosi's 1956 death, the character actor Martin Landau won an Academy Award for Best Supporting Actor for portraying him in the film *Ed Wood*.

Comments: The fact that Bela Lugosi was not proficient in English in the early sound period and still had to read lines phonetically actually added to his appeal. The painstakingly slow line delivery and odd enunciation, combined with his smooth baritone, certainly seemed to be in character for a long-dead vampire.

Lugosi brought much of his early persona as an intensely romantic figure and considerable personal charisma to his Dracula. He was still handsome in his early middle age and possessed striking blue eyes. Unfortunately that potent combination of eroticism and evil was not sufficiently understood by the studio moguls and was not really utilized again.

Instead Lugosi was turned into an all-purpose menace who was often a figure of fun. Realizing that he had made an error in rejecting the tour-de-force *Frankenstein*, which had made a star of Boris Karloff, he soon began taking anything offered to him, an equally egregious error.

Ironically, when he no longer had any say in the matter, Lugosi played several roles in which he barely spoke and had his features hidden or at least coarsened. Unfortunately, he seemed willing enough to become a parody of himself, and his own identification with at least the outward trappings of Dracula became more grotesque with every passing year.

Bela Lugosi's final act of being buried in the vampire's cape had an air of inevitability. Rarely has an actor been so taken over — in a very real way himself vampirized — by a fictional creation.

Reviews

Dracula: It is difficult to think of anybody who could quite match the performance in the vampire part of Bela Lugosi, even to the faint(!) flavor of foreign speech that fits so neatly. He makes the part extremely convincing and horrible. *Variety* 2/18/31, *Harrison's Reports* 2/21/31.

White Zombie: Bela Lugosi, as Murder, is the dominant figure with not too horrifying make-up and a sinister air he never loses. He gives an exceptionally good performance. *Variety* 8/2/32.

The Black Cat: Because of the presence in one picture of Boris Karloff and Bela Lugosi, that suave fiend, this picture probably has box office attraction. They are sufficiently sinister and convincingly demonic.

(Actually Lugosi's Dr. Werdegast was a sympathetic figure, albeit a weak one until the gory climax.) *Variety* 5/22/34.

The Raven: With both Karloff and Lugosi in the cast, it should get them to the box-office in spades. Lugosi, as the psychopathic doctor, contributes the shock aspects forcibly. *Variety* 7/10/35.

Ninotchka: Lugosi is adequate in a supporting role. *Variety* 10/11/39.

Scared to Death: This fails to cause the goose pimples expected by a Bela Lugosi vehicle. About all he has to do is to stand around and look mysterious. *Variety* 7/16/47.

Lunt, Alfred, Milwaukee, Wisconsin, 1892/93–1977

Silent: One of the most renowned theater stars of his generation after his success in *Clarence* (1919), Alfred Lunt made just five silent films. They were *Backbone* and *The Ragged Edge* (1923), *Second Youth* in 1924 and, finally, two the next year, the first of which was D. W. Griffith's *Sally of the Sawdust*, probably his best-known silent today. His wife and acting partner, Lynn Fontanne, was also seen in *Second Youth*. Last silent: *Lovers in Quarantine* (1925).

Sound: Lunt's sound output was even more sparse than his silent one. He made only two films, 1931's *The Guardsman*, a sophisticated comedy based on his 1924 stage success co-starring Fontanne, and *Stage Door Canteen*, in which he had a cameo appearance.

From the '30s to 1958's *The Visit* Lunt continued to be one of Broadway's most popular actors, winning two Tony awards. In one of their final performances together he and his wife did *The Magnificent Yankee* on television in 1965.

Comments: Half of one of the greatest acting teams in theater history, Alfred Lunt made his stage debut about 1912 and became a top star in 1924. Ultimately he appeared with Fontanne in 28 plays including *Reunion in Vienna*, *Design for Living*, *There Shall Be No Night*, *Elizabeth the Queen*, *O Mistress Mine* and *I Know My Love*.

Lunt and Fontanne were not only near-legends but seemingly two parts of one entity: "Lunt-fontanne." As such they were perhaps too "big" for the movie screen. Rumor has it that the film of *The Guardsman* was enough of a success to cause MGM to offer Lunt and his wife almost half a million dollars to continue appearing in their films. Their witty and now-legendary demurrer was, "We can be bought but we can't be bored."

REVIEWS

The Guardsman: Reviews did not agree. One opined that the screen took kindly to Lunt and Fontanne and that they had a sophistication that was not only camera proof, but was enhanced by close-up inspection. Another said that Lunt was not a rage as a picture actor, whatever his popularity had been on the stage. *Variety* 9/15/31, *Harrison's Reports* 9/19/31.

Lynn, Sharon (sometimes Lynne; D'Auvergne S. Lindsey), Weatherford, Texas, 1904/10–1963

Silent: Entering films as an extra, Sharon Lynn signed with Fox in the late 1920s and made appearances in numerous films beginning in 1927. She was generally to be found midway down the cast list although she had an occasional lead, as in the Tom Mix oater *Son of the Golden West*.

Among Lynn's pictures were *The Cherokee Kid*, *Clancy's Kosher Wedding*, *None but the Brave*, *Aflame in the Sky*, *The Coward* and *Jake the Plumber*. She also appeared in two-reelers. Last silent: *The One Woman Idea* (1929), with synchronized music, made after her first talkie.

Sound: The late–1928 *Give and Take* was Lynn's first, and Universal's second, talkie. Most of her '29 films were sound and included the musical hits *Fox Movietone Follies of 1929* and *Sunny Side Up*, the first full talkie of the romantic team of Charles Farrell and Janet Gaynor.

Other early Lynn pictures were *Speakeasy* and another musical, *Happy Days*, in which she had a cameo. Sound proved to pose no problem for her voice and she appeared in six pictures in 1930, among them *Crazy That Way*, *Lightnin'* and *Up the River*. After that year her appearances decreased inexplicably and she made fewer than ten films for the rest of her career.

No doubt Lynn is best remembered today for her portrayal of Lola Finn, the saloon keeper's wife, in one of Laurel and Hardy's best features, *Way Out West* (1937). Other pictures included *Men on Call*, *The Big Broadcast*, *Big Executive*, *Enter Madame*, *Go into Your Dance* and *West Point Widow*, her last in 1941.

REVIEWS

Speakeasy: Sharon Lynn portrays a fickle cafe singer and is allowed to warble a full chorus of a pop number. *Variety* 3/13/29.

Sunny Side Up: Lynn seems to be a new name but she plays a socialite debutante extremely well and looks the part. She should be worth watching. *Variety* 10/9/29, *Harrison's Reports* 10/19/29.

Man Trouble: Lynne sings but no one will mention it. *Variety* 9/10/30.

Big Executive: Sharon Lynne, as the boss's secretary, is okay but the story offers her little. *Variety* 10/3/33.

Way Out West: Sharon Lynne, a comely blonde, works hard to gain prominence in a role of which more could have been made.

(This review is difficult to understand considering how Lynne's character worked to get the deed to a gold mine away from Stan Laurel. This feat was climaxed by one of the most famous tickling scenes in cinema.) *Variety* 5/5/37.

Lyon, Ben, Atlanta, Georgia, 1901–1979

Filmography: List of films in *Silent Picture* (Spring 1971)

Silent: Nineteen seventeen appears to be the year Ben Lyon made his screen bow; *Morgan's Raiders* and *The Transgressor* were among his earliest efforts. Other early films included *The White Moth*, *The Savage*, *The Prince of Tempters*, *Lily of the Dust* and *Bluebeard's Seven Wives*.

Flaming Youth in 1923 was Lyon's breakthrough to popularity as a leading man. *So Big* and *The Wages of Virtue* were some of his other major films. He co-starred with Gloria Swanson, Colleen Moore,

Clara Bow and Blanche Sweet, among others. Last silent: *The Quitter* (1929).

Sound: Lyon's first and only 1929 talkie was *The Flying Marine.* His most famous film, *Hell's Angels,* came a year later. Others of his films were *I Cover the Waterfront, Night Nurse, Indiscreet, Hat Check Girl, Frisco Waterfront* and *Dancing Feet.*

Lyon made his last American films in 1936. He subsequently went to England with his wife Bebe Daniels, whose starring career was also flagging. There they made additional pictures and were active on radio and television in the *Hi Gang* and *Life with the Lyons* series. His final film was the English-made *The Lyons in Paris* (1956).

Comments: Ben Lyon proved to be "okay for sound." He worked in numerous films after talkies came in and his role as the "bad" brother in *Hell's Angels* certainly provided impetus. He was never a major star, though, and after 1933 his career was not going well.

Lyon and Bebe Daniels became well known in England for their popular radio programs, but more especially for their steadfast support for that country during the Second World War. In the 1940s Lyon became a talent director for Twentieth Century–Fox, in which capacity he provided a career boost for Marilyn Monroe, among others.

REVIEWS

Hell's Angels: For his performance Ben Lyon will catch most of the public attention and credit. Playing an unsympathetic character, Lyon gives his all to make this his best celluloid effort to date. *Variety* 6/4/30.

Frisco Waterfront: The weakness of the story lies in the uneven performance turned in by Ben Lyon. *Variety* 12/25/35.

Lytell, Bert, New York, New York,
1884/85–1954
Filmography: Films in Review (Aug.-Sept. 1983); *Classic Images* (Sept. 1989)

Silent: By the time Bert Lytell made his first film as the title character in *The Lone Wolf* in 1917, he was already a distinguished stage star. He appeared in almost 25 motion pictures for Metro from 1917–22 alone; a major hit with *The Right of Way* (1920) was the impetus for him to continue to make films throughout the 1920s.

Among Lytell's prestigious efforts were *The Eternal City, Rupert of Hentzau* and *Lady Windermere's Fan.* Besides the Lone Wolf, he portrayed other gentleman crooks like Jimmy Valentine. He did several more in the "Lone Wolf" series, two of which, *The Lone Wolf Returns* and *Alias the Lone Wolf,* were silents.

Other Lytell pictures included *The Spender, The Lion's Den, Born Rich, Eve's Lover, Kick In* and *Steele of the Royal Mounted.* Among the studios for which he appeared were Warner Bros., Universal, Columbia and Preferred. Last silent: *Women's Wares* (1927).

Sound: Lytell successfully brought his smooth voice to the talkies. His first talkie, and only 1928 film, was *On Trial,* the fourth all-sound picture produced at Warner Bros. In it he played a man accused, and ultimately acquitted of, murder.

This was followed by Lytell's sole 1929 film *The Lone Wolf's Daughter,* a part-talkie. There were only three more starring roles to follow: a dual role in *Brothers, The Last of the Lone Wolf,* both 1930, and *The Single Sin* in 1931. His last appearance on-screen was a cameo in *Stage Door Canteen* (1943).

Comments: The Lone Wolf role that began Bert Lytell's film career was originally offered to John Barrymore. Because they were both theater matinee idols, the studio undoubtedly thought one was as good as the other, and indeed Bert Lytell became a screen matinee idol as well.

Although his stage-trained voice was suitable for sound, Lytell's age mitigated against his becoming an important talkie leading man. He certainly would have made a handsome older man or father figure but he undoubtedly decided the theater audience's eye was less merciless than that of the camera. He went back to the stage.

REVIEWS

On Trial: This proves that talkies are a medium for older Hollywood players; they have resuscitated some careers. In this respect Bert Lytell comes out like a new piece of goods. His voice lends him personality even greater than in his silent heyday. *Variety* 11/21/28, *Harrison's Reports* 11/24/28.

The Lone Wolf's Daughter: The dialogue opening does considerable harm to Lytell's vocal reputation. That Lytell can talk is no secret but you can't prove it by this picture. It is a case of poor recording. The sound quality is so poor that it is unintelligible. One hears nothing but booming, as if the characters talked through their noses. Lytell is as good in the Lone Wolf's part as he has always been. *Variety* 3/6/29, *Harrison's Reports* 3/9/29.

Last of the Lone Wolf: This should draw good crowds on account of the popularity of this series in which Bert Lytell takes the part of the clever romantic crook. He gives his customary good performance but the "Lone Wolf" here is limited. It is a cut-and-dried role. *Harrison's Reports* 9/20/30, *Variety* 10/22/30.

Brothers: Lytell does well as either of the brothers. *Variety* 10/18/30.

McAvoy, May, New York, New York, 1901–1984

Filmography: Films in Review (Oct. 1968)

Silent: Following a modeling career and extra work, May McAvoy had her first featured role in *Hate* (1917). She then played ingenue roles for a couple of years before signing with Pathe. Her breakthrough part came in *Sentimental Tommy* in 1921. In 1923 she was the first person to be named what is now the Rose Queen in the New Year's Day Rose Parade.

McAvoy reached stardom when she signed with Realart, a Paramount subsidiary, and then with Paramount itself. Her major films included *The Enchanted Cottage, Ben-Hur, Lady Windermere's Fan* and *The Road to Glory*. Others were *Morals, The Bedroom Window, Slightly Used, My Old Dutch* and *Clarence*. Last silent: *The Little Snob* (1928), made after her first part-talkie.

Sound: May McAvoy's first foray into talkies was epochal: She was Al Jolson's leading lady in the late 1927 Vitaphone part-talkie *The Jazz Singer,* although she had no spoken dialogue. She made only one full-sound film, *The Terror* (1928), and a handful of other part-talkies. They were *Caught in the Fog* and *The Lion and the Mouse* in 1928; *Stolen Kisses* and *No Defense* in 1929.

Besides the sound features, McAvoy also made the Vitaphone short *Sunny California* in 1928. She became one of the better-known casualties of the talkies and was off the screen completely during the '30s, returning in 1940 at MGM to appear in bit roles and as an extra throughout the decade.

Comments: May McAvoy was a most popular star in the 1920s. Small (4'11") with startlingly blue eyes, she was a good actress and appeared in some top-notch pictures. There was, however, the problem of The Voice. Almost as well-known as John Gilbert's talkie travails were those of Miss McAvoy, and the Legend of the Lisp has gone down in film annals.

The question of whether or not she actually had a lisp seems still to be an open one. She always denied it vehemently (in a voice presumably lipless) and Warner Bros. did dub her "The Vitaphone Girl" so they must have had some faith in her ability to speak. In her various interviews over the years, it also did not seem to be noticeable.

McAvoy certainly did not succeed in talkies. Her voice was not heard at all in *The Jazz Singer* (as might be expected, Jolson had all the spoken lines) and his dominance in their scenes together made it a certainty that she did not fully register. Its success no doubt did rub off on her and provided her the opportunity to make further talking pictures.

It was in *The Terror* (aptly named for its effect on her career) that McAvoy presumably uttered the immortal "I'm thick of thuth thilly antichth." However, reviews indicated her enunciation was not quite so bad. The impression that she lisped may have been caused by the sibilance created by the Vitaphone recording device. It certainly was a phenomenon much commented upon by reviewers of the time.

But the question remains: Did she or didn't she?

REVIEWS

The Jazz Singer: May McAvoy has little to do and there is no love angle to help, but she plays opposite Al Jolson with charm. The picture is better with the Vitaphone than without it. *Variety* 10/12/27, *Harrison's Reports* 10/22/27.

The Lion and the Mouse: Reviews disagreed somewhat. One stated that at first McAvoy's voice hardly carried to the back of the theater, giving the impression it was not robust, but in a later sequence it became clear and strong. A second review from the same source opined that her voice was high, thin and out of all proportion to that of her co-stars. The film would have been better off without her speaking or perhaps a voice double should have been used. Her voice had little or no tonal shading.

Another review said that McAvoy handled her part very well even though she had never acted on the stage. *Variety* 5/20/28 (first review), 6/20/28 (second review), *Harrison's Reports* 6/23/28.

The Terror: Reviews of McAvoy's voice differed again. One said it was shy and shrinking, merely a lisping peep but another thought that her voice registered better in this picture than it did in *The Lion and the Mouse*.

(This was one of the first all-talking films and perhaps the first to feature screaming.) *New York Times* 8/16/28, *Harrison's Reports* 8/25/28.

Caught in the Fog: Yet again, reviewers heard things differently, perhaps because of different theaters' recording. One said that nothing seemed to be able to improve McAvoy's voice but the other stated that her voice registered very well and that she acted and talked with grace. *Variety* 12/5/28, *Harrison's Reports* 12/8/28.

Stolen Kisses: McAvoy is a pleasing heroine insofar as her physical appearance but she is lost in speaking lines. *Harrison's Reports* 4/27/29, *Variety* 5/8/29.

No Defense: McAvoy does good work. Her voice registers better than it has registered in any other talking picture in which she has so far appeared. *Harrison's Reports* 7/6/29, *Variety* 7/10/29.

McCoy, Tim, Saginaw, Michigan, 1891–1978

Filmography: Films in Review (Apr. 1968)

Silent: Tim McCoy worked his way into a film career somewhat through the back door. He was a consultant on Native American customs for the epic *The Covered Wagon* in 1923 and accompanied the film to theaters, delivering a spoken prologue.

His first film before the cameras was *The Thundering Herd* (1925) in which he was billed as Colonel T. J. McCoy. The next year he was signed by MGM for a series, his first film being *War Paint.* Some of his movies there were historical melodramas rather than straight westerns, a genre that MGM did not seem to favor.

Other McCoy films included *Winners of the Wilderness,* co-starring Joan Crawford, *Beyond the Sierras, Law of the Range, Foreign Devils* and *Sioux Blood.* Last silent: *The Desert Rider* (1929). He was released by MGM that year.

Sound: A Night on the Range, a 1929 short, was McCoy's first talkie effort. This was followed by the 1930 serial *The Indians Are Coming,* one of the first sound serials as well as perhaps the last silent one. Another serial *Heroes of the Flames* came in 1931. His maiden sound feature was that year's *One Way Trail.*

McCoy was signed by Columbia for a series of adventure-melodramas and westerns. After the mid–'30s, when his career was slipping, he worked for such Poverty Row studios as Puritan, Monogram, Victory and PRC.

Among McCoy's films were *End of the Trail, Hold the Press, Square Shooter, Outlaw Deputy, The Traitor, Gun Code, Outlaws of the Rio Grande* and *Down Texas Way.* He was on-screen fairly steadily to 1942; his final starring role was in *West of the Law.*

McCoy returned in the 1950s for cameos in *Around the World in 80 Days* and *Run of the Arrow* and finally was one of the numerous old-time oater stars in *Requiem for a Gunfighter* (1965). Altogether he made over 70 sound films.

During the 1930s, McCoy had his own Wild West show and in the late '50s and early '60s traveled with a circus. He also produced a documentary about Native American sign language called *The Silent Language of the Plains.*

Comments: The hallmark of Tim McCoy's films was authenticity. He really did know Native American life intimately and had lived closely with them in the "wild" West. He was also a real colonel, at least a lieutenant colonel, having been discharged with that rank in 1919.

Although far from conventionally handsome, McCoy made a convincing western hero with his gimlet-eyed gaze and air of incorruptibility. Although he was somewhat too old to play the hero when his last films were made, he always maintained his military dignity and authority.

MacDermott, Marc (sometimes McDermott), Goldbourne or Sydney Australia, or London, England, 1880/81–1929

Silent: Marc MacDermott was hired on at Edison about 1908 after theater experience; he later went to Vitagraph. He was in the seminal serial *What Happened to Mary?* and feature appearances as a leading man and supporting player began about 1915 with *The Destroying Angel* and *Shadows from the Past.*

MacDermott's later pictures, for MGM, Fox and other studios, included *Whom the Gods Destroy, Babette, While New York Sleeps, Footlights, Dorothy Vernon of Haddon Hall, Graustark, Kiki, Flesh and the Devil* and *The Yellow Lily.* Last silent: *The Whip* (1928), with synchronized music and sound effects.

Sound: MacDermott's only sound film was the part-talkie *Glorious Betsy* (1928), a tale of the Napoleon family, in which he played the father of heroine Dolores Costello. It is not certain he was in the sound portion of the picture.

REVIEWS

Glorious Betsy: McDermott does well as Dolores Costello's somewhat haughty and high-living father. *New York Times* 4/27/28.

McDonald, Francis, Bowling Green, Kentucky, 1891–1968

Filmography: List of films in *Classic Images* (June 1983); *Eighty Silent Film Stars*

Silent: From about 1912, in over 100 silent features and many one- and two-reelers, Francis McDonald played a variety of roles including villains. He worked at such pioneering studios as Sennett, Pathe, Imp and Triangle. His career was so long that moviegoers saw him evolve from his youthful matinee idol looks to hollow-cheeked old age over a period of some 45 years.

McDonald had many leading roles in the 'teens and only a handful (*Hearts and Masks, Puppets of Fate, The Desert's Toll*) in the '20s, but he continued to appear in many films. They included *The Price of Power, The Crystal, Trilby, Mary of the Movies, Bobbed Hair, Battling Butler, Satan in Sables, Legion of the Condemned, Madame Sphinx* and *Paid to Love.* Among his serials were *The Voice on the Wire* and *The Grey Ghost.* Last silent: *The Dragnet* (1928).

Sound: McDonald made two feature films in 1929, both part-talkies, *The Carnation Kid* and *Girl*

Overboard. His career continued apace, although frequently in very small parts (and some shorts) with *A Farewell to Arms, Viva Villa!, Mississippi, The Plainsman, Under Two Flags, If I Were King, The Buccaneer, Spoilers of the North, The Sea Wolf, The Paleface, Duel in the Sun* and countless others.

Among the studios for which McDonald appeared were Universal, Fox, MGM, Paramount, Warner Bros., Columbia, RKO and Republic. As he aged he was often cast as grizzled old codgers, loony prospectors and similar characters. There was also one leading role, in 1932's *Trailing the Killer,* although a dog was actually top-billed.

McDonald made at least four serial appearances, including *The Mystery of the Riverboat.* He left films about 1958, after *The Saga of Hemp Brown,* but returned for a last role in *The Great Race* (1965).

REVIEWS

Bar 20: Francis McDonald plays a henchman. *Variety* 7/21/43.

Gene Autry and the Mounties: McDonald is capable. *Variety* 1/24/51.

MacDonald, J(ohn) Farrell (some
sources say Joseph), Waterbury, Connecticut, 1875/80–1952

Filmography: Academy of Motion Picture Arts and Sciences

Silent: In the early 'teens J. Farrell MacDonald was both actor and director; in the latter capacity he helmed such features as *The Patchwork Girl of Oz* and *Samson,* as well as several one- and two-reelers. He began his screen career possibly as early as 1908 playing leads. Eventually he became a character actor, one of Hollywood's most respected.

Among the studios for which MacDonald worked were Imp, Triangle, Sennett, American and Pathe. His films included *The Heart of Maryland, Molly of the Follies, Hitchin' Posts, This Hero Stuff, Trailin', The Young Rajah, The Signal Tower, Bertha, the Sewing Machine Girl* and *Colleen.*

MacDonald also played Jiggs in *Bringing Up Father,* based on the popular comic strip. One of his most celebrated roles was in *The Iron Horse,* the John Ford railroad epic of 1924. Last silent: *Masked Emotions* (1929), with synchronized music and sound effects, released after his first talkies.

Sound: The early '29 part-talkie *Abie's Irish Rose* marked MacDonald's sound bow; he was the Irish patriarch. He appeared in several others that year including *In Old Arizona, Masquerade, Happy Days* (a cameo) and *The Painted Angel.* Having supposedly sung in opera, his voice proved to be just fine.

In the '30s MacDonald was omnipresent, sometimes being seen in more than 20 pictures a year, and he was still on-screen as late as 1951. His total of films may have exceeded 300 for such major and minor studios as First National, Majestic, Tower, Tiffany, Chesterfield, Monogram, Mascot, Victory, Republic, United Artists, PRC, Lippert and Fox.

The films of J. Farrell MacDonald, in which he not unsurprisingly often played Irishmen, included *The Maltese Falcon* (1931 version), *Madame Racketeer, I Loved a Woman, The Cat's Paw, Northern Frontier, Riffraff, Maid of Salem, Come On, Rangers, Prairie Law, A Tree Grows in Brooklyn* and *Mr. Belvedere Rings the Bell.* A favorite of John Ford, he was often seen in his westerns such as *My Darling Clementine.* His final venture may have been 1951's *Here Comes the Groom.*

REVIEWS

Abie's Irish Rose: J. Farrell MacDonald is splendid, giving a dignified interpretation. *New York Times* 4/20/28.

Men Without Women: MacDonald makes his lines count as one of the submarine crew in this John Ford production. *New York Times* 2/1/30.

No Man of Her Own: MacDonald stands out from the others in smaller character roles. *Variety* 1/3/33.

McDowell, Claire, New York, New York,
1877–1966

Filmography: Classic Images (Nov.-Dec. 1985, Apr. 1992)

Silent: Handsome Claire McDowell was not always the Eternal Mother. She began as a leading lady with Biograph about 1908 after a stage career which included *The Clansman.* Some of her early films were *The Female of the Species, The Primal Call, Men and Women, Her Dormant Love, Her Renunciation, Mixed Blood* and *A Romany Rose.* She later went to Universal to play leads.

At some point in the late 'teens, McDowell began her "nurturing" career, notably as Mary Pickford's mother in *Heart o' the Hills* (1919). Her major films included *Ben Hur, Ponjola, The Mark of Zorro, Black Oxen* and *The Big Parade.* Other films were *Mother o' Mine, Penrod, Tillie the Toiler, Human Wreckage, The Restless Sex* and *Don't Marry.* Last silent: *The Viking* (1929), with synchronized music and sound effects.

Sound: Only one of McDowell's several 1929 films was in sound, the part-talkie *Four Devils.* She went on to appear in numerous sound films to 1944 but many were in bit roles. Among them were *The Big House, Paddy, the Next Best Thing, Imitation of Life, Three Comrades, Black Market Rustlers* and her last, *Are These Our Parents?* By the time McDowell made her final film, she had appeared in hundreds, including shorts.

Comments: In talkies there was little opportunity for Claire McDowell to display the signature maternal suffering for which she was so famous in the silents. Leave-taking and homecoming scenes were her forte, as epitomized in MGM's *The Big Parade.* Well into middle age she retained the vestiges of a mature beauty and, with soulful dark eyes smoldering and ample chest heaving, she was a mother anyone would love to come home to.

McGregor, Malcolm, Newark, New Jersey, 1892–1945

Silent: Handsome and clean-cut, Malcolm McGregor was a popular leading man in silents from 1922. Among his major films were *All the Brothers Were Valiant* and *The Prisoner of Zenda.* Others included *The Social Code, The Bedroom Window, Smouldering Fires, Don Juan's Three Nights, The Girl from Gay Paree* and *Buck Privates.* Last silent: *Tropical Nights* (1928).

Sound: Sound quickly spelled the end of McGregor's starring career. He made two 1929 part-talkies, *The Girl on the Barge* and *Whispering Winds,* and was seen in 1930's *Murder Will Out* in a supporting role. He also appeared in the 1933 serial *The Whispering Shadow.*

McGregor returned in 1935 for several supporting and small roles in such films as *Diamond Jim, Happiness C.O.D., I'll Name the Murderer, The Reckless Way* and *Agent K-7,* apparently his last, in 1937.

REVIEWS

The Girl on the Barge: Malcolm McGregor's talking seldom seems spontaneous but his interpretation is competent. *New York Times* 2/26/29, *Harrison's Reports* 3/2/29.

Whispering Winds: McGregor makes an attractive hero. *Harrison's Reports* 9/28/29.

McGuire (also Maguire), Kathryn, Peoria, Illinois, 1897/1903–1978

Silent: Best known for being the somewhat unhelpful leading lady of Buster Keaton in *The Navigator* and also the object of his heart's desire in *Sherlock Jr.* (both 1924), Kathryn McGuire also co-starred with Tom Mix. Her feature debut came in 1921; among her earliest were *The Silent Call, Bucking the Line* and *The Crossroads of New York.*

Among McGuire's studios were Fox, First National, Metro and Sennett. Others of her films included *The Love Pirate, The Shriek of Araby, The Gold Hunters, Buffalo Bill on the U.P. Trail, Naughty*

but Nice and *Lilac Time.* By the end of the silent era her career was beginning to fade. Last silents: *The Big Diamond Robbery* and *The Border Wildcat,* released at about the same time in 1929.

Sound: The pretty Irish-colleen face of Kathryn McGuire appeared in but two 1929 talkies. *The Long Long Trail,* a Hoot Gibson western, was the first; it was also Gibson's. The other was *The Lost Zeppelin.* In neither did she have more than a small part.

REVIEWS

The Long, Long Trail: Kathryn McGuire has just a bit role. *Variety* 11/6/29.

The Lost Zeppelin: Although McGuire is billed fairly high she is limited to one speech which she gets a laugh on. *Variety* 2/5/30.

Mackaill, Dorothy, Hull, England, 1903/04–1990

Filmography: Films in Review (Dec. 1977)

Silent: Dorothy Mackaill's first movie appearance was a bit in an English film. After arriving in America she worked in a Ziegfeld musical and then made her first credited feature, 1921's *Bits of Life.* It was her subsequent roles in comic Johnny Hines's popular two-reel "Torchy" series which brought her notice.

Mackaill was featured in both comedy and drama, co-starring with Jack Mulhall in several films as well as with Richard Barthelmess. After she signed with First National, stardom came in *Chickie* (1925). Other films included *Shore Leave, The Crystal Cup, The Fighting Blade, Joanna, Subway Sadie, Man Crazy* and *The Dancer of Paris.* She made almost 35 silent films in all. Last silent: *Children of the Ritz* (1929), with synchronized music and sound effects, made after her first part-talkie.

Sound: Dorothy Mackaill's sound debut came in the popular part-talkie *The Barker* in 1928. Other part-talkies were *His Captive Woman* and *Two Weeks Off,* both 1929. Her first full-sound film that year was *Hard to Get,* the others *The Love Racket* and *The Great Divide.*

The Office Wife, made in 1930, proved to be a hit and led to Mackaill securing a place in the talkies, at least temporarily. She appeared in such other films as *Safe in Hell, No Man of Her Own* (supporting Clark Gable and Carole Lombard), *Love Affair* (a pre-famous Humphrey Bogart was her leading man), *The Chief* and *Picture Brides.*

Following Mackaill's last American films in 1934, she made one final picture in England, *Bulldog Drummond at Bay* (1937). Among the studios for which she worked in talkies were First National, MGM, Fox, Columbia, PDC/Majestic and Liberty.

Comments: By the time sound arrived, Dorothy Mackaill had lost a good deal of her English accent and it was detectable only upon close listening. Although attractive, she was not a conventionally soft-looking blonde and thus was most suited to assertive, even brassy roles.

Mackaill was equally at home in serious or light roles but, for the most part, those offered to her in talkies did little to sustain a long-term career. Although she made a successful transition, any recognition factor her name may still possess is no doubt due largely to her co-starring with those who would become some of the biggest names in Hollywood.

REVIEWS

The Barker: The picture is well supplied with "It" by Dorothy Mackaill as a circus performer. Her voice records well. *Variety* 12/12/28, *Harrison's Reports* 12/15/28.

Hard to Get: The dialogue is well handled. Mackaill plays her role in a manner which brings her closer to the audience with each sequence. *Variety* 10/2/29.

The Office Wife: Critical opinion differed slightly. One pointed out that Mackaill got a new Warners contract on the strength of this picture and that might tell more about her performance than the critics could. Another thought the audience would feel no sympathy for the heroine. *Variety* 10/1/30, *Harrison's Reports* 10/4/30.

Safe in Hell: Mackaill has little chance to do anything but act tough, but she manages to get through the film without stepping over the boundary and getting over-emotional. *Variety* 12/22/31.

Love Affair: This hardly provides Mackaill with an opportunity commensurate with her talents. *Variety* 4/19/32.

Cheaters: Dorothy Mackaill has been cast for her name but her role is a mere walk-through. *Variety* 5/1/34.

MacKenna, Kenneth (Leo Mielziner, Jr.),

Canterbury, New Hampshire, 1899–1962

Silent: Stage actor Kenneth MacKenna, the scion of a well-known theater family (his brother was famed stage designer Jo Mielziner), played supporting roles and a second lead in a few silent films. The first was 1925's *A Kiss in the Dark*. His others were *Miss Bluebeard* the same year and *The American Venus* in 1926. Last silent: *Lunatic at Large* (1927).

Sound: Talkies found MacKenna in leading roles. His first was *Pleasure Crazed* (1929), followed by *South Sea Rose*. Nineteen thirty was his busiest year on-screen; he appeared in seven films which included *Men Without Women, Sin Takes a Holiday, Temple Tower* and *The Three Sisters* (no relation to the Chekhov play).

MacKenna was also cast opposite Mary Pickford in the first sound version of *Secrets*. However, she grew unhappy with the film and although it was nearly completed she scrapped it. A later version co-starring Leslie Howard in the male lead appeared to little excitement in 1933 and proved to be Pickford's final film.

MacKenna apparently was more interested in a career behind the scenes. After a few other films in 1931 and '32, like *The Man Who Came Back* and *Those We Love*, he began to direct and, eventually, to write for the screen.

MacKenna ultimately returned to the stage but almost 30 years later was back before the cameras to play a handful of small roles in films like *High Time* (1960) and *Judgment at Nuremburg* (1961). His final film may have been 1962's *13 West Street*.

REVIEWS

Pleasure Crazed: Although Kenneth MacKenna is no Adonis he's not really bad-looking, but he has a wonderful voice that will make you forget everything else. He sings the words in his own way; it's a dramatic way of talking that goes over forcefully. *Variety* 7/17/29, *Harrison's Reports* 7/20/29.

South Sea Rose: MacKenna, as the doctor, is satisfactory but the voices sometimes trembled. *Variety* 12/11/29, *Harrison's Reports* 12/14/29.

Those We Love: MacKenna gets few chances but makes the most of them. *Harrison's Reports* 9/17/32, *Variety* 9/20/32.

McLaglen, Victor, Tunbridge Wells, England, 1886–1959

Filmography: List of films in *Film Dope* (June 1987); *Stars* (Dec. 1988); *Eighty Silent Film Stars*

Silent: As probably could be guessed at the first sight of him, Victor McLaglen had been a boxer before turning to the English cinema in 1920. His first film was *Call of the Road* and he appeared in several more British films including *The Glorious Adventure* in 1922. A decline in industry production brought him to America in 1924.

McLaglen's premiere film in the U.S. was a starring one, *The Beloved Brute*, in which he convincingly played a wrestler. Other early pictures included *The Hunted Woman, The Unholy Three*, as the circus giant, and *Winds of Chance*. In 1925 he made his first film with John Ford, *The Fighting Heart*.

Nineteen twenty-six proved to be McLaglen's banner year in silents with the very successful *Beau Geste* and *What Price Glory?*, co-starring Edmund Lowe, which was to generate several sequels.

Others of his films included *The Loves of Carmen*, *The Isle of Retribution* and two additional Ford films, *Mother Machree* and *Hangman's House*, both 1928. Last silent: *Strong Boy* (1929), with synchronized sound effects and music, made after his first talkie.

Sound: McLaglen made his sound debut in the 1928 part-talkie *The River Pirate*. In it he was top-billed, as he was in most of his films around this time. The next year he re-teamed with Edmund Lowe in *The Cock-Eyed World*, a sequel to and an attempt to recreate the success of *What Price Glory?* with the squabbling Quirt and Flagg characters from that film.

Others that year included *The Black Watch* and *Hot for Paris*. Although there was little slackening in McLaglen's output of pictures in the early '30s, their quality began to erode noticeably. His career seemed to be on the wane and he returned to Britain for *Dick Turpin*, which was a failure.

It was his old mentor/antagonist John Ford who rescued McLaglen with 1934's Foreign Legion picture *The Lost Patrol*, and then raised him to the heights with his role of Gypo Nolan in the classic *The Informer* (1935). For that bravura bit of emoting he won the Academy Award for Best Actor.

The mid-to-late 1930s proved to be the apex of McLaglen's career except for additional Ford resuscitations in the late 1940s and early '50s with *Fort Apache*, *She Wore a Yellow Ribbon*, *Rio Grande* and *The Quiet Man*. He was nominated for a Best Supporting Actor Oscar for the latter. Other McLaglen motion pictures included *Women of All Nations* (the second sequel to *What Price Glory?*), *Dishonored*, *King of the Khyber Rifles*, *Wee Willie Winkie*, *The Foxes of Harrow*, *Gunga Din*, *The Princess and the Pirate*, *Prince Valiant*, *Bengazi* and *Lady Godiva*.

In the 1940s and '50s McLaglen generally made only one or two films per year. He had spent several years at Fox and after leaving that studio in 1933 freelanced at Paramount, RKO, MGM, United Artists, Columbia and Republic.

Among McLaglen's final films were *The Abductors* (directed by his son Andrew) in 1957 and the British-made *Sea Fury* in 1958. He also made occasional television appearances. In the early '40s he had a radio show which again featured the redoubtable Quirt and Flagg.

Comments: Given his 6'3" height and somewhat battered face, it was easy to cast Victor McLaglen in "dumb brute" roles. It took more vision to see the sensitivity beneath the exterior, a side of him rarely shown on-screen.

McLaglen's voice, with its rushed, sometimes indistinct enunciation, perfectly fit his image as a rough roisterer. He convincingly portrayed military men, generally of the NCO ranks, who took "nothing from nobody" and were always ready to use their "dukes."

McLaglen occasionally also played menacing villains, as in 1940's *South of Pago Pago*. In the 1940s his casting became simplistic typecasting. He generally was a caricature comic tough guy with little chance to display any shading of character.

Although McLaglen and John Ford had a rocky relationship—the infamous Ford needling was very much in evidence with the lumbering actor—the director brought out his best work. When he was teamed with someone like John Wayne who was an ideal match for him, his acting, rather than mugging, ability shone out.

REVIEWS

The Cock-Eyed World: A low comedy in which Victor McLaglen does excellent work. *Harrison's Reports* 8/10/29.

Wicked: Although McLaglen has just a bit, for pure (but unintentional) high comedy nothing is better than the semi-climax speech given by him. *Variety* 9/22/31.

Hot Pepper: In this sequel to *What Price Glory?*, McLaglen's English accent in a U.S. marine's role is harder to take now that this series has lost its kick. He's a good enough actor to handle that handicap. *Variety* 1/24/33.

The Informer: McLaglen is so completely convincing that audiences will wonder at his being squandered in roles as a dumb detective. This performance is certainly the apex of his career to date. *Variety* 5/15/35.

Klondike Annie: McLaglen puts perfume behind his ears and uses breath aids to increase his appeal with Mae West. He is clearly uncomfortable and under wraps. *Variety* 3/18/36.

Powder Town: McLaglen fails to surmount the paucity of suitable material. *Variety* 5/13/42.

MacLaren, Mary (Mary MacDonald), Pittsburgh, Pennsylvania, 1900–1985

Filmography: Films in Review (Apr. 1985)

Silent: After signing with Universal about 1916, Mary MacLaren's first film may have been *Where Are My Children?* One of her first, the Lois Weber–directed *Shoes* (1916), proved a major success and she was to appear in several more films directed by Weber. Beside *Shoes*, MacLaren's most famous film was probably Douglas Fairbanks's *The Three Musketeers* (1921).

Other MacLaren movies included *Rouge and Riches*, *The Wild Goose*, *Creaking Stairs*, *The Pointing Finger* and *Bread*. MacLaren left Universal in 1920 and thereafter freelanced. Her older sister

Katherine MacDonald, renowned for her great beauty, was also a silent star. Last silent: *The Courageous Coward* (1924).

Sound: MacLaren returned to the screen about 1933 for extra work and numerous small roles. She was seen throughout that decade, into the 1940s, and possibly beyond. Among the films in which she appeared were *Charlie Chan's Courage, Harmony Lane, The Reckless Ranger, A Day at the Races, In Name Only* and *We Who Are Young.*

Comments: Aside from an occasional nostalgia piece, Mary MacLaren was virtually forgotten. She came back to public attention in a most unfortunate way in the 1970s and '80s following several newspaper stories. She was described as living in squalor in her once-imposing mansion, and as a result of several legal wrangles she was threatened with loss of her home and being placed in a conservatorship.

Most poignant was a photograph of the former actress, now heavily wrinkled, posed with a 1920s movie magazine cover which featured her as a young red-haired beauty. Mary MacLaren was not a victim of the talkies because her starring career had ended years before. But somehow her story seemed emblematic of those cast off by the industry to which they had given so much.

MacLean, Douglas, (also McLean)

Philadelphia, Pennsylvania, 1890/97–1967
Silent: Beginning about 1914, light comedian Douglas MacLean appeared in features like *As Ye Sow, The Fair Barbarian, Fuss and Feathers, Mary's Ankle, The Rookie's Return, The Hottentot* (1922 version), *Mary of the Movies* and *Seven Keys to Baldpate* (1925 version). He made fewer films after 1923, mainly for his own production company. Last silent: *Soft Cushions* (1927).

Sound: MacLean appeared in only two talkers: the part-sound *The Carnation Kid*, in which he played a noiseless typewriter salesman, and the all-talking *Divorce Made Easy*, both 1929. He continued to be top-billed.

MacLean's voice was apparently no obstacle to his continuing before the camera but he chose not to. After his on-screen career ended, he became an associate producer beginning in 1931 and ultimately a producer as well as a screenwriter.

Reviews

The Carnation Kid: What it doesn't do for the picture itself the talking does for Douglas MacLean. Formerly a fairly popular juvenile, he now is a great light comedian with a good voice. If he was 100 percent before talking, MacLean is now 200 percent because of his voice. He is highly impressive

throughout, and more so when talking. *Variety* 2/27/29.

Divorce Made Easy: MacLean has a very pleasing voice. *Harrison's Reports* 7/20/29.

Maloney, Leo, San Jose, California,

1888–1929
Silent: As a stuntman and bit player, burly Leo Maloney was in films by 1914. He later appeared in the "Range Rider" series for Pathe. Among his earlier features were *Judith of the Cumberlands, The Manager of the B. and A.* and *Whispering Smith.*

In the '20s, Maloney became popular in a long string of westerns that included *Ghost City, The Western Musketeer, Riding Double, Ranchers and Rascals, Blind Trail, Don Desperado* and *Flash o' Lightning.* That popularity was on the wane when he made the serial *The Vanishing West* in the late '20s and it somewhat restored his box office value.

Earlier serials in which Maloney had appeared were *The Hazards of Helen, A Lass of the Lumberlands, The Railroaders, The Lost Express* and *The Fatal Sign.* Later in his career he had his own production company and directed several pictures as well. Last silent: *Yellow Contraband* (1928).

Sound: Maloney made a single talkie, the "B" western *Overland Bound.* He was in New York attempting to market it at the time of his death and it did obtain a release in late 1929. Although it was definitely a cheapie production, it bore the distinction of being the second all-sound western following the popular *In Old Arizona.*

Reviews

Overland Bound: Leo Maloney is the hero in a better story than any he has so far put into pictures. His voice has registered well. *Harrison's Reports* 10/12/29.

Marion, George (later Sr.), 1858/60–1945

Silent: From 1903 to 1920, stage actor George Marion largely eschewed performing for theater directing. His 1920 appearance as the title character's sea captain father in Eugene O'Neill's *Anna Christie* marked the beginning of his return to an acting career. He had already made a couple of silent features in the mid-'teens, *Excuse Me* and *Madame X,* and may have been in two-reelers a bit earlier.

In 1921 Marion embarked on a string of silents including *Gun Shy,* the 1923 film version of *Anna Christie, Clothes Make the Pirate, Tumbleweeds, Rolling Home, The King of Kings, Bringin' Home the Bacon* and *Loco Luck.* Last silent: *A Texas Steer* (1927).

Sound: Marion's first part-talkie was 1929's

Evangeline. The second year of Marion's sound career, 1930, was an active one. To no one's surprise he reprised his stage and silent roles as the title heroine's father in the talkie version of *Anna Christie.* She was played by Greta Garbo and it was the film that trumpeted "Garbo Talks!" In it he repeated his character's famous speech about "Dat ole debbil sea."

Marion made several that same year including *Man to Man, The Big House, A Lady's Morals* and *The Sea Bat.* From 1931 to 1935, his final year on the screen, he made fewer than ten films, among them *Laughing Sinners, Six Hours to Live, Her First Mate, Port of Lost Dreams, Rocky Mountain Mystery* and *Metropolitan.* He was the father of well-known screenwriter George Marion, Jr.

REVIEWS

Anna Christie: Marion gives a very good performance. *Variety* 3/19/30, *Harrison's Reports* 3/22/30.

Port of Lost Dreams: The waterfront characters including George Marion reflect good choices on the part of the casting director. *Variety* 4/3/35.

Metropolitan: George Marion Sr. plays his volatile Latin role with all the gusto that's usually ascribed to this type of temperament. *Variety* 10/23/35.

Markey, Enid, Dillon, Colorado,
1891/96–1982

Silent: Although primarily a stage performer, Enid Markey made about 25 films from 1915 to '18 and a couple in the following decade. She is most famous today for her portrayal of the first cinema Jane opposite that swinger through the jungle, Tarzan, as played by Elmo Lincoln. Their films were 1918's *The Romance of Tarzan* and *Tarzan of the Apes.*

Markey also was a sometime co-star of William S. Hart and Tom Mix. Other movies included *The Captive God, The Cup of Life, The Iron Strain, Civilization, The Female of the Species, The Curse of Eve, Six Shooter Andy* and *Sink or Swim.* Last silent: *Foolish Mothers* (1923).

Sound: After returning to the theater, Markey made only three sound pictures thereafter, the first being a recreation of her stage role in *Snafu* in 1945. Only two followed: *The Naked City* (1948) and finally, two decades later, *The Boston Strangler,* in which she had a small role. She appeared on television and was still performing in the 1970s.

REVIEWS

Snafu: Enid Markey shines in the role of Aunt Emily. *Variety* 1/2/46.

Marlowe, June (Gisela Goetten), St. Cloud, Minnesota, 1903/07–1984
Filmography: Classic Images (Mar.-May 1985)

Silent: After bit parts in the "Fighting Blood" series, June Marlowe had her first substantial role in *When a Man's a Man* in 1924. She was signed by Warner Bros. for Rin Tin Tin's *Find Your Man,* the first of several appearances with the canine star which included *The Night Cry, Below the Line, Clash of the Wolves* and *Tracked in the Snow Country.*

Marlowe also "co-starred" with another dog, Silverstreak, in *Fangs of Justice.* Others of her films were *A Lost Lady, The Life of Riley, Alias the Deacon, The Old Soak, Free Lips* and *The Eternal Silence.* She also played a small role in John Barrymore's *Don Juan.* Last silent: *Code of the Air* (1928).

Sound: At the end of the silent era, June Marlowe went to Germany to appear in films and radio broadcasts there. Upon her return to the United States she made only about five talkie features and probably is better remembered for her role as the teacher Miss Crabtree in several "Our Gang" shorts of 1930–32.

Marlowe's first lengthy talkie appearance was in the serial *The Lone Defender,* once again with Rin Tin Tin. Among her features were Laurel and Hardy's *Pardon Us, The Devil on Deck* and *Riddle Ranch* (1935). After many years' hiatus, her last bit part may have been in *Slave Girl* (1947). There was also an appearance in an Argentinian picture.

Comments: June Marlowe was undeniably a pretty addition to the silent screen. Named a Wampas Baby Star in 1925, she was dubbed "The Girl with the Soulful Eyes" and "The Most Beautiful Girl on the Screen." Of course, numerous others had equal claim to that honor.

Marlowe's career may well have been on the wane before silents ended and she never gained a strong foothold in talkies. If her minuscule role in *Pardon Us* is any indication, her voice recorded as high-pitched and without tonal color.

REVIEWS

Pardon Us: June Marlowe is the only female on-screen, and for only about three or four minutes, in which she speaks about a dozen words in all. *Variety* 8/25/31.

Marsh, Mae (Mary Marsh), New Madrid, New Mexico, 1895–1968
Filmography: Films in Review (June-July 1958); *Silent Picture* (Autumn 1969)

Silent: One of D. W. Griffith's favored actresses, Mae Marsh began at Biograph in 1912, possibly in a Mary Pickford film. Her first lead was in the one-reeler *Man's Genesis*. She had major roles in both *Birth of a Nation* and *Intolerance* and also appeared in *The Avenging Conscience, The Battle of Elderbush Gulch* and *Judith of Bethulia*. Robert Harron was a frequent co-star.

Marsh starred for Goldwyn in 1917–19 but many of her films there were not successful and her career took a downward turn. Among her films in the 'teens were *Hoodoo Ann, The Wharf Rat, Polly of the Circus, All Woman, The Face in the Dark* and *Spotlight Sadie*.

In the '20s Marsh's output fell dramatically; she was seen in but one film a year from 1920–25. *The White Rose* (1923), again for Griffith, probably gave her her outstanding role of the decade. She went to England for a few pictures that included *Paddy, the Next Best Thing*. Last U.S. silent: *Tides of Passion* (1925); last U.K. silent: *The Rat* (1925).

Sound: Marsh's first and only starring film in the talkies was a 1931 remake of the 1920 success *Over the Hill (to the Poorhouse)*. In it, at the age of only 36, she essayed the role of an aged mother. Despite its genuinely heart-tugging quality and her praised performance, it was not successful in those Depression days when people wanted escapist entertainment.

From 1932 to the early '60s Marsh appeared in small roles in many movies, including *Black Fury, Young People, Dixie Dugan, Girls in Prison, Cry Terror, Night Without Sleep* and *Impact*. She was a favorite of John Ford's and was cast in several of his pictures: *Fort Apache, The Grapes of Wrath, Three Godfathers, How Green Was My Valley* and *Sergeant Rutledge*. Her last film appearance was in *Two Rode Together* (1961).

Comments: Mae Marsh did not succeed as a star in the talkies. Her voice did seem adequate, if a bit high-pitched. The greater question, possibly, is why she did not succeed in *silents* after she left Griffith. An actress of major talent, charm and all–American prettiness, she nevertheless floundered and had few vehicles worthy of her.

The reasons why Marsh did not fulfill her great potential in the silents also may hold the answer for the sound era. She perhaps needed a strong hand to guide her; alone, she apparently did not have the drive it took to sustain a starring career. She herself claimed that raising a family came first and that may have been a partial reason.

At 35 Marsh was too old at the beginning of the talkie era to begin again as a romantic leading lady but she might have had a bigger career nonetheless. Whatever the cause of her disappointing later career and the failure to fulfill her potential, her shining talent is still available on film to be admired.

REVIEWS

Over the Hill: Marsh is extraordinarily competent and always natural. Her characterization is lifelike and her acting is compelling and subdued. She is the perfect choice for the mother role. People could be heard sobbing. *New York Times* 11/21/31, *Variety* 11/24/31, *Harrison's Reports* 11/28/31.

Black Fury: Mae Marsh, silent screen star, has a bit. *Variety* 4/17/35.

Three Godfathers: Marsh makes a choice assignment out of her part. *Variety* 12/1/48.

Marshall, Tully (William Phillips), Nevada City, California, 1864–1943

Filmography: List of films in *Films in Review* (Nov. 1966); *Classic Images* (Jan.-Feb., May 1991); *Eighty Silent Film Stars*

Silent: After his screen debut in *Paid in Full* (1914), stage actor Tully Marshall seemed to be in every other film made in the silent era. He made at least 110 of them, including *Intolerance, The Squaw Man* (1918 version), *The Covered Wagon* (one of his major roles), *The Hunchback of Notre Dame, The Cat and the Canary, Queen Kelly* and *Broken Hearts of Broadway*. Last silent: *Redskin* (1929), with synchronized music and sound effects, made after his first talkies.

Sound: The Perfect Crime, a 1928 part-talkie, was Marshall's first foray into sound. It was followed that year by the fully sound *Conquest*. He appeared in nine films in 1929, most of them also talking, and in 1930 he was seen in 12 films. He continued to be very active through the mid-'30s, often as a bad man.

Although at some point in the 1930s Tully Marshall claimed to be semi-retired, he still made film appearances until the year of his death. His 70 or so talkies included *Mammy, Corruption, Ball of Fire, Cabin in the Cotton, Diamond Jim, Grand Hotel, Souls at Sea, Go West* and *Hitler's Madman*, his last in '43.

Marshall's later roles were by no means insignificant. As Alvin Brewster, the smarmy industrialist-traitor in *This Gun for Hire* (1942), he gave one of his most memorable performances. He also made at least one serial, appearing as a red herring suspect in the 1932 John Wayne serial *The Hurricane Express*.

Comments: A character actor supreme was Tully Marshall. His thin, leering face, often emphasized by lighting, and his cadaverous physique made him a natural for the villainous roles which he was still playing into his old age. The utter foulness of his treasonous industrialist in *This Gun for Hire* showed he still could snarl, menace (and almost slaver) with the best of them, although he played the part in a wheelchair.

Sound added the dimension of Marshall's stage-trained voice. It was somewhat reedy in age but it enhanced his characterizations, both good and bad. He could easily play benign old men and codgerly characters but somehow you always expected him to throw off his meek sheep's clothing to reveal the wolf beneath.

REVIEWS

Burning Up: Tully Marshall is one of the confederates of the villain. *Harrison's Reports* 2/15/30.

She Asked for It: Marshall, who hasn't been around much lately, plays the murderer's victim. *Variety* 9/1/37.

Youth Will Be Served: Marshall is convincing as the ornery old man with the tender heart. *Variety* 11/20/40.

This Gun for Hire: Marshall plays the wealthy head of a chemical concern and a fifth columnist. *Harrison's Reports* 3/21/42.

Behind Prison Walls: Tully Marshall is a steel magnate. *Harrison's Reports* 3/6/43.

Mason, Shirley (Leonie Flugrath), Brooklyn, New York, 1900/01–1979

Filmography: Films in Review (March 1976), additional filmography (June 1976)

Silent: One of three child actress sisters (Virginia [Viola Dana] and Edna were the others), Shirley Mason made her screen bow about 1910 with Edison, possibly in *A Christmas Carol*. The studio dubbed her "The Remarkable Girl Actress." She continued appearing in movies under her real name while also acting on the stage. Her many features during the 'teens included *Vanity Fair, Envy, The Little Chevalier, The Rescuing Angel* and *Come On In*.

The tiny Mason (4'11") became a popular leading lady working at Fox in 1920–25 and subsequently at Paramount, First National and FBO. Among her 1920s silents were *Lord Jim, Little Miss Smiles, The Eleventh Hour, Desert Gold, Stranded* and *What Fools Men*. She made at least 90 features and also was seen in the serial *Vultures of the Sea* (1928). Last silent: *Anne Against the World* (1929).

Sound: Mason made three talkies, all in 1929, none of which did anything for a successful continuation of her career. One of the films was the all-star Warner Bros. extravaganza *The Show of Shows*, in which she appeared in ensemble numbers, including the sharing of a snippet of song and dance with Viola Dana in "Meet My Sister."

Mason also had the femme lead in two independent quickie melodramas: *The Flying Marine* and *Dark Skies*. Some sources refer to the latter as *Darkened Skies* and question whether she appeared

in it at all. The reviews make it clear that she did. There perhaps has been some confusion with Evelyn Brent's *Darkened **Rooms*** the same year.

REVIEWS

The Flying Marine: Shirley Mason is the heroine and adds to the interest of the film. *Harrison's Reports* 7/20/29, *Variety* 8/7/29.

Maynard, Ken, Vevay, Indiana, 1895–1973

Filmography: List of films in *Eighty Silent Film Stars*

Silent: Ken Maynard was a daredevil rider with Ringling Brothers circus and the holder of the All-Around Cowboy title before essaying films. His first billed appearance was in 1923's *The Man Who Won* and he subsequently was seen as Paul Revere in Marion Davies's *Janice Meredith*. His western career was launched in 1924's *$50,000 Reward* and stardom followed in a series for Davis Distributing in 1925–26.

Among Maynard's films were *The Demon Rider, Señor Daredevil, The Red Raiders, The Phantom City, Somewhere in Sonora, The Unknown Cavalier* and *Cheyenne*. Like many another western star he had his own production unit. Last silent: *Lucky Larkin* (1930), with synchronized music and sound effects, made after his first talkies.

Sound: The Wagon Master, a 1929 part-talkie, marked Ken Maynard's sound bow. Made late that year, *Señor Americano* was his first almost-full-talkie. Among his other early sound pictures were *The Fighting Legion, Mountain Justice, Parade of the West* and *Song of the Caballero*.

Other Maynard films included *Hellfire Austin, Dynamite Ranch, In Old Santa Fe*, which marked Gene Autry's fleeting screen debut in 1934, *Fargo Express, The Lone Avenger, Western Frontier, Strawberry Roan* and *Wheels of Destiny*.

Maynard also made the popular serial *Mystery Mountain*. Among the studios for which he appeared were Universal, Tiffany, Ascot, Columbia, Grand National and KBS/World Wide.

Finding his career in decline in the latter '30s, Maynard departed Hollywood and toured the country with his own circus. When it went bankrupt he returned to the screen in 1941, becoming a part of Monogram's "Trail Blazers" series with Bob Steele and Hoot Gibson.

Maynard's final leading roles in his 150 film career were in the mid–1940s but he returned for a brief appearance in *Bigfoot*, made about 1970. In the '40s he again toured with circuses and Wild West shows.

Comments: Handsome and rugged, Ken Maynard was enormously popular from the mid–1920s to the middle of the following decade. He was a natural athlete who performed many of his own stunts; others were doubled by his brother Kermit. He even could claim to be the precursor of the singing cowboys because he occasionally sang and fiddled in his films, although his voice may have been dubbed.

More than any other star of the oaters, Maynard was seen in films whose plots often strayed from straight western melodrama to far-out fantasy and points in between. Credibility was frequently strained but his primarily juvenile fans did not seem to mind.

Maynard's speaking voice was not particularly good, being somewhat high-pitched, and sound revealed his acting not to be on a par with his athletic abilities. Another problem which may have hastened the end of his career was his weight and considerable drinking — the two very possibly being related. He was also becoming somewhat long in the tooth for his customary roles.

Besides that, no studio had much of an incentive to keep employing Maynard because his prickly real-life personality notably lacked the affability of his screen persona. Again that was possibly alcohol-related. He became roundly disliked; the unsympathetic character of Tex in the novel *The Carpetbaggers* supposedly is partly based on him.

REVIEWS

Wagon Master: Maynard speaks distinctly and with the intonation one expects from a kind-hearted he-man of the wide open spaces. Besides speaking he instrumentalizes on the guitar and violin. *Variety* 10/2/29.

Señor Americano: About the best fare Ken Maynard has appeared in. He is better as an actor because he is more reserved. He speaks well. *Variety* 1/1/30.

Sons of the Saddle: Maynard and his cowboys sing without accompanying music and in one spot he even strums on his guitar while he is singing. He doesn't have much of a voice but in his characterization it's okay. He is improving histrionically and vocally. *Variety* 8/20/30.

In Old Santa Fe: One of the best Ken Maynards to date. *Variety* 3/20/35.

Six Shootin' Sheriff: Maynard shows the effect of real life good living, being about 30 pounds heavier than he can comfortably conceal. It slows him up a bit and may have something to do with his horse Tarzan growing thinner from picture to picture. *Variety* 8/17/38.

Flaming Lead: Maynard has lost about 25 pounds from his paunch since he was last seen but could stand a bit more training to get rid of some more weight. *Variety* 11/15/39.

Mehaffey, Blanche (also known as Janet Morgan and Joan Alden), Cincinnati, Ohio, 1905/07–1968

Filmography: List of films in *Sweethearts of the Sage*

Silent: One of her earliest films was the one-reeler *Powder and Smoke* and, after being named a 1924 Wampas Baby Star, Blanche Mehaffey became a supporting player in major productions and a "B" leading lady.

Among Mehaffey's films were *A Woman of the World*, a Pola Negri starrer, *The White Sheep*, *The Princess from Hoboken* and *His People*, in which she played an Irish colleen in love with a Jewish boy.

Mehaffey's co-stars were not always of the two-legged variety. In *Marlie the Killer* she co-starred with the title character played by Klondike, a dog. She also was seen in Hoot Gibson westerns like *The Texas Streak*, *The Denver Dude* and *The Silent Rider*. Last silent: *Smilin' Guns* (1929).

Sound: Mehaffey continued to play some leads in quickie melodramas and westerns, including those of Hoot Gibson, starting in 1931 and '32. During those years she made about a dozen movies. There was also the 1931 serial *The Mystery Trooper*. She returned in 1935 for a few more and then made her last two in 1938, *Held for Ransom* and *The Wages of Sin*.

Among Mehaffey's other pictures were *Dancing Dynamite*, *Mounted Fury* (starring the ill-fated John Bowers in his last film), *Sunrise Trail*, *Dynamite Denny*, *Sally of the Subway*, *North of Arizona* and *Wildcat Saunders*. Somewhere along the way she changed her name at least twice in ill-fated attempts to resuscitate a flagging career. In the late '40s she sued to prevent her films from being shown on television but lost the suit.

REVIEWS

Dancing Dynamite: Blanche Mehaffey did okay with a dizzy dame part. *Variety* 8/25/31.

Held for Ransom: The topliner is Blanche Mehaffey who is cute. She stars for the first time and is unknown.

(Considering this was just about Mehaffey's *last* film, this served as an ironic commentary on her almost 15-year career.) *Variety* 7/20/38.

Meighan, Thomas, Pittsburgh, Pennsylvania, 1879–1936

Filmography: Films in Review (Apr. 1974); *Classic Images* (May 1991); List of films in *Eighty Silent Film Stars*

Silent: After making one film in England in 1914, stage actor Thomas Meighan signed with Famous Players–Lasky in 1915 as a leading man and ultimately became a major Paramount star throughout most of the silent era. During the course of his almost 75 silents, he partnered many of the leading actressesof the era, among them Mary Pickford, Gloria Swanson, Blanche Sweet and Norma Talmadge.

The Miracle Man (1919) proved to be Meighan's breakthrough and DeMille's *Male and Female* and *Why Change Your Wife?* confirmed his stardom. Other films included *The Storm, Peg o' My Heart, Manslaughter, Tin Gods, The Canadian, The Racket* and *The Alaskan.* Last silent: *The Mating Call* (1928).

Sound: Meighan's first talkie was *The Argyle Case* for Warner Bros. in 1929. He made five more, some in the lead but later playing supporting roles. They were *Young Sinners* and *Skyline* (1931), *Cheaters at Play,* in which he had top billing, and *Madison Sq. Garden* (1932) and, finally, *Peck's Bad Boy* (1934).

Comments: Despite already being mature (over 35) when he made his initial films, Tommy Meighan rose to the very top echelon of silent leading men in popularity as well as salary. The latter was certainly high, allowing him to live a baronial life on a Long Island estate.

Meighan specialized in rugged but romantic roles of the type that Clark Gable later played, and he favored stories that took his characters to the great outdoors. His value to Paramount was clearly demonstrated by their willingness to let him live and work in the East. In fact, their New York studio was kept open primarily to accommodate him.

Meighan departed Paramount when they seemed unwilling to cast him in a talkie, a recalcitrance they showed with other players as well. He was 50 in 1929 and his career had already begun to decline slightly so the studio may well have wanted him to terminate his expensive contract. Also, he was not in top health, made worse by his rumored alcoholism.

Meighan's first talkie was well-received, his theater-trained voice was fine and he remained a star, however temporarily. But on the other hand he was rich, he enjoyed his off-screen lifestyle, and he probably felt he had little reason to actively pursue a career which promised only father roles in the future.

REVIEWS

The Argyle Case: This has the added significance of being Thomas Meighan's first talker. He more than sustains his end, even lending conviction to an occasional banality. Judging by the work he does in it, it will not be his last one; his work is excellent. His voice registers well and his lines are clear. *Variety* 9/4/29, *Harrison's Reports* 9/7/29.

Young Sinners: They've given Meighan a brogue, which seems unnecessary but doesn't interfere with his performance. V*ariety* 5/13/31.

Skyline: Meighan couldn't do anything with the part except give a workmanlike performance without any frills. All that is believable about the character is to be attributed to him. He makes his role human. *Variety* 10/6/31, *Harrison's Reports* 10/10/31.

Cheaters at Play: No outstanding performances to speak of; everybody seems to drift through the picture. As the father, Meighan acts stern and self-reliant. *Variety* 3/1/32, *Harrison's Reports* 3/5/32.

Peck's Bad Boy: It is an ideal role for Meighan's comeback. *Variety* 10/9/34.

Menjou, Adolphe, Pittsburgh, Pennslyvania, 1890–1963

Filmography: Films in Review (Oct. 1983); List of films in *Film Dope* (Oct. 1989)

Silent: Mustachioed Adolphe Menjou played in stock productions and vaudeville before trying his fortunes in film. Starting in 1914 he was an extra and bit player with Vitagraph. Among his early features from 1916 were *The Kiss, The Reward of Patience* and *The Valentine Girl.*

Menjou arrived in Hollywood in 1920, his first important role coming in the next year's *The Faith Healer.* Nineteen twenty-three ushered in his starring career when he played the Parisian roué in the Charles Chaplin–directed *A Woman of Paris.* In 1924 he consolidated that stardom with the sophisticated *Sinners in Silk* and *The Marriage Circle.* He was seen in ten motion pictures that year alone.

Other popular silent films among the 60 or so credited to Menjou included Rudolph Valentino's *The Sheik, The Three Musketeers, Rupert of Hentzau, The King on Main Street, The Grand Duchess and the Waiter* and *Are Parents People?* Last silent: *His Private Life* (1928).

Sound: The coming of sound put Menjou's career in some jeopardy. To accommodate his established screen image as a boulevardier, he spoke with a French accent in his first talkie, 1929's *Fashions in Love.* Apparently some critics were fooled into thinking he was actually French-born.

One of Menjou's 1930 efforts was indeed a French-language version of *Slightly Scarlet* and he also made a picture in France. His one English-language film that year, *Morocco*, put him back on the path towards stardom.

The Front Page in 1931 was a huge hit and a personal one for Menjou as well, probably the apex of his film career. It not only revealed his flair for sound comedy but earned him an Academy Award nomination for Best Actor.

It was the first of many significant films in various genres for Menjou in that decade, including *A Farewell to Arms, 100 Men and a Girl, Morning Glory, Little Miss Marker, The Milky Way, Stage Door* and *A Star Is Born.*

Going into the 1940s, Menjou's films, with few exceptions, became somewhat less prestigious and they were fewer in number. Among them were *You Were Never Lovelier, Step Lively, State of the Union, Sweet Rosie O'Grady* and *Father Takes a Wife.* Perhaps only *The Hucksters* and *The Bachelor's Daughters* showed him to best advantage.

In later years Menjou's output declined even further but he scored a comeback of sorts with his very well-acted, albeit unsympathetic, role as General Broulard in the Stanley Kubrick picture *Paths of Glory* (1957). Set during World War One, it provided him with an unlikely but brave piece of casting.

Other Menjou pictures that decade included *The Fuzzy Pink Nightgown, The Ambassador's Daughter, To Please a Lady* and *Across the Wide Missouri.* The last of his approximately 80 talkies for studios like RKO, MGM, Universal, Warner Bros., Fox and United Artists was 1960's *Pollyanna.*

Comments: The persona that Adolphe Menjou established in silents, in both comedy and drama, was as a highly sophisticated man of the world and sometime seducer of unwary women. He was usually morally ambiguous and often a downright villain. In both silents and talkies, the word "suavity" became a synonym for "Menjou."

Given his deep, well-modulated voice, it is difficult to understand why Menjou was considered risky for talkies, but he succeeded hugely. His change of persona to a sometimes shady but ultimately sympathetic character in comic and serious talkie roles was essential to his success. He became an expert at fast-talking frenetic comedy, but whether he totally understood his gift for humor is not entirely clear.

In later years Menjou's reputation rested as much on his vaunted sartorial splendor and deeply held (and publicly expressed) conservatism as on his film performances. Because of his loudly proclaimed anti–Communism he perhaps ironically (some would say deservedly) fell victim to a backlash against blacklisting. But when called upon, he was still capable of giving an effective performance.

REVIEWS

Fashions in Love: Adolphe Menjou's first talkie proves the star has a diction tailored to his silent screen personality. Sophisticated audiences will find many laughs in the Menjou touches. He impersonates the role to perfection and does as good work as he did in *A Woman of Paris.* He has a slight French accent but it is not unpleasant. His voice registers well. *Variety 7/3/29, Harrison's Reports 7/6/29.*

Morocco: Menjou has a brief role, done with his accustomed suavity. *Variety 11/10/30.*

The Front Page: A standout performance is given by Adolphe Menjou. The usually suave heavy plays softer here but without letting up. *Variety 3/25/31.*

Morning Glory: It is a characteristically suave performance. *Variety 8/22/33.*

Little Miss Marker: Menjou turns in a very good performance. *Variety 5/22/34.*

The Goldwyn Follies: Menjou seems to be a producer's idea of how a producer should look. *Variety 2/2/38.*

Paths of Glory: Menjou, in an offbeat bit of casting, is excellent. *Variety 11/20/57.*

Miljan, John, Lead, South Dakota,

1892/93–1960

Silent: Saturnine John Miljan made the first of his hundreds of films in 1924 and later in the decade was appearing in as many as 20 films a year. Occasionally he played the lead but mostly was seen in supporting roles, often as the villain.

Miljan's pictures were in a wide variety of genres and included *The Painted Lady, The Phantom of the Opera, My Official Wife, Sailor Izzy Murphy, The Unchastened Woman, Old San Francisco, Romance Ranch* and *Lovers?* Last silent: *Speedway* (1929), with synchronized sound effects and music, made after his first talkies.

Sound: Miljan appeared in the now risible trailer for *The Jazz Singer* in 1927; that could be considered his sound bow. *Tenderloin,* a 1928 part-talkie, was his first actual feature. He made several sound or part-sound films that year including *Glorious Betsy, The Home Towners, The Terror, Land of the Silver Fox* and the Vitaphone short *His Night Out.* Most of the 13 pictures he made in 1929 were sound as well.

Miljan kept rolling along through the early '40s in both features and shorts, and then was seen in fewer during the last part of that decade and the 1950s. Most of his roles were in support but he still was infrequently top-billed, such as in *Twin Husbands.* His final effort was 1958's *The Lone Ranger and the Lost City of Gold.*

Other Miljan movies included *Our Blushing*

Brides, The Unholy Three, The Wet Parade, Belle of the Nineties, The Ghost Walks, If I Were King, Bombardier, The Killers, Samson and Delilah and *The Ten Commandments.*

Comments: It is apparent that Hollywood producers thought John Miljan's syrupy-smooth voice was something special. This is obviously why he was selected to make the *Jazz Singer* trailer and why, of his nine 1928 films, six were sound or part-talking. This is a probable record for the most appearances in very early sound films. He also made a widely seen trailer which extolled the talking film and which may well have been the basis for the spoof trailer in *Singin' in the Rain.*

Miljan's career lasted all the longer for his never having become a talkie star. His lean and frequently mustachioed face was seen in at least 200 films, in many of which his villainy was unbridled but generally unavailing. He was said to have had the distinction of being "killed" more often than any other character actor.

REVIEWS

Under the Pampas Moon: Miljan manages to play a heavy without going overboard. *Variety 6/5/35.*

Pirates of Tripoli: Miljan is satisfactory as the villain. *Variety 1/26/55.*

The Lone Ranger and the Lost City of Gold: Miljan portrays an old Indian chief. *Harrison's Reports 6/7/58.*

Miller, Patsy Ruth (Patricia Miller), St. Louis, Missouri, 1904/05–1995

Filmography: Filmograph (nos. 1-2, 1971)

Silent: Before her first lead in 1922's *Watch Your Step*, brunette Patsy Ruth Miller had a bit in *Camille* (1921) and perhaps appeared briefly in a few other films. Her most famous motion picture, Lon Chaney's *The Hunchback of Notre Dame*, came in 1923, the year after she was named a Wampas Baby Star.

Among Miller's 55 silent films were westerns with Tom Mix, William S. Hart and Hoot Gibson. Her pictures included *The King of the Turf, The Breaking Point, Singer Jim McKee, The Fighting Edge, The Girl I Loved, Red Hot Tires* and Ernst Lubitsch's *So This Is Paris*, probably her other best-known work. Last silent: *Tropical Nights* (1928).

Sound: All of Miller's 1929 films were talking or part-talking. Of her 12 talkies, in some of which she proved herself adept at comedy, eight were made that year. Among them were *The Fall of Eve, Twin Beds, The Show of Shows, So Long Letty* and *The Hottentot.* Her output fell to two in 1930. Her final film after a 20-year hiatus was *Quebec* (1951), in which she had little more than a walk-on, apparently just for fun.

REVIEWS

The Fall of Eve: Miller's role, although the center of the complications, is less impressive than those of other cast members. *Variety 6/19/29, Harrison's Reports 6/22/29.*

Twin Beds: Miller plays without verve but is pleasingly sexy. *Variety 7/17/29, Harrison's Reports 7/20/29.*

Wide Open: A very good farce comedy aided by the work of Patsy Ruth Miller. *Harrison's Reports 3/9/30.*

Lonely Wives: Miller inclines a bit too much to the boisterous as the drunk. *Harrison's Reports 2/21/31, Variety 3/18/31.*

Miller, Walter, Dayton, Ohio, 1892–1940

Filmography: List of films in *Eighty Silent Film Stars*

Silent: The man who was to become the greatest male serial star of the '20s (and perhaps of all time) began his film career about 1910 with Reliance, after having been in vaudeville and stock. Walter Miller was in numerous one- and two-reelers for such studios as Biograph, Rex and Edison. His films of the 'teens included *The Spider and the Fly, The Cloud, Tangled Lives, The Eleventh Commandment, Thin Ice* and *The Return of Tarzan.*

During the early part of the next decade, Miller worked for small studios like Salient, Gilbert, Dependable, Encore, Barker and Arrow in films like *The Shadow, The Bootleggers* and *The Tie That Binds.* His career seemed to be heading nowhere rapidly until he was teamed with Allene Ray to make the first of their serials together. He was to appear in 17 during the silent era, most of them extremely popular.

Among Miller's serial appearances, many co-starring Miss Ray, were *Way of a Man, Sunken Silver, The Green Archer, House Without a Key, Hawk of the Hills, The Man Without a Face, Snowed In* and *The Terrible People.* Last silent feature: *Manhattan Knights* (1928). The 1929 release *Hawk of the Hills* was a feature version of his serial.

Sound: With the advent of sound, Miller's starring career was no more although he did occasionally play the lead in a quickie. He continued to appear in many serials as well but again he had the lead in only a couple, including *King of the Kongo* (1929), made in both talkie and silent versions.

Miller worked steadily throughout the '30s as a supporting player, including many a western as a sheriff or villain. Among his numerous sound films (he made over 20 in 1937 alone) were *Rough Waters, Hell's Valley, The Ghost City, Central Airport, Rocky Rhodes, The Raven, The Invisible Ray,*

Boss of Lonely Valley, Kentucky, Each Dawn I Die and *Bullet Code*. He was still in harness at the time of his death, a contributory cause of which may have been a strenuous fight scene.

REVIEWS

Rocky Rhodes: Walter Miller is the menace, employing the same tactics as they used in the old days. It is a good type, however, and well played. *Variety* 1/1/35.

Bullet Code: Miller provides suitable menace as a heavy. *Variety* 2/28/40.

Mix, Tom, Mix Run, Pennsylvania, 1880–1940

Filmography: Classic Images (Jan. 1980), Selig films only (July-August 1987); List of films in *Classic Film Collector* (Fall 1975); *Film Dope* (Mar. 1990)

Silent: After careers in law enforcement, the military and Wild West shows, Tom Mix began working behind the scenes for the Selig studio which used his Oklahoma ranch for the documentary *Ranch Life in the Great Southwest*.

Eventually Mix drifted to the other side of the camera and between 1911 and '17 made over 70 one- and two-reelers that included *Chip of the Flying U, Sagebrush Tom* and *Why the Sheriff Is a Bachelor*. His initial roles mostly were in support of Selig star Kathlyn Williams.

There also were occasional features like *In the Days of the Thundering Herd* (1914), but the studio favored shorter films and Mix decided to sign with Fox. This proved to be the making of his career and by 1920 he was the most popular western star on the screen.

Mix became Fox's biggest moneymaker in films like *The Riders of the Purple Sage, Three Jumps Ahead, Rough Riding Romance, The Lone Star Ranger, The Rainbow Trail, Sky High* and *Just Tony*. The latter film featured his horse, which was almost as famous as its master.

After about 60 features, among which were non-westerns like *Tom Mix in Arabia* and *Dick Turpin*, Mix signed with FBO for a brief silent series in 1928 and '29, including *King Cowboy, The Drifter* and *Outlawed*. Last silent: *The Big Diamond Robbery* (1929).

Sound: After ostensibly retiring, Mix returned to the screen in 1932 for a nine-film Universal series, the first of which was *Destry Rides Again*. This was reasonably well-received, but as a whole they were not outstandingly successful. The succeeding films were *My Pal the King, The Texas Badman, The Fourth Horseman, Hidden Gold, Riders of Death Valley, Flaming Guns, Terror Trail* and *Rustler's Roundup*.

Mix appeared just once more on-screen in the 1935 Mascot serial *The Miracle Rider*, which had a science-fiction theme. He then began touring with the Tom Mix Wild Animal Circus but after a couple of successful years it went bankrupt in 1938. This marked the end of his career but his name was kept before the public in the '40s via a long-running radio show in which he was portrayed by another actor.

Comments: Tom Mix was a new kind of cowboy star. Instead of the apparent gritty realism of actors like William S. Hart and Broncho Billy Anderson, he favored slick, streamlined and action-filled stories which catered to younger audiences. His heroes neither smoke, drank nor swore — unlike his hard-playing off-screen self — and he tried to capture rather than kill the villains. It was a model most western stars followed thereafter.

Although the money Fox made on Mix's films allowed them to make more prestige works like *Sunrise*, they eventually became more concerned with their dramatic films and he took his leave of the studio. There probably was also a question in the moguls' minds as to how well he could make the transition to talkies. The question was answered in 1932: It was only fair.

The talkies were not Tom Mix's medium; he was not a trained actor and he was over 50 by then. His words tended toward slurring and occasional indistinctness. (A story that his vocal cords had been damaged during a stunt may or may not be true.) He pretty much sounded and looked his age and eventually his stunts were almost always performed by others.

After his time as a star had passed, the flamboyant Mix did remain a major personality. He was bigger than life even without his much-publicized, and mainly overblown, exploits which supposedly included fighting in the Spanish-American War, the Philippine Insurrection, the Boxer Rebellion and the Boer War.

Mix lived on a grand scale and was truly a character who thrived on and invited publicity, which he always received. He was involved in numerous scraps — marital and otherwise — as well as lawsuits of various kinds. His death in an automobile accident was big news. The cinema did not see his like again.

REVIEWS

Destry Rides Again: The fear that Mix's voice would not record well will be dissipated by this picture. He again plays his old part of being kindly and of setting no bad example for children. He is also the same hard-riding star as of old and delivers when he gets a chance, but he gets too little chance. *Harrison's Reports* 4/16/32, *Variety* 6/21/32.

My Pal the King: With Mickey Rooney as a co-star, Mix has a chance to show a good part of his Wild West show and gets ample opportunity to do many tricks. *Harrison's Reports* 10/1/32, *Variety* 10/11/32.

The Texas Bad Man: Tom Mix scores strongly. The role fits him nicely and is the best he has had since his return to the screen. He plays adroitly. *Variety* 9/27/32.

The Fourth Horseman: This is another good Mix western. *Harrison's Reports* 10/22/32.

Terror Trail: Like all Tom Mix stories this offers excitement and thrills. There is plenty of shooting and riding horses at top speed. *Harrison's Reports* 2/11/33.

Montgomery, Peggy (Baby Peggy) (later
Diana Serra), Rock Island, Illinois, or Merced, California 1917/18–

Filmography: *What Ever Happened to Baby Peggy?*

Silent: For a comparatively brief period, until she did the unforgivable and got older, Baby Peggy was the major child actress in silent movies. A daughter of the industry (her father was a stuntman), she was in pictures by the age of three; her first appearance probably was in the two-reel Century comedy *Playmates* about 1920.

An appealing little girl with a Jackie Coogan haircut (later called the Baby Peggy haircut) and dark button eyes, the wee Miss Montgomery created a sensation. Eventually her father set up the Baby Peggy Film Company and she appeared in a phenomenally popular series of shorts in which she spoofed the major films and personalities of the day, like Valentino, Pola Negri, Mae Murray and Chaplin.

Baby Peggy began her feature career with the successful *The Darling of New York* (1923). Others were *Captain January, Helen's Babies* and *The Family Secret*. However, the inevitable happened and by the age of six or seven the once-lionized little girl found herself a has-been. For the next four years she toured in vaudeville. Last silent: *April Fool*(?) (1926).

Sound: In her adolescence (1932), Peggy Montgomery returned to the screen in the two-reeler *Off His Base*. Her first feature role was as one of the *Eight Girls in a Boat* in 1934. Until 1938 she had small and bit parts in a few other films, among them *Souls at Sea, True Confession, Having a Wonderful Time* and the serial *The Return of Chandu*. She may also have been in others as an unbilled player.

As an adult, Peggy Montgomery changed her name to Diana Serra and became a serious writer of articles and books about the movies, including *Hollywood Posse* and *Hollywood's Children*, a study of child actors and their generally unfortunate fates. Needless to say, she included her own sad story.

NOTE: Montgomery's mother, previously an extra, adopted the name Peggy Montgomery after her daughter's career had virtually ended. From 1924 to 1929 she co-starred in several "B" westerns and melodramas. Her credits are sometimes confused with those of her daughter by many of the important sources of such data.

Comments: As with Jackie Coogan, the other major '20s child sensation, Peggy Montgomery's story is one of exploitation and subsequent oblivion. Pushed by her parents and movie moguls into being an obedient baby-adult for their profit, she became "one-take Peggy" who did many of her own stunts and took direction like a trouper. It paid off handsomely for the adults; she made $10,000 a week when she was making two-reelers and earned $1.5 million a year in features.

Like Shirley Temple a decade later, Baby Peggy was a cottage industry with dolls, games and clothes bearing her likeness or name. Unlike Temple, all that she earned was lost by the greed or naiveté of those around her. Even her name was appropriated by her mother. As a teenager she felt that she had let her parents down by her "failure" and so returned to films for a comeback which no one seemed to notice.

It no doubt took many years for the adult Diana, *née* Peggy, to overcome the feeling that she, and not others, were to "blame." Judging by her perceptive writings and interviews, she is the ideal person to tell the world about the real life, as opposed to the "reel" life, of many of the envied tots of Tinseltown. Hers is a cautionary tale indeed.

Moore, Colleen (Kathleen Morrison), Port
Huron, Michigan, 1900/03–1988

Filmography: *Films in Review* (Aug.-Sept. 1963); List of films in *Film Dope* (Mar. 1990)

Silent: Colleen Moore was the actress who was to embody the quintessential flapper in the so-called Jazz Age. She began her career modestly enough in 1917, possibly with *The Bad Boy*, made comedies for Christie and played supporting roles in Tom Mix westerns.

There were other programmers for Moore until stardom beckoned with First National's *Flaming Youth* (1923), which gave its name to a decade of high-spirited, high livers. She became one of that studio's major stars for the remainder of the silent era. About her, author F. Scott Fitzgerald made the famous remark: "I was the spark which lit up flaming youth; Colleen Moore was the torch."

Among Moore's popular successes were *So Big*, *Lilac Time*, a World War One drama co-starring Gary Cooper, and *Ella Cinders*. Others of her almost 55 films, most comedies but some dramas, were *Oh, Kay!*, *Irene*, *We Moderns*, *Naughty but Nice*, *Happiness Ahead* and *The Perfect Flapper*. Last silent: *Why Be Good?* (1929).

Sound: Moore appeared in only six sound films. The first two, coming in 1929, were *Smiling Irish Eyes* and *Footlights and Fools*. She was then off-screen until 1933's *The Power and the Glory*, with Spencer Tracy; Moore played his first wife. This was her best talkie and was known, and later appreciated, for its innovative use of "narratage." At the time, it apparently confused viewers and was not very successful.

Moore's final three pictures were a poky remake of *The Scarlet Letter* and the dramas *Success at Any Price* and *Social Register* in 1934. While the latter two were well-mounted productions, her voice was only adequate and she was perhaps getting too mature for the parts she was given.

Moore was later back in the public eye when she displayed her widely publicized and fabulously appointed doll house in museums and other venues. Her 1968 autobiography *Silent Star* also introduced her to a new generation of film fans.

Comments: Although some of Colleen Moore's sound pictures were no better than mediocre, *The Power and the Glory* is now considered a minor classic. Unfortunately her first two sound vehicles did not get her off to a promising start. They were apparently selected with the idea that speaking with an accent (Irish and French) would highlight her acting ability.

Moore's signature persona as "The Flapper" was becoming passé by this time but she had successfully appeared in a variety of roles in both comedy and drama. Her long absence from the screen in the early 1930s certainly did not help. She was having serious domestic problems and was disappointed by the indifferent success of the first two films. That hiatus allowed other, newer faces to take her place.

The fact seems to be that Colleen Moore was perceived just as a silent star, as she herself acknowledged in the title of her popular autobiography. She was also at an age where she might have had to play character roles and this may have been something she was not willing to undertake.

There are many "ifs." If Moore's films had been better, and if she had continued appearances in the early days of sound, she might have lengthened her career. She certainly was capable of charming performances. But perhaps there was no real cure for the fatal perception that her day had simply passed.

REVIEWS

Smiling Irish Eyes: This is a personal triumph for Colleen Moore whose piquant personality of silent cinema dovetails charmingly with her talking personality. *Variety* 7/31/29, *Harrison's Reports* 8/3/29.

Footlights and Fools: Moore will draw the audience on her personality and past achievements. She does a good bit of acting; she is and always was a beautifully sincere performer. There is some pathos and plentiful comedy provoked by her acting. Her English spoken *à la* French should bring laughter. *Variety* 11/13/29, *Harrison's Reports* 11/16/29.

The Power and the Glory: Moore's comeback is a distinguished one. *Variety* 8/22/33.

Social Register: Moore struggles with a part that is wholly unsuited to her, a chorus girl. It is supposed to be the means of bringing her back to stardom but she's no longer appropriate for ingenue roles and this story makes that emphatic. She almost saves the day but the load is too heavy to carry. She is not always convincing but in spite of her handicaps she often projects herself well. *Harrison's Reports* 3/24/34, *Variety* 10/9/34.

Success at Any Price: Reviews differed. One thought that Moore was the most sympathetic character but another said she rated a weak third among those in support. *Harrison's Reports* 3/24/34, *Variety* 5/8/34.

The Scarlet Letter: Again critical opinion was divided. One review stated that the film had no entertainment value except for a sincere performance by Colleen Moore who was wasted on a creaky story. Another thought it would be difficult to imagine a more happy choice for Hester than Colleen Moore. Her work had a gentle humility which gave the part dignity and appeal and she acted with both reserve and with power. *Harrison's Reports* 8/4/34, *Variety* 9/25/34.

Moore, Matt, County Meath, Ireland, 1888–1960

Silent: Matt Moore was the next-to-youngest of the four acting Moore Brothers; Owen, Tom and Joe were his siblings, and the former two were important stars. After stage experience he made his cinema debut in 1913, one of his first features being *Traffic in Souls*. He worked mostly in one- and two-reelers during the early years and wrote and directed some of his films at Universal.

Moore's films included *20,000 Leagues Under the Sea* (1916 version), *Pride of the Clan*, *Don't Ever Marry* (he didn't), *The Glorious Lady*, *The Unholy Three* (1925 version), *The Passionate Pilgrim* and *Tillie the Toiler*. Last silent: *Phyllis of the Follies* (1928).

Sound: Mary Pickford's maiden talkie *Coquette* (1929) was also Matt Moore's. His other 1929 effort was *Side Street*, the only time he co-starred with brothers Owen and Tom. He went on to appear in numerous, mostly supporting, roles until the mid–1950s in films such as *The Hoodlum Saint, Bad Boy, Such Women Are Dangerous, Plymouth Adventure, Seven Brides for Seven Brothers* and *I Bury the Living* (1958), his last.

Comments: Although he played leading roles in the silents, Matt Moore was not the major star his two brothers had been early in their careers. He remained in films the longest, however, even though he was off-screen in some years after the mid-'30s and his roles gradually grew sparser.

Moore was a solid supporting player in talkies. Although born in Ireland, he had a fine voice without the noticeable brogue of his brothers and therefore could play a somewhat wider range of characters.

REVIEWS

Coquette: Matt Moore is woefully out of place. *Variety* 4/10/29.

The Squealer: Moore is the hero's friend, and the role is a walk-through. *Harrison's Reports* 8/30/30, *Variety* 9/10/30.

Rain: Moore seems rather quizzical about his role. *Variety* 10/18/32, *Harrison's Reports* 10/22/32.

I Bury the Living: A person in the cast who is helpful to the story is Matt Moore. *Variety* 7/2/58.

Moore, Owen, County Meath, Ireland,
1886–1939

Silent: Theater-trained Owen Moore was in films by 1908 with Biograph and he was a busy performer in both comedy and drama. His films included *Honor Thy Father, The Escape, A Coney Island Princess, The Poor Simp, The Silent Partner, Code of the West, The Taxi Dancer* and *Oh Mabel, Behave.* He also made two films with Lon Chaney, *The Blackbird* and *The Road to Mandalay.* Last silent: *Stolen Love* (1928).

Sound: Owen Moore made few talkies, although a couple were memorable. His first was *High Voltage* (1929) and he also appeared that year with his brothers Matt and Tom in *Side Street.* Among his others were *Cannonball, As You Desire Me* with Greta Garbo, *She Done Him Wrong, Extravagance, What a Widow!* (Gloria Swanson's second talkie) and his final effort, the classic *A Star Is Born* (1937), in which he had a small role.

Comments: Owen Moore's voice was not very suitable for talkies although he made some prestigious ones. He did have a brogue which was not in itself inhibiting. The problem was, at least on-

screen, that he tended to speak rapidly and slur his words badly.

While this style of speech might have sufficed for certain types of roles, like wisecracking reporters or even gangsters, it limited his possibilities.

Also unhelpful was Moore's well-publicized love of alcohol. This was one problem that was of long standing. Mary Pickford, once secretly married to Moore, cited it in her divorce petition.

REVIEWS

Side Street: A high-class crime drama in which Owen Moore is given the part of a bootlegger chief. *Harrison's Reports* 8/24/29.

What a Widow!: Moore does a good job. *Variety* 9/17/30.

As You Desire Me: Moore grabs the acting honors among the male performers with his jaunty handling of a minor part. *Variety* 6/7/32.

She Done Him Wrong: Owen Moore plays a former lover of Mae West; he is never permitted to be anything more than just background. *Harrison's Reports* 2/4/33, *Variety* 2/14/33.

Moore, Tom, County Meath, Ireland,
1884/85–1955

Silent: Probably the most popular of the four Moore Brothers was Tom, who came to films about 1912 after working in the theater. His debut was at Kalem and his early films included *The Cinderella Man, One of the Finest, Mary of the Movies, Officer 666, The Vampire's Trail* and *Brown of Harvard* (1917 version).

With the closing of Kalem, Moore worked at Selig, Lasky and thence to Goldwyn from 1918–21. He hit the peak of his popularity as a mature leading man in the early and mid-'20s in films like *A Kiss for Cinderella* and *Manhandled.* Last silent: *The Yellowback* (1929).

Sound: *Side Street* (1929), co-starring brothers Owen and Matt, was Tom Moore's first talkie. His other films included *The Costello Case, The Last Parade, Neighbor's Wives, Reunion* and *Ten Laps to Go.* He gave up performing in the '30s — or it possibly gave him up — to work as a drama coach for Twentieth Century–Fox.

Moore returned to the other side of the camera, beginning in 1946, for character roles in *Behind Green Lights, Moss Rose, Forever Amber, The Fighting O'Flynn* and his last in the early '50s, *The Redhead and the Cowboy.*

REVIEWS

Mr. Broadway: His role is very amateurishly carried out by Tom Moore. *Variety* 9/19/33.

Moran, Lois (Lois Darlington Dowling),
Pittsburgh, Pennsylvania, 1908/09–1990
Filmography: Classic Images (Sept. 1990)

Silent: Lois Moran appeared in two French films before playing her highly praised role as the daughter in 1925's *Stella Dallas*. Subsequent silents, all of lesser quality, included *The Reckless Lady*, *Whirlwind of Youth*, *Sharp Shooters*, *The Prince of Tempters* and *The Road to Mandalay*. Last silent: *Joy Street* (1929), with synchronized music and sound effects, made after her initial talkie.

Sound: The part-talkie *The River Pirate* (1928) was Moran's first sound effort. Among her others were *Behind That Curtain*, *Making the Grade*, *Not Damaged*, *Mammy* and *West of Broadway*, her last, in 1932. The poor reviews of that John Gilbert film no doubt helped her to make the decision to leave Hollywood.

It was Broadway that next claimed Moran. She went there to appear and vocalize in the prize-winning musical *Of Thee I Sing*, in which she portrayed the President's wife. She also was cast in its less successful sequel *Let Them Eat Cake*. In the 1950s she appeared on the TV series *Waterfront*.

Comments: Lois Moran was perhaps most famous for supposedly being the model for the character of Rosemary in F. Scott Fitzgerald's novel *Tender Is the Night*. However, she proved in her first American film that she was already a sensitive actress at the young age of 16.

Moran's youth became the basis of the publicity which portrayed her as an old-fashioned, innocent girl. Her contract even stated that she was to remain "unmodern and unsophisticated" and she was dubbed the "The Fragile Cameo" and "The Naive Child Wonder."

Moran may or may not have been those things but the image limited her to virginal ingenue roles and, in time, she tired of the restriction. Partly to assuage her, she was given more sophisticated films with titles like *Joy Street*, *The Whirlwind of Youth* and *The Men in Her Life* but they were undistinguished. In fact, none of her subsequent films matched the quality of Goldwyn's *Stella Dallas*, so she took her considerable talents elsewhere.

REVIEWS

The River Pirate: Lois Moran makes a charming heroine. *Harrison's Reports* 9/29/28.

Behind That Curtain: Moran shows more promise as an actress of emotional ability than in any other picture in which she has appeared to date. Occasionally her voice gets high during a dramatic moment but her performance is one of superb sincerity. *Variety* 7/3/29, *Harrison's Reports* 7/6/29.

A Song of Kentucky: Moran is a charming heroine. *Harrison's Reports* 12/28/29.

Mammy: The heroine, Lois Moran, looked all right and was charming but had little to do. *Variety* 4/2/30, *Harrison's Reports* 4/5/30.

The Spider: Moran has little to do for someone who is top-billed. *Harrison's Reports* 8/22/31, *Variety* 9/8/31.

West of Broadway: Lois Moran seems far below standard, handicapped by one of the poorest make-up jobs in modern films. *Variety* 2/2/32, *Harrison's Reports* 2/6/32.

Moran, Polly (Pauline Moran), Chicago, Illinois, 1884/86–1952

Silent: Polly Moran may have been in films as early as 1913 for Mack Sennett and she appeared in his "Sheriff Nell" series, spending the next five years or so in one- and two-reelers. A very physical roughhouse comedienne, she was also a vaudeville monologist.

Moran departed the movies in the late 'teens but returned in 1921 to make a few features like *The Affairs of Anatol*, *Skirts* and *Two Weeks with Pay*. Her feature career began in earnest in 1927 and she appeared in about 15 in two years, including *The Callahans and the Murphys*, the first teaming with future co-star Marie Dressler.

Other Polly Moran movies were *London After Midnight*, *Bringing Up Father* (again with Dressler), *Rose-Marie*, *Show People*, *Telling the World* and *The Divine Woman*, technically a silent but with singing sequences. Last silent: *Speedway* (1929), with synchronized sound effects and music, made after her first talkie.

Sound: Because it seemed she was often being cast as a maid, it could not be said that Moran's career was proceeding spectacularly well. That is until she was again teamed with the increasingly popular Marie Dressler. The frenetic 1929 short *Dangerous Females* reunited them in sound and they became an extremely popular duo in the first years of the talkies. She had previously made the 1928 Vitaphone short *The Movie Chatterbox*.

No doubt the combination of the short, pugnacious Polly Moran and the tall and pseudo-dignified Dressler was an appealing one. Their first feature appearance together was in MGM's *The Hollywood Revue of 1929* in which they performed a couple of extended musical sketches, including the nostalgic "Strolling Through the Park One Day."

Nineteen twenty-nine also found Moran in *Hot for Paris*, *So This Is College* and *The Unholy Night*. In 1930 she appeared with Dressler in *Caught Short* and was also seen in *Chasing Rainbows*, *Paid* and

Way for a Sailor, among others. The pair teamed again in 1931 and '32 for *Prosperity, Reducing* and *Politics.*

Other films in which Moran appeared before she left Hollywood in 1941 were *The Passionate Plumber, Down to Their Last Yacht, Alice in Wonderland, Ambush* and *Tom Brown's School Days.* She also made some comedy shorts at Columbia. In 1949 she was back with a memorable cameo in *Adam's Rib,* followed by *The Yellow Cab Man* the next year.

Comments: While Marie Dressler soon became Hollywood's top talkie female character star, Polly Moran's one-note raucousness seemed to pall on audiences. Although she was on-screen throughout the 1930s, and had some leading roles, she did not become a major screen presence.

There was a short-lived attempt to recreate the Dressler magic by teaming Moran with Alison Skipworth late in the 1930s in *Two Wise Maids* and *Ladies in Distress.* Her well-received, albeit brief, role in *Adam's Rib* seemed to indicate that she could profitably pursue a career as a latter-day character actress but she apparently did not wish to do so.

REVIEWS

Hot for Paris: Although Polly Moran has just a bit she makes it count. *Variety* 1/8/30.

Way Out West: Moran has a bit which doesn't give her any opportunity. *Variety* 8/20/30.

Reducing: The Dressler-Moran name on the marquee insures crowds and profit, and the film gives Moran a chance to develop some of those human interest touches she manages so well. *Variety* 1/21/31.

Prosperity: Moran's new nose, which made her look a bit too handsome in the past, lends realism to the smugness which this role calls for and she's very effective too. *Variety* 11/29/32.

Two Wise Maids: Moran more or less plays it straight and she doesn't have the laugh lines she usually gets. *Variety* 3/10/37.

Ambush: Polly Moran gives an effective account of herself as a lunchroom operator. *Variety* 2/15/39.

Moreno, Antonio (Antonio Garido or Garrido Monteagudo), Madrid, Spain, 1887/88–1966

Filmography: Films in Review (June-Sept. 1967); *Classic Images* (May-June 1990); List of films in *Eighty Silent Film Stars*

Silent: Rex-Universal was the studio for which Antonio Moreno made his screen bow about 1912. It was the start of a career in which he made 100 silents, and which included co-starring with Mary

Pickford, the Gish sisters, the Talmadges, Pearl White, Pola Negri, Gloria Swanson, Colleen Moore, Greta Garbo and Clara Bow.

Moreno appeared in all genres, including westerns, and at one period was in so many serials he was known as "The King of the Cliffhangers." Among these serials were *The House of Hate, Perils of Thunder Mountain, The Veiled Mystery* and *The Invisible Hand.*

Among Moreno's features were *The Spanish Dancer, Mare Nostrum, The Temptress, Beverly of Graustark, It, The Tarantula, The Exciters* and *Venus of Venice.* He worked for studios like Mutual-Reliance, Biograph, Vitagraph, Paramount, First National and MGM. Last silents: *Synthetic Sin,* with synchronized music score, and *The Air Legion,* released about the same time in 1929.

Sound: Nineteen twenty-nine's *Careers* marked Moreno's sound debut. His own career in the next years, with a few exceptions, consisted of Hollywood-made Spanish-language versions of American films. He also was seen in some early Mexican talkies.

In the latter '30s Moreno again began appearing in English-language films, which he continued to do sporadically until the 1950s. They included *One Mad Kiss, Ambush, Tampico, Thunder Bay, Saskatchewan, Wings of the Hawk, Creature from the Black Lagoon* and *The Bohemian Girl.* His last American film, *The Searchers,* appeared in 1956. His actual final picture was made in Cuba and not released in the U.S.

Comments: Whether he liked it or not, Antonio Moreno was looked upon as a "Latin lover" by Hollywood in the 1920s. He was probably the most successful in that niche after Valentino and Ramon Novarro. Previously he was somewhat of an action hero and had portrayed Americans with no difficulty, and was to do so again when the Valentino craze had spent itself.

Although he was over 40 at the end of the silent era, Moreno retained his good looks well into advanced age, so that was not an immediate problem. But he obviously could not play the "all–American boy" in talkies because he did have an accent. Although he spoke pleasingly enough, his career was undeniably curtailed. When he did return to American films, it was generally in character and "ethnic" roles to which he lent an innate dignity.

REVIEWS

Careers: Antonio Moreno, as the hero, appeared a bit self-conscious at times. *Variety* 6/12/29, *Harrison's Reports* 6/22/29.

Storm Over the Andes: Antonio Moreno has the

part of an army major and he is excellent. *Variety* 10/2/35.

Dallas: Moreno is capable as the ranch owner. *Variety* 11/22/50.

Morgan, Frank (Francis Wupperman), New York, New York, 1890–1949

Filmography: Academy of Motion Picture Arts and Sciences (silent films only)

Silent: After some Broadway experience, Frank Morgan, using his real name, made his first foray into the silent cinema with *The Suspect* (1916). In subsequent roles he acted under his stage name. *The Daring of Diana* and *The Girl Philippa* were two other early efforts.

About ten more motion pictures with Morgan followed to 1919, including *A Child of the Wild*, *Who's Your Neighbor?*, *At the Mercy of Men* and *The Gray Towers Mystery*. In these he sometimes had the lead and at other times appeared in support.

After more theater appearances, Morgan returned in 1924 and '25 for character roles in another handful of films among which were *Manhandled*, *The Crowded Hour* and *The Man Who Found Himself*. He also was seen in vaudeville. Last silent: *Love's Greatest Mistake* (1927).

Sound: The talkies first heard Morgan's distinctive voice in mid–1930 beginning with *Dangerous Nan McGrew*. The others that year were the well-received *Laughter* with Nancy Carroll, *Queen High* and *Fast and Loose*. He thereafter remained a staple in character support and lead performances until the time of his death.

Morgan's movies included *Secrets of the French Police*, *Reunion in Vienna*, *The Great Ziegfeld*, *Rosalie*, *Boom Town*, *Broadway Melody of 1940*, *Green Dolphin Street*, *Lady Luck*, *Any Number Can Play* and his last, *Key to the City*, released posthumously in 1950.

Morgan is certainly known best to modern audiences as the befuddled title character in 1939's *The Wizard of Oz*. In fact, on-screen befuddlement seemed to be the actor's most frequent stock-in-trade. He also could play affectingly, as in *The Shop Around the Corner* and *The Human Comedy*.

Best Supporting Actor Academy Award nominations were earned by Frank Morgan for *The Affairs of Cellini* and *Tortilla Flat*. Among his occasional leads was *The Cockeyed Miracle* in 1946. In addition to his picture work, he was often heard on the radio beginning in 1938.

Comments: Nobody could "dither" like mustachioed Frank Morgan. He was often cast as a somewhat lightweight type who wished for but lacked authority. It was a persona which his sometimes quavery voice enhanced beautifully. Although in private life he was rumored to be a hard-drinking man, with the personality type that entailed, his screen image was one of likable sweetness, albeit well hidden on occasion.

Morgan once in a while played a less likable character and it would have been interesting to see him play against type more often. He is so thoroughly identified with one role that to see him is to think only of the Wizard. Interestingly, he inherited that part only after W. C. Fields proved unavailable. His brother Ralph Morgan was also a well-regarded film actor.

REVIEWS

Laughter: Frederic March steals the picture, dominating everyone, even Frank Morgan as a dignified banker. *Variety* 10/8/30.

Bombshell: Morgan gives his all to his comic role as Jean Harlow's father. It is a bit different from his usual type but well done. *Variety* 10/24/33.

A Lost Lady: Morgan has played the middle-aged Lothario opposite young leading ladies so often that he must be hardened to it by now. He does about as much as could be done with this assignment. *Variety* 10/9/34.

Dimples: Frank Morgan excels opposite Shirley Temple. He is so good that he almost steals the picture. *Harrison's Reports* 10/10/36.

Paradise for Three: Top-billed Morgan has seldom had a better opportunity for his drolleries. *Variety* 1/19/38.

The Mortal Storm: Frank Morgan does a fine characterization of the non–Aryan (i.e., Jewish) professor. *Variety* 6/12/40.

The Human Comedy: Morgan clicks solidly as the veteran telegrapher. *Variety* 3/3/43.

The Cockeyed Miracle: The leading role is made for Frank Morgan and he gives a solid performance. *Variety* 7/17/46.

Mulhall, Jack, Wappingers Falls, New York, 1887/90–1977

Filmography: Classic Images (Oct.-Nov. 1991); List of films in *Eighty Silent Film Stars*

Silent: Jack Mulhall had his first credits about 1913 but 1910 may have been the year he made the first of his 160 silents. Previously, he had been in vaudeville and also worked as a model. During his career he appeared in all genres including farce comedy and serials, among which were *Into the Net*, *The Brass Bullet*, *The Social Buccaneer* and *The Wild West*. As a very popular leading man, he worked at many different studios including Realart, Metro, Fox, Pathe, Warner Bros., Paramount and RKO.

Mulhall's features included *Madame Spy*, *Whom the Gods Would Destroy*, *Waterfront*, *The Poor Nut*,

The Midnight Man, Lady Be Good, Joanna and *Subway Sadie.* Among his co-stars were Alice Terry, Colleen Moore, Corinne Griffith, the Talmadge sisters and Bebe Daniels. Last silent: *Children of the Ritz* (1929), with synchronized music and sound effects.

Sound: Most of Mulhall's 1929 output were part- or full talkies. They included the popular *Dark Streets,* in which he played a dual role, *The Show of Shows, Twin Beds* and *Two Weeks Off.* He went on to appear in over 150 talkies.

Until the early 1930s Mulhall retained his star status but was soon appearing in many bit roles or even as an extra.

Among Mulhall's sound films were *The Golden Calf, Show Girl in Hollywood, The Old Fashioned Way, Sweet Adeline, The Spy Ring, First Love, Cheers for Miss Bishop, Sin Town* and *100 Men and a Girl.* He portrayed "himself," i.e., a former silent star, in 1936's *Hollywood Boulevard.*

Jack Mulhall was also seen in shorts and 13 serials including *The Clutching Hand, Adventures of Captain Marvel, Mystery Squadron, Burn 'Em Up Barnes* and *The Three Musketeers.* His last-known film appearance came in *The Atomic Submarine* (1959).

Comments: Jack Mulhall was a most popular star in the 1920s and talking pictures seemed to pose no threat to him. Although his voice perfectly matched the persona he projected, his fall from stardom to near-obscurity in the early 1930s was swift and complete. While his age could have been a contributing factor, so rapid a decline was usually due to "personal" problems or offending some studio executive.

Whatever the cause, it will no doubt remain just speculation. Mulhall managed to remain a presence in Hollywood one way or another and he never seemed to lose his optimism that he could "come back." He never really did but was certainly seen, however briefly, in numerous pictures.

REVIEWS

Dark Streets: The viewer thinks that Mulhall is surely two different people. He does excellent work. *Harrison's Reports* 9/7/29, *Variety* 10/9/29.

The Fall Guy: Mulhall is inclined at times to overdo the wisecracking. The role frequently takes on an unnatural aspect and ruins his otherwise capable characterization. *Variety* 5/28/30.

Crime Ring: Jack Mulhall lends strong support. *Variety* 7/27/38.

First Love: A former star of silent pictures, Jack Mulhall, does capably as the family chauffeur. *Variety* 11/8/39.

Desperate Cargo: Jack Mulhall, former silent star, contributes an important secondary role with polish. *Variety* 10/8/41.

Murray, Charles (sometimes Charlie), Laurel, Indiana, 1872–1941

Silent: A "professional" Irishman, Charles Murray was at Biograph in 1911 and soon became a Sennett stalwart, including a stint as a "Keystone Kop." He already had achieved fame in vaudeville as part of the popular team of Murray and Mack, and before that was in circus and medicine shows.

Nearly all Murray's pre–1920 films were one- and two-reelers. His features included *Puppy Love, A Small Town Idol, The Gorilla, The Cohens and Kellys* (he, of course, portrayed Kelly opposite George Sidney as Cohen), *Irene, McFadden's Flats, The Boob* and *Vamping Venus.* Last silent: *Do Your Duty* (1928).

Sound: Murray did not appear in the 1929 part-talkie *The Cohens and Kellys in Atlantic City* (in it he was replaced for the only time by Mack Swain). His sound feature debut came in 1930 with two films released just days apart: *Clancy in Wall Street* and *The Cohens and the Kellys in Scotland,* the latter part of the continuing series.

Murray went on to make somewhat scattered appearances throughout the '30s. Among his few features were *The Cohens and Kellys in Africa, …in Trouble* and *…in Hollywood.* Other films were *Hypnotized, Dangerous Waters* and *Breaking the Ice.* He also made shorts, some with George Sidney.

Comments: In his early cinema days, Charlie Murray was famous for his chin whiskers and patented grimace, but the "map of Ireland" was on his face and he rarely broke away from playing rambunctious Irishmen. The most famous of these was Kelly but even when not playing that role his characters invariably were called Hogan, Clancy, Riley or McFadden.

Murray was less active in talkies, perhaps because his type of exaggerated characterization was out of fashion. The longer his bread-and-butter "Cohens and Kellys" franchise went on, the more it became the subject of critics' ire. But in his few chances he continued to give worthy character performances.

REVIEWS

The Cohens and the Kellys in Africa: Murray isn't provided with any kind of a chance. *Variety* 12/24/30, *Harrison's Reports* 12/27/30.

Caught Cheating: Charlie Murray performs in his accustomed manner. *Variety* 3/11/31.

The Cohens and Kellys in Trouble: Murray is more natural here than in many of the previous films in the series. He doesn't try to force the laughs. *Variety* 4/18/33.

Murray, James, the Bronx, New York,
1901–1936

Filmography: Films in Review (Dec. 1968)

Silent: James Murray's first film was apparently *The Pilgrims*, made on Long Island in 1923. About 1927 he went to Hollywood for extra and bit roles and some leading parts in films such as *In Old Kentucky* and *The Lovelorn*. He received some billing in about ten silents altogether.

It is, of course, for the 1928 MGM classic *The Crowd* that he is known. Director King Vidor was looking for a relatively unknown actor with the right look and he settled on Murray. His co-star was the director's wife, Eleanor Boardman. Other leading roles were in *Rose-Marie* and *The Big City*. Last silent: *Thunder* (1929), with synchronized sound effects and music, made after his first talkie.

Sound: The Little Wildcat, a 1928 part-talkie, was Murray's introduction to sound. In 1929 he appeared in another part-talkie, *The Shakedown*; *Shanghai Lady* was his first full-sound film. He made about 15 talkies, in some of which he played bits.

Murray's movies included *The Rampant Age*, *High Gear* (lead), *Bachelor Mother*, *Frisco Jenny*, *Heroes for Sale* and *Skull and Crown* (1935), his final effort. He also may have appeared in two comedy shorts. After leaving MGM, he made films for Universal, Warner Bros. and independent studios.

Comments: In *The Crowd* James Murray plays a blue-collar Everyman whose life with its joys and sorrows (mostly the latter) is lived anonymously. It is apparently the way he wanted his own life to be lived for he could not seem to deal with celebrity, however minor.

Murray had no problem making a transition to sound. He had a good voice for his established persona and he might have found a niche as a convincing action hero in "B" films, as he was in *High Gear*. But he was an alcoholic and hence unreliable while shooting a film.

Murray's stardom was about as brief as it could be; many of his later sound roles were little more than background appearances. His suicide or accidental death by drowning perhaps was not unexpected.

Reviews

Shanghai Lady: Very well acted by all including James Murray as the hero. *Harrison's Reports* 11/16/29.

Kick In: Murray is merely the cause to permit a plot development. *Variety* 5/20/31.

Air Hostess: His role is pleasantly acted by James Murray. *New York Times* 1/23/33.

High Gear: As a car racer, Murray plays the lead with an effective simplicity and is better than the film. *New York Times* 4/15/33, *Variety* 4/18/33.

Murray, Mae (Adrienne Marie Koenig),
Portsmouth, Virginia, 1886/90–1965

Filmography: Films in Review (Dec. 1975)

Silent: After a dancing career and an engagement with the Ziegfeld Follies, Mae Murray signed with Famous Players-Lasky. *To Have and to Hold* (1916) was her first screen appearance. Among the earlier films of the little "Girl with the Beestung Lips" were *The Mormon Maid*, *The Right to Love*, *Idols of Clay*, *Her Body in Bond*, *What Am I Bid?* and *The Delicious Little Devil*.

After Murray signed with Tiffany-Metro in the early '20s, her screen image began to change and her fame increased accordingly. She had found her niche. The innocent Mae became the sophisticated Mae and a major star in such films as *On with the Dance*, *The French Doll*, *Peacock Alley*, *Jazzmania*, *Circe the Enchantress* and especially *The Merry Widow* (1925).

With that film the apex of Mae Murray's career had been reached and a swift decline set in almost immediately. She insisted on playing roles meant for much younger women (a baby spotlight was always on her to minimize skin lines) and she battled with Louis B. Mayer, always a dangerous foe.

Thereafter Murray made only three starring silents. Last silent: *Altars of Desire* (1927). She later made the briefest of guest appearances as "herself" in Marion Davies's 1928 comedy *Show People*.

Sound: Murray appeared in only three sound films, the first being *Peacock Alley* (1930), her final starring role. Although it bore the title of her 1922 film, the plot was dissimilar. The other films, both from 1931, in which she had supporting roles were *Bachelor Apartment* and *High Stakes*, her last. She thereafter remained on the fringes of show business lecturing and performing in night clubs.

Comments: Perhaps more than any other actress, Mae Murray came to epitomize the eccentric silent film star so well captured in *Sunset Blvd.* As her fame grew, so did the difficulty in working with her. It is rumored that she was finally blackballed from the industry by Louis B. Mayer, who was fed up with her temperamental demands.

Murray was probably a better dancer than an actress and dancing did figure in several of her roles, notably in *The Merry Widow*. Her acting, restrained in the early days of her career, became more highly emotive later on and lavish costumes seemed as important as plot lines.

In talkies, Mae Murray revealed a somewhat high-pitched, affected voice and an exaggerated performing style. Although this was not suitable in her first talkie role (as a chorus "girl"), her mannerisms did not seem so out of place in her two last films. These were directed by Lowell Sherman, who gave them the right amount of "tongue in cheek" (and who perhaps gave the actress the work out of friendship). She played unsympathetic roles in both.

The sad story of Mae Murray's later life is well-known. The year before her death she was found wandering in the streets, disheveled and little aware of her surroundings. Yet in those later years she still considered herself, and demanded to be treated as, a star. Even though her day had long, long passed, she was still "The Self-Enchanted," as the title of her biography so aptly put it. But she had brought a vivacity to the screen that few other actresses could match.

REVIEWS

Peacock Alley: A good society drama in which Mae Murray does good work. *Harrison's Reports* 1/25/30.

Bachelor Apartment: Murray is the married woman who pursues the hero and she looks just as if the silly role befits her. *Harrison's Reports* 3/21/31, *Variety* 5/20/31.

High Stakes: Murray, as the scheming gold digger, does good work. *Harrison's Reports* 5/30/31.

Myers, Carmel, San Francisco, California,
1899–1980

Silent: Carmel Myers is best-remembered for donning a white-blonde wig and "vamping" it up as Iras in *Ben-Hur.* She entered films about 1917 as an ingenue and worked steadily thereafter as a popular leading woman throughout the entire silent era.

Myers's films included *A Society Sensation* (with a callow pre-fame Valentino), *The Gilded Dream, The Famous Mrs. Fair, Beau Brummell, Sorrell and Son, The Gay Deceiver* and *Mary of the Movies.* Last silent: *The Red Sword* (1929).

Sound: All but one of Myers's 1929 pictures were part- or full-sound. They included her first, *The Ghost Talks,* as well as *Careers, Broadway Scandals* and *The Careless Age.* She also was one of the many Warners players in *The Show of Shows.*

Myers's career began to decline about 1930 but she had a supporting role in one memorable film, John Barrymore's *Svengali* (1931). Her others were routine programmers like *Ship from Shanghai, Chinatown After Dark, No Living Witness, Nice Women* and *The Mad Genius,* a follow-up to *Svengali.*

With 1934's *The Countess of Monte Cristo* Myers bowed out of films but returned for a few later small roles including shorts in the '40s (*Lady for a Night, Whistle Stop*) and a cameo (along with other old-timers) in *Won Ton Ton, the Dog Who Saved Hollywood.*

Comments: Carmel Myers did not just disappear into contented (or discontented) retirement. She became a successful businesswoman with her own line of perfume and was a frequent, and chatty, guest on talk shows. She always took the opportunity to remind the world who she had once been.

REVIEWS

Svengali: Carmel Myers is acceptable in a minor role. In a singing sequence she shows she has a voice and is presumably not doubled. *New York Times* 5/1/31, *Variety* 5/6/31.

Countess of Monte Cristo: As the flower girl, Myers has just a bit but she sings a song interestingly. *Harrison's Reports* 3/24/34, *Variety* 4/3/34.

Myers, Harry, New Haven, Connecticut,
1882/86–1938

Silent: In vaudeville and stock from 1900, Harry Myers may have begun his film career as early as 1906 with Lubin. He also worked at Universal, Sennett, Christie and MGM, appearing in, directing and writing many one- and two-reelers as well as full-length films. Among the early features in which he played supporting parts were *The Earl of Pawtucket, The Man of Shame, Conquered Hearts* and *Out of the Night.*

Myers was seen in numerous character roles in the 1920s in pictures that included *On the High Road, The Beautiful and Damned, Brass, The Marriage Circle, Tarnish, Monte Carlo, Getting Gertie's Garter* and *Dream of Love.* Last silent: *City Lights* (1931), with synchronized sound effects and music, made after his first talkie.

Sound: The 1929 part-talkie *The Wonder of Women* was Myers's first; his next feature appearance came in 1931. It is possible he also made some shorts in between. The frequency and size of his roles became smaller, especially toward the end of the decade.

Myers's motion pictures included *Convicted, The Savage Girl, Police Call, We Live Again, Hollywood Boulevard* and *Stand-In.* His final films, *Zenobia* with Oliver Hardy and *I'm from Missouri,* were posthumously released.

Comments: It is of course for his final, and almost *the* final silent film, that Harry Myers is remembered at all. In *City Lights* he was the millionaire who, in equal measure, befriends and rebuffs Charlie Chaplin's Tramp, depending on whether he is sober or in his cups. He made somewhat of a career out of being intoxicated on the screen but never again so memorably.

REVIEWS

Savage Girl: Myers essays his familiar drunk impersonation. He tries hard, but such acting honors as there are go to another cast member. *Variety* 5/2/33.

Nagel, Conrad, Keokuk, Iowa, 1897–1970

Filmography: Films in Review (May 1979); List of films in *Eighty Silent Film Stars*

Silent: First he was a stage actor and then Conrad Nagel turned to the screen in 1919; *Little Women* may have been his premiere film. In the course of his 50 or so silents he co-starred with some of the leading actresses including Blanche Sweet, Gloria Swanson, Marion Davies, Norma Shearer, Pola Negri and Bebe Daniels.

Nagel worked in several DeMille pictures. His films included *Saturday Night, Three Weeks, Nice People, Pretty Ladies, The Waning Sex, Sinners in Silk, Singed Wings* and *Quality Street.* Among his more prestigious efforts were *Sun-Up* and *Tess of the D'Urbervilles.* Last silent: *The Kiss* (1929), with synchronized music, made after his first talkies. This was one of the last silent films produced by MGM.

Sound: Nagel's mellifluous baritone was heard in several part-talkies beginning with *Tenderloin* in 1928. Other early sound or part-sound films were *The Thirteenth Chair, Glorious Betsy, Redemption, Dynamite* and *Kid Gloves.* The very early 1930s marked the height of his career but he worked steadily until about 1937.

Nagel's appearances were somewhat sporadic thereafter into the 1950s, but he still occasionally topped the cast, as in 1948's *The Vicious Circle.* He was also frequently on television in the '50s. The last of his four films in that decade was *The Man Who Understood Women* (1959).

Among Conrad Nagel's other films were *Hell Divers, The Marines Are Coming, I Want a Divorce, Hidden Fear, Yellow Cargo* and *DuBarry, Woman of Passion.* He also was one of the founders of the Academy of Motion Picture Arts and Sciences.

Comments: Although he was a competent enough actor, Conrad Nagel seemed to be at his best in the silents when making his leading ladies look good. Tall, with marcelled hair (later a hairpiece) and bland good looks, he never made much of a strong impression on his own.

It took the talkies to boost Nagel's career. Producers clamored for him, with his fine voice, and he was extremely active in the early days of sound, appearing in about 20 films in a two-year period. He had the distinction of being in one of the last major silents and some of the very first part-talkies.

Nagel was reputed to have said that even he was tired of seeing himself in every theater, but that changed quickly enough. The fact is that he could not surmount his lack of charisma. He was a somewhat colorless (and seemingly humorless) actor and his career waned after his initial talkie success into supporting roles and quickie films.

REVIEWS

Tenderloin: The hero, played by Conrad Nagel, is not only a crook but also a liar. His talking is natural. *Harrison's Reports* 4/21/28.

Red Wine: Nagel gives a splendid performance. *Harrison's Reports* 2/16/29.

The Idle Rich: Nagel is excellent. *Variety* 6/19/29.

Free Love: Conrad Nagel plays a comic drunk scene. He doesn't do that well but is capable the rest of the time. *Variety* 12/17/30.

Kongo: Although Nagel tries hard to play his difficult assignment well, it becomes silly. *Variety* 11/22/32.

Girl from Mandalay: The top-billed Nagel struggles with a role that offers only fleeting opportunities. He is seldom photographed well and some of the silly scenes do not enhance his performance. *Variety* 5/13/36.

Wedding Present: Nagel plays a stodgy suitor. (A matinee idol of the '20s gave way to one of the '30s, as Cary Grant stole the girl [Joan Bennett] away from Nagel.) *Harrison's Reports* 10/31/36.

All That Heaven Allows: Nagel is fine in a supporting role as a middle-aged suitor of Jane Wyman. *Variety* 10/26/55.

Nazimova, Alla (Adelaide Leventon), Yalta, Russia, 1878/79–1945

Filmography: Films in Review (Dec. 1972, June-Sept. 1985); List of films in *Film Dope* (Mar. 1991)

Silent: Alla Nazimova was one of the most distinguished of the theater actresses who essayed silent films. The first of her 17 silents was the popular *War Brides* (1916), based on the stage play in which she had starred. She went on to make 11 films with Metro, including *An Eye for an Eye, The Red Lantern, Revelation* and *Madame Peacock.*

Nazimova's years with that studio ended with the failure of *Camille* in 1921, a highly stylized, even bizarre film for its day. The next two, which she herself financed, were *A Doll's House* and *Salome*; they also flopped, the latter ruining her financially. There were a few more in the '20s, including *The Redeeming Sin* and *Madonna of the Streets*, before she returned to the stage. Last silent: *My Son* (1925).

Sound: After more notable theater successes,

among them Eugene O'Neill's *Mourning Becomes Electra* and Ibsen's *Ghosts*, Nazimova was back in films in 1940. Her first was the Norma Shearer drama *Escape*, in which she played the supporting role of a concentration camp inmate smuggled out of Europe.

Nazimova's subsequent pictures were few. They were the 1941 remake of Rudolph Valentino's famous *Blood and Sand*, this time with Tyrone Power, *The Bridge of San Luis Rey* which was another remake, *In Our Time* (she played Paul Henreid's mother, a Polish countess) and a brief final role in the "all-star" *Since You Went Away* (1944).

Comments: Alla Nazimova, for whom the famous Hollywood apartment complex The Garden of Allah was named, was a paradox. In stage and early film appearances her acting was praised for being restrained and natural. Much of her enormous popularity stemmed from that. Personally, she was the embodiment of a temperamental Russian diva and brooked little contradiction.

This trait contributed to the failure of Nazimova's ill-advised early '20s films. Possibly against better advice, she decided that her popularity gave her carte blanche to experiment. Although seen today as interesting failures, the pictures were not what her fans expected and they deserted her. Their lack of success was almost certainly not attributable to their homoerotic subtexts which perhaps was not quite so clear to contemporary audiences.

The fear of Nazimova's temperament perhaps partly explains her late appearance in the talkies. However, by then she was not quite the mighty stage star she once had been and her foreign background limited the type of roles she could play. In her best talkie role, that of the matador's mother in *Blood and Sand*, she revealed some of her old authority.

REVIEWS

Escape: Nazimova is seen again in a film with a war background. It recalls her success during the first World War in *War Brides*. *Variety* 10/30/40.

Blood and Sand: Nazimova will get a major share of audience attention. She gives a wonderful performance. *Variety* 5/21/41.

The Bridge of San Luis Rey: Nazimova plays a scheming aristocrat. *Harrison's Reports* 2/5/44.

In Our Time: Nazimova plays a patrician mother reminiscent of her very best *Cherry Orchard* style. *New York Times* 2/12/44.

Negri, Pola (Barbara Apollonia Chalupec or Chalupiec), Yanowa, Poland, 1894/99–1987

Silent: In many ways Pola Negri embodied the later popular conception of a silent star. Off the screen she was flamboyance personified, and Hollywood's ubiquitous publicity machine played that up in an unending stream of stories pairing her with every important star, including Chaplin and Valentino. Her "performance" as grief-stricken paramour at the latter's 1926 funeral made worldwide news.

After a successful German career on-stage and in films like *Madame DuBarry* and *Carmen* (*Gypsy Blood*), Negri's eagerly awaited American debut came in 1923 with *Bella Donna*. She was thereafter cast in a series of Paramount melodramas and for a few years was an extremely popular star and rival to the studio's other diva, Gloria Swanson.

Negri's American motion pictures included *Men*, *The Spanish Dancer*, *A Woman of the World*, *Lily of the Dust* and *The Secret Hour*. One of her most popular was *Hotel Imperial*. Last silent: *The Woman from Moscow* (1928).

Sound: Fearful about her accent, Hollywood did not present Negri in her sound debut until 1932 in the unsuccessful *A Woman Commands*, co-starring Basil Rathbone. It was a story based on events in the former kingdom of Serbia and included the song "Paradise," performed in the star's throaty contralto.

Negri's other American sound films were the farce-comedy *Hi Diddle Diddle* (1943) and the adventure *The Moonspinners* (or *The Moon-Spinners*) in 1964. After the failure of her talkie comeback, she had gone to Germany where, under the Nazi regime, she became a popular star from 1933 until 1937. She also appeared in some French and British films.

Comments: In contrast to Pola Negri's over-the-top public image, her silent screen portrayals were generally restrained and realistic. Her persona was that of a world-weary woman who had really lived. As the films became poorer and less popular in the late '20s, her image was changed to that of a more average person.

Given the fact that Negri's beauty was of an extremely exotic kind, this persona hardly fit; such casting served to finish her starring career. There were numerous actresses who could have played "average" roles so her unique qualities were not utilized. When talkies revealed a heavy (but not unpleasant) accent, there was little for her to do in films but parody her own image.

REVIEWS

A Woman Commands: Negri is attractive but her accent is strongly foreign. She never manages to portray the character with a vital personality. The highlight of her performance is when she sings two verses of a torch song in an agreeable contralto. *New York Times* 1/28/32, *Variety* 2/2/32.

Hi Diddle Diddle: This comeback picture for Negri, who has been off the screen for many years, is a good vehicle for her reentry. As the wife of Adolphe Menjou, she gives a very good account of herself as a glamorous and temperamental opera star. *Variety* 8/4/43, *Harrison's Reports* 8/7/43.

The Moonspinners: Negri makes a late entrance as a weird, wealthy widow. It's novelty casting and not likely to initiate a new screen career for the silent screen siren. She looks appropriately exotic and sounds like a road company Maria Ouspenskaya.

(Ouspenskaya was a tiny Russian actress with an almost indecipherable accent, so the allusion to her is not intended as a compliment.) *Variety* 6/24/64.

Nilsson, Anna Q(uerentia), Ystad, Sweden, 1888/90–1974

Filmography: Films in Review (Feb. 1976)

Silent: After a modeling career, blonde beauty Anna Q. Nilsson debuted for Kalem in 1911. The first of her approximately 140 silents may have been *Molly Pitcher*. Among her other films were *Miss Nobody, The Lotus Eater, The Marked Woman, Adam's Rib, Ponjola, The Spoilers* (1923 version), *The Toll Gate, Cheating Cheaters* and *Sorrell and Son*. She also appeared in the "Who's Guilty?" series.

Nilsson was an important star but her starring career was ended prematurely when she was thrown from a horse and subsequently became bedridden for two years. Last silent: *The Whip* (1928), with synchronized music and sound effects.

Sound: The only sound film in which Nilsson had the lead was *Blockade*, a 1928 part-talkie. During the transition to sound she went back to Europe but by 1933 she had returned and began appearing in small roles. The first was possibly in *The World Changes*.

Nilsson continued to play in shorts and character parts throughout the '30s and '40s, notably as Loretta Young's mother in *The Farmer's Daughter* (1947). One of her last films was *Sunset Blvd.* (1950) in which she had a cameo as one of the "waxworks" who plays bridge with the mad Norma Desmond. She may have ended her career in *Seven Brides for Seven Brothers*.

Reviews

Blockade: Anna Q. Nilsson, who plays three characters, is quite good. *Harrison's Reports* 5/25/29.

The World Changes: Excellent performances by the supporting cast that includes Anna Q. Nilsson. *Harrison's Reports* 11/4/33.

Prison Farm: Anna Q. Nilsson, of silent film days, is fine as an unbending, cruel farm matron. *Variety* 7/20/38.

Girl's Town: Anna Q. Nilsson of silent film fame plays the mother and injects some realism into a poorly conceived role. *Variety* 4/15/42.

Nissen, Greta (Grethe Ruzt-Nissen), Oslo, Norway, 1906–1988

Filmography: Films in Review (Jan. 1981)

Silent: Beautiful blonde Greta Nissen signed with Paramount in 1924 after a film in Norway where she had trained as a ballerina and stage actress. Her first American film role was in *In the Name of Love* (1925), but *Lost — A Wife* was the first one released.

Nineteen twenty-six proved to be Nissen's busiest year in silents as well as the year she appeared in the Ziegfeld revue *No Foolin'* in New York. After her Paramount contract ended in '27, the screen appearances decreased. Her silent films included *The King on Main Street, The Wanderer, The Lucky Lady, The Lady of the Harem, The Popular Sin, Fazil* and *Blonde or Brunette*.

Ironically, the film for which Nissen is best known is one which was not widely seen: the silent version of *Hell's Angels*. It was completed but overtaken by the sound revolution and remade by Howard Hughes with Jean Harlow in her role. Last silent: *The Butter and Egg Man* (1928).

Sound: Nissen's career was not completely destroyed by sound. She took English lessons and learned to speak the language competently, albeit with an accent. The first of Nissen's 12 American talkies was 1931's *Women of All Nations* in which she ironically was made to speak with a heavier accent. Among her others were *Life in the Raw, Ambassador Bill, The Silent Witness, Rackety Rax, The Circus Queen Murder* and *Hired Wife*.

In 1934, when her U.S. career seemed to be ending, Nissen went to England where she appeared in several undistinguished motion pictures, including *Luck of a Sailor, Honours Easy* and *Spy 77*. Her final appearance came with *Danger in Paris*. She also did theater work in the United Kingdom.

Reviews

Women of All Nations: Nissen, who has been out of pictures for some time, looks well but does not have good talkie skills. *Variety* 6/2/31, *Harrison's Reports* 6/6/31.

The Unwritten Law: Nissen has what amounts to a bit in spite of the fact she tops the bill. *Harrison's Reports* 12/3/32, *Variety* 12/20/32.

Life in the Raw: Nissen has a bit part but she looks good. *Variety* 11/7/33.

Hired Wife: Nissen plays a charming German

girl. Her accent fits the part nicely and her performance is above average. *Variety* 5/13/34.

Nixon, Marion (sometimes Marian), Superior, Wisconsin, 1904/06–1983

Filmography: Classic Images (Jan.-Feb. 1986); List of films in *Sweethearts of the Sage*

Silent: Little Marion Nixon got her start as an extra in 1922 and she was a bit player in films such as *Rosita* (1923). She went on to appear in westerns with Tom Mix and Hoot Gibson and was one of the 1924 crop of Wampas Baby Stars.

Among Nixon's films were *Durand of the Badlands, The Auctioneer, What Happened to Jones, Just Off Broadway, Red Lips, The Saddle Hawk* and *Honeymoon Flats.* Last silent: *The Red Sword* (1929), made after her first part-talkie.

Sound: Marion Nixon made nine films in 1929, most of them all or part-talking. The first of her part-talkies had been *Geraldine* in late 1928; other early sound efforts were *Say It with Songs, The Show of Shows* and *General Crack.*

Nixon continued to appear almost without a break, alternating leads in mostly minor films and supporting parts in better ones, until 1936 when she made her last, *Captain Calamity.* Other pictures included *Scarlet Pages, The Lineup, By Your Leave, Women Go On Forever, Too Busy to Work* and *Rebecca of Sunnybrook Farm,* supposedly her personal favorite and probably her best remembered.

Comments: "Elfin" is the word that comes to mind for Marion Nixon. She somewhat resembled Janet Gaynor and was possibly intended by the Fox studio to keep that actress in line. She was almost always cast as an ingenue even toward the end of her career and rarely had a chance to flex any acting muscles.

Nixon's voice was only fair, being somewhat high-pitched and lacking in power, but it was good enough to enable her to make over 40 talkies, more than her silent output.

REVIEWS

Geraldine: Nixon is a good little actress and the only name in the cast with any box office appeal. She is always kept looking her best. *Harrison's Reports* 12/22/28, *Variety* 3/6/29.

General Crack: Marion Nixon is pretty and her voice is soft but she seems miscast. *New York Times* 12/4/29.

Courage: Nixon has a vixenish, unsympathetic role. *Variety* 6/11/30.

Ex-Flame: Neither Nixon nor the screenwriter seemed to have much of an idea of the role. *Variety* 1/28/31.

Rebecca of Sunnybrook Farm: Nixon's acting provides a certain freshness to the saccharine role. She establishes the naive leading character impressively from the start. *Harrison's Reports* 7/16/32, *Variety* 8/2/32.

Strictly Dynamite: Sympathy is felt for Marion Nixon in this comedy. *Harrison's Reports* 5/12/34.

Tango: Sympathy is aroused for Marion Nixon, the heroine. The surprise of the picture is her performance and she brings nice contrasting moods into the characterization. *Harrison's Reports* 1/11/36, *Variety* 2/19/36.

Nolan, Mary (also known as Imogene "Bubbles" Wilson; Mary Robertson), Louisville, Kentucky, 1905–1948

Filmography: Films in Review (May 1980)

Silent: After working as a Ziegfeld Follies showgirl and appearing in several German silents, "Hard Luck Girl" Mary Nolan made her U.S. film debut in a small role in *Topsy and Eva* (1927). Her real break came the same year with *Sorrell and Son.* Among her few other silents were *West of Zanzibar, Good Morning Judge, The Foreign Legion* and *Silks and Saddles.* Last silent: *Desert Nights* (1929), with synchronized music and sound effects.

Sound: Nolan's sound career got off to a worthy beginning with *Charming Sinners,* a 1929 Ruth Chatterton vehicle. Her other '29 talkie *Shanghai Lady* foreshadowed the downward direction her career would go.

Other Nolan talkies, some made for Poverty Row studios after Universal released her, included *Undertow, Outside the Law, X Marks the Spot, The Big Shot, Docks of San Francisco* and *Midnight Patrol* (1932), her last.

Comments: Mary Nolan's sobriquet of the "Hard Luck Girl" was not lightly given. She was a beautiful blonde and probably talented but she had a penchant for self-destructive behavior. Although other Hollywood performers might well have had the same problems, most of them were not quite as public about it.

As a Follies stunner under the name of Imogene "Bubbles" Wilson, Nolan attracted much positive attention. She changed her name in order to assume a film career but this reinvention did not bring her any real lasting success. Her career slid steadily downhill with each sordid revelation of drug abuse, physical abuse and "illness" of various sorts.

Even after Mary Nolan's career was over, virtually thrown away, there were still numerous stories about legal problems and potential comebacks but she ended her days in obscurity.

Charming Sinners: Mary Nolan has a suitable role and is very good as the fluffy blonde. *Variety* 7/10/29, *Harrison's Reports* 7/13/29.

Shanghai Lady: The acting of Mary Nolan is artistic. She plays so well that she wins sympathy even though her part is basically unsympathetic. *Harrison's Reports* 11/16/29.

Young Desire: A great deal of sympathy is felt for the heroine played by Mary Nolan as the carnival dancer. In her attempt to seem sophisticated, however, she spoke too slowly and slurred her words, giving the impression of being drunk. *Harrison's Reports* 7/5/30, *Variety* 7/30/30.

Midnight Patrol: Nolan has just a bit part. *Variety* 5/10/32.

Norton, Barry (Alfredo Biraben or de Biraben), Buenos Aires, Argentina, 1905–1959

Silent: Handsome Barry Norton entered films in 1926 with such vehicles as *What Price Glory?* and *The Lily*. Others included *Ankles Preferred, Sunrise, The Wizard, Legion of the Condemned* and *Fleetwing*. Generally portraying sensitive youths, he occasionally was cast in a lead but more frequently as second lead or supporting player. Last silent: *The Exalted Flapper* (1929), with synchronized music, made after his first part-talkie.

Sound: The 1928 part-talkie *Mother Knows Best* was Norton's first. His sole 1929 part-talkie role came in *Four Devils* and in the early '30s he was making Spanish-language versions of Hollywood films like *Dracula*. He also appeared in an occasional English language film such as *Dishonored*.

Norton's busiest sound period was 1933–37 when he had roles in films like *Cocktail Hour, Nana, Anna Karenina, Storm Over the Andes* and *I'll Take Romance*. There were single films in 1938 and '39 (*The Buccaneer, Should Husbands Work?*) and then he became a performer in Mexican films. His last American film role was a cameo in *Around the World in 80 Days* (1956). He also appeared on television.

Mother Knows Best: Norton looks good on screen and gives his role quite a bit of spirit. He acts superbly. *Variety* 9/19/28, *Harrison's Reports* 10/6/28.

Dishonored: Norton's talking ability is all right. *Variety* 3/11/31, *Harrison's Reports* 3/14/31.

The Grand Canary: Barry Norton, as a missionary, plays the one part that could have been dramatic, but is never allowed to be. *Variety* 7/24/34.

Novak, Eva, St. Louis, Missouri, 1898–1988

Filmography: Classic Images (Jan. 1985); List of films in *Sweethearts of the Sage*

Silent: One of the beautiful Novak sisters (Jane was the other), Eva Novak debuted at Fox in 1919. Among her films, many westerns with Tom Mix and William S. Hart, were *Trailin', Sky High, 30 Below Zero, Missing Daughters, The Smart Sex, Irene* and *O'Malley of the Mounted*.

Novak was a very busy actress through 1927, making in some years eight or ten films. Toward the latter part of her silent career, her roles were in support. Last silent: *Duty's Reward* (1927).

Sound: When Novak returned in the sound era it was in small parts. Her first talkie was *The Medicine Man* (1930), one of Jack Benny's early pictures, and she was seen very sporadically thereafter until the mid–1960s.

Novak's motion pictures, some directed by John Ford, included *Four Faces West, Sergeant Rutledge, Wild Seed, Ride a Violent Mile* and *Three Godfathers*.

Novak, Jane, St. Louis, Missouri, 1896–1990

Filmography: Classic Images (Spring 1969, Mar.-Apr. 1983); List of films in *Sweethearts of the Sage*

Silent: The more successful of the Novak sisters (Eva was the other), Jane Novak was first seen onscreen about 1913. Her first films were Vitagraph one-reelers. She was an early leading lady of Harold Lloyd's and went on to appear in westerns with William S. Hart (e.g., *Three Word Brand*).

Other Novak films included *Thelma*, which was one of her most successful, in 1922, *The Lullaby, The Temple of Dusk, Man's Desire, One Increasing Purpose, Divorce* and *The River's End*. She also appeared in *Graft*, a 1915 serial. Last silent: *Redskin* (1929).

Sound: Novak's starring career ended with sound. She did not return to the screen until 1936 and then she played off and on small roles in films which included *Ghost Town, Hollywood Boulevard, The Yanks Are Coming, Desert Fury* and *The File on Thelma Jordon*. Her last films, *About Mrs. Leslie* and *The Boss*, were made in the 1950s.

Ghost Town: Jane Novak is still attractive, but she has a thick speaking voice and talks like an inexperienced ingenue. Also, the former silent-day star has gotten heavier in places where she does not carry it well. *Variety* 1/6/37 (first review), *Variety* 1/27/37 (second review).

Novarro, Ramon (Jose Ramon Gil

Samaniegos), Durango, Mexico, 1899–1968
Filmography: Films in Review (Nov. 1972)

Silent: MGM star Ramon Novarro was a dancer and singer before he entered films as an extra about 1917. He worked for Sennett in 1921 (dancing in *A Small Town Idol*) and gained recognition in *The Prisoner of Zenda* (1922) under his real name, which was changed soon thereafter.

Novarro was placed under contract by MGM as a "Latin lover" type but proved his versatility in other roles. His films included *The Arab, Scaramouche, The Student Prince, The Red Lily, A Lover's Oath, Across to Singapore* and his greatest role, the title character in *Ben-Hur* (1925). Last silent: *The Pagan* (1929), technically a silent with singing sequences including the popular "Pagan Love Song."

Sound: Devil-May-Care (1929) was Novarro's first talkie. His easy-to-take singing voice ensured that he would be seen in several musicals. Among his other films were *Call of the Flesh* (he also did the Hollywood-made French and Spanish versions), *The Barbarian, The Cat and the Fiddle, The Son-Daughter, Laughing Boy* and *Mata Hari* with Greta Garbo (1932), perhaps his best-known sound effort.

After 1934's *The Night Is Young*, Novarro was released by MGM and was seen in two minor Republic efforts which parodied his image as a lover. They were *The Sheik Steps Out* in 1937 and *A Desperate Adventure* the following year. Thereafter he was inactive on-screen for many years, except for a French and a Mexican film in the early '40s.

Ramon Novarro returned for a handful of character roles beginning in 1949. These included *The Big Steal, Crisis* and *Heller in Pink Tights* (1960), his final film. He also appeared on television.

Comments: Ramon Novarro rose above his typecasting in the 1920s to give sensitive performances in several films, but most of his material was not worthwhile. After the smashing success of *Ben-Hur*, for which he was not the first choice, he seldom was cast in good films. He was, however, frequently assigned strong and popular leading ladies.

Talkies did not find Novarro's fortunes improving too much but the popularity of musicals in the very early sound period did give his career a chance to branch out. His lightly-accented speaking and singing voices were adequate and he did appear in some popular talkies, but there also were several clinkers.

Ultimately MGM did not seem to know what to do with Novarro and he was sometimes miscast in generalized "exotic" roles. Unfortunately his quiet and uncharismatic acting style did not suit them. Certainly *Mata Hari* was an example of this.

Novarro's star declined rapidly and by the late '30s he was reduced to self-parody, no matter how gentle. His later supporting roles were not an unworthy farewell to the screen, but he might have been largely forgotten had it not been for the publicity surrounding his brutal murder by two hustler-brothers.

REVIEWS

Devil-May-Care: Novarro sings well but with an accent. He handles dialogue nicely and his singing voice is not unlike Maurice Chevalier's. *Variety* 12/25/29, *Harrison's Reports* 1/4/30.

Mata Hari: Novarro gives an excellent performance. *Harrison's Reports* 1/9/32.

The Barbarian: Novarro's flair for romantic light comedy shows to advantage during the first half hour but then he and the story both go wrong together. The burden is entirely on Novarro and the results aren't happy. *Variety* 5/16/33.

The Cat and the Fiddle: Novarro sings well and does a good job with the lines. *Variety* 2/20/34.

The Night Is Young: Novarro fails to ignite any real romantic fire and gives a stilted performance. *Variety* 1/15/35.

A Desperate Adventure: The former Metro star doesn't sing in this film and acts only fairly well. *Variety* 8/10/38.

Crisis: Among the interesting, typical Latin types is Ramon Novarro who is very good. *Variety* 6/21/50.

Oakman, Wheeler (Vivian Eichelberger),

Washington, D.C., 1890–1949

Filmography: Classic Images (July-September 1983); Academy of Motion Picture Arts and Sciences (through 1929 only)

Silent: Wheeler Oakman appeared in his first major film *The Spoilers* in 1914, after several years in repertory and then as an extra and supporting player. His starring role in 1916's *The Ne'er-Do-Well* began a career as a leading man that lasted into the early '20s. During the rest of the decade he was increasingly offered roles that featured him as a villain.

Among Oakman's major early 1920s pictures were *Outside the Law* and *The Virgin of Stamboul*. Other of his numerous films included *The Tragedy of Ambition, Chip of the Flying U, The Black Orchid, Revenge, What Women Love, The Half Breed* and *The Danger Patrol*.

Oakman's picture output declined during the 1920s but by the latter part of the decade he had become increasingly busy on-screen. Last silent: *Devil's Chaplain* (1929), made after his first talkies.

Sound: Although he became best-known in talkies as a fearsome mustachioed villain in "B" westerns, Oakman made sound films in various genres including musicals. Of his eleven 1929 films, all but one had at least some talking sequences, including *The Donovan Affair, Little Johnny Jones, The Show of Shows, On with the Show* and *Handcuffed.* He had made his sound debut with the first all-talking picture *Lights of New York* (1928).

During the '30s Oakman hit his stride with innumerable bad man portrayals in westerns, serials and melodramas. Among his films were *Roarin' Ranch, Guilty or Not Guilty, Undercover Man, The Mysterious Avenger, In Old Montana, What a Man, The Ape Man, Three of a Kind, Rough Ridin' Justice* and *The Bank Alarm.*

From 1945 to the time of his death, Oakman was seen almost exclusively in serials. His many chapterplays included *The Phantom Empire, The Airmail Mystery, The Phantom of the Air, The Lost Jungle, The Adventures of Rex and Rinty, Brick Bradford, Buck Rogers, Flash Gordon's Trip to Mars* and *Hap Harrigan.* His last film appearance was in the serial *Superman* (1948).

REVIEWS

The Gorilla Ship: Wheeler Oakman has a tough time playing the villain. *Variety* 8/2/32.

O'Brien, George, San Francisco, California,
1900–1985

Filmography: Films in Review (Nov. 1962)

Silent: After being behind the camera as an assistant, as well as doing stunt and extra work, George O'Brien began getting screen billing in 1922. He became a Fox romantic star in the 1924 railroad epic *The Iron Horse*, directed by John Ford.

O'Brien's other films included *East Side, West Side, The Man Who Came Back, Three Bad Men, Fig Leaves, The Johnstown Flood, Paid to Love* and his most memorable, the classic Murnau production of *Sunrise* (1927) co-starring Janet Gaynor. Last silent: *Masked Emotions* (1929), with synchronized music and sound effects, made after his first part-talkie.

Sound: O'Brien was first heard on-screen in the part-talkie *Noah's Ark* (1928); *Salute* (1929) was his first full sound film. Losing his status as an "A" leading man, for ten years (1930–1940) he appeared in a long series of "B" westerns and adventure-melodramas for Fox and RKO beginning with *The Lone Star Ranger.*

Among these O'Brien actioners were *Daniel Boone, Racketeers of the Range, The Dude Ranger,*

Wings Over Wyoming, The Seas Beneath, The Marshal of Mesa City, Park Avenue Logger and *Windjammer.*

After distinguished Navy service during the Second World War, O'Brien returned to films in 1947 for character roles in *My Wild Irish Rose* and *Fort Apache.* He also appeared in what might be considered his final starring role, *Gold Raiders* with the Three Stooges. He was last seen in *Cheyenne Autumn* (1964).

Comments: George O'Brien's designation as "The Chest" and "The Torso" was part of Fox's effort to publicize him as a "man's man" in contrast to the "Latin lover" type then so popular. Despite O'Brien's sensitive acting in *Sunrise* and other silents, the publicity eventually won out and he was typecast as an action hero.

Although O'Brien's voice was just fine for talkies, he rarely had a chance to do anything but ride and fight. Over half his films were westerns. In them, his persona was breezy and bantering; he teased his leading ladies rather than putting them up on a pedestal like many of his cowboy confreres.

In his later supporting roles, O'Brien again showed what a dependable actor he could be. He retained his youthful appearance well into middle age and possibly could have sustained a really worthwhile career in films had he been given the opportunity.

REVIEWS

Noah's Ark: O'Brien is surprisingly good in the talking sequences. He has a pleasing voice, clear diction and enunciation. This part is possibly his best. *Variety* 11/7/28, *Harrison's Reports* 3/23/29.

Mystery Ranch: O'Brien does some hard riding and good work generally. *Variety* 11/5/32.

Hard Rock Harrigan: The film gives O'Brien an opportunity to get away from a saddle into a melodrama. He fits the role well. *Variety* 7/31/35.

Gun Law: O'Brien fits the hero's part very well. Not only does he act with naturalness but he is well suited to parts of this type because of his powerful physique. *Harrison's Reports* 5/14/38.

Triple Justice: It is certain to satisfy George O'Brien fans for he plays his typical part, that of a courageous hero. *Harrison's Reports* 9/14/40.

Gold Raiders: O'Brien is somewhat stiff. *Variety* 6/18/52.

O'Day, Molly (sometimes Mollie; Susan or
Suzanne Noonan), Bayonne, New Jersey,
1911/12–

Filmography: List of films in *American Classic Screen* (May-June 1983)

Silent: After appearing in some Hal Roach

two-reelers, Molly O'Day had her first starring role in *The Patent Leather Kid* (1927), a popular film with Richard Barthelmess. Her other silent features were *Hard-Boiled Haggerty*, *The Lovelorn* (with her sister Sally O'Neil) and *Shepherd of the Hills*. Last silent: *The Little Shepherd of Kingdom Come* (1928).

Sound: By the time sound arrived, Molly O'Day had begun fighting the weight problem that, at least temporarily, derailed her career. Her only 1929 appearance was a brief one, part of the "Meet My Sister" musical number performed with her actual sister in *The Show of Shows*. *Sisters*, again with O'Neil, was her only 1930 effort.

Other O'Day films, after she had gotten her weight under control, included *Sob Sisters*, *Gigolettes of Paris*, *The Life of Vergie Winters*, *Lawless Border* and her last film *Skull and Crown* in 1935.

Comments: Molly O'Day, with her pretty Irish colleen face, was a promising ingenue but her growing chubbiness and its attendant publicity completely overshadowed her career. She was released by First National. Her first talkie appearance, brief though it was, amply revealed her excess girth. She then had experimental surgery which apparently caused some (unseen) disfiguring.

Eventually O'Day conquered her problem but the momentum was lost from her career. Her talkie appearances were few and generally in quickies. In her one major sound film, *The Life of Vergie Winters*, starring Ann Harding, she showed she could be a sensitive actress. But it was a supporting role.

REVIEWS

Gigolettes of Paris: The acting is stilted. Molly O'Day plays the husky and sometimes too noisy roommate. *Harrison's Reports* 7/29/33, *Variety* 10/17/33.

Oland, Warner (Warner Ohlund; some
sources say Johan or Johann Ohlund),
Umea, Sweden, 1880–1938

Filmography: Films in Review (June-July 1985); List of films in *Eighty Silent Film Stars*

Silent: After appearing on the stage, Warner Oland may have debuted in films as early as 1912; he is known to be in two 1915 Theda Bara films, *Destruction* and *Sin*. He soon found himself playing the devious "Oriental" and other villains for which he became well-known in Pearl White serials (e.g., *The Fatal Ring*) and numerous features.

Among Oland's other serials were *Patria*, *The Yellow Arm*, *The Lightning Raider*, *Hurricane Hutch* and *The Phantom Foe*. His features included *The Witness for the Defense*, *Don Juan*, *The Naulahka*, *Curlytop*, *So This Is Marriage*, *Infatuation* and *Don Q. Son of Zorro*. Last silent: *The Faker* (1929), made after his first sound film.

Sound: Oland's first part-talkie was, of course, the first successful part-talkie, *The Jazz Singer* (1927). As the cantor father of star Al Jolson, he spoke only one word aloud from the screen, and any singing he may have done in his role was most certainly dubbed.

Oland was not to speak until 1929's *Chinatown Nights*, another part-talkie. His first full sound effort was *The Studio Murder Mystery*; others that year were *The Mighty* and *The Mysterious Dr. Fu Manchu*, in which he played the first incarnation of that evil genius.

During the remaining eight years in which he appeared in films, Oland played a variety of roles but he became identified with the Chinese detective Charlie Chan in a series of 16 pictures which began with *Charlie Chan Carries On* in 1931.

Further titles in the series included *Charlie Chan in London, …in Paris, …at the Opera, …in Egypt, …at the Circus, …on Broadway* and, lastly, *…at Monte Carlo*.

Other films in which Oland appeared were *Shanghai Express*, *Bulldog Drummond Strikes Back*, *The Painted Veil*, *Werewolf of London* and *Before Dawn*. Nineteen thirty-five's *Shanghai* was his last non–Chan film.

Comments: Warner Oland was a distinguished theater actor when he decided to essay films. He had translated, with his actress wife Edith Shearn, several works of the playwright August Strindberg into English. Unfortunately for him, his eyes did have a slight slant to them and this was all unimaginative producers needed to see.

The frequent casting of Oland, a suave Swede, as an Asian villain and other exotics may not have seemed strange in Hollywood but such typing rarely allowed him to stretch his acting muscles.

Oland's transition to talkies was without effort. His well-modulated, stage-trained voice, with its slight and unidentifiable accent, was an asset. His typecasting continued, the only difference being that he metamorphosed from evildoing to beneficence after he began playing Charlie Chan.

Even when Oland was in another type of role, reviews tended to bring up the Chinese detective gratuitously. Whether this restrictive box contributed to his alcoholism is only conjecture. At the last he refused to report to the studio for work on another Charlie Chan film, fled to Sweden and there was taken with his final illness.

REVIEWS

Chinatown Nights: Warner Oland does exceedingly well. His previous accomplishments are fortified anew with the addition of a decisive speaking voice. *Variety* 4/3/29.

The Mysterious Dr. Fu Manchu: It would not have been half as good were it not for the artistic acting of the incomparable Warner Oland. The Chinese impersonations of Lon Chaney cannot approach the artistic work of Oland. He is a smooth and finished actor. *Harrison's Reports* 7/27/29.

Daughter of the Dragon: Oland sounds more like Charlie Chan, the Chinese detective, than Fu Manchu, which makes it look like the actors got cast wrong. *Variety* 8/25/31.

Before Dawn: The villain is played by Warner Oland. He portrays the physician and moves in his accustomed "Chan" fashion through the film. *Harrison's Reports* 10/21/33, *Variety* 10/24/33.

Charlie Chan in Shanghai: Oland, the merry Swede who has won himself an international reputation as a Chinese man, handles the Chan assignment with competence and assurance. *Variety* 10/16/35.

Charlie Chan at Monte Carlo: Oland plays Charlie Chan as skillfully as ever. *Harrison's Reports* 12/25/37.

Oliver, Edna May (Edna May Nutter),
Malden, Massachusetts, 1883–1942

Filmography: Film Fan Monthly (Nov. 1972); *Focus on Film* (May-June 1992); partial filmography in *Films in Review* (Jan.-Feb. 1962)

Silent: As a singer and actress, Edna May Oliver appeared in stock and then on Broadway from 1916. Her most famous role was that of Parthy Ann in Jerome Kern's 1927 success *Show Boat,* in which she played for three years. By that time it had already been four years since her screen debut in *Three O'Clock in the Morning* and *Wife in Name Only.* Other films in which Oliver had supporting roles included *Icebound,* a repeat of her Broadway success, *Restless Wives, Lucky Devil, Lovers in Quarantine* and *The American Venus.* Last silent: *Let's Get Married* (1926).

Sound: Oliver's introduction to sound came in Clara Bow's *The Saturday Night Kid* (1929), in which her voice proved to be an ideal match for her persona. After signing with RKO she supported the zany comedy team of Wheeler and Woolsey in a few pictures; the first time was in their 1930 film. *Half Shot at Sunrise.*

Although a character actress par excellence, Oliver was occasionally top-billed, notably in *Fanny Foley Herself, Ladies of the Jury* and *My Dear Miss Aldrich,* as well as in the "Hildegarde Withers" series. She also appeared in the early talkie *Cimarron* with Richard Dix, an actor with whom she co-starred several times.

In the mid–'30s Oliver went to MGM where she

was to make some of her most prestigious films. All together she appeared for various studios in more than 40, among them *David Copperfield* (a signature role as Aunt Betsey Trotwood), *Alice in Wonderland, Parnell, Little Women* (Aunt March), *Romeo and Juliet* (the Nurse), *A Tale of Two Cities* (Miss Pross), *The Story of Irene and Vernon Castle,* and *Pride and Prejudice* (Lady Catherine De Bourgh).

The Technicolor picture *Drums Along the Mohawk* brought Oliver an Academy Award nomination for Best Supporting Actress in 1939. During her career she specialized in playing characters who could be both haughty and down-to-earth, roles enhanced by her equine face, piercing glare and imperious "sniff." Her final role came in 1941's *Lydia.*

Comments: Like all great character people, Edna May Oliver's screen persona had very distinctive attributes. The famous sniff and haughty manner were the outward manifestations of an overbearing and vinegary know-it-all who was almost always a spinster and probably an unhappy one. (She had been briefly married in real life.) But, like many movie "meanies," her characters had hearts of gold.

It is reported that Oliver was not particularly happy with a face most often described as "horsy." And who could doubt that she would have preferred to be beautiful? She was realistic about it though, saying, "No one realizes more than I do that this face of mine is my fortune."

Although the few films in which she had an opportunity to star were either minor efforts or unsuccessful, Edna May Oliver's face *was* her fortune as a character actress. So was her voice and so was a certain less definable quality. It is no coincidence that she appeared in many adaptations of classic literature. Her character was redolent of an earlier time when people seemed to stand for something — perhaps decency?

REVIEWS

The Saturday Night Kid: The supporting cast is good, especially Edna May Oliver playing the director of personnel as a sonorous, schoolteacherish type. Her domineering nature brings many a laugh. *Variety* 11/20/29, *Harrison's Reports* 11/23/29.

Half Shot at Sunrise: Oliver makes something out of the role as the colonel's wisecracking, worldly wife. *Variety* 10/15/30.

Fanny Foley Herself: Edna May Oliver, a fine stage comedienne, is starred but she has two handicaps. She is not well known by the nation's film fans, and her first starring film won't advance her much further. No one will disagree that she is an artist and does her work artistically, but she is miscast. *Variety* 10/27/31, *Harrison's Reports* 10/31/31.

Murder on the Blackboard: If it were not for some of the comedy of Edna May Oliver it would be very tiresome. It's a perfect role for her and she overshadows everyone else.

(This was one of the three Hildegarde Withers films in which Oliver appeared. As the spinster schoolteacher she solved murders that had baffled the police.) *Harrison's Reports* 6/16/34, *Variety* 6/26/34.

David Copperfield: Oliver does low comedy in a high comedy manner and shows flashes of the underlying tenderness of the character. Of all the women in the film she drew the only burst of applause; it was well earned. *Variety* 1/22/35.

A Tale of Two Cities: There is some non-obtrusive comedy, mostly contributed by Oliver, who does valiant service. Although she never gets quite the chances she had in "David Copperfield," she makes every line count. *Variety* 1/1/36.

My Dear Miss Aldrich: Edna May Oliver comes through with one of the funniest performances. *Variety* 10/6/37.

Pride and Prejudice: Oliver, domineering as Lady Catherine, comes in late in the story and supplies some much needed merriment. *Variety* 7/10/40.

Olmsted, Gertrude (sometimes Olmstead),
Chicago, Illinois, 1897/1904–1975

Filmography: List of films in *Sweethearts of the Sage*

Silent: Gertrude Olmsted was one of the few beauty contest winners who made a respectable career in silent films. In 1920 she won a *Chicago Herald-Examiner* contest with a Universal contract as the prize. After appearing in some two-reelers, her feature debut came in 1921 with small roles in *Shadows of Conscience* and *The Big Adventure*.

Olmsted's other films, many quite respectable, included *Cobra* (with Rudolph Valentino), *The Monster* and *Mr. Wu* (with Lon Chaney), *The Torrent* (with Greta Garbo), *California Straight Ahead, Time, the Comedian, The Boob* and *Cameo Kirby*. Last silent: *Hey Rube!* (1928).

Sound: Hit of the Show, a 1928 part-talkie, was Olmsted's introduction to sound. She was to make only four other sound features, all in 1929: *The Lone Wolf's Daughter* (part talking), *Sonny Boy* and *The Time, the Place and the Girl.* Her last, brief appearance was in the all-star *The Show of Shows* in 1929.

REVIEWS

Hit of the Show: Reviewers were split. One thought that Olmstead had never appeared to better advantage and she was a real artist. Another thought she was miscast and looked too sophisticated for the role. *Harrison's Reports* 6/30/28, *Variety* 7/11/28.

The Lone Wolf's Daughter: The sound quality is so poor that it is unintelligible. There is an irritating booming noise as if the characters talked through their noses. Gertrude Olmstead is the heroine. *Harrison's Reports* 3/9/29.

The Time, the Place, the Girl: Olmstead is charming as the heroine. *Harrison's Reports* 7/13/29.

O'Malley, Pat, Forest City, Pennsylvania,
1890/92–1966

Silent: In films from about 1907, working for studios that included Edison, Essanay, Universal and Kalem, Pat O'Malley was a popular leading man, generally in rugged romantic roles. He entered features about 1915 with *Gladiola* and *On Dangerous Paths*; other early ones were *Hit-the-Trail Holliday, The Prussian Cur, False Evidence* and *The Love That Lives*. There was also a serial, *The Red Glove*.

O'Malley remained busy in leading and supporting roles through the 1920s in such vehicles as *Bob Hampton of Placer, Brothers Under the Skin, The Man from Brodney's, The Virginian* (1923 version), *Proud Flesh, My Old Dutch* and *A Bowery Cinderella*. Last silent: *The House of Scandal* (1928), in which he was top-billed.

Sound: The talkies reduced O'Malley to almost permanent supporting and even bit player status; in his first talkie, *Alibi* (1929), he did have a lead. His career lasted, with breaks, until 1962, or some 55 years. This certainly made him one of the contenders for longest career honors. He also made movies in Ireland and appeared on television.

Besides the 1930 Vitaphone short *The People Versus —,* O'Malley's many films included *The Fall Guy, Night Life in Reno, Klondike, Broadway Bill, Hollywood Boulevard, East of the River, Over My Dead Body, Mule Train* and *Invasion of the Body Snatchers.*

NOTE: Not to be confused with the Hollywood-based British character actor J. Pat O'Malley.

REVIEWS

Alibi: The hero, Pat O'Malley, is a detective sergeant and he stands out as a talent for talkies. *Variety* 4/10/29, *Harrison's Reports* 4/27/29.

It's a Date: A large group of old-time film stars

are briefly paraded before the camera, including Pat O'Malley. *Variety* 10/16/40.

O'Neil, Nance, Oakland, California,
1874/75–1965

Silent: A famous Broadway star from about 1909, Nance O'Neil specialized in classical roles such as Shakespeare and the Greek tragedies as well as Ibsen. She first essayed the cinema in 1915 with *The Kreutzer Sonata*, *Princess Romanoff* and *A Woman's Past*.

Most of O'Neil's roles were starring ones but there were a few supporting parts as well. During the next two years she made several more films including *The Iron Woman*, *Souls in Bondage*, *Hedda Gabler*, *Those Who Toil* and *The Seventh Sin*. Then she returned to the theater. Last silent: *The Fall of the Romanoffs* (1918).

Sound: In the clamor for stage-trained actors at the dawn of the talkies, O'Neil was called back to the screen. Her first picture was the ill-fated John Gilbert starrer *His Glorious Night* (1929). Several more followed over the next three years, including *Call of the Flesh*, *The Floradora Girl*, *Cimarron*, *Transgression*, *Resurrection* and *The Rogue Song*.

In 1932 O'Neil made what were probably her final films, *False Faces* and *Westward Passage*. *NOTE:* The Nance O'Neil who made films in England in 1935 (*Brewsters Millions*, etc.) and thereafter appears to be a different and younger actress. Her credits are often found included with those of the American actress.

Comments: One interesting fact about Nance O'Neil was her improbable friendship with Lizzie Borden, the Massachusetts spinster immortalized for apparently killing her stepmother and father with an ax. (Borden was acquitted.) Their association began after Miss Borden inherited her father's money and bought a Fall River mansion. Borden apparently was a great fan of O'Neil's and entertained her in style.

REVIEWS

The Royal Bed: Second-billed Nance O'Neil always remains the stern Queen. *Variety* 2/4/31.

Transgression: An expert performance is turned in by Nance O'Neil, splendid in a small part. *New York Times* 6/15/31, *Variety* 6/16/31.

O'Neil, Sally (sometimes O'Neill; Virginia
Noonan), 1908/12–1968

Filmography: List of films in *Films in Review* (Feb. 1972); *American Classic Screen* (May-June 1983)

Silent: Pert Sally O'Neil made her film debut in MGM's *Don't* (1925) and very shortly thereafter became a star in *Sally, Irene and Mary*, co-starring Joan Crawford and Constance Bennett. She was released by the studio toward the end of the decade and then freelanced.

Other O'Neil pictures included *Mike*, *Frisco Sally Levy*, *Battling Butler* with Buster Keaton, D. W. Griffith's *The Battle of the Sexes* and *Slide, Kelly, Slide*. Last silent: *Broadway Fever* (1929).

Sound: *The Girl on the Barge*, a 1929 part-talkie, was O'Neil's first sound film. Her first all-talker was the popular color musical *On with the Show*, of which *42nd Street* was a partial remake. That year she was also seen in *The Show of Shows* (in which she did a brief song and dance with her sister Molly O'Day in the "Meet My Sister" number), *Jazz Heaven* and *The Sophomore* among others.

The next year O'Neil was on-screen in four films including *Sisters* (again with her real sister) and *Girl of the Port*, a South Seas melodrama. After 1930 her career began to decline.

Among O'Neil's other films were *Kathleen Mavourneen* (her final film, *Kathleen*, made in Ireland in 1937, was based on the same story), *Salvation Nell*, *Convention Girl*, *Too Tough to Kill* (her last U.S. film in 1935) and the John Ford–directed *The Brat*, based on her Broadway play. She also made other stage appearances

Comments: In silents Sally O'Neil established a persona as a gamine, a role for which her cute face, with its "map of Ireland," well-suited her. She repeated it several times. Although she claimed to have gotten tired of it, the public may well have tired of it first. The resultant dip in her popularity led to her release by MGM.

O'Neil made the transition to talkies and during the first year retained some popularity. Her voice, though, was high in pitch, even grating, and very redolent of her New Jersey roots. She was by no means a subtle actress in talkies and before too long she found herself in quickies.

O'Neil did not work for lengthy periods of time. With each of her films after 1930 there was talk of a comeback and she struggled through until 1937, but she was long past her peak.

REVIEWS

On with the Show: Sally O'Neil has the sympathetic ingenue part and she sings the theme song. (It is more than likely that the singing attributed to O'Neil was dubbed.) *Variety* 6/5/29.

The Girl of the Port: O'Neil does excellent work as the heroine. *Harrison's Reports* 1/25/30.

The Brat: Sally O'Neil handles the assignment with skill and the diminutive actress wins the spectator's sympathy. *New York Times* 8/25/31, *Variety* 8/29/31.

By Appointment Only: Most of the picture is centered around Sally O'Neil but her terrible makeup and amateurish mugging make her hard to accept. *Variety* 11/21/33.

Too Tough to Kill: O'Neil does a satisfactory job. *Variety* 12/25/35.

Kathleen: O'Neil is satisfactory in the title role although some camera angles are not flattering. She has not lost her acting ability and is right at home with the Irish contingent. *Variety* 1/26/38.

Owen, Seena (Signe Auen), Spokane, Washington, 1894/96–1966

Silent: Seena Owen was probably best known for roles at opposite ends of her career: The Princess Beloved of Babylon in *Intolerance* (1916) and the mad Queen who whipped Gloria Swanson down the halls of the palace in 1928's *Queen Kelly.* Her feature debut came about 1915 in films such as *The Fox Woman, The Lamb* (an early Doug Fairbanks vehicle) and *Martha's Vindication.*

Others of Owen's pictures, in which she usually was the leading lady, included *Branding Broadway, The Gift Supreme, Lavender and Old Lace, Unseeing Eyes, Faint Perfume* and *The Blue Danube.* Last silents: *Sinners in Love* and *His Last Haul,* released about the same time in 1928.

Sound: Owen apparently made only two sound appearances, the first being 1929's *The Marriage Playground* in which she was billed seventh. The other was a small role in *Officer 13* (1933). In the early '30s she began a screenwriting career that lasted into the latter 1940s, and she also was credited with contributing to the scripts of several more films.

REVIEWS

The Marriage Playground: Seena Owen is very good. *New York Times* 7/14/29, *Harrison's Reports* 12/21/29.

Officer Thirteen: Seena Owen contributes good acting. *Harrison's Reports* 2/4/33.

Page, Anita (Anita Pomares), Flushing, New York, 1910–

Silent: Blonde Anita Page came late to the silents, her first featured role coming in 1928 after a few appearances as an extra. She made a literal splash (or at least a splat) in one of her earliest — *Our Dancing Daughters* — by falling dramatically down the stairs.

Other Page silents included *Telling the World, While the City Sleeps* (with Lon Chaney), *The Flying Fleet* and *Our Modern Maidens.* Last silent: *Speedway* (1929), with synchronized sound effects and music, made after her first talkie.

Sound: Page made a smashing sound debut top-billed in 1929's *The Broadway Melody,* which ultimately won the Academy Award for Best Picture. Other talkies that year were *The Hollywood Revue of 1929* and *Navy Blues.* It was also the year she was named a Wampas Baby Star.

Among Page's subsequent films through 1933, in which she sometimes appeared in second leads or support, were *Free and Easy* (Buster Keaton's first starring talkie), *Our Blushing Brides, Reducing, Prosperity* (the latter two Marie Dressler-Polly Moran comedies), *Jungle Bride* and *The Little Accident.* She returned for a final supporting role in *Hitch Hike to Heaven* (1936).

Comments: Anita Page never again had a vehicle to match *The Broadway Melody* and her career waned thereafter. Perhaps she was not given a comparable film because her talents really did not merit one; although she gave a competent-enough performance, she was out-emoted by Bessie Love. The very popular film, with its music and color sequences, probably would have been as popular without her.

Undeniably blonde and beauteous, but with a voice which lacked flexibility and training, Page was not a particularly strong actress. In fact, her subsequent talkies revealed her to be a rather colorless emoter. In the MGM stable of stars, she did not shine and she was eventually released by the studio.

REVIEWS

The Broadway Melody: Page's performance will make a splash. It's natural all the way and she looks great. Her only handicap is that she can't dance but the remainder of her performance easily suffices. *Variety* 2/13/29, *Harrison's Reports* 2/16/29.

Our Blushing Brides: The picture is helped by the good acting of Anita Page. *Harrison's Reports* 8/9/30.

Gentleman's Fate: Page plays a girl involved with a gang; she looks very good. *Harrison's Reports* 3/14/31, *Variety* 6/30/31.

Pallette, Eugene, Winfield, Kansas, 1889–1954

Filmography: List of films in *Films in Review* (Nov.-Dec. 1967); *Classic Images* (Nov.-Dec. 1989); *Eighty Silent Film Stars*

Silent: After appearing in stock, Eugene Pallette came to films about 1910 for such studios as American and Mutual-Reliance. He also co-starred opposite Norma Talmadge in two-reelers at Triangle. His feature career began about 1916 and included the romantic lead in the "Huguenot" story of *Intolerance.*

Other early Pallette films were *Going Straight, The Winning of Sally Temple* and *Breakers Ahead.* By now putting on the weight that was to be so much a part of his persona, in the 1920s he began playing supporting roles in many films, including westerns. Some of his major pictures were *The Three Musketeers, Chicago* and *Mantrap,* with Clara Bow.

Among Pallette's others were *To the Last Man, Whispering Smith, The Light of Western Stars* and *The Good-Bye Kiss.* He also appeared in Hal Roach two-reel comedies, most notably with Laurel and Hardy. Last silent: *Out of the Ruins* (1928), made after his first talkie.

Sound: Pallette's distinctive voice may have first growled from the screen in the first all-talkie, Warner Bros.' *Lights of New York* (1928), or it may have been in that year's Vitaphone short *The Swell(ed) Head.* All his 1929 films, including *The Greene Murder Case, The Studio Murder Mystery* and *The Canary Murder Case,* were sound. That year he also polished his sidekick image in *The Virginian* and appeared in *The Love Parade.*

As the 1930s progressed, Pallette became one of the screen's leading character actors and he was cast in important films like *My Man Godfrey, The Ghost Goes West* and *Mr. Smith Goes to Washington.* The epitome of his career was probably his born-to-play role as Friar Tuck in 1938's *The Adventures of Robin Hood.* (Pallette played an almost-identical role two years later in *The Mark of Zorro.*) He had also made some shorts earlier in the decade.

Pallette's '40s films were generally less important (e.g., *The Gang's All Here, Heavenly Days* and *Lake Placid Serenade*), with a few better efforts like *The Male Animal* and Preston Sturges's *The Lady Eve,* in which he delivered a very fine comic performance.

He remained a "large" presence on the screen until his last films in 1946: *In Old Sacramento* and *Suspense.* In all he had made hundreds of silent appearances and over 100 talkies.

Comments: After seeing rotund, 300-pound Eugene Pallette in his trademark blustering talkie parts, it is most difficult to envision him as he was in the early silents: slim and romantic in dramatic roles. He was not the frog who turned into a prince but the reverse.

Even if Pallette had been slimmer and younger when sound came, it is highly unlikely that his *basso profundo,* froglike croak would have suited him for anything but character parts. His *métier* was as the ineffectual minor authority figure, often a policeman, or, at the other end of the scale, a rich but often henpecked man. Either way he played his roles to perfection.

REVIEWS

Easy to Take: Pallette's performance is superlative; he shows what he can do when he is given a break. *Variety* 12/23/36.

Clarence: Pallette plays one of his typical roles capably. *Variety* 3/10/37.

The Cheaters: Pallette, as the financially embarrassed tycoon, contributes a splendid performance. *Variety* 7/4/45.

Panzer, Paul (Paul Panzerbeiter), Wurzberg, Germany, 1872–1958

Silent: Paul Panzer, the darkly glowering, bushyhaired villain of the legendary 1914 Pearl White serial *The Perils of Pauline,* claimed to have started at Vitagraph as early as 1903. He also professed to have made over 900 films, most of them split- and one-reelers. (A very early effort may have been 1904's *Stolen by Gypsies.*) Even if both these claims are highly exaggerated, his modest place in cinema history is assured.

Panzer entered features starting about 1914 or '15 with such films as *The Last Volunteer, Under Southern Skies* and *The Woman Who Lied.* Other motion pictures of the teens included *The Woman the Germans Shot* (about nurse Edith Cavell), *Broken Fetters, The Unchastened Woman* and *Who's Your Brother?*

Although he may have played leads in his earliest films, Panzer's roles in features were usually in top support and he also menaced Pearl White in the serials *The House of Hate* and *The Clutching Hand.* Not for nothing had he been dubbed "Pathé's Popular Villain."

Panzer worked steadily through the 1920s playing character parts in films like *When Knighthood Was in Flower, Under the Red Robe, East Lynne, The Johnstown Flood, City of Purple Dreams* and *Sally in Our Alley.* In 1925's *The Ancient Mariner* he essayed the title role, although toward the end of the decade some his roles were small.

Panzer also appeared in the serials *The Mystery Mind, The Black Book* and *Hawk of the Hills.* Last silent: *Redskin* (1929) with synchronized music and sound effects, made after his first part-talkie.

Sound: The 1928 part-talkie *Glorious Betsy* was Panzer's first. He made no sound films in 1929 and his only 1930 appearance was in a Hollywood-made German-language version of *Those Who Dance.* Although he eventually did appear in many pictures of the 1930s, including "B" westerns, his roles were usually small.

Among Panzer's films were *Cavalier of the West, Secrets, Bolero, Moonlight on the Prairie, San Quentin, Torchy Blane in Panama* and *Devil's Island.* The onset of World War Two gave the aging German-accented actor a slightly new lease on life playing bits as Nazis in films like *Beasts of Berlin, Casablanca, Action in the North Atlantic* and *Hotel Berlin.*

Panzer made a few others in the late '40s including *Cry Wolf* and the 1947 film that purported to be, but fell far short of, a reasonable version of Pearl White's life. It was, of course, titled *The Perils of Pauline.* He may also have had a bit in 1948's *A Foreign Affair.*

Pearson, Virginia, Louisville, Kentucky, 1879/88–1958

Silent: For a brief time, Virginia Pearson (she of the "perfect back") was one of the leading contenders at Fox for the "vampire" title held by Theda Bara, whom she physically resembled. However, most of her starring career was spent in more conventional romantic melodramas.

Among Pearson's earlier roles from 1914 were *Aftermath, The Turn of the Road, Thou Art the Man, When False Tongues Speak* and *Her Price.* Her starring career did not survive beyond the early '20s and she made fewer than 15 films, mostly in supporting roles, during the decade.

Among Pearson's later motion pictures were *The Phantom of the Opera,* as Carlotta, the rival diva, *The Wizard of Oz, Silence, Wildness of Youth* and *The Actress.* She also appeared in the 1926 serial *Lightning Hutch.* Last silent: *Smilin' Guns* (1929). Her 1930 silent film, *The Danger Man,* with synchronized music and sound effects, was a feature version of *Lightning Hutch.*

Sound: Although she may have done other bits and extra work, Pearson's only known appearances in the talkies came in small roles in *Primrose Path* (1931) and *Back Street* (1932).

Pennington, Ann, Wilmington, Delaware or Camden, New Jersey, 1893/94–1971

Silent: One of the most popular dancers in the teens and '20s was Ann Pennington, famed as "The Girl with the Dimpled Knees," a Broadway attraction since 1911. A Ziegfeld Follies and George White Scandals favorite, she popularized the dance called "The Black Bottom."

Because she was extremely petite, Pennington was able to portray very young girls well into her 20s in films like *Sunshine Nan, The Rainbow Princess, The Antics of Ann, The Little Boy Scout* and *Susie Snowflake,* made between 1916 and 1918.

Pennington returned in 1924 and '25 to play both major and minor roles, sometimes just doing a dance specialty, in a string of films including *Manhandled, Pretty Ladies, The Mad Dancer* (top-billed), *Madame Behave* and *A Kiss in the Dark.* Last silent: *The Golden Strain* (1925).

Sound: In 1929 Pennington went back before the cameras for a few early musical films. Among them were *Tanned Legs, Gold Diggers of Broadway, Is Everybody Happy?* and 1930's *Happy Days.* She also had a brief role in the melodrama *Night Parade.* After making the Vitaphone musical short *Hello Baby,* in 1930, she was not seen on-screen again for ten years but continued to dance in Broadway musicals until the early '30s.

Although Pennington did film a dance for 1936's *The Great Ziegfeld,* it was cut from the film. After a bit in the 1940 "B" western *Texas Terrors,* she may have had roles in *Unholy Partners* (1941) and, lastly, *China Girl* in 1943. She appeared in touring shows and vaudeville until the mid–1940s.

REVIEWS

Gold Diggers of Broadway: Technicolor brings out the beauty of Ann Pennington. She doesn't dance so much or distinguish herself in acting but her name is worth something. *Variety* 9/4/29.

Is Everybody Happy?: Pennington, as the little Hungarian snob, engenders little sympathy. *Variety* 11/6/29.

Tanned Legs: Pennington is featured in the billing but does not have the lead in the picture. She shows more than her legs, wearing some summery bathing apparel. At times she looks like a kid but at other times seems older than the girl she plays. From the chin down she is always a knockout. *Variety* 12/11/29.

Texas Terrors: The credits list a "dancer." The role is just an on-and-off song and dance bit for atmospheric purposes but it is done by Ann Pennington. *Variety* 11/12/40.

Percy, Eileen (also Persey) Belfast, Ireland, 1899/1901–1973

Silent: Eileen Percy's first film years were probably her most memorable. She co-starred with Doug Fairbanks in 1917 in several of his breezy comedies including *Wild and Woolly, Reaching for the Moon* and *The Man from Painted Post.* Other early co-stars were Bert Lytell, Lew Cody and William Russell.

Percy's films, in many of which she had the lead, included *Told in the Hills, Husband Hunter, Pardon My Nerve, Hollywood, Cobra, Souls for Sables, Why Trust Your Husband?* and *Lovey Mary.* After 1927 her films became sporadic. Last silent: *Telling the World* (1928).

Sound: The Broadway Hoofer (1929) was Percy's first sound film. She was down in the cast list where she was to remain for the remainder of her career, which ended in the mid–'30s except for at least one short. Her other talkies were *Wicked, The Cohens and the Kellys in Hollywood,* and *The Secret of Madame Blanche.*

Missing Daughters, which had very limited play in 1933 and in which Percy had a leading role, was actually a re-release of a 1924 silent film with added talking sequences, music and sound effects.

REVIEWS

Wicked: The silent screen actress Eileen Percy is hidden beneath trick makeup and serves as a bad moral example in the prison scenes. *Variety* 9/22/31.

Perrin, Jack (also briefly known as Richard Terry), Three Rivers, Michigan, 1896–1967

Filmography: Classic Images (June 1991); Academy of Motion Picture Arts and Sciences; List of films in *Eighty Silent Film Stars*

Silent: Jack Perrin may have been one of the (minor) Keystone Kops before he worked in Triangle one-reelers and then in two-reel westerns. One of his first features was Erich von Stroheim's *Blind Husbands* (1919) and that year he also made his first serial, *The Lion Man*.

During the 1920s, Perrin appeared in numerous film genres, including melodramas, but his *métier* was to be the western. Many of the 1920s films made by the tall and handsome actor were two-reelers, including a series showcasing the Northwest Mounties.

Among Perrin's films were *The Rage of Paris, Mary of the Movies, The Dangerous Little Demon, Fire and Steel, Coyote Fangs* and *Canyon Rustlers.* His serials included *The Fighting Skipper, Santa Fe Trail* and *The Vanishing West.* Last silent feature: *Romance of the West* (1930), made after his first talkies.

Sound: The voice of Jack Perrin was first heard from the screen in *Overland Bound*, one of the earliest sound westerns in late 1929. Once established in "B" westerns, he remained an oater star until 1936's *Wildcat Saunders.* He also had the lead in a series of three-reelers, segueing into second leads and then smaller roles and bits well into the 1960s.

Perrin's motion pictures included *Hell-Fire Austin, Dynamite Ranch, The Great Jewel Robbery, Son of Oklahoma* and *Jaws of Justice.* In his latter days he was seen in such films as *Calamity Jane, The Spoilers* (1956 version), *The Young Philadelphians* and *Ocean's Eleven.* Possibly the last of his 150 or so sound films was *Flower Drum Song* in 1961.

Perrin was also a staple of many serials of the '30s such as *Mystery Squadron, The Jade Box, The Sign of the Wolf, The Painted Stallion, The Mysterious Pilot, The Lone Ranger, The Great Adventures of Wild Bill Hickok* and *The Secret of Treasure Island.*

In the 1940s Perrin's serial appearances included *The Green Hornet Strikes Again, The Shadow, Rid-* ers of *Death Valley, Holt of the Secret Service* and *Adventures of the Flying Cadets.* Among the studios for which he appeared were Aywon, Reliable, Syndicate, Anchor and Rayart.

REVIEWS

Overland Bound: Jack Perrin acts with ease and naturalness in his cowboy role. It sets him far ahead of the average slick-haired young fellow. *Harrison's Reports* 10/12/29, *Variety* 4/23/30.

Philbin, Mary, Chicago, Illinois, 1903–1993

Silent: Mary Philbin was yet another beauty contest winner who made good. She won a Universal contract after entering a *Chicago Herald-Examiner* contest and was in films by 1921. Some of her earlier roles were in *The Blazing Trail, False Kisses* and *Human Hearts.*

Among Philbin's more prestigious pictures were *Merry-Go-Round*, the title role in *Stella Maris* (a 1925 remake of the Mary Pickford picture), *The Man Who Laughs* and, most famous of all, the Lon Chaney classic *The Phantom of the Opera* (1925).

Other films in which Philbin appeared were *Penrod and Sam, Fools' Highway, Surrender* and *Fifth Avenue Models.* Last silent: *Love Me and the World Is Mine* (1928).

Sound: All of Philbin's talkie appearances came in 1929. She was in two part-talkies, *Girl Overboard* and *The Last Performance.* The latter film originally may have been made some time earlier and re-released with talking sequences. Her two all-sound films, which premiered about the same time, were *The Shannons of Broadway* and *After the Fog.*

Comments: Mary Philbin was a pretty and adequately talented actress who would not be much thought about were it not for her role as Christine in *The Phantom of the Opera.* For that she does hold a place in cinema history, most especially for the iconographic scene where she unmasks Erik, the Phantom, in the catacombs of the Paris Opera. This may, in fact, be in serious contention for the best-remembered scene in all of silent cinema.

REVIEWS

Girl Overboard: Philbin sings the theme song and does very well no matter what one thinks of her singing or speaking voice. *Variety* 8/14/29.

The Last Performance: Due to the heroine Mary Philbin's captivating charm, this picture holds the audience's attention. *New York Times* 11/4/29, *Harrison's Reports* 11/23/29.

The Shannons of Broadway: Philbin plays the usual ingenue part and plays it well as always. *Variety* 12/25/29.

After the Fog: The naivete of Philbin's acting

and other factors make this risky. The voices of the cast record uniformly with no variations of tonal value. If Philbin's name means anything, that provides the best chance to draw crowds. *Variety* 1/29/30.

Pickford, Jack (Jack Smith), Toronto, Canada, 1896–1933

Filmography: Films in Review (Mar. 1986)

Silent: Jack Pickford toured in stock companies with his older sister Mary, soon to be America's Sweetheart, and he joined Biograph at the same time as she. His screen debut came about 1912 in a one-reeler on loanout to Selig. He followed Mary from studio to studio and appeared in many of her films. He also co-directed two pictures.

Pickford's best films were probably those he made for Paramount in which he portrayed wholesome all–American boys. They included *Seventeen, Tom Sawyer, Huck and Tom* and *Freckles*. Other films were *Great Expectations, The Varmint, Poor Little Peppina* and *The Little Shepherd of Kingdom Come* (1920 version).

In the '20s Pickford's sybaritic lifestyle was beginning to catch up with him and he made fewer films. Among them were *The Hill Billy, My Son, Hollywood* and *Brown of Harvard*. Last silent: *Exit Smiling* (1926).

Sound: Pickford's career had seriously declined because of illness and scandal when he made his final full-length picture and his sole feature with sound. It was the 1928 part-talkie *Gang War*, which had a talking prologue. He was the leading man but his voice may not have been heard in it. He may also have appeared in *All Square*, a 1930 short.

Comments: The beneficiary, or perhaps the victim, of Mary Pickford's enormous clout, Jack Pickford experienced a career he might not otherwise have had. His was a "double whammy" in that his formidable mother was *the* stage mother of all times.

Pickford's screen persona was of course much different from that of the real person. He lived high, even recklessly, and seemed always to be trying to elude the control of the Pickford women. In this he was unsuccessful. Even during his marriages, two of which were to actresses Olive Thomas and Marilyn Miller, he was not out of their grasp.

Unfortunately, the publicity surrounding his troubled life overshadowed the fact that Jack Pickford was a sensitive actor and he more than held his own against the innocent screen heroes of the day.

REVIEWS

Gang War: Jack Pickford makes a good hero in this underworld drama. *Harrison's Reports* 7/28/28.

Pickford, Mary (Gladys Smith), Toronto, Canada, 1892/93–1979

Filmography: Tribute to Mary Pickford

Silent: After appearances on the stage, including Broadway, from the time she was a small girl, Mary Pickford began in one-reelers about 1909 at D. W. Griffith's Biograph studio. By the mid-'teens, with her blonde curls and spunky persona, she had become the premier female star in films and was America's — and the entire world's — "Sweetheart."

Pickford appeared in numerous one- and two-reelers. Among her early features from 1913 were *In the Bishop's Carriage, Cinderella, A Good Little Devil* and *Rags*. Other immensely popular films, for which she received an equally immense salary, included *Poor Little Rich Girl, Suds, Stella Maris, Tess of the Storm Country* (two versions), *Little Lord Fauntleroy* (a dual role), *Daddy Long Legs, Rebecca of Sunnybrook Farm* and *Sparrows*.

Mary Pickford became even more of a cultural icon after her marriage to the also-enormously-popular Douglas Fairbanks, Sr. They were at the very top of the Hollywood pantheon as arbiters of movieland social life and were considered all but equal to actual royalty, being dubbed the "King" and "Queen" of Hollywood.

A shrewd businesswoman, Pickford eventually had her own film company under the aegis of Adolph Zukor and in 1919 was one of the founders of United Artists with Fairbanks, Griffith and Charles Chaplin. In the 1920s her output of films declined greatly and she made only about ten features.

Pickford's attempts at establishing a more adult persona in the mid–1920s costume films *Rosita* and *Dorothy Vernon of Haddon Hall* did not succeed well; they were disappointments at the box office. The latter, Ernst Lubitsch's first Hollywood film, was an artistic failure as well.

Pickford's symbolic and highly publicized act of having her curls cut off in 1928 caused a not-unexpected furor from her legions of fans. It was perhaps the last act of her silent career and her hopeful declaration that little girl roles were over. Last silent: *My Best Girl* (1927), a major success co-starring her husband-to-be Buddy Rogers, in which she played a 17-year-old girl.

Sound: Given her strong desire to put the little girl behind her, Pickford wanted a contemporary story for her first talkie, one which would not be compared with her previous films. She claimed to be enthusiastic about sound. "It is amazing how the new medium rounds out personality," she was quoted as saying.

Pickford ultimately selected the role of Norma

Besant in *Coquette*, although the character was about half her actual age. It had been done as a stage play by Helen Hayes and some of the rawer elements were toned down for the film. For the director she made the offbeat choice of Sam Taylor, who had directed her last silent and who was primarily known for his work on several Harold Lloyd comedies.

Because the story was set in Alabama, Pickford decided to essay a Southern accent; English grande dame Constance Collier was hired as her dialogue coach. The picture did not proceed without problems, however. She fired her longtime cameraman Charles Rosher in the middle of filming and it was rumored that she preferred Karl Struss for his ability to make older actresses look young.

Pickford later averred that Taylor contributed little or nothing to her performance. "It was left to me to make my role come alive... Mr. Taylor seemed to think the important thing was to show me off in a sound movie." Although there were some critical quibbles about Pickford's accent and the unsavory character of the story, *Coquette* was a major success and earned about $1.5 million, a good return in those days.

For her performance, Pickford won the second Academy Award for Best Actress but there was not universal acceptance of this. Some believed she had won it more for her social status than her acting and that either Ruth Chatterton for *Madame X* or Jeanne Eagels for *The Letter* would have been a better choice.

Pickford's next film, also in 1929, was *Taming of the Shrew* with Sam Taylor again at the helm. It was the first sound film based on Shakespeare's works and Douglas Fairbanks's full-sound debut. She later maintained she had been talked into doing the film against her better judgment. "The making of the film was my finish," she stated. "My confidence was completely shattered and I was never again at ease in front of the camera."

According to Pickford, part of the problem lay with Fairbanks. She claimed he was undisciplined, read the dialogue from cue cards and was snappish with his wife when she tried to remonstrate with him. His idea that filming should be fun also was not in synch with her notion of saving as much money as possible.

Also, she claimed, Sam Taylor had wanted her performance to be played for broad comedy and asked her to use her "Pickford bag of tricks." In retrospect, she felt her performance had been too gentle; in her words, more like a "spitting kitten than a forceful tiger cat."

Seeming to bear this out, one wag later actually referred to Mary Pickford in this film as a "Shrewette." Apparently she was still brooding over her perceived poor performance 30 years later and she recorded some lines from the film as she thought she should have spoken them.

Despite Pickford's frequently repeated statements in later years that Fairbanks was unprepared and difficult on the set, others on the scene thought that she was envious of his ability to overwhelm her on the screen. In any event, the film was not a success despite some good reviews. A silent version was shown overseas and in American theaters not wired for sound.

In 1930 Pickford began work on *Secrets*, a remake of one of Norma Talmadge's most successful films. It was scrapped, and the negative burned, after being half completed at a cost of $300,000. Although she claimed that it was simply not working—for one thing, leading man Kenneth MacKenna was too young—others have hinted that her use of alcohol was beginning to affect her work.

Nineteen thirty-one's *Kiki*, another remake of a Talmadge film, was a picture in which Pickford hoped to once and for all change her image. Her role as a French chorus girl trying to lure her married lover away from his adulterous wife was ill-considered, however. This time she used a French accent and again Sam Taylor directed.

The popular fan magazine *Photoplay*, something of a drumbeater for the movie industry, rhetorically asked, "Where has Mary been hiding all this fire?" But to Pickford, and seemingly most everyone else, it was more of a misfire. *Kiki* was dismissed in her autobiography with literally four words: "It was a misadventure."

Pickford decided to try again to make *Secrets*. Although she wanted Gary Cooper for the male lead, Leslie Howard finally played it. The action of the film spanned a 50-year period and gave her a chance to age from young womanhood to old age. No expense was spared in its making and Frank Borzage was hired on as director.

Now considered Pickford's best sound film, *Secrets* opened to generally respectful notices in 1933, but the public did not respond and it was a box office disappointment. It was to be her final motion picture although from time to time it was announced or rumored that she would again go before the cameras.

In the late 1940s Pickford was close to signing on for the role of Lavinia Day in *Life with Father*. It went to Irene Dunne instead. The role of Norma Desmond in *Sunset Blvd.* was said to be hers for the asking as well but she apparently asked for script changes that were not forthcoming. The role went to Gloria Swanson. She did make some stage and radio appearances after her film career ended.

Comments: There were no doubt several factors in the relative failure of Mary Pickford's talkie career although she tended in later life to point the finger at external reasons and other people. She blamed the hapless Sam Taylor for the perceived failure of *Taming of the Shrew* and the certain failure of *Kiki.* As mentioned, Doug Fairbanks came in for his share of the blame as well.

Although Pickford had been a stage actress when very young, her adult speaking voice was somewhat high and thin, or reedy. It certainly was not a forceful instrument and it retained the flat inflection of her native Canada. This was probably most apparent in *Taming of the Shrew* and was perhaps one reason she chose to disguise it by undertaking accents in two of her talkies.

Pickford was undeniably too old for both *Coquette* and *Kiki*, although she managed to get away with it passably in the former film. She was also plainly miscast in the latter. It was a role more suitable for one of the "jazz babies" of the '20s although they, too, were having their problems in talkies.

At bottom, Pickford had simply had her day. She had tired of, and aged out of, her silent persona and she was not really right for a melodrama like *Coquette* either. She had lost her uniqueness. In 1930, *The New York Times* stated: "Mary is slipping as a box-office attraction... A grown-up Mary — alas, perhaps too well grown! — has taken the place of what seemed inexhaustible youth incarnate."

Pickford later said, looking back at the time she cut her golden curls: "You would have thought I had murdered someone and perhaps I had, but only to give her successor a chance to live." And: "I left the screen because I didn't want what happened to Chaplin to happen to me. When he discarded the Tramp, the Tramp turned around and killed him. The little girl made me. I wasn't waiting for the little girl to kill me."

Although she may have been less perceptive about the reasons for Chaplin's slow decline, Pickford was more so about her own career loss. In fact, she poignantly may have gotten it just about right. The little girl did kill her and there was absolutely nothing to be done about it.

REVIEWS

Coquette: Reviewers generally liked Pickford but differed slightly. One stated that she saved the picture despite the fact that in some scenes she appeared to be Mary Pickford more than Norma Besant. Whether the role is suited to her was a matter of opinion, although she handled dialogue well. In close-ups she looked a trifle too mature and sophisticated for the part of a young impetuous girl. Other reviews said she gave an excellent performance, in fact the best dramatic acting of her career. She filled the part of the young girl as would a girl still in her teens. *New York Times* 4/6/29, *Variety* 4/10/29, *Harrison's Reports* 4/13/29.

Taming of the Shrew: Again reviews differed. One said that although Pickford's playing was admirable in its intention, physically she did not look the part, and could never hope to look it. She could not be both the world's sweetheart and the world's worst-tempered woman, but it was enormously to her credit that she tried to forget she was the former and pretended to be the latter. She tried extremely hard, but you can see that she was trying.

Other reviewers were somewhat more charitable. One said she sometimes resembled the purse-lipped Mary of years gone by but if it be entertainment one sought she provided it. She was delightful in her fits of fury and also in those moments when she trembled at Petruchio's wrath. Most of the comedy in the first part of the picture was caused by her slapstick comedy work.

(The film was and still is the object of hilarity because of the [in]famous credit line: "Written by William Shakespeare. Additional dialogue by Sam Taylor.") *The Tatler*, 1929, *New York Times* 11/30/29, *Variety* 12/4/29, *Harrison's Reports* 12/7/29.

Kiki: Once more reviews differed. One stated that Mary Pickford was the whole show, a tribute to her inexhaustible energy and verve. There were not the soulful interludes that Norma Talmadge brought to her characterization on the silent screen. Pickford was too busy raising general havoc and did as good an acting job as she had ever done.

Another thought that it was a just middling film despite the Pickford name. In characterizing what was meant to be a rough chorus girl she acted more like an innocent, tempestuous child. The result was that she was "cute" and that many may wonder why she did "Kiki."

(Legend has it that a very young Betty Grable doubled Pickford in the scenes where she danced in the chorus.) *New York Times* 3/6/31, *Variety* 3/11/31, *Harrison's Reports* 3/14/31.

Secrets: Pickford is vivacious and charming in the New England scenes of the picture but her acting elsewhere is not always convincing. She is at her best in the lighter interludes where her flair for light comedy is seen. *New York Times* 3/16/33, *Variety* 3/21/33.

Pidgeon, Walter, St. Johns, New Brunswick, 1897–1984

Filmography: Films in Review (Nov. 1969)

Silent: Supposedly discovered by Fred Astaire in

the mid–1920s singing at a party, tall and dapperly handsome Walter Pidgeon became an actor/singer in stock companies and ultimately on Broadway. He came to Hollywood in 1926 for about 15 undistinguished silents.

The first of Pidgeon's motion pictures was *Mannequin*; others included *Old Loves and New*, *Miss Nobody*, *The Heart of Salome*, *The Girl from Rio*, *The Gorilla* and *The Thirteenth Juror*. In them he played some supporting roles, among which were villainous characterizations, but there were leading roles as well. Last silent: *Clothes Make the Woman* (1928).

Sound: Pidgeon made the first of his 90 or so talkies with *Melody of Love* (1928), in which he was cast as a songwriter. In that role he could legitimately burst into song and he did in that film and in several that followed, including the 1930 operettas *Bride of the Regiment*, *Sweet Kitty Bellairs* and *Viennese Nights*. For a while he was First National's resident baritone.

During the early 1930s, Pidgeon alternated between generally non-prestige film work (*Fatal Lady*, *Journal of a Crime*, *She's Dangerous*, *Rockabye*) and an occasional theater role. His appearance as a gangster in the 1935 stage melodrama *Night of January 16th* resulted in his signing by Universal for a series of programmers.

Pidgeon's major break came when he was offered a contract by MGM, who first cast him in a second lead in 1937's *Saratoga*. He had his initial top-billed role there in *Society Lawyer* and then played detective Nick Carter in a three-film "B" series.

After many unimportant second leads, Pidgeon's first teaming with then-popular Greer Garson in *Blossoms in the Dust* proved to be a breakthrough. His best roles came in the early 1940s, two of them on loanout to Twentieth Century–Fox in 1941's *How Green Was My Valley* and *Man Hunt*. The former, in which he essayed the role of the Reverend Mr. Gruffydd, won the Best Picture Oscar.

Other teamings with Garson included the patriotic and very successful *Mrs. Miniver* (for which Pidgeon got an Academy Award nomination for Best Actor), *Madame Curie* (another nomination) and *Mrs. Parkington*. His career began declining in the latter 1940s and his continued teamings with Garson in such films as *The Miniver Story*, *Julia Misbehaves* and *Scandal at Scourie* apparently grew tiresome to the public.

Although there was an occasional strong showing in a picture like *Command Decision*, Pidgeon's transition to a character actor was inevitable. In this capacity he acquitted himself well in major productions such as *The Bad and the Beautiful*, *Executive Suite* and *Forbidden Planet*.

After Pidgeon's MGM contract expired in 1956 his on-screen roles grew rarer. *Voyage to the Bottom of the Sea*, *Advise and Consent*, *Funny Girl*, *Harry in Your Pocket*, *Two Minute Warning* and *Skyjacked* were some of his later films into the 1970s. He made television appearances in the '50s and '60s and returned to the stage in such musicals as *Take Me Along* and *The Happiest Millionaire*.

Comments: Walter Pidgeon had a beautifully modulated baritone voice which brought him some measure of fame as a singer. Indeed, he is credited with being the first one to record two all-time standards: "All Alone" and "What'll I Do?"

With the advent of talkies, Pidgeon's voice stood him in excellent stead but with the glut of musicals in the late '20s and early '30s his career hit one of its periodic valleys. His dramatic movie roles during the early 1930s left little impression on moviegoers.

Overall, it must be admitted that Pidgeon was among the least charismatic of the important leading men of his day. While he could play decency and dependability very believably, he needed a strong female star to add some zest to his films. The flame-haired Greer Garson supplied that strength.

Pidgeon's popular co-starring films with Garson hit the right note with war-weary audiences. He represented the quietly heroic average man most creditably, especially in *Mrs. Miniver* and *Man Hunt*. In the latter picture he almost assassinated Hitler himself.

When Hollywood's need for simple and uncomplex leading men gave way to postwar complexity and moral shades of gray, Walter Pidgeon's persona was out of style. Ultimately he was perhaps more suited to the later character roles in which he always acquitted himself well.

Reviews

The Melody of Love: In Universal's first all-sound film, Pidgeon's voice sounds rather metallic, except when he sings. His piano playing is convincing as is his playing of the lead role. *Variety* 10/17/28.

Fatal Lady: Pidgeon shows excellent promise and has the appearance and voice for the current trend of he-man lovers. *Variety* 7/15/36.

Sky Murder: Pidgeon fails to make much of an impression as the master sleuth Nick Carter. *Variety* 9/25/40.

Man Hunt: Pidgeon performs well throughout. *Variety* 6/11/41.

Madame Curie: Pidgeon lives the part, making Curie warm, humane and lovable. *Harrison's Reports* 11/20/43.

Command Decision: As the general, Walter

Pidgeon has never been better. He even manages to make a scene where he recites a long history of the Air Force something more than a tiresome solo reading. *Variety* 12/29/48.

Pitts, ZaSu, Parsons, Kansas, 1898/1900–1963

Filmography: Films in Review (June-July 1980); List of films in *Monthly Film Bulletin* (Sept. 1978)

Silent: ZaSu Pitts had her first major film role in Mary Pickford's *The Little Princess* (1917), but she had probably debuted about a year earlier in small roles at Universal. She became a busy actress in over 60 silents, alternating between drama and comedy, mostly in support but with occasional leading roles such as in 1919's *Better Times*.

Among Pitts's motion pictures were *Poor Relations, West of the Water Tower, Monte Carlo, The Fast Set, Pretty Ladies, Wife Savers, Casey at the Bat* and *Daughters of Today*. Her greatest role came as the ill-starred Trina in Erich von Stroheim's 1925 classic *Greed*, and she also appeared in his *The Wedding March* (1928). Last silent: *Sins of the Fathers* (1928), with synchronized sound effects, music and a singing sequence.

Sound: Pitts appeared in the first nine of her more than 100 talking pictures in 1929 alone, most of them melodramas or comedies. Among them were *Paris, Twin Beds, The Squall, The Locked Door* and *Oh, Yeah!*. Her role in *The Dummy* set a pattern for her future screen persona — as twittery and even scatterbrained.

Pitts was cast in a deeply dramatic role, as a German mother in *All Quiet on the Western Front* (1930), but her role in the sound version had to be recast with Beryl Mercer because preview audiences expected her to be funny and they laughed inappropriately.

Pitts teamed with Thelma Todd in the early '30s for a well-received series of 17 comedy shorts, including *On the Loose, Sneak Easily, Maids à la Mode* and *Strictly Unreliable*. (She was replaced later in the series by Patsy Kelly.) She also continued her feature appearances with numerous films well into the 1940s.

Among Pitts's pictures were *Broken Lullaby, Blondie of the Follies, Meet the Baron, Naughty but Nice, So's Your Aunt Emma, Mrs. Wiggs of the Cabbage Patch, Ruggles of Red Gap* and *Life with Father*. In the early '30s she was teamed with lanky comic Slim Summerville in a series of second features. She also played the detective Hildegarde Withers in a couple of that series' entries.

Pitts's film output dropped in the 1940s and screen roles in later decades were few, including a couple in the "Francis, the Talking Mule" series. She made thousands of stage appearances, touring

for many years in *Ramshackle Inn, Everybody Loves Opal* and other plays.

Pitts also was a television stalwart in the '50s in *The Gale Storm Show* and *Oh Susanna*. Both of her last films, *The Thrill of It All* and *It's a Mad Mad Mad Mad World*, were made near the time of her death.

Comments: One of the archetypal comic actresses with the heart of a tragedienne, ZaSu Pitts was condemned by typecasting in the talkies to a career playing spinsters and maids. But she appears to have bought into it by developing a set of mannerisms including fluttery hands and a continual string of "Oh dears!" which perpetuated the stereotype. This made it even harder to break out even if she had so desired. Even her name militated against her.

Given her interestingly "comic" face as she aged and the somewhat oddly-pitched voice, it is doubtful whether Pitts could have made it for long in talkies solely in dramatic roles. She no doubt exaggerated her vocal tones for many of her parts but the quavering voice certainly fit a comic persona.

This is not to say that ZaSu Pitts did not essay some worthy roles in sound films, one being in *Ruggles of Red Gap*. She really did not need to despair of her career for she had already proved herself a fine dramatic actress. Just think of the doomed Trina McTeague clandestinely counting her hoarded gold in *Greed*.

REVIEWS

Finn and Hattie: A winner for ZaSu Pitts who is always good and is the only consistent cast member. She causes several laughs. *Variety* 2/4/31, *Harrison's Reports* 2/7/31.

Is My Face Red?: The laughs come in great measure from ZaSu Pitts as a telephone operator. *Variety* 6/14/32, *Harrison's Reports* 6/18/32.

Her First Mate: The laughs are brought about by the way ZaSu Pitts and Slim Summerville work at cross-purposes. They have more story background and support than they've been accustomed to. *Harrison's Reports* 8/5/33, *Variety* 9/5/33.

She Gets Her Man: Pitts, who can be extremely funny, finds it difficult to handle the poor material she is given but squeezes every possible laugh out of the commonplace lines. *Variety* 9/11/35.

Miss Polly: Pitts does the best she can in the title role but she is aided by a struggling cast. *Variety* 11/5/41.

Francis Joins the Wacs: Pitts is seen again as the screwy nurse she created for the first Francis film. She delivers a slick performance. *Variety* 7/7/54.

Pollard, Snub (Harry Pollard; Harold Frazer or Fraser), Melbourne, Australia, 1889–1962

Silent: After appearing in Australian variety, Snub Pollard was a Roach player from 1915–19 and he may have appeared on-screen as early as 1914, possibly for Essanay. He was instantly recognizable by his lavishly drooping walrus mustache and downward slanting eyes.

Pollard supported Charles Chaplin and most frequently Harold Lloyd in numerous of the latter's Lonesome Luke characterizations. After Lloyd's severe injury in 1919, Pollard was awarded his own series and between that year and 1922 he made over 100 starring one-reelers and several two-reelers as well.

Pollard set up his own production company about 1926 but his pictures were becoming less successful and by the latter part of the decade his popularity in knockabout two-reelers had waned. As far as is known, during the silent era he did not appear in features.

Sound: Besides making numerous sound shorts, generally as a supporting player, Pollard had small roles in a number of features and he played the sidekick to oater star Tex Ritter in several western films. His first full-length sound film was apparently 1931's *Ex-Flame*.

Pollard's feature career was at its height in the '30s when he appeared in pictures that included *Midnight Patrol, Stingaree, The Laramie Kid, Anything Goes, Headin' for the Rio Grande, Riders of the Rockies* and *Hollywood Cavalcade*.

Among Pollard's declining number of 1940s films were *Murder on the Yukon, The Perils of Pauline,* as one of the numerous old-time silent performers, and *The Crooked Way*. He continued to be seen in occasional bit roles in films like *Man of a Thousand Faces, Pocketful of Miracles* and *The Errand Boy* up to the time of his death.

NOTE: Not to be confused with American director Harry Pollard.

REVIEWS

Midnight Patrol: Pollard has a very small part. *Variety* 5/20/32.

Starlight Over Texas: Pollard, as Pee Wee, is apparently featured in the series to provide comedy but he has to struggle through unfunny situations and lines. *Variety* 9/21/38.

Polo, Eddie, San Francisco, California, 1875/76–1961

Filmography: List of films in *Eighty Silent Film Stars*

Silent: Eddie Polo had been a circus acrobat and aerialist before he began appearing in small film roles about 1913. He then signed with Universal for supporting roles in serials such as *The Broken Coin, Graft, The Adventures of Peg o' the Ring* and *The Gray Ghost*.

Even though he was physically unprepossessing, being small, dark and wiry, Polo eventually became known as "The King of the Serials" himself. Among his popular starring serials, in which he displayed his great acrobatic skills, were *The Bull's Eye, The Lure of the Circus, The Vanishing Dagger, The King of the Circus* and *Do or Die*.

The often-injured Polo also made a series of "Cyclone Smith" two-reel westerns as well as features like *A Kentucky Cinderella* and *The Plow Woman*. He left Universal in 1921, established an unsuccessful production company and appeared in a few more features. After making some German films he returned to find the industry had forgotten him. Last U. S. silents: *Dangerous Hour* and *Prepared to Die*, released about the same time in 1923.

Sound: Polo tried his luck in Europe again during the 1930s and apparently played some bit roles. He then returned to American films about 1940 for a series of small parts in pictures which included *La Conga Nights, Between Us Girls, The Son of Roaring Dan* and *It's a Date*. His last film may have been *Around the World in 80 Days*.

Powell, William, Pittsburgh, Pennsylvania, 1892–1984

Filmography: Films in Review (Nov. 1958)

Silent: After stage experience, including Broadway, William Powell made his screen debut billed as William H. Powell low down in the cast list of *Sherlock Holmes* in 1922. He played a henchman of Professor Moriarty. Primarily a Paramount player, he often was cast in his 34 silent films as a villain, both foreign and domestic, sometimes as a gangster.

Among Powell's more prestigious films were *Beau Geste, The Great Gatsby, Beau Sabreur, Romola* and *The Last Command*. He also was in such lesser efforts as *Too Many Kisses, Nevada, Paid to Love, Feel My Pulse* and *My Lady's Lips*. Last silent: *The Four Feathers* (1929), with synchronized music and sound effects.

Sound: With the coming of the talkies, William Powell's smooth voice allowed him to shed the mantle of villainy and become the leading man he was to remain for almost all the rest of his 60 sound pictures.

In 1929 Powell played suave detective Philo Vance in *The Canary Murder Case* and *The Greene Murder Case*, as well as appearing in the popular drama *Interference*. It was his first talkie and in it he was top-billed.

Powell labored at Paramount until 1931 and then went to Warner Bros. While there, he co-starred in several with Kay Francis, one of their films together being *Street of Chance*. This was perhaps his breakthrough film. Another of their popular pictures was *One Way Passage*.

In 1934 Powell was felicitously signed by MGM where his second role was as detective Nick Charles in 1934's *The Thin Man*, co-starring Myrna Loy. The rest, as they say, is history. Basically a "B" film, *The Thin Man* was extremely successful and made bankable stars of both its leads, generating an Academy Award nomination for William Powell.

There were eventually five sequels, none quite as good as the original, including *The Song of the Thin Man*, *After the Thin Man* and *The Thin Man Goes Home*. The two compatible stars worked together 13 times in all, almost always in comedies.

Among Powell's most memorable '30s films were the "screwball" comedy *My Man Godfrey*, *Libeled Lady* with his then-lover Jean Harlow, and *The Great Ziegfeld*, in which he had the title role. Due to serious illness, he was off the screen for almost two years at the end of the decade.

Powell's efforts in the 1940s did not compare with those of the previous decade until he made what is probably his signature film, the superior *Life with Father* (1947). It led to another Academy Award nomination.

Powell's other films into the 1950s included *Private Detective*, *Fashions of 1934*, *Reckless*, *Double Wedding*, *The Heavenly Body*, *The Hoodlum Saint*, *The Senator Was Indiscreet*, *Mr. Peabody and the Mermaid* and *The Treasure of Lost Canyon*.

In the late '40s the now-aging Powell became primarily a character actor. He was part of a distinguished ensemble of players in his final films *How to Marry a Millionaire* (1953) and *Mister Roberts* (1955). The latter film proved a worthy farewell to the screen. Although never winning an Academy Award he did receive two New York Film Critics awards.

Comments: William Powell brought a talent to talkies which few other actors did. His charming, debonair and suave characters often seemed to lack real substance but, while they were delivering their delightful banter, there really was something going on beneath the surface. Nick Charles might seem like a dilettante but he really had the smarts to solve the crime.

Much of Powell's popularity was certainly due to his almost syrupy voice with its oh-so-precise enunciation. He certainly was not conventionally handsome. Many of his silent bad man roles played up his somewhat reptilian countenance with its startlingly blue, almost hooded eyes.

That Bill Powell overcame this image was a tribute to his abilities. In the talkies he developed a seemingly effortless acting style that worked well in both comedy and drama. He was dubbed "the virtuoso of the vocalized pause" and could make stammers and hesitations as meaningful as words.

In some of his earlier sound films Powell could come across as somewhat aloof and imperious, but that changed as he got older and his features grew more avuncular. He became more of a solid citizen but one could always imagine there was still a lively twinkle in those pale blue eyes even when he was blustering as the formidable Clarence Day in *Life with Father*.

William Powell always had the knack of keeping the audience's sympathy and attention even in his least worthy pictures. There was an innate decency in his talkie persona that always shone through. He had very few peers at what he did best and there were none to top him. It is most fitting that he went out at the peak of his form.

REVIEWS

Interference: Powell reads his lines with the easy authority of a stage-trained actor. *Variety* 11/21/28.

The Canary Murder Case: Another hit for Powell who is right now a leading name in talkers and perhaps the best straight dramatic actor on the sound screen so far. Two such performances should lift him into the starring class. He has accomplished all this in a year. A year ago he was the meanest, most treacherous villain in films and now he is a player of respectable roles. Perhaps he still may play heavies, but with a greater range, in the talkies. He is a good actor and has a voice that registers well. *Variety* 3/13/29, *Harrison's Reports* 3/16/29.

Lawyer Man: Powell, by his good performance, makes more of the role than it is worth; he is quite believable as the lawyer. In fact he is the entire picture. *Harrison's Reports* 12/31/32, *Variety* 1/3/33.

The Thin Man: It is a pleasure to watch the grand companionship between William Powell and Myrna Loy as his wife. They both give fine performances and the studio couldn't have done better than to pick them. They shade their semi-comic roles beautifully. *Harrison's Reports* 6/23/34, *Variety* 7/3/34.

The Great Ziegfeld: Powell's portrayal is excellent. Preserving the audience's sympathies, he endows the role with all the qualities of the man without sacrificing the shades and moods called for. *Variety* 4/15/36.

My Man Godfrey: Powell brings normality and comic breeziness to the madcap household. The role doesn't require stretching for him. *Variety* 9/23/36.

Another Thin Man: The return of William Powell to the screen after nearly two years absence provides strong marquee value. He is again effective. *Variety* 11/15/39.

Love Crazy: Once again co-starring with Myrna Loy, Powell scores as an ever-loving husband who gets into jams. He is tops in farce performance. *Variety* 5/14/41.

Life with Father: To a considerable extent, Powell has captured the play's charm. *Variety* 8/20/47.

Mister Roberts: Powell plays the role of the ship's doctor with an easy assurance that makes it stand out. *Variety* 5/25/55.

Power, Tyrone (later Sr.; Frederick T.

Power), London, England, 1869–1931

Silent: After appearing in stock, dark and handsome Tyrone Power became a Broadway matinee idol and then a leading man in films from about 1914 to 1921. Among his earlier films were *Aristocracy, A Texas Steer, The Eye of God, Where Are My Children?, Thou Shalt Not Covet* and *Lorelei of the Sea.* His last starring film was 1921's *Footfalls.*

Power was off the screen for over a year in the early '20s. When he returned it was for character roles, sometimes as a villain, and an occasional second lead in such films as *Bright Lights of Broadway, Janice Meredith, The Lone Wolf, Braveheart, Red Kimono, Damaged Hearts* and *Wife in Name Only.* Last silent: *Hands Across the Border* (1926).

Sound: Tyrone Power, Sr., completed only one talkie, Raoul Walsh's *The Big Trail* (1930). He had begun work on *The Miracle Man* (1932) but died during filming. His son and namesake (1913–1958), who resembled him closely, began his starring movie career not too long thereafter.

Prevost, Marie (Mary Bickford Dunn or

Gunn), Sarnia, Ontario, 1898/1901–1937

Filmography: Focus on Film (Autumn 1974)

Silent: From Mack Sennett bathing beauty to Ernst Lubitsch star: so went Marie Prevost. After her apprenticeship with Sennett from 1917–21, she signed with Universal and starred in several romantic comedies, ultimately appearing in three Lubitsch films, *The Marriage Circle, Three Women* and *Kiss Me Again.*

In 1926, Prevost joined PDC for a series of bedroom farces, among which were *Getting Gertie's Garter, Up in Mabel's Room* and *His Jazz Bride.* A role in the 1928 crime melodrama *The Racket* broke this chain of fluffy comedies. Her other films included *The Dark Swan, Bobbed Hair, East Lynne, Don't Get Personal, A Small Town Idol* and *Tarnish.* Last silent: *The Sideshow* (1928).

Sound: Prevost's first sound film was the unsuccessful and somewhat odd 1929 part-talkie *The Godless Girl,* directed by Cecil B. DeMille. Her two other films that year were *The Flying Fool* and *Divorce Made Easy,* in which she sang. About this time, she began battling a weight problem that relegated her to supporting roles.

Prevost appeared in films steadily until 1933. A comeback of sorts came in 1935 with the Carole Lombard starrer *Hands Across the Table* but she made only two more after it, the last being *Thirteen Hours by Air* (1936). Among her films were *The Sin of Madelon Claudet, Paid, It's a Wise Child* and *Tango.*

Comments: The story of Marie Prevost is one of the sadder Hollywood sagas. After modest film beginnings, she had attained stardom in the mid–1920s only to see it dissipate with a series of popular but inconsequential films. Her well-publicized weight and other problems began to overshadow her career and then essentially ended it.

Prevost did make a successful transition to talkies. Her voice was pleasant and fit her usual sound film role as the wisecracking best friend of the heroine. But these roles alternated between major and minor in size and she ultimately was considered washed up.

Unfortunately, just as it seemed she might again have a place in the movies, Prevost was found dead under rumored horrible circumstances. Ironically, at her death the plump actress was found to have been suffering from severe malnutrition.

REVIEWS

The Godless Girl: Although the acting is undistinguished throughout, Marie Prevost is as human as her part permits but her character is notably confusing. *Variety* 4/3/29.

Ladies of Leisure: The plump gold digger is nicely played by Marie Prevost. She has a number of good scenes which she does not overplay. *Harrison's Reports* 4/19/30, *Variety* 5/28/30.

Paid: Well acted by the cast, among whom is Marie Prevost. *Harrison's Reports* 1/10/31.

Reckless Living: Marie Prevost is so changed that if it weren't for a careful perusal of the cast few would know that it is she playing the part of a female drunk. *Harrison's Reports* 10/10/31, *Variety* 12/8/31.

Parole Girl: The characters are unsympathetic, among them the one played by Marie Prevost who has a piquant bit. *Harrison's Reports* 3/4/33, *Variety* 4/11/33.

Hands Across the Table: Well acted by a cast including Marie Prevost who stages a convincing comeback in a Dumb Dora assignment. *Harrison's Reports* 11/2/35, *Variety* 11/6/35.

Pringle, Aileen (Aileen Bisbee), San Francisco, California, 1895–1989

Filmography: Films in Review (Oct. 1979)

Silent: Aileen Pringle was a stage actress in London and New York before she began appearing in films about 1919. She carved a niche for herself as a modern "vamp," especially after being chosen by English authoress Eleanor Glyn (the popularizer of "It") to star in the perfervid melodrama *Three Weeks* (1924).

Pringle was a versatile actress, though, and also made a series of popular MGM comedies teamed with Lew Cody. Among her 35 or so silent films were *Souls for Sale, His Hour, Tin Gods, Name the Man, The Christian, Wife of the Centaur* and *Wickedness Preferred*. Last silent: *A Single Man* (1929).

Sound: Nineteen twenty-nine's *The Night Parade* was Pringle's first talkie. By this time her roles were beginning to be in support and she rarely had leading roles again (one of them was in 1931's *Murder at Midnight*). Eventually her parts dwindled into bits, although she worked steadily for various studios until 1937.

After a hiatus, Pringle returned in 1939 but then she was seen no more until 1943 for her last two films, *The Youngest Profession* and *Happy Land*. Others of her 30 sound films were *Wall Street, Soldiers and Men, Jane Eyre* (1934 version), *Piccadilly Jim* and *The Women*.

Comments: Although Aileen Pringle became a popular MGM player, the studio did not seem to know what to do with her and she was loaned out as often as she made films for her home studio. Her own opinion was that because of her outspokenness and independence the moguls did not like her. She also was rumored to be an *intellectual*—another quality not endearing to them.

The theater-trained Pringle had a good speaking voice and she retained her attractive brunette looks for a while. All in all she had a respectable sound career but little more than that, mostly typecast in rather unsympathetic roles. Basically she was considered by Hollywood to be just another silent star and she appeared in mostly forgettable films.

Reviews

The Night Parade: As a siren, Aileen Pringle is seen in a somewhat different role than usual, but she plays it with uncommon finesse. *Variety* 11/13/29, *Harrison's Reports* 11/16/29.

Wall Street: Pringle shows little emotion and her dialogue is delivered with an accent so cultured that it becomes almost a burlesque. *New York Times* 11/25/29.

Once to Every Bachelor: Had the character of the married vamp been given more screen time she might have stolen the picture, but she probably would have saved it. As played by Aileen Pringle it is the outstanding villain role, but there are too few opportunities. *Variety* 9/25/34.

John Meade's Woman: Included in the roles which are practically bits is that played by Aileen Pringle, but it is ably acted by her. *Variety* 2/24/37, *Harrison's Reports* 2/27/37.

Ralston, Esther, Bar Harbor, Maine, 1902–1994

Filmography: Classic Images (Sept.-Oct. 1984); List of films in *Sweethearts of the Sage*

Silent: In the seven years before Esther Ralston achieved stardom, she worked as an extra from 1917 and had parts in features like *Oliver Twist* (1922 version) and *The Kid*. There were also serials like *The Phantom Fortune* and *Wolves of the North*. Previously, she had been a child actress traveling with her family in stock.

Ralston's breakthrough came with the popular success *Peter Pan* (1924) in which she played Wendy Darling's mother. She became a Paramount star from that year to 1929 in such films as *A Kiss for Cinderella, Old Ironsides* and *The American Venus*. The title of the latter film gave her a well-publicized sobriquet.

Among Ralston's other films were *Pals of the West, Ten Modern Commandments, The Sawdust Paradise, Children of Divorce* and *Womanhandled*. Her penultimate silent, *The Case of Lena Smith* (1929), directed by Josef von Sternberg, was considered her finest work but is apparently a lost film. Last silent: *Betrayal* (1929), co-starring Emil Jannings, with synchronized sound effects and music.

Sound: As with many of its other high-priced stars, Paramount was reluctant to put Ralston into a talkie. Finally the mediocre *The Wheel of Life* became her first in 1929. Her starring career began to decline almost immediately and she went on an extensive vaudeville tour.

When Ralston returned to Hollywood, she was cast in a succession of supporting roles or second leads for various studios. Her films included *Strange Wives, Lonely Wives, Reunion, As Good as Married* and *Slander House*.

Although Ralston was eventually signed by MGM, she made few pictures there, *Sadie McKee* being one. Later in her career she was more likely to be found in quickies turned out by Poverty Row studios. She also was seen in some English films and did more serials, *Jungle Menace* and *The Mysterious Pilot*.

Esther Ralston was off-screen in the very last

years of the '30s but she returned for two final films in 1940, *Tin Pan Alley* and *San Francisco Docks*, in which she played the wife of a gangster. Later she appeared on radio and television. One of her roles was in the soap opera *Our Five Daughters* in the 1960s.

Comments: Esther Ralston was a tallish, cool and beautiful blonde who personified her other publicity name, "The Golden Girl of the Silver Screen." She was one of the highest-paid Hollywood stars (and lived like one) and her rapid fall might be attributed, at least in part, to the desire of Paramount to save money. Her voice was very fine and her beauty certainly undiminished at the "ripe old age" of 27.

The vaudeville tour which so many former stars undertook to prove they could "talk" was both unnecessary and unsuccessful, as far as the studios were concerned, in Ralston's case. She later said that her time at MGM was marred by a disagreement with Joan Crawford, presumably about similar eye makeup (!), during the shooting of *Sadie McKee* (1934) and she was loaned out for most of her contract.

Ralston had no problem adapting to talkies. In one of her last films she gave a nice performance as Nora Bayes, the legendary singer, and she was still most attractive as well. But she really never could surmount being a "silent" actress.

Reviews

The Wheel of Life: It's doubtful if any star, even one as popular as Esther Ralston, the heroine, could carry such a burden. *Variety* 6/26/29, *Harrison's Reports* 6/29/29.

Lonely Wives: Ralston is pleasant as the lawyer's wife in this bedroom farce. *Harrison's Reports* 2/21/31, *Variety* 3/18/31.

Shadows of the Orient: The top-billed Ralston is a coy heroine and does not become the role. *Variety* 1/13/37.

Ralston, Jobyna (Jobyna Raulston?), South
Pittsburg, Tennessee, 1900/04–1967
Filmography: Classic Images (Sept. 1983)
Silent: Best known for being Harold Lloyd's leading lady in some of his popular later silents, Jobyna Ralston had her apprenticeship in Hal Roach one-reelers. She had had a few other minor feature roles previous to appearing with Lloyd as well. Her stint with him lasted from 1923–26 and included roles in *Why Worry?*, *Hot Water*, *The Freshman*, *Girl Shy* and *The Kid Brother*.

Ralston's other films included *Gigolo*, *Little Mickey Grogan*, *The Three-Must-Get-Theres*, *Lightning*, *The Power of the Press* and, most famous of all, the aviation epic *Wings* (1927), in which she had a small role opposite her husband-to-be Richard Arlen. Last silent: *Some Mother's Boy* (1929).

Sound: Ralston's sound career was brief and her few films were in no way comparable to her best silent ones. After her first talkie *The College Coquette* in 1929, she made only two others: *Rough Waters* (1930), in which she "co-starred" with Rin-Tin-Tin, and *Sheer Luck* (1931), a low-grade quickie.

Reviews

The College Coquette: Reviews differed. One said that possibly because of bad recording, the voice of Jobyna Ralston appeared to be curiously childish and frequently indistinct. Another said that her performance showed that her stage experience came in handy in those hectic talkie days. She turned in an effective characterization and her voice was most acceptable. *New York Times* 8/26/29, *Variety* 8/28/29.

Rough Waters: Ralston appears unconvincingly as a well-dressed and soft-spoken girl in a dingy fishing hut, where she is supposed to have drudged a long time. *Harrison's Reports* 7/26/30, *Variety* 7/30/30.

Sheer Luck: The film is a sheer waste with no story, no action and no interest. One of the most nonsensical films seen. *Variety* 6/9/31.

Randolph, Anders (also Randolf), Denmark, 1875/76–1930
Silent: A veteran of stock companies, Anders Randolph came to Vitagraph as a leading actor and in the mid-'teens began numerous feature appearances in supporting roles. He also appeared for Goldwyn and Famous Players. Among his earlier films were *Mother's Roses*, *The Girl Philippa*, *Sins of Ambition*, *The Splendid Sinner* and *Too Many Crooks*.

Randolph was a busy top character actor throughout the 1920s, often in "bad man" parts in comedies and dramas such as *Sherlock Holmes*, *Madonna of the Streets*, *Old San Francisco*, *Dorothy Vernon of Haddon Hall*, *Her Market Value*, *Me, Gangster* and *The Love of Sunya*.

Last silents: *The Viking*, with synchronized sound effects and music, and *The Kiss*, with synchronized music, released about the same time in 1929, and made after his first talkies.

Sound: Nineteen twenty-eight's *Women They Talk About* and *Noah's Ark* both contained talking sequences, and several of Anders Randolph's 1929 films were talkies. They included *The Show of Shows*, in which he sing-songed in a musical number, *Dangerous Curves, Shanghai Lady* and *Young Nowheres*.

Randolph continued making features such as *Going Wild, Sons of the Gods* and *The Way of All Men*, and also was seen in shorts, at least one starring Laurel and Hardy. It seemed as if he had made the transition to talkie character actor very successfully when death intervened. His last film *Call of the Rockies* was posthumously released.

REVIEWS

Shanghai Lady: Very well acted by the cast which includes Anders Randolph as the Mandarin. *Harrison's Reports* 11/16/29.

Rawlinson, Herbert, Brighton, England, 1885/86–1953

Filmography: Classic Images (Jan.-Mar. 1985, June 1986); List of films in *Eighty Silent Film Stars*

Silent: In films since 1911, Herbert Rawlinson had his first big roles in the serial *The Black Box* and the feature *Damon and Pythias*, both 1915. He appeared for numerous studios in one- and two-reelers as well as features like *The Bugle Call, The Sea Wolf, The Victor, Mary of the Movies, Men of the Night, Wealth* and *Stolen Secrets*.

The suave Rawlinson also was seen in other serials which included *The Carter Case, The Flame Fighter* and *Trooper 77*. Last silent: *Wages of Conscience* (1927).

Sound: Rawlinson made a Vitaphone short in 1928 in which he was dubbed the monologist of the screen. He was then off-screen for several years, returning in character roles and making his feature debut in 1933's *Moonlight and Pretzels*.

Rawlinson worked until the '50s in films like *Bullets or Ballots, Dark Victory, Colt Comrades, Convention Girl, Lost Canyon, Accomplice* and *Nobody's Baby*. He also appeared in more serials, including *Robinson Crusoe of Clipper Island, SOS Coast Guard, King of the Texas Rangers* and *Superman*. His last film was director Ed Wood's *Jail Bait*; he supposedly died the day after he finished shooting.

Comments: Like other gentlemanly matinee idols of the early silents, Herbert Rawlinson found his later career in supporting or bit roles in westerns, quickies and serials. He was not really distinctive enough in personality to be a memorable character actor but he lent his gray-haired, smooth-voiced dignity to many a role, both worthy and unworthy.

REVIEWS

Moonlight and Pretzels: Herbert Rawlinson indicates he isn't finished in pictures by any means. *Harrison's Reports* 8/26/33, *Variety* 8/29/33.

The People's Enemy: Rawlinson does not do an impressive job. *Variety* 5/1/35.

Flying Wild: Rawlinson, as a plantation owner, manages to remain sincere and credible despite the lines he speaks. *Harrison's Reports* 4/26/41, *Variety* 7/16/41.

Arizona Cyclone: Rawlinson has a minor part as a freight line owner who gets murdered. *Variety* 3/11/42.

Ray, Allene (Allene Burch), San Antonio, Texas, 1901–1978

Filmography: List of films in *Sweethearts of the Sage*

Silent: As Pearl White was *the* serial queen of the teens, Allene Ray was *the* serial queen of the 1920s. Before her chapterplay fame, she had appeared in two-reel westerns. It had been the second prize in a Fame and Fortune contest which brought her to Hollywood.

Among Ray's serials, in many of which she was teamed with Walter Miller, were *The Way of a Man, The Fortieth Door, Ten Scars Make a Man, The Terrible People, Hawk of the Hills, Sunken Silver, Play Ball* and *The Green Archer*.

Ray also appeared in features like *Honeymoon Ranch, West of the Rio Grande* and *Your Friend and Mine*. Last silent feature: *Times Have Changed* (1923). A feature version of *Hawk of the Hills* was released in 1929.

Sound: The Indians Are Coming (1930) was both Ray's last silent serial and her first sound one; it was released in both versions. She made only a few features, the first of which was *Overland Bound* in 1929. *Westward Bound* followed the next year and then 1931's *The Phantom*. There is also a possibility she made at least one other talkie.

REVIEWS

Overland Bound: The leading lady is serial favorite Allene Ray. Her voice is a disappointment to fans, who can remember back to her starring days. Maybe it's the recording, which was generally poor, but more likely it's Miss Ray's voice.

(This is reputed to have been the second all-talking outdoor western after *In Old Arizona*.) *Harrison's Reports* 10/12/29, *Variety* 4/23/30.

Westward Bound: The heroine as played by Allene Ray is a bust. On film she is an insipid blonde who possesses a faltering voice without screen quality. *Variety* 3/18/31.

Ray, Charles, Jacksonville, Illinois, 1891–1943

Filmography: Films in Review (Nov. 1968); *Classic Images* (Sept. 1980).

Silent: Following stage experience, Charles Ray's

first known credit was in 1913; *The Coward* (1915) was his first notable film. From the mid-'teens to the early 1920s he was an enormously popular silent star for Triangle, Paramount and ultimately for his own production company.

With films like *The Hick, Homer Comes Home, The Clodhopper* and *Hay Foot, Straw Foot*, Ray established the persona of a simple (if not slow-witted) country boy who overcomes all odds and gets the girl. Many of Ray's 120-plus romantic comedies and melodramas dealt with the Civil War, baseball and rustic life.

Among Ray's other films were *The Son of His Father, The Busher, An Old Fashioned Boy, The Old Swimmin' Hole, Forty-Five Minutes from Broadway, A Tailor Made Man* and *Greased Lightning*. He was still going strong with his production company in the early '20s when he had a big hit with *The Girl I Loved* (1923).

Ray overreached himself in attempting to make his expensive magnum opus *The Courtship of Miles Standish* in 1924 and went deeply into debt after the film failed. Although he continued on until the end of the silent era with a new persona as a man of the world (e.g., *Getting Gertie's Garter, Paris* and *Vanity*), he never found great success again. Last silent: *The Garden of Eden* (1928).

Sound: Charles Ray returned in 1934 to bit and small roles in films like *Ladies Should Listen* (he was a doorman), *Hollywood Boulevard* (with many other silent screen old-timers), *A Little Bit of Heaven, Welcome Home* and *By Your Leave*. He did have a final leading role in the little-seen *Just My Luck* and a fair-sized part in *A Yank in the RAF*.

After becoming one of the MGM "stock company" of former (and down on their luck) silent stars, Ray apparently made no films or was an extra from 1937 to 1940. His last known film appearance came in *The Magnificent Dope* in 1942. He had also made a 1932 short, *The Bride's Bereavement*.

Comments: Charles Ray achieved fame and fortune playing his signature bumpkin role in overalls and chewing on a piece of grass, with an unruly lock of hair straggling out from under his straw hat. He was the quintessential country lad. It was no doubt his characters' qualities of earnestness, honesty and modesty which touched a chord with the audience.

As is so often the case with an established persona, when Ray tried other roles as, for instance, a spoiled rich boy, he was less successful. In real life, Ray did live splendiferously. He had a mansion with numerous servants and threw lavish parties. All this was lost with the failure of *The Courtship of Miles Standish*.

Although he essayed a film or two with his familiar persona in the mid–'20s, by then Charles Ray was more often cast as a sophisticated (even villainous) character, his now receding hair slickly brushed back.

Part of Ray's problem, apparently, was that he seldom took advice and believed that only he knew what was best for his career. As a result he did not see that the moviegoing public of the '20s had different tastes than that of the teens. They were tiring of him. He was not a victim of the talkies; his long fall came long before.

REVIEWS

Welcome Home: Charles Ray, a veteran of the silents, has just a bit. *Variety* 8/28/35, *Harrison's Reports* 9/7/35.

It's a Date: Many old-time film stars are paraded briefly before the camera, including Charles Ray. *Variety* 10/16/40.

Reed, Donald (Ernest Guillen or Gillen),
Mexico City, Mexico, 1902/05–1973

Silent: In 1925 and '26, Donald Reed made a handful of pictures playing supporting roles under his real name, e.g., *His Secretary* and *Brown of Harvard*. Beginning in 1927 he appeared under his new name as leading man to such actresses as Dolores Del Rio, Sally O'Neil (twice), Colleen Moore and Billie Dove. His films included *Naughty but Nice, Mad Hour, The Night Watch* and *Show Girl*. Last silent: *Hardboiled* (1929).

Sound: The talkies reduced Donald Reed to supporting roles in which his characters usually had names like "Pancho," "Nick," "Ramon" and "Pedro." He also had a lead or two in quickies. His first sound film was the part-talkie *Evangeline*, followed by *A Most Immoral Lady* and *Little Johnny Jones*.

Among Reed's other films through 1937 were *The Texan, Flame of Mexico, Man from Monterey, Happy Landing, Ramona, Law and Lead* and *Slaves in Bondage*. He also played a role in the 1936 serial *Darkest Africa*.

REVIEWS

The Man from Monterey: Reed is handicapped by stilted lines as the villain in this John Wayne western. *Variety* 8/22/33.

Revier, Dorothy (Doris Velarga, Velagra, Velegra and other variations of the name),
San Francisco, California, 1904–1993

Filmography: Classic Images (Nov. 1989); List of films in *Sweethearts of the Sage*

Silent: Dancer Dorothy Revier, soon to be one of the silent screen's greatest "vamps," debuted in

1922. Among her earliest films were *The Broadway Madonna* and *Life's Greatest Question*, the only time she may have used her real name. Her new screen name came from her marriage to director Harry Revier.

Revier was to work for studios such as Universal, Paramount, Fox, Columbia and United Artists. Her films, in which she frequently co-starred with Jack Holt, included *The Other Kind of Love*, *The Drop Kick*, *Submarine*, *Sealed Lips*, *Stolen Pleasures*, *The Tigress*, *Steppin' Out* and *When the Wife's Away*. Last silent: *The Quitter* (1929).

Sound: Revier continued her wicked ways playing the villainess Milady de Winter in her first part-talkie *The Iron Mask* (1929). Of the eight films she made that year, all but one were sound or part-sound. They included *The Donovan Affair*, *The Dance of Life*, *The Mighty* and *Tanned Legs*.

Among Revier's other films, in which she increasingly essayed standard romantic leads, were *Anybody's Blonde*, *Raffles*, *The Bad Man*, *Graft*, *Green Eyes*, *By Candlelight* and *The Lady in Scarlet*. Revier also appeared in many westerns with Buck Jones, who was the lead in her final film *The Cowboy and the Kid* in 1936.

Comments: One of the most beautiful blondes in silents, Dorothy Revier came to be known as the "Queen of Poverty Row" because of her association with Columbia Pictures. As a leading "bad" girl she had a secure niche in the silent era but in talkies, to which she made an effortless transition, she more often than not was cast as a bland leading lady in quickies.

Deprived of her more interesting "baddie" roles, Revier lost her edge and became just another pretty blonde who was often loaned out to studios like Chesterfield and Monogram, her career obviously going nowhere. She claimed that a falling-out with Columbia's vindictive boss Harry Cohn, with whom she had been romantically involved, hastened her decline. When she began playing largely unseen leading ladies in horse operas, the former vamp had had enough.

Reviews

The Donovan Affair: Revier, as the love interest, is putting on weight. Her voice is all right. *Variety* 5/1/29.

The Secrets of Wu Sin: Revier has just a bit as a foil to the lead. *Variety* 2/28/33.

The Cowboy and the Kid: Revier overacts a little as a school teacher. *Variety* 7/29/36.

Reynolds, Vera (Norma?), Richmond, Virginia, 1900/05–1962

Silent: Having paid her dues in comedy shorts, pert ex-dancer Vera Reynolds had her first supporting roles in 1923 features like *Prodigal Daughters* and *Woman-Proof* and eventually graduated to leads. She was a favorite of C. B. DeMille for a while in such films as *The Golden Bed*, *Feet of Clay* and *The Road to Yesterday*.

Among Reynolds's other films were *Flapper Wives*, *Icebound*, *Corporal Kate*, *The Little Adventuress*, *Divine Sinner* and *Jazzland*. Last silent: *Back from Shanghai* (1929), with synchronized sound effects and music.

Sound: For the most part Reynolds retained her leading lady status in talkies but her films were mostly quickies for Poverty Row studios. They included her first, *Tonight at Twelve* (1929), in a supporting role, *Borrowed Wives*, *Gorilla Ship*, *Hell Bent for Frisco*, *The Monster Walks* and *Dragnet Patrol*. There were about a dozen altogether, after which she vanished from the screen before 1933.

Reviews

The Last Dance: Reynold's name provides limited publicity value. Nobody gets any acting honors but the nod goes to her. *Variety* 4/2/30.

Rich, Irene (Irene Luther), Buffalo, New York, 1890/97–1988

Filmography: Classic Images (July 1988); List of films in *Sweethearts of the Sage*

Silent: Irene Rich's first screen credits came in 1918; she may have started as an extra in *Stella Maris* the same year. She went on to make numerous films in which her expressive dark-eyed beauty was prominently featured in roles through which she suffered nobly.

Rich's pictures included *Lady Windermere's Fan*, *The Desired Woman*, *Behold This Woman*, *Don't Tell the Wife*, *Rosita*, *Boy of Mine* and *A Lost Lady*. She also made some two-reelers. Last silent: *The Exalted Flapper* (1929), with synchronized music score, made after her first talkies.

Sound: *The Perfect Crime* and *Women They Talk About*, released about the same time in 1928, were Rich's first part-talkies. That year she also appeared in two Vitaphone sound shorts, *Lead Kindly Light* and *The Beast*.

Rich's debut in an all-sound feature came in *Ned McCobb's Daughter* in 1929. One of the films for which she is best remembered, *They Had to See Paris* with Will Rogers, was her other '29 talkie. She also co-starred with him the next year in *So This Is London*. In 1931's *The Champ* she played Wallace Beery's wife.

In an apparent effort to convince studio moguls that her voice was suitable for sound, Rich undertook a vaudeville tour and was off the screen for a few years in the mid–'30s. She returned for a handful in 1938–42, including a good role in *The Mortal Storm*.

Rich appeared in her last films beginning in 1947. Among her pictures were *Check and Double Check*, *Her Mad Night*, *Manhattan Tower*, *Keeping Company*, *Fort Apache* and *This Time for Keeps*. Her final one was *Joan of Arc* in 1948. She was also a renowned radio and stage star.

Comments: Although she played numerous roles in silents, Irene Rich's forte was the misunderstood wife in domestic dramas and flat-out tearjerkers. Her mature beauty seemed to lend itself well to this type of role. She had a fine voice but for some reason the success of her sound career seemed to be in doubt, hence the vaudeville tour.

In talkies Rich played some unsympathetic characters, notably as the wife of national icon Will Rogers, with whom she also had appeared in silent two-reelers. Eventually she established a respectable record of sound films but her roles were frequently small and her best screen days were in the silent era.

REVIEWS

They Had to See Paris: Rich, as the wife, handles a slightly unsympathetic part well and is most impressive in her transition from Oklahoma wife to Parisian chump. *Variety* 10/16/29, *Harrison's Reports* 10/19/29.

The Champ: Rich is excellent as the mother, but the role is little more than a bit. *Harrison's Reports* 11/14/31, *Variety* 11/17/31.

Everybody's Hobby: The presence of Irene Rich, who has garnered an enhanced reputation from doing radio, goes far in making the film worthwhile. She makes an attractive matron. *Variety* 9/27/39.

The Lady in Question: Rich is excellent as the wife. *Variety* 8/7/40.

Calendar Girl: Rich is good as the kindly landlady. *Variety* 2/12/47.

Rich, Lillian, London, England, 1900–1954

Silent: Beginning in 1919, Lillian Rich made over 40 silent films, including *The Blazing Trail*, *Ship of Souls*, *Cheap Kisses*, *Empty Hearts*, *Braveheart*, *The Isle of Retribution*, *Man to Man* and *Web of Fate*. Her starring role in Cecil B. DeMille's *The Golden Bed* in 1925 marked the height of her career. Last silent: *The Old Code* (1928).

Sound: When Rich returned to the screen in 1931 it was for small supporting roles in at least a dozen features and some two-reel comedy shorts. Among her films were *The Devil Pays*, *Mark of the Spur*, *Riptide*, *She Married Her Boss*, *Arsène Lupin*

Returns and 1940's *Doctor Kildare's Crisis*, which may have been her last film.

Rin Tin Tin (also Rin-Tin-Tin), near Lorraine, France, 1918–1932

Silent: No two-legged star was ever discovered in so dramatic a fashion as was Rin Tin Tin: on a World War One battlefield. The German Shepherd pup came to California with his discoverer, ex-pilot Lee Duncan, and was trained in dog jumping. Apparently a film made of one such record jump was sold to a film company for exhibition and the rest, as they say, is history.

Warner Bros. saw in "Rinty" a canine star quality and they were proved correct. His heroics kept the studio solvent during the '20s and he even had his own production unit. Although he started in support, by 1924 he was definitely "top dog."

Rin Tin Tin's films from 1922 included *The Man from Hell's River*, *Where the North Begins*, *Find Your Man*, *Tracked in the Snow Country*, *The Night Cry*, *A Dog of the Regiment* and *Jaws of Steel*. Last silent: *Rinty of the Desert* (1928).

Sound: Nineteen twenty-eight's all-talking Vitaphone feature *Land of the Silver Fox* marked Rin Tin Tin's barking debut. That year he also was seen in the Vitaphone short *Rin-Tin-Tin and His Owner and Friend Lee Duncan*. All of his 1929 pictures were either part- or all-sound, including *Frozen River* and *The Million Dollar Collar*.

There was also the all-star *The Show of Shows*, in which Rinty briefly added his hoarse basso voice to the all-singing, all-dancing festivities. He had a rare supporting role in *Tiger Rose* that year but he recovered his accustomed top billing in three 1930 barkfests: *Rough Waters*, *The Man Hunter* and *On the Border*.

Rinty appeared in two serials: 1930's *The Lone Defender* (released in a feature version in 1934) and *Lightning Warrior* (1931). That chapterplay was his farewell to the screen but his offspring, Rin Tin Tin, Jr., carried on the family name and honor in several films of the '30s. Another progeny was seen on television in a popular series of the 1950s.

Comments: Although challengers yapped at his heels in the silent days (Thunder, Wolfheart, Silverstreak, Klondike and Dynamite were but a few), Rin Tin Tin remained at the top of the canine heap. Many a pretty starlet supported him on her way up and/or down and his films always had top production values. Not for nothing did Warners refer to him as "the mortgage lifter."

Rin Tin Tin's great success is the more surprising because, physically, he was not what one could call beautiful. He was a dark colored shepherd of a type not very much in favor. Like many a star, his public persona was far from the reality; he had a temperament that was, to say the least, snappish.

Rinty was a one-man dog, that man was Lee Duncan, and he had trained Rinty well. The dog obeyed numerous commands and seemed almost to assume a human expression at times. He also mastered many tricks, one of which was climbing a seemingly vertical wall (there were disguised pawholds) and jumping through transoms.

As for Rin Tin Tin's voice, it was a bit growly but "okay for sound." If silent cues had to replace previously spoken commands, there was little evidence of any difference in the dog's "performance."

Although there have been many dogs, and indeed other fauna, in films going back to the pit bull Teddy at Keystone, only Lassie in the 1940s matched Rin Tin Tin's popularity. In the 1970s the film *Won Ton Ton, the Dog Who Saved Hollywood* satirized his ascent to fame. That says something *about* his fame.

REVIEWS

Frozen River: His bark rings out huskily and his almost human acting is, as usual, appealing. Although it is little better than Rinty's silents he does his usual job as the beast who is savage until the right people come along. *Harrison's Reports* 6/22/29, *Variety* 7/3/29.

On the Border: Dialogue has seemingly not had the slightest impact on Rinty's work, and whatever cueing is necessary in directing the dog. *Variety* 2/5/30.

Rough Waters: There were differences of opinion about Rin Tin Tin's performance. One review pointed out how he made beautiful high dives and climbed over rocks and hills; everything except actually talk. Another thought that directing him in the matter-of-fact way that is done in this film would injure his appeal. The dog too obviously responded to orders. *Harrison's Reports* 7/26/30, *Variety* 7/30/30.

Robards, Jason (later Sr.), Hillsdale, Michigan, 1892–1963

Silent: Before there was well-known stage and screen star Jason Robards, Jr., there was his father: well-known stage and screen star Jason Robards. Considered to be one of the leading performers in the theater of his day, the senior Robards may have made more than 150 films, perhaps beginning at Vitagraph in the days of two-reelers.

Robards's first credited features were *The Gilded Lily* and *The Land of Hope* (as leading man) in 1921. In the 1920s he alternated stage and cinema appearances and was off the screen until mid-decade. He returned for leads and top supporting roles in films

such as *Stella Maris, Footloose Widows, The Heart of Maryland, Irish Hearts, Polly of the Movies* and *Tracked by the Police.* Last silent: *Trial Marriage* (1929), with synchronized music and sound effects, made after his first talkie.

Sound: Robards's only full-length film in 1928 *On Trial,* was also his first talkie, and he also appeared in the Vitaphone short *The Death Ship* that year. His stage-trained voice was just fine for sound and several 1929 talkies followed: *The Flying Marine, The Gamblers, The Isle of Lost Ships* (top-billed) and *Paris.*

Robards went into the '30s alternating leads and supporting roles in such motion pictures as *Abraham Lincoln, Peacock Alley, Lightnin'* and *Jazz Cinderella* (lead). During the 1930s, Robards devoted himself entirely to the screen, often appearing in eight or nine films a year, increasingly in villain roles.

Robards's 1930s movies, many of "B" caliber, included *Law of the Tong, Slightly Married, All of Me, Corruption, The Crusades, San Francisco, The Firefly, The Rage of Paris* and *Range War.* He also made the serials *Burn 'Em Up Barnes* and *Scouts to the Rescue* and was seen in several shorts.

In the following decade Robards continued his frequent appearances, mostly at RKO, where he was under contract. Among his pictures were *The Fatal Hour, The Master Race, What a Blonde, Isle of the Dead, Ding Dong Williams, Wild Horse Mesa, Mr. Blandings Builds His Dream House* and *South of Death Valley.*

Starting in the late 1940s, he was unable to work because of blindness, but then in 1957 he underwent a series of operations which restored his sight. He made one film in the 1950s (*The Second Woman*) and then was on the screen only once more, in 1961's *Wild in the Country.* In the meantime, he had played his first (and last) stage role in 36 years, opposite his son, in 1958's *The Disenchanted.* He also appeared on television.

REVIEWS

The Isle of Lost Ships: Robards is manly and natural as the hero. *New York Times* 10/28/29.

Jazz Cinderella: Robards is the hero and he sings a few songs in a pretty good tenor voice. *Variety* 10/1/30.

Roberts, Edith, New York, New York, 1899–1935

Silent: Stage actress Edith Roberts became a leading lady in films about 1918 and remained one until the end of the silent era. Her early films included *Beans, The Love Swindle, Sue of the South* and *Her Five-Foot Highness.*

Among Roberts's other pictures, in which she

specialized in playing spirited heroines, were *The Fire Cat, The Dangerous Age, Thorns and Orange Blossoms, Roaring Rails, Seven Keys to Baldpate* (1925 version), *Shameful Behavior?* and *Man from Headquarters*. Last silent: *Two O'Clock in the Morning* (1929), made after her part-talkie.

Sound: Either by choice or happenstance, Roberts appeared in only one part-talkie, the 1929 Ken Maynard western *The Wagon Master*.

REVIEWS

The Wagon Master: A typical Ken Maynard western in which Edith Roberts is a pleasing heroine. *Harrison's Reports* 9/28/29.

Roberts, Theodore, San Francisco, California, 1861–1928

Filmography: Films in Review (Apr. 1972)

Silent: Dubbed "The Grand Duke of Hollywood" and "The Grand Old Man of the Screen," Theodore Roberts had a lengthy theater career (including *The Squaw Man*) before he essayed films. *The Call of the North* (1914) was his first one and in that year's *The Circus Man* he had his first starring role. He then alternated between leading and supporting roles and, in the early days, sometimes played the "heavy."

Generally Roberts's characterization was that of the gruff old man with a warm heart. *Grumpy* (1923) was a typical role of that type. His more than 100 films, among which were 23 for C. B. DeMille, included *The Girl of the Golden West, The Arab, Saturday Night, The Woman Thou Gavest Me, Too Much Speed* and *Forty Winks*.

Among Roberts's more prominent pictures were *Miss Lulu Bett, Male and Female, The Affairs of Anatol* and his best-remembered role, that of Moses, in the 1923 version of *The Ten Commandments*. Illness forced him off the screen in 1924 and he made but few films thereafter. Last silent: *The Masks of the Devil* (1928), with synchronized sound effects and music score.

Sound: The only two sound films in which Roberts appeared were released posthumously in 1929: *Ned McCobb's Daughter* and *Noisy Neighbors*, the latter a part-talkie. They proved that his stage-trained voice would have been just fine for a continuing stint in talkies.

REVIEWS

Noisy Neighbors: It is uncanny to hear the late Theodore Roberts talk. His little bit of dialogue proves that he possessed a splendid voice and was able to put his old stage experience to good use. He showed the class of actor he was and made one realize what the movie world lost. *Harrison's Reports* 2/23/29, *Variety* 7/24/29.

Rogers, Charles ("Buddy"), Olathe, Kansas, 1904–

Filmography: Film Fan Monthly (Dec. 1970); *Films in Review* (Dec. 1987)

Silent: The short-lived Paramount Pictures School of Acting was Buddy Rogers's entree into films. His first role, along with other "graduates," came as a juvenile lead in *Fascinating Youth* (1926). Other early films were W. C. Fields's *So's Your Old Man* and *More Pay-Less Work*.

Nineteen twenty-seven proved to be a banner year for Rogers. Both the flying epic *Wings* and *My Best Girl*, in which he co-starred with a "grown-up" Mary Pickford, were great successes. (The latter was Pickford's final silent.) Other films were *Red Lips* and *Get Your Man*. Last silent: *Someone to Love* (1928).

Sound: The 1928 part-talkie *Varsity* was Buddy Rogers's first. All his 1929 movies were sound or part-sound, including *Abie's Irish Rose, Close Harmony* and *River of Romance*. With college musicals in vogue he went on to make several. His subsequent films included *Illusion, Follow Thru, Paramount on Parade, Along Came Youth, Safety in Numbers, Best of Enemies, Old Man Rhythm* and *Heads Up*.

When his career began to falter in the U.S., Rogers went to England in the mid–'30s. Among his pictures there were *Once in a Million* and *Let's Make a Night of It*. Later American films included *This Way Please*, three in the 1940s' "Mexican Spitfire" series and *An Innocent Affair* (a.k.a. *Don't Trust Your Husband*). His last film was 1957's *The Parson and the Outlaw*.

Rogers was also an orchestra leader, which was often reflected in his films. His group The California Cavaliers was popular for many years and this eventually became the major part of his career. The orchestra was also involved in some musical shorts he made in the '30s and '40s.

Comments: Wings was a career-maker for Buddy Rogers and he was never able to outdo it. In it he presented the clean-cut all–American boy image which was the hallmark of most of his later, and generally inferior, efforts. When he tried to diverge from this persona, as in 1931's *The Lawyer's Secret*, his limited acting ability was not up to the task.

When, as "America's Boyfriend," Rogers married "America's Sweetheart," Mary Pickford, it seemed only fitting despite the difference in their ages. By then his film career had waned and he was devoting more time to the orchestra. (The amount of time he spent away from home was to prove a bit of a thorny issue later on.)

Although he was handsome and likable, Rogers

was never more than a journeyman actor in talkies. Sometimes he would be top-billed (e.g., *Old Man Rhythm*) but would have little to do. It seemed apparent, as some reviews pointed out, that his studio was not particularly concerned about his ongoing picture career. Nor possibly, after some years, was he.

It would be unfair merely to call Rogers a "pretty boy." To audiences, at least for some while, he did typify the idealized "average" American youth of his day. In later life he did much, and still does, for the Hollywood film community but on-screen he rarely rose above his mundane film roles.

REVIEWS

Varsity: Reviewers did not agree. One said that Rogers was vocally colorless and that as his first talkie it was not strong. Another thought he did very well. *Variety* 10/31/28, *Harrison's Reports* 11/3/28.

Close Harmony: It is about the best thing Rogers has done since his fan mail jumped after *Wings*. He is still doing his shy, modest, clean-cut American boy act, but it fits this role. His acting is good. *Variety* 5/1/29, *Harrison's Reports* 5/4/29.

The Lawyer's Secret: Rogers plays a ne'er-do-well with as much brazenness as he can muster, but it is not much help. Paramount seems to be playing him down because he is only one of a featured cast. He gives a fairly good performance despite the fact that he is miscast. *Variety* 6/2/31, *Harrison's Reports* 6/6/31.

This Way Please: Rogers has done pretty well via personal appearances around the country with his band. If he had been given more suitable material than this picture he might mean something to exhibitors. As it is he is lost in an insignificant part that lacks sympathy. *Variety* 9/15/37, *Harrison's Reports* 10/23/37.

An Innocent Affair (Don't Trust Your Husband): As a tobacco tycoon, Buddy Rogers makes a belated return to the screen and retains much of the boyish charm and personality of his former film days.

Rogers, Will, Oolo(a)gqah or Claremore,

Indian Territory, later Oklahoma, 1879–1935
Filmography: Classic Images (Spring 1978)
Silent: Will Rogers began his climb to world acclaim humbly enough as a rancher and cowhand. He was an expert with a lariat and eventually developed the skill into a career as an international performer with his roping act. He first toured with circuses and Wild West shows, went into vaudeville and then found stardom in several editions of the Ziegfeld Follies.

Rogers developed a line of homespun patter to accompany his rope tricks in the Follies and soon found audiences wanting more. He was performing there when he appeared in his first film *Laughing Bill Hyde* (1918) for Sam Goldwyn. In pictures he established the character of Jubilo, a rural clown who constantly gets into trouble. His spectacular lariat skills were prominently featured in some of his movies, especially *The Ropin' Fool* (1922).

Among Rogers's films for Pathe, Roach and Goldwyn were *Jes' Call Me Jim, Jubilo, Honest Hutch, Boys Will Be Boys, The Headless Horseman, Doubling for Romeo* and *Our Congressman*. On a European trip he also made a series of glorified travelogues that showcased himself in various cities like Dublin and Paris.

In the 1920s, Rogers appeared in several Broadway shows and wrote a column that was published in over 500 papers. He traveled abroad extensively to observe major events of the day and his comments were eagerly read by millions. When he had the time for anything else, he also was a much sought-after dinner speaker.

Rogers was probably best known for his amusing spoofs of currently popular films. Among them were *Two Wagons — Both Covered, Big Moments from Little Pictures* and *Uncensored Movies*. Last silent: *A Texas Steer* (1927).

Sound: It was with the first of his over 20 talkies, *They Had to See Paris* (1929), that Rogers came into his own in motion pictures as an up-and-coming Fox star. His studiedly drawling voice and Southwestern accent was a perfect accompaniment to his persona. That year he also appeared in the all-star musical *Happy Days* as "himself."

Rogers cast aside his silent persona and assumed a new one as a kind of innocent who overcomes a variety of external problems while contending with emotional problems closer to home; e.g., nagging wives usually played by Irene Rich or Louise Dresser.

Rogers's films during this period included *So This Is London, Lightnin', A Connecticut Yankee, Young as You Feel, Down to Earth* and *Business and Pleasure*. He was to become even more of a major film star during the last few years of his life.

Starting with *State Fair* (1933), many of Rogers's films hearkened back, at least in spirit, to an earlier and more serene time where the old rural values still reigned supreme and he was their champion. Three of these nostalgic pieces were directed by John Ford and were among his best. They were *Judge Priest*, containing what was perhaps Rogers's finest performance, *Doctor Bull* and his last, *Steamboat 'Round the Bend*.

Other Rogers motion pictures included *Life*

Begins at Forty, *David Harum*, *The County Chairman*, *Handy Andy* and *In Old Kentucky*. The latter was released posthumously, as was *Steamboat*, after his death in an airplane crash. In 1934 he was the top box office attraction of the cinema.

Comments: Will Rogers was, of course, much more than a mere movie star although he certainly was that, and the highest-paid actor in the cinema to boot. Through his daily syndicated newspaper columns, books, the radio and his far-flung travels he became the beloved conscience of America and the greatest of home philosophers.

Rogers knew and appeared to be at ease with presidents, kings and power brokers of all kinds, yet he seemed to remain a plain man of the people imbued with great decency. In his films he played "himself" or at least the persona he wanted people to see. He was seen as a simple man speaking out against more powerful and less scrupulous men.

The fact that Rogers was very wealthy and probably had to be extremely sophisticated to pull it all off was beside the point. He knew how to always guard his public persona. In actuality he was an intensely private individual who was far more complex, and perhaps dark, than was realized.

As an actor Rogers was perhaps better than he seemed although he denigrated his own abilities and indeed the movies themselves. He amusingly called sound films "the noisies." Some of his on-set shenanigans, such as ad-libbing, were certainly less than professional, although some directors, including John Ford, encouraged his improvisations at times.

Many of Will Rogers's pictures depended on his persona and had little else to recommend them. There is no question that audiences brought to his films their knowledge of him as a public person and probably ignored any deficiencies in his emoting. And he wisely stayed within the narrow range of his established persona.

Whether Rogers was truly as beautiful a human being as he seemed, or whether he really ever met a man he "didn't like," will never be known. What is certain is that at his death a whole nation mourned. They felt he was so much more than, as he facetiously put it, a "cowhand gone wrong."

About Will Rogers, President Franklin Roosevelt said, "We pay grateful homage to the memory of a man who helped the nation to smile…. Above all things, in a time grown solemn and somber, he brought his countrymen back to a sense of proportion." How many other mere actors would have received such a tribute?

Perhaps the fact that he was so much a man of his time has resulted in Rogers's films being so little revived today. In this more cynical age it is unlikely that any actor or indeed any other person could assume the role he played in more naive times: a symbol of the best in humankind.

Reviews

They Had to See Paris: There was critical disagreement. One review said that Will Rogers in silent pictures was like an orator with his tongue cut out. With speech he is completely the person who has made a fortune out of being archetypically American, and he gets all the laughs. Another review thought that the film was nothing to brag about and that Rogers rarely was given an opportunity to display his brilliance. *Variety* 10/16/29, *Harrison's Reports* 10/19/29.

Young As You Feel: Rogers plays his usual homely routine but outside of him there's little to recommend the film. *Variety* 8/11/31.

Business and Pleasure: Rogers has always depended on a special type of homespun low comedy, but his characters nearly always had some depth and truth. Here he has all the low comedy but little legitimate characterization. *Variety* 2/16/32.

Too Busy to Work: The box office draw of Will Rogers is not what it used to be but he will have to sell the picture. He is the whole picture. *Variety* 12/6/32.

State Fair: There is just enough of Will Rogers's quaint humor but those who are accustomed to his quips will find them missing here.

(For perhaps the only time in talkies Rogers was not top-billed. He was listed below Janet Gaynor in the cast of this nostalgic Henry King–directed picture.) *Variety* 1/31/33, *Harrison's Reports* 2/4/33.

Judge Priest: Rogers has made the character completely his own and gives one of the best performances of his career. He does as well in serious moments as in comedy ones, and he holds the audience's absolute attention. He invests the character strongly with his personality.

(The character of Priest was based upon several of humorist Irvin S. Cobb's stories. Although not the same physical type as the actor, the character proved a perfect fit for Rogers. The film was also noteworthy for Rogers's interplay with African-American actor Stepin Fetchit.) *Variety* 10/16/34.

In Old Kentucky: It's no less than fitting that Will Rogers's last picture should be one of his best. It will merit attention whenever Rogers revivals are played. *Variety* 12/4/35.

Roland, Gilbert (Luis Alonso), Ciudad

Juarez, Mexico, 1905–1994

Filmography: Classic Images (Fall-Winter 1971); *Films in Review* (Nov. 1978)

Silent: After extra work and some bit parts, handsome Gilbert Roland had his first larger role in 1925's *The Plastic Age*. He received billing in relatively few silents, the most famous being *Camille* (1927) starring Norma Talmadge, his great and good friend.

Among Roland's films were *The Blonde Saint*, *The Campus Flirt*, *The Dove*, again with Talmadge, *The Love Mart* and *Rose of the Golden West*. Last silent: *The Woman Disputed* (1928), also with Talmadge, with synchronized music and sound effects.

Sound: Talkies revealed Gilbert Roland to have a slight but by no means unpleasant accent. His — and again Norma Talmadge's — first sound film, *New York Nights*, came in late 1929. He was kept busy thereafter making Spanish-language versions of Hollywood films.

Roland also had leads in several lesser English-language pictures as well but his career had seemingly stalled by the time he became a featured player in 1937's *Last Train from Madrid*. Although he was rarely top-billed after the mid–'30s, he made almost 100 talkies.

Roland played the Cisco Kid in a Monogram series of 1946–47 and he appeared in several other westerns. Among his films were *Call Her Savage*, with Clara Bow, *She Done Him Wrong*, starring the inimitable Mae West, *Life Begins*, *Ladies Love Danger*, *Rangers of Fortune*, *The Gay Cavalier*, *The Sea Hawk* and *The Other Love*. He was also in the 1944 serial *The Desert Hawk*.

Roland's strong character role in 1949's *We Were Strangers* revived his career again and he was seen in such films of the 1950s as *Bullfighter and the Lady* (top-billed), *The Bad and the Beautiful*, *My Six Convicts*, *Beneath the 12-Mile Reef* and *The French Line*. Later appearances came in *Cheyenne Autumn*, *Islands in the Stream* and several Italian-made westerns. He was also seen much on television.

Comments: In the silents, Gilbert Roland was not particularly stereotyped as a "Latin lover" although he was dark and handsome and certainly could be smolderingly romantic. It was perhaps his status as Norma Talmadge's lover and protégé which kept him from that kind of typecasting.

The talkers proved Roland to have a fine and deep, though slightly "foreign" voice, and his possibilities became somewhat limited. Throughout his career, much of the actor's publicity came from his active love life rather than his acting ability but he never claimed to be a great actor — in fact, quite the reverse.

Roland was, however, undeniably masculine and charismatic. This was a quality that apparently not only Talmadge found exciting but his later wife Constance Bennett as well. He retained his mature good looks well into late middle-age and was thus able to extend his career. He also brought a self-deprecating quality to his later roles and knew how to give creditably understated, even laid-back, performances within his limited range.

REVIEWS

New York Nights: Roland does well in an unpleasant story. *Harrison's Reports* 2/8/30.

Ladies Love Danger: In the part of the playwright/amateur sleuth, Roland is a pleasing choice. *Variety* 9/11/35.

Last Train from Madrid: Roland is the heavy-hero and is good. *Variety* 6/23/37.

Crisis: The film is full of interesting, typical Latin types like Ramon Novarro and Antonio Moreno. Roland is very good. *Variety* 6/21/50.

The Bullfighter and the Lady: A particular standout is Roland who, without overplaying, gives his matador character color and vigor, bravery without bravado, and dignity. *Variety* 5/2/51.

That Lady: Roland looks right for the role of the great lover but he doesn't quite live up to it. *Variety* 3/30/55.

The Christian Licorice Store: Veteran actor Gilbert Roland is charmingly reflective and nostalgic, and because of his own film career, an appropriate representative of old Hollywood. *Variety* 1/21/71.

Roland, Ruth, San Francisco, California, 1892–1937

Filmography: Classic Images (Jan. 1992); List of films in *Eighty Silent Film Stars*; *Sweethearts of the Sage*

Silent: Red-haired Ruth Roland made over 200 one-reel and split-reel films, mostly comedies, for Kalem starting about 1911. In 1915 she appeared in her first serial *Who Pays?* and was thus launched as one of the era's premier serial queens even though she did not do any of her own stunts.

Other popular Roland serials, in which her first name sometimes appeared, included *Hands Up!*, *The Tiger's Trail*, *Ruth of the Range*, *Ruth of the Rockies*, *The Adventures of Ruth* and *The Timber Queen*. Her last, *The Haunted Valley*, was made in 1923.

Among Roland's features during the teens were *The Sultana*, *The Devil's Bait*, *Comrade John* and *Cupid Angling*. She also appeared in the "Girl Detective" series. Her latter features made in the 1920s, *Dollar Down* and *Where the Worst Begins*, were not particularly successful. Last silent: *The Masked Woman* (1927), in which she had a supporting role.

Sound: Roland was to appear in only two talkies. Her acting style did not prove suitable for sound and the pictures were not successful. The first was *Reno* in 1930; the other, done not too long before her death, was the Canadian-made and little-seen *From Nine to Nine*.

Comments: Ruth Roland was a popular star but also a shrewd woman of business. She bought up hundreds of acres of bean fields that were later to become Beverly Hills, an increasingly popular locale for the great stars' homes of the 1920s. It is therefore doubtful that she was too crestfallen at the end of her picture career.

REVIEWS

Reno: Roland's character awakens sympathy, but at times she speaks her lines mechanically. Obviously she finds working in talking pictures vastly different from the way it was in the silent days. She looks remarkably young and does several interpolated songs in a charming parlor contralto. However, her acting is hopelessly old-fashioned. *Harrison's Reports* 10/18/30, *Variety* 11/5/30, *Photoplay*, 1930.

Rubens, Alma (Alma Smith), San Francisco, California, 1897–1931

Silent: Sultry Alma Rubens was in films by 1915 and had her first co-lead in Doug Fairbanks's *The Americano* (1917). She co-starred with him again in *Reggie Mixes In* and *The Mystery of the Leaping Fish*. Her other films included *Humoresque*, *Under the Red Robe*, *Cytherea*, *The World and His Wife*, *The Painted Lily*, *The Gilded Butterfly* and the ironically titled *The Price She Paid*.

Presumably because of her damaging lifestyle, Rubens's output of films dropped after 1925 and she made only a few between 1926 and '28. Last silent: *The Masks of the Devil* (1928), with synchronized music and sound effects, directed by Victor Seastrom (Sjostrom).

Sound: Rubens appeared in only two part-talkies, both in 1929. In *Show Boat* she portrayed the unfortunate Julie, played in the theater by Helen Morgan. *She Goes to War* was her last.

Comments: Alma Rubens made a career out of playing "vamps" and "other women" despite her serene, almost Madonna-like beauty. That beauty, so often admired and commented upon, ultimately was destroyed, as was the woman who possessed it, by drug addiction. Her appearance at the end of her brief life was shockingly changed.

Although there were no doubt many drug-addicted stars, Wallace Reid being a notable example, most of them were kept well-hidden by the studios' public relations machinery. Probably because of her violent behavior, it was not possible to completely conceal Rubens's affliction. Her life and death became a cautionary tale of too much adulation and too much ill-used wealth.

REVIEWS

Show Boat: Rubens has a short role but is good in it. *Variety* 4/24/29, *Harrison's Reports* 4/27/29.

She Goes to War: Probably the best thing in the film is the work of Alma Rubens, the last role she did before her collapse. As Rosie Cohen from Flatbush she does well, even singing a song. *Variety* 6/12/29, *Harrison's Reports* 6/15/29.

Russell, William (William Leach or Lerche), Bronx, New York, 1884/86–1929

Filmography: *Classic Images* (Sept. 1990); List of films in *Eighty Silent Film Stars*

Silent: Rugged action hero William Russell was one of the cinema's earlier leading men, having debuted at Biograph about 1909 or '10. He made almost 140 films, among them *New York Luck*, *Bare Knuckles*, *Times Have Changed*, *The Still Alarm*, *Beloved Brute*, *Colorado Pluck*, *Robin Hood* (1913 version) and *Brass Buttons*. He also appeared in the famed serial *The Diamond from the Sky* and its sequel.

During Russell's career he co-starred with such actresses as Mary Pickford, Blanche Sweet, Lillian Gish and Florence Lawrence. Besides his action melodramas, he was seen in westerns and comedies and he sometimes (especially in latter years) played a villain. Last silent: *Girls Gone Wild* (1929), with synchronized sound effects and music, made after his first talkies.

Sound: Nineteen twenty-eight's *The Midnight Taxi* and *State Street Sadie*, both part-talkies, were the only sound films in which Russell appeared. He continued to play leading roles up to the time of his death.

REVIEWS

State Street Sadie: Usually a hero, Russell is on the wrong side of the law this time. His voice does not register well but his acting is fine and he is an asset to the talkies. Vitaphone actors cannot pronounce the letter "S" well and it is odd when the characters start talking after they acted silently before. The change from one to the other is unsettling to the spectator, destroying the illusion for several seconds. *New York Times* 9/3/28, *Variety* 9/5/28, *Harrison's Reports* 9/15/28.

The Midnight Taxi: Russell is not as good as other cast members when it comes to talking. *Variety* 10/31/28, *Harrison's Reports* 11/3/28.

St. John, Al, Santa Ana, California,
1892/93–1963

Filmography: Classic Images (May-June 1988), additions and corrections (Sept. 1988)

Silent: It is very likely that being Roscoe "Fatty" Arbuckle's nephew provided a boost to Al St. John's career. After a stint in vaudeville, he joined the Keystone Kops and appeared in innumerable Keystone one-reelers before establishing a moderately successful reputation in two-reelers for Paramount, Fox and Educational. Unlike his famous uncle, he was on the skinny side and much of his comedy sprang from his skill as an acrobat and trick bicycle rider.

Although St. John appeared for many years in comedies as a "bumpkin," in mid-'20s two-reelers he changed his image completely to that of a tuxedoed dandy. He also began branching out into features such as *Casey Jones, Hello Cheyenne, The Garden of Weeds* and *American Beauty.* Last silent feature: *Painted Post* (1928).

Sound: Al St. John's sound feature debut came in the 1929 part-talkie *She Goes to War.* This was followed by *The Dance of Life.* Although he worked in sound shorts, the main emphasis of his talkie career was as a sidekick in numerous "B" westerns with such stalwarts as Buster Crabbe, Bob Steele, William "Hoppy" Boyd and Lash LaRue.

Because he had grown a scraggly beard, his character was often named "Fuzzy Q. Jones" and he frequently received billing as Al "Fuzzy" St. John. A few of the westerns revolved about his character and featured the name in the title.

Among St. John's films were *Law of the North, West of Nevada, Gunsmoke Trail, Texas Justice, The Kid Rides Again, Call of the Yukon, Rustler's Hideout, Pioneer Justice* and *My Dog Shep.* His often toothless, and as often witless, persona was seen on-screen up to the end of the quickie western era, his last film possibly being *The Frontier Phantom* (1952).

REVIEWS

She Goes to War: Al St. John is a standout as a comedy doughboy, far overshadowing the male lead. *Variety* 6/12/29.

Hell Harbor: Al St. John sneaked in a couple of giggles with a certain nimbleness. *Variety* 4/9/30.

Border Badmen: Kids will probably go for the too obvious humor inserted by Al St. John.... Acting in the film is so-so, with Buster Crabbe and St. John carrying the bulk of the plot in their usual routine manner. *Variety* 11/21/45.

Gentlemen with Guns: Al St. John's slapstickery dates back to silent films. *Variety* 3/13/46.

Sais, Marin (May Smith?), San Rafael, California, 1888/90–1971

Filmography: List of films in *Sweethearts of the Sage*

Silent: After her debut at Vitagraph in 1909 or '10 Marin Sais became a star and remained one until about 1917. She primarily was known for her many westerns but appeared in various genres, mainly in one- and two-reelers, for Kalem and Biograph. Her films included *The City of Dim Faces, The Barnstormers, The Vanity Pool, His Birthright, The Hellion, Man of Daring, A Son of the Desert* and *Rough and Ready.*

Sais also made the popular series "The Girl from Frisco" and "The American Girl." Among her serials were *Stingaree, The Further Adventures of Stingaree, Thunderbolt Jack, The Social Pirate* and *Deadwood Dick.* Last silent: *Come and Get It* (1929).

Sound: In talkies, Sais grew plump and gray before the cameras. She was seen in small character parts, again mostly in "B" westerns, through the late '40s and probably longer. Her first-known sound film was *The Fighting Cowboy* (1933). Her final one may have been 1953's *The Great Jesse James Raid.*

Others Sais pictures included *Juarez, Oath of Vengeance, Ride, Ryder, Ride, The Fighting Redhead, Along the Navajo Trail* and *Sierra Sue.* Among the oater stars with whom she appeared were Roy Rogers, Gene Autry and Buster Crabbe.

Santschi, Tom (Paul Santschi?), Kokomo,
Indiana or Lucerne, Switzerland,
1876/79–1931

Filmography: Classic Images (Jan.-Feb. 1990); List of films *Eighty Silent Film Stars.*

Silent: Tom Santschi appeared in over 275 silent films starting about 1908, most of them one- and two-reelers for Selig. Among the other studios for which he worked were FBO, First National, Fox, Warner Bros., Universal, Tiffany, RKO, Pathe, Rayart and Metropolitan.

Santschi appeared in numerous features as well but he is best known for one film, and especially one scene in that film: the epochal fight with William Farnum in *The Spoilers* (1914). He also was seen in the seminal serial *The Adventures of Kathlyn.*

Other films in which Santschi played either leads or supporting roles (sometimes as the villain) included *The Hell Cat, Little Orphan Annie, Are You a Failure?, Two Kinds of Women, Frivolous Sal* and *The Third Degree.* Last silent: *The Yellowback* (1929), made after his first talkie.

Sound: In sound films Santschi rarely had leading roles. *Land of the Silver Fox,* a 1928 Rin-Tin-Tin starrer, was his first talkie. Three of his four '29 films were also part-sound or sound: *In Old Arizona*, *The Shannons of Broadway* and *The Wagon Master*.

Santschi was a character player in such other films as *The River's End*, *Paradise Island*, *Ten Nights in a Barroom*, reunited with William Farnum, and *The Utah Kid*. There were also the serials *King of the Wild* and *The Phantom of the West*. His last film was the aptly named and posthumously released *The Last Ride* in 1932.

REVIEWS

Ten Nights in a Barroom: William Farnum and Tom Santschi have another barroom fight, albeit less fiercely than in the old days, in this melodrama. The acting is capable. *Variety* 3/4/31, *Harrison's Reports* 3/14/31.

The Last Ride: The acting is terrible but there is a nice bit by Tom Santschi *Harrison's Reports* 1/30/32, *Variety* 2/16/32.

Schildkraut, Joseph, Vienna, Austria,
1896–1964
Filmography: Films in Review (Feb. 1973)

Silent: The son of distinguished actor Rudolph Schildkraut, Joseph Schildkraut appeared in several German silents, sometimes with his father, from 1908 to 1921. He also frequently performed on the stage before making his American film debut for D. W. Griffith in *Orphans of the Storm* (1921).

In the 1920s and '30s Schildkraut alternated between stage and screen. In the latter medium, his almost 15 silent films included *The Song of Love*, *The Road to Yesterday*, *Meet the Prince*, *Young April*, *His Dog* (a distinct departure for him), *The Heart Thief* and *The King of Kings*, as Judas. Last silent: *Tenth Avenue* (1928).

Sound: The part-talkie *Show Boat* (1929) was Schildkraut's first (as Gaylord Ravenal) but he may not have appeared in the sound portion. His mellifluous, albeit slightly accented, voice was definitely heard in his other film that year, *The Mississippi Gambler*.

The 1930s proved to be Schildkraut's outstanding screen decade. He made some German-language versions of Hollywood films and appeared in a few English pictures. He was seen in prestige vehicles like *Viva Villa!*, *The Crusades*, *Cleopatra*, *Marie Antoinette*, *The Shop Around the Corner* and *Idiot's Delight*. He appeared in at least one short, 1941's *The Tell-Tale Heart* (as the tormented murderer).

For his portrayal of the wronged Alfred Dreyfus in *The Life of Emile Zola*, Schildkraut garnered an Academy Award for Best Supporting Actor of 1937.

In the late 1930s and '40s he found himself increasingly cast as a sneering villain (*Monsieur Beaucaire*, *The Man in the Iron Mask*, *The Lady of the Tropics*).

Schildkraut's career can be said to have reached bottom after he signed with Republic in the '40s and was put into a series of westerns, some with Wild Bill Elliott, including *Old Los Angeles*. He had one or two well-received roles in that decade, Republic's 1945 *The Cheaters*, being one.

After a hiatus from the screen that had lasted almost ten years after 1948, Schildkraut returned with acclaim to recreate his notable stage role as Otto Frank in *The Diary of Anne Frank*. His last screen appearance was in 1965's *The Greatest Story Ever Told* (released after his death). He also had a television series and was much seen on early live television as well as later series.

Comments: Joseph Schildkraut was certainly handsome enough for romantic leads but his type of looks, accent and Continental suavity also made him a convincing heel. With few exceptions Hollywood did not really know what to do with him. The gamblers and other smooth bad guys he portrayed generally wasted his talents. He perhaps was seen to better advantage on the stage.

In Molnár's popular theater success *Liliom*, Schildkraut, playing a morally ambiguous character, gave a signature performance. His last stage role, in *The Diary of Anne Frank*, may have been his best. With his dashing handsomeness largely faded and his head shaved to better resemble the real-life Otto Frank, he played a role somewhat akin to his screen Dreyfus: a man horribly trapped in a circumstance he could never hope to comprehend.

REVIEWS

The Mississippi Gambler: The looks of the romantic pair, Schildkraut and Joan Bennett, place appearance above the rest of the film. The acting is very good except when Schildkraut overdoes being conceited. *Variety* 10/30/29.

Night Ride: Reviews differed. One thought that Schildkraut was too often theatrical in the more dramatic scenes but later on in the film his acting assumed a more realistic flavor. Another review stated that as the hero he did some powerful acting. *Variety* 1/22/30, *Harrison's Reports* 1/25/30.

The Life of Emile Zola: Schildkraut makes a deep impression. *Variety* 6/30/37.

Lancer Spy: Schildkraut impersonates a German martinet with good comedy resulting. *Variety* 10/6/37.

Phantom Raiders: Schildkraut is capable as the heavy. *Variety* 5/29/40.

The Cheaters: The top-billed Schildkraut gives

one of the best performances of his career, displaying artistry and a tongue-in-cheek humor throughout. *Variety* 7/4/45.

Northwest Outpost: Schildkraut looks too well got up for a convict but he handles the role satisfactorily. *Variety* 5/14/47.

The Diary of Anne Frank: Joseph Schildkraut repeats his marvelous stage performance, bringing dignity and wisdom to the role. In his restrained way he is a tower of strength and there is not a false note in his performance, only warm beauty and understanding.

(To Schildkraut went the well-known final line "She puts me to shame," after he had found Anne's diary with its determined optimism in the face of disaster.) *Variety* 3/18/59.

Sebastian, Dorothy, Birmingham, Alabama, 1903/06–1957

Silent: After her debut in 1924's *Sackcloth and Scarlet,* Dorothy Sebastian eventually became a popular second lead and minor leading lady at MGM. She superficially resembled the up-and-coming Joan Crawford, but lacked her determination, a fact which ultimately may have hurt her career.

Sebastian's films included *Bluebeard's Seven Wives, Twelve Miles Out, Isle of Forgotten Women, Our Dancing Daughters, Their Hour* and *Spite Marriage.* Of her eight 1929 films, six were silents. Last silent: *The Single Standard* (1929), with synchronized music and sound effects.

Sound: Sebastian's two 1929 talkies were *The Unholy Night,* her first, and *His Last Command,* in which she co-starred with her husband-to-be William Boyd. She made eight films in 1930 but after she was released by MGM her career declined sharply. The pictures she made later had her mainly in supporting or bit roles (e.g., "Woman in cafe" in *Among the Living*).

Sebastian was on-screen until at least 1942, including some further appearances with Boyd. Her films included *Ladies Must Pay, Montana Moon, Brothers, The Big Gamble, The Ship of Wanted Men, The Life of Vergie Winters, Rough Riders Roundup* and *Reap the Wild Wind,* possibly her last. She also appeared in some comedy shorts and she was seen in *The Mysterious Pilot,* a 1937 serial.

REVIEWS

His First Command: Reviewers differed. One said that while Sebastian was usually a competent performer she appeared to be uninterested in the proceedings. Another thought that as the heroine she did very good work. *New York Times* 12/23/29, *Harrison's Reports* 12/28/29.

The Lightning Flyer: Sebastian is overshadowed by the male lead James Hall. *Variety* 4/8/31.

Ship of Wanted Men: Although her acting is good, Sebastian should have complained about the cameraman. She doesn't get photographed well and she needs good lighting. *Variety* 11/21/33.

The Arizona Kid: A satisfactory performance is given by Dorothy Sebastian, a featured player of the silents. *Variety* 10/11/39.

Shearer, Norma (Edith N. Shearer), Montreal, Canada, 1900/04–1983

Filmography: Films in Review: (Aug.-Sept. 1960)
Silent: The winning of a beauty contest, modeling, and song plugging in a music store ultimately led Norma Shearer to extra work at Universal. She had her first significant role in 1920's *The Stealers* and also could be glimpsed in that year's D. W. Griffith production *Way Down East. Channing of the Northwest* (1922) provided her with her first lead.

Much of Shearer's silent and later career was fostered by her husband-to-be Irving Thalberg, a rising young executive in motion pictures and soon to be a major power at MGM as head of production. She was cast in a series of programmers with an occasional better film like *He Who Gets Slapped* (1924).

Among Shearer's 30 or so credited silent films were *The Wanters, Trail of the Law, Excuse Me, His Secretary, The Waning Sex, The Student Prince in Old Heidelberg, The Tower of Lies* and *Waking Up the Town.* Last silent: *The Actress* (1928).

Sound: The part-talkie *A Lady of Chance* (1928) was Shearer's first. All her 1929 films were sound, including her very successful first all-talkie *The Trial of Mary Dugan.* Others that year were *Their Own Desire* and *The Last of Mrs. Cheyney.* Foreshadowing her later role in *Romeo and Juliet* she played a truncated balcony scene in slang(!), with John Gilbert, in a color segment of *The Hollywood Revue of 1929.*

Shearer appeared in about 20 sound films, for one of which, 1930's *The Divorcee,* she won an Academy Award. From the mid–'30s her output dropped considerably; she made eight pictures in as many years. Her films were among MGM's most prestigious (and sometimes most pretentious), if not their most successful.

Private Lives contained one of Shearer's better roles. Other pictures included *Strange Interlude, The Barretts of Wimpole Street, Romeo and Juliet* and the title role in *Marie Antoinette.* She was Oscar-nominated for the latter three, as well as for the earlier *A Free Soul,* for which Lionel Barrymore won an Oscar.

One reason for Shearer's screen inactivity was Thalberg's early death. She seemed to have lost her zest for acting — or perhaps, with her protector gone, MGM lost its zest for *her*. Her performances in her last films were a mixture of good (*The Women*), mediocre (*Escape, Idiot's Delight*) and poor (*Her Cardboard Lover, We Were Dancing*), the final two in 1942.

Comments: As the story goes, at some point early in Norma Shearer's career Irving Thalberg saw her in a film. He became enamored of her screen image and was determined to promote her career. Whether this is literally true or not, he certainly became enamored of more than her screen image and did promote and ultimately marry her.

As filmtown wags so wittily put it, speaking about such moguls as Carl Laemmle, Jr., and David O. Selznick: "The son (or son-in-law) also rises." In this case, the wife also rose. While other MGM actresses like Joan Crawford and Marion Davies fumed, Shearer usually got the roles they thought they should have had. Some were indeed beyond her range, although in fairness they were perhaps also beyond the other actresses' range as well.

MGM immodestly touted Norma Shearer as "The First Lady of the Screen" but during the silent days she was not considered a particularly good actress. She was strikingly pretty, however, and her acting did gradually improve, although she never did become the actress her fame indicated she was. From the standpoint of diction, her voice proved to be fine, but on occasion it could be unpleasantly shrill in the higher register.

If Shearer never got to the point of really being up to such roles as Elizabeth Browning and fair Juliet, for which she was much too old, she at least gave them a respectable try. It somewhat cruelly, and perhaps unfairly, was said that everyone could steal scenes from her, even the spaniel in *The Barretts of Wimpole Street*.

Shearer began as a standard heroine but later switched to sophisticated roles in which her hairstyle and Adrian-designed clothes were commented on as often as her performances. From the latter 1920s to the mid–'30s her characters generally were women who flouted convention and often paid a heavy price for it.

When Shearer switched from those kinds of roles to the over-produced so-called "prestige" pictures, her career also paid a heavy price. When she played an "ordinary" woman she was still capable of contributing a worthwhile performance, as in *The Women*. In it she succeeded in making a basically good woman also an interesting one.

Shearer's reputation has not endured through the years well. When she retired, she dropped out of the public eye and did so with grace. Not for her was the relentless pursuit of a place in cinema history. She was neither as good as her publicity nor as bad as her detractors claimed. She was, simply, a star whose day came and went.

REVIEWS

The Trial of Mary Dugan: Audience comment was heavily in favor of Shearer. She doesn't look as well as usual but considering that it's her first time at the microphone her performance is highly creditable. It proves that she is a first rate actress. Her voice registers well and her ability to express emotion is great. *Variety* 4/3/29, *Harrison's Reports* 4/20/29.

The Divorcee: Shearer has captured much of the spirit of the heroine but has been restricted in her interpretation of the part because of censorship. She is charming and does excellent work. *Variety* 5/14/30, *Harrison's Reports* 5/17/30.

Strangers May Kiss: Shearer is back with a sweet film and gives an unusual performance. *Variety* 4/15/31.

Strange Interlude: Reviews varied. One said the picture would not improve the standings of its stars, Shearer and Clark Gable, and that she gave a vacillating characterization. Another thought she rose to new dramatic heights and was not only convincing but actually superb. *Variety* 9/6/32, *Harrison's Reports* 9/10/32.

The Barretts of Wimpole Street: Shearer is sincerely compelling in her role. *Variety* 10/2/34.

Marie Antoinette: In the title role Shearer gives a superb interpretation after a two-year hiatus. In every respect she shows progress as an artist and reveals capabilities hitherto unknown. *Variety* 7/13/38.

The Women: Shearer delivers a sparkling performance and performs in some poignant scenes. *Variety* 9/6/39.

We Were Dancing: In what is virtually a comeback for Norma Shearer (who hasn't appeared in a film for well over a year), it is instead a sad shambles. *Variety* 1/21/42.

Sherman, Lowell, San Francisco, California, 1885–1934

Filmography: Focus on Film (Winter 1975/76)
Silent: Lowell Sherman had been in the theater from the time he was a child when he made his film debut about 1914. He continued to intersperse stage appearances with those in such films as *The Better Woman, The New York Idea, Yes or No, The Divine Woman, The Spitfire, Molly O', Monsieur Beaucaire* and, most famous, *Way Down East* (1920).

During the teens, Sherman appeared sporadically and from 1916 to '19 apparently made only a single film. But he was active during most years of the 1920s in his patented persona as a gigolo. In 1928 alone he made eight films. Last silent: *The Whip* (1928), with synchronized sound effects and music.

Sound: The 1928 part-talkie *A Lady of Chance* was Lowell Sherman's first. His initial all-sound effort was apparently a short called *Phipps* (1929); the first sound feature was *Evidence* that same year. Other films included *General Crack, Mammy, Ladies of Leisure, The Payoff, High Stakes* and the George Cukor classic *What Price Hollywood?*, in which he portrayed the washed-up, alcoholic director.

During the last few years of his life, Sherman became a respected director with such credits as *Morning Glory* (Katharine Hepburn's Oscar-winning performance), *She Done Him Wrong* with Mae West and *Broadway Thru a Keyhole*. His acting career ended in 1932 with *False Faces*, but he continued directing. His last film *Night Life of the Gods* was released posthumously in 1935.

Comments: In silents, Lowell Sherman became expert at portraying what then passed for sophisticated lechery. His sharp-featured face, sometimes heavily made up, and his flowery (unheard) words apparently could drive innocent heroines into fearful indiscretions. (Lillian Gish in *Way Down East* was a prime victim.) His performances could be mannered, flamboyant and even hammy but they usually had a saving tongue-in-cheek quality.

In the sound era, Sherman's lechery was transmogrified into a more benign charm which was usually filtered through his characters' alcoholic hazes. His voice was fine and he certainly was becoming one of the more interesting actors of early talkies when directing took his fancy. At the time of his death, he had the potential of becoming a top director of comedy.

REVIEWS

Evidence: An outstanding bit is provided by Lowell Sherman who gives a splendid performance as the villain. *Variety* 10/9/29, *Harrison's Reports* 10/12/29.

Ladies of Leisure: Sherman is not a very vicious villain but is presented as a roué. The Frank Capra film is vastly aided by his playing in one of those parts for which he seems to be made. *Harrison's Reports* 4/19/30, *Variety* 5/28/30.

Bachelor Apartment: It is a shame that Lowell Sherman is not a great drawing card in pictures because his work entitles him to be one. His acting makes one laugh heartily now and then, and he has developed into a first-class director. *Harrison's Reports* 3/21/31, *Variety* 5/20/31.

What Price Hollywood?: An excellent performance is given by Lowell Sherman as the director. *Harrison's Reports* 6/15/32, *Variety* 7/19/32.

False Faces: As usual Lowell Sherman is the whole show and he gives an excellent performance. The picture is less of a picture than a monologue for him. *Harrison's Reports* 11/12/32, *Variety* 11/29/32.

Short, Antrim, Cincinnati, Ohio, 1900–1972

Silent: The major part of Antrim Short's career occurred when he was a teenager and he appeared in many films from 1914 through '20. His roles were generally supporting ones, although he had an occasional second lead, in films like *The Gambler of the West, Amarilly of Clothes-Line Alley* (with Mary Pickford), *The Flirt, Tom Sawyer* (1917 version), *Huck and Tom, Romance and Arabella, The Yellow Dog* and *Old Lady 31*.

Once into adulthood, Short had supporting roles in a relatively few 1920s films. They included *O'Malley of the Mounted, Beauty's Worth, Classmates, The Pinch Hitter* and *Married?*. Last silent: *Jack o' Hearts* (1926).

Sound: From 1934 to '37 Antrim Short played bits in a large number of films, and at least one short including *The Big Shakedown, College Scandal, The Big Show, The Case Against Mrs. Ames, Artists and Models, The Devil Is Driving* and *Rose Bowl*. When his on-camera career ended, he became a casting director at Goldwyn, Republic and Universal.

Sidney, George (Samuel Greenfield), Hungary or New York, New York, 1876/77–1945

Silent: After lengthy stage and vaudeville experience, rotund George Sidney entered films in 1924's *In Hollywood with Potash and Perlmutter*. Jewish-stereotype humor was his specialty so he tended to be cast in such roles in films like *Clancy's Kosher Wedding* and especially in the "Cohens and Kellys" series that usually co-starred Irish comedian Charlie Murray.

On the stage, Sidney had created the character of "Busy Izzy," which he repeated in several shows. Among his films, in which he was often top-billed, were *Millionaires, For the Love of Mike, The Cohens and the Kellys in Paris* (with J. Farrell MacDonald as Kelly), *The Auctioneer, Sweet Daddies* and *The Latest from Paris*. Last silent: *We Americans* (1928).

Sound: Sidney's ersatz Jewish inflection was first heard in 1928's *Give and Take*, a part-talkie. His next part-talkie and only 1929 feature was *The Cohens and Kellys in Atlantic City*, with Mack Swain playing Kelly for the only time. That year he made the Vitaphone short *Cohen on the Telephone* and may have appeared in others as well.

Two of Sidney's four 1930 features also showcased

the Cohens and Kellys (...*in Scotland* and ...*in Africa*), with Charlie Murray returning as Kelly. By now he and Murray were considered part of a comedy team. His other starring appearance that year was again with the Irish comedian in *Around the Corner*, as was the subsequent *Caught Cheating*.

In 1930 and '31 Sidney and Murray made a series of shorts, e.g., *Discontented*, *All Excited* and *Divorce à la Carte*. They also completed the last two renditions of the "Cohens and Kellys" saga which took place ...*in Hollywood* (1932) and ...*in Trouble* (1933), an apt title for a tired series.

The diminutive comedian's career was also in trouble. Audiences of the '30s were not too receptive to Sidney's stock-and-trade Jewish humor and he made only a few more films after the series ended. His final films *Manhattan Melodrama*, *Diamond Jim* and *The Good Old Soak* saw him in supporting roles. The last one in 1937 cast him, ironically, as an Irish character. There were some later shorts as well. His namesake nephew became a prominent Hollywood director.

Reviews

Give and Take: Sidney impersonates a German and his voice registers very well as does his performance. Unfortunately, wisecracks as old as the pyramids are given to him to recite. *Harrison's Reports* 1/5/29, *Variety* 1/9/29.

The Cohens and Kellys in Atlantic City: Jewish-Irish hokum as low-grade as this can hardly mean much but George Sidney handles most of the talk very ably. *Variety* 3/20/29.

The Cohens and Kellys in Hollywood: Sidney causes a laugh or two with his portrait of a fish out of water. *New York Times* 4/22/32.

The Cohens and Kellys in Trouble: Sidney is more natural here than in many of the previous episodes. He doesn't try to force the humor. *Variety* 4/18/33.

Sills, Milton, Chicago, Illinois, 1882–1930

Filmography: Films in Review (Dec. 1971-Jan. 1972); List of films in *Eighty Silent Film Stars*

Silent: Stage actor Milton Sills made his maiden film *The Pit* in 1914. He soon became a most popular leading man in numerous films like *The Isle of Lost Ships*, *The Honor System*, *Satan Jr.*, *Behold My Wife*, *The Eyes of Youth*, *The Spoilers* (1923 version) and *The Unguarded Hour*.

Among Sills's better-known pictures were *Adam's Rib*, *Miss Lulu Bett* and *The Sea Hawk*. He also appeared in the serial *Patria*. Last silent: *Love and the Devil* (1929), with synchronized music and sound effects, made after his first part-talkie.

Sound: Sills made a smashing sound debut with the very successful part-talkie *The Barker* in 1928.

This was followed by the part-sound *His Captive Woman*; *Man Trouble* was his first fully sound feature in 1930. His final film and a major success was 1930's *The Sea Wolf*, in which he essayed the villainous Wolf Larsen.

Comments: Nearing 50, Milton Sills departed at the top but he probably could not have sustained leading man status very much longer. It is likely, though, that he could have found a continuing career in major character roles. This is the route such contemporaries as George Bancroft took with some success. He was a charismatic performer with a fine voice and would have made a convincing man of the law or even a gangster.

Reviews

The Barker: Sills dominates the film by his acting. All voices record well; he has no worries with sound. *Variety* 12/12/28, *Harrison's Reports* 12/15/28.

His Captive Woman: As the hero, Sills talks well enough, even with a Tenth Avenue brogue. He did look a little peaked. *Variety* 4/10/29, *Harrison's Reports* 4/20/29.

Man Trouble: Sills does good work. His voice registers well and he has the face for the role. *Harrison's Reports* 8/2/30, *Variety* 9/10/30.

The Sea Wolf: It is too bad that Milton Sills died after doing the best acting of his career. His performance stands out. He succeeded in making Wolf Larsen's part, despicable as it is, somewhat sympathetic. It is a most fitting climax to his career and one of his best he-man characterizations. He dominates every scene. *Harrison's Reports* 9/20/30, *Variety* 10/1/30.

Sleeper, Martha, Lake Bluff, Illinois, 1907/11–1983

Silent: As a young girl, Martha Sleeper had a role in the melodrama *The Mailman* (1923). She may also have appeared in some two-reelers before her spate of co-starring 1928 features, among them *Danger Street*, *Skinner's Big Idea* and *Taxi 13*. Last silents: *The Voice of the Storm* and *The Air Legion*, released about the same time in 1929.

Sound: Sleeper's first talkies came in 1930 with *Madam Satan*, *Our Blushing Brides* and *War Nurse*. In all of these she was well down in the cast list as she was to be in most of her sound efforts. When she did have leads it was generally for lesser outfits such as Monogram and Republic in films like *Two Sinners*, *Tomorrow's Youth* and *Great God Gold*.

In 1934 Sleeper discovered her true acting future: the Broadway theater. For the next ten years or so she appeared in a series of plays which established her as a fine stage actress. She did make a full slate of films in 1935 but only two the rest of the decade,

Rhythm on the Range (1936) and *Four Days' Wonder* (1937).

Among Sleeper's other motion pictures were *Confessions of a Coed, Ten Cents a Dance, Penthouse, West of the Pecos* and *Spitfire.* She returned in 1945 for a supporting role in *The Bells of St. Mary's* and soon thereafter left acting entirely.

REVIEWS

War Nurse: Sleeper is convincing in a brief scene. *Variety* 10/29/30.

Huddle: Sleeper has been given more footage than previously by MGM and she does well by it as an on-the-make young woman. *Variety* 6/21/32.

Great God Gold: First place for acting honors from the female end of the supporting cast goes to Martha Sleeper. *Variety* 5/8/35.

Two Sinners: The cast headed by Martha Sleeper is thoroughly capable. *Variety* 9/18/35.

Four Days Wonder: Sleeper renders nice support. *Variety* 12/23/36.

The Bells of St. Mary's: Martha Sleeper gives an adequate performance. *New York Times* 12/7/45.

Sojin, Kamiyama (billed as Sojin or So-Jin), Sendai, Japan, 1871–1954

Silent: A veteran of the Japanese theater, Sojin is perhaps best remembered for his first American role as the Mongol Emperor in Douglas Fairbanks's *The Thief of Bagdad* (1924). He went on to appear in numerous silents, most often as a villain, and also was the earliest celluloid Charlie Chan, having played that eminent detective in 1927's *The Chinese Parrot.*

Occasionally Sojin had a major role and, rarely, even received top billing. Among his numerous pictures were *Proud Flesh, Eve's Leaves, The King of Kings* (as a Prince of Persia), *Streets of Shanghai, Chinatown Charlie, Foreign Devils, China Slaver* (top-billed) and *The Lady of the Harem.* Last silent: *Back from Shanghai* (1929), made after his first part-talkie.

Sound: Sojin made his talkie debut in the part-talking melodrama *Seven Footprints to Satan* (1929). That year he had a walk-on in the all-singing, all-talking, all-dancing *The Show of Shows* and had roles in *The Unholy Night* and *Painted Faces* as well. All of them were small.

Kamiyama Sojin's American career did not long outlast the silents; his final film was the 1930 operetta *Golden Dawn* in which he had a minor role. He thereupon returned to play in Japanese films.

Comments: Kamiyama Sojin (nicknamed "Sloe Gin" by Hollywood wags) was mostly used as an all-purpose "exotic," serving as general back-ground color and often as a red herring in mysteries. He also played elderly Chinese men and mystics when not being hissably evil.

His appearance certainly enabled Sojin to portray screen villainy with panache. He was excruciatingly thin, had high cheekbones, and often sported a sparse droopy mustache. He also may have been, or was made up to be, somewhat snaggletoothed. His U.S. career was ended by his accent and the lack of interest in real Asian actors, as opposed to Americans or other nationalities who impersonated "Orientals."

REVIEWS

The Unholy Night: Sojin's melancholy tones are heard for the first time from the screen in a bit part as a medium. *New York Times* 10/12/29, *Variety* 10/16/29.

Southern, Eve, Texas, 1898–

Silent: Eve Southern had small roles in at least two films of the late teens (*Conscience* and *Broadway Love*) before appearing in about 20 films of the 1920s, mainly in support. She did have some leads later in the decade. Her most important picture was probably Douglas Fairbanks's *The Gaucho* (1927), although she was again in a secondary role.

Some other Southern films were *The Rage of Paris, Souls for Sale, The Dangerous Blonde, Morals for Women, Resurrection, Clothes Make the Woman* and *A Woman of the Sea*, a 1926 film made by Charles Chaplin to showcase Edna Purviance, but not released. Last silent: *The Haunted House* (1928), with synchronized sound effects and music.

Sound: Southern appeared in two 1929 part-talkies, *The Voice Within* and *Whispering Winds.* In the former film she was top-billed for the last time. Her other 1930s appearances were few; among them were *Morocco, Lilies of the Field, Fighting Caravans, Law of the Sea* and *The Ghost Walks.* Nineteen thirty-six's *The King Steps Out*, in which she played a gypsy fortuneteller, was perhaps her last but there also may have been some unbilled appearances.

REVIEWS

Whispering Winds: Eve Southern is beautiful as the other woman. If it is her voice singing the theme song she rates praise but she should lay off acting. She's too pretty to be a flop at that. *Harrison's Reports* 9/18/29, *Variety* 10/2/29.

The Law of the Sea: Southern is scarcely more successful than the leading lady with a good-bad girl part. *Variety* 5/3/32, *Harrison's Reports* 5/7/32.

Starke, Pauline (Pauline Stark?), Joplin, Missouri, 1900/01–1977

Silent: After extra work in 1916's *Intolerance* and other films, wide-eyed beauty and Wampas Baby Star Pauline Starke began playing supporting roles and leads in almost 50 silent films such as *Until They Get Me*, *Irish Eyes*, *Alias Mary Brown* and *The Eyes of Youth*. Her best known was probably 1921's *A Connecticut Yankee in King Arthur's Court*. She was subbed the "Sad-Glad Girl" for her weepy roles.

Starke's other pictures, most of which were run-of-the-mill dramas, included *Soldiers of Fortune*, *The Little Shepherd of Kingdom Come* (1920 version), *Eyes of the Forest*, *Sun-Up*, *The Man Without a Country* and *War Paint*. Last silent: *The Viking* (1929), in color with synchronized sound effects and music.

Sound: Starke made only the merest handful of talkies, the first being *A Royal Romance* in 1930. She had apparently been set to play the lead opposite Erich von Stroheim in 1929's *The Great Gabbo* but was replaced by Betty Compson to the undoubted detriment of her career.

The only other Starke films were *What Men Want* (1930) and *$20 a Week*, her last in 1935. *Missing Daughters*, a 1933 film, was actually a re-release by a Poverty Row studio of a 1924 silent with added talking sequences, music and sound effects.

Stedman, Myrtle (also Steadman), Chicago, Illinois, 1885/89–1938

Filmography: Classic Images (July–Aug. 1984); List of films in *Sweethearts of the Sage*

Silent: A veteran of Selig one-reelers, including westerns, from 1911 (*When Women Rule*, *The Opium Smugglers*, *Roped In*), blonde Myrtle Stedman entered features in *The Sea Wolf* (1913). She also co-starred with Hobart Bosworth in other Jack London stories such as *The Valley of the Moon* and *Martin Eden*. Another 'teens leading man was Sessue Hayakawa in *The Soul of Kura-San*.

In the 'teens and very early '20s Stedman occasionally had starring roles in films like *The Wild Olive*, *The Silver Horde* and *The American Beauty*, but most often she played supporting parts. Earlier features included *The Caprices of Kitty*, *Jane*, *As Men Love*, *The Call of the Cumberlands* and *In the Hollow of Her Hand*.

Almost entirely a supporting actress for most of the 1920s, Stedman was seen in *Sex*, *Reckless Youth*, *Lilies of the Field*, *Flaming Youth*, *Sally*, *The Life of Riley* and *Alias the Deacon*. Last silent: *The Sin Sister* (1929).

Sound: The 1929 picture *The Jazz Age*, a part-talker, was Stedman's entree into sound. Although she remained before the cameras until the year of her death, her output of films declined as did the size of her parts. Among her early talkies were *Lummox*, *The Wheel of Life*, *The Love Racket* and *The Truth About Youth*.

Others of Stedman's motion pictures were *Widow in Scarlet*, *School for Girls*, *Song of the Saddle* and *Green Light* (billed last in the credits as "A Nurse"). Among her very last were *The Life of Emile Zola*, *Hollywood Hotel* and *A Slight Case of Murder*. Although she appeared in many films in 1937 and '38, her appearances in most of them were little more than uncredited bits.

REVIEWS

Lummox: Myrtle Stedman will be remembered from years ago for her fine performance as "The Famous Mrs. Fair." She does well in a minor role. *New York Times* 3/24/30.

Steele, Bob (Robert Bradbury, Jr.), Pendleton, Oregon, 1906/07–1988

Silent: Bob Steele appeared in vaudeville as a child and with his brother made a series of "Bill and Bob" adventure shorts for Pathe in 1921 and '22. Their father Robert Bradbury, Sr., was the director.

Later Steele also had roles in features such as *The College Boob*, *Sitting Bull at the Spirit Lake Massacre*, *Come and Get It*, *The Amazing Vagabond* and *Davy Crockett at the Fall of the Alamo*.

In 1927 Steele began a series of starring western films for FBO and Syndicate. Among them were *The Bandit's Son*, *Driftin' Sands*, *Headin' for Danger*, *The Trail of Courage* and *A Texas Cowboy*. Last silent: *The Oklahoma Sheriff* (1930), made after his first talkie.

Sound: Near the Rainbow's End marked Steele's sound bow in 1930. Once established in talkies, he made numerous westerns for many studios including Amity/Tiffany-Stahl, Monogram, Republic, PRC, Metropolitan, Sono-Art/World Wide, Supreme and Republic. In 1937–38 he was among the top ten western stars.

Steele's oaters included *Riders of the Desert*, *Man from Hell's Edges*, *Border Phantom*, *Tombstone Terror*, *Powdersmoke Range*, *Death Valley Rangers* and *Northwest Trail*. He was part of the "Trail Blazers" and "Three Mesquiteers" series for a while and also was the hero of the serial *Mystery Squadron* in the early '30s.

Steele's final starring films came in the mid–1940s and he made the transition to character actor that he had begun in 1939 with *Of Mice and Men*. He made a convincing villain in that film as the jealous rancher whose wife is killed by the retarded Lenny (Lon Chaney, Jr.). He also shone as a gunsel in *The Big Sleep* (1946) and appeared in such motion pictures as *Killer McCoy*, *The Steel Jungle*, *Revenge of the Zombies*, *South of St. Louis* and *The Enforcer*.

From 1965–67 Steele revealed his comic side as Trooper Duffy in the popular television western-comedy series *F Troop*; in 1966 *The Hollywood Reporter* erroneously printed (and one day later retracted) his obituary. He made several other television appearances and also continued to play small roles in films like *The Skin Game* and *Something Big*. His last was 1973's *Charley Varrick*.

Comments: Despite, or perhaps because of, his small stature, Bob Steele's pictures were full of hard fighting and non-stop action. He had a fine deep voice for talkies and though he never attained the fame of some western stars, his multitude of "B" films never let his young audiences down.

As Steele aged, his face hardened in a way that enabled him to play villainous roles quite believably. Interestingly, as he aged even *more* his face again softened into a more kindly aspect that allowed him to portray likable old men. His role as the garrulous and boastful cavalry trooper in *F Troop* brought him a new measure of visibility.

REVIEWS

Border Phantom: Steele displays his usual good form. *Variety* 2/7/37.

The Red Rope: Steele is the cowboy hero. He shines most in action scenes but dialogue does not help much because he is not that good with it. *Variety* 7/21/37.

Killer McCoy: Steele stands out as a fighter. *Variety* 10/29/47.

Sterling, Ford (George Stitch), LaCrosse, Wisconsin, 1880/83–1939

Silent: Ford Sterling found fame playing the befuddled chief of the Keystone Kops for Mack Sennett. Before he joined the studio in 1911, he had been a circus, vaudeville and stage performer. He appeared mostly in one- and two-reelers during the 'teens in support of, among others, Charlie Chaplin, Mabel Normand and Fatty Arbuckle.

A Sterling feature of the 'teens was *Yankee Doodle in Berlin*. In the '20s his full-length films included comedies and dramas such as *The Stranger's Banquet*, *The Destroying Angel*, *So Big*, *He Who Gets Slapped*, *The Show Off*, *Casey at the Bat* and *Gentlemen Prefer Blondes*. Last silent: *Oh, Kay!* (1928).

Sound: All of Sterling's 1929 films were talkies: *The Fall of Eve*, *The Girl in the Show* and *Sally*. His 1930 films were musicals which included *Bride of the Regiment*, *Kismet* and *Spring Is Here*. After that year he was in only a few more pictures through 1935, among them *Alice in Wonderland*, *Her Majesty Love*, *Behind Green Lights*, *Black Sheep* and *The Headline Woman*. After he lost a leg he was forced to end his career.

REVIEWS

The Fall of Eve: Ford Sterling makes his debut with a good voice, doing far better in this than he has in most of his latter-day silent parts. Whether there is any color to his tones is a matter of opinion but he succeeds in talking as if he meant what he was saying. He does excellent work. *New York Times* 6/18/29, *Variety* 6/19/29, *Harrison's Reports* 6/22/29.

Sally: Sterling is the outstanding comedy performer as a restaurant owner. *Variety* 12/19/29, *New York Times* 12/24/29.

Spring Is Here: Considerable comedy is provoked by Ford Sterling, who plays the heroine's irate father. *Harrison's Reports* 5/10/30.

The Bride of the Regiment: Sterling, as a posing Count, performs his comedy assignment exceedingly well. *Variety* 5/28/30, *Harrison's Reports* 5/31/30.

Her Majesty Love: Sterling does yeoman service in a low comedy stooge part. *Variety* 12/1/31.

Stevens, Charles, Solomonsville or Solomansville, Arizona, 1893–1964

Silent: Charles Stevens was a Native American and one of Douglas Fairbanks's favorite villains. Supposedly a grandson of Chief Geronimo, he specialized in Indian, Mexican and other "exotic" roles during a lengthy career. In films from about 1914, during the 'teens he appeared with Fairbanks in *The Man from Painted Post* and *Wild and Woolly*. Another of his early features was *Six Shooter Andy* with Tom Mix.

In the '20s Stevens was in just about every film that Fairbanks made, including *The Mollycoddle*, *The Mark of Zorro*, *The Three Musketeers*, *The Thief of Bagdad*, *Don Q, Son of Zorro* and *The Black Pirate*. Among his other pictures were *Captain Fly-By-Night*, *Where the North Begins*, *The King of Kings*, *The Vanishing American*, *Recompense* and *Mantrap*. Last silent: *Diamond Handcuffs* (1928).

Sound: Stevens continued to play an assortment of "native" types well into the sound era. His 1929 talkies were *The Mysterious Dr. Fu Manchu* and *The Virginian*; he also appeared in Fairbanks's *The Iron Mask* which had brief talking sequences. His 1930s films were a mixture of the major and minor and included *The Cisco Kid*, *Viva Villa!*, *Chandu the Magician*, *The Lives of a Bengal Lancer* and *The Renegade Ranger*.

Still active in the 1940s, Stevens was seen increasingly in "B" westerns but was also in the remakes of *The Mark of Zorro* and *Blood and Sand* as well as *My Darling Clementine*. In the following decade he appeared in fewer pictures, many of them quickie westerns, including those of Gene Autry. Besides the remake of *The Vanishing American*, he was seen in *Indian Territory*, *Escape from Fort Bravo*, *Ride, Vaquero* and *Last Train from Gun Hill*, among others.

Stevens also made serials in the '30s and '40s such as *Red Barry*, *Winners of the West*, *Flaming Frontiers* and *Overland Mail*. He remained sporadically before the cameras through the 1950s; his last film may have been 1962's *The Outsider*.

Stewart, Roy, San Diego, California, 1884/89–1933

Filmography: Partial filmography *Classic Images* (Fall 1977)

Silent: Burly Roy Stewart made his film bow about 1913 with American and later appeared for Hal Roach, Majestic and Masterpiece studios before signing with Triangle. There he became a western star but also worked in other genres.

Among Stewart's co-stars were Mary Pickford and Lillian Gish. His films included *The Sagebrusher*, *The Lone Hand*, *Wolves of the Border*, *Prisoners of Love*, *Her Social Value*, *Sparrows*, *Life's Greatest Question* and *Trimmed in Scarlet*. In 1925–26 he made some independent historical dramas which included *Kit Carson Over the Great Divide* and *Buffalo Bill on the U. P. Trail*.

Stewart also appeared in the serials *The Diamond from the Sky*, *Liberty, a Daughter of the USA* and *The Radio King*. Toward the end of the '20s he began being cast in supporting roles. Last silent: *The Viking* (1929) in color, with synchronized music and sound effects.

Sound: All of Stewart's 1929 films were silent except for *In Old Arizona*, in which he was way down the cast list. He continued working in small parts to the time of his death. Among his films were *The Lone Star Ranger*, *Fighting Caravans*, *Exposed*, *Mystery Ranch*, *King Kong* and his last, *Zoo in Budapest* (1933).

Stone, Fred, Denver or Valmont, Colorado, 1873–1959

Silent: Ex-acrobat Fred Stone and his vaudeville partner Dave Montgomery formed one of the most popular teams on Broadway in the first decade of the 1900s and in the 'teens. They appeared in several popular musicals including *The Wizard of Oz* and *Chin-Chin* and also in operettas like *The Red Mill*.

The year after Montgomery's death (1917), Stone made his starring film debut in *The Goat*. He previously had a small role in 1915's *Destiny*. Others of his few and scattered silent pictures were *Johnny Get Your Gun*, *Under the Top*, *The Duke of Chimney Butte* and *Billy Jim*. Last silent: *Broadway After Dark* (1924), in a cameo role.

Sound: Primarily a stage actor — he was called "The Grand Old Man of American Theater"— Fred Stone returned to the cinema in the 1930s for some worthy character roles, notably as Katharine Hepburn's impecunious but sympathetic father in *Alice Adams* (1935). During 1936 and '37 he was also top-billed in several of lesser cachet: *Hideaway*, *Quick Money* and *Konga, the Wild Stallion*.

Stone's homely, open face, so representative of the common man, was seen in a dozen or so talkies including *The Farmer in the Dell*, *My American Wife*, *The Trail of the Lonesome Pine* and *The Westerner*, his last, in 1940. He returned to the stage where he was active until about 1950. His daughters Carol and Paula also appeared in the theater.

REVIEWS

Alice Adams: Throughout, Stone is a human and sympathetic delineator of a role that's typical of many not very successful fathers. *Variety* 8/21/35.

Grand Jury: Stone is buried under by the feeble-mindedness of the character he plays. *Variety* 8/5/36.

My American Wife: Stone adds much to the interest and worth of the picture. He has been hurt by his recent assignments but gets a much better chance here. He is a very interesting character and is missed when not in the picture. *Variety* 8/26/36.

Hideaway: Stone heads up the cast. Given his long and distinguished record on the stage and in pictures he deserves something better than this trashy, incredible and irritating story. *Variety* 7/21/37.

Quick Money: A mediocre potboiler to which Fred Stone isn't much help. *Variety* 2/16/38.

Konga, the Wild Stallion: Stone, who has been out of films for some time, comes back and his characterization is well drawn. *Variety* 11/15/39.

No Place to Go: An ingratiating performance is given by Fred Stone. It gives the impetus that carries the vehicle over its more trying moments. *Variety* 12/6/39.

Stone, Lewis (Louis Stone), Worcester, Massachusetts, 1878/79–1953

Filmography: Films in Review (Mar. 1981); Academy of Motion Picture Arts and Sciences; List of films in *Eighty Silent Film Stars*

Silent: After working in the theater, Lewis Stone came to films in 1916 as a leading man, making his debut in *Honor's Altar*. Other early pictures were *According to the Code, Inside the Lines* and *Man's Desire*. His first major hit came with 1922's *The Prisoner of Zenda* in which he was starred opposite Alice Terry. Many of his early films were made for First National.

Stone went on to appear in about 50 silents, increasingly in character roles, including *Scaramouche, The Lost World, The Private Life of Helen of Troy, A Fool There Was* (1922 version), *A Woman of Affairs, Why Men Leave Home* and *Lonesome Ladies*. He received a Best Actor Academy Award nomination for *The Patriot* (1928), beating out that film's star Emil Jannings for a nomination. Last silent: *Wild Orchids* (1929), a Greta Garbo starrer, with synchronized music and sound effects.

Sound: Stone was by now an MGM stalwart, and all but one of his 1929 movies had some sound, including *Madame X, The Trial of Mary Dugan* and *Wonder of Women*, in which he received top billing. The next year he again co-starred opposite Greta Garbo in *Romance*.

Among Stone's '30s talkies were *Grand Hotel* (as Dr. Otternschlag he spoke the famous tag line "People coming, people going — always coming and going — and nothing ever happens"), *New Morals for Old, The Mask of Fu Manchu, China Seas, Suzy, Queen Christina, Treasure Island* (1934 version) and *Letty Lynton*.

Stone first portrayed Judge Hardy, the role with which he became strongly identified, in 1938's *You're Only Young Once*. The character had been created the previous year by Lionel Barrymore in *A Family Affair*. There were at least a dozen sequels in which Stone played the idealized eternally calm and wise father of Mickey Rooney as Andy Hardy.

Aside from "Hardy" movies, from 1942 to 1948 Stone was seen infrequently on the screen (*The Hoodlum Saint, The Bugle Sounds*); from 1949 he was somewhat more active up to the time of his death, but many of his roles were small. The final one of his almost 100 talkies was *All the Brothers Were Valiant* (1953) but he was seen briefly in a flashback sequence in *Andy Hardy Comes Home* (1958), the last of the series.

Comments: Lewis Stone was certainly one of the grand old men of MGM and of Hollywood in general. Although he had essayed some early villain roles, he was a courtly leading man to many of the great actresses of his day, notably Greta Garbo, in both silent and sound films. With his smooth stage-trained voice, he made the transition to talkies with no problem.

Stone had grayed and aged considerably by this time, however, and his future lay in character roles. He became somewhat typecast as the kindly father figure (a persona no doubt much to the liking of family-minded Louis B. Mayer), especially as paterfamilias to the Hardy clan.

Stone also appeared in many prestige productions in which he was known for his "natural" style of acting. About that he was quoted as saying: "Acting is never actually natural. You must act all the more to give the effect of naturalness."

Stone seemed to be genuinely admired by his colleagues. His frequent co-star Mickey Rooney said about him that acting with Lewis Stone was all the residuals he needed from the Hardy series. He seemed like a genuine gentleman — and hopefully that was no job of acting.

Reviews

The Trial of Mary Dugan: Lewis Stone does a nice piece of work. It is a cute studio trick to foist the generally heroic or martyred Stone on an unsuspecting public as the villain. *Variety* 4/3/29, *Harrison's Reports* 4/20/29.

Romance: Stone, who is featured, gives a magnificently restrained performance as a clergyman loved and rejected by Greta Garbo. *Variety* 8/27/30, *Harrison's Reports* 8/30/30.

Grand Hotel: A mere bit is allotted to Lewis Stone but it is cameo-like in polish and authority. *Variety* 4/19/32.

The Hoodlum Saint: Stone, sharing featured billing, has only a small bit. *Variety* 2/6/46.

The Sun Comes Up: Stone is a familiar face but only has two scenes. *Variety* 1/5/49.

Bannerline: Stone's brief portrayal of a newspaper morgue-keeper goes over well. *Variety* 9/19/51.

Stuart, Nick (Nicholas Prata, Bratza, Brata and other versions), Romania, 1904–1973

Silent: One of the archetypal "students" in the college films of the late 1920s, Nick Stuart began his on-camera career in 1927, often co-starring with his wife-to-be Sue Carol. Previously he had been behind the scenes in various capacities including assistant cameraman.

Stuart remained a minor Fox star through the end of the silent era in such films as *The Cradle Snatchers, High School Hero, Why Sailors Go Wrong, The News Parade* and *Girls Gone Wild*. Last silent: *Joy Street* (1929), with synchronized sound effects and music, made after his first part-talkie.

Sound: The part-sound *The River Pirate* (1928) was Stuart's first. Other early talkies included *Chasing Through Europe, Why Leave Home?, Happy Days* and *Swing High*. From 1930 he began appearing in quickie melodramas and an occasional western such as *The Fourth Alarm, Sundown Trail, Police Call, A Demon for Trouble* and *Blake of Scotland Yard*.

Stuart's acting career declined and he made only four films from 1934 to 1940, the last a bit role in a "Dead End Kids" film. He also made some shorts. He had formed his own band in the mid–1930s and this became his chief vocation for many years. He returned for a few small film roles in the 1960s, including *It's a Mad Mad Mad Mad World* and *This Property Is Condemned.*

REVIEWS

The River Pirate: The simple and natural work of Nick Stuart is notable. *Variety* 9/19/28, *Harrison's Reports* 9/29/28.

Chasing Through Europe: It is nothing more than a series of good newsreels subjects taken by Nick Stuart while on a trip to Europe. *Harrison's Reports* 9/21/29.

Police Call: The performance of Nick Stuart has a staccato style that is usually characteristic of amateurs. *Variety* 8/29/33.

Rio Grande Romance: Stuart, who is barely a memory to fans, has only a minor role. *Variety* 5/12/37.

Summerville, George ("Slim"; George Somerville), Albuquerque, New Mexico, 1892/96–1946

Filmography: Classic Images (Oct. 1988); Academy of Motion Picture Arts and Sciences; List of films in *Eighty Silent Film Stars*

Silent: Reputedly one of the original "Keystone Kops," tall (6'3"), sad-faced and rangy Slim Summerville appeared in well over 100 one- and two-reelers during the silent era beginning about 1913. With his mournful mien and studiedly blank stare, he was adept at playing country bumpkins.

In the '20s, Summerville eschewed acting for several years to work as a gagman and director at Sennett, Paramount and Fox. He established a feature career when he returned to face the camera in 1926 and he was the sidekick, often named "Slim," in several Hoot Gibson westerns.

Summerville also appeared in non-westerns such as *The Beloved Rogue* and *The Chinese Parrot.* Among his other films were *The Denver Dude, Riding for Fame, Hey! Hey! Cowboy, King of the Rodeo* and *The Texas Streak.* Last silent: *Strong Boy* (1929), with synchronized sound effects and music, made after his first part-talkie.

Sound: Summerville broke out of the western sidekick mold when he made his sound bow in the 1929 part-talkie *The Last Warning.* Other talkies that year included *One Hysterical Night, The Shannons of Broadway* and *Tiger Rose.* His best-remembered role, that of the German soldier Tjaden, came the next year in *All Quiet on the Western Front.* In it he deftly intermixed comedy and pathos. He repeated the role in the 1937 sequel *The Road Back.*

Alternating numerous short and feature appearances, George "Slim" Summerville's busiest decade was the 1930s. His films included *The King of Jazz, Rebecca of Sunnybrook Farm, Out All Night, White Fang, Western Union, I'm From Arkansas, Way Down East, Niagara Falls* and *Tobacco Road.* He was co-starred with fluttery comedienne ZaSu Pitts in a series of films in which their comedy styles meshed well.

In the 1940s, Summerville's screen appearances grew sparse and his last film was *The Hoodlum Saint* (1946). He had made over 70 talkie features and perhaps several hundred shorter pictures during his career.

REVIEWS

Troopers Three: Summerville, a gawky, hick type, almost steals the picture. He is a perfect comedy type and has a good chance to step ahead. *Variety* 2/19/30, *Harrison's Reports* 2/22/30.

All Quiet on the Western Front: It is hard to inject comedy into the greatest tragedy the world has ever known but they get it in, mostly through Slim Summerville as a hard boiled veteran. He is second only to Louis Wolheim in the cast. There are many situations in which he causes hearty laughter. *Variety* 5/7/30, *Harrison's Reports* 5/10/30.

Out All Night: Summerville and ZaSu Pitts romp through their assignments well. *Variety* 4/11/33.

Winner Take All: Summerville scores nicely in the humor department. *Variety* 4/5/39.

Swain, Mack, Tacoma, Washington, 1876–1935

Silent: After long theater experience, hefty Mack Swain joined Keystone in 1913 and soon appeared with Charles Chaplin and other Sennett luminaries. Among his co-starring one-reelers with Chaplin were *Caught in a Cabaret, A Busy Day,* and *His Trysting Place,* and the feature *Tillie's Punctured Romance.*

The years from 1915 to 1917 were probably the busiest of Swain's career. He worked for Triangle and L-KO where he had his own series as Ambrose (*Ambrose's Lofty Perch, …Sour Grapes, …Icy Love,* etc.). He even had his own production company, the Mack Swain Photo-Comedy Company.

From 1918 Swain worked at Herald and Fox but then his career was put on hold, perhaps because he quarreled with a producer who blackballed him. Whatever the reason, he was rescued by Chaplin with roles in *The Idle Class, Pay Day, The Pilgrim* and the famous *The Gold Rush*, in which he had the part of a lifetime as the prospector Big Jim.

The latter film opened the door for numerous worthy character roles during the remainder of the decade. Swain's films included *Hands Up!*, *The Torrent*, *Kiki*, *Gentlemen Prefer Blondes* (one of his greatest successes), *My Best Girl*, *Mockery* and *The Beloved Rogue*. Last silent: *Tillie's Punctured Romance* (1928).

Sound: Caught in the Fog (1928) was Swain's first part-talkie and 1929's *Marianne* his first fully sound film. Others included *The Locked Door*, *The Last Warning*, *Finn and Hattie*, *The Sea Bat* and *Redemption*.

Swain replaced Charlie Murray in *The Cohens and the Kellys in Atlantic City*, a 1929 part-talkie, and one of a series co-starring George Sidney. His output slowed after 1930 and he played small parts in very few films thereafter.

REVIEWS

Caught in the Fog: Mack Swain is amusing as the insufferable dumb detective. Most of the comedy is contributed by him and he talks in a few situations. *New York Times* 12/3/28, *Harrison's Reports* 12/8/28.

The Last Warning: Swain has been cast as comedy relief but he doesn't do anything with it. *Variety* 1/9/29, *Harrison's Reports* 1/12/29.

The Cohens and the Kellys in Atlantic City: Swain was padded both in his stomach and in his role. He fits the part well. *Variety* 3/20/29, *Harrison's Reports* 3/23/29.

Finn and Hattie: Swain affords chuckles as a Frenchman. *New York Times* 1/31/31, *Harrison's Reports* 2/7/31.

Swanson, Gloria (Gloria Swenson or

Svenssen ?), Chicago, Illinois, 1898/99–1983
Filmography: Films in Review (Apr. 1965)
Silent: After working as an extra, Gloria Swanson became an Essanay bit player and then a featured player about 1914. Later appearing in Mack Sennett comedies — although, she claimed, not as one of his "bathing beauties" — she worked with her then-husband Wallace Beery in several knockabout one-reelers.

Swanson moved on to Triangle in 1918 for a group of dramas. Among her features there were *Everywoman's Husband*, *Society for Sale* and *Shifting Sands*. Her hiring by Cecil B. DeMille in 1919 was the entree to her starring period with such films as *Male and Female*, *Why Change Your Wife?*, *Don't Change Your Husband* and *The Affairs of Anatol*.

Swanson was now on the track of Paramount superstardom which she maintained throughout the 1920s despite some mediocre efforts. She was adept at both comedy and melodrama but one of her chief geniuses was for self-publicity, a not insignificant talent in those days of god-like stars.

Swanson's extensive and exotic wardrobe, her made-up feuds with other divas, and her marriage to a presumably genuine French nobleman were the stuff of Jazz Age legend. Among her better-known films were *Zaza*, *Madame Sans-Gêne*, *Beyond the Rocks* with Rudolph Valentino, *Manhandled* and *The Wages of Virtue*.

Swanson seemed to go from strength to strength as the 1920s wore on. She also became entangled both professionally and personally with Joseph P. Kennedy, then a film mogul and founder of the famous Kennedy clan. Her first Academy Award nomination as Best Actress came for 1927's popular and profitable *Sadie Thompson*. The Oscar was won by Janet Gaynor.

Swanson's run of luck came to an abrupt end when she produced the not-successful *The Love of Sunya* for her own production company, and then became entangled with manic director Erich von Stroheim on *Queen Kelly* in 1928. The now-legendary aborted film virtually ended his directing career.

In all, Swanson made more than 50 silent films, including two-reelers. Last U.S. silent: *Sadie Thompson* (1927); *Queen Kelly* in its abbreviated form had a later European and South American release.

Sound: Swanson had been off the screen for about a year-and-a-half when she made her talkie debut with the melodrama *The Trespasser* in 1929. It was a major hit and made hers one of the most successful transitions of any of the top silent stars. The film premiered in London and New York to delirious crowds and glowing reviews.

For this film Swanson received her second nomination for an Academy Award as Best Actress; it was won by Norma Shearer for *The Divorcee*. Besides her emoting, she was praised for her singing and one song became a standard: "Love, Your Magic Spell is Everywhere." Two songs from the film were later recorded by her for RCA Victor, presumably proof her singing had not been dubbed.

The Trespasser was made by Swanson's own production company, as all her films had been since *The Love of Sunya*. (The financial power behind the company was none other than sometime lover Joe Kennedy.) She chose frothy comedies for her next vehicles. *What a Widow!* (1930), *Indiscreet* and *Tonight or Never* (1931) were moderately successful.

Swanson's next endeavor, *Perfect Understanding*, made in England in 1933 and co-starring a very callow Laurence Olivier, marked the end of her company and gave rise to speculation that her career was finished. One further effort, Fox's *Music in the Air* (1934), did not change this perception. She was then signed by MGM but made no films there.

Swanson was off the screen for seven years when she was cast in a co-starring role in the minor comedy *Father Takes a Wife* in 1941. Although she was praised for her performance in this slight film, the remainder of the 1940s passed with no further screen appearances.

Swanson regained the spotlight with a vengeance upon her return as the faded silent star Norma Desmond in 1950's *Sunset Blvd.*, directed by Billy Wilder in his trademark sardonic style. This led to her third Best Actress Award which she again lost, this time to Judy Holliday for *Born Yesterday*. She was not the first choice for the role; that was apparently Mary Pickford.

There were three subsequent film roles for Swanson, one in each of the next three decades. *Three for Bedroom C* came in 1952; the Italian-made *Nero's Mistress* (it had various other titles as well) ten years later, and her final film, in which she played a cameo role, *Airport 1975* (1974). That same year she appeared in a made-for-television film, *The Killer Bees*. She also performed frequently on the stage and was often seen on TV.

REVIEWS

The Trespasser: Swanson is going to wow picturegoers with her singing voice; she sings like a prima donna. The film will do so much for her as a talker star that she should make two or three more as quickly as possible. It reveals that she is an excellent actress; in dramatic moments she can rise to great heights. She speaks her lines naturally and without unnecessary pantomimic gestures. Her work is restrained, particularly in the emotional scenes.

(Swanson played a stenographer in this contemporary melodrama of mother love. According to her later accounts it was shot in just 21 days and she felt her adjustment to sound films was not difficult. It was also, supposedly, her least expensive film since becoming a star. She also claimed that Clark Gable was tested for the male lead but that "he looked like a truckdriver and spoke like a private eye." Because the male lead had to be someone who seemed at home in Chicago society, suave Broadway and film actor Robert Ames was cast.) *Variety* 9/18/29, *New York Times* 11/2/29, *Harrison's Reports* 11/16/29.

What a Widow!: In the talkies Swanson has blossomed. Her performance is all lighthearted and in an altogether different direction from her first talkie. Sometimes her violent attempts to draw laughs makes one think that she is trying to emulate her early efforts in pictures under Mack Sennett. *Variety* 9/17/30, *New York Times* 10/4/30.

Indiscreet: Swanson is at her best during the farcical interludes. *New York Times* 5/7/31.

Tonight or Never: Reviews disagreed. One opined that Swanson's portrayal of the opera singer fell short of Helen Gahagan's stage performance and that Melvyn Douglas's interpretation overshadowed hers. Another thought that she did some extremely effective acting and that she gave a capital performance. *New York Times* 12/18/31, *Variety* 12/22/31.

Perfect Understanding: Swanson is by no means at her best, showing no particular talent for acting. She never once rises above the mediocre material with which she has supplied herself and seems like a stock actress struggling with the futilities of an old-fashioned society drama.

(When shooting had been almost completed on this ultimately unsuccessful comedy the film lab which was processing the negative burned down. This was an ominous omen for the problems faced by this ill-starred film.) *New York Times* 2/23/33, *Variety* 2/28/33.

Music in the Air: Reviews again did not agree. One thought that Swanson made an agreeable return to the screen and possessed a pleasing voice and a gift for light comedy. Others said that she did not possess a voice that thrilled anyone and that she was not well cast. *New York Times* 12/14/34, *Harrison's Reports* 12/15/34, *Variety* 12/18/34.

Father Takes a Wife: The film is highlighted by the return of Gloria Swanson. She shows her age to some extent but can be termed only *semi*-matronly. Moviegoers will be well pleased both by her performance and her appearance; she acts with charm. She has been provided with an amusing comedy which permits her to run the familiar gamut without ever taxing her capabilities as an actress. *Variety* 7/16/41, *Harrison's Reports* 7/26/41, *New York Times* 9/5/41.

Sunset Boulevard: Swanson gives an exceptional performance, using silent acting techniques to put over the decaying star she is called upon to portray. She is as glamorous as ever and makes the most of the histrionic opportunities of her femme fatale role. Many filmgoers will want to see her return to the screen. It is inconceivable that anyone else might have been considered for the role. She dominates the picture; it is a classic screen creation. She plays it not just to the hilt, but right up to the armpit, and magnificently.

(Billy Wilder, who had co-written the script for *Music in the Air*, directed this story of a half-mad — and ultimately completely mad — silent screen actress, Norma Desmond. Montgomery Clift was originally approached to be the leading man, but he turned it down. [It was thought by some that the screen relationship uncomfortably mirrored his real-life affair with singer Libby Holman who was 30 years his senior.] The film was immensely popular upon its release and was nominated for several Academy Awards, besides Best Actress. It won three: for screenplay, score and art direction.) *Variety* 4/19/50, *Harrison's Reports* 4/22/50, *New York Times* 8/11/50, *New Yorker* 8/19/50, *Fortnight* 9/1/50, *Esquire* 12/50, *Agee on Film.*

Three For Bedroom C: Swanson acts demure but it does not fit her personality; she should have stuck to *Sunset Blvd.* Her emoting smacks of the old silent Sennett days, using passé techniques with enthusiasm but not proving that coy looks and fluttering eyelashes can successfully substitute for acting. Whatever possessed her to make such wickedly silly junk is her secret but another such vehicle may find her switching professions. She contributes a kittenish, inconsistent caricature of her unforgettable Norma Desmond role that is plain embarrassing.

(This was Swanson's first color film. She played an actress traveling to Hollywood by train with her young daughter. A young professor is mistakenly assigned the same compartment and the unfunny complications ensue.) *Variety* 6/11/52, *New York Times* 6/27/52.

Comments: Gloria Swanson's talkie career began, almost literally, on a high note but she failed to follow up on her triumph. In an apparent effort to demonstrate her versatility, she chose insubstantial vehicles, all comedies, for her subsequent movies and they soon sent her on a downward spiral. This pattern repeated itself after *Sunset Blvd.* as well so her judgment must be questioned.

Swanson's speaking and singing voices were mellifluous and her looks still appealing in her early 30s, albeit she was possibly a bit exotic for Depression-era audiences. There also was about her the unmistakable attitudes of a *silent* movie star — too much the grande dame for the more gritty '30s. And there was the question of how good an actress she actually was.

Swanson's smashing, almost legendary, return in *Sunset Blvd.* was certainly unique amongst all the silent actresses but it left her with virtually nowhere to go in terms of a further film career. In her autobiography, she claims to be afraid that people would think she and Norma Desmond were the same person and that she might be irrevocably typecast.

"I had a huge specter in the spotlight with me," Swanson wrote. "She was just about ten feet tall, and her name was 'Norma Desmond.' During my years of obscurity, the public had forgotten Gloria Swanson. In order to spring back to them in one leap I had to have a bigger than life part. I had found it, all right. In fact my present danger seemed to lie in the fact that I had played the part too well."

This was, in fact, probably true as far as the 1950 moviegoing public was concerned. The role was almost made for parody (Carol Burnett's hilarious *Nora* Desmond springs to mind) but some of the lines uttered by Norma Desmond are still oft-repeated: "We didn't need dialogue; we had faces!" and "I'm still big; it's pictures that have grown small."

Some film writers have called *Sunset Blvd.* a cruel film. The suspicion is that Wilder really did use aspects of Gloria Swanson's own personality and life in it. He had been, after all, the co-writer of *Music in the Air* at a time when she was in reality a fading star. Whatever the truth may be, her wonderful performance — a measured admixture of pathos and bizarreness — stands proudly on its own.

It would have been more auspicious for Swanson had she departed at the top. Unfortunately, her handful of subsequent efforts were indeed in "small" films that were minor and even embarrassing. Critics all but stated that her emoting in *Three for Bedroom C* was the kind that hammy Norma Desmond herself would have done had she achieved her dreams of a comeback.

Gloria Swanson had to be content thereafter with being a stage and television personality. Her widely publicized nutritional beliefs and opinions on a wide range of other, sometimes esoteric, subjects made some regard her as an eccentric. But at least she did not fade out of the public eye as did most of her contemporaries. Not for her was seclusion behind the crumbling walls of a rococo Hollywood mansion.

Sweet, Blanche (Sarah B. Sweet), Chicago, Illinois, 1895/96–1986

Filmography: Films in Review (Nov. 1965); *Classic Images* (May-June 1989); List of films in *Sweethearts of the Sage*

Silent: Blanche Sweet was a stage actress and dancer before becoming one of the premier leading women of the cinema. Beginning at Edison about 1909, she soon joined D. W. Griffith's Biograph Studio to play small roles, eventually becoming known as "The Biograph Blonde." *The Long Road* may have been her first lead.

Sweet went on to appear in *The Lonedale Operator*, *The Avenging Conscience*, *The Goddess of Sagebrush Gulch* and other classic two-reelers. The feature *Judith of Bethulia* (1914) was the film which made her a major star.

In 1915, Sweet migrated to Lasky and worked for C. B. DeMille in *The Warrens of Virginia* and *The Captive*. She made about 115 films through 1927 but, except for a couple of years in the mid-'20s, was seen less frequently after 1920. She also appeared in a few British films.

Sweet's films included *The Lady from Hell*, *The Sporting Venus*, *Bluebeard's Seven Wives*, *Those Who Dance*, *In the Palace of the King* and *Quincy Adams Sawyer*. Nineteen twenty-three's *Anna Christie* and *Tess of the D'Urbervilles* the following year were among her best-regarded roles of the 1920s. Last U.S. silent: *Singed* (1927). Last U.K. silent: *The Woman in White* (1929).

Sound: The 1929 Vitaphone short *Always Faithful* was apparently Sweet's introduction to sound. She was to make only three sound features, all in 1930. The first, in which she sang, was *Showgirl in Hollywood*. It was followed by *The Woman Racket* and *The Silver Horde*. In the first and the latter pictures she played only supporting roles.

Sweet turned to vaudeville in the 1930s and then remained active on the stage and in other creative arenas until her retirement. Some filmographies also list Danny Kaye's *The Five Pennies*, made in the late '50s, in her credits. If she does appear, she is unbilled.

Comments: Although she made a few memorable films in the 1920s, it is fair to say that Blanche Sweet's career had peaked earlier. But that peak was high. She was a Griffith favorite and certainly one of the most fondly-remembered of the early silent players.

The blonde and beauteous Sweet was a talented and naturalistic actress who often underplayed in an era when gestural excess was considered great screen acting. Playing virginal heroines was not really to her taste. To her credit she always sought, but did not always find, interesting and offbeat roles.

In the talkies, Sweet's accomplishments were negligible. In her last role, in *The Silver Horde*, she played what seemed to be a prostitute with an ersatz "tough girl" accent. Although it may have been one of her favored offbeat roles, it was not a very fitting finale to a great career.

Reviews

The Woman Racket: Blanche Sweet is the heroine. *Harrison's Reports* 3/8/30.

Showgirl in Hollywood: Sweet plays her part so well that she overshadows the star, Alice White. However, the tragic story of the character played by Sweet is dragged in without conviction. Her attempted suicide is incompetently handled but she does the best of any of the cast. *New York Times* 5/5/30, *Variety* 5/14/30.

Taliaferro, Mabel, New York, New York, 1887/89–1979

Silent: For a short while in the 'teens, Mabel Taliaferro was a popular star, as was even more briefly her sister Edith. She was a prominent stage actress before and after her film career which began with one-reelers at Selig about 1911, possibly in *Cinderella*.

Among Taliaferro's films, some for the Rolfe Film Company, were *The Snowbird*, *Her Great Price*, *God's Half Acre*, *A Magdelene of the Hills* and *The Barricade*. Last silent: *Sentimental Tommy* (1921).

Sound: The one and only talkie in which Mabel Taliaferro is known to have appeared was *My Love Came Back* in 1940. She continued on the stage thereafter.

Talmadge, Norma, Jersey City, New Jersey (older sources say Niagara Falls, New York), 1893/97–1957

Filmography: Films in Review (Jan. 1967)

Silent: Norma Talmadge, she of the luminous dark eyes, made well over 200 one- and two-reelers for Vitagraph in New York beginning about 1910. She appeared in a variety of genres including comedy; it was not until later that she gained her reputation as the queen of the "weepies."

Probably the first film in which Talmadge received notice was the 1911 version of *A Tale of Two Cities*. Her first major feature was *The Battle Cry of Peace* (1915). She ultimately went to Hollywood and appeared in films for D. W. Griffith's company, although in none directed by him.

Marrying shrewd mogul Joe Schenck proved to be fortuitous for Talmadge's career, if not for her personal fulfillment. He set up a production company through which her popular films were distributed, thus maximizing profits. (He did the same for her sister Constance and her brother-in-law Buster Keaton, who was married to Natalie, the non-star Talmadge.)

By the 1920s, Talmadge had built her career, as she herself described it, on "sobs and smiles." She had become the epitomization of noble suffering. Often co-starring with Conway Tearle and Eugene O'Brien, some of her successes included *Yes or No?*, *The Voice from the Minaret*, *Smilin' Through*, a major hit, and *Secrets*.

The latter motion picture (remade by Mary Pickford in 1933) was considered to be the apex of Talmadge's screen career. By the time she made her final silents, including *The Dove*, her popularity was somewhat on the wane. Last silent: *The Woman Disputed* (1927).

Sound: A talkie hit was deemed to be vital for Talmadge's continued stardom. Her voice apparently did not register well in tests and she was off the screen for well over a year, supposedly taking daily voice lessons. Unfortunately, *New York Nights*, her first sound film, released in late 1929 and co-starring her off-screen lover Gilbert Roland, was not the success she had hoped for.

The melodramatic film turned out a very static affair, apparently using only a single stationary camera. The sole action sequence unfolded in one underworld scene. An entirely different setting was therefore thought to be needed for Talmadge's second attempt in the sound medium.

This turned out to be the ill-advised *DuBarry, Woman of Passion* (1930). The costume melodrama was generally considered to be a film full of stilted performances with few dramatic highlights and it proved to be Talmadge's final screen appearance. Although moviegoers had already made the decision for her, in 1934 she announced her "official" retirement from the screen. She later was heard on the radio.

Comments: After Norma Talmadge's relative lack of success in *New York Nights*, sister Constance Talmadge, who herself essayed no talkies, supposedly sent her a telegram reading "GET OUT NOW."

Whether or not this is an apocryphal story as some suppose, it is probably wise that Talmadge soon ended her career. Although she had been a very successful actress for much of the 1920s, she was not necessarily a great one and her voice was untrained. Her last silent films seemed to show a decline in her popularity.

Time magazine stated of Talmadge in *DuBarry*: "In her first film she talked like an elocution pupil. This time she talks like an elocution teacher.... [It is hoped] this will be the last attempt to establish her as a great figure in sound pictures." It was.

Although Talmadge's voice was not as redolent of the streets of Brooklyn (or Jersey City) as it was rumored, her sound vehicles certainly were poorly selected and she was already at the dangerous age, her later 30s, for a leading woman of her type. Also, the kind of exaggerated melodrama in which she had specialized was not as much in style in the '30s.

Rightly or wrongly, Talmadge has been held up as the prototype of the silent star who could not

"talk." Re-evaluating her gifts, or lack thereof, is not an easy task these days. Of all the major actresses, save perhaps Theda Bara, her output is the least available for reconsideration.

Norma Talmadge's reputation — and it was considerable — must speak for her. One final tweak to that reputation did come in the use of her first name in a classic film. Norma Desmond was of course the crazed has-been heroine of *Sunset Blvd.* Perhaps this was a coincidence — but perhaps not.

REVIEWS

New York Nights: If Norma Talmadge has retained her drawing power from former days, this picture will need it. She looks good and acts and talks well.

(The storyline of *New York Nights* was a triangle consisting of an alcoholic songwriter [Gilbert Roland], his loyal wife [Talmadge] and a lecherous gangster. Perhaps ominously the *The New York Times* reviewer failed to mention that Miss Talmadge was in the film.) *Variety* 2/5/30, *Harrison's Reports* 2/8/30. *Variety* 2/5/30, *Harrison's Reports* 2/8/30.

Dubarry, Woman of Passion: Although reviews generally were poor, one held out a ray of light. Most were along the lines that Talmadge was evidently the victim of Sam Taylor's none too brilliant direction. Her voice had no flexibility and her facial expressions were not so good. The acting was overloaded with misdirected enthusiasm. One review, though, opined that the acting was artistic.

(Sam Taylor was the director whom Mary Pickford blamed for her lack of success in the talkies, particularly for his direction of *Taming of the Shrew*. He soon faded from the industry.) *New York Times* 11/3/30, *Variety* 11/5/30, *Harrison's Reports* 11/8/30.

Talmadge, Richard (Ricardo Metezzeti or Sylvester Metzetti), Munich, Germany or Switzerland, 1892/96–1981

Filmography: List of films in *Eighty Silent Film Stars*

Silent: Richard Talmadge was a stuntman in the serial *The Million Dollar Mystery* and other films before becoming a leading actor in about 30 silents from 1921. Many were made for Goldstone and FBO. His mentor was Douglas Fairbanks, for whom he frequently worked and whom he presumably doubled.

The titles of some of Talmadge's action melodramas tell it all: *Taking Chances*, *Danger Ahead*, *Speed King*, *The Fighting Demon*, *Tearing Through* and *Doubling with Danger.* Last silent: *The Poor Millionaire* (1930).

Sound: Richard Talmadge's initial talkies *Scareheads, The Yankee Don* and *Dancing Dynamite* were not made until 1931. Others included *Speed Madness, Get That Girl, On Your Guard, Fighting Pilot, Now or Never* and *Never Too Late,* the latter two among his penultimate pictures in 1935.

Talmadge was seen in his final starring role in 1936's *The Speed Reporter.* He appeared before the cameras at least once more in a small role in *Black Eagle* (1948), with perhaps some unbilled bits as late as the mid–1960s.

Before his on-camera career ended, Richard Talmadge also appeared in the 1934 serial *Pirate Treasure.* Beginning in the latter '30s he became a second unit director on about 70 films like *Beau Geste, The Greatest Story Ever Told* and *How the West Was Won.* He also continued doing stunt work.

Comments: Richard Talmadge was among the most athletic of actors, possibly the equivalent of 1990s action stars like Jean-Claude Van Damme, Jackie Chan, Steven Seagal and their ilk. He was famous for his leaps from great heights, and stunts such as these compensated for any lack of acting ability. The late release, in April 1930, of his final silent film was an indication that there were some concerns about his speaking voice.

These concerns were not unjustified. Talmadge had a noticeable Germanic accent, his voice was weak (or at least recorded weakly) and it was high-pitched. He may have overcome these problems to some extent but his greatest contributions in the talkie era were to other people's pictures.

Reviews

The Yankee Don: The acrobatics of Richard Talmadge help what would otherwise have been a run-of-the-mill western. When he started to sing a love song, the audience giggled. *Variety* 5/20/31.

Scareheads: Talmadge's acting is of low caliber. He would do better to stick to westerns; he does less talking while injecting more action. Here it's vice versa and not so good. *Variety* 10/27/31.

Speed Madness: Although it is a society drama, Talmadge doesn't exactly suggest the social register. The film contains some of his gymnastics but he is agile rather than able in the lead. *Variety* 10/11/32.

Tashman, Lilyan (Lillian Tashman), Brooklyn, New York, 1899–1934

Silent: Blonde Follies girl Lilyan Tashman was in a couple of films in 1921 and '22 but her career was truly launched with 1924's *The Garden of Weeds.* Tall, cool and elegant, she became popular in numerous silents as the hard-boiled but sometimes good-hearted "other woman."

Among Tashman's films were *Declassee, Pretty Ladies, Camille* (1927 version), *For Alimony Only, Craig's Wife, Phyllis of the Follies* and *The Woman Who Did Not Care.* Last silent: *Hardboiled* (1929).

Sound: All but one of Tashman's eight 1929 releases were talkies, the first of which, *The Lone Wolf's Daughter,* was part-talking. She worked steadily until the time of her death in films like *New York Nights, Millie, Up Pops the Devil, Those We Love* and *Too Much Harmony.* In *Wine, Women and Song,* one of her last, she had the top-billed role.

Comments: Perhaps Lilyan Tashman was known as much for her sartorial elegance as for her acting. This could also be said of her husband Edmund Lowe. But she was a more than competent and always watchable actress who carved a niche for herself as a "bad girl" and wisecracking heroine's friend in numerous films.

When Tashman stole someone's husband, it was usually done in a self-mocking tongue-in-cheek manner and she was never really all bad even at her worst. She played some leads in silents but shone mainly in supporting roles in talkies. At the time of her early death, it seemed as if a career in character leads might be in the offing.

Reviews

Bulldog Drummond: Tashman is the she-devil and the sex symbol. *Variety* 5/8/29, *Harrison's Reports* 5/11/29.

The Cat Creeps: The comic character who provides the meat of the piece is Lilyan Tashman, who does her usual workmanlike job of it. *Variety* 11/12/30, *Harrison's Reports* 11/15/30.

Finn and Hattie: Tashman was allowed to overplay the gypsy girl too often. *Variety* 2/4/31.

The Road to Reno: The picture's biggest fault is top-billed Lilyan Tashman as the mother; she is badly miscast. *Variety* 10/13/31, *Harrison's Reports* 10/17/31.

The Wiser Sex: Tashman plays the girlfriend excellently. Probably the picture's most valuable asset are the clothes of Claudette Colbert and Tashman. *Variety* 3/15/32, *Harrison's Reports* 3/19/32.

Too Much Harmony: As a gold digger, Tashman shows what the well-dressed menace wears and she contributes a first-rate performance. *Variety* 9/26/33, *Harrison's Reports* 9/30/32.

Wine, Women and Song: The only really worthwhile feature of the picture is the love Lilyan Tashman shows for her daughter. *Harrison's Reports* 1/20/34.

Taylor, Estelle (Ida Estelle [or Estella] Boylan), Wilmington, Delaware, 1899/1903–1958.

Silent: Dark-eyed Estelle Taylor made her reputation as a bad girl in films like the 1922 remake of *A Fool There Was*, but she also played conventional romantic leads. Her career began about 1919 with supporting and leading roles in films such as *The Golden Shower*, *The Return of Tarzan* and *The Adventurer*. After 1924 her output grew sparser; during part of that time she was appearing in a Broadway play with her then-husband Jack Dempsey.

Among Taylor's films were *Only a Shop Girl*, *Desire*, *Mary of the Movies*, *The Alaskan*, *Manhattan Madness*, *Lady Raffles*, *The Ten Commandments* and *The Whip Woman*. In *Don Juan* (1926), the first full-length feature with Vitaphone-accompanied sound effects and music, she again played a villainess. Last silent: *Where East Is East* (1929).

Sound: Taylor appeared in few talkies, her first being *Liliom* in 1930. She had important roles in two popular 1931 films: the epic western *Cimarron* (as Dixie Lee, Richard Dix's discarded first wife) and in *Street Scene*, as Sylvia Sidney's mother. Small, if not bit, roles came later in *Call Her Savage*, *The Frisco Kid* and *Bachelor Mother*.

Taylor received her final top-billing in a 1932 Monogram release, a quickie mystery melodrama called *Western Limited*. Her last, and only 1940s film, was *The Southerner* (1945). She also made some vaudeville and stage appearances.

Comments: "Sultry" is a word that could have been coined for pretty Estelle Taylor. She certainly could portray the innocent heroine but somehow it seemed a waste of her talents; smoldering was more in her line. In real life, though, she apparently received, rather than gave, the figurative blows.

Taylor was somewhat of a hard luck case and well-publicized illnesses, injuries and a rocky, fight-filled marriage with Jack Dempsey came to overshadow her career. That career was a worthwhile one even in talkies where her output was meager. Her voice was just fine and her major talkie performances were well-received.

It was perhaps ominous, however, that by her early 30s Taylor already was being cast as a mother. Her sound career probably did not prosper for a variety of reasons; surely her fragile emotional and physical health were chief among them. But she did not have any cause to be ashamed of her legacy.

REVIEWS

Cimarron: Taylor somewhat overshadows Irene Dunne in their portrayals of the young and old wife, the latter played by Taylor. She has few scenes but she makes them impressive. *Variety* 1/18/31, *Harrison's Reports* 2/7/31.

Street Scene: Taylor does creditable acting. *New York Times* 8/27/31, *Harrison's Reports* 9/5/31.

Tearle, Conway (Frederick Levy), New York, New York, 1878–1938.

Filmography: List of films in *Eighty Silent Film Stars*

Silent: Stage performer Conway Tearle (a half-brother of British actor Godfrey Tearle) entered films about 1914. His first-known credits were *The Nightingale* and *Shore Acres*. He continued to appear on the stage while making such films as *Stella Maris*, *Seven Sisters*, *The Common Law* (two versions), *Heart of the Hills*, *Morals for Women* and *Her Game*.

Tearle enjoyed a fairly distinguished silent film career. Among his major co-stars were such luminaries as Mary Pickford, the Talmadge sisters, Marion Davies, Corinne Griffith, Mae Murray and Colleen Moore. The studios for whom he worked included First National, Famous Players-Lasky, MGM, Warner Bros., FBO, Columbia and Victory.

The 1920s were Tearle's busiest film years but for at least a year near the end of the decade he made no motion pictures. He claimed to have been blackballed by a producer, following a quarrel. Last silent: *Smoke Bellew* (1929).

Sound: Tearle made almost 25 talkies, the first of which was *Gold Diggers of Broadway*. His other 1929 sound films were *Evidence* and *The Lost Zeppelin*. Although he began the sound era as a leading man, he gradually slipped into supporting roles, including some quickie melodramas and even westerns.

In the 1932 Mascot serial *The Hurricane Express*, Conway Tearle was unmasked as the villain, a part he was to play more often in talkies. Among his feature films were *Vanity Fair*, *Day of Reckoning*, *Sing Sing Nights*, *The Preview Murder Mystery*, *Klondike Annie*, *Desert Guns* and his last, *Romeo and Juliet* (1936).

REVIEWS

The Lost Zeppelin: Top-billed as the Zeppelin commander, Conway Tearle, whose return to screen acting is still of recent date, gives one of his best performances. When given a restrained, dramatic part his stage training comes out. *Variety* 2/5/30.

The Truth About Youth: Tearle's performance couldn't be improved on but it was a mistake to give him so many close-ups. *Variety* 12/17/30.

Man About Town: Tearle is hardly the forceful

type he is supposed to be with that broad enunciation he uses in speaking. Considering his long absence from pictures, his comeback bodes well for more work. His voice is clear and he looks young and interesting. *Variety* 5/31/32.

Sing Sing Nights: In the lead, Tearle chews the scenery as the crooked newspaper correspondent. *Variety* 1/29/35.

Tell, Alma, 1894/98–1937

Silent: Stage performer Alma Tell, sister of actress Olive Tell, appeared in scattered films in the 'teens (*Simon the Jester, Nearly Married*) and she made a few more during the '20s. They included *On with the Dance, The Iron Trail, Broadway Rose, The Silent Command* and *Paying the Piper*. In these she was usually to be found down in the cast list. Last silent: *San Francisco Nights* (1928).

Sound: *Saturday's Children*, a 1929 part-talkie, marked Tell's sound debut. She is known to have appeared in only two other talkies: *Love Comes Along* in 1930 and *Imitation of Life* (1934), in which she played a very minor part.

REVIEWS

Saturday's Children: Alma Tell does well. *New York Times* 4/29/29.

Tell, Olive, New York, New York, 1894–1951

Silent: The sister of actress Alma Tell, and probably the more successful of the two, stage performer Olive Tell entered films as a star about 1916. Her earlier pictures included *Her Sister, The Smugglers, The Unforeseen* and *The Girl and the Judge*.

Tell's appearances after 1920 were sporadic, probably because of her theater work, and only occasionally did she have the leading role. Among her pictures in that decade were *Worlds Apart, Chickie, The Prince of Tempters, Slaves of Beauty* and *Sailors' Wives*. Last silent: *Soft Living* (1928).

Sound: All three of Tell's 1929 films were talkies: *Hearts in Exile, The Very Idea* and *The Trial of Mary Dugan*. Her roles were in support as they would be for the remainder of her career.

Tell was fairly active until 1936 in such films as *Lawful Larceny, False Faces, Strictly Personal, The Scarlet Empress, Four Hours to Kill* and *Brilliant Marriage*. Another film, possibly her last, *Zaza*, was made in 1939.

Tellegen, Lou (Isidor Van Dameler or Van Dammeler), The Netherlands, 1881–1934

Filmography: Films in Review (Apr. 1988)

Silent: In the early years of the century handsome Lou Tellegen was Sarah Bernhardt's leading man, both on-stage and off-, and he appeared with her in the French films *Camille, Queen Elizabeth* and *Adrienne LeCouvreur* from 1911–13. His U.S. film debut came in 1915's *The Explorer* for Lasky.

Among Tellegen's other films were three he made with his then-wife Geraldine Farrar: *Flame of the Desert, The World and Its Woman* and *The Woman and the Puppet*. After the latter film in 1920, he made no more until 1924. He appeared in 37 silents, in some of which he was cast as the "other man" or villain.

Tellegen's pictures included *Between Friends, After Business Hours, East Lynne* (1925 version), *Parisian Nights, Three Bad Men* and *Those Who Judge*. He also directed some movies in the 'teens and again in 1928. Last silent: *Married Alive* (1927).

Sound: Tellegen was severely burned in late 1929 and had to undergo plastic surgery. His sound debut did not come until 1931 with *Enemies of the Law*, a quickie for Regal Pictures. There was only one further role, and that a small one, in the posthumously released *Together We Live* (1935).

Comments: Lou Tellegen was an extremely popular matinee idol but his ability as an actor was perhaps less than great. What is certain is that he parlayed his appeal for women into torrid affairs with many actresses who could aid his career. He acknowledged this in his autobiography, which was bluntly entitled *Women Have Been Kind*.

When Tellegen's physical attractions faded, so did his stardom. The inevitable aging process, coupled with his unfortunate accident, apparently led to feelings that ultimately resulted in a messy suicide.

REVIEWS

Enemies of the Law: Among the best-known cast names is Lou Tellegen. He gives an unusually bad performance; it is an amazing display of overacting. *Variety* 7/14/31, *Harrison's Reports* 7/18/31.

Together We Live: Just a so-so performance is turned in by the late Lou Tellegen. *Variety* 10/23/35.

Theby, Rosemary (Rose Masing), St. Louis, Missouri, 1885–?

Silent: Possibly as long ago as 1910 Rosemary Theby made her film debut (it could have been as "late" as 1913). By the latter year she was at Reliance appearing in numerous one- and two-reelers, some with comedian Harry Myers (who later became her husband).

The couple went to Universal in 1914 for a comedy series and then to Vim in '16. The next year, Theby began appearing in supporting and leading roles in features and at least one serial. She continued in films through the end of the silent era but by then she was seen in support only.

Theby's pictures included *The Sacrifice, The Mills of the Gods, The Great Love, A Connecticut Yankee in King Arthur's Court, Rich Men's Wives, The Red Lily* and *Fifth Avenue Models*. Last silent: *The Peacock Fan* (1929).

Sound: Theby's feature sound bow was in *Midnight Daddies*, a 1930 comedy. She continued playing small and then bit roles until the beginning of the 1940s or possibly somewhat longer.

Among Theby's films were *Ten Nights in a Barroom, The Man on the Flying Trapeze, Yours for the Asking, The Devil is Driving* and *One Million B.C.* (1940), which may have been her last. She also appeared in shorts, a memorable one being *The Fatal Glass of Beer*, in which she played the wife of W. C. Fields.

Thomson, Kenneth (sometimes billed as Thompson), Pittsburgh, Pennsylvania, 1899–1967

Silent: Handsome Kenneth Thomson was a stage actor who made his first films *Man Bait, Corporal Kate* and *Risky Business* in 1926 as a romantic leading man. Others included *Almost Human, The King of Kings, Turkish Delight, White Gold* and *The Secret Hour*. Last silent: *The Street of Illusion* (1928).

Sound: Thomson transitioned to talkies without a beat being missed. All his seven 1929 films had some talking; among them were *The Careless Age, The Girl from Havana, Say It with Songs* and *The Bellamy Trial*. The most important was *The Broadway Melody* which was his first full-sound film and in which he was the second male lead.

Although Kenneth Thomson maintained a full complement of films through 1935, he soon found himself mostly in supporting roles, including some as villains. He still also was seen in occasional second leads; one was in Harold Lloyd's 1932 comedy *Movie Crazy*.

Thomson's films during this period included *Just Imagine, Sweet Mama, Up for Murder, Her Mad Night, Hop-a-Long Cassidy, Daring Daughters* and *Behold My Wife!* He played his last two small roles in *Criminal Lawyer* and *Jim Hanvey, Detective* in 1937.

Possibly more important than the rather mediocre pictures Kenneth Thomson made was his role in the founding of the Screen Actors Guild and his longtime service as its Executive Secretary.

Reviews

Reno: Even the young, personable actor Kenneth Thomson couldn't make the film attractive. *Variety* 11/5/30.

Movie Crazy: Thomson is the heavy but he possesses something which the ladies go for. A semi-sinister brunette, if he were more sympathetically cast he would appeal to women. *Variety* 9/20/32.

Todd, Thelma (also known as Alison Loyd), Lawrence, Massachusetts, 1905–1935

Filmography: Film Fan Monthly (Sept. 1966); *Hot Toddy*

Silent: From 1926, Thelma Todd was a minor player in about a dozen silent features such as *Fascinating Youth, The Gay Defender, Nevada, Rubber Heels, The Crash* and *The Haunted House*.

Todd supposedly had been discovered by mogul Jesse Lasky from unsolicited photographs and was chosen to attend the Paramount School of Acting (Buddy Rogers was a classmate). Last silent: *Trial Marriage* (1929), with synchronized sound effects and music.

Sound: With the exception of the talkie *Her Private Life*, 1929 was a year of silents and part-talkies for Todd. Among the latter were *Seven Footprints to Satan, The Bachelor Girl* and *Careers*. Her voice proved just fine for sound and she made about 40 talking features.

Todd's career lasted to the time of her most untimely death. Among her other features were *Follow Thru, The Maltese Falcon* (1931 version), *Command Performance, Monkey Business, Horse Feathers* (the latter two as a foil to the Marx brothers), *Counsellor-at-Law* and *Lightning Strikes*.

Todd also appeared in two of Laurel and Hardy's operettas, *The Devil's Brother* and *The Bohemian Girl*. The latter was her last, posthumously released in 1936. Her occasional use of the name Alison Loyd apparently was intended to separate her work as a dramatic actress from that as a comic actress.

Todd was even better known for the lengthy series of perhaps 40 comedy shorts (a few posthumously released) which she made with Charley Chase, ZaSu Pitts and finally Patsy Kelly. She was also seen in a couple of shorts with Laurel and Hardy. Among these comedies were *Chickens Come Home, On the Loose, Maids a la Mode, One Track Minds, Done in Oil, Top Flat* and *Sing Sister Sing*.

Comments: A very pretty blonde (and presumably a natural one), Thelma Todd proved to be much more than a stereotypical Hollywood "dumb" blonde. She was an actress of some charm and within her range a most winning and intelligent one; e.g. the "College Widow" in *Horse Feathers*. Although she never reached stardom, she always was a dependable supporting player. Her voice, though somewhat high-pitched, perfectly matched her persona.

Unfortunately, the mysterious manner of Todd's death at 30 and the ultimately unsatisfactory resolution of it — determined at the time to be an accident or suicide, but most likely murder — has come to overshadow her historically modest but real screen accomplishments.

REVIEWS

Her Private Life: Thelma Todd plays the hero's sister. *Harrison's Reports* 11/30/29.

Monkey Business: Todd, always an eyeful, is the subject of cracks by Groucho Marx. She takes part in some funny scenes. *Variety* 10/13/31, *Harrison's Reports* 10/17/31.

Horse Feathers: Todd plays the college widow. She's a luscious eyeful and great foil for the Marx's boudoir manhandling. She can remain looking serious no matter how ridiculous the situations may be. *Variety* 8/16/32, *Harrison's Reports* 8/20/32.

Speak Easily: Todd rounds out the lead trio with Buster Keaton and Jimmy Durante. She is a natural leading lady for the pair and her stripping down to her undies doesn't hurt. She is an eyeful of lines and curves. *Variety* 8/23/32.

Two for Tonight: Todd's role as a vamp is more decorative than anything else. *Variety* 9/4/35.

Torrence, Ernest (Ernest Tayson or
Thoyson), Edinburgh, Scotland, 1878–1933

Filmography: Classic Images (May 1992); List of films in *Eighty Silent Film Stars*

Silent: Ernest Torrence came to films after a career as a singer and actor in musical comedies. His first role as the frightening bully Luke Hatburn in Richard Barthelmess's *Tol'able David* (1921) was a world away from his previous experience but it set a pattern for many villain roles to follow.

Others of Torrence's nearly 40 silent films were *Singed Wings*, *The Heritage of the Desert*, *The Side Show of Life*, *Night Life of New York*, *The Cossacks* and *Captain Salvation*. Besides his first, Torrence made some memorable motion pictures that included *Peter Pan* (as Captain Hook), *The King of Kings*, *The Covered Wagon*, *The Hunchback of Notre Dame*, *Steamboat Bill Jr.* and *Mantrap*.

Torrence worked primarily for Famous Players and MGM in the 1920s but also made films for Vitagraph, Universal, Warner Bros., Pathe and Goldwyn. Last silent: *Speedway* (1929), with synchronized music and sound effects.

Sound: The part-sound *The Bridge of San Luis Rey* (1929) was Torrence's first. Others that year were *Untamed* and *The Unholy Night*, his first full talkie. He was busy until the time of his death in a variety of parts in such films as *Hypnotized*, *Call of the Flesh*, *Shipmates*, *Fighting Caravans*, *Sherlock Holmes* (1932 version as Doctor Moriarty) and his last, *I Cover the Waterfront* (1933).

Comments: It was far from unusual for Hollywood to cast — and typecast — people in unlikely roles. Because of his background and training, the very cultured Ernest Torrence would seem to have been miscast. The expressive face atop his 6'4" inch frame bespoke "villainy," however, and he certainly played some memorable ones.

Torrence could of course also play comedy, which he did — notably — in *The Covered Wagon* (as the scout Jackson) and in Buster Keaton's *Steamboat Bill Jr.* (he was Bill Sr.). In the talkies, in true Hollywood style, his pleasant Scots burr was transmuted into that of various other nationalities but somehow was never completely submerged. Nor was he ever anything but a center of attention in every scene in which he appeared.

REVIEWS

The Bridge of San Luis Rey: The cast is of high quality; especially excellent is the playing of Ernest Torrence. *Variety* 5/22/29, *Harrison's Reports* 5/25/29.

Call of the Flesh: Torrence, as a Spanish maestro, keeps his Scottish burr fairly well concealed. He provides capable support. *Variety* 9/17/30, *Harrison's Reports* 9/20/30.

Sherlock Holmes: Torrence is a rather benevolent menace as arch-villain Professor Moriarty. *Variety* 11/15/32.

I Cover the Waterfront: As a smuggler of Chinese into the United States, the late Ernest Torrence has the meaty part. His performance is in keeping with the standard he had set for himself and he'll be sorely missed on the screen. *Harrison's Reports* 5/20/33, *Variety* 5/23/33.

Truex, Ernest, Rich Hill, Missouri,
1889/90–1973

Silent: Diminutive Ernest Truex was a Broadway actor from 1908; he had been on the stage from the age of five. By 1913 he was also a film player in *Caprice*. Off and on until 1919 he starred or appeared in support in such films as *An American Citizen*, John Barrymore's first, and *A Good Little Devil*, co-starring with Mary Pickford.

Other Truex silents were *Dope*, *Artie the Millionaire Kid* (title role), *Good-Bye, Bill* and *Oh, You Women* (top-billed). He was also in some two-reelers with popular actress Shirley Mason. Last silent: *Six Cylinder Love* (1923), in which he was starred.

Sound: Continuing to be primarily a stage actor, Truex returned to the screen for a few in 1932 including *If I Had a Million* and *The Warrior's Husband*. Then it was back to the theater. From 1938 to '46 he concentrated on movies, appearing in many, mostly in supporting roles but with an occasional lead, as in *Mama Runs Wild*.

Only 5'3" as an adult and with an expressive "everyman" face, Truex specialized in timid, henpecked husbands. Among his films were *The Adventures of Marco Polo, Bachelor Mother, Slightly Honorable, His Girl Friday, Lillian Russell* (as a youngster he had appeared with the *real* Lillian Russell), *Star Spangled Rhythm* and *Life with Blondie.*

Truex was more or less absent from the movie screen for about ten years until the latter 1950s when he returned for a handful, including *The Leather Saint, All Mine to Give, Twilight of the Gods* and lastly, in 1965, *Fluffy.* He was, however, very much a part of television, a medium in which he frequently appeared until the late '60s.

REVIEWS

The Warrior's Husband: Truex leaves something to be desired. Either he's not effeminate enough or he takes too many comedy falls in the wrong spots. *Variety* 5/16/33.
Freshman Year: Truex clicks as a professor. *Variety* 9/2/38.
Ambush: Truex takes tight hold of the audience's attention with his portrayal of a pint-sized mastermind. He carves out a good chunk of kudos for himself. *Variety* 2/15/39.
Little Orvie: Truex is excellent as an indulgent father. *Variety* 3/27/40.
The Leather Saint: Truex, as the elderly priest, does all he can to imitate Barry Fitzgerald. *New York Times* 1/16/56.

Tryon, Glenn, Julietta, Idaho, 1894/99–1970

Silent: *The Battling Orioles* (1924) was fresh-faced Glenn Tryon's first-known feature. A former stage actor, he was top-billed, as he would be for most of the silent era in a series of light comedies. He made one other picture that year and then returned in 1927 for a full complement of films.

Tryon's films included *The Poor Nut, A Hero for a Night, The Gate Crasher, How to Handle Women* and *The Denver Dude.* Last silent: *The Kid's Clever* (1929), made after his first talkie.

Sound: Lonesome, a part-talkie, was Tryon's first in 1928. All but one of his 1929 films were "talkers" as well. Among them were *Barnum Was Right, Broadway* and *Skinner Steps Out.* His later film appearances included *Tangled Destinies, The Widow in Scarlet, Neck and Neck, Daybreak, Dames Ahoy* and *The King of Jazz.*

Tryon's on-screen career waned after 1932 and he eventually became a screenwriter, director and producer. He returned for a few small roles in 1940s pictures such as *George White's Scandals* and *Variety Girl* and a 1951 film, *The Hometown Story,* which may have been his last.

REVIEWS

Broadway: It is obvious that the first song sung by Glenn Tryon is done by a double; the other songs are probably sung by him. His acting is superb. *Variety* 6/8/29.
Barnum Was Right: Tryon supports the plot in a likable fashion. Without him the picture would be a sleep inducer. *Variety* 10/30/29.
Skinner Steps Out: Tryon is more enjoyable in his lighter moods than in his serious ones. His facial expressions help in the fun. He overacts at times and the net result is not as hilarious as some of his other work. What laughs he evokes come from his own personality and natural antics. *New York Times* 12/7/29, *Variety* 12/11/29.
Dames Ahoy: Tryon is spontaneous and has a flair for comedy. He does excellent work as the hero. *New York Times* 3/29/30, *Harrison's Reports* 4/5/30.
Neck and Neck: The humor is caused mostly by the wisecracks of the hero, Tryon. He plays a smart-aleck in a superficially amusing manner. *Harrison's Reports* 11/14/31, *Variety* 11/17/31.

Tucker, Richard, New York or Brooklyn, New York, 1884?–1942

Silent: On-screen from 1913 or '14 in Edison one-reelers, Richard Tucker graduated to top supporting roles and leads in numerous features beginning in 1915 with *The Ring of the Borgias* and *Vanity Fair.* Among his other early films were *The Law of the North, Threads of Fate, Babbling Tongues* and *The Royal Pauper.*

Tucker was off the screen in 1918 and '19, possibly for war service, but returned in 1920 for a lengthy string of supporting roles in such motion pictures as *The Branding Iron, The Old Nest, Remembrance, Cameo Kirby, Beau Brummell, The Man Without a Country, The World at Her Feet* and *Captain Swagger.* He also was seen in the serial *King of the Kongo.* Last silent: *Daughters of Desire* (1929), made after his first talkies.

Sound: Tucker was now a distinguished-looking gray-haired man with a voice that perfectly fit his authoritative image. His roles were usually those of a man in a high position in life: military officer, bank president, district attorney. He continued to appear in film after film, sometimes more than a dozen a year, as a dependable character actor.

Tucker's first part-talkie was *the* first part-talkie *The Jazz Singer* (1927), although his voice was not heard. His next sound effort was 1928's *On Trial.* Among his 1929 sound or part-sound films were *Half Marriage, Lucky Boy, The Squall* and *This Is Heaven.*

Tucker was seen until 1940 in films that included *Seed*, *Baby Take a Bow*, *Diamond Jim*, *The Great Ziegfeld*, *Something to Sing About*, *Test Pilot*, *The Great Victor Herbert* and *Road to Singapore*. Before he was through he had appeared in over 200 films as well as the serials *The Shadow of the Eagle*, *Flash Gordon* and *Jungle Menace* and some shorts.

REVIEWS

On Trial: Tucker is quite successful as the prosecuting attorney. His talking is only weakened by the Vitaphone lisp and he is more convincing and saleable in sound. His performance exacts some mirth. *New York Times* 11/15/28, *Variety* 11/21/28.

The Squall: Tucker, usually an excellent actor, is out of his element. His performance seems to have been cramped by the director. *New York Times* 5/10/29, *Variety* 5/15/29.

Turner, Florence, New York, New York,
1885–1946

Silent: Known as "The Vitagraph Girl," Florence Turner made scores of one- and two-reelers for that studio beginning about 1910. Enormously popular for her generally understated acting style in an era of theatrical emoting, she went to England in 1913 and founded her own production company.

Turner remained abroad until the outbreak of World War One and when she returned to America her popularity had decreased. In 1919 she directed and starred in a series of one-reel comedies for Vitagraph and also began appearing in features both in the U.S. and, in the first part of the 1920s, in England once again.

Among Turner's early full-length films, in which she played supporting roles, were *Fool's Gold*, *Blackmail* and *The Ugly Duckling*. Other roles, many quite small, came intermittently during the '20s. Toward the end of the decade she was seen in such pictures as *The Mad Marriage*, *Flame of the Argentine*, *Padlocked*, *Jazzland*, *Marry the Girl* and *College*. Last silent: *The Kid's Clever* (1929).

Sound: Turner made her sound debut in *The Rampant Age*, a low-budget 1930 film. She then played small roles in a few pictures in 1931–33 including *The Ridin' Fool*, *The Animal Kingdom*, *The Trial of Vivienne Ware* and *The Sign of the Cross*. Eventually she became a member of the MGM "stock company" as a bit player and extra.

Turpin, Ben (Bernard Turpin), New Orleans,
Louisiana, 1869/74–1940

Filmography: Films in Review (Oct. 1977); *Classic Images* (Dec. 1988-Jan. 1989); List of films in *Eighty Silent Film Stars*

Silent: After working in repertory, Ben Turpin came to Essanay and literally worked his way up from the ground floor. He was a janitor and clerk before he not too successfully essayed crude slapstick comedy on the screen. In 1909 or so he left the movies to tour for several years in his "Happy Hooligan" act.

Turpin returned to films, and to a little greater success, in 1914 with Essanay, where he appeared with Chaplin and other comics of the studio. He supplied some of the comedy relief in Broncho Billy films and then worked at Vogue studios. He did not find his special niche until he came to Sennett and stumbled upon the hilarity inherent in parodying the successful films of the day.

Well-known Ben Turpin parodies included *Uncle Tom Without the Cabin*, *East Lynne with Variations*, *The Shriek of Araby* and *Three Foolish Weeks*. Among his features were *A Small Town Idol* (considered a comic masterwork), *The College Hero*, *Hogan's Alley* (a dramatic role), *Yankee Doodle in Berlin*, *Down on the Farm* and *Married Life*.

In several of Turpin's films, in what amounted to a running gag, he played the "suave" lady-killer Rodney St. Clair. He also appeared in a series of Pathe two-reelers. Last silent: *The Wife's Relations* (1928).

Sound: Ben Turpin made minuscule appearances in two 1929 musicals, *The Show of Shows* and *The Love Parade*. His roles in 1930s features were small, sometimes bits, and were few and far between. He did appear in shorts for Paramount, Educational and Vitaphone, as well as in some Laurel and Hardy films.

Turpin's features included *Cracked Nuts*, *Hypnotized*, *Hollywood Cavalcade* and *Saps at Sea*, his last in 1940. His final major role came in the serial *The Law of the Wild* (1934) and he made no full-length films between 1935 and 1939.

Comments: The success of Ben Turpin's parodies came from his characters' total obliviousness about the incongruity between their physical appearance (short and scrawny physique, wagging Adam's apple, ill-trimmed mustache, large head and one crossed eye) and their swaggering derring-do. Actually, before the adulthood misfortune which caused his eye to turn inward, he had been a not-unhandsome man.

Despite his unprepossessing looks, Turpin was an athletic man who performed the famous "108," a back somersault from a standing position from which he landed on all parts of his anatomy except the feet. This and other stunts led to many injuries which may have been one reason for his long screen absences.

While it is unlikely that Ben Turpin could have

carried an entire talkie feature, his gravelly voice was certainly suitable for character roles. However, he was reputedly a difficult man to work with; this might explain his paucity of roles and their generally minute size.

REVIEWS

The Love Parade: Although Ben Turpin is in the cast he has so little to do he could almost as well have been out of it. He is billed last as "cross-eyed lackey." *Variety* 11/27/29.

Make Me a Star: Turpin is cast as himself, a cross-eyed slapsticker. *Variety* 7/5/32.

Million Dollar Legs: Turpin plays a bit part in a cast that has everything but good material. *Variety* 7/12/32.

Saps at Sea: The film includes some old-timers, among them Ben Turpin.

(Turpin's "role," playing on his cross-eyedness for the final time, consisted of less than a minute of screen time and a few words.) *Variety* 5/1/40, *Harrison's Reports* 5/4/40.

Tyler, Tom (Vincent Markowski), Port
Henry, New York, 1903–1954

Filmography: Filmograph (vol. 1, no. 1, 1970); List of films in *Eighty Silent Film Stars*

Silent: Beginning as an extra in the early '20s, Tom Tyler became a western star in a series of FBO westerns. The first was *Let's Go Gallagher* in 1925. Among his films were *The Cowboy Musketeer, The Arizona Streak, Tom and His Pals, The Flying U Ranch, The Avenging Rider, Idaho Red* and *'Neath Western Skies.* Young Frankie Darro was his frequent sidekick. Last silents: *Call of the Desert* and *The Canyon of Missing Men,* released about the same time in 1930, both with synchronized music.

Sound: Tyler finally made his talkie feature bow in 1931's *West of Cheyenne,* but the first time his voice actually may have been heard was in the serial *Phantom of the West.* There followed a long series of westerns for Syndicate, Reliable, Monogram, Bell, Victor, Monarch and other indies. He also began taking supporting roles in major films.

Tyler was one of a rotating band of western performers who appeared in "The Three Mesquiteers" series; he made his final starring "B" western, *Sing Me a Song of Texas,* in 1945. Prior to that, he had appeared in his now best-known role, that of Captain Marvel, in the 1941 serial *Adventures of Captain Marvel.* It is considered one of the best sound serials.

Another of Tyler's prominent roles was as "The Mummy" in *The Mummy's Hand.* A man of muscular physique, he was perfect physical casting. Among his other westerns were *Powdersmoke Range, Frontier Marshal, Coyote Trails, Stagecoach* (as a villain) and *Valley of the Sun.*

Other features in which Tyler appeared included *King of Alcatraz, The Dude Goes West, The Grapes of Wrath, They Were Expendable* and *What Price Glory?* He also made serial appearances in *Clancy of the Mounted, The Jungle Mystery, The Phantom of the Air, Battling with Buffalo Bill* and *The Phantom.*

About 1943, Tyler began experiencing the arthritis attacks that were ultimately to disable him. He left films for several years and when he returned in the late '40s it was in bit parts. As the disease progressed, his radically changed appearance limited him to villain roles. His final films came in the early 1950s: *The Great Missouri Raid, Outlaw Women* and *Cow Country.* He also was seen on television.

REVIEWS

West of Cheyenne: The only good thing in the film is Tom Tyler's voice. Otherwise it's the same old brand of western. *Variety* 3/4/31.

Man from New Mexico: Tyler gives a nice performance. *Variety* 8/30/32.

War of the Range: Tyler is starred and does his best but he does not get much help from the writer and director. *Variety* 12/12/33.

Ulric, Lenore (Lenore Ulrich), New Ulm,
Minnesota, 1892–1970

Silent: Later to be a famous stage star in plays like *Lulu Belle, Kiki* and *The Son-Daughter,* Lenore Ulric made her cinema debut for Essanay about 1911 and appeared in many one- and two-reelers. She was immodestly billed as "The Magic Mistress of a Thousand Emotions." Her feature bow came in 1915's *Kilmeny* and for the next couple of years she starred for Triumph and other studios.

Ulric showed at least a few of her "thousand" emotions in a handful of rather perfervid melodramas like *The Better Woman, The Heart ofPaula, The Intrigue, The Road to Love* and *Her Own People.* After 1917 she returned to the cinema only twice in the silent era, the first time being in 1919's *Roses and Thorns.* Last silent: *Tiger Rose* (1923).

Sound: Like many theater divas, Ulric came West to face the cameras in the early talkies. Her 1929 starring vehicles *South Sea Rose* and *Frozen Justice,* in which she was called upon to be exotic and/or sultry, were not hugely successful.

Thereafter, Ulric limited herself to the theater and supporting roles in a smattering of films like *Camille* in 1936, and ten years later *Notorious, Temptation* and *Two Smart People.*

Frozen Justice: Ulric plays a good-looking Eskimo woman in her first talking picture. She might have had a better chance in a part calling for some clothes and a little romance. In one scene she sings in a talk-sing way. She is not impressive as a vocalist, but in talking she's always impressive and should be built into an important talking picture name. She has all of the requisites. *Variety* 10/30/29.

South Sea Rose: As a French girl in the South Sea islands Ulrich again has the opportunity to show her stuff and she does. *Variety* 12/11/29.

Camille: Ulric has been away from the screen for several years. She has a major part and gives it real importance in the story. She looks well and handles her scenes excellently. *Variety* 1/27/37.

Temptation: In a minor role Lenore Ulric contributes very well playing a lady's maid. *Variety* 12/11/46.

Valli, Virginia (Virginia McSweeney),
Chicago, Illinois, 1895/1900–1968

Silent: Virginia Valli began her career with Chicago-based studios about 1915 and she was in features by 1917 for Essanay. Among her early ones, in which she alternated between leading and supporting roles, were *The Fibbers*, *The Midnight Bride*, *Satan's Private Door* and *Ruggles of Red Gap*.

Valli eventually went to Hollywood and became a popular leading woman (or occasionally played in support) in many 1920s films including *Wild Oranges*, *Sentimental Tommy*, *Tracked to Earth*, *The Lady Who Lied*, *Paid to Love*, *The Escape* and *The Signal Tower*. Last silent: *Behind Closed Doors* (1929).

Sound: Valli appeared in only five talkies. *Mr. Antonio* was the first in 1929. The other two the same year were *The Isle of Lost Ships* and *The Lost Zeppelin*. They were followed by *Guilty?* in 1930 and *Night Life in Reno* (1931). In each she was the lead.

Comments: Already at the "dangerous" age of about 35 in 1931, Virginia Valli let it be known that she was leaving the screen for marriage to actor Charles Farrell. It is evident from reviews that her voice was satisfactory, so perhaps the reason offered was the actual one.

It is also probable that Valli, never a major star, would have been in the predicament so many of her contemporaries were. Soon she would have been playing in quickies for minor studios and then there would be ever smaller and fewer supporting roles. That fate, understandably, she may not have desired.

The Isle of Lost Ships: As the heroine, Valli's performance is stiff and too "English." She also lacks warmth, although her only female competitors are two elderly women. *Variety* 10/30/29, *Harrison's Reports* 11/2/29.

Mr. Antonio: Valli's acting makes the heroine sympathetic. She is charming and her speaking voice is pleasant. *Variety* 12/11/29, *Harrison's Reports* 12/14/29.

The Lost Zeppelin: The performance of Virginia Valli is not especially worthy of praise, but she must struggle with the silly dialogue. *New York Times* 2/1/30.

Guilty?: Valli is a good heroine in this melodrama. *Harrison's Reports* 3/22/30.

Varconi, Victor (Mihaly Varconyi),
Kisvard(a), Hungary, 1891–1976

Filmography: List of films in *Film Fan Monthly* (Jan. 1973)

Silent: Victor Varconi was a film star in Hungary and he also appeared in the Italian, German, Polish and British cinemas. Under the name Michael Varconi (almost immediately supplanted by his new Christian name) he made his American debut in *Poisoned Paradise* (1924). A favorite of Cecil DeMille, he was seen in several of the director's films like *Triumph*, *Feet of Clay*, *The Volga Boatman* and *The King of Kings*, in which he played Pontius Pilate.

Among Varconi's other pictures were *Worldly Goods*, *Chicago*, *Silken Shackles*, *The Forbidden Woman* and *The Angel of Broadway*. Last silent: *Eternal Love* (1929), with synchronized music and sound effects. His earlier 1929 film *The Divine Lady* was technically a silent although it contained singing sequences.

Sound: It soon became clear that Varconi's accent would hamper his talkie career. He did not make his first sound film, in the title role of the poorly-received *Captain Thunder*, until late 1930. In it he played a Mexican bandido. His career thereafter was mainly in supporting roles, some in good but many in indifferent films.

Varconi also seemed a natural for Nazi roles during World War Two (e.g., *They Raid by Night*), even portraying the hapless Rudolph Hess in *The Hitler Gang*. His films included *Roberta*, *The Plainsman*, *Strange Cargo*, *My Favorite Blonde*, *Samson and Delilah*, *Suez*, *Mr. Moto Takes a Vacation*, *For Whom the Bell Tolls* and *The Sea Hawk*. After a considerable hiatus he made his final movies, *The Man Who Turned to Stone* and *The Atomic Submarine*, in the late 1950s.

REVIEWS

Captain Thunder: The acting is something awful. *Variety* 5/13/31.

The Black Camel: Varconi always looks guilty under the right circumstances, helped by his accent and his scowls. *Variety* 7/7/31.

King of the Newsboys: Varconi plays the role of a sinister racetrack tout. *Variety* 3/30/38.

The Atomic Submarine: Although none of the featured players have marquee value, most have good acting ability, e.g., Victor Varconi. *Variety* 2/17/60.

Vaughn, Alberta, Ashland, Alabama,
1905?–1992

Silent: Pixieish Alberta Vaughn was a Wampas Baby Star of 1923 and a leading lady in Sennett two-reelers and features. Among her other studios were Fox, Universal and Vitagraph.

Vaughn's films from 1923, many of them comedies, included *A Friendly Husband, The Adorable Deceiver, Ain't Love Funny?, The Drop Kick, Forbidden Hours, Skyscraper* and *Sinews of Steel.* She also appeared in serials. Last silent: *Points West* (1929), made after her first part-talkies.

Sound: The part-talkies *Noisy Neighbors* and *Molly and Me,* both 1929, were Vaughn's first, followed by *The Show of Shows.* In this musical melange she was seen briefly in the "Meet My Sister" number singing and dancing with sister Adamae.

Vaughn's talkie career was not memorable. She made no features in 1930 and for the next few years she was cast in quickie melodramas and then increasingly in westerns.

Among Vaughn's films were *Dancers in the Dark, Midnight Morals, Alimony Madness, Dance Hall Hostess, Randy Rides Alone* (a John Wayne "B" western) and lastly, *The Laramie Kid* and *The Live Wire* in 1935.

REVIEWS

Noisy Neighbors: Vaughn contributes to this comedy's entertainment values by her youthfulness and acting ability. *Harrison's Reports* 2/23/29.

Molly and Me: Alberta Vaughn does well in an unsympathetic role. *Harrison's Reports* 4/20/29.

Midnight Morals: Vaughn does as well as can be expected in her role as the dancer, but is given little opportunity. *New York Times* 9/13/32.

Veidt, Conrad, Potsdam, Germany,
1893–1943
Filmography: Focus on Film (Summer 1975)
Silent: Conrad Veidt appeared in many German films from 1917 before he played the role of Cesare, the killer-somnambulist in the expressionist classic *The Cabinet of Dr. Caligari* (1919). Earlier he had been a stage actor with Max Reinhardt.

Veidt also had French and Swedish films to his credit when he made his American debut as a decadent Louis XIV in 1927's *The Beloved Rogue.* His other motion picture that year was *A Man's Past.* Last silent: *The Man Who Laughs* (1928), with synchronized music and sound effects.

Sound: Although Veidt made an American part-talkie, *The Last Performance,* released in 1929, he was considered too exotic for American audiences and he returned to Germany. There he made numerous films until the Nazis came to power in 1933. He prudently departed along with his half–Jewish wife and England became his home for the rest of the decade.

Veidt appeared in both French and English pictures including *Under the Red Robe, Dark Journey* and *The Thief of Bagdad* before returning to the United States in 1940. Not surprisingly, beginning with that year's *Escape,* he was cast in a series of Nazi and other villain roles, the most famous of these being Major Strasser in the 1942 classic *Casablanca.*

Veidt's other American movies, in which his villainy occasionally had a comic cast, were *A Woman's Face, Whistling in the Dark, The Men in Her Life, Nazi Agent, All Through the Night* and, lastly, *Above Suspicion* in the year of his death.

Comments: In Germany, Conrad Veidt had made a specialty of appearing in gothic-type fantasy films (*The Student of Prague, The Hands of Orlac*) which very much fed into the World War One and postwar German psyche. He was praised as an outstanding actor who thoroughly immersed himself in his characters, a prototype early "Method" actor. He came to be considered the "Lon Chaney" of Germany.

Extremely thin with a long, gaunt face, Veidt could convincingly play romantic heroes but he was not Hollywood's vision of an ideal leading man. He spoke English well and his accent was not at all unpleasant but American moguls saw him as a villain and a villain he remained during his brief return in the '40s. No doubt he strongly felt the irony of playing Nazis after his experiences with the genuine articles, but that was Hollywood.

REVIEWS

A Woman's Face: Veidt plays his typically suave villain. *Variety* 5/7/41.

All Through the Night: As a smooth but ruthless Nazi agent, Conrad Veidt is first rate. *Variety* 12/3/41.

Above Suspicion: The late Conrad Veidt does solid work in a major supporting role. *Variety* 4/28/43.

Velez, Lupe (Guadalupe Velez Villalobos),
San Luis de Potosi, Mexico, 1909–1944
Filmography: Films in Review (Nov. 1977)

Silent: After brief stage experience, Lupe Velez began her equally brief silent career in 1927. She appeared in at least a couple of two-reel comedies, including Laurel and Hardy's *Sailors Beware*, and made her feature debut second-billed to Douglas Fairbanks in *The Gaucho* (1928). That year she also was named a Wampas Baby Star.

Velez's other silents were *Stand and Deliver* and 1929's *Wolf Song*, technically a silent but with singing sequences, in which she co-starred with Gary Cooper. Last silent: *Where East Is East* (1929), co-starring Lon Chaney, made after her first part-talkie.

Sound: The D. W. Griffith part-talkie *Lady of the Pavements* was Velez's first and *Tiger Rose* her first full-sound picture. Talkies revealed her considerable accent and she was more or less consigned to a range of "exotic" portrayals that included characters who were French-Canadian, Indian and even Chinese.

Velez also made some Spanish-language versions of Hollywood pictures. Among her '30s films were *Hell Harbor*, *The Storm*, *The Broken Wing*, *Strictly Dynamite*, *High Flyers* and *The Girl from Mexico*, which launched the "Mexican Spitfire" series. She also began appearing in Broadway revues and made a few British films in 1935 and '36.

In the '40s the "Spitfire" series continued on with entries such as *Mexican Spitfire('s) Elephant ...Baby ...Sees a Ghost ...at Sea*, etc. In these, Velez's invariable co-star was Leon Errol in his dual roles as Uncle Matt and Lord Epping. She also was seen in other "B"s such as *Six Lessons from Madame LaZonga* and *Redhead from Manhattan* (1943), her final U.S. picture. Her last film, *Nana*, was made in Mexico the year of her death.

Comments: Almost inevitably, Lupe Velez was typecast in fiery señorita roles, an image just begging for hackneyed Hollywood publicist designations like "bombshell" and "firecracker." A competent if somewhat fevered dramatic actress (*Resurrection*, *The Squaw Man*), she was relegated later in her career mostly to silly comedies.

Unfortunately the five-foot Velez lived up (or down) to her publicity, making it less likely she would ever break away from her stereotyping. She led a hectic and well-reported love life with the likes of Gary Cooper and Johnny Weissmuller (with whom she had a stormy marriage). Her death by suicide provided more copy than her fading career had for many years.

REVIEWS

Tiger Rose: This will add nothing to the reputation of Lupe Velez, who plays a half-caste French girl, but it will not hurt her either. *Variety* 1/1/30, *Harrison's Reports* 1/4/30.

The Storm: The name of Lupe Velez will add box-office value. She has an accent that is a cross between Spanish and French, half the time playing a flashing Spanish señorita, the other half a French girl. Her voice records nicely throughout; the accent adds something to the part rather than detracting from it. It will not harm her career unless the studio casts her in an English drawing room role. *Variety* 8/27/30.

Hot Pepper: Velez provides a better than usual reason for the conflict between the heroes (Quirt and Flagg from *What Price Glory?* and its sequels.) She is seen in panties once, and does an almost indecent cooch dance that would make the girls at Minsky's burlesque go back to their previous professions. *Variety* 1/24/33, *Harrison's Reports* 1/28/33.

Laughing Boy: As a Navajo Indian Velez steals the picture, being far ahead of Ramon Novarro in handling the dialogue. *Variety* 5/15/34.

High Flyers: Velez appears just as miserable as the stars, Wheeler and Woolsey, but helps things along by singing a few songs and imitating different stars. *Variety* 11/10/37, *Harrison's Reports* 11/6/37.

The Girl from Mexico: The film will make up for Velez's less successful screen roles, despite the fact that for her comeback she's been given a corny story. She is given free rein and mugs, sings and dances, revealing an excellent flair for comedy in her stylized bombshell manner. *Variety* 5/24/39.

Mexican Spitfire: Where the name of Lupe Velez has nominal marquee value, the picture will do well enough. She occupies the starring spot, but the attention is focused on Leon Errol. *Variety* 12/13/39.

Vidor, Florence (Florence Cobb, later Arto),
Houston, Texas, 1895–1977
Filmography: Films in Review (Jan. 1970)

Silent: Florence Vidor appeared in almost 60 silent films from 1916. Her career began with bit parts at Vitagraph, her first notable role being in the 1917 version of *A Tale of Two Cities*. Also in that year Vidor had her first lead opposite Sessue Hayakawa in an uncharacteristic comic role. This led to appearances in C. B. DeMille films and then Thomas Ince productions.

Vidor also appeared under the aegis of her then-husband director King Vidor. Her playing of the title role in 1923's *Alice Adams* was probably the highlight of her career prior to a breakthrough in Ernst Lubitsch's *The Marriage Circle*. Her signing with Famous Players-Lasky in 1925 ushered in her golden age, three years that proved to be her final ones as a film actress. Highlights of this period included *Are Parents People?*, *The Grand Duchess and the Waiter*, *You Never Know Women* and *The Popular Sin*. Last silent: *The Patriot* (1928), co-starring Emil Jannings, with synchronized music and sound effects.

Sound: Vidor's first and only talkie, *Chinatown Nights*, was released in 1929 with only about 60 percent of the sound version containing spoken dialogue. Reviewers of the day suspected that at least some of her talk had been dubbed. It was a somewhat sleazy melodrama co-starring Wallace Beery and Warner Oland. Vidor's role in it was completely atypical of the kind of roles she had been playing during her starring career. The film did not meet with success from either the critics or the public.

Comments: The story of a society woman slumming in Chinatown, being caught in a tong war, and then becoming no better than a woman of the streets was unsavory. It seems an odd choice for a Florence Vidor vehicle and she claims to have hated it. Perhaps the studio was trying to convey a message to her, or, more charitably, perhaps herself wanted a change of image which she later regretted.

Vidor's voice certainly did not register well and some of her dialogue presumably had to be dubbed because it recorded poorly. In any event, the combination of the silly story line and poor "talk" was enough to finish her career, either in her own eyes or that of the studio. Indeed, she had spoken about retiring in the latter years of silents; perhaps the inevitability of character roles did not interest her.

In 1928, Vidor had married violinist Jascha Heifetz and begun living the life of a Beverly Hills society matron. She was quoted as saying that she was never an actress, she just did what she was told. She underestimated herself. With the proper vehicle and director, the luminously lovely silent star was indeed a most welcome screen presence.

REVIEWS

Chinatown Nights: It is astonishing that Florence Vidor should have been asked to act this unedifying part in an absurd story. Her voice does not register well and it is patently clear that in some sequences another voice is doubling for hers. *New York Times* 4/1/29, *Variety* 4/3/29, *Harrison's Reports* 4/6/29.

Von Eltz, Theodore, New Haven, Connecticut, 1894–1964

Silent: Theodore Von Eltz was in a couple of mid-'teens silents (*His Wife* and *The Traffic Cop*), but his cinema career seriously began in 1921. Although he played occasional leads, he most often was found in solid supporting roles which continued throughout the decade.

Von Eltz made films in all genres, including *Extravagance*, *The Glorious Fool*, *Manslaughter*, *Hearts of Oak*, *Paint and Powder*, *Red Kimono*, *Bardelys the Magnificent*, *The Sea Wolf* (1926 version) and *The Way of the Strong*. Last silent: *The Four Feathers* (1929), with sound effects and music.

Sound: The Awful Truth (1929) was Theodore Von Eltz's first talkie and was followed that year by *The Very Idea*. For the next 20 years or so he remained a fixture as a character actor, often in bad man parts, in such pictures as *Susan Lenox: Her Fall and Rise*, *Luxury Liner*, *Bright Eyes*, *Private Worlds*, *I Cover Chinatown*, *Devil's Island*, *Dr. Ehrlich's Magic Bullet*, *Sergeant York* and *Since You Went Away*.

One of Von Eltz's interesting sound roles came in Mary Pickford's final film *Secrets* in 1933. With three other silent film performers he played one of Pickford's greedy middle-aged children. Another juicy role was that of the sleazy blackmailer in the film noir classic *The Big Sleep* in 1946. His final film was made in the early '50s.

REVIEWS

Red-Haired Alibi: Von Eltz acts more gentlemanly than any gang leader has the right to be. *New York Times* 10/24/32.

von Stroheim, Erich (Erich Stroheim), Vienna, Austria, 1885–1957

Filmography: Films in Review (June-July 1967)

Silent: Although many of the facts of Erich von Stroheim's life are open to question, it seems likely that from about 1914 to '17 he worked for D. W. Griffith as an actor, assistant director, art director and perhaps as a military advisor. It is known that his actual military experience was limited.

As an actor, von Stroheim appeared in such 'teens films as *Old Heidelberg*, *The Birth of a Nation* (a bit), *The Social Secretary*, *The Hun Within*, *For France*, *Hearts of the World* and *The Heart of Humanity*. A victim of the usual Hollywood typecasting, he convincingly portrayed terminally heinous Huns and similar roles.

In 1919, von Stroheim directed his first film *Blind Husbands*, in which he also appeared. Stylistically it was to set the pattern for all the pictures he directed thereafter. The '20s proved to be the period of both his greatest triumphs and most grievous defeats, both extremes often stemming from the same film. The latter generally came about as a result of his legendary spending habits and Prussian autocratic manner.

"Von," as he was called, helmed and acted in *Foolish Wives* and he directed *The Devil's Passkey*, *Merry-Go-Round* (which was completed by another director), the (in)famous classic *Greed*, *The Merry Widow*, *Queen Kelly* (never completed but released abroad in an abbreviated form) and *The Wedding March*.

Only *Passkey* and *Widow* were issued substantially as von Stroheim had directed them, the latter being his biggest commercial hit. He also worked on the screenplay of 1928's *Tempest*. Last silent (as an actor): *Souls for Sale* (1923), in which he made a cameo appearance.

Sound: From 1929 to 1935 von Stroheim acted in several American talkies, the first of which was *The Great Gabbo* (1929). It was a routine melodrama with musical numbers shot in color. Others included *Three Faces East*, *Crimson Romance*, Greta Garbo's *As You Desire Me*, *The Lost Squadron*, *The Crime of Doctor Crespi* and *Friends and Lovers*.

"Von" also directed his final American film, 1932's *Walking Down Broadway* which was, familiarly enough by this time, recut and released as the unsuccessful *Hello, Sister*. From 1937 to '39 he was active in France where he starred in the classic antiwar drama *La Grande Illusion* as well as *L'Affaire Lafarge*, *Le Monde Tremblera*, *Menace* and *La Danse de la Mort*, among others.

The onset of World War Two brought Erich von Stroheim back to the United States, his first film being 1940's *I Was an Adventuress*. Several more followed including *Five Graves to Cairo*, as the Desert Fox Erwin Rommel, *The North Star*, *The Lady and the Monster* and *Scotland Yard Inspector* before he returned to France in 1946.

In 1950 von Stroheim came back once again to appear with Gloria Swanson, the unhappy star of the grimly legendary *Queen Kelly*, in *Sunset Blvd.* They were both nominated for Academy Awards which neither won. Then, once again, it was back to France where he acted in more films and where he spent his remaining years.

Comments: For Erich von Stroheim, life and art seemed to merge dramatically. As an actor he made a specialty of playing Huns and other villains. He was "The Man You Love to Hate" and as a director he continued to live up to the characterization. He was roundly loathed by film casts and crews for his rigid perfectionism and dictatorial behavior which led to the widely repeated motto that it was "Von's way or no way."

Von Stroheim's performance as the maniacal director in *The Lost Squadron* was seemingly so close to the real-life director that it is surprising he agreed to play the part. He also was much from beloved by studio moguls. His idea of "art" was far different from theirs and he fought hard for his version of honesty on the screen rather than resorting to what he considered stylistic tricks.

As a result, "Von's" penchant for shooting vast amounts of film while spending mind-boggling sums of money on costumes, settings and retakes ultimately got him fired from some films. Others were drastically edited. *Greed* and *The Wedding March* are examples which have become the stuff of legend.

The former is considered a butchered masterpiece although what is left after MGM cut it down is admirable enough. Von Stroheim had filmed almost every page of the source novel *McTeague*. The second part of the latter film was never released in the United States at all. Typically, he said that he hated the one solid success he did have, 1925's *The Merry Widow*.

In many ways, von Stroheim's life — and all his exaggerations and outright falsehoods about it — was more interesting than most movies. He certainly was not descended from a noble family (his father was a Jewish hat maker) and he provably did not have an exemplary military career.

It is sometimes tempting to believe that von Stroheim was not the humorless martinet he seemed to be but was knowingly putting on the entire film industry. Whether he was really the person he seemed or a tongue-in-cheek creation, he did live his life in the most colorful way possible. He was often his own worst enemy but he remains a true legend.

REVIEWS

The Great Gabbo: Reviews differed somewhat. One said that von Stroheim dominated the screen with his role as an eccentric and arrogant ventriloquist. His voice, at times frenzied and then soft, strongly compelled the audience's concentration. Another review opined that his acting was self-conscious at times, but admitted his personality was impressive. *Variety* 9/18/29, *Harrison's Reports* 9/21/29.

The Lost Squadron: Von Stroheim plays the part to the hilt. As the domineering, militaristic Prussian film director it was a smart casting. *Variety* 3/15/32.

Crimson Romance: Von Stroheim has a minor role as a captain with a sadistic love of death. Although he looks considerably fatter, he still is an unusual type and does the best acting job in the film. *Variety* 10/16/34.

Five Graves to Cairo: Affording a vivid picture of Rommel, Stroheim does a great job. The characterization is tailor-made for him. *Variety* 5/5/43.

The Great Flamarion: Von Stroheim has one of his better screen roles, one that he makes plausible. *Variety* 1/7/45.

The Mask of Diijon: As a murderous hypnotist in this cheaply made film, von Stroheim is aided by his sour countenance. *Variety* 1/20/46.

Sunset Blvd.: Von Stroheim, as Norma Desmond's butler and original discoverer, delivers an excellently restrained performance. *Variety* 4/19/50.

Wales, Wally (later known as Hal Taliaferro)
(Floyd Alderson), Montana or Wyoming, 1895/96–1980

Silent: Beginning as an extra, perhaps as early as the mid-'teens, Wally Wales segued his talents as an expert rider into a career as a hero in westerns. From 1925 he worked at Action Pictures.

Among Wales's films were *Tearin' Loose, Double Daring, Vanishing Hoofs, Soda Water Cowboy* and *Saddle Mates.* In the early pictures his character was usually named Wally. Last silent: *The Flying Buckaroo* (1928).

Sound: In 1930, Wales began alternating leading and supporting roles for the Big 4 Company, both in shorts and features. Among his early talkies that year were *Breed of the West, Overland Bound* (the second outdoor sound western) and *Canyon Hawks.*

By the mid–1930s Wales had metamorphosed into Hal Taliaferro and was now primarily a supporting actor, eventually working for Republic, Paramount, United Artists and Columbia. Under this new name he sometimes was seen in villain roles.

Among Taliaferro/Wales's numerous pictures that decade were *Heir to Trouble, Flying Lariats, Fighting Through, Between Men, Daughter of the Tong* and *Rio Grande.* His 1930s serials included *The Lone Ranger* and *The Painted Stallion.*

Taliaferro remained as busy as ever in the 1940s, mostly in "B" westerns, but with small roles in an occasional prestige movie. His films included *Bullets for Rustlers, Sheriff of Tombstone, Idaho, Duel in the Sun, Lumberjack, Ramrod* and *Red River.*

Taliaferro's career ended in the early 1950s with the end of "B" oaters. His last films were *The Savage Horde, The Sea Hornet* and *Junction City.* By then he had appeared in hundreds of features and had also been in the serials *Adventures of Red Ryder, Haunted Harbor, Zorro's Black Whip, Federal Operator 99* and *The Phantom Rider.*

Walker, Charlotte, Galveston, Texas, 1878–1958

Silent: Charlotte Walker was a respected theater actress when she made her film debut for C. B. DeMille in *The Kindling* (1915). This role made her a star. Other early films included *Mary Lawson's Secret, Pardners, Every Mother's Son* and *Sloth.*

Walker's career as a leading lady ended in 1919 with *Eve in Exile* and when she returned to the cinema in 1924 it was for supporting roles. Among her later silent pictures were *The Manicure Girl, The Sixth Commandment, The Savage* and *The Clown.* Last silent: *Annapolis* (1928), with synchronized sound effects and music.

Sound: Paris Bound (1929) marked Charlotte Walker's sound debut. Her other film that year was *South Sea Rose.* She was seen on-screen steadily through the mid–'30s and then sporadically thereafter.

Walker's films, in which she often played very minor roles, included *Scarlet Pages, Hotel Variety, Three Faces East, Salvation Nell, Millie* and *Scattergood Meets Broadway* (1941), her final film.

REVIEWS

Three Faces East: Charlotte Walker's performance is somewhat theatrical. *New York Times* 9/6/30.

Salvation Nell: Walker is the Salvation Army woman who does a lot for the good will of that group in the way she handles the saloon bunch. *Variety* 7/7/31, *Harrison's Reports* 7/11/31.

Walker, Johnnie (sometimes Johnny), New York, New York, 1894/98–1949

Silent: Johnnie Walker's film career began about 1915 in films such as *Cohen's Luck, Destruction, Brown of Harvard* and *The Man from Nowhere.* He did not reach his screen stride until about 1921 when he attained leading man status in a series of adventure melodramas and comedies. His best-known films were probably *Over the Hill (to the Poorhouse)* (1920) and *Old Ironsides* (1926).

Others of Walker's films were *Live Wires, Captain Fly-By-Night, The Fourth Musketeer, The Spirit of the U.S.A., Held by the Law, The Snarl of Hate, Fangs of Justice* and *Wolves of the Air.* He also appeared in the 1928 serial *Vultures of the Sea.* Last silent: *The Matinee Idol* (1928).

Sound: Walker made no films in 1929 but was back in 1930 for several, among them *Ladies in Love, Ladies of Leisure, The Girl of the Golden West, The Swellhead* and *Up the River.* In most of these he had supporting roles for which his pronounced New York accent was suitable. He also appeared in at least one short.

Walker's acting career came to an end with 1931's *Enemies of the Law* but he tried his hand at producing and also directed one film, *Mr. Broadway* in 1933. It was not a success and later he turned to screenwriting.

REVIEWS

The Swellhead: The only defect is that Johnnie Walker, the hero, looks too soft to be a convincing prize fighter. No muscles are seen on his body. *Harrison's Reports* 4/12/30.

Ladies in Love: Reviews did not agree. One said that Walker's characterization as the man from Vermont fell flat. Another thought that he played the hick role very well and spoke with a characteristic small town twang. He never forgot to stay in character. *New York Times* 6/14/30, *Variety* 6/18/30.

Enemies of the Law: Walker gives an unusually bad performance in an amazing display of overacting. *Variety* 7/14/31, *Harrison's Reports* 7/18/31.

Walsh, George, New York, New York,
1889–1981

Filmography: Silent Picture (Summer/Autumn 1971); *Films in Review* (Apr. 1982); *Classic Images* (June 1990); List of films in *Eighty Silent Film Stars*

Silent: Rugged George Walsh made many romantic comedies and action films for Fox and was one of that studio's major stars from 1916 to early '21. *Blue Blood and Red* was his first major role. He previously had been an extra and had appeared in two-reelers, his first-known credit being 1915's *The Hunting Master.*

Walsh went to Universal in 1921 and then, in what seemed to be a good career move, he was hired for the leading role in *Ben-Hur* for Metro. While that troubled production languished in Italy, he was off the screen for a year and a half. Ultimately replaced by Ramon Novarro, he found that his career had stalled irretrievably and he went to work for the independent Chadwick studio.

Among Walsh's 65 silent films were *Intolerance, The Serpent, The Beast, Luck and Pluck, Number 17, The Miracle Makers, Striving for Fortune, Brave and Bold, Sink or Swim, Rosita* (Mary Pickford's leading man) and *The Plunger.* He also was seen in the 1922 serial *With Stanley in Africa.* Last silent: *Inspiration* (1928).

Sound: The advent of talkies found Walsh out of films. He worked for his director-brother Raoul Walsh behind the scenes in *The Big Trail* in 1930, and eventually returned to acting in small supporting roles, most all of them in his brother's films.

Walsh's ten sound films included *Out of Singapore, Me and My Gal, Belle of the Nineties, Under Pressure, Rio Grande Romance* and *The Bowery,* in which he portrayed famous fighter John L. Sullivan. His last picture was *Put on the Spot* in 1936.

Comments: At one time George Walsh's athletic derring-do was compared to that of the great Doug Fairbanks himself. Although he was not considered more than a journeyman actor, his films were very popular for a time. Adding to this popularity, no doubt, was the fact that he wore as little as possible in some of his films and that he occasionally posed (artistically) in the nude.

It is ironic that his potentially most important role, that of Ben-Hur, proved to be the one that sent Walsh's star plummeting. He apparently was not compensated for his time off the screen and was even unfairly blamed for some of the film's problems. Its subsequent great success when his own career was fading must have been even more galling.

REVIEWS

Me and My Gal: The villain is George Walsh, who has changed a lot since the silent days and the athletic roles he played. *Variety* 12/23/32, *Harrison's Reports* 12/24/32.

Black Beauty: In a supporting role as the junk man, George Walsh turns in a good performance. *Variety* 8/29/33.

Walthall, Henry B(razeal), Shelby City,
Alabama, 1876/78–1936

Silent: Always to be remembered as *The Birth of a Nation*'s Little Colonel, Henry B. Walthall was first a stage actor. He made his debut for D. W. Griffith about 1909 (possibly in *The Convict's Sacrifice*) and appeared in numerous two-reelers in supporting and leading roles. Among his costars were Mary Pickford, Blanche Sweet and Lillian Gish.

For Essanay, Walthall appeared in the serial *The Misleading Lady* (1916) as well as several features. In 1917 he formed his own production company and interspersed film and theater appearances. By the early 1920s he was no longer a leading man but he made numerous appearances in character roles.

Among Walthall's films were *The Avenging Conscience, Judith of Bethulia, Blind Justice, Home Sweet Home, The Great Love, The False Faces* (as the Lone Wolf), *Simon the Jester, One Clear Call, The Confession* and *The Unknown Purple.* Last silent: *Black Magic* (1929), with synchronized sound effects and music.

Sound: Walthall apparently made his sound bow in the 1928 Vitaphone short *Retribution.* Of his ten 1929 films, nearly all were part- or full talkies. The first of these were *Stark Mad* and *Speakeasy,* both released early that year. Others included *The Tres-passer*, Gloria Swanson's sound bow, *The Bridge of San Luis Rey* and *River of Romance*. He had one of his last starring roles in *In Old California*.

Throughout the remainder of his life Walthall was a valued and busy character actor in a wide variety of films, among which were *Viva Villa!, A Tale of Two Cities, Men in White, The Last Outlaw, Judge Priest, Police Court* and his last, *China Clipper*. He also made at least one other short, *The Pay Off* in 1930.

Comments: Some performers have played one great role and have never lived up to it subsequently, usually to their great frustration. If Henry B. Walthall felt that way, he at least had the satisfaction of knowing that his was one of *the* greatest, and in one of the most epochal of films. D. W. Griffith thought his performance in *The Birth of a Nation* to be the most outstanding by any actor in the history of the cinema.

Walthall was short of stature and he aged noticeably. This was possibly due to the alcoholism from which he was rumored to suffer. His days as a romantic leading man were therefore fairly brief. Even then he was not really considered washed up in silents.

Sound, however, made Henry B. Walthall an even more sought-after character actor. His stage-trained voice was perfectly fine and he could still deliver a powerful performance. Just as important, he had brought to the talkies his considerable ability to deliver an understated performance.

Many of Walthall's sound films were quickies, but they were generally uplifted by his presence. Others were of course prestigious, made more so by his participation. The old cinema pioneer died as he undoubtedly wanted to: in harness.

REVIEWS

Police Court: The picture holds the audience's interest because of the good acting of H. B. Walthall as a broken-down actor. *Harrison's Reports* 4/9/32.

Viva Villa!: In a worthy and gentle "Christ fool" character, Henry B. Walthall's acting stands out. *Variety* 4/17/34.

Judge Priest: Walthall plays a minister and makes the courtroom scene outstanding. He seems to make no effort at dramatics but his voice is thrilling throughout. *Harrison's Reports* 8/25/34, *Variety* 10/16/34.

Ward, Fannie (sometimes Fanny; Fannie
Buchanan), St. Louis, Missouri,
1868/72–1952
Filmography: Films in Review (Dec. 1985)
Silent: Before she signed with Famous Players-

Lasky in 1915, Fannie Ward was a singer and stage actress both in the U.S. and England. Her first film was *The Marriage of Kitty*; her second the sensationally successful melodrama *The Cheat*.

It was in that C. B. DeMille film that Ward's character received the (in)famous shoulder branding administered by Sessue Hayakawa. None of her films was more sensational, however, than the constant publicity barrage (it now would be called hype) about her supposed ability to retain a youthful appearance well into middle age.

Ward went to Pathe in 1918. Among her 25 silents, mostly all before 1920, were *The Narrow Path, The Profiteers, The Yellow Ticket, Unconquered, Common Clay* and *The Winning of Sally Temple*. Her last two films were made in France. Last U. S. silent: *Our Better Selves* (1919); last silent: *The Hardest Way* (1922).

Sound: Ward's sole sound effort was the Vitaphone short *The Miracle Woman* (1929). She afterwards returned to the stage, often appearing with her husband Jack Dean. The din of the public relations machinery did not abate.

Comments: Ward was a competent enough actress whose career was both boosted and overshadowed by her effort to look "eternally" young. Indeed, she was at least 43 when her screen career began and she always played much younger women.

Ward's face was undeniably smooth and in certain lighting she could look younger, but it was all done by plastic surgery which she did much to popularize. Some still photographs clearly revealed her unnaturally lineless and "pulled back" skin. Therefore she may have preferred the concealments of a less revealing and thus less cruel movie set, even with its somewhat primitive lighting.

Inevitably cruel — and undeniably humorous — were the barbs of Fannie Ward's contemporaries like Anita Loos who said, "When a girl is cute for fifty years, it really gets to be historic."

Warner, H(enry) B(yron) (one source
says real surname was Lickfold), London,
England, 1876–1958
Filmography: Classic Images (Jan.-Feb. 1987);
List of films in *Eighty Silent Film Stars*
Silent: H. B. Warner had been a longtime stage actor when he made his first top-billed films for Famous Players-Lasky in 1914, *The Ghost Breaker* and *Lost Paradise*. He returned to the theater for a while but was back in front of the cameras by 1916. Thereafter he interspersed his cinema appearances with stage acting.

Among Warner's 35 silents were *Wrath, Haunting Shadows, Whispering Smith, Zaza, Romance of a Rogue, The Seventh Sin* and *Below the Dead Line*.

In 1927 he appeared in two of his best-known: *Sorrell and Son* and DeMille's *The King of Kings* in which he played the title role. Last silent: *The Divine Lady* (1929), technically a silent although it contained singing sequences, made after his first talkie.

Sound: Conquest, a late 1928 film, was Warner's first sound effort. Eight of his nine 1929 pictures were also either part- or fully sound. Among his talkies that year were *The Show of Shows, The Gamblers, The Argyle Case* and *The Trial of Mary Dugan*.

There were some very distinguished films among Warner's 90-plus talkies including *Mr. Deeds Goes to Town, Lost Horizon* (for which he received an Academy Award nomination), *It's a Wonderful Life, A Tale of Two Cities, Mr. Smith Goes to Washington* and *Sunset Blvd.*, in which he was one of the so-called "waxworks."

Warner also was seen in the "Bulldog Drummond" series and other less than prestigious efforts like *Savage Drums* and *The Princess and the Plumber*. In *Supernatural* he played a kind of mad scientist. He had a long and distinguished career, appearing on the screen regularly until 1951. His last film was the 1956 version of *The Ten Commandments*.

Comments: H. B. Warner managed to avoid being typecast solely as a good (if not holy) man after his portrayal of Jesus in *The King of Kings*. He grew older gracefully with his gray hair and lean physique and went on to play a wide variety of parts in talkies, both sympathetic and villainous. Certainly one of his strongest assets was a distinctive theater-trained voice.

REVIEWS

The Trial of Mary Dugan: In his part as the district attorney, it can almost be said that this is H. B. Warner's picture. He is as strong here as he was at a disadvantage in a previous talkie and he does a nice bit of acting. *Variety* 4/3/29, *Harrison's Reports* 4/20/29.

The Argyle Case: In this mystery melodrama Warner is good as the counterfeiter. *Harrison's Reports* 9/7/29.

Lost Horizon: H. B. Warner does excellent work. *Harrison's Reports* 3/20/37.

Journey into Light: Warner provides some fine characterization in several brief scenes. *Variety* 8/29/51.

Warwick, Robert (Robert Bien), Sacramento, California, 1878–1964

Silent: In 1914 Robert Warwick transferred his fame as a stage matinee idol to films in *The Dollar Mark* and he had a major success with the first version of *The Argyle Case* (1917). He was one of Famous Players-Lasky's "Famous People in Famous Stories." Among his other pictures were *Alias Jimmy Valentine, Secret Service, Jack Straw, Hell Hath No Fury, Thou Art the Man* and *All Man*.

Much was made of Warwick's distinguished service during World War One when he was off the screen for over a year. He returned to continuing success but, apparently as a result of a legal suit against Famous Players-Lasky, he was blacklisted and made only two films in the 1920s. He went back to the theater. Last silent: *The Spitfire* (1924).

Sound: Nineteen twenty-nine's *Unmasked*, in which he was top-billed as the scientific detective Craig Kennedy, was Warwick's first talkie. Starting in 1931 he returned full time to films for a distinguished and lengthy career as a supporting player in all genres. His sound films included *I Am a Fugitive from a Chain Gang, The Awful Truth, Juarez, Tennessee Johnson, Romeo and Juliet, The Buccaneer* and *Sutter's Gold*.

Among Warwick's serial appearances were *The Three Musketeers, Fighting with Kit Carson, The Whispering Shadows, The Fighting Marines* and *Ace Drummond*. He continued to be seen on-screen as late as 1959 with his final films *The Night of the Quarter Moon* and *It Started with a Kiss*. He also worked on television.

REVIEWS

The Adventures of Don Juan: In this lush melodrama, the ambassador to Spain is played by Robert Warwick. *Harrison's Reports* 12/25/48.

Sword of Monte Cristo: Warwick is a wealthy marquis. *Harrison's Reports* 3/17/51.

Night of the Quarter Moon: Veteran actor Robert Warwick is persuasive as the Judge. *Variety* 2/11/59.

Washburn, Bryant (Franklin B. Washburn), Chicago, Illinois, 1889–1963

Filmography: Classic Images (Dec. 1987-Feb. 1988); List of films in *Eighty Silent Film Stars*

Silent: A matinee idol during much of the 'teens and early '20s, Bryant Washburn first had been a stage actor. He began with Essanay about 1911 playing villains and character roles at a relatively young age. His starring career commenced about 1915, perhaps in *The Little Straw Wife*.

Washburn went to Pathe in the late 1910s and then founded his own production company. His more than 190 silent films included *It Pays to Advertise, The Prince of Graustark, Skinner's Dress Suit* (and its sequels), *Too Much Johnson, Rupert of Hentzau* and *Temptation*. In the mid–1920s, he began appearing in supporting roles but still had an occasional lead. Last silent: *Honeymoon Flats* or *Jazzland*, released about the same time in 1928.

Sound: Washburn's sound debut may have been in a 1929 short entitled *The Unkissed Man*. He also made the Vitaphone shorts *Christmas Knight* and *Niagara Falls* in 1930. His first feature was that year's *Swing High*. Some of his other films were *Mystery Train, What Price Innocence?, Bridge of Sighs, Paper Bullets, West of the Pecos* and *Sutter's Gold*.

Washburn was also much seen in serials like *The Clutching Hand, Tailspin Tommy and the Great Air Mystery, Jungle Jim, The Black Coin* and *Adventures of Captain Marvel*. Nineteen forty-seven marked his last appearances in films: There was the short *Do or Die* and the quickie *Sweet Genevieve*.

REVIEWS

The Curtain Falls: The screen veteran Bryant Washburn contributes a nice bit. *Variety* 5/22/35.

The Law Rides Again: Washburn, a leading man of the silent screen days, has a minor bit. *Variety* 8/11/43.

Westover, Winifred, San Francisco, California, 1900–1978

Silent: Pretty Winifred Westover was probably better known for being the co-star William S. Hart finally got to marry (he apparently proposed to all of them) than for her screen performances. The marriage was extremely brief but did result in the birth of William S. Hart, Jr.; the career was somewhat longer.

Westover appeared in *Intolerance* in 1916. Other early efforts included *The Microscope Mystery, Cheerful Givers, Hobbs in a Hurry* and *John Petticoats*, the film in which she first co-starred with Hart. She was active until 1922 in such films as *Forbidden Trails, The Village Sleuth, Is Life Worth Living?* and *Anne of Little Smoky*.

After becoming a leading lady, Westover appeared several times with action star William Russell and also partnered Buck Jones, Charles Ray and Conway Tearle. She also made a couple of films in Sweden. Last silent: *Love's Masquerade* (1922).

Sound: Westover came back before the cameras in 1930 to make her one and only talkie, the poorly-received *Lummox*. In it she played an immigrant maid. Its uneasy and unsuccessful melding of brutish naturalism and attempted poetic mysticism proved a loser.

REVIEWS

Lummox: Westover commands serious attention by the sincerity of her portrayal. Although she has not appeared in pictures for nine years her performance would lead one to believe that she has studied acting. She plays a blonde amazon of great physical and mental breadth. *New York Times* 3/24/30, *Variety* 3/16/30, *Harrison's Reports* 3/29/30.

White, Alice (Alva White), Paterson, New Jersey, 1906/08–1983

Silent: Alice White was working behind the Hollywood studio scenes as a secretary when she was tapped for her first role in *The Sea Tiger* (1927). She then alternated between leads and supporting roles in films that included *Breakfast at Sunrise, Show Girl, Gentlemen Prefer Blondes, Harold Teen* and *The Mad Hour*. Last silent: *Naughty Baby* (1929), with synchronized sound effects and music.

Sound: White entered talkies as a leading lady, a status she maintained for a few more years. It was widely believed that she was intended by the Paramount studio to be a threat to Clara Bow in case that star got too "temperamental."

Hot Stuff, a 1929 part-talkie, was White's sound bow. Other films that year were *Broadway Babies* and *The Girl from Woolworth's*. She continued on in films, most of them quickies, until the late '30s.

White's films included *Employees Entrance, Cross Country Cruise, Picture Snatcher, Sweet Music, The Big City* and *King of the Newsboys*. By the mid-part of the decade she was back in supporting roles.

White also appeared in a few pictures during the 1940s, her last role coming in 1949's *Flamingo Road*. By that time she had made about 20 talkies to add to her silent film total of about 15.

Comments: Whether blonde or brunette, Alice White was undeniably cute and she brought an infectious pep to her roles. Unfortunately she was no great shakes as an actress and was characterized as a "second-string" Bow and just another flapper. This was not only unfair to Bow, who was a much superior actress, but it also had a chilling effect on White's career as well.

White did make the transition to sound and eventually appeared in more talkies than silents so it could be said that her transition was a "success." By 1930 her type and day had passed, however, and her appearances in cheapie melodramas and comedies soon brought her starring career to a halt.

As more than one review boldly hinted, it is possible that White's signs of temperament gave the studio heads the excuse they sought to give her a push on the slippery slope downward.

REVIEWS

Hot Stuff: White does well in her part. *Harrison's Reports* 5/4/29.

Sweet Mama: The film is horribly miscast and just about washes up Alice White. She has been let down by the studio and there is a suspicion that the miscasting is deliberate so she can be dismissed. In the scene where she attempts to sing she is terrible. *Variety* 7/16/30, *Harrison's Reports* 7/19/30.

The Widow from Chicago: At the theater, the name of the leading lady Alice White is omitted from the billing, nor does she appear in any of the stills. Her performance is barren and her exaggerated eye-rolling is bad. *Harrison's Reports* 11/15/30, *Variety* 12/24/30.

Luxury Liner: Reviews did not agree. One stated that Alice White, as a gold digger, was inept but the script was to blame. Another said that she gave a good comedy performance. *Variety* 2/7/33, *Harrison's Reports* 2/11/33.

Secret of the Chateau: The stars have little to do and Alice White, in a comic role, is no more successful. *Harrison's Reports* 12/15/34, *Variety* 2/5/35.

Whitman, Gayne (also known as Alfred Whitman) (Alfred Vosburgh), Chicago, Illinois, 1890–1958

Silent: Under his real name of Alfred Vosburgh, Gayne Whitman appeared in supporting roles in several motion pictures in 1916 and '17, including *Her Father's Son*, *The Divorcee*, *Money Madness* and *Shackles of Truth*. As Alfred Whitman he became a leading man in many more over the next three years, among them *The Flaming Omen*, *Desert Law*, *Tongues of Flame* and *A Trick of Fate*.

From 1919 to 1925 he appeared in the Los Angeles theater and it was in the latter year, as Gayne Whitman, that he began playing supporting roles in such films as *His Majesty Bunker Bean*, *Three Weeks in Paris* and *The Love Hour*. Whitman later was the leading man in a few but mostly continued to be seen in support. Other films included *Hell-Bent fer Heaven*, *A Woman's Heart*, *Stolen Pleasures* and *Wolves of the Air*. Last silent: *The Adventurer* (1928).

Sound: Although Whitman's only 1929 film, George Jessel's *Lucky Boy*, was a part-talker, his voice was not heard. It took 1930's *Reno* to reveal that he was the possessor of a fine speaking voice which was heard on the radio during most of that decade and well into the 1940s. One of his shows was *Chandu the Magician*.

Whitman continued making movie appearances in the '30s as a character actor, often a villain, in films like *The Yankee Don*, *Igloo*, *Page Miss Glory*, *The Return of Jimmy Valentine*, *A Star Is Born* and *The Texas Rangers*. He was seen in the serials *Finger Prints* and *Adventures of Red Ryder* and heard in the serial *The Masked Marvel* (he provided the voice of the crime-fighting hero).

There were a few feature roles for Whitman in the 1940s in *Tennessee Johnson*, *My Gal Loves Music* and *The Sickle and the Cross*. He also was heard in some films as the narrator, as well as narrating and writing numerous short subjects. His on-screen career ended in 1952 after *Big Jim McLain* (as a Communist agent) and *Dangerous Crossing*.

Williams, Kathlyn, Butte, Montana, 1888?–1960 (some sources state that she was considerably older)

Filmography: Films in Review (Feb. 1984); List of films in *Sweethearts of the Sage*

Silent: A Hollywood pioneer, Kathlyn Williams made her first films about 1909, and from 1910 to 1917 she was a top Selig star. She was in the original *The Spoilers* (1914) and in about 150 other silents including *The Ne'er-Do-Well*, *The Coming of Columbus*, *Conrad in Quest of His Youth*, *Locked Doors*, *Our Dancing Daughters*, *The Whispering Chorus* and *Clarence*.

Among Williams's leading men were the popular stars Tom Mix, Harold Lockwood and Wallace Reid. She was probably most famous for her starring role in what is considered to be the first true serial, *The Adventures of Kathlyn*. She left Selig to work at Paramount and other studios and as the 1920s drew on was seen more frequently in supporting roles. Last silent: *The Single Standard* (1929), with synchronized music and sound effects.

Sound: Williams made her sound debut down in the cast list of *Wedding Rings* in 1929. She made only a few other sound films, among them *Road to Yesterday*, *Daddy Long Legs* (1931 version), *Unholy Love*, *Blood Money* and *Rendezvous at Midnight*, her last in 1935.

Comments: Kathlyn Williams was a talented actress who also directed at least one two-reeler and wrote some of her own films. She is best-remembered for her role in the seminal serial that bore her name and for what is referred to as her "sudden aging" in the early 1920s.

Williams's appearance changed from that of a fairly young-looking leading lady to that of a middle-aged woman seemingly "overnight." This led to widespread speculation by her contemporaries that she was considerably older than her publicized age. It may also have been because of the personal tragedies that dogged her life.

REVIEWS

Unholy Love: In a lesser part is Kathlyn Williams. *Variety* 8/30/32.

Rendezvous at Midnight: Williams gives an okay performance. *Variety* 4/24/35.

Wilson, Ben, Clinton (?), Iowa, 1876 — 1930

Silent: One of the silents' premier serial "kings" was Ben Wilson. He was in the first pseudo-chapterplay, *What Happened to Mary*, in which each episode had self-contained endings rather than cliffhangers. That was 1912 and there was a sequel, *Who Will Marry Mary?*, the next year.

In Wilson's later "true" serials he was teamed frequently with actress Neva Gerber beginning in 1917. They included *The Voice on the Wire, The Mystery Ship, The Trail of the Octopus, The Screaming Shadow, The Branded Four* and *The Mysterious Pearl.*

Wilson had gotten his show business start in stock companies and he made numerous one- and two-reelers after joining Edison in 1911. Later he worked for Rex and Universal. His more than 100 films included *Idle Wives, Even As You and I, Castles in the Air, Sheriff's Girl, Tonio, Son of the Sierras* and *The Range Riders.*

Between 1925 and 1929 Wilson appeared in numerous westerns and adventure-melodramas but his roles got progressively smaller. He also directed some films. Last silent: *China Slaver* (1929).

Sound: Wilson appeared in only two talkies: the little seen part-talkie *Bye Bye Buddy* in 1929 and *Shadow Ranch*, a 1930 Buck Jones western.

Wilson, Lois, Pittsburgh, Pennsylvania,
    1896/98–1988

Filmography: Films in Review (Jan. 1973), additional filmography (Mar.-July 1973); List of films in *Sweethearts of the Sage*

Silent: Undoubtedly the most successful of the beauty contest winners (Miss Alabama, 1915) to have a film career, Lois Wilson debuted about 1916. In *The Dumb Girl of Portici*, her first, she played several small roles. Other early pictures included *Alimony, The Bells, Gates of Brass* and *The Morals of Hilda.*

A Wampas Baby Star of 1922, Wilson co-starred with many of the prominent leading men of the day including J. Warren Kerrigan, Wallace Reid, Rudolph Valentino and Tommy Meighan. Among her major films were *Miss Lulu Bett, The Covered Wagon, Only 38, What Every Woman Knows, Manslaughter, Monsieur Beaucaire, The Great Gatsby* and *Bella Donna.*

Others of Wilson's 80 silents for Paramount, Universal and other studios were *Broad Daylight, Ruggles of Red Gap, North of 36, Fascinating Youth, New York* and *Alias the Lone Wolf.* She also appeared in some westerns. Last silent: *Object — Alimony* (1928), also known as *Object — Matrimony.*

Sound: The 1928 Vitaphone short *Miss Informa-* *tion* was Wilson's first sound effort. Her initial feature was *On Trial*, the fourth all-sound film produced by Warner Bros. that same year. In it she amply demonstrated her suitability for the talking screen.

Wilson made shorts in 1929 as well and her features included *The Gamblers, The Show of Shows* and *Kid Gloves.* Others of her almost 50 talkies included *Seed, There's Always Tomorrow, Bright Eyes* (as Shirley Temple's mother), *Wedding Present, The Crash* and *Deluge.*

Wilson worked steadily until 1936, made a few more in 1939–41, and then returned for her final picture, *The Girl from Jones Beach*, in 1949. Among the studios for which she appeared were First National, Fox, Columbia, RKO, Liberty, Invincible, Republic, Paramount, MGM and Universal. She made her Broadway debut in 1937 and besides many other stage appearances was seen on television, including a soap opera.

Comments: Lois Wilson was one of the top stars of the 1920s. She was an understated and intelligent actress who sometimes appeared in unglamorous character parts, among them many mother roles, as well as being a conventional leading lady. Her most outstanding physical feature were those expressive dark eyes through which she so convincingly could portray emotion.

Wilson was not a trained actress before her arrival in films but her voice was perfectly satisfactory. Although she made a fine transition to talkies, it did her subsequent career little good. It seems the operation was a success but the "patient" died anyway.

Although not all of Lois Wilson's talking films were poor, many of them certainly were. It seemed that Hollywood considered her as just another ex-silent star and her career was slowly killed off by the studios' disinterest. Broadway's gain was definitely Hollywood's loss.

REVIEWS

On Trial: Lois Wilson is more convincing and saleable in sound; her performance is outstanding. The voices of the characters, with the exception of Wilson, sound muffled but her lines will remain in the viewer's memory. *Variety* 11/21/28, *Harrison's Reports* 11/24/28.

The Furies: As the heroine, Wilson is appealing and her acting is artistic but the script makes her role a bewildering one. *Variety* 4/23/30, *Harrison's Reports* 4/26/30.

Bad Little Angel: The acting of Lois Wilson gives the film a wholesome quality. *Harrison's Reports* 11/4/39.

Windsor, Claire (Clara Cronk), Cawker
City, Kansas, 1897/98–1972

Silent: Renowned for her blonde beauty, Claire Windsor appeared in numerous romantic melodramas during the 1920s. She had begun as a Lasky extra before being discovered by director Lois Weber for whom she made several films in the early '20s. Her initial efforts included *What Do Men Want?*, *The Blot*, *One Clear Call* and *The Stranger's Banquet*.

Windsor appeared for Goldwyn for five years and then signed with Tiffany-Stahl. Among her films were *Nellie the Beautiful Cloak Model*, *A Son of the Sahara*, *The Denial*, *Dance Madness*, *Souls for Sables* and *Fashion Madness*. Last silent: *Captain Lash* (1929), with synchronized music and sound effects.

Sound: The part-talkie *Midstream* (1929) was Windsor's first. She was then off-screen until 1932 when she appeared in the quickies *Self-Defense*, *The Constant Woman*, *Kiss of Araby* and *Cross Streets*.

A supporting role in 1938's *Barefoot Boy* followed and Windsor's last was apparently the 1945 "B" mystery-comedy *How Do You Do?* She also toured with Al Jolson's musical *Wonder Bar* in the '30s.

Comments: Claire Windsor's voice was not deemed suitable for the talkies. Her return to the screen in 1932 most certainly was a result of the well-publicized legal proceedings in which she was involved at that time. Accused of being a "love pirate," she was entangled with a married man who was being sued by his wife. The resultant headlines no doubt awakened Hollywood's interest in her; after the trial ended, so, largely, did her "comeback."

REVIEWS

Barefoot Boy: Claire Windsor portrays the cold wife. *Variety* 8/31/38.

Winninger, Charles, Athens, Wisconsin,
1884–1969

Silent: There was a hardly a branch of show business in which diminutive Charles Winninger did not appear. First he was a boy soprano billed as "The Boy Prodigy" touring with his family's medicine show. Then came the circus, stock, Broadway (including the Ziegfeld Follies) and films.

Winninger first essayed the medium of film about 1915 in some one- and two-reelers, and then in the '20s he made three features in which he had character roles. The first was *Pied Piper Malone* (1924). Last silents: *The Canadian* and *Summer Bachelors*, released about the same time in 1926.

Sound: Winninger's greatest stage role, as Cap'n Andy in Jerome Kern's *Showboat*, came in 1927 and he remained with it until 1930. In that year he returned to the screen in the farce comedy *Soup to Nuts*, which was also the first film of The Three Stooges.

Among Winninger's relatively few and scattered '30s talkies were *Bad Sister*, *The Sin of Madelon Claudet* and *Showboat* (1936 version), in which he recreated his stage role. Late in the decade he received his best screen opportunities in *Three Smart Girls*, *Destry Rides Again* and *Nothing Sacred*. In the latter he played the incompetent sawbones who incorrectly diagnoses Hazel Flagg with radiation poisoning.

Some later Winninger films were *Little Nellie Kelly*, *Coney Island*, *Sunday Dinner for a Soldier*, *Give My Regards to Broadway* and *Raymie*, perhaps his last film, which came in the early 1960s. He also had a radio show in the 1930s and was seen on television.

REVIEWS

Soup to Nuts: Winninger is turned into a straight man in what was intended to be a comic performance. His character plays a trombone, but not too comically either. *Variety* 10/29/30.

Night Nurse: What good performances there are belong to Joan Blondell and Winninger as the hospital head. *Variety* 7/21/31.

Social Register: Winninger gets two chances and takes both of them successfully. *Variety* 10/9/34.

Three Smart Girls: This is one of Winninger's best performances. *Variety* 1/27/37.

Destry Rides Again: Of the male actors, Winninger, as the inept sheriff, makes the next deepest impression after Jimmy Stewart in the title role. *Variety* 12/6/39.

Little Nellie Kelly: In a dual role, Winninger scores with his portrayal of an irascible Irish drunkard. *Variety* 11/20/40.

The Sun Shines Bright: Playing the Will Rogers role in this remake of *Judge Priest*, Charles Winninger makes as much as possible of the character and is the principal figure around whom the story revolves. *Variety* 5/6/53.

Winton, Jane, New York, New York,
1905/06–1959

Silent: Jane Winton was "The Green Eyed Goddess of Hollywood," at least according to her publicists. She was certainly striking in a feline way but the designation ultimately did little for her career. From 1925 she played small roles in major films like *Sunrise*, *Don Juan*, *The Beloved Rogue* and *The Patsy*.

In minor pictures such as *The Love Toy*, *Why*

Girls Go Back Home, The Poor Nut, Bare Knees and *Nothing to Wear*, Winton's parts were larger. She rarely rose above supporting player, however. Last silent: *Captain Lash* (1929), with synchronized music and sound effects, made after her first talkie.

Sound: Winton's sound career consisted of a handful of supporting roles. Most of them were as the "bad girl," casting to which her exotic looks consigned her. *Melody of Love* (1928) was her first effort followed by two 1929 part-talkies: *The Bridge of San Luis Rey* and *Scandal.* Winton appeared in three 1930 films, the epochal *Hell's Angels* (in a very small role), *The Furies* and *In the Next Room.* There was to be only one more, 1934's *Hired Wife.* She made some stage appearances in the early 1930s and apparently did operatic performing as well. In the 1950s she published two novels.

REVIEWS

Scandal: Jane Winton, as the jealous and scheming villainess, is good in her part. *New York Times* 4/22/29, *Harrison's Reports* 5/4/29.

In the Next Room: Winton appears in the short prologue and handles it nicely. *Variety* 4/9/30.

Withers, Grant (Granville Withers), Pueblo, Colorado, 1904–1959

Silent: Grant Withers began his film career in 1926 with a supporting role in the Buck Jones western *The Gentle Cyclone.* By the next year the ruggedly handsome 6'3" actor was a leading man in films such as *The Final Extra, In a Moment of Temptation* and *Upstream.*

Withers also began receiving top billing in a few pictures. Last silents: *Bringing Up Father, The Road to Ruin, Golden Shackles* and *Tillie's Punctured Romance,* all released about the same time in 1928.

Sound: Sound presented Withers with no problems insofar as his voice was concerned. He appeared in nine films during 1929 and all of them had at least some talking. He was top-billed in *In the Headlines* and *The Time, the Place and the Girl.* But he never attained important leading man status and gradually drifted into supporting roles. His 1930 marriage to actress Loretta Young was annulled in 1931.

Throughout the 1930s, Withers appeared in numerous motion pictures most of which were "B" quickies. His films in that decade included *Swanee River, The Secrets of Wu Sin, Goin' to Town, Let's Sing Again, Telephone Operator, Three Loves Has Nancy, Tomboy* and the "Mr. Wong" series. He also made such serials as *The Red Rider, The Fighting Marines, Jungle Jim, Radio Patrol* and *The Secret of Treasure Island.*

As the 1940s arrived, Withers's facial features and physique were both noticeably thickening. He found himself in supporting roles in films like *Road to Alcatraz, Blackmail, The Vampire's Ghost* and numerous westerns of the stripe of *Throw a Saddle on a Star* and *In Old Oklahoma.* There also were brief appearances in *Fort Apache, My Darling Clementine, Tennessee Johnson* and other more prestigious pictures.

Withers worked in films almost to the time of his death and was also seen on television. The movies which he made in the '50s generally did not rise above the quality of *Hoedown, Utah Wagon Train, Hoodlum Empire, The Outlaw's Daughter, Hidden Guns* and *I, Mobster,* which may have been his last in 1958.

REVIEWS

The Time, the Place and the Girl: Withers gives a fine characterization as the conceited bond salesman. *Variety* 7/10/29.

Tiger Rose: Withers is believable and makes the most of his part. *New York Times* 12/25/29.

Red-Haired Alibi: Withers does what he can with a weak role. *Variety* 10/25/32.

Wolheim, Louis, New York, New York, 1880–1931

Silent: In 1916 Louis Wolheim began amassing film credits, generally in small parts, after a stint as an extra. His early films included *The Sunbeam, A Pair of Cupids, The Darkest Hour* and *The Eternal Mother.* His first major role came in 1920's *Dr. Jekyll and Mr. Hyde,* starring John Barrymore.

Wolheim also began a stage career in 1919 and he interspersed film and theater roles for many years thereafter. He proved to be a most distinguished stage star, although given his physiognomy perhaps an unlikely one. Among his plays were the enduring classics *The Hairy Ape* and *What Price Glory?*

Wolheim's 30 silent films (not counting unbilled bits) included *Orphans of the Storm, Sherlock Holmes* (1922 version), *America, Lover's Island, Sorrell and Son* and *The Racket.* He also was seen in the serials *The House of Hate,* with Pearl White, and *The Carter Case.* Last silent: *Wolf Song* (1929), technically a silent film with singing sequences.

Sound: Wolheim made five films in '29, all but one of them were fully or part-talking. The first was *The Shady Lady;* others were *Square Shoulders, Frozen Justice* and *Condemned.* Nineteen thirty, his penultimate year of life, brought him his greatest (and top-billed) film role as Katczinsky in the anti-war epic *All Quiet on the Western Front.*

Wolheim made about 10 or 11 talkies that included *Danger Lights, The Silver Horde, The Sin Ship* (which he also directed), *The Ship from Shanghai* and *Gentleman's Fate* (1932), his last, released posthumously.

Comments: Wolheim's battered face made him a natural for villainous roles in the silents. With the addition of his deep, authoritative voice in talkies, he had a little more opportunity to diversify and show his mettle as an actor.

Hollywood, of course, generally responded in its customary way and Wolheim continued to play some "bad" or just unsympathetic roles. He also showed his benign side on occasion and never more so than in the classic *All Quiet on the Western Front* wherein he portrayed the gruff sergeant with a heart of gold.

Except for *All Quiet* and one or two others, Wolheim's talkie roles were not promising, being mostly in melodramas. No doubt had he lived he would have continued to be stereotyped and cast extensively in the gangster roles just then becoming popular. Even so, he probably would have brought an extra dollop of humanity to them.

Reviews

Square Shoulders: Wolheim wins sympathy but his voice is, at times, throaty and indistinct, possibly due to poor reproduction. *Harrison's Reports* 6/15/29, *Variety* 7/3/29.

Frozen Justice: Wolheim is a sympathetic villain but the sound is so poor that the voices of the actors become sharp and shrill. *Variety* 10/30/29, *Harrison's Reports* 11/2/29.

The Ship from Shanghai: Wolheim manages to make his villainous steward role the strongest and most interesting in the production. *Variety* 4/30/30, *Harrison's Reports* 5/3/30.

All Quiet on the Western Front: In a group of standout performances Wolheim leads. He contributes considerable comedy and does excellent work. *Variety* 5/7/30, *Harrison's Reports* 5/10/30.

Danger Lights: Wolheim brings the force of his unusual personality to getting laughs but in this instance he's more warm-hearted than comic. His performance is excellent. *Variety* 11/19/30.

Gentleman's Fate: Although it ranks as John Gilbert's best talking picture so far, the late Louis Wolheim, as his brother, nearly steals the picture from him. *Harrison's Reports* 3/14/31.

Wong, Anna May (Wong Liu-Tsong), Los
Angeles, California, 1902/07–1961
Filmography: Films in Review (Mar. 1987)

Silent: In 1921, after working as an extra, Anna May Wong began appearing in supporting and a few leading roles. *Bits of Life* and *The Toll of the Sea*, an early color film, were among her first features.

In 1924 she was seen in two major successes, *The Thief of Bagdad* and *Peter Pan*.

Wong's 25 silent films included *The Alaskan, The Devil Dancer, A Trip to Chinatown, Old San Francisco, Mr. Wu* and *The Desert's Toll.* Late in the decade she went to England and Germany to make some films. Last U. S. silents: *Chinatown Charlie* and *The Crimson City*, released about the same time in 1928. The British-made *Piccadilly* (1928) may have been her last silent.

Sound: One of Anna May Wong's earliest sound films was the British-made *Elstree Calling* in 1930. She also appeared in *The Flame of Love* in the U.K. before returning to America in 1931 to portray Fu Manchu's daughter in *Daughter of the Dragon.* (It was also Sessue Hayakawa's first American talkie.) She made the prestigious *Shanghai Express*, directed by Josef von Sternberg, before she once again departed for England in 1933.

From 1937 to 1942 Wong was back in this country to appear in several minor films. Among her pictures during that time were *Daughter of the Orient, Java Head, Bombs Over Burma, Dangerous to Know* (in which she was top-billed), and *Ellery Queen's Penthouse Mystery.*

Anna May Wong made radio appearances in the 1930s and staged a very mild "comeback" in 1949 with a small role in *Impact.* She also did some television in the 1950s. Her last two films were *Portrait in Black* and *Savage Innocents* in 1960.

Comments: At times during her career, Anna May Wong benefited from the movies' use of "exotic" actresses. In the late '20s, for instance, there was a vogue for "Oriental" mysteries. For a while she was the most famous ethnic Asian actress in the world, but, on balance, her ethnicity proved a major drawback. Performers of that day seldom were cast in a "color blind" way. There obviously also was prejudice, as amply revealed in the careless racism, as some would now consider it, of many film reviews.

Although very attractive, Wong just did not fit Hollywood's idea of a leading lady. By the late 1920s her roles had diminished and she had to try to revive her career abroad. Her later roles as evil "Oriental" villainesses, red-herrings in "B" mysteries and servants ensured that she never reached her full potential.

As far as the quality of Wong's voice was concerned, latter-day audiences heard her beautifully cultured tones. But apparently it was originally somewhat flat and without much color in its tone. She was Laurence Olivier's co-star in an English play in the late 1920s and her voice was panned by the critics. She subsequently may well have taken voice lessons.

REVIEWS

The Flame of Love: It is doubtful that Anna May Wong has any drawing power with her flat American accent. Maybe she did sing the songs she seemed to sing but it will not help. As an actress she probably did as well as she could. *Variety* 11/5/30, *Harrison's Reports* 11/22/30.

Daughter of the Dragon: Anna May Wong and other Oriental actors will find it tough going in the talkies because they can't synchronize the action with the white man's tongue. *Variety* 8/25/31, *Harrison's Reports* 8/29/31.

King of Chinatown: The top-billed Wong provides a nice portrait of a Chinese girl turned doctor. *Variety* 3/22/39.

Ellery Queen's Penthouse Mystery: As a mysterious Oriental, Wong handles a minor role with ease. *Variety* 3/12/41.

Impact: Nice support is rendered by Anna May Wong as a maid. *Variety* 3/16/49.

Portrait in Black: Wong returns to the screen after a ten-year absence but she has chosen the thankless, unnecessary part of a suspicious housekeeper. Her appearances are accompanied by annoying, hackneyed 'Oriental' music designed to make her seem mysterious. *Variety* 6/15/60, *Harrison's Reports* 6/25/60.

Wray, Fay, Cardston, Alberta, Canada, 1907–

Filmography: Film Fan Monthly (Nov. 1974), *Classic Images* (July-Aug. 1983), *Films in Review* (Feb. 1987); List of films in *Sweethearts of the Sage*

Silent: After doing extra work from about 1923, Fay Wray began appearing in Hal Roach comedies and numerous westerns, including two-reelers, at Universal. In 1926 she was designated a Wampas Baby Star and potential stardom did unexpectedly loom with her role in Erich von Stroheim's 1928 epic *The Wedding March.* But like many of that director's films, it was not shown in its entirety and was financially unsuccessful.

Most of Wray's silent motion pictures were lesser efforts. They included *The Coast Patrol, The Man in the Saddle, Lazy Lightning, Legion of the Condemned, The Street of Sin, The First Kiss, One Man Game* and *Spurs and Saddles.* Last silent: *The Four Feathers* (1929), with synchronized sound effects and music.

Sound: Wray made her talkie debut in 1929's *Thunderbolt; Pointed Heels* came later that year. She came into her own in 1932, assuming the unofficial mantle of the scream queen of horror films with *Doctor X, Mystery of the Wax Museum, The Vampire Bat* and *The Most Dangerous Game.*

Wray hit her cinema high point as the menaced and frequently screaming heroine and heart's desire of *King Kong* in 1933. For that film, the brunette actress became a blonde and remained one for some time thereafter. *Kong* brought her a large measure of fame but also somewhat overshadowed the rest of her career.

Although Fay Wray was ever after to be the beauty who killed the beast, to paraphrase the famous final line of the film, she also appeared in a few dramas of quality such as *Viva Villa!, The Affairs of Cellini* and *One Sunday Afternoon.* In the mid–'30s she starred in some films in the United Kingdom, one of the best being *The Evil Mind* with Claude Rains.

Upon returning, Wray found her career in decline. Afterwards her future lay mainly in "B" films and an occasional "A," the latter generally in small roles, e.g., 1941's *Adam Had Four Sons.* For about ten years from the mid–'40s she was off the screen entirely but during that hiatus made stage and radio appearances.

Wray returned to the cinema in character roles in the 1950s. Among her films for such studios as Paramount, RKO, Columbia, Universal and Monogram were *The Texan, Below the Sea, The Woman I Stole, White Lies, Come Out of the Pantry, Navy Secrets, Melody for Three, Rock Pretty Baby, Dragstrip Riot* and *Summer Love,* her last, in 1958. She was seen on television and as late as 1980 appeared in a made-for-television film.

Comments: As the leading lady of the "tallest, darkest leading man in Hollywood," Fay Wray became a movie immortal if not an important star. The image of that leading man, the great ape King Kong, climbing the Empire State Building and depositing her thereon is surely one of the cinema's enduring iconographic images.

In the years since, many interesting interpretations have been placed on the relationship between the dark "hero" and the virginal, blonde heroine. It is a film that has kept both film writers and psychologists quite active.

After Wray's brief breakout role in *The Wedding March,* an effort was made to co-star her with more important leading men such as Ronald Colman and Gary Cooper. With the latter there seemed to be a short-lived attempt to make them into a romantic team.

Fay Wray was a pretty and appealing actress but she was essentially a rather bland one with little charismatic quality. Her voice was somewhat high-pitched (suitable for the frequent screaming she needed to do) but certainly not unpleasant. Her screen persona projected what might be termed virtuous sex appeal, perhaps not a formula for long-lasting stardom.

REVIEWS

Pointed Heels: As the heroine, Wray makes no more than an ordinarily pleasing impression in her scattered appearances. *Variety* 1/1/30, *Harrison's Reports* 1/4/30.

King Kong: Neither the story nor the cast gains more than secondary importance; they're not even close. The light hair is a change for Wray. *Variety* 3/7/33.

Cheating Cheaters: Wray plays a mob moll-detective with grace and effectiveness; at all times she photographs well. *Variety* 12/11/34.

They Met in a Taxi: Wray is all right except for the slight British accent she has developed. *Variety* 9/16/36.

Smashing the Spy Ring: Wray is merely acceptable in another stooge role, and she has received doubtful help from the makeup people. *Variety* 1/18/39.

Young, Clara Kimball, Chicago, Illinois, 1890/91–1960

Filmography: Films in Review (Aug.-Sept. 1961), additional filmography (Oct. 1961); *Classic Images* (Nov. 1988-Jan. 1989)

Silent: Clara Kimball Young entered films at Vitagraph about 1909, after stock experience, and was a frequent co-star of matinee idol Maurice Costello. *My Official Wife*, a 1914 feature, was the vehicle that brought her fame. Known as "The Dark Madonna," she ultimately left Vitagraph to sign with Selznick and established her own production company.

From 1918 to 1921 Young was an international star and a top moneymaker. Unwisely, she bought her way out of the Selznick contract and turned her business affairs over to an inexperienced "friend." This proved to be the start of a precipitous decline in her fortunes and 1923 was the last year she made a full slate of films.

By 1925 Young was off the screen. Among her films had been *Eyes of Youth* (a young Valentino played a villain), *Camille* (1916 version), *The Woman of Bronze, Magda, The Common Law, The Easiest Way* and *The Yellow Passport*. Last silent: *Lying Wives* (1925).

Sound: Noticeably older and plumper, Young returned to films in 1931, generally in small character parts. She did have at least a couple of leads, one being in *Women Go on Forever* (1931). Until 1938 she was seen in such films as *Kept Husbands, Fighting Youth, His Night Out, I Can't Escape* and *Atlantic Adventure*.

Young also played in her share of "B" westerns including those featuring William Boyd's "Hopalong Cassidy." Among them were *The Frontiersman, Hills of Old Wyoming* and *Oh, Susanna!* Among her serial appearances were *The Return of Chandu, The Mysterious Pilot, The Black Coin* and *The Secret of Treasure Island*. She also made at least one Three Stooges short. Her last film was 1941's *Mr. Celebrity*.

Comments: To see Clara Kimball Young cavorting in a witless Three Stooges comedy, chintzy serial or "B" western is to realize how far she had fallen from her days atop the pinnacle of success. She was a major world star in the late 1910s and her films, generally romantic melodramas, were eagerly awaited by millions.

Young was not conventionally pretty but she was tall, even stately, and had a dignity which allowed her to suffer sympathetically through countless crises as the wronged woman. Her real-life crises unfortunately overshadowed those of the cinema but she managed to acquit herself, even in unworthy roles, with good grace.

In the talkies, reviews of Young's work differed widely. Physically, she had matured in a way which made her ideal for casting as a society woman. Sometimes she did play that type of role and sometimes, as in westerns, she was seen in a lower stratum of life. Either way her great cinema days were long over.

REVIEWS

Kept Husbands: The cast looks like a revival of silent days with Clara Kimball Young and others in supporting roles. Most are seen rarely in talkies but there is no reason why they shouldn't be seen more often. *Variety* 3/25/31.

Women Go On Forever: Disagreement was seen among reviewers. One said that the value of the story was heightened by the excellent acting of Clara Kimball Young. It seemed as if she had not lost the art of acting, even though she had been away from pictures for years. Another said that her appearance caused some interest but she never was and probably never would be a character actress. In her hands the leading role did not stand up. It was false and she seemed inattentive. She didn't give it flesh and blood at any time. *Harrison's Reports* 8/29/31, *Variety* 10/20/31.

File 113: Young is less than spellbinding and, in an intentionally heavy mother part, does not get the part over. *New York Times* 2/20/32, *Variety* 2/23/32.

Hills of Old Wyoming: Young, a one-time favorite, has a small character part. *Variety* 6/9/37.

Mr. Celebrity: Many people will be touched at seeing the old favorites Francis X. Bushman and Clara Kimball Young appearing throughout the picture. *Harrison's Reports* 10/25/41.

Young, Loretta (Gretchen Young or Jung),
Salt Lake City, Utah, 1912/13–
Filmography: Films in Review (May 1969)

Silent: Loretta Young worked as a child extra along with her two sisters Polly Ann and Betty Jane, later to be known as Sally Blane. She returned to films as a teenager, making her debut in a bit in *Naughty but Nice* in 1927.

The following year the strikingly pretty Young began getting a few larger roles, most notably in *Laugh, Clown, Laugh* with Lon Chaney, and also in *The Head Man*, *The Magnificent Flirt* and *The Whip Woman*. Last silent: *Scarlet Seas* (1929), with synchronized sound effects and music.

Sound: The Squall (1929) was Loretta Young's sound bow. Although she played a supporting role in that picture her ascent was a rapid one. She was soon co-starring, frequently with Douglas Fairbanks, Jr., and then receiving top-billing.

To cement her budding stardom, Young was named a Wampas Baby Star. Other 1929 films included *The Show of Shows*, in which she sang and danced in the "Meet My Sister" number with older sister Sally, *The Careless Age* and *The Fast Life*.

During her first few years at Fox Young's films were mostly program grade and in them she frequently portrayed downtrodden working girls. As the 1930s progressed, her pictures became more prestigious and she became a top Hollywood star. By this time she had far outpaced both her actress sisters who were mired in second features.

Young's films during that decade included *The Man from Blankley's*, *Zoo in Budapest*, *A Man's Castle*, *House of Rothschild*, *Clive of India*, *The Call of the Wild*, *Ramona* and *Eternally Yours*. For the only time the three sisters and half-sister Georgianna appeared together in 1939's *The Story of Alexander Graham Bell*.

The next decade saw a decline in the quality of Young's films. Such movies as *China*, *Bedtime Story* and *And Now Tomorrow* made little impact. Although she was the female star of the interesting Orson Welles melodrama *The Stranger* in 1946, it too was not particularly successful.

It was not until 1947 that Young made a mini-comeback with *The Farmer's Daughter* for which she won a Best Actress Academy Award. Ingrid Bergman had been slated to star in it. This was followed by such well-respected films as *Come to the Stable*, *Rachel and the Stranger* and *The Bishop's Wife*.

Although it had been given impetus by her Oscar, Loretta Young's film career petered out in the early 1950s with lukewarm efforts like *Half Angel*, *Cause for Alarm*, *Paula* and *It Happens Every Thursday*, her final motion picture.

The ever-ambitious Young then turned successfully to television. *The Loretta Young Show* ran for several years, garnering an Emmy award for her. She also did radio work and in the 1980s she returned for a couple of roles in made-for-television movies.

Comments: For most of her career, even at the height of her stardom, Loretta Young was considered at best a journeyman actress. Undeniably beautiful, with strikingly large and luminous eyes, she made a decorative and serviceable leading lady when teamed with some of the screen's most popular leading men like Clark Gable and Spencer Tracy.

It is instructive that Young's reviews sometimes were directed more at her appearance and her clothes than her emoting. She certainly was parodied during her television days for her lavish outfits and swirling skirts but she was undeniably popular for a time. Toward the end of her film career she began to gain more respect for her acting ability, but by that time she was at the dangerous age for leading women.

As is the case with many screen divas, Loretta Young was not as popular among her co-workers as she was with the public. Known variously as "The Steel Butterfly," "The Iron Madonna" and even "Gretch the Wretch" (a play on her real first name), she was the subject of a "Mommie Dearest"–type biography written by her daughter.

REVIEWS

The Squall: Young looks beautiful but her voice sounds like it is reciting commencement exercises in a grammar school. *Variety* 5/15/29.

The Fast Life: As the heroine Loretta Young shows more promise with each production. She is not only one of Hollywood's prettiest ingenues but is also gifted with an excellent speaking voice. *Variety* 8/21/29, *Harrison's Reports* 8/24/29.

The Truth About Youth: Young is a charming heroine and satisfactorily plays a part that suits her. *Variety* 12/17/30.

Taxi!: Young does better than usual, putting more solidity in her portrayal than is generally true. More depth is still to be desired to go with that beautiful face. *Variety* 1/12/32.

Zoo in Budapest: The role of the terror-stricken orphanage refugee proves a happy selection for Loretta Young's talents. *Variety* 5/2/33.

Ramona: Young, in a coal black wig, makes a lovely Indian girl and the Technicolor adds to her attractiveness. *Variety* 10/14/36.

Eternally Yours: Young is excellent. Only through her ability is she able to remain untouched by the poor story. *Variety* 10/4/39.

The Farmer's Daughter: Young has difficulty with the Swedish accent which occasionally lapses into straight Americanese. But that is the only flaw in Young's performance; otherwise she breezes through with finesse. *Variety* 2/19/47.

Cause for Alarm: Despite the presence of Loretta Young it is still a secondary feature. She provides it with some marquee value and her usual excellent acting. *Variety* 1/31/51.

Appendix I
Some Silent Stars Who Did Not Appear in Talkies

Art Acord
Claire Adams
May Allison
Linda Arvidson
Mabel Ballin
Theda Bara
Viola Barry (Peggy Pearce)
Constance Binney
True Boardman (d. 1918)
Priscilla Bonner
John Bunny (d. 1915)
Catherine Calvert
June Caprice
Marguerite Clark
Marguerite Clayton
Miriam Cooper
Ward Crane (d. 1928)
Dorothy Dalton
Grace Darmond
Marjorie Daw
Carol Dempster

Elliott Dexter
June Elvidge
Dustin Farnum (d. 1929)
Margarita Fischer
Helen Gardner
Louise Glaum
Dagmar Godowsky
Elaine Hammerstein
Robert Harron (d. 1920)
Madeline Hurlock
Arthur Johnson (d. 1916)
Edith Johnson
J. Warren Kerrigan
Winifred Kingston
Florence LaBadie (d. 1917)
Barbara LaMarr (d. 1926)
Harold Lockwood (d. 1918)
Louise Lovely
Katherine MacDonald
Violet Mersereau
Mary Miles Minter

Nita Naldi
Mabel Normand
Eugene O'Brien
Olga Petrova
Billy Quirk (d. 1926)
Wallace Reid (d. 1923)
Billie Rhodes
Eileen Sedgwick
Larry Semon (d. 1928)
Marguerite Snow
Anita Stewart
Ruth Stonehouse
Edith Storey
Valeska Suratt
Constance Talmadge
Alice Terry
Olive Thomas (d. 1920)
Fred Thomson (d. 1928)
Rudolph Valentino (d. 1926)
Pearl White
Earle Williams (d. 1927)

Appendix II
The One- and
Two-Shot Wonders

The following actors and actresses included in this book are believed to have appeared in only a single talking or part-talking American feature film:

G. M. (Broncho Billy) Anderson	*The Bounty Killer* (1965)
Francelia Billington	*The Mounted Stranger* (1930)
Lon Chaney	*The Unholy Three* (1930)
Davenport, Dorothy (Mrs. Wallace Reid)	*Man Hunt* (1933)
Dorothy Dwan	*The Fighting Legion* (1930)
Elsie Ferguson	*Scarlet Pages* (1930)
Harrison Ford	*Love in High Gear* (1932)
Gilda Gray	*Rose Marie* (1936)
Raymond Griffith	*All Quiet on the Western Front* (1930)
Georgia Hale	*The Lightning Warrior* (1931 serial)
Hope Hampton	*The Road to Reno* (1938) (also appeared in a short)
Juanita Hansen	*Sensation Hunters* (1933)
Elsie Janis	*Women in War* (1940) (also appeared in shorts)
Marc McDermott	*Glorious Betsy* (1928)
Leo Maloney	*Overland Bound* (1930)
Jack Pickford	*Gang War* (1928)
Tyrone Power, Sr.	*The Big Trail* (1930)
Edith Roberts	*The Wagon Master* (1929)
Ruth Roland	*Reno* (1930) (also appeared in a Canadian film)
Edith Taliaferro	*My Love Came Back* (1940)
Florence Vidor	*Chinatown Nights* (1929)
Winifred Westover	*Lummox* (1930)

The following actors and actresses included in this book are believed to have appeared in only two talking or part-talking American films:

Vilma Banky	*This Is Heaven* (1929)
	A Lady to Love (1930)
John Bowers	*Skin Deep* (1929)
	Mounted Fury (1931)
Alice Calhoun	*Bride of the Desert* (1929)
	Now I'll Tell (1934)
Sam DeGrasse	*Wall Street* (1929)
	Captain of the Guard (1930)
Helen Ferguson	*In Old California* (1929)
	Scarlet Pages (1930)
Jetta Goudal	*Lady of the Pavements* (1929)

	Business and Pleasure (1932)
Wanda Hawley	*Trails of the Golden West* (1931)
	The Pueblo Terror (1931)
Cullen Landis	*Lights of New York* (1928)
	The Convict's Code (1930)
Alfred Lunt	*The Guardsman* (1931)
	Stage Door Canteen (1943)
Douglas MacLean	*The Carnation Kid* (1929)
	Divorce Made Easy (1929)
Theodore Roberts	*Noisy Neighbors* (1929)
	Ned McCobb's Daughter (1929)
Alma Rubens	*Show Boat* (1929)
	She Goes to War (1929)
William Russell	*State Street Sadie* (1928)
	The Midnight Taxi (1928)
Norma Talmadge	*New York Nights* (1930)
	DuBarry, Woman of Passion (1930)
Lou Tellegen	*Enemies of the Law* (1931)
	Together We Live (1935)

The following performers included in this book appeared only in sound shorts:

Roscoe (Fatty) Arbuckle (1932–33)
Fannie Ward (1929)

The following performer included in this book appeared only in a prologue:

William S. Hart	Talking prologue (1939) to a re-release of his last silent *Tumbleweeds* (1925)

Bibliography

Film Reviews

Harrison, Peter. *Harrison's Reports and Film Reviews*. Reprint edition. Hollywood, Calif.: Hollywood Film Archive, 1991–1994. Covers film reviews from 1919 to 1962.
New York Times Film Reviews. Reprint edition. New York: New York Times, 1970–.
Variety Film Reviews. Reprint edition. New York: Garland; Bowker, 1983–. Covers film reviews from 1913.

Film Periodicals

Classic Images. Muscatine, Iowa: Muscatine Journals, 1962?–. Began as *8mm Collector*, then became *Classic Film Collector* and then *Classic Film/Video Images*.
Film Comment. New York: Film Society of Lincoln Center, 1962–.
Film Dope. London: Film Dope, 1972–.
Film Fan Monthly. Teaneck, N.J., 1950s?–1970s.
Films and Filming. London: Hansom Books, 1954–1990.
Films in Review. New York: National Board of Review of Motion Pictures, 1950–.
Focus on Film. London: Tantivy, 1970–.
Hollywood Studio Magazine. Studio City, Calif.: R.B. Productions, 1957–.
The Silent Picture. New York: First Media Press, 1968?–.
Stars. Mariembourg, Belgium, 1970s?–.

Catalogs

Catalog of Motion Pictures Produced in the U.S. New York: Bowker; Berkeley, Calif.: University of California Press, 1971–.

General Books

Agate, James. *Around Cinemas*. 2nd series. New York: Arno, 1972. Reprint of the 1948 edition.
Agee, James. *Agee on Film: Reviews and Comments*. New York: McDowell Obolensky, 1958.
Anderson, Robert G. *Faces, Forms, Films: The Artistry of Lon Chaney*. So. Brunswick, N.J.: Barnes, 1971.
Astor, Mary. *A Life on Film*. New York: Dell, 1972.
Balio, Tino. *United Artists: The Company Built by the Stars*. Madison, Wis.: University of Wisconsin Press, 1976.
Beck, Calvin T. *Heroes of the Horrors*. New York: Macmillan, 1975.
Carey, Gary. *Doug & Mary: A Biography of Douglas Fairbanks and Mary Pickford*. New York: Dutton, 1977.
Cary, Diana Serra. *What Ever Happened to Baby Peggy?* New York: St. Martin's, 1996.
Cushman, Robert. *Tribute to Mary Pickford*. Beverly Hills, Calif.: American Film Institute Theatre, 1970.
Edmonds, Andy. *Hot Toddy: The True Story of Hollywood's Most Sensational Murder*. New York: Morrow, 1989.
Everson, William K. *The Films of Laurel and Hardy*. New York: Citadel, 1967.
Farber, Manny. *Negative Space: Manny Farber on the Movies*. New York: Praeger, 1971.
Greene, Graham. *Graham Greene on Film: Collected Film Criticism, 1935–1940*. New York: Simon and Schuster, 1972. Reissued as *The Pleasure-Dome*. Oxford, England: Oxford University Press, 1980.

Griffith, Richard, Arthur Mayer and Eileen Bowser. *The Movies*. Revised and updated edition. New York: Simon and Schuster, 1981.

Hale, Georgia. *Charlie Chaplin: Intimate Close-Ups*. Metuchen, N.J.: Scarecrow, 1995.

Harvey, James. *Romantic Comedy in Hollywood from Lubitsch to Sturges*. New York: Knopf, 1987.

Herndon, Booton. *Mary Pickford and Douglas Fairbanks: The Most Popular Couple the World Has Ever Known*. New York: Norton, 1977.

Higashi, Sumiko. *Virgins, Vamps and Flappers: The American Silent Movie Heroine*. Montreal, Canada: Eden Press, 1978.

Katchmer, George A. *Eighty Silent Film Stars: Biographies and Filmographies of the Obscure to the Well Known*. Jefferson, N.C.: McFarland, 1991.

Kreuger, Miles, ed. *The Movie Musical from Vitaphone to 42nd Street*. New York: Dover, 1975.

Maltin, Leonard. *The Great Movie Comedians*. New York: Harmony Books, 1982.

Mast, Gerald. *A Short History of the Movies*. Indianapolis, Ind.: Pegasus, 1971.

Meade, Marion. *Buster Keaton: Cut to the Chase*. New York: Harper Collins, 1995.

Norman, Barry. *The Hollywood Greats*. New York: F. Watts, 1980.

Parish, James R. and William T. Leonard. *Hollywood Players: the Thirties*. New Rochelle, N.Y.: Arlington House, 1976.

Parish, James R. *The Paramount Pretties*. New Rochelle, N.Y.: Arlington House, 1972.

Pickford, Mary. *Sunshine and Shadow*. New York: Doubleday, 1955.

Rainey, Buck. *Sweethearts of the Sage: Biographies and Filmographies of 258 Actresses Appearing in Western Movies*. Jefferson, N.C.: McFarland, 1992.

Schickel, Richard. *Harold Lloyd: The Shape of Laughter*. Boston, Mass.: New York Graphic Society, 1974.

Shales, Tom, Kevin Brownlow et al. *The American Film Heritage: Impressions from the American Film Institute Archives*. Washington, D.C.: Acropolis Books, 1972.

Shipman, David. *The Great Movie Stars: The Golden Years*. New York: DaCapo, 1985. Reprint of the Hill and Wang edition, 1979.

Spears, Jack. *Hollywood: The Golden Era*. South Brunswick, N.J.: Barnes, 1971.

Steinbrenner, Chris and Burt Goldblatt. *Cinema of the Fantastic*. New York: Saturday Review Press, 1972.

Swanson, Gloria. *Swanson on Swanson*. New York: Random House, 1980.

Thompson, Frank T. *William A. Wellman*. Metuchen, N.J.: Scarecrow, 1983.

Walker, Alexander. *Stardom: The Hollywood Phenomenon*. Philadelphia, Pa.: Stein and Day, 1970.

Windeler, Robert. *Sweetheart: The Story of Mary Pickford*. New York: Praeger, 1974.

Index